CONTEMPORARY E[N]

1914-1964

[with] epilogue 1964-1974

CONTEMPORARY ENGLAND

1914–1964

with epilogue 1964–1974

W. N. MEDLICOTT

LONGMAN

Longman Group Limited
Longman House, Burnt Mill, Harlow
Essex CM20 2JE, England
Associated companies throughout the world

*Published in the United States of America
by Longman Inc., New York*

© W. N. MEDLICOTT 1967

First published 1967
First appearance in paperback (with epilogue) 1976
Fifth impression 1986

ISBN 0-582-48487-1

Produced by Longman Group (FE) Ltd
Printed in Hong Kong

INTRODUCTORY NOTE

ONE of the effects of two world wars and of fifty years of ever-accelerating industrial and social revolution has been the growing interest of the citizen in the story of his land. From this story he seeks to learn the secret of his country's greatness and a way to better living in the future.

There seems, therefore, to be room for a rewriting of the history of England which will hold the interest of the general reader while it appeals at the same time to the student. This new presentation takes account of the recent discoveries of the archaeologist and the historian, without losing sight of the claims of history to take its place among the mental recreations of intelligent people for whom it has no professional concern.

The history will be completed in a series of ten volumes. The volumes are of medium length, and are intended to provide a readable narrative of the whole course of the history of England and give proper weight to the different strands which form the pattern of the story. No attempt has been made to secure general uniformity of style or treatment. Each period has its special problems, each author his individual technique and mental approach; each volume is meant to stand by itself not only as an expression of the author's methods, tastes, and experience, but as a coherent picture of a phase in the history of the country.

There is, nevertheless, a unity of purpose in the series; the authors have been asked, while avoiding excessive detail, to give particular attention to the interaction of the various aspects of national life and achievement, so that each volume may present a convincing integration of those developments—political, constitutional, economic, social, religious, military, foreign, or cultural—which happen to be dominant at each period. Although considerations of space prevent minute investigation it should still be possible in a series of this length to deal fully with the essential themes.

A short bibliographical note is attached to each volume. This is not intended to supersede existing lists, but rather to call attention to recent works and to the standard bibliographies.

W. N. MEDLICOTT

A HISTORY OF ENGLAND
IN ELEVEN VOLUMES

General Editor: W. N. Medlicott

THE PREHISTORIC AGE IN BRITAIN

ROMAN BRITAIN

THE ANGLO-SAXON AGE*
BY D. J. V. FISHER

THE FEUDAL KINGDOM OF ENGLAND*
BY FRANK BARLOW

ENGLAND IN THE LATER MIDDLE AGES*
BY B. WILKINSON

THE TUDOR AGE*
BY JAMES A. WILLIAMSON

THE STUART AGE*
BY BARRY COWARD

EIGHTEENTH CENTURY ENGLAND*
BY DOROTHY MARSHALL

THE AGE OF IMPROVEMENT*
BY ASA BRIGGS

ENGLAND 1868–1914*
BY DONALD READ

CONTEMPORARY ENGLAND 1914–1964*
BY W. N. MEDLICOTT

* Already published

Some of the titles listed above are provisional

PREFACE

As this volume is the last in a series dealing with some 2,000 years of English history it has fallen to me to find a closing date for the whole story. I have chosen the year 1964, well aware that time alone will show whether the fall of the Conservative government in that year is anything more than a convenient stopping place for the historian: whether it was the beginning of a new era or merely the end of a phase. There can be no serious doubt, however, that the opening date, 1914, is fundamental.

The book is based throughout on the published sources, primary and secondary, which are abundant; I did not feel that its scale would justify reference to any unpublished documents to which I might have had access. I have followed the practice in recent volumes of this series of giving some reference in the footnotes to books for further reading, although these cannot claim to be exhaustive. They are published in London unless otherwise stated.

While writing the book I have enjoyed and benefited from discussions with many friends and colleagues, including the members of my seminar on interwar history at the London School of Economics and my next-door neighbour there, the late Professor Reginald Bassett. Professor Asa Briggs has read the whole manuscript, and made helpful suggestions. Mr. H. Duncan Hall of Bethesda, Maryland, Professor A. C. F. Beales, and Dr. L. S. Pressnell have read and given most useful advice about parts of the manuscript. My wife has given me practical aid at many points, and my secretary, Mrs. P. Joseph, has coped admirably with the preparation of the manuscript for publication.

W. N. MEDLICOTT

London School of Economics,
November 1965.

ACKNOWLEDGEMENTS

We are grateful to the following for permission to reproduce copyright material:

The Controller of Her Majesty's Stationery Office for an extract from Neville Chamberlain's speech, 24 March 1938 and Sir Winston S. Churchill's speech, 3 June 1940, printed in *Hansard* (Crown copyright), and the Proprietors of *The Times* and *Daily Express* for a letter by Bonar Law printed in issues 6 October 1922.

CONTENTS

Contents

Contents

MAPS

LIST OF ABBREVIATIONS

A.N.Z.U.S.	Australia, New Zealand, United States (pact).
B.D.	*Documents on British Foreign Policy, 1919–1939.*
B.S.P.	British Socialist party.
C.I.D.	Committee of Imperial Defence.
C.I.G.S.	Chief of the Imperial General Staff.
C.O.S.S.A.C.	Chief of Staff to the Supreme Allied Commander.
D.G.F.P.	*Documents on German Foreign Policy, 1918–1945*
D.O.R.A.	Defence of the Realm Act.
E.E.C.	European Economic Community.
E.F.T.A.	European Free Trade Association.
E.H.R.	*English Historical Review.*
E.R.P.	European Recovery Programme.
F.E.A.	Foreign Economic Administration.
F.O.	Foreign Office.
F.R.U.S.	*Foreign Relations of the United States.*
H.M.S.O.	His (Her) Majesty's Stationery Office.
I.L.P.	Independent Labour party.
I.M.F.	International Monetary Fund.
I.R.A.	Irish Republican Army.
I.R.B.	Irish Republican Brotherhood.
J.M.H.	*Journal of Modern History.*
K.A.N.U.	Kenya African National Union.
LlGM	*War Memoirs of David Lloyd George.*
N.A.T.O.	North Atlantic Treaty Organization.
N.E.D.C. (Neddy)	National Economic Development Council.
P.D.	Parliamentary Debates.
P.E.P.	Political and Economic Planning.
R.A.F.	Royal Air Force.
R.I.C.	Royal Irish Constabulary.
S.D.F.	Social Democratic Federation.
S.E.A.T.O.	South East Asia Treaty Organization.
T.G.W.U.	Transport and General Workers' Union.
T.U.C.	Trades Union Congress.
U.D.C.	Union of Democratic Control.
W.O.	War Office.

INTRODUCTION

IT is sometimes said that the historian of recent times is handicapped by both a lack of perspective and a lack of material. It is true that many public men who have moulded the history of the last half century are still alive, and quite capable of adding to, or contradicting, their own earlier revelations. It is also true that among very recent events there are many that seem relevant and interesting to us and will be considered by later historians to have no significance at all. Events and movements, in so far as they are the antecedents of developments in the future, must be left for a final assessment to what the Victorians kindly called the voice of impartial posterity.

But debate and even passion are not unknown among those who write about more remote ages and problems, and for no period of history is the documentation complete. It is certainly not the case that the fifty years of history covered by this volume is just a shapeless mass of unrelated facts, or that we cannot discern many powerful and important trends, or define the major problems that the men and women of the age tried to solve. And as it is usual today for historians to deprecate their capacity for true objectivity we may well doubt whether the voices of posterity will speak with any more unanimity than our own. The contemporary historian has, on balance, many advantages. His subject has a wide and natural appeal; his material is, in point of fact, abundant; he is himself a living witness; and he has little excuse for forgetting that there are two sides to every public question.

The year 1914 marks an obvious turning point after the previous ninety-nine years of ostensible peace and it also sees the beginning of the modern phase of many familiar developments, domestic and foreign. I have chosen to call this book simply 'Contemporary England' for it is difficult to think of any quite satisfactory alternative label for this crowded and rather terrifying era. Dr. David Thomson calls the years of the twentieth century down to 1945 'the age of violence', and the term could also be used in some measure of the period after 1945, although not in the domestic field, which has really been very peaceful since 1926. The interwar years have been called 'the age of illusion' and 'the age of Baldwin'; the 1945–51 period has been described as an 'age of austerity', which it was, but so too was the decade of the nineteen-twenties in many fields. Sir Oliver Franks calls the period of forty years after 1921 'the great retreat'. We might say that the half century was an age of organized welfare, and the altruistic element in colonial and international policy would allow us to apply this term to many aspects of external as well as of domestic activity. In comparison with the pre-1914 era it was also an age of collectivism, not only in the regulation of the citizen's daily life but also in the international arena, where the *ad hoc* combinations of the old diplomacy have been replaced by a great range of permanent, formalized groupings; it is within their complicated framework that most of the problems of foreign policy have now to be worked out. But terms such as these, useful in their way, are not all-embracing.

The theme of a history of Britain since 1914 is, however, easy to define. It must be the impact of an almost continuous series of external crises on the domestic outlook, economy, and national policy of the country. The landmarks are the two world wars (1914–18 and 1939–45), followed in each case by a period of emotional deflation and economic difficulty and also perhaps by some lapse of will power and mental vigour. The government hesitated, both in the nineteen-thirties and in the nineteen-fifties, to take the lead in European affairs, although a more positive phase started in 1939 with the challenge to Hitler, and in 1961 with the decision to seek entry into the European Common Market. After these five decades of almost unbearable tension and hot party controversy a certain stability then seemed to have been achieved in the country's affairs, for in spite of fierce argument in the general election of October 1964 over the choice of economic expedients there was a remarkable absence of basic disagreement between the two leading parties as to the future handling of problems, domestic and foreign, facing the country.

While this long period has an obvious unity of its own it would be quite misleading to assume that the First World War meant a complete break with the past. The country was already facing new challenges and problems before the end of the nineteenth century;

the year 1914 is a turning point only in the sense that the more pressing difficulties could no longer be ignored. The extent of these unsolved problems was, however, partly concealed from the prewar generation by its sense of the unshakeable character of its daily life and institutions. The façade of high politics and high society showed no modification of traditional authority and splendour, apart perhaps from the more sober note which King George V and Queen Mary had introduced into Court life, and which public opinion and at least the older aristocracy were thought to welcome. The country as a whole, although not unaware of foreign competition and foreign enmity, had no serious forebodings of the great war and the great economic setbacks that were to follow it; it took for granted King, Lords, and Commons (with some coolness towards the Lords), the capitalist system, the free and established churches, progress, the poor, and the British Empire; but it was the possibility of fundamental change, rather than the case for social and other reform, which was in doubt. Industrial strikes and suffragette violence were evidence of the frustration of any serious hope of upsetting the established order in industry or politics, rather than of the absence of criticism. Onlookers thought that the country faced difficulties, but could successfully meet them. 'It'll take a long time to bankrupt England', a friendly American ambassador wrote in February 1914; nevertheless, the thought had crossed his mind. Earlier, after admitting that the British people had 'an awful slum' and 'an idle class' he had waved aside the idea of decadence. 'The world never saw a finer lot of men than the best of their ruling class. . . . I meet such men everywhere—gently bred, high-minded, physically fit, intellectually cultivated, patriotic.' But the war when it came did not so much end an idyll as close some paths, and, as it seemed to many of the postwar generation, the more attractive ones.

We can summarize under four heads—diplomatic, economic, social-political, and imperial—the problems which were aggravated rather than created by the war. After the turn of the century there were growing doubts as to whether isolation, so long regarded as a happy evasion of other people's troubles, might not leave the British Empire the prey of every predatory power in Europe and beyond. The all-sufficiency of the Royal Navy was challenged by the rise of German sea power and also, for the first time in history, by two potentially first class naval powers outside European waters, Japan

and the United States. Alliance with Japan, the concession of all
American demands in the Caribbean and Alaska, and the settlement
of outstanding colonial issues with France in 1904 and Russia in
1907, were attempts to simplify the issues rather than to solve the
basic problem of German rivalry, which it was hoped to alleviate
by a naval agreement, colonial concessions, and the absence of such
provocative gestures as conscription or a French alliance. The
irrevocable commitment to France came only in August 1914;
the relative advantages of isolation, mediation, and commitment
were still unsolved problems after the war.

In a somewhat similar way the balance of economic power was
shifting; the facts were known, but it still seemed better to try to
maintain an eminently advantageous system than to seek some
not very obvious alternative. Great Britain was facing the unique
problem of the influence of new industrialization on an old industrial
state. She exported about one-third of her national industrial output in order to maintain heavy imports of food and raw materials. In
her merchandize trade, imports had normally exceeded exports for
several generations, a favourable balance being preserved by income
from shipping, overseas investment, and insurance. But for a decade
after 1900 the terms of interchange were deteriorating—imports
were costing relatively more than the equivalent amount of exports.
Her exports, moreover, were being driven out of certain traditional
markets by foreign competitors and out of the domestic markets of
the foreign competitors themselves. This aroused some popular
resentment at unfair foreign practices, and counter-recriminations
about British jealousy of legitimate competition and hypocrisy in
equating Britain's advantage with the general good. Nevertheless
Britain had probably been a net gainer from the industrialization of
the world since the eighteen-seventies; in steel, pig-iron, coal,
engineering, and textile production her output was steadily increasing, although at a slower pace than that of her leading rivals,
Germany and the United States. Her share of world trade had
dropped from 23 to 17 per cent between 1870 and 1913, but she
still had more than the U.S.A. with 15 per cent, and Germany with
12 per cent. She still possessed 40 per cent of the world's carrying
trade. Moreover the years 1909–13 were a boom period of full
employment and expanding foreign trade and investment, continuing a general process of improvement since 1903.

In these circumstances the government and business world,

while by no means unaware of the chillier winds that were blowing, believed that they had more to lose than to gain by countermeasures, which might provoke retaliation. It seemed too early to reject free trade and belief in the stimulus of foreign competition. Nevertheless, certain measures, ranging from the Merchandizing Marks Act of 1887 to the government decision to hold half the shares in the Anglo-Persian Oil Company in 1914, were departures from *laissez-faire* of varying utility and unorthodoxy. Joseph Chamberlain's tariff programme foundered for many reasons including the general recovery from the depression of the nineties, the fact that protection could not be extended to world markets, fear of dearer food, and the swing of the political pendulum in 1906. But from this point onwards the tariff reformers were in the ascendant in the Tory ranks, and Victorian self-sufficiency had again been challenged.

The modern phase of working class action in the form of industrial strikes and political representation was a product of the depression of the late eighties and the nineties, by which time both the older parties had let slip the chance to keep it within their own orbits. Long hours, squalid housing, poor food, and the prospect of complete destitution in unemployment or illness were still the lot of the lowest ranks of labour. The aristocracy of labour in the form of the skilled workers and artisans in regular employment were able to look after themselves through their unions, but there was a permanent if diffused state of dissatisfaction among them too, coloured by rising costs, the relatively slow expansive rate of British industry, and the size of employers' profits. The result was the general sense of a major problem which received ample attention and no permanent solution. On the Labour side or in sympathy with Labour there appeared a wide range of bodies from new or strengthened trade unions to the Fabian Society (1884); there were also less influential groups such as H. M. Hyndman's Social Democratic Federation (1883), and then came the Independent Labour Party, or I.L.P. (1893), the Labour Representation Committee (1900), and the Labour party, taking its place in the Commons as an independent party heavily dependent on Liberal support in 1906. The majority of its members were plain Liberals or old-fashioned Radicals, but some already called themselves Socialists, and from 1900 onwards the word was a threat and a puzzle to their opponents. Syndicalism and Industrial Unionism began to be discussed, the Second International linked international working class solidarity with pacifism, and militancy increased at home, encouraged by the example of Ulster, Tory, and suffragette die-hards. The older parties and local authorities made great efforts by municipal slum clearance programmes, educational expansion, and national insurance to remedy social evils. The Liberal government after 1906 launched a campaign of expanding social benefits, and the 'people's budget' followed in 1909. All this is the beginning of a story that is resumed, to become the dominant theme in domestic politics, after 1918. It is sufficient to note here that the Liberals did not solve the problem, and Asquith failed, as Attlee was to fail in somewhat similar circumstances after 1951, to provide the intellectual leadership which would give a new reformist programme to his party after the fulfilment of its earlier mission.

The country became conscious of the Empire in the eighties, proud of it in the nineties, and increasingly self-conscious about it after the turn of the century. A sense of guilt, stimulated and confused by theories of exploitation of Liberal-Radical, pacifist, and Marxist-Leninist origin, and based on much bad history and wishful economic thinking, began to undermine belief in the unmixed blessings of the civilizing mission and the *Pax Britannica*. The Englishman, easily embarrassed by recollections of his brief display of emotion and flagwagging and the unexpected warnings of Rudyard Kipling (of all people) against wild tongues and boastings, tended at first to assume that it was his own pride, and not the Empire, that was at fault. This indeed is what Kipling appears to have meant. The three dilemmas of policy which were facing British statesmen and their advisers were, however, of a more specific character. The first was that of assessing the strength of the centripetal urge towards a more closely knit Commonwealth based on imperial federation and some system of empire free trade; partly linked to this were the views of the racialists who dreamed of the inclusion of America and Germany in an Anglo-Saxon alliance. Then there was the problem of imperial defence and an imperial foreign policy, and of reconciling the inclination of the self-governing Dominions to play their part with their reluctance to abandon the initiative permanently to the Mother Country. The Committee of Imperial Defence was a step towards a solution as soon as the idea of including imperial representatives was accepted. A third problem was that of preparing the dependent empire for self-rule, in the face of those who doubted the capacity or the loyalty of the

---

inhabitants. Except in some measure in the case of Ireland the full impact of these problems was postponed until after the war, but this merely increased their weight.

The war accentuated all these diverse problems and difficulties. While the economic situation worsened, the organization and self-confidence of the Labour movement improved, the citadel of capitalism no longer seemed unassailable, and the predominantly Conservative administrations of the interwar years faced a complex of practical criticisms with many ideological and class-conscious undertones. But to the governments of the interwar period the lack of any basic solution of the country's external problems was the essential obstacle to great progress at home, and this view the Labour party as a whole, with its fierce insistence on domestic improvement, for long refused to take seriously. Ramsay MacDonald and Snowden left the party over this issue in 1931. There can certainly be no question that the existence of chronic external embarrassment, political and economic, hampered domestic progress both in the interwar years and after 1945. Could the country's leaders, faced after 1918 with far greater difficulties than their critics usually recognized, really have done much better than they did? Or were they in fact a succession of rather mediocre and un-enterprising or self-seeking men, who failed to make the best of their opportunities?

To ask these questions is to ask whether England was not being assigned by those who made demands on her a rôle beyond her strength. The period ends with widespread assertions of England's decline in both stature and status. 'Gone are the days when the British lion roared and everything trembled', said Mr. Khrushchev in April 1958. 'Now it can frighten no one.' Mr. Dean Acheson, a former American Secretary of State, said more politely on 5 December 1962, 'Great Britain has lost an empire and has not yet found a rôle', and President Nasser on 23 December 1961 happily informed an audience at Port Said that 'next year Britain will become a fourth-rate country and later a fifth-rate one'. She seems to have been spared this rapid descent and Mr. Harold Macmillan rightly remarked in May 1963 that in absolute terms she had never been so prosperous and her military power had in absolute terms never been so greater. Mr. Harold Wilson spoke in similar but more guarded terms in March 1964.

Comparisons of the relative strengths of countries are in fact very difficult to make when influence, the ability to affect the immediate decisions of other governments, may bear no very close relation to power, measured by more long-term standards of economic and military strength. There is no doubt that the numerous assertions as to Britain's recent loss of power and status oversimplify the issue by attributing to her far greater ability to rule or dominate the world at the beginning of the century than she in fact possessed. They also err in assuming that the decline, such as it is, began only after 1945. The 'great retreat' starts in the early twenties with acquiescence in the surrender of naval primacy, in the demilitarization of British possessions in the Pacific, in the granting of virtual independence to Eire, and in the destruction of the British textile market in India by hostile tariffs. And yet if we view the period as a whole we find much to support a rather different interpretation from that of a net decline. At the beginning of the century she had a position of influence in the world beyond her strength, and what has followed has been a continuous process of adjustment to the realities of the modern world, complicated and delayed by the fact that in the interwar years there were strong forces of public opinion pushing her into an unaccustomed rôle of international leadership.

For this reason the record of fluctuating influence and authority is at times confusing, but we are justified on balance in thinking of the story in terms of achievement, with a wide range of (on the whole) beneficial developments; we shall be able to follow their course over the years.

At home at least five of these are notable. The first was the successful democratization of British politics; the history of the Labour party as one of the two main parties of the state belongs entirely to this period. The second was the achievement of a welfare state of Liberal design in a community which had accepted Liberal political institutions so unquestionably as to make the Liberal party superfluous. The third was a social revolution, extensive but preserving some beloved anomalies. The fourth was a new industrial and commercial revolution, which by the nineteen-sixties had reversed the decline threatening the country's economy in the interwar years. The fifth was the revolution in mass communication media, which included not only the enormous spread of wireless broadcasting and television, but also the network of local omnibus companies which, together with the ubiquitous private motor car, largely abolished rural isolation.

There were also five distinctive and noteworthy developments abroad. The first was the country's successful performance in two great wars and in subsidiary fighting and crises, the result of a vast military and economic effort and of the courage, toughness, and military aptitude of its population, combined with a more skilful use of diplomacy than the Foreign Office is usually given credit for. The second was the transformation of the British Empire into the British Commonwealth of Nations. The third was the successful fostering of international organizations for peace, the League of Nations and the United Nations; the League was as much British as American in its origin and conception and Britain has remained the most faithful and, with France, the only continuous member of these organizations among the great powers. The fourth was the achievement of a special relationship with the United States, a consistent aim of the British government since the beginning of the century. The fifth was the maintenance of Britain's rôle as the central banker of the sterling area.

Probably the effect of external pressures and preoccupations on the domestic life of the country has been in the long run to hasten rather than retard change. The country's broader demands for a form of post-Liberal social democracy, which were already emerging as the dominating reformist objectives before 1914, have been substantially achieved, even if progress has been slow at times. There was a remarkable absence of deeper social antagonism and of genuine political rivalry in 1964; it is a proof rather than a disproof of this statement that English writers were never more prone to prickly reminders of the vestigial snobbishness thought to be lurking in some corners of the social edifice. Differentials in social status as well as in employment conditions continued to provide peripheral tensions. A grievance at the absence of grievance irked would-be crusaders, and young men seem angry because there was so little to be angry about. The prevailing sub-acid tone of popular journalism had killed hero worship in public life (except in the case of Winston Churchill, whose reputation survived all traditional reactions). But it had also left little room for the cultivation of monsters; even when these appeared fleetingly abroad they had a disconcerting habit of transforming themselves into the most respected of Commonwealth prime ministers, or into the best Soviet premier that the country could afford.

Thus our period ends on a marked, but no doubt quite transitory, note of fulfilment; the broader ends of domestic policy which were beginning to emerge at its start had been substantially achieved, although Labour's retreat from nationalization and the Conservatives' new enthusiasm for planning were too opportunistic to suggest permanent programmes. Certainly too the popular mood was less one of fulfilment than of a curious sense of uneasiness before the prospect of new problems inherent in the solution of the old.

I

THE FIRST WORLD WAR

1. INTO BATTLE

THE impact of the First World War on the British people was
violent but confused. For perhaps the majority of Englishmen
it never lost the character of a vast but temporary interruption
of the normal business of life. It was always easier to understand as
a war that would end war than as a war that would end for ever the
prewar England or the prewar world. Even the German menace,
frightening enough at the time, was accepted by many people as
the product of essentially transitory forces, the spirit of militarism,
the megalomania of ambitious individuals, or the arrogance aroused
by Bismarck's startling successes. So it was possible, and reassuring,
to believe that the chastening effects of defeat would bring the
German people back to earth and to normality. To the Frenchman,
on the other hand, German conduct more readily assumed the
aspect of a permanent barbarism, and for large sections of the
British people too the first spontaneous outburst of strong feeling
developed into a settled and deepening animosity which survived
the war.

Sir Edward Grey's handling of the international crisis in late
July and early August 1914 owed much of its success to his close
accord with the public mood. His strong desire for peace was in
partial conflict with his desire to honour what he considered his
country's commitment to France; he wished to do nothing to
precipitate war, both because he disliked war and because the commitment was largely a personal one. He tried to mediate. The
immediate cause of German action was the decision of the German
Emperor and his Chancellor, Bethmann Hollweg, on 5/6 July, that
they could bring off a great diplomatic coup, and ensure the success
of Austria's policy towards Serbia, without a general war; and they

had only themselves to blame for a gamble that failed.[1] Nevertheless, they could say that the British were the most elusive and reserved of all the early participants. For years the cabinet had followed almost blindly Grey's lead in foreign affairs. Grey now waited scrupulously for the cabinet to lead him.

The German invasion of Belgium swept the country into war before the voice of pacifism or calculations of expediency could provide an alternative; the cabinet made its decision twenty-four hours ahead of public opinion. John Morley, who had no sense of a German menace, had asked his colleagues whether they liked the prospect of a Europe dominated by Russia, with Cossacks as 'victorious fellow-champions for Freedom, Justice, Equality of man (especially Jew man), and respect for treaties (in Persia for instance)'.[2] Obviously they did not, but they liked the prospect of domination by Germany even less. When the decisive meeting of the cabinet took place at 11 a.m. on 3 August, the opposition had sunk to two. The Conservative leaders had no doubt about the need to resist Germany, and Bonar Law gave Asquith a promise of 'unhesitating support' on 2 August, but the Labour party showed at first, and in a more extreme form, the same divisions as the Liberals. Public demonstrations culminated in the Trafalgar Square meeting of 2 August, with the demand that the British government should work only for peace. Big industrialists and financiers were also reported to be solidly opposed to intervention. Men of light and leading in the City, cotton men, steel and coal men in the North, as Lloyd George told the cabinet on 29 July, 'were all *aghast* at the bare idea of our plunging into the European conflict'.[3]

Yet by Monday, the 3rd, the change was complete. The City, like the country, had been 'set on fire' by the threat to Belgium. But what after Belgium? Grey, in his unforced, unemotional, and completely convincing speech to the Commons on the 3rd reminded them of the basic dilemma that faced the country: with her imperial

[1] L. Albertini, *The Origins of the War of 1914* (1953), vol. II, pp. 137–64. On Germany's longer term plans, see Fritz Fischer, *Griff nach der Weltmacht* (Düsseldorf, 1962), pp. 56–99, and the critical comments of Gerhard Ritter, 'Eine neue Kriegsschuldthese' in *Historische Zeitung*, vol. 194 (iii), pp. 646–68; I. Geiss, *Julikrise und Kriegsausbruch 1914* (1963), vol. I, pp. 19–47.

[2] John Viscount Morley, *Memorandum on Resignation August 1914* (1928), pp. 3–6, 31. The future Lord Beveridge (*Power and Influence*, 1953, p. 120), wrote in a private letter on 3 August: 'it's all against the grain with us to go against Germans with French and Russians'.

[3] Morley, p. 5; Albertini, vol. III, p. 370; LlGM (Lloyd George, *War Memoirs*), vol. I, p. 65.

commitments, could she afford to throw herself into a European war? On the other hand, could she afford not to do so?

> ... with our enormous responsibilities in India and other parts of the Empire, or countries in British occupation, with all the unknown factors, we must take very carefully into consideration the use which we make of sending an Expeditionary Force out of the country ...

Nevertheless,

> the Belgian Treaty obligations, the possible position in the Mediterranean, with damage to British interests, and what may happen to France from our failure to support France—if we were to say that all these things mattered nothing and to say we would stand aside, we should, I believe, sacrifice our respect and good name and reputation before the world and should not escape the most serious and grave economic consequences ...[1]

Ramsay MacDonald, who immediately followed, said that Grey was wrong, the government he represented was wrong, and it had not been proved that the country was in danger. But on the following day the Labour party decided to support the government, and in the country's first statement of war aims, on 6 August, Asquith was content to give the Commons only two: to fulfil a solemn international obligation (to Belgium), and to vindicate the principle that 'small nationalities were not crushed, in defiance of international good faith'. Security, the most urgent of war aims, he perhaps thought it needless to mention.

Grey's alternatives posed, although in an incomplete form, the problem that was to underlie British strategical and political planning throughout the war. Great Britain was a world power which had hitherto maintained a far-flung empire and equally far-flung lines of trade by naval supremacy, by keeping her European commitments to a minimum, by great mobility in the employment of her limited armed forces throughout the world, and by a high level of export–import trade as the source of her financial predominance. The highest merit of her statesmen had consisted in the shrewdness and caution whereby simultaneous challenges to her interests had been avoided and there had always been a margin of strength—whether in men, money, or diplomatic friendship—to meet any individual threat that might arise. How far should the

---

[1] P.D., 5 Ser. HC., vol. 45, 3 August 1914, cols. 1824-25.

slowly accumulated wealth and resources of the Empire now be thrown into a brief European holocaust?

This was not a question which could be fully answered, or even very clearly formulated, in August 1914. The war, or at any rate its first phase, had been visualized as one of limited military commitments. In a prolonged war a greater contribution would have to be made, but it might still be best to limit the British contribution to a relatively small continental army, with an effective use of her diversified resources elsewhere. Blockade, diversionary expeditions, financial aid and armament supplies resulting from her vast industrial strength, were contributions for which she was clearly well suited. The choice of objectives soon raised difficulties. Should young skilled engineers be sent to the trenches or to the munitions factories? Could the war be financed without a flourishing export trade to keep up supplies of foreign exchange? Could the export industries be kept going if there were drastic cuts in labour supply? 'Business as usual' might be the highest patriotism. On the other hand Great Britain was the one belligerent with ample reserves of fresh manpower, and it might be best, or at any rate politically essential, for her to make the raising of great armies her first objective. In fact, with the 1916 Conscription Act she made a fatal attempt to achieve dominance in both fields; this was, in the view of one American historian, the beginning of the end of her long preponderance as a world power.[1]

In practice these issues were largely solved in the tide of events without any comprehensive decision ever being made in the sphere either of grand strategy or even of diplomacy. The concentration of the German effort in France made the French battlefield always the main preoccupation, and the great armies were raised; but almost to the end of the war the problem of their use remained, the munitions industry absorbed manpower, and the case for a bolder use of peripheral attack was being pressed. In diplomacy the aim was defensive, and it was far more the need to keep in step with other powers than the desire for fresh power or territory which led to the staking out of claims in the Middle East or elsewhere. One result was the appearance of temperamental differences between the 'push-and-go' and the 'wait-and-see' elements among the nation's leaders. Asquith's tact and skill, his massive intellect and imper-

[1] Hanson W. Baldwin, *World War I* (1963), p. 73.

turbability combined with long established prestige, fitted him ideally to guide the country through the first period of the war. But in the short breathless phase of incredible achievement to which a country dedicates itself in a great war the leader must show that he has the ruthless and reckless will to win at any cost. It gradually became evident that Asquith would never learn to strike these dynamic and often delusive notes. Nevertheless, his elimination in 1916 did not remove the basic dilemma.[1]

In the opening months of the war, while the government struggled with its unaccustomed tasks, he was indispensable. His relations with Grey, 'of that distant but friendly kind which an ocean might have with a contiguous mountain peak',[2] and the fact that decision was forced on the Liberal leaders as the administration in office, meant the automatic support of the Liberal party for the war; this was no doubt a fortunate circumstance, for in opposition many of the waverers might have committed themselves to a pacifist line. The Labour party's support of the government was also facilitated by the earlier cooperation with the Liberals, although it was not unqualified; it involved Ramsay MacDonald's resignation from the leadership and the election of Arthur Henderson, together with an evident desire in its early pronouncements to prove that the government was not without blame for the war. The Unionists displayed none of the Liberal or Labour party hesitations. They were pleased by Lord Kitchener's appointment as Secretary of State for War, for at this stage they fully accepted the Kitchener legend and felt sure that if the great imperialist could have brought his remote eyes to view the English political scene he would have been a Tory.[3] They were, nevertheless, alarmed at first by the cabinet's 'pitiable vacillation', including its apparent reluctance on 4 August to despatch the Expeditionary Force, and they were not ready for coalition. They were both alarmed and annoyed when the government interpreted the political truce as meaning that it should put the Irish Home Rule Bill on the statute book, while suspending its operation for the war period. But this wise move ensured the support of the cause by the Irish Nationalist party; when the bill passed on 19 September Will Crooks, the Labour member for

---

[1] J. A. Spender and C. Asquith, *Life of Lord Asquith and Oxford* (1932), chaps. 28–30.
[2] Lord Beaverbrook, *Politicians and the War, 1914–1916* (1928), p. 246.
[3] Some of the Liberals were less enthusiastic. Margot Asquith thought him 'a natural cad', a great poster rather than a great man. Roy Jenkins, *Asquith* (1964), p. 343. Cf. P. Magnus, *Kitchener* (1958), p. 232, and chap. 14 generally.

Woolwich, led the singing of 'God Save the King', and called for three cheers, exclaiming 'God Save Ireland'; Mr. Redmond responded by crying 'God Save England'.[1]

While the country awaited the first news of the fighting the cabinet, having survived its initial hesitations, quickly won confidence with some drastic emergency legislation. This was made easy by the meticulous planning directed by Major Maurice Hankey and the Committee of Imperial Defence. On 6 August the Commons voted an addition to the army of 500,000 men, and on the 8th a credit of £100 million for war purposes. A State Insurance Scheme for shipping provided against risks at sea and their threat to wartime trade. A press bureau was set up under F. E. Smith. The government also took powers to control the railways, shipping, houses, and transport. The first edition of D.O.R.A., the Defence of the Realm Act, was carried on the 8th, and gave the government general powers to regulate the conduct of affairs under war conditions.

'Money,' as Lloyd George wrote in after years, 'was a frightened and trembling thing'; not because the masters of money were timid or pacifist as men but because the delicate financial cobweb of the world's greatest credit centre seemed likely to be 'torn into shreds by the rude hand of war'. However, as J. M. Keynes remarked later, the financial crisis of 1914 was due, 'not to our being unable to pay what we owed abroad, but to foreigners being unable to pay us'. It was not sterling that crashed at that time, but the dollar. On 1 August the Bank of England was authorized to exceed the prescribed fiduciary issue of notes; the bank rate was raised to 10 per cent; and a moratorium of one month was granted to accepting houses. But after the holidays the risk was taken of reducing the bank rate to 6 per cent; government notes of the value of £1 and 10s. were printed with great speed; the Bank Act was suspended. When the banks reopened on the 7th business was resumed smoothly, without domestic panic. The government's subsequent decision to stand behind the accepting houses did much to reestablish the normal machinery for financing international trade; still uneasy about their position, they were unwilling without it to engage in

---

[1] This astonishing scene is recorded in *The Annual Register, 1914*, pp. 208-9. At an inter-party recruiting rally on 11 September at the London Opera House Crooks had said that 'he would rather see every living soul blotted off the face of the earth than see the Kaiser supreme anywhere' (p. 203).

fresh business. This was a successful beginning to an unprecedented extension of Treasury activity during the war.[1]

The Army was ready, superbly ready indeed for a rather different war and much more limited tasks than those that were soon to engulf it. Haldane's reorganization (greatly assisted at the War Office by General Haig) had prepared, for a continental war on the French left flank, an expeditionary force of about 160,000 men, a professional army with a higher standard of individual training and more diversified fighting experience than that of any of its continental neighbours. But it is now evident that its strategical thinking had been stultified by its subordinate rôle, its lack of precise knowledge of the French grand strategy (including the controversial Plan XVII), and the assumption that its most likely function would be to turn the scale in a short but vital campaign.

The expeditionary force, commanded by Sir John French, and consisting of one cavalry and four infantry divisions, appears to have had its first skirmish with the advancing German army on 22 August. Along with the ten divisions of the French Fifth Army it was expected to surge forward and envelop the German right flank, which however soon had thirty-four divisions and was preparing to carry out a vastly more successful envelopment of the Allies. The German sweep through Belgium was greatly facilitated by the *élan* of the main French forces in throwing themselves into battle in the opposite direction. While Joffre with four French armies was fighting the 'battle of the frontiers' in Lorraine and Luxembourg from 14 to 25 August and suffering 300,000 casualties, the Belgian frontier was sketchily defended. The British forces had advanced as far as Mons on the 22nd and then heard that General Lanzerac on their right had already been repulsed at Charleroi. The battle of Mons next day was a delaying action which had to be followed by retreat when the French, without notifying their ally, fell back to avoid envelopment by fresh German forces from the east.[2]

In this rather hit-or-miss fashion the main forces of both sides

---

[1] L1GM., vol. I, pp. 74, 100–110; R. F. Harrod, *The Life of John Maynard Keynes* (1951), p. 205.

[2] The story of the opening clash is told graphically in Barbara W. Tuchman, *August 1914* (1964). Good short histories of the war are numerous; they include Liddell Hart, *A History of the World War, 1914–1918* (1934); C. R. M. F. Cruttwell, *A History of the Great War, 1914–1918* (1934); J. E. Edmonds, *Short History of World War I* (1951); Cyril Falls, *The First World War* (1960); Hanson Baldwin, *World War I* (1963).

came clumsily to grips. For the British the first great phase of the fighting ran from Mons on 23 August to the end of the first battle of Ypres on 11 November; when the fighting died down in cold and filthy November weather the British sectors of the line were still grimly held by the weary and dogged remnants of the old army, but over 50,000 had fallen. French reinforcements had shared the defence, and General Foch, by his flattery, self-confidence, and inexhaustible good will, had captivated the touchy British commander and established a happier collaboration between the two forces.

In other spheres the lines still held at the end of 1914, after some dreadful setbacks. Churchill's somewhat embarrassing presence did not prevent the fall of Antwerp on 9 October, but the Belgian army retained a foothold on native soil. The Russian advance in East Prussia met with disaster and vast losses at Tannenberg at the end of August, but the best Russian generals were in the south, where the Austrians were everywhere defeated. Serbia survived the first Austrian attack, and smashed the second in a great victory early in December.

It could be said that at sea the Royal Navy had established its expected mastery. Yet the great battleships and battle cruisers were dangerously vulnerable to mine, submarine, and torpedo, and even, as experience was to prove, to superior enemy gunnery. One really disastrous great battle might destroy the Allied preponderance: perhaps there was truth (although the French could never see it) in Churchill's comment that the Commander-in-Chief was the one man on either side who could lose the war in an afternoon.[1] As it happened the Germans preferred the advantages, which were partly political and partly psychological, of a fleet in being to a gamble which might send it, and not the British, to the bottom. There was to be no major clash of surface vessels apart from Jutland (1916), which left the British still ruling the North Sea, and before the end of 1914 nearly all the German warships that had found themselves outside European waters on the outbreak of war were disposed of. The *Emden*, most deadly and chivalrous of commerce raiders, was destroyed by the Australian cruiser *Sydney* on 9 November, and Count von Spee's powerful squadron, after sinking two ships of Admiral Cradock's weaker squadron on 1 November, was itself destroyed by Sir Doveton Sturdee's battle cruisers on 8 December

[1] W. S. Churchill, *The World Crisis* (1931), p. 680.

off the Falkland Islands. But the menace of mine and submarine was constant and unsolved.

There was no great success in the diplomatic field to balance the generally depressing news from the fighting fronts. In their immediate aim in the Near East the three *entente* powers were agreed. Germany's hold on Turkey, or rather on the triumvirate of Young Turks who dominated the government (Enver, Djemal, and Talaat Pashas) had been consolidated by virtual control of the Turkish army and the position to offer exciting territorial bribes, which the *entente* could not match. Secret Turco-German agreements were signed on 2 and 6 August. The *entente* diplomatists knew enough to realize that the best they could hope for would be Turkish neutrality, and their aim was to maintain this as long as possible. Russia had no desire to precipitate a scramble for Constantinople in which she might be anticipated by Greece or Bulgaria while she was fighting in central Europe, Britain had no desire to alienate Muslim feeling in the Empire by picking a quarrel with Turkey (if the Turks took the offensive it would look a little less bad), and France was opposed to any diversion of forces from the European battlefield.

While Germany still hoped for a quick victory it was sufficient for her that Turkey's ambiguous neutrality severed the flow of supplies between Russia and her allies. The Turks hesitated, belatedly conscious of their bargaining position and of the fact that they could not now limit their fighting to Russia. Two Turkish battleships, built in English shipyards, were seized on the outbreak of war, and the German ships, the *Goeben* and *Breslau*, were allowed to slip into the Dardanelles by the British and French naval forces which were busy in the western Mediterranean protecting the transport of French troops from Africa. At the end of October the triumvirate forced war on their reluctant colleagues by arranging for the bombardment of Russian ports and the invasion of Egypt. The *entente* ambassadors asked for their passports on 1 November.[1]

Perhaps no more could have been done, but somehow several chances of swaying the issue in Constantinople seemed to have been missed. The need to open the Straits became at once a major objective, and meanwhile the neutral Balkan states watched closely the

---

[1] The factors, including the complicated economic issues involved in the *entente* decisions, are admirably analysed by W. W. Gottlieb, *Studies in Secret Diplomacy During the First World War* (1957), although the suggestion that the western powers encouraged Turkish belligerency in order to goad Russia to continue fighting seems fanciful: pp. 47–8, and chaps. 2, 3, generally.

swaying prospects of their own aggrandizement. So too did the strongest of the Mediterranean neutrals, Italy, whose bargaining with both sides was linked with extensive and confused secret negotiations by the *entente* diplomats about the whole future of the Balkans and Middle East.

The considerations, perhaps ill-judged, which had inhibited a forceful line with Turkey also hampered the use of blockade. When war began the ruling ideas on this subject were those of the Declaration of London of 1909, a strange document to which the British delegates had subscribed as a result of some mistaken notions as to the nature of a future war.[1] The House of Lords, which in those days threw its weight about, threw out the bill ratifying the Declaration in 1911, and as a result neither Britain nor any other leading power had ratified the Declaration by August 1914. The obvious danger that Germany would start to bolster her war economy by drawing supplies through Holland and the adjacent neutral countries led to the Order in Council of 20 August 1914 which accepted the proposals of the Declaration of London only with certain exceptions. The lists of contraband goods were extended in stages, with much uneasiness as to the American attitude. Grey felt that he must move cautiously; among other things, Kitchener had secured an undertaking from the Bethlehem steel company to sell its entire output of arms and munitions to the British. The State Department, while asserting the alleged legal trading rights of neutrals in a series of notes between 1914 and 1917, was willing to examine practical solutions.

But cotton had to be left free to pass through the Allied blockade to Bremen until March 1915. Germany also bought it extensively in adjacent neutral countries, and exports of cotton even from Great Britain to these countries increased to about fifteen times the normal figure. Yet cotton was an essential item in the manufacture of explosives; about four-tenths of a pound of cotton was used to manufacture a pound of cordite. There had, however, been a record cotton crop in the States after two years of slump, and to stop the exports to Germany would have meant ruin throughout the South. The United States had declared its neutrality, and the issues of the war were genuinely remote to the majority of Americans. But the remainder included large groups that were sympathetic to the

[1] The best study is the forthcoming work by M. R. Pitt, *Maritime Rights and Economic Warfare: British Policy, 1854-1914.*

Allied cause, and smaller but determined groups that were aggressively neutralist or actively anti-British (through pro-German, Irish-American, or other connexions). The policy of pro-German elements was to cry for the freedom of the seas, and failing that an embargo on exports to all belligerents. In March 1915, when it was at last decided to declare cotton contraband, arrangements were made for Great Britain to buy the American surplus.[1]

Germany meanwhile had announced on 4 February 1915 its intention to sink merchantmen by submarine in waters surrounding the British Isles without warning and without guaranteeing the immunity of neutrals. As a reprisal an Order in Council of 11 March 1915 provided for the seizure of all German exports. The most spectacular incident in the German submarine campaign was the sinking of the *Lusitania* on 7 May 1915, with the loss of 1,100 lives, including 114 Americans. Each side justified its actions by reference to the mounting severity of the other, but the Allied practices remained more humane—at least they did not destroy ships or lives.

2. KITCHENER, MYTH AND SCAPEGOAT

In three fields, each vitally dependent on Kitchener's judgment and initiative, the government had now to consider urgently a fundamental change of approach, involving a departure from the assumption of early victory and a quick return to normality. These were the conduct of war in France, munitions supply, and war aims involving a major reconstruction of European and Near Eastern boundaries. Everyone looked to Kitchener, and he could look only to the future, which was not immediately encouraging. The original expeditionary force had failed to turn the balance in France, and had been largely destroyed; by the end of 1914 there were some 270,000 British troops on the western front, but there had been nearly 100,000 casualties. He had acted decisively on the outbreak of war in calling for a large enlistment of 500,000 volunteers for the regular army; but these would take time to train and he did not anticipate that the full weight of the British effort could be thrown in until perhaps the middle of 1916. To the new regulars, however, could be added the Territorial Army of some 250,000 men, who should undoubtedly have been used earlier. They were, however,

[1] W. E. Arnold-Forster, *The Economic Blockade, 1914–1919*, chap. 8 (the Admiralty's official history, printed in 1920, and made available to the public in 1963). A good recent American study, embodying new material, is by Marion C. Siney, *The Allied Blockade of Germany* (Ann Arbor, 1957).

being used more extensively in the trenches after the beginning of 1915, and twenty-one divisions of 'Kitchener's Army' had gone overseas by the end of the year. Already by the spring of 1915 this ardent, heroic young force, 'the most splendid material that ever went out to fight from this country',[1] had been thrown into battle.

But the cabinet, the country, and the French, still deluded in some degree by belief in the possibility of a speedy victory, looked for more dramatic action than the War Office could provide. Although Sir John French may not have shared Joffre's belief that victory might come from one more great effort he obviously had exaggerated hopes of the limited operations into which he proceeded to hurl his inadequate forces. In February and March 1915 Joffre launched two vast, expensive, and unsuccessful preliminary attacks in Champagne. This prevented French cooperation with what had been intended as a combined operation in Artois, in the north. The British attacked alone at Neuve Chapelle (10–13 March), captured the village, lost 13,000 men, and made no real progress. This was the prelude to the main 1915 fighting, which continued in Artois and Champagne with heavy losses and virtually no progress until it died down in the following October. In the process the British bore the shock of the first gas attack at Ypres on 22 April. In May, jointly with the French, they attacked north and south of Neuve Chapelle, but again with minute gains and severe casualties.

The lesson drawn from these operations was the need for increased fire power. The solution seemed to be to blow the enemy's wire and trenches to smithereens in order to prepare the way for the infantry to advance without excessive loss. Enormous casualties and invariable failure to break through did not prevent repetitions of these methods in 1915, 1916, and 1917, while the trench defence system, with deeper and stronger dug-outs, wire, pill-boxes, and concentrated machine-gun fire, repeatedly proved its ability to seal off breaches in the line and annihilate attackers. The shell crisis of the early months of 1915, which did not become public knowledge until May, arose from the first cries of the British Command for more fire power.

The handling of industry was one of the linked problems which were diminishing the government's reputation and straining its internal loyalties in the first winter of the war. Kitchener still combined at this stage what were soon to become the three separate

[1] Cruttwell, p. 138.

functions of civilian war minister (spokesman of the War Office in Parliament and the cabinet), Minister of Munitions, and director of military strategy. Under him General von Donop, Master General of Ordnance, believed sincerely that the necessary high skill and experience needed for the manufacture of guns, rifles, and shells could not be improvized, but it seems that he and Kitchener were thoroughly aware of the mounting demands of the western front and did everything possible to meet it within these rigid limits. Kitchener in any case could have argued that it was Britain's prewar government which had failed to provide a modern armaments industry, it was Joffre and the wartime French government which made France the main theatre of Anglo-French land fighting, and it was the generals who failed in the field.[1] In the cabinet, however, Kitchener did not argue, and although he gave the Prime Minister his full confidence Asquith did not make any special effort to become his spokesman when the great man was maintaining his injudicious silences, perhaps through mere shyness, perhaps through sheer lack of words. Lord Esher believed that he failed not in prevision but in self-assertion.[2] In Asquith and Kitchener the busy, managing, competitive genius of Lloyd George had already found the principal obstacles to the pushful, ruthless direction of the war. Asquith himself, however, had come to recognize by March 1915 that the task of harnessing the industry and labour of the country to the great armament tasks was not one that could fairly be expected of professional soldiers.

The cabinet was alarmed by the report of shortages, but it also had to listen to the two most vociferous of the civilian strategists, Churchill and Lloyd George, who were both easterners. Both saw, although no more clearly than Kitchener himself, that it might be easier to turn the flanks of the central powers elsewhere than in France. Lloyd George favoured an attack on Austria through Dalmatia or Salonika, or an attack on Turkey by means of a landing in Syria which would cut the communications of the Turkish forces threatening Egypt; geographical difficulties in both cases would

[1] Magnus, pp. 284–8, 309–14.

[2] 'Asquith can be trusted.' Kitchener's comment, recorded in Robert Blake, *The Private Papers of Douglas Haig* (1953), p. 128 (cited as *Haig Papers*); *Journals and Letters of Reginald Viscount Esher* (1938), vol. IV, pp. 5, 11. Later F. E. Smith seems to have tried to act as Kitchener's spokesman, without much success. Haldane might have done so, but he was displeased by Kitchener's neglect of the Territorials. Sir F. Maurice, *Haldane, 1856–1915* (1937), vol. I, pp. 360–61; vol. II, pp. 114–19. Spender and Asquith, vol. II, pp. 131–33, 136–43.

have been formidable. The Dardanelles attack, of which Churchill was the powerful sponsor in the War Committee, seemed more practicable than the first and more profitable than the second.

There is no doubt that a conquest of Gallipoli and seizure of Constantinople with the consequent opening of the Straits would have profoundly altered the course of the war. It would have separated Turkey completely from her allies, opened up lines of supply with Russia, and decisively influenced the alignment of the Balkan states. Russia had asked for such a diversion on 2 January 1915, and Churchill had promised it on the 19th. On the 28th the government accepted the Admiralty plan for the forcing of the Dardanelles by ships alone. But it is difficult to see what could have been done without a land attack, and in any case the naval attack failed. By 22 March Admiral de Robeck had decided that the aid of all the available troops would be necessary to complete the task, and the troops were now, but already too late, being made available. An offer of three divisions by the Greek government at the beginning of March had been promptly vetoed by the Russian government. The landing of British forces, under Sir Ian Hamilton, did not begin until 25 April, by which date the Turkish troops under German command had already begun to strengthen their defensive dispositions. Even so, a swift advance from the beachhead at Gaba Tepe would probably have opened the road to Constantinople. The Turkish defences rallied just in time; and the chance did not recur.

These operations were closely linked with the intense negotiations which led to Italy's entry into the war, the first dramatic success for the Allies in the diplomatic field. But the bargaining was hard, and the Italian appetite healthy. On 12 March 1915 Britain and France announced their agreement to Russian annexation of Constantinople and the Straits, after reserving their claims in the Ottoman empire and elsewhere. By the end of March Asquith noted that the Italians were 'slightly contracting the orifice of their gullet', the result it appears of Russian firmness, combined with the fear that Italy would be left in the cold by a separate Russo-German peace. The secret treaty of London, signed by Grey and the ambassadors of Italy, France, and Russia on 28 April 1915, gave Italy Austro-Hungarian territory from the Trentino to Northern Dalmatia, together with control of Albanian foreign relations, the twelve Dodecanese islands, the province of Adalia in the event of a partition of Turkey, and a promise of colonial gains in Africa if France and Britain extended their own possessions at Germany's expense. Italy declared war on Austria on 23 May, but not on Germany until August 1916.[1] There is no doubt that the British ministers regarded the successive provisions for the destruction of the Mediterranean and Near Eastern *status quo* with secret dismay, and in spite of their reservation of British interests were not at all clear as to what these were. The result was reflected in the conflicting agreements with the Arabs made during the following twelve months.[2]

And meanwhile the government's difficulties on the home front were mounting; the unimpressive Allied record needed to be balanced by more dramatic evidence of furious, bold planning than Asquith and company seemed able to supply. The war on the other hand had had a dreadfully sobering effect on domestic politics: the hasty patching up of political and industrial truces had in it an element of expiation for the prewar excesses of strikes and suffragette tantrums and Irish violence.

For a time the Tories loyally desisted from the carefree excesses of uninhibited opposition; but this was a silent service which the rank and file of the party soon found highly irksome. As the winter went on the two leaders, Bonar Law and Lansdowne, were inundated with memoranda from their members on proposals for winning the war and demands for debates, and Tory M.P.s became a convenient repository for complaints from Sir John French's headquarters against the War Office and the government. Curzon complained of the 'exiguous memoranda of platitudes' with which Kitchener, his old antagonist, fobbed off the House of Lords and won respectful eulogies in the Liberal press. Discontented Tories could also point out that while they remained silent the government was not spared Liberal and Labour criticism.[3]

The Labour movement, in this still early stage of its rapid growth, had neither a unifying creed nor a tight, inclusive organization;

---

[1] Gottlieb, pp. 312–98; A. Salandra, *Italy and the Great War* (1932), pp. 214–345; Grey, vol. III, pp. 179–82.

[2] Complicated by the fact that the Foreign Office (through Sir Henry MacMahon) and the India Office were negotiating with different Arab potentates. By the Sykes-Picot agreement of 16 May 1916 France secured a zone of influence in Syria which had been promised by MacMahon to the Emir Hussein of the Hejaz. The British zones included Mesopotamia and, on the Syrian coast, Haifa and Acre. E. Monroe, *Britain's Moment in the Middle East, 1914–1956* (1963), pp. 29–34 and chap. 1 generally.

[3] Earl of Ronaldshay, *The Life of Lord Curzon* (1928), vol. III, pp. 122–5; Robert Blake, *The Unknown Prime Minister* (1955), pp. 231–3, 237–9.

and where its political strength was strongest it was least dogmatic. Groups and parties, diminishing in size as they receded towards Marxist extremism, were loosely linked and tended to drift apart in face of the tremendous issue of war; but because the federal link was an easy one this situation did not lead to irrevocable breaches. In the end, after the war, both the critics and the supporters of the war effort found that their diverse activities had, somehow or other, strengthened them in the public esteem.

After shedding Ramsay MacDonald and four of the other seven I.L.P. members on the outbreak of war, the Labour party followed the industrial truce (24 August) by agreeing with the other parties on the 29th to an electoral truce; it also agreed to place the party machine at the service of the recruiting campaign, and in a manifesto of 15 October came out in support of wholehearted participation in the national effort, laying the entire blame for the war on the German government. This was in part a reply to the pronouncements of the I.L.P., which blamed rulers, diplomats, and militarists for the war, proclaimed German Socialists their faithful friends, and declared against any aid to recruiting. The I.L.P., however, was by no means united; while the largest section, pacifist rather than revolutionary, continued to refuse support for the war, there were a few left-wing extremists who sought, implacably and ineffectually, the social revolution; J. R. Clynes and James Parker supported the Labour party's attitude, and a considerable section, including the three leaders—Keir Hardie, MacDonald, and Snowden—thought that the war must be fought, although they felt that the government had a grave measure of responsibility for it. In the two other affiliated groups, the leaders of the Fabian Society and the *New Statesman* were in general strong believers in the justice of the Allied cause and the badness of the German government; while in the small British Socialist party (B.S.P.), to all appearances doctrinaire, Marxist, and extremist, the founder, H. M. Hyndman, together with Robert Blatchford, Belfort Bax, Ben Tillett, and others soon showed themselves to be strongly pro-war, and ultimately in March 1916 withdrew with about one-fifth of the membership to form the National Socialist party. In spite of divisions, the leaders of all the groups generally managed to keep on speaking terms with one another; all agreed that the war must be followed by a just and moderate peace.

Far more effective and down to earth was the defence of working class interests. By November 1914 the typical wartime situation of a deficiency of workers in essential industries had made its appearance, as a result on the one hand of enlistment and on the other of the expansion of the armament industry, which was likely to grow and grow now that the hope of a speedy victory was fading. The situation was almost bound to lead to clashes with the government. The bargaining position of the workers would improve. The employers and the government could offer increased wages, but with the persistent and imperative demand for greater and greater output. This would raise both the prospect of 'dilution' and coercion and the prospect (in some quarters) of pushing extremist demands. If the patriotic inclinations of the Labour leaders led them to join or support the government in its demands they would be suspect; steering his melancholy course in qualified disagreement with almost everyone, Ramsay MacDonald might still emerge from the war as the least tainted of Labour politicians. All these complications had made their appearance by the summer of 1915.

It was, however, the unpromising opening of the 1915 fighting which supplied the real, although not the ostensible, cause of the formation of the first wartime coalition in May 1915. Two crises faced the government in the middle of the month—the resignation of Lord Fisher, the First Sea Lord, and *The Times* campaign over the shell shortage. Having with 'short-sighted extravagance'[1] fired away 100,000 rounds of the B.E.F.'s limited ammunition supplies on the gamble of Neuve Chapelle, Sir John French supplied Lloyd George, Opposition leaders, and Colonel Repington of *The Times* with harrowing details of the shell shortage at Festubert on 9 May, making it plain where he considered responsibility to lie. *The Times* published the story under headlines on 14 May, and during the next fortnight Northcliffe bombarded the government with demands for action. This campaign, which gave the public its first dramatic view of the munitions problem, certainly supplied a compelling additional reason for coalition, but the immediate cause was Fisher's resignation on the 15th. It was announced to his colleagues in the oddest way, but one thing was clear: the old sailor could no longer tolerate the passionate single-mindedness of the First Lord. He now discovered doubts about the Dardanelles expedition which he had not hitherto made clear, and the unique prominence of

---

[1] Cruttwell, p. 150; LlGM, vol. I, pp. 199–200.

Kitchener seemed a further depreciation of his own legitimate standing.[1]

When news of the resignation reached Bonar Law he decided, with the agreement of his principal Conservative supporters, that the opposition would now have to join the government or publicly attack it. Asquith at once agreed; the essential structure of a coalition government was settled with Bonar Law in fifteen minutes on 17 May 1915. The Tory decision to take office was an assertion of their own ability to do better than the Liberals and of their confidence in the experts.[2] Accordingly they backed Fisher against Churchill over the Dardanelles, and did not condemn Kitchener over the shell shortage. The issue, however, was not exactly a choice between Fisher and Churchill. The First Sea Lord seemed determined not to be persuaded to withdraw his resignation, and the First Lord was not acceptable to the Conservatives whether Fisher stayed or went. It is difficult to say how far the coolness which Bonar Law had long felt towards Churchill coloured his judgment; he undoubtedly viewed the Dardanelles expedition with misgiving, and did not know enough about its inner complications to lay the blame where it really belonged. It was indeed a great political and strategical conception, ruined not by the Admiralty which had done all it could, but by the War Office which carried out the concentration of troops too slowly and too ostentatiously to gain the dvantage of surprise.

So ended the last Liberal Government in British history, with no fuss—and few regrets? At any rate, Lloyd George seems to have had none, and found no place for them in his voluminous wartime memoirs. Now, as he moved adroitly between the leaders, he had the goodwill of all, and he was the chief beneficiary of the change: coalition opened a path to the leadership which would never have been available to him in a purely Liberal administration before Asquith's retirement. So far there was no sign of a rift between them. Haldane, like Churchill, who went to the Duchy of Lancaster, was a victim of Conservative hostility, and, in Lloyd George's opinion, of the willingness of Asquith and Grey to sacrifice friendship to expediency; but they saved McKenna, who was useful in keeping Bonar Law out of the Treasury. It was decided that Lloyd George should become the temporary head of a new Ministry of ⌐

---

[1] Blake, pp. 242–3; R. H. Bacon, *Lord Fisher* (1929), vol. II, pp. 235–78.
[2] P. Guinn, *British Strategy and Politics, 1914–1918* (1965), pp. 78–9.

Munitions, that he should vacate the Exchequer only during this tenure of office, and that McKenna should become Chancellor in the meantime.[1]

Thus Bonar Law was excluded from two offices for which he seemed a likely choice; he was offered and modestly accepted the Colonial Office, in spite of the dissatisfaction of his friends. Asquith may well have believed that this relatively lowly office was bound to have an adverse effect on the consolidation of Bonar Law's position as the undisputed leader of the Tories; and there seems no doubt that he was not greatly impressed by Bonar Law's abilities.[2] Balfour went to the Admiralty, but otherwise the key positions in the new government—Treasury, Foreign Office, Home Office, Munitions, and the War Office, as well as the prime ministership—were kept out of Tory hands. Labour was represented by Arthur Henderson, who found himself, somewhat uncomfortably, at the Board of Education.[3]

With this fresh start, with the shocks of the opening phase of the war behind them and the proportions of the task becoming clearer, the government had now to lay broader foundations of victory than before. A War Committee of three to five members, announced by Asquith on 2 November 1915, succeeded the earlier War Council and Dardanelles Committees, to discuss general questions of state and strategy referred to it by the cabinet. On 11 November Asquith named himself, Balfour, Lloyd George, Bonar Law, and McKenna; Kitchener (at the moment out of England) and Grey normally sat with it. Hankey says that Asquith had not intended to include Bonar Law at first. Hankey as secretary kept copies of 'Conclusions', which were circulated to all members of the cabinet, an innovation of great importance for the future.[4]

3. MUNITIONS AND CONSCRIPTION

Asquith kept the reins well in hand during 1915. Having sent Lloyd George to the new Ministry of Munitions, a belated but decisive step in war preparation, he gave him the vital support that he needed in this challenge to the War Office. The Order in Council

[1] Blake, pp. 248–57, 259–60; LlGM., vol. I, pp. 223–38; Sir F. Maurice, *Haldane*, vol. I, pp. 363–4. The William Jacks case at this moment made it impossible for Law to take either the Exchequer or Munitions. Roy Jenkins, *Asquith*, p. 371.

[2] Cf. Blake, p. 251.

[3] Two other Labour M.P.s joined the Ministry, William Brace as Under-Secretary for Foreign Affairs and G. H. Roberts as junior Lord of the Treasury.

[4] Lord Hankey, *The Supreme Command, 1914–1918* (1961), vol. II, pp. 439–43.

defining the minister's powers directed him to supply whatever
might be required by the Army Council or the Admiralty, and also
what might 'otherwise be found necessary', a vital additional clause
which gave the minister the opportunity to decide for himself
what was wanted. The War Office took this hardly, although
Kitchener's attitude to Lloyd George was one of Olympian courtesy
throughout. One side of the story is of the War Office's ill-judged
hesitancy and ostentatious reserve, which Lloyd George could
triumphantly parade as proof that the 'rigid and hardened mentality
of the War Office refused to bend or give to any facts that were not
stale with age'.[1] He succeeded in his task because he could outbid
them with vast programmes which he largely achieved, thereby
discrediting their technical pretensions, and he could justify his
programmes by quoting the demands of the army in France. For
the soldiers were divided among themselves, and the War Office
was too inarticulate to make much of its case, such as it was. And
yet it had not been standing still. Supplies to the B.E.F. were in
fact steadily increasing during the summer and autumn of 1915,
and this production was due entirely to War Office orders down to
October.

Apart from the official history, Lloyd George's own memoirs
give the best available account of the building of the new ministry.[2]
His immediate achievement lay in the ample supplies that reached
the battlefields after 1915; but the ultimate importance lay in his
demonstration of the vast possibilities of economic planning to
secure rapid national advantages, provided that certain conditions—
such as priority in the use of labour and materials, guaranteed by the
moral and legal authority of the state—were granted. Thus the
success of the Ministry of Munitions was to have results far beyond
the battlefields; the case of the peacetime planners was also being
won. It was also the fact that the economic purpose was destructive,
that some cannibalizing of less essential industries was necessary,
that a rapid inflation of wage and price levels at the national expense
was an indispensable condition, and that success was due to the
highly individualistic efforts of some ninety men of first-class
business experience. But if the lessons were in some ways ambiguous,

---

[1] LlGM., vol. II, p. 549.
[2] *Ibid.*, vol. I, chap. IX; vol. II, chap. XIX; the twelve-volume official *History of the
Ministry of Munitions* (H.M.S.O., 1920–4), can be consulted in various libraries, but
was not put on sale. Cf. also Christopher Addison, *Politics from Within* (1924), vol. I,
pp. 226–42; *Four and a Half Years* (1934), vol. I, pp. 78–112.

the industrial revolution was a real one. Labour's programme was carried a long way towards respectability by it.

Lloyd George's instinctive preference for the bolder alternatives was soon proved to be justified by the capacity of the country to supply, and of the armed forces to get rid of whatever they received. The heavy gun programme was increased and then increased again, in spite of the scepticism of the War Office. After Kitchener had committed himself on paper to the assertion that anything above four machine guns to a battalion could be counted a luxury, Lloyd George promptly fixed the alternate target at sixty-four per battalion. The output rose from 6,102 in 1915 to 33,507 in 1916, 79,746 in 1917, and 120,864 in 1918. The expansion involved a decision to place the main reliance on the Lewis gun, superior to rival models for its lightness and mobility. Other innovations, including the adoption of newer forms of high explosives and of an invaluable quick-firing light mortar, the Stokes gun, were claimed by Lloyd George; he also helped along the development of the tank, production of which was taken over from the Admiralty.

By the end of 1915, seventy-three emergency national factories for manufacture or repair of munitions had been set up, and the number had risen to 218 by the end of the war. In addition, the Ministry came to control mines, quarries, storage depots, and similar establishments, and to make use, under varying degrees of control, of a great number of private firms. Control of plant led in turn to the control of the supply of materials. In fact, the materials and the plant and the labour were available, but a vast effort of tact, hard work, and ingenuity was needed to dovetail everything together.

Organized labour played its part readily enough in these developments, although it demanded certain assurances. The problem of labour supply was now to turn as many trained engineering workers as possible from private to armaments industries, to bring in unskilled (and particularly female) labour where possible, to make everyone work as hard as possible, and (in Lloyd George's view), 'to ensure a more rigid control of drinking facilities'. Skilled workers, being increasingly in demand, could raise their terms, relax their efforts, oppose dilution, and waste their substance in riotous living. Some, it seemed, were already doing so. Apart from some deliberate slacking and playing-up of harassed employers there was a deliberate attempt in certain quarters to consolidate permanent gains for the unions, and a mixture of uneasiness and resentment at the mounting profits of the armament firms. The basis of a farreaching solution was laid in the 'Treasury Agreement' of 19 March 1915, signed by Lloyd George and Runciman on behalf of the government, and by Henderson and William Mosses[1] on behalf of the trade unions. A similar agreement was signed by representatives of the Amalgamated Society of Engineers a week later. These agreements provided for dilution, with the same wage scales for unskilled and semi-skilled labour as for skilled, arbitration in place of strikes in industrial disputes, and the limitation of manufacturers' profits. But it did not prove easy to find an agreed basis for the voluntary limitation of profits, and the Munitions of War Bill, which became law on 2 July, provided both for compulsory limitation and for government control of munitions work.[2] During the remainder of 1915 the great expansion continued, although not without further labour trouble. Dilution was still resisted in some quarters (such as the machine tools industry), and in the munitions works the shop stewards seemed to be deliberately fostering discontent, particularly on the Clyde. Lloyd George was the government's most effective spokesman.[3]

The leaders of labour played their part loyally in striving to honour the wartime industrial agreements. They showed less certainty towards conscription, but they shared these doubts with others. For more than two centuries British politics had condemned the control of large armed forces by the Crown. Furthermore, in wartime, military conscription might lead to industrial conscription. Conscription was thus the second great issue, in addition to the supply of munitions, which had to be faced and solved at this stage of the war. Paradoxically, the very success of the voluntary system prepared the way for its supersession: for it committed the country to the raising of great armies. And yet the first unregulated rush of volunteers, while it was depriving industry of key workers, would probably not be sufficient to meet the new army's ultimate needs. The recruiting campaign, elaborately organized and conducted with

---

[1] 1858–1943: General Secretary, Federation of Engineering and Shipbuilding Trades from 1890: Director of the Labour Enlistment Complaints Section of the Ministry of Munitions during the war.

[2] V. L. Allen, *Trade Unions and the Government* (1960), pp. 131–3; S. Pollard, *The Development of the British Economy* (1962), pp. 78–80.

[3] For the Clydesiders' case against the Munitions Act, and Lloyd George's speeches: R. K. Middlemas, *The Clydesiders* (1965); D. Kirkwood, *My Life of Revolt* (1935), pp. 81–120; S. J. Hurwitz, *State Intervention in Great Britain . . . 1914–1919* (New York, 1949), pp. 262–6.

expert publicity, continued to bring in volunteers, although the rate of enlistment slackened after the end of 1914. The new government's plans for a National Register, which would give a comprehensive picture of the national manpower resources, met with opposition from some Liberal and Labour M.P.s when it was laid before Parliament in July 1915. The cabinet had to recognize in August that the men were available for the army of seventy divisions which Kitchener considered indispensable, but that not more than half of these could be secured by voluntary recruitment.

Yet it was not until the following May, 1916, that universal military service was finally adopted, after a curious and sometimes disingenuous public debate, which had important effects on party alignment. In the government the Conservatives were more ready for it than the Liberals, although Lloyd George was by now a strong supporter. Kitchener was still struggling with doubts (mainly it would seem on the score of timing). Simon and, unexpectedly, Grey, were opposed on principle, McKenna because of the financial burden, and Runciman because of the drain on industry.[1] Arthur Henderson was a convert by the end of the year, but did not know whether he could carry the Labour party with him. In the meantime Lord Derby had been entrusted with a last attempt to make the voluntary system work. But the 'Derby scheme', in spite of strong publicity, was a failure. Of 2,179,231 unenlisted single men, 1,029,231 had not attested by the closing date in mid-December 1915.[2] Accordingly on 5 January 1916 Asquith introduced a Military Service Bill to compel the attestation of all unmarried men and widowers without dependants between the ages of eighteen and forty-one, and this half-measure, which spared the married men but not the voluntary principle, became law after much heart-searching in Liberal and Labour ranks.

It had indeed nearly driven Labour out of the coalition.[3] Opposition was varied: it certainly included fears that industrial conscription would follow the passing of the bill. There were also some unrealistic cries that it was unnecessary, and complaints that it was not accompanied by a corresponding conscription of wealth; and underlying the whole debate was the near-pacifist assumption that it was all right to take life if you volunteered to do so, but not if the

[1] Jenkins, pp. 387-9.
[2] Randolph S. Churchill, *Lord Derby, 'King of Lancashire'* (1959), pp. 184-208.
[3] C. F. Brand, *British Labour's Rise to Power* (1941), pp. 33-8.

government commanded you. A special national conference at Bristol, on 6 January, recommended opposition to the bill at all stages, but on the 12th Asquith gave the Labour leaders assurances against industrial compulsion, and as a result the Labour M.P.s were left free to speak and vote as they saw fit. Henderson supported the bill. MacDonald, Philip Snowden, and J. H. Thomas spoke against it, but it was carried by a decisive majority, and became law on 27 January 1916. In some rather contradictory voting the Bristol conference of the Labour party, meeting immediately afterwards, accepted the situation. The government had taken a risk, and won; forced to choose and to weigh the alternatives, the Labour and Liberal dissentients had opted for the most part for national unity and an intensified war effort. But there were substantial minorities, partially concealed in the block voting of the Bristol meeting, and it had still to be seen whether the final step to complete military conscription would be possible.

The case for this could be based on the depressing state of the war; but there were those who argued that it was from the leadership as well as from the rank and file that more was needed. Sir John French gave a final push to his tottering reputation by his handling of the reserves at Loos on 25 September 1915; Haig complained privately to Kitchener on the 29th. The fighting went on, increasingly to the Allies' disadvantage, and with the French forces deliberately holding back, until it petered out in the mud and cold of November. Asquith decided that French must be brought home, and after prompting from Lord Esher, the little field marshal resigned on 17 December 1915, and was appointed commander of the home forces. He was succeeded by Haig, who entered on his new responsibilities convinced that France had the manpower for only one more offensive, and that 'the war must be won by the Forces of the British Empire'.[1]

Confidence in Kitchener continued to wane. By the end of October 1915 both Bonar Law and Lloyd George were pressing for changes at the War Office.[2] To gain a little time Kitchener was sent to report on Gallipoli, although Sir Charles Monro, who had replaced Ian Hamilton, had already given an emphatic recommendation in favour of evacuation. This was carried out without loss at the end of the year. A report in the *Globe* that Kitchener had

[1] *Haig Papers*, pp. 105, 125; Esher, *Journals and Letters*, vol. III, pp. 281–93.
[2] LlGM, vol. I, pp. 499–526; Blake, pp. 269 ff.

resigned raised a storm which convinced Asquith that Kitchener must stay, but he returned to the War Office with sadly diminished powers, after an offer of resignation had been refused. The solution had been to appoint Sir William Robertson C.I.G.S., and to give him powers which virtually took the direction of the higher strategy of the war out of Kitchener's hands. With munition supply in the comprehensive grasp of Lloyd George, and strategy directed by Robertson, the Secretary of State for War could still for some months give the government the prestige of a great name: he could offer little else. Carson resigned on 12 October, and Churchill on 15 November; both, although for rather different reasons, deplored the government's decisions in the Aegean.[1]

Thus the year 1916 opened with better prospects for manpower and munitions, with Haig and Robertson planning victory in Artois, and with Asquith still firmly holding the first place at home. England was approaching her maximum effort; she was imposing on herself proportionate tasks. She virtually rejected United States proposals for a negotiated peace. Colonel House, Wilson's personal representative, reached agreement with Grey on 22 February 1916 on a programme according to which Alsace-Lorraine would be restored to France, a Polish state would be revived, and Germany would be compensated outside Europe. The document contained the astonishing statement that if Germany refused these terms the U.S.A. would leave the conference as a belligerent. But Wilson cautiously inserted the word 'probably' before this assertion, and although Lloyd George shared his belief in the possibility of a genuine reconciliation with Germany, Balfour doubted whether the Germans would ever keep a bargain. The proposal was killed for the time being by Grey's note of 12 May saying that a conference would be premature.[2] And yet as the year advanced another gloomy record of frustrated endeavour intensified the search for scapegoats. This was always a likely development under the uneasy partnerships of a coalition government, but the basic problems remained.

The two outstanding domestic issues of the first half of 1916— conscription and Ireland—ended with some decisive action and a weakening of the position of both party leaders. Under the existing arrangements, the continued demand for recruits could mean only the call-up of groups of the older attested married men. The Liberal

[1] P. Guinn, pp. 80-3.
[2] E. H. Buehrig, *Woodrow Wilson and the Balance of Power* (1955), pp. 218-26.

leaders for the most part were still hostile to universal conscription, and the Conservatives increasingly insistent that it should be enforced. Bonar Law had done his best to preserve cabinet unity, but he was shaken by the Army Council's note of 15 April 1916, which estimated that there would be a deficit of 179,000 men by 30 June. He warned Asquith on the 17th that his followers might now be expected to insist on full compulsion, and that it should be easier for Asquith to persuade the Liberals than for him to dissuade the Tories. After secret sessions on 25 and 26 April Walter Long brought in a Bill with the compromise proposals of the cabinet, but these were swept away by the rising impatience of the House and on 2 May Asquith announced his decision in favour of immediate compulsory military service for all able-bodied men between eighteen and forty-one. The decision was a triumph for the bolder spirits; opposition from the handful of followers of Sir John Simon and Ramsay MacDonald was negligible, and the Bill received the Royal Assent on 25 May. Lloyd George had supported full conscription throughout. Asquith once again had been forced to follow the lead of more single-minded colleagues.

4. Ireland: The Easter Rising

The Irish crisis of April 1916 was to shake Bonar Law's position as a party leader more than Asquith's, and it threatened for a time to destroy the coalition itself. It inevitably revived something of the tension which had existed between the parties as they faced the prospect of fighting in Ireland in the prewar months. This was deepened by older apprehensions of a stab-in-the-back delivered by a foreign enemy from Irish soil.

Southern Ireland it is true had responded satisfactorily enough to the war; for a time it had even been possible to hope that in spite of the Ulster deadlock the essential basis of a permanent settlement now existed. The land question had been solved over the years, the Department of Agriculture in Dublin was showing the farmer the benefits of competent administration, and the country was prosperous with the wartime demand for farm products.[1] The Nationalist party through its leader, John Redmond, had pledged its support of the war and its loyalty to the Allied cause. Irish

---

[1] Presumably for this reason the extremist demand for economic as well as political nationalism was underrated in Whitehall: cf. N. Mansergh, *The Irish Free State, Its Government and Politics* (1934), pp. 17–22.

volunteers had enlisted in large numbers. The Home Rule Bill was on the statuté book even although its operation was suspended. A short war, a quick victory, and the speedy implementation of the act might have achieved the orderly transition to self-government when emotions of loyalty and goodwill were at their height (although the Nationalists had not yet accepted the principle of partition). This prospect faded with the prolongation of the war.

Immediately after war began in August 1914 the Supreme Council of the Irish Republican Brotherhood decided that 'Ireland should make use of the opportunity of the European War to rise in insurrection against England'. This highly secret body, originally founded in the United States in 1858, had been reorganized at the end of the century, and was financed throughout its existence by the powerful Irish-American organization, the *Clan na Gael*. In the years before 1914 it remained small, uncompromising, pledged to the ultimate achievement of an independent Irish republic, and ready for a resort to physical force as soon as the opportunity arose. Along with it there had developed a number of other small nationalist groups; none made any great impression on the Ireland of the prewar years, with its growing prosperity and hopes of Home Rule through the Parliamentary party. The body known as Sinn Fein had been founded by Arthur Griffith in 1905; at this time he advocated a dual monarchy, with a policy of non-recognition of British institutions. The formation of the Ulster Volunteers had been followed not surprisingly by the inauguration of the Irish Volunteers in November 1913, under the ostensible leadership of Professor Eoin MacNeill, but with the secret instigation of the I.R.B. The tramway strike in Dublin led members of the Transport and General Workers' Union to form the 'Citizen Army', which drilled and retained its formation after the collapse of the strike early in 1914. Thus the I.R.B. had some fighting men at its command from the beginning of the war. But the vast majority of the Volunteers, who numbered perhaps 180,000 in August 1914, endorsed Redmond's policy towards the war and became known as the 'National Volunteers'; only some 10,000, who continued to be known as the 'Irish Volunteers', followed MacNeill in affirming loyalty 'to Ireland, and to Ireland alone'.[1]

In the circumstances an insurrection in wartime could be no

---

[1] I have followed Dorothy Macardle, *The Irish Republic* (1937), pp. 59-126, as my basic guide for these earlier developments.

more than a desperate political gesture, and it was the view of MacNeill and his associates that it should not be attempted unless the German army invaded Ireland, or the British government attempted to enforce conscription. Unknown to MacNeill the I.R.B. leaders were, however, determined to strike before the war was over. Even in defeat they could hope to galvanize the cause, establish the nation's separate identity, and secure admission to the peace conference. What this really meant was that they foresaw the possible extinction of their own extremism in a compromise settlement, which might very well be achieved in the mood of Anglo-Irish goodwill created by the war. This type of nationalist extremism (the British Empire was to see many more examples during the next forty years) assumed a unique understanding of the need and duties of the nation, and therefore the right to speak for it: the small numbers of those with the true vision merely increased their responsibility to the people, who seemed positively to enjoy their servitude.[1]

During the winter of 1914-15 republican journals openly advocated physical force, denounced recruiting, and vigorously propagated the views of the Brotherhood. When some of these papers were suppressed as seditious literature, others took their place. The Irish Volunteers marched about and made demonstrations while secretly manufacturing explosives. The O'Rahilly organized gun running. In America the *Clan na Gael* provided money and purchased arms. Its Executive drew up a petition asking for the Kaiser to include the freedom of Ireland among German war aims, and Sir Roger Casement took it to Berlin, where on 27 December 1914 he signed with Von Zimmermann a document promising German support and equipment for an Irish Brigade recruited from Irish prisoners of war. Only fifty-two responded to the invitation, but in March 1916, after the Clan had discovered the practical difficulties of smuggling arms into Ireland through the blockade, the German authorities promised to send 20,000 rifles, with machine guns, ammunition, and explosives between 20 and 23 April.

Meanwhile the majority in Southern Ireland, whether passively or warmly supporting the war, were subject to its normal dis-

---

[1] 'Not again, they believed, for many generations, would such an opportunity recur, nor could an organization such as theirs, if it disintegrated now without action, ever be recreated again. Unless a blow was struck soon, if only as a protest, the Irish people would sink beyond redemption into despair, or, worse, into contentment with servitude.' Macardle, p. 149.

contents. Speakers on Irish recruiting platforms, with their calls to duty and hints of conscription, were believed to have struck the wrong note. Kitchener had denied the Irish Division a flag with the Green Harp of Ireland, although the Ulster Division had been allowed one with the Red Hand of Ulster. Eight Unionists, including Bonar Law, Carson, and F. E. Smith, were included in the Coalition Government in May 1915. Were these happenings really significant? Augustine Birrell, the Chief Secretary, testified later to the shock created by the Coalition appointments, which seemed to many to mean the end of Home Rule. What was certainly important was that a natural and tragic selection had taken the actively loyal overseas. While 135,000 (or more) Irishmen volunteered to fight Germany during the war, only 2,000 fought against the British government in 1916, and the active rebels probably did not number much more than 15,000 at any time: but they were on the spot and uncompromising. No priest had declared for Sinn Fein up to the end of 1914. In 1915 some were said to be praying for a German victory.

It is generally agreed that the government handled the situation ineffectively, although it is not easy to see what it should have done. There were no serious attempts to stop street demonstrations, anti-war propaganda, and other extremist manifestations. There was even less attempt to silence the intransigent declarations of Ulster Unionists. The authorities knew what was going on. They preferred to rely on Redmond's influence and assurances, instead of risking the unpopularity of rigorous preventive measures. It was considered imperative that anti-British feeling should not be aroused in America.

James Connolly, the leader of the Citizen Army, was the only person outside the secret, oath-bound group of I.R.B. leaders to know the final plan. The rising was planned for Easter Monday, for on that day the Fairyhouse Races were expected to attract many of the officers of the Dublin garrison away from town. Three thousand volunteers were to seize strategical points in Dublin, while 13,000 in the provinces prevented the movement of British troops to the capital. The German arms, in a ship called the *Aud*, were to be landed in Tralee Bay, not earlier than the night of Easter Sunday (the 23rd). This was a change of plan which was not known to the German skipper, but was known to the British Admiralty; they took appropriate measures. Casement was to be landed on the Kerry coast by a German submarine.

The Easter rising as a military enterprise was a fiasco; but in defeat it achieved its political ends.[1] On the evening of Thursday, 20 April, the *Aud* was intercepted and blown up by her German crew; Casement was landed, and arrested soon afterwards; so too was Austin Stack, Commandant of the Kerry Brigade of Volunteers. MacNeill, discovering the plan belatedly, hesitated, and finally issued orders countermanding all 'parades, marches, or other movements' planned for Easter Sunday. On Sunday morning, the Revolutionary Council of the I.R.B., what with the *Aud* disaster and the Kerry arrests and MacNeill's countermand, were in a state of gloom; should the whole enterprise be called off? Had it now lost its already faint chance of military success? To the extremists, to turn back was unthinkable; better a simple protest (against what?) and death than retreat. Finally all agreed. The rising took place on Monday as planned, starting with the Proclamation of an Irish Republic by Padraic Pearse in Dublin on the steps of the Post Office.

But only some 1,500 volunteers turned out; and although the initial surprise was complete and buildings were seized, the government forces soon gained the upper hand. Artillery was brought up, there were bayonet charges, one by one the rebel strongpoints were captured, and at 3.45 p.m. on 29 April Pearse announced the unconditional surrender of his forces in both Dublin and the country districts. Outside Dublin indeed prompt action by the R.I.C. and the troops had already stifled any chance of successful action.

The failure had been too complete to serve as much of an advertisement for the Republican cause; and there were many in Ireland who, following Redmond, did not wish an Irish issue to conflict with the major war effort. Some of Redmond's Volunteers fought in Dublin on the government side. The general unpopularity of the rising was seen when the captured 'rebels' were booed through the streets of Dublin on their way to prison, often by women whose menfolk were serving in the trenches in France.[2] Nothing, however, did more to force the still uncommitted Irish opinion to identify itself with the extremists than the executions of leaders which General Sir John Maxwell now considered necessary. P. H. Pearse, T. MacDonagh, and T. J. Clarke were sentenced by field court martial and shot on 3 May; twelve other executions were announced

---

[1] A recent account is that of Max Caulfield, *The Easter Rebellion* (1964).
[2] Caulfield, pp. 354–60.

at intervals up to 12 May, the last two being those of Sean Mac-
Dermott and James Connolly. There were protests in the London
press and the House of Commons, and appeals by John Dillon and
John Redmond to Asquith; and although the Prime Minister
stopped the executions and hurried to Dublin himself the Nationalist cause had been given its martyrs.

The result was that an Irish settlement, which was really only
possible on the basis of partition, had once more to be examined in
conditions less favourable in some respects even than those immediately preceding the war. In July 1914 Bonar Law and Carson had
been prepared, after Lord Murray of Elibank's mediation, to
accept Home Rule subject to the exclusion by plebiscite of an area
in Northern Ireland, and although Redmond at this stage could still
not bring himself to agree to permanent partition he had reached
the point in the Buckingham Palace conference (21–24 July 1914)
of discussing the extent of the plebiscite area. Now in 1916 the
terms of the problem had changed, for one side had shed blood for
unity and independence, and the other was preoccupied with the
problems of security and survival in an international conflict. After
making what investigations he could in Dublin Asquith returned;
he called on Lloyd George to 'take up Ireland' and told the House
of Commons on 25 May that the machinery of government in Ireland had broken down and the time for a new departure had come.[1]

Lloyd George had not hitherto played a prominent part in Irish
discussions. Home Rule was a Gladstonian heritage whose logic and
necessity he had accepted but seemingly with no great warmth of
feeling for Irishmen or the Irish cause. He had 'a good deal of the
protestant' in him,[2] and it is to be remembered that the first flowering of the Welsh nationalist movement before 1895 had been the
product of a militant nonconformity which was careful to dissociate
itself from the cause of the Catholic Irish.[3] He had had doubts
before the war as to the expediency of a fight with the Lords over
Home Rule—he was all for a fight, but would have preferred victory
on a safer issue. Now after an outstanding success at the Ministry
of Munitions he was called on to achieve a miracle of reconciliation
which would bring together the extremists on both sides; and it

[1] Jenkins, pp. 395–9.
[2] Lucy Masterman, 'Recollections of David Lloyd George', *History Today*, vol.
IX(4), p. 274.
[3] K. O. Morgan, *Wales in British Politics* (Cardiff, 1963), pp. 68–70.

soon became clear that neither the Nationalist leaders nor the Die-Hard peers were susceptible to the charm and bustle of the Welsh wizard.

The essential point of Lloyd George's proposals, drafted in London and forwarded to Redmond and Carson on 29 May, was that Home Rule should be introduced at once, with the Six Counties remaining in the United Kingdom until after the war. All Irish M.P.s would continue to sit in the Imperial Parliament at Westminster, and after the war an Imperial conference would decide the future relationship between all the Empire countries. It was a statesmanlike attempt to move forward from the point of the Buckingham Palace conference, and at first the prospect seemed fair; Redmond and Carson both accepted the plan in principle. Carson in particular was impressed by the urgent need for a settlement in view of the delicate state of the political balance in the United States; the Irish-American vote might otherwise follow the Clan leaders in support of Germany and ensure the defeat of pro-Allied policies at the Presidential election in November. The first step was a round table conference attended by Carson, James Craig, Joseph Devlin (leader of the Ulster Catholics), John Dillon, T. P. O'Connor, and Redmond. There seemed genuine anxiety for agreement, although Lloyd George was to discover subsequently that one of the six, Dillon, was unconverted. After this the party leaders had to convince their followers. Redmond addressed meetings in Dublin on 10 June and Belfast on the 23rd; at the latter, which consisted of representatives of the Ulster Nationalists, he secured a majority in support of the plan after a threat that he, Dillon, and Devlin would otherwise resign the leadership. Carson also went to Belfast and after a similar struggle secured the acceptance of the proposals by his followers on 12 June.

The plan, however, was anything but watertight, and it was shipwrecked in storms of denunciation from the extremists on both sides. The discussions revealed a fundamental ambiguity: was the exclusion of Ulster to be temporary or permanent? Redmond's supporters believed, or professed to believe, that the proposals provided an instalment of Home Rule which left open the means of 'carrying on the fight for a united self-governing Ireland'. Carson's followers on the other hand authorized him to negotiate on the basis of the 'definite exclusion' of the Six Counties. Of course, the Nationalist extremists were out to wreck even a temporary exclusion;

protests were poured out by the press, public meetings, and individuals. Unionist extremists for their part wanted no Home Rule Parliament at all. The proposals finally died in the Commons debate in July. After it had been made clear that 'without a new bill' Ulster would remain excluded from Home Rule after the war, and that during the war General Maxwell's military régime would have to continue, Redmond withdrew his assent on 24 July. Lloyd George as a negotiator had weakened Redmond's difficult position by concessions to the Unionists; all to no avail, but everything had to be tried. The government now withdrew the proposals, which were only published in their entirety on 27 July.

5. ASQUITH PASSES

To understand the complexity of the struggle over the Irish situation we must remember that it coincided with the climax of parliamentary discontent over the conduct of the war, and that this discontent, even without the Irish issue, might have split the Conservative party. Bonar Law had already had serious differences with his Conservative colleagues over conscription. The fighting, as far as available news from the fronts was able to show, still hovered between stalemate and near disaster; as time went by, 1916 looked less and less like the anticipated year of victory. In France, the German assault on Verdun had begun on 21 February, and the French had to hold on with increasing desperation and enormous losses until the British offensive on the Somme relieved pressure after 1 July. In Mesopotamia the defence of the oilfields near the Persian Gulf, a necessary precaution, had led to an over-optimistic offensive which ended in the siege of General Townshend's small force by the reinforced Turks at Kut-el-Amara from 8 December 1915. He surrendered on 29 April 1916, before relief could reach him. The battle of Jutland, a confused engagement on 31 May between almost the full strength of the British Grand and the German High Seas Fleets, resulted in the Germans hurrying back to harbour after inflicting heavier damage than they received, and sounded like a near defeat in the colourless factual communiqué issued by Balfour on 2 June. And on 5 June Kitchener, sailing to Russia in the cruiser *Hampshire*, was drowned with all the crew when the ship struck a mine in heavy seas. The public depression might have been even greater if Britain's first great wartime personality had gone down with the second; for it was only the call to take charge of the Irish negotiations which had prevented Lloyd George from sailing with Kitchener to Russia.[1]

Shorn of most of his original responsibilities, Kitchener had still been a comfort to the public. Now he was dead. The central direction of the war rested for some time with Asquith, Robertson, and Haig. Asquith became acting Secretary of State for War, and he does not seem to have had any serious thought about occupying the position permanently; but he did not like the demand, which the press voiced loudly and some Tories echoed, for a freer hand for the soldiers, in short for a repetition of the Kitchener experiment. A strong civilian minister must therefore go to the War Office. This pointed to Lloyd George, and Asquith does not appear to have shared his wife's qualms as to his own fate if the ambitious man secured this key position. A prompt offer to Bonar Law might have been accepted. But Asquith delayed his decision; Bonar Law and Lloyd George put their heads together; and when the offer was made to Bonar Law he replied that he had promised not to stand in the way of Lloyd George's appointment. Lloyd George accordingly became Secretary of State for War on 6 July 1916.

But he took office under conditions which he found exasperating and even depressing. He who had done so much to whittle down Kitchener's authority now found himself in office on the same restricted terms. The delay in making the appointment had been due to Asquith's insistence on this point.[2] Even during his short period at the War Office his personal intervention produced one major achievement in France; by arranging for Sir Eric Geddes to undertake a thorough reorganization of communications behind the British lines he removed a transport chaos which had seriously worried Haig. But whereas Kitchener and Robertson had worked in harmony, no one, least of all Robertson, expected Lloyd George to play a self-effacing rôle. He took the worst view of the four months of carnage on the Somme, which seemed to him a dreadful waste of lives without any compensating advantage.

It is possible today to say that, unlike the 1915 fighting, the Somme made a serious contribution to the ultimate Allied victory.[3] The Allied losses were certainly enormous—over 400,000 British, and nearly half that number of French. The German losses were

---

[1] J. M. Keynes was also saved by a last-minute change of plan from sailing in the *Hampshire*: Harrod, p. 216.
[2] Jenkins, pp. 407–10; Blake, pp. 288–90.
[3] Cf. Cruttwell, pp. 275–9.

probably less, but not much less. When the heavily laden British troops made their deliberate advance in line and in bright sunlight on 1 July, they were dreadfully blasted by machine gun fire; there were 60,000 casualties by the evening. But in the later fighting the British tactics improved, and the Germans began to suffer heavily. The new German line was longer and more vulnerable than the old; Ludendorff wrote later that the army's morale was exhausted by the end of the year. The German divisions which had to be detached for the eastern front prevented a counter-offensive in the west, and placed an almost intolerable strain on those that had to hold on desperately there. The British threw their first tanks into battle on 15 September; there were too few for a decisive result, but the superiority of Allied resources, already emphasized by complete mastery in the air, was confirmed.

Nevertheless the accumulation of frustrations and near disasters proved fatal to Asquith, and finally brought Lloyd George to power as the head of a new coalition government on 6 December 1916. The one sure fact was a general conviction among politicians of Lloyd George's unique powers, not necessarily of judgment but of decision; it was evident that while several Tory leaders distrusted him as a colleague they distrusted Asquith even more as a leader. Labour made the same choice, after also balancing objections. Lloyd George's most useful ally in the Liberal ranks was Dr. Addison, whose soundings revealed that 136 Liberals would probably support him as premier. This in the end brought him Conservative support, and meanwhile the Northcliffe press hounded Asquith to his political grave with reiterated jeers of 'wait and see'.

Lloyd George does not appear at any stage to have asked in as many words for the premiership. He professed a willingness to act under Asquith or Bonar Law. What did gradually emerge was a demand for the chairmanship of a very small committee, which could include Asquith, to direct the war. It would replace the former War Council, and Asquith would retain the nominal leadership, while surrendering control of war policy. Asquith thought the plan a further proof of Lloyd George's personal ambition, which would soon be followed by a demand for yet more power. The decisive fact was that Bonar Law, who was not without his own doubts about Lloyd George, began in his rather diffident way to back the plan after 19 November, and was able after a fortnight of confused negotiation to secure the reluctant agreement of Lloyd

George's chief Tory critics, Chamberlain, Curzon, Cecil, and Long. There is some reason to believe that Asquith might have reconstructed his government with Conservative support and without Lloyd George, or with Lloyd George while retaining considerably more than a nominal leadership. But he simplified the issue by refusing either to serve under another leader, or to surrender the 'supreme and effective control of War policy'. He resigned; and Bonar Law advised the King to send for Lloyd George.[1]

The day of the cottage-bred man had dawned. Let us recognize, however, that all the basic British preparations for victory (except the convoy system) had been initiated before Asquith left office; during his administration the men (including Lloyd George) were appointed who made the preparations. But he lacked Lloyd George's unique capacity for dissociating himself from other people's failures, while absorbing their successes as a natural by-product of his own statesmanship. Lloyd George's assets also included individual achievements as a wartime minister (particularly at the Ministry of Munitions) which Asquith could not show, and a formidable appeal to the masses as a natural extremist—a man who needed watching in peacetime, but one who, in a bitter war, would see things through. Fantastic stories of the beguiling and impassioned oratory of the Welsh wizard helped many people, who had never heard him speak, to see him as a leader of fanatical ardour. Asquith seemed rational, rather tired, without much drive or plan. It would appear, however, that he was losing ground more rapidly with his colleagues than with the general public in the last months.

6. THE DECISIVE YEAR

The new government took office at a moment when the possibility of victory was being questioned. When Lloyd George had told an American correspondent on 28 September 1916 that he repudiated the idea of an immediate or compromise peace some of his Liberal colleagues had feared that such intransigence would lose the country President Wilson's support, and Lansdowne took the same

---

[1] The crisis, so briefly summarized here, is described at length by many of the participants. Lloyd George and others accept Lord Beaverbrook's pungent account in *Politicians and the War* (1932), vol. II, as authoritative for many of the vital Tory decisions. Cf. LlGM, vol. III, pp. 1030–44; Addison, *Politics from Within*, vol. I, pp. 264–76; Blake, pp. 328–39; Spender and Asquith, vol. II, chap. 49. The best and fullest account is now, however, that of Jenkins, *Asquith*, chaps. 26 and 27, based on the Asquith papers.

view in a memorandum circulated to the cabinet in mid-November. Although the Asquith government stoutly rejected both Lansdowne's doubts as to the possibility of victory and the expediency of any peace negotiations with Germany before final victory the case for pessimism was not removed.[1] Under the new arrangements Lloyd George kept himself free to devote his whole attention to the war, while Col. Hankey, as Secretary of the Cabinet, helped matters by systematic minuting and circulation of papers.[2]

Disaster seemed imminent in a number of fields. There was, to begin with, shipping. Germany's first submarine offensive had been drastically modified in May 1916 after a virtual ultimatum from President Wilson, and for a time German–American relations improved, while the British continued to irritate the President by the continuance of the blockade, their unresponsiveness to his peace proposals, and the stirring up of Irish–American intransigence. But the 'restricted' or cruiser warfare to which the German submarines were now limited was itself proving highly dangerous to Allied and neutral shipping. Admiral Jellicoe felt it necessary to warn the cabinet on 29 October 1916 that food and other shortages might drive the Allies out of the war by the early summer of 1917.

The German government thought the same. The total German submarine fleet was probably six times larger than it had been in 1915, and although this included numbers of mine-laying and even transport U-boats the general effectiveness of the force in range and hitting power was vastly greater. German hesitations were political. Should a decision be taken that would bring the United States into the war with vast (if unmobilized) resources? Bethmann Hollweg was too experienced and disillusioned an administrator to trust his experts completely; it was as much the pessimism of the army leaders, who could not promise victory on land, as the optimism of the navy which brought about his hesitating agreement, strengthened by the conviction, which the appointment of Lloyd George reinforced, that a compromise peace was impossible. It was a gamble with time. On 1 February 1917 Germany announced her intention to sink at sight any vessel found in the approaches to the

---

[1] A memorandum by Lord Buckmaster, written a few weeks after Asquith's fall and printed by R. F. V. Heuston, *Lives of the Lord Chancellors* (1964), attributed the final collapse of confidence in his leadership to his action in circulating the Lansdowne document to the cabinet. On the earlier peace plans generally: H. I. Nelson, *Land and Power* (1963), pp. 5–16; G. R. Crosby, *Disarmament and Peace in British Politics, 1914-1919* (Harvard, 1957), pp. 27–37.

[2] Hankey, vol. II, pp. 582–91.

British Isles, the French west coast, and the Mediterranean. Allied and neutral shipping losses rose to 866,610 tons in April. On 6 April the United States declared war.[1] This meant, among other immediate advantages, the endorsement and reinforcement of British blockade practices by the Washington authorities.[2]

The new government had also to face the prospect of a sudden deterioration of Allied strength from two other causes—the Russian revolution and finance. The view that the *entente* powers could secure victory through their greater overall resources depended statistically on Russia and Rumania remaining effectively in the war; Lloyd George had not been alone in his uneasiness on this score, but tells us that he had hitherto secured little support for urgent proposals (not necessarily practicable) for more effective coordination between east and west. He failed at the end of September 1916 to persuade Robertson to undertake the mission to Russia on which Kitchener had embarked at the time of his death; Robertson perhaps saw in the ambitions of his departmental chief sufficient reason why he should stay at home. But by the beginning of December the Rumanian armies had been overwhelmed before Bucarest; the last great Russian offensive had been halted in September by the transport chaos and shortage of munitions; at meetings in Paris and Chantilly in November the Allied soldiers and politicians had been too absorbed in plans for the next offensive in the west to give much thought to the ominous news from the east, but Lloyd George's proposal for an Allied conference in Russia to make final arrangements for the 1917 offensive was accepted. The three western allies finally sent a delegation to Russia in February 1917; Lord Milner, Sir Henry Wilson, Lord Revelstoke, and Sir Walter Layton represented England. At the Petrograd conference plans were laid at last for closer cooperation and the pooling of resources; but all too late. The revolution (the imminence of which was not obvious to any of the British delegates) began just over a week after the delegation returned home.

And it now appeared that to the collapse of Britain's food supplies and her Russian ally might be added the collapse of her finances. This was a crisis of external credit: her domestic finances had been handled, as soon as the proportions of the task were understood,

[1] Fritz Fischer, pp. 353–95; K. E. Birnbaum, *Peace Moves and U-Boat Warfare* (Stockholm, 1958) is the fullest account.
[2] T. A. Bailey, *The Policy of the United States towards the Neutrals 1917–1918* (Baltimore, 1942), pp. 41–63.

with sufficient strictness to meet the enormous demands of the war without placing an intolerable burden of debt on posterity. During McKenna's term as Chancellor in 1916 the principle had been established that the budget should cover both the normal expenditure outside war debts and the charges resulting from these debts. To the expediency of this course for ultimate national solvency there was added the more immediate necessity of keeping the trade unions in a good temper by ensuring that the masters should not profit unduly by the war. The resulting Excess Profits Duty thus served a double purpose. As far as possible, however, the traditional tax system was retained, the income tax rising from 1*s* 3*d* in 1914 to 3*s* in 1915, 5*s* in 1916, and 6*s* by the end of the war. Increases in indirect taxation and heavy borrowing, which had raised the National Debt from £654 million on the outbreak of war to £3,856 million by March 1917, had not so far caused the experts any serious qualms as to the ability of the country to master the domestic problem. There could be no complacency, however, about the problem of foreign credits.

The dollar crisis, so well publicized through the country after the Second World War, was a permanent element in British policy from the middle of the First. The problem was not so much that of securing United States financial assistance as of securing it without unduly onerous terms. One thing was clear, however, by the beginning of 1917: the British Treasury was no longer in a position to continue the enormous purchases of food, munitions, shipping, and other necessities of war which she had been making for her own use and that of her Allies. These had been paid for in gold, or by dollar earnings on British export trade, or by the sale of securities, or by private loans; but by this stage of the war the yield from these sources was no longer adequate. The Treasury, which had no confidence in the understanding of the new ministers, tried not to sound alarmist. Exchange policy, which was the immediate responsibility of a temporary civil servant of genius, John Maynard Keynes, was still based on the assumption that the Treasury must pay out 'free exchange' to the limit of the demand. The dollar rate was pegged by the Treasury in agreement with its New York agents, J. P. Morgan and Co., and there were enormous, although fortunately intermittent, runs on the dollar reserves, fluctuating according to war needs and even war news. There was a particularly severe run in December 1916, just after the new government took office.

The drain dried up just in time, but the Treasury continued with no more than a week or two's cash in hand until the following March.

The distrust that Lloyd George aroused among his professional advisers was mainly due to the fear that the country, deprived in its highest direction of the steadying intellectual power of Asquith, would take risky short cuts that might end in disaster. This led, for example, to the concealing by the Treasury officials of the true proportions of the dollar situation; they feared an impulsive decision to abandon the 'pegged' rate of exchange, with consequential disaster to British credit and chaos to business.[1] It led, also, to a steady if somewhat inarticulate resistance by the great soldiers and sailors to Lloyd George's strategical flashes. However, the unorthodox course, attractive perhaps merely because of its novelty, did sometimes prove to be startlingly right. He certainly hankered after swift brilliant strokes; but he had come to the conclusion that the Allies were sadly lacking in military genius and that attrition—a second best solution—was the key to victory. 'The issue of the War now depended on exhaustion. Whose strength would give out first? Morale, food, man-power, war material and transport—the belligerent group that failed first in one of these essential elements would lose the War.'[2]

The first stage was the reorganization of the government, in accordance with the plan which had caused the Liberal *Hari-kiri*. The new 'War Cabinet' had five members of whom four—Lloyd George, Curzon, Milner, and Arthur Henderson—were entirely free from departmental duties, and the fifth, Bonar Law, as Chancellor of the Exchequer and leader of the House, was not expected to attend regularly. Balfour went to the Foreign Office—in many ways a clever appointment; Carson, a rather less felicitous choice, succeeded him at the Admiralty. There were two Labour ministers in addition to Henderson, George Barnes (Pensions) and John Hodge (Labour). They were well balanced by big business. Lloyd George created some entirely new ministries, and brought in 'men of exceptional capacity who had never held any office in any Govern-

---

[1] Cf. Harrod, pp. 204-5, 218. ' "Well, Chalmers, what is the news?" said the Goat. "Splendid," Chalmers replied in his high quavering voice; "two days ago we had to pay out $20,000,000; the next day it was $10,000,000; and yesterday only $5,000,000." He did not add that a continuance at this rate for a week would clean us out completely.' Sir Robert Chalmers was Joint Secretary to the Treasury.

[2] LlGM, vol. III, p. 1084.

ment' to run these and some of the older ones, which they did with varying success. Even the universities supplied a man in the hour of crisis; H. A. L. Fisher, Vice-Chancellor of Sheffield University, became President of the Board of Education.

The new men were judged by results. Speedy success was expected of them. Sir Joseph Maclay, a great Glasgow shipowner, did well with shipbuilding; Lord Devonport, another eminent business man, was less successful with food. Neville Chamberlain was called from a busy career in the municipal and business life of the Midlands to become Director of National Service. Lloyd George was himself making eloquent appeals for volunteers for unspecified tasks, and did not realize perhaps the extent to which the departments which already controlled most of the labour supply would be unwilling to surrender their powers. It would thus seem that Chamberlain had from the start a rather hopeless task in his attempts to establish a redistribution of labour on strictly voluntary lines. Conscientious and hard-working, sensible and humourless, he revealed little aptitude for headway in the inspired jungle of Lloyd George's wartime administration. He resigned on 8 August 1917. Lord Rhondda and Auckland Geddes, who succeeded Devonport and Chamberlain, did better; they could learn some useful things from their predecessors' experience.[1]

But the ultimate purpose of all the new government's endeavours was victory in the field, and Lloyd George at once put forward plans which he had himself drawn up at the War Office in November 1916. His feeling for Allied cooperation had some recognition in the setting up of a joint standing committee of Allied prime ministers, which held its first meeting in Rome early in January 1917. Here he again urged his views on diversionary strategy, putting forward bold plans with all his formidable well-argued oratory. He now favoured an Italian offensive, with suitable artillery reinforcements. He did not, however, receive much help from the Italians; General Cadorna argued that tactical surprise, under modern conditions, was not practicable, and was unimpressed by Milner's retort that they were always told that they could not surprise the enemy, but the enemy always surprised them. The British and French generals were determined to stick to Joffre's plan for a great offensive in

---

[1] Cf. C. Addison, *Four and a Half Years*, vol. II, pp. 341–54; Francis Williams, *A Pattern of Rulers* (1965), pp. 141–4, and K. Feiling, *The Life of Neville Chamberlain* (1946), chap. 7; Lord Salter, *Memoirs of a Public Servant* (1961), pp. 91–3.

France. Joffre himself had now gone: he had resigned on 12 December 1916 when it had been made abundantly clear that France was tired of him. But the plan remained, with modifications by his successor, General Nivelle, which appeared to Lloyd George to bring at last the authentic touch of genius to the uninspired western strategy.

No one who contemplates the story of Haig's stubbornly direct methods and the appalling British losses that resulted from it during 1916 can fail to understand Nivelle's appeal to Lloyd George. Haig's mind, he wrote later with characteristic malice, only worked well, like a primitive tank, when the objective was limited.[1] Nivelle's programme, which reached Lloyd George on Christmas Day 1916, placed its main emphasis on an overwhelming attack by a powerful reserve army, a 'mass of manoeuvre' which would be hurled at an unexpected point in the German line (on the Aisne) after his main forces had been tied down by simultaneous British and French attacks in the Arras-Bapaume and Oise-Somme areas. Nivelle talked well in fluent English, which is more than one could say of Haig. The essential new feature of the plan which captivated Lloyd George was the element of surprise. The plan failed in execution rather than in conception. The Germans themselves effectively confused the situation by withdrawing on 5 February 1917 to the new, straighter 'Hindenburg' line of well-sited fortifications at the base of their vulnerable salient from Arras to Soissons. Haig did not accept the plan with any warmth, and he liked even less a proposal of the War Cabinet for his own subordination to Nivelle; after a good deal of argument, in which Robertson was an even more stubborn resister, the arrangement was limited to the period of the forthcoming battle.[2] But worse than delay was the fact that Nivelle's secret, his general strategy and even his detailed battle orders, had fallen into the German hands before the French attack was launched in mid-April.

The unexpected result of these developments was that the British were, after all, called on to bear the main burden of the fighting in France in 1917. Many things went wrong with Nivelle's attack, which did however in the end give the French command of most of the Chemin des Dames. Indeed, it compared not unfavourably in its

[1] LlGM, p. 1467. Haig also was impressed by Nivelle: *Haig's Papers*, pp. 190–7; cf. Duff Cooper, *Haig* (1936), vol. II, pp. 110–60.
[2] R. S. Churchill, pp. 245–88.

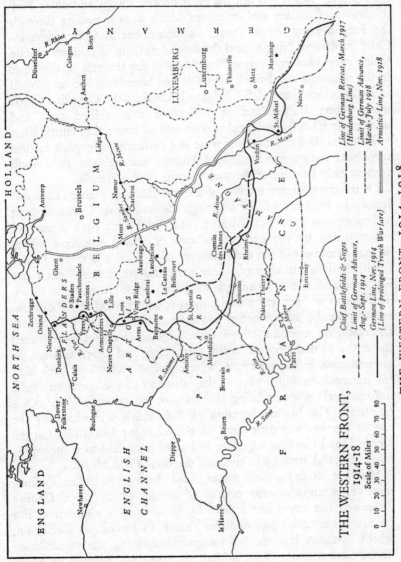

THE WESTERN FRONT, 1914-1918

results with Joffre's efforts in 1915 or with the British opening on the Somme.[1] But it was not the great breakthrough, and on 15 May the waves of mutiny and defeatism which were spreading through the French army led to Pétain's appointment as Commander-in-Chief in place of Nivelle, and the careful nursing of military morale which precluded any major French effort for the rest of the year. In the meantime the British offensive had been launched on 9 April at Arras under General Sir Edmund Allenby; the Canadian Corps seized Vimy Ridge, and at Ballecourt a combined tank and infantry attack achieved local success and an interesting anticipation of Cambrai. But the reserves were not sufficient to exploit tactical successes; losses mounted, and Haig continued the fight until 23 May only because of the parlous state of the French.

Of the three supreme crises of the war this was perhaps the most serious in British eyes, for although the immediate German threat in France was greater in August 1914 and March 1918 it was not accompanied by the general collapse of Allied resources which seemed imminent in the early summer of 1917. For at this point the British had to visualize not only the paralysis of the French and Russian armies, but imminent starvation by German submarines. The month of May was also the most serious period of Labour unrest during the war. America was now in the war, but long before she could do anything effective the submarine might have forced the Allies to make peace. In this crisis Haig and Lloyd George, so incompatible in temperament, were equal in resolution; each bent his tremendous will power to the salvation of the common cause, unfortunately without being able to give the other full confidence or credit. The higher direction of the British war effort for the rest of the war was dependent on this uneasy relationship. On the whole Lloyd George, a greater and abler man, had to conform his ideas of grand strategy to those of the dour Field Marshal.

Haig got his way in the summer of 1917 because he had an obvious, massive, straightforward course of action which Lloyd George distrusted but could not replace by an acceptable alternative. But he drove his colleagues and the French to prolonged discussion, which certainly had the advantage of exploring the possibilities. Shortly after taking office he had summoned a meeting of representatives of the Dominions and India which became known as the

[1] This was the view of the committee of enquiry (Foch, Gouraud, Bruyère) appointed by the French Chamber; cf. Cruttwell, p. 412; LlGM, vol. III, pp. 1523-8; E. Ludendorff, *Meine Kriegserinnerungen 1914-1918* (Berlin, 1920), pp. 332-41.

Imperial War Cabinet, and held fourteen sessions, under his chairmanship, between 20 March and 2 May.[1] General Smuts was sent to France in April 1917 to find out the exact intentions of the French, whose difficulties were becoming known to Robertson and Haig and the British cabinet. His report gave no support to Lloyd George's diversionary plans in the east. But Lloyd George was by no means so opposed at this point to further heavy fighting in France as his *War Memoirs* were later to suggest. He was still backing Nivelle's plans, and at the Paris conference on 4 and 5 May made a powerful appeal to the French in favour of a continuance of the operations throughout the summer, whatever the losses. With the idea of preventing a German initiative against the French, Haig launched an attack on the Messines Ridge which was carried out with complete success by General Plumer early in June. This complete though limited victory straightened out the Ypres salient, boosted morale, and brought the War Cabinet face to face with Haig's plan for a further prolonged offensive in Flanders. In support of this repetition of the Somme nightmare Haig could argue that the capture of the Belgian ports would be a major blow to the German submarine campaign.

As it happened the convoy system was about to solve the submarine problem, although some time was needed to make sure. Whether Lloyd George was justified in claiming all the credit for this triumph over naval conservatism has been questioned. He had certainly convinced himself by April that Carson as First Lord had not the knack of overriding the Board of Admiralty. When he threatened to descend on the Admiralty and take peremptory action there appeared to be a hasty but thorough re-examination of the problem, and agreement to give the convoy plan a trial.[2] Although after this the Admiralty still moved with what seemed to the country to be maddening deliberation, regular convoys were running on the dangerous Gibraltar route by the end of July, and it soon became evident that the worst of the crisis was over.[3] The

[1] See pp. 293-4.
[2] This is Lloyd George's version of the convoy story: LlGM, vol. III, pp. 1130-82; Hankey, vol. II, pp. 641-51, agrees in substance with Lloyd George's account, although he says that the Prime Minister did not seem to grasp the danger of the submarine question until 22 April (p. 649).
[3] This again is Lloyd George's version. The Admiralty's answer is that convoying had been made practicable only by America's entry into the war, and had been already decided on in principle before Ll. G.'s visit on 30 April, at which the convoy system was not discussed. R. H. Bacon, *The Life of John Rushworth Earl Jellicoe* (1936), pp. 357-62; 368-71.

marked fall in sinkings which followed was helped by many other expedients in addition to the convoy system, which remained however the vital discovery. Soon Sir Eric Geddes, on Haig's suggestion, replaced Carson as First Lord. He stipulated that Jellicoe should remain, at any rate for the time being; but tension between Jellicoe and Admiral Beatty, the commander of the Grand Fleet, made further changes advisable, and after some reshuffling the pleasant, tactful, rather mediocre Admiral Sir Rosslyn Wemyss became First Sea Lord on 26 December 1917.[1]

In the meantime a new body, the War Policy Committee (Lloyd George, Curzon, Milner, and Smuts) had been appointed by the cabinet to examine the overall strategy. It gave Haig's plans a somewhat reluctant endorsement after Jellicoe had testified to the vital importance of capturing the Belgian ports before winter and Haig had promised this and more. There would be a three-stage advance, first to the Passchendaele-Staden ridge; secondly to a line running from Ostend through Thourout to Roulers; thirdly an advance to Blankenberg and Bruges. The first objective had no value in itself, but it was in fact as far as the sodden troops managed to go—four miles in four months. When the battle was called off on 10 November it had apparently failed in every respect: Germany still held the ports; there had been no breakthrough; even the battle of attrition had gone, on balance, against the British army, although not to the extent that Lloyd George claims in his memoirs.[2] But if Lloyd George was right to be pessimistic, he was right for the wrong reasons. The impossible terrain, the simple horrible fact of the nightmarish mud: it was this which no one among the British planners had adequately anticipated. In mid-August General Gough, commanding the Fifth Army, had told Haig that it was impossible to go on, but he was ordered to continue. Further south a well planned surprise attack with 400 tanks did achieve complete tactical success at Cambrai on 20 November. They were indeed too successful: infantry and cavalry in support did not move forward quickly enough to consolidate the victory, and during the next ten days the Germans recovered most of the ground in counterattacks.

What was the overall picture at the end of 1917? In spite of remarkable successes the Germans had not won the war, and the

---

[1] Bacon, chap. XXIII; LlGM, vol. III, pp. 1178-80; Lady Wester Wemyss, *The Life and Letters of Lord Wester Wemyss* (1935), pp. 361-71.

[2] For a more favourable verdict: Duff Cooper, *Haig*, pp. 133-76; C. Falls, *The First World War*, pp. 250-6.

point had been passed at which they could hope to do so. The French army and the British merchant navy had been husbanded to recovery after the threatened collapse of April and May 1917. America was now in the war, with vast resources. Even without these, the superiority of Allied equipment was beginning to be marked, and its relative weight was increased by the strain of the blockade inside Germany. Russia it was true was finished as a fighting force, and the Italians, after fighting commendably in eleven futile offensives on the Isonzo for two years, had collapsed before the combined German–Austrian offensive at Caporetto in the last week of October. But General Cadorna, an able if unsympathetic leader, had established a satisfactory defensive position on the Piave by the time of his dismissal on 9 November, and French and British divisions, the latter under Plumer, relieved sections of the weary Italian troops in December. In March General Maude had captured Baghdad, and after much obstruction by the War Office a new commander in Egypt, General Allenby, was given substantial reinforcements and captured Jerusalem on 9 December. On 2 November the Balfour Declaration, favouring the establishment of a national home in Palestine for the Jewish people, was a bid for the support of world Jewry but the forerunner of endless complications with the Arab world. So the war entered its last phase.

7. Labour and the Peace Movement

Middle-class opinion was solidly behind the government, accepting the war's human sacrifices and its domestic privations, and the vision of a monstrous enemy who must be utterly vanquished. This was the essential element in the 'general public' which was determined to see the thing through, and found confirmation as much as inspiration in the daily press. The broad mass of working class opinion also accepted the need to fight the war to a victorious end, but with less readiness to identify its own condition with that of the country at large. Germany was one opponent, but another, the employer, remained. The class enemy could even be serving the ends of the national enemy in a conscious or unconscious desire to keep the war going for profit. Alternatively the propertied classes, seeing the need for a united front against a workers' revolution, might seek the wrong sort of compromise peace.[1] After widespread strikes in May 1917 the government appointed a series of commis-

[1] LIGM, vol. IV, pp. 1950–55.

sions on industrial unrest which reported through George Barnes, the Minister of Labour, in July. The three more or less 'universal grievances' were shown to be food prices in relation to wages; the operation of the Munitions of War Acts in restricting the mobility of labour; and the effect of the Military Service Acts, which by calling up those previously exempt gave strength to the suspicion that government pledges had been broken. There was general animosity against the profiteer.[1]

Victory in this mass struggle of nations would go to the side which maintained the safest margin between grumbling and defeatism, and in the May strikes the margin seemed to be narrowing dangerously. Compulsory arbitration under the 1915 Munitions of War Act had worked well during 1916, in the sense that stoppages were comparatively few. But it bottled up some grievances, and increased the importance of the shop stewards, who were also called on to represent the new bodies of workers brought into the shops by dilution. This rank-and-file movement attracted some ambitious men and was almost bound to develop a certain truculence with a strong leaning to revolutionary syndicalism.[2] Nevertheless, the government did enough to keep discontent at a minimum. When Winston Churchill succeeded Dr. Addison as Minister of Munitions on 18 July 1917 he at once introduced a Munitions of War Act (1917) which enabled him to carry out with some success the recommendations of the Barnes commission.

The two streams of pacifist and syndicalist criticism now began to merge, with reactions on the Labour party which were complicated and confused by contradictory currents in America and Russia. In the process of promoting peace talks in the winter of 1916–17 President Wilson had impressed himself on the world as the apostle of an equitable peace and a league of states to enforce it; he had publicly associated himself with the league cause in May 1916 and in a speech of 22 January 1917 calling for 'peace without victory' had pleased the I.L.P. and U.D.C.[3] groups in Britain, and no one else for the moment. After the Russian revolution in March 1917 the Kerensky régime endeavoured to carry on the war, while the Petrograd Soviet demanded a negotiated peace based on 'peace

[1] Brand, pp. 89–90; Addison, *Four and a Half Years*, vol. II, pp. 115–44; Hurwitz, pp. 258–76.
[2] B. Pribićević, *The Shop Stewards' Movement and Workers' Control, 1910–1922* (1959), pp. 83–102; Hurwitz, pp. 278–80.
[3] See below, p. 110.

without annexation or indemnities, on the basis of the self-determination of peoples', in its formula of 15 May. Having entered the war Wilson could not but adopt a 'fight until victory' programme, although he seems to have persuaded himself at the same time that the dogged ardour of the British government proved their insensitiveness to the 'progressive forces' which he sought to lead. The British pacifists and Labourites were sadly disappointed, and could only observe that America's entry had strengthened 'aggressive jingoism'.[1] The Russians replaced Wilson as the chief hope for a negotiated peace.[2]

A large and enthusiastic but essentially unrepresentative gathering at Leeds under MacDonald's somewhat embarrassed chairmanship passed resolutions on 3 June hailing the Russian revolution, calling for immediate British acceptance of the Russian foreign policy and war aims, demanding the release of labour from all forms of compulsion and restraint, and urging the establishment in every urban and rural district of Councils of Workmen's and Soldiers' delegates. However, nothing much happened. The government wisely declined to dramatize the conference by banning it, and Ramsay MacDonald, who didn't really wish to become the British Kerensky, was glad to accept the Labour party's suggestion that he should go to Russia to report. Unfortunately for this plan to get himself out of the way the Sailors' and Firemen's Union finally refused to allow him to sail.

The cabinet sent Henderson to Russia to report, and if possible to keep Russia in the war; but there was little he could do. Plans for an international socialist conference at Stockholm had in the meantime left the Labour party hopelessly divided, and to his cabinet colleagues it seemed that even the good, sober Arthur Henderson was behaving more and more oddly. 'He had more than a touch of the revolutionary malaria', wrote Lloyd George later. 'His temperature was high and his mood refractory.'[3] After he had insisted on conferring with French socialists in Paris against the cabinet's wishes, he was asked to wait in the Secretary's room while his colleagues discussed his conduct. This increased instead of reducing his embarrassment. However, he seems to have swallowed his indignation at this seemingly cavalier treatment, and the cabinet,

---

[1] G. R. Crosby, pp. 43–52; A. J. Mayer, *Political Origins of the New Diplomacy, 1917–1918* (New Haven), pp. 110–12; E. Windrich, *British Labour's Foreign Policy* (1952), pp. 13, 14; Cole, pp. 31–3; Brand, p. 87.

[2] R. W. Postgate, *The Life of George Lansbury* (1951), pp. 662–71.

[3] Cole, pp. 34–5; LlGM, vol. IV, p. 1900, and chap. LVIII generally; Postgate, pp. 173–9; Mrs. M. Hamilton, *Arthur Henderson* (1938), pp. 121–62.

which did not want either to be associated with MacDonald and Stockholm or to quarrel with the Labour party, readily accepted his hint that the party might solve the problem of the conference by refusing to attend. But he himself strongly urged Labour participation at an emergency Labour conference on 10 August, and resigned from the cabinet next day. Swaying loyalties and emotions aroused by the Russian prospect had left him it would seem without any clear policy. He was replaced in the government by G. J. Wardle; William Adamson became leader of the party in the Commons. Henderson now discovered that he wished to remain free to work for the resumption of international socialist relations, and to reorganize the party machine; but he was a valuable recruit for Labour's fence-sitting patriots.

Although the Labour conference protested against the government's decision to refuse passports for Stockholm, the voting at the resumed meeting of the conference on 21 August and at the inter-allied socialist conference in London on the 28th virtually killed the Stockholm plan.[1] But Labour was moving leftward, a process accelerated by the Bolshevik revolution in Russia in November.[2] The call from within its ranks for a negotiated peace was encouraged by the Pope's peace proposal which had been before the world since August, and by Lord Lansdowne's letter in *The Daily Telegraph* on 29 November. This was the first revelation to the public of belief in exalted Tory circles of the possibility of a satisfactory peace by compromise; and although the criticisms of most of the London press were violent, there was a noticeable readiness in Liberal journals in London and the provinces to assume that the letter had in some undefined way made a satisfactory peace more easily attainable. In December the Bolsheviks published the text of the 1915 secret treaties, and in secret peace discussions with General Smuts on 18–19 December 1917 Count Mensdorff, an Austrian envoy, urged the expediency of a statement of Allied peace terms.

Lloyd George claims that the cabinet was impressed by this recommendation.[3] It was, no doubt, much more impressed by the Labour swing. Henderson, who was now working closely with

---

[1] They were also disheartened by the stout refusal of Samuel Gompers and the American Federation of Labour to take part in any negotiations with 'Socialists' or 'the enemy'. Pelling, pp. 112–3; Brand, pp. 92–3.

[2] S. R. Graubard, *British Labour and the Russian Revolution, 1917–1924* (1956), pp. 44–63.

[3] LlGM, vol. V, p. 2482.

MacDonald and the I.L.P. group, produced a memorandum on peace aims which was accepted by a decisive majority at a further Labour conference in London on 28–29 December. The significance of the meeting was that the I.L.P.–U.D.C. viewpoint was now that of the majority; it was the right-wing group, represented by men like Havelock Wilson and Stephen Walsh, who found themselves in a hopeless minority when they opposed any peacemaking before victory. But of even greater urgency from the government's point of view was the need at this moment to secure agreement to the Man-power Committee's proposals for the recruitment of a further 150,000 unwilling men of 'A' category, and 100,000 of lower categories, from the existing industrial population. The time had come for Lloyd George to talk persuasively to Labour.[1]

Some of the assumptions underlying the talk of a compromise peace only made sense in terms of a change of heart or of government in Germany; but such a peace would be more likely to save the existing German régime. While imperialistic aims, annexations, and indemnities were readily condemned, it seemed reasonable to demand of the enemy guarantees of future security, the freeing of conquered territories and submerged peoples, and reparations. Was there any substantial difference? At any rate, the Allies had an ample array of objectives which verbal ingenuity could display in a reasonably respectable light, and when Lloyd George addressed himself to this task he did it very adequately. After the cabinet had agreed to a statement of terms he secured the assent of Asquith and Grey at breakfast at Asquith's house, and had received the approval of the Dominions to his statement before addressing the Labour conference at Caxton Hall on 5 January 1918.

The delegates were impressed by his grave and moderate tone. 'I made it clear that our one object in the War was to defend the violated public law of Europe, to vindicate Treaty obligations and to secure the restoration of Belgium', he wrote in his memoirs. They were not fighting to destroy Austria–Hungary or to deprive Turkey of her capital, or of areas predominantly Turkish in race. The Straits should be internationalized and neutralized. Belgium must be completely restored: but such reparation was not the same as a war indemnity. After that must come the restoration of Serbia, Montenegro, and the occupied parts of France, Italy, and Rumania. The success of the speech was due as much to what it left unsaid

[1] Brand, pp. 101–2; Cole, pp. 39–40; LlGM, vol. V, p. 2656; Crosby, pp. 55–60.

as to its specific promises. For the same reason, while it secured his immediate objectives, it failed to establish itself as the basic Allied peace programme: this distinction fell to Wilson's Fourteen Points, issued three days later on 8 January 1918. These were more systematically formulated, more strikingly phrased, and even more skilful than Lloyd George's in presenting a heavy and unilateral programme of enemy concessions as a stern emanation of international justice. The circumstances of its delivery had forced the Prime Minister to put his own statement in a more argumentative and even defensive form than Wilson's, and comparisons favourable to the President were soon being made by some of the Labour critics. But, except on the question of the freedom of the seas, there was no essential difference between the two programmes.[1]

The immediate result, for the government, was satisfactory enough. The Labour party wished to help win the war while preserving an independent position in the postwar domestic struggle. When Lloyd George spoke to the conference again on 18 January 1918, commending the government's manpower bill by reference to Allied aims and needs, he secured full support; the bill then went quickly through Parliament, and received the royal assent on 6 February.[2]

Balfour followed up the proposal which Wilson had made in his 14th Point for 'a general association of nations' by appointing early in 1918 a committee under Sir Walter (later Lord) Phillimore 'on the League of Nations', which reported on 20 March.[3] Although Wilson captured the headlines as the sponsor of the League, it was not until after the armistice that the British government had any precise idea as to what he wanted, and indeed Wilson himself remained rather vague on the point throughout. The idea had had its origins in unofficial discussions, shortly after the beginning of the war, in the Fabian Society and in a committee under Lord Bryce. The method that gained most support in the early discussions was for a body providing machinery to facilitate the peaceful settlement of international disputes, but the Fabian Society's scheme, as expounded by J. A. Hobson, visualized the provision of means

---

[1] H. I. Nelson, *Land and Power*, pp. 33–9, shows the priority of Lloyd George's views on many points; cf. Mayer, pp. 353–67, 376. LlGM, vol. V, pp. 2486, 2515–27, gives the full text of Lloyd George's speech.

[2] Brand, pp. 106–9; LlGM, vol. V, pp. 2657–64.

[3] The committee included three historians (A. F. Pollard, Julian Corbett, and Holland Rose) and three Foreign Office seniors (Eyre Crowe, William Tyrell, and Cecil Hurst).

to enforce a decision.[1] Parallel American discussions were conducted by the 'League to Enforce Peace' founded in June 1915.[2] The Phillimore report was to become the basis of British–American proposals on the subject at the peace conference.

8. THE LAST PHASE

Germany was as yet far from accepting the view that Wilson's Fourteen Points offered her a mild and honourable settlement. She had now no alternative to one vast final offensive in the West which would mean early defeat if it failed, and which might not mean victory even if it succeeded. Having decided in November 1917 to launch this offensive in the spring, Ludendorff fiercely opposed the idea of a negotiated peace, advocated by Prince Max of Baden with some influential support. Thus Germany, like the *Entente* powers, feared to show any sign of weakening. Her position was deteriorating, nevertheless; war weariness and declining resources would prevent Turkey, Bulgaria, and Austria–Hungary from continuing much longer, and she herself was feeling the pinch of shortages which were generally, but not always correctly, attributed to the blockade. She should, indeed, have been more or less self-supporting in foodstuffs. The near famine conditions that appeared at certain points, and particularly in the 'turnip' winter of 1916–17, were partly due to such causes as hoarding by local producers, failure to build up stocks of imported fertilizers, the too lavish feeding of animals, and conscription; the call-up of farm labourers for the armed forces led to a drop in production greater than the loss of supplies from abroad. Things had improved in 1917 through careful husbandry; some supplies could be extracted from the Ukraine (although it needed forty divisions to do so). The factories continued to pour out war material. Civilian morale could be maintained a little longer. By withdrawing good divisions from the east Ludendorff could build up a 10 per cent superiority in manpower in the west. But he knew that the enemy would soon enjoy, with American participation, a rapidly growing quantitative and qualitative superiority. The war must be won in 1918.

Yet there was no disposition in any Allied capital to anticipate

[1] H. Winkler, *The League of Nations Movement in Great Britain* (New Brunswick, 1952); Alfred Zimmern, *The League of Nations and the Rule of Law* (1939 edn.), pp. 160–89; J. A. Hobson's proposals in *Towards International Government* (1915), especially chap. 6; Viscount Bryce and others, *Proposals for the Prevention of Future Wars* (1917).
[2] Ruhl J. Bartlett, *The League to Enforce Peace* (Chapel Hill, 1944), pp. 35–9.

an early victory. Lloyd George, thoroughly shocked by Passchendaele, thought that the Allied advantage, slight at best, might
easily be thrown away by stupid generalship. Depressed by the
'optimistic slosh' that flowed from G.H.Q. during the battle, he
now distrusted his own generals so much that he sought a united,
which meant a French, command. He would have got rid of Haig
if he could have found a satisfactory alternative. Given extra troops,
would not Haig throw them away in another Passchendaele-type
attack, instead of staying on the defensive until the arrival of
American troops made the victorious offensive practicable? 'The
thing is horrible, and beyond human nature to bear, and I feel I
can't go on any longer with the bloody business,' he said to C. P.
Scott in December; 'I would rather resign.'[1]

Haig might be frustrated, but he could not be removed. He had
to accept some conditions that he disliked, but got his way on the
things he thought vital. In short, the war continued to be fought,
on the whole, as the soldiers desired. Lloyd George was not a
great war leader in the field of grand strategy; he did not have the
unquestioned command of every aspect of the supreme planning of
the war that Winston Churchill received by general consent in
World War II. The frequent parliamentary storms, culminating in
the Maurice debate in May 1918, the uncertain but ominous thunder
of the press, and continued coolness towards him in sections of the
Tory party, were all reminders of the insecurity of a wartime
coalition prime minister. He had been appointed to get results; to
give the leadership that would ensure victory. He would be the
first scapegoat in defeat. While victory was uncertain, his position
was uncertain too. On the other hand, there was no doubt about the
reality of his leadership; the question that faced his critics was
whether he was not taking on too much, trying to dominate even
the generals.

The Supreme War Council, consisting of the Prime Minister, a
cabinet member, and a military representative of each of the three
allied countries (Britain, France, and Italy), was set up in November
1917 at Rapallo on his initiative and under the shock of Caporetto,
but achieved very little. A few days later, in one of his great parliamentary triumphs, he routed the critics, political and journalistic,

[1] Lord Buckmaster objected that that would mean 'a purely War Government'.
Lloyd George said that there was a good deal of feeling in the War Cabinet towards
peace, Milner the most inclined of anybody. J. L. Hammond, *C. P. Scott* (1934), p. 222.

who had sprung to the defence of the British generals; the defence was, however, partly a retreat, for he repudiated anything but an advisory rôle for the military members (Foch, Wilson, and Cadorna) of the Council. He again triumphed in a beautifully planned and delivered speech on 12 February 1918, and it was announced four days later that Robertson had resigned.[1] Offered the choice of either continuing as C.I.G.S. without authority over Wilson, or going as the British representative to Versailles in Wilson's place, he had rejected both alternatives. On the following day Haig showed that he, for his part, had no intention of resigning. His refusal nevertheless to supply divisions for the general reserve frustrated the only major plan that the Supreme Council had produced up to this point. Lord Derby, who had been frequently on the point of resignation, was sent as ambassador to Paris, and Milner, Lloyd George's staunchest supporter in the Robertson row, became Secretary of State for War in April 1918.[2]

The great German attack, launched against General Gough's Fifth Army on 21 March 1918, was astonishingly successful, although strategically indecisive; the German army enjoyed four months of unexampled triumphs which brought it the more rapidly to defeat. Gough had only seventeen divisions (three of cavalry). There was a heavier concentration of divisions north of Arras because here the British forces, with their backs to the sea in Flanders, could scarcely risk even a few miles of retreat. The Germans could make little headway against the right wing of Byng's Third Army, and on large sections of Gough's front the resistance was equally determined. But the turning of the southern flank above La Fère forced Gough to order a retreat behind the Crozat Canal on the 22nd and, on the 23rd, a general retreat to the Somme. After three years of attack the British forces had had no training in orderly retreat, and it looked (and not only to Ludendorff) as if the whole British army was on the verge of annihilation.

This supreme crisis of the war was to put to the test the character and policies of all the leading men, and if on the British side there was no lack of resolution, equally there was no one who came out

---

[1] This followed the article by Col. Repington in *The Morning Post* of 11 February, which revealed the whole plan of a General Reserve under Foch; Robertson must have been the source of this information. M. Thomson, *David Lloyd George, The Official Biography* (1949), pp. 280–81. Haig told Robertson on 11 February that 'it was his *duty* to go to Versailles or anywhere else if the Government wished it'. *Haig Papers*, p. 284. P. Guinn, p. 294.
[2] R. S. Churchill, pp. 295–352.

of it entirely without blame. For Haig and his advisers it could be said that in their concentration of strength in Flanders they had taken a calculated risk, but the fact remains that they guessed wrong, and it is difficult to find an answer to Lloyd George's exasperated criticism of Haig's decision to allot most of his engineers and labour battalions for work on the Passchendaele defences. Nor can he be acquitted of some irresponsibility—or a lack of sophistication—in relying on immediate French help. Gough, with depleted forces and inadequate reserves, had perhaps an impossible task, but the Fifth Army had lost much of its confidence in his leadership in the Passchendaele battles, and he failed to keep a tight hold on his forces during the critical week after 21 March. The situation was dark enough, but it was made worse by precipitate retirements and a consequent failure to carry out demolitions or to evacuate vast quantities of wounded men and of material. Lloyd George for his part threw himself with magnificent spirit into the crisis; on 23 March, when the extent of the disaster was first understood in London, he went to the War Office and himself took charge, hurrying all available reinforcements to the front.[1] On the other hand, he must bear his share of responsibility for the fact that they were not available before the battle started.

The crisis quickly settled the problem of the supreme command. At the memorable conference at Doullens under Poincaré's presidency Haig was agreeable and Pétain acquiescent, and Foch, at first charged only to coordinate the action of the Allied armies on the Western front, at once justified his appointment by refusing to listen to further talk of retreat. On 14 April he was finally given the title of Commander-in-Chief. In spite of his pessimism, on 24 March Pétain had begun to send French divisions forward; by the 26th, twenty-one were on their way. A fresh attack by Ludendorff against the British First Army on 28 March failed completely, and although the advance further south continued until Montdidier was captured and Amiens threatened, the stiffening resistance had brought it to a standstill by the beginning of April. However, a second vast offensive began on 7 April, launched this time against the British position in Flanders, and was only halted on the 13th, after desperate fighting, just short of the vital railway centre of Hazebrouck. This advance, although shorter in actual mileage, was in the area in which, owing to the proximity of the coast, it was

[1] LlGM, vol. V, pp. 2284–8.

strategically dangerous to yield any ground at all. It is significant perhaps that it was this crisis, and not the much more extensive German penetration towards Amiens in March, which called forth Haig's most famous battle order on 12 April, with its noble but ominous appeal:

> ... Every position must be held to the last man : there must be no retirement. With our backs to the wall and believing in the justice of our cause, each one of us must fight on to the end ...

The line held on the most critical day, the 13th, and it was fortunate that Ludendorff did not know how thin the line was, and how impervious was Foch to Haig's angry demands for French reinforcements. The Germans gained no real success in this area, and this phase of their offensive died down at the end of April. The total British losses since 21 March were over 300,000, although those of the Germans were even greater.

Lloyd George's leadership was now openly attacked; his critics felt that the chance was too good to be missed. The cabinet's first reaction to the German offensive was a desperate search for more recruits; after his morning at the War Office on 23 March, Lloyd George presided at a meeting of the War Cabinet in the same building which decided to conscript men up to fifty, clergy, and the Irish, and to send conscientious objectors abroad for labour service. The calamitous decision to extend recruiting to Ireland seems to have been due primarily to the fear that Labour would otherwise make difficulties. Bonar Law promised that the government would try to bring a Home Rule measure into operation simultaneously with the enforcement of conscription. But neither course proved practicable, and in the end the government had the worst of both worlds. After the Commons had passed the Military Service Bill on 16 April, all the Nationalist members under John Dillon withdrew to Ireland to organize opposition, and joined with the Sinn Fein and Irish Labour leaders in a joint protest. Thus the measure helped to consolidate the extremist position, thereby making even more difficult any modified Home Rule programme with the reservations desired by the government; at the same time Lloyd George was not prepared to introduce conscription without it.

In the Irish conscription debate Asquith refrained from voting, although he disagreed with the government's policy. But such abstentions in the national emergency became impossible when the

Prime Minister's opponents found the way to an open challenge. This came through Sir Frederick Maurice, a reserved, conscientious, and, quite obviously, very angry soldier, who after silent consideration relieved only by a talk with his mother and his wife, wrote to several newspapers on 6 May 1918 calling the Prime Minister a liar. He described as 'not correct' Lloyd George's statement in a speech on 9 April that the British Army in France was considerably stronger on 1 January 1918 than it had been on 1 January 1917. Also 'not correct' the further statement that there was only one white division in Mesopotamia and only three in Egypt and Palestine. He mentioned other 'misstatements'. Haig himself estimated in November that British infantry in France would be about 250,000 below establishment on 31 March 1918.[1] We have seen that Lloyd George took the view that Haig's forces were adequate for a defensive rôle. Maurice, however, did not raise these broader issues. He limited himself to specific figures and in fact chose very disadvantageous ground for his fight.

Lloyd George was convinced that this was the culmination of a widespread campaign against the government and himself, inspired largely by military leaders in France and at the War Office who were supplying the press; his opponents in Parliament moreover were, he believed, seeking an opportunity for an open attack on the war leadership. Although Bonar Law's own admiration for Lloyd George was at its height as he contemplated his splendid handling of the crisis he knew that there were influential critics of the Prime Minister inside the Conservative ranks. Among Asquith's followers there was a strong conviction that Lloyd George's hour of retribution had come. Asquith gave them a lead by moving that a select committee be appointed to inquire into Maurice's charges, and rejecting the government's offer on 7 May of a judicial inquiry, a course which would have ensured a thorough examination of the facts.[2] The appalling weakness of Maurice's position lay in the fact that he himself, as Director of Military Operations at the War Office, had supplied the figures that Lloyd George had used in his speech on 9 April, so that Lloyd George was able to trounce him with zest in a masterly speech on 9 May.[3] He also had some hard things to say about his political opponents, including the Cadbury

[1] Cruttwell gives the decrease in the British army in March 1918 as 180,000 men, if compared with the same date in the previous year.
[2] Spender-Asquith, vol. II, pp. 299–309.
[3] P.D., 5 Ser., HC, vol. 105, 9 May 1918, cols. 2355–73.

press, which had drenched him 'with cocoa slop' for years. The debate was ineffectual, although Asquith refused to withdraw his motion. When it was put to the vote it was defeated by 293 to 106.[1] Haig thought it 'terrible to see the House of Commons so taken in by a clap-trap speech by Lloyd George'.[2]

The Maurice debate was from every point of view a disaster for the Liberal party. The real Liberal split had taken place in December 1916, but the formal vote against the government on 9 May consolidated it, and on the other hand, with the tide of war soon turning in favour of the Allies, Lloyd George and the coalition government were triumphantly vindicated in popular esteem. Thus Asquith lost the faint possibility of Liberal reunion and the even fainter possibility of re-establishing the fortunes of the party under his wing as leader of an alternative government. Although Lloyd George appealed to Asquith not to press the Maurice issue to a division he was quite ready for an electoral battle, for which he had been preparing for some months, and in the coupon election in November the couponless Asquithian Liberals were to be largely annihilated.

The tide turned in July. There was a lull in the fighting in May, and then Ludendorff's third stroke, directed this time against the French on the 29th, brought the Germans back to the Marne by 1 June; but this was an embarrassing victory, for what had been meant only as a diversion had created an extremely awkward salient and tied down divisions which had really been intended for operations further north. After initial success the Germans were held and then driven back in a vigorous counter-offensive under General Mangin, while the Americans in their first considerable action near Chateau-Thierry demonstrated their gusto and courage, if also their

---

[1] Guinn, p. 304. The Opposition had no help from Maurice, who withdrew into the country after writing his letter. Lord Beaverbrook, in *Men and Power 1917–1918* (pp. 262–3) prints an extract from the Diary of Countess Lloyd George stating that Maurice sent to Lloyd George a paper containing modifications and corrections of the figures used by Lloyd George in his speech on 9 April. By some mischance this was left unnoticed in the W.O. box, and subsequently burnt by J. T. Davies, Lloyd George's secretary. Maurice, it must be assumed, believed that his letter would make some sort of public enquiry inevitable, and that the discrepancy would then be revealed. In a pamphlet which he published in 1922, with the title *Intrigues of the War*, Maurice stated that the error had been due to the inclusion of the strength of the British forces in Italy in the strength of the armies in France. In his pamphlet, however, it is the statement of 18 April that Maurice claims to have corrected. Cf. Thomas Jones, *Lloyd George*, p. 151. Lloyd George does not show any awareness of this error in the account in vol. V of his *War Memoirs*, although he defends himself quite effectively by quoting examples of the repeated divergences between the W.O. figures.

[2] *Haig Papers*, p. 309. On Asquith's rôle: Jenkins, pp. 467–74. Cf. M. Thomson, pp. 288–90.

inexperience. Thus checked, Ludendorff now took a whole month to collect his forces for a final supreme stroke. Foch, anticipating the German plans correctly, was massing reserves for his great counter-offensive, and Haig, with excellent courage, took the risk on Foch's urgent request of sending four divisions and a Corps Headquarters to the French front, declining the War Cabinet's offer to back him in refusal. The Germans attacked on 15 July; on the 18th Foch launched his counter-offensive in a second battle of the Marne, a great victory which continued with heavy German losses of men and territory until 7 August. Then the British Fourth Army under Rawlinson launched a limited, brilliantly concealed, and overwhelmingly successful attack on a fourteen mile front east of Amiens on the 8th, 'the black day of the German army' in Ludendorff's much quoted phrase.

The British army's contribution to the final victory in France did much to restore the reputation of its generals. Even Lloyd George, who found it hard to say a good word for Haig, admits that he earned high credit, although only as 'second in command to a strategist of unchallenged genius'. Foch's planning of a continuous attack, with successive hammer blows to allow the enemy's weakening forces no rest, certainly achieved in brilliant fashion the French ideal of an irresistible offensive, but earlier this had inspired Joffre and Nivelle; it had failed in their case through the dourness and power of the German defence, rather than through any lack of spirit on the part of the French commanders. What the British were now able to contribute was a reserve of fresh vigour in the final stage which equalled that of the Americans, and a mastery of tank movements which, suddenly produced at this late stage in the war, had a correspondingly disconcerting effect on the weakening German army. This moral victory was achieved by the perfection of the tactics first tried out at Cambrai in November 1917. A great concentration of 456 tanks, complete air supremacy, the absence—which the tank attack made possible—of preliminary artillery bombardment, and a heavy ground mist gave the Fourth Army a complete breakthrough on 8 August, which was, however, discontinued and replaced by successive advances further north by the Third and First Armies when resistance began to harden.[1]

Haig's will to victory, frustrated to the detriment of his troops

---

[1] *Official History of the War, Military Operations 1918* (1947), vol. IV, p. 512, suggests that Foch contributed little as generalissimo to the result.

in the stalemate of trench warfare in 1916 and 1917, now served the
Allies well. The fighting from 8–12 August was the greatest British
success of the war and one of the decisive battles of history, not
because of the extent of the advance or even the numbers of prisoners
captured, but because its character suddenly and finally destroyed
Germany's hopes of further effective resistance. Ludendorff was
still busily refurbishing plans for fresh attacks, including the long
postponed offensive in Flanders, up to the eve of the battle. The
advance continued all along the front; the enemy was allowed no
rest; and it fell to the British forces to storm the Hindenburg Line,
the decisive action on 29 September being fought once again by the
valiant Fourth Army. Ludendorff's loss of nerve after this battle and
his insistence on armistice negotiations were due to fears of an
immediate collapse of all German resistance, and although this did
not happen the spell was broken; the appeal to Wilson for an
armistice now made it plain to all Germans that the war was lost.[1]

The armistice, signed on 11 November, was for Germany a prelude to peace which was also a prelude to revolution; the red flag
appeared with the white. Foch and Admiral Wemyss met the
German delegates; the distinctive British contribution was to insist
on the internment of a large part of the German fleet and the
continuation of the blockade, although with a promise to feed
Germany 'as shall be found necessary' while the armistice and the
blockade continued. Germany signed the armistice as a preliminary
to peace on the basis of Wilson's fourteen points. The ambiguities
of that vaguely worded document had been partly resolved in the
'interpretation' by F. I. Cobb and Walter Lippmann, which was
ready by 29 October; but although this was satisfactory to Wilson
it was not given to the Germans, who were thus left with ample
opportunity for argument over the meaning of the clauses. Lloyd
George, however, objected to Point 2, and was neither reassured nor
enlightened by Colonel House's assurance that while demanding
the acceptance of the principle of the Freedom of the Seas the
President did not object to the principle of blockade.[2] On British
insistence the Germans were told that the Allies reserved this point

---

[1] *Ibid.*, pp. 88–92, on the German position; Ludendorff, p. 547.

[2] The woolliness of Wilson's ideas on this point is made clear by the Cobb-Lippmann
commentary which recognizes that in a blockade during a 'limited' war—one in which
the League of Nations was neutral—the rights of both neutrals and belligerents must
be maintained after being clearly and precisely defined. H. R. Rudin, *Armistice 1918*
(1944), pp. 267, 412–13.

for further discussion at the peace conference. The Germans were also told, on the French initiative, that the 'restoration' of invaded territory included compensation for all damage done to the civilian population of the Allies and their property. Otherwise they accepted the Fourteen Points as they stood, and were soon able to convince themselves that it was a benign and idealistic charter far different from the subsequent harsh reality of Versailles.

So ended the first world war. 'La France a remporté la victoire!' declared Clemenceau after announcing the armistice terms to the Chamber of Deputies; on this and subsequent occasions there was no tribute to the share of Britain or the other Allies.[1] But in a sense it was Britain's victory, for she was the strongest power in the alliance in 1918; her mobilization of resources was at its peak, and she had even been able to call on a final reserve of fresh energy and zest for the culminating victory. By comparison, France had shot her bolt in 1916, and the war was over before the United States was fully involved. It had now to be seen whether this costly predominance, which she could not hope to maintain, would enable her to impose worthwhile conditions of peace.

[1] Lord Derby was annoyed. Viscountess d'Abernon, *Red Cross and Berlin Embassy, 1915–1926* (1946), pp. 49–50.

2

POSTWAR PROBLEMS AND MOODS

1. COUNTING THE COST

Postwar Britain must have contained a great many people who were profoundly grateful for the fact of victory and the state of peace. But there was little sign of it in political discussion and the tone of the press. On the contrary, the country seemed to be full of demobilized heroes and expectant civilians who did not accept peace as its own reward. It is evidently not easy to be satisfied for long with mere survival. It soon appeared that the losses, animosities, and general dislocation were too extensive for the prompt transition to a peace of goodwill and plenty; the war had created a consciousness of new needs and at the same time made it harder for the country to meet them.

Some of the material losses can be measured with a fair degree of accuracy. The total number of deaths of Army and Royal Navy personnel from Great Britain and Ireland is usually estimated as 744,000; 14,661 sailors of the British mercantile marine also lost their lives. The total number of deaths for the British Empire (including India) was 947,000. These were heavy losses, although they were exceeded by those of France, Russia, Germany, and Austria–Hungary. A relatively small but ominous figure, new to warfare, was that of 1,117 civilians killed, and 2,886 wounded, in airship and aeroplane raids over England. The total number of deaths in all countries during the war was probably about 13 million, although this figure includes nearly 3 million deaths from disease; in the case of the Americans, for example, deaths from disease were as great as the losses in action (57,460 out of a total of 115,920). Influenza, so inadequately named, was a major plague which spread through the world and took a heavy toll of populations lowered in vitality and resistance; there were 150,000 deaths in England and

Wales, including over 15,000 in London alone. The epidemic began in England in June 1918 and reached its peak in the week before the armistice; there was a second heavy outbreak in the early months of 1919.[1]

Some of the damage and dislocation caused by the war to the country's wealth and property can also be measured statistically. As a preliminary to the great reparations' struggle there were various attempts to fix a figure for the physical damage suffered by Great Britain and her allies through enemy action. J. M. Keynes suggested £2,120 million, of which the British share would be £570 million.[2] He thought the sum actually demanded in 1921— £767 million—'very high'.[3] The main item among the British claims was for merchant shipping lost through enemy action— 2,479 vessels, of 7,759,090 gross tonnage. For some reason he did not include in this estimate 675 fishing vessels of 71,765 gross tonnage, nor 1,885 vessels of over 8 million tonnage damaged or molested but not sunk. A relatively small sum—not more than £10 million—would cover damage to civilian property through air raids and bombardment from the sea. To these figures must be added those for military supplies and other goods which were lavishly produced only to be rapidly destroyed in war; these were, however, outside the reparations' calculations. Ten years later, Professor A. J. Bowley put the overall Allied figure at £2,000 million at prewar prices, and the aggregate capital of the United Kingdom in 1914 at some £13,800 million; the value of this civilian income-yielding property probably grew between 1 and 2 per cent annually, so that the wartime losses represented the destruction of perhaps 2 to 4 years of its normal growth, or one-thirtieth of its whole value.[4] Then too the concentration on production for war

---

[1] *Statistics of the Military Effort of the British Empire during the Great War* (H.M.S.O., 1924); J. Brophy, *The Five Years, 1914–18* (1936), statistical tables, pp. 225–307; C. L. Mowat, *Britain Between the Wars* (1955), pp. 22–4.

[2] J. M. Keynes, *The Economic Consequences of the Peace* (1919), pp. 120–3. The other items were, Belgium, £500m; France, £800m; other allies, £250m. Earlier, Germany's losses, direct and indirect, in the Franco-Prussian war had been estimated at about £115m; France was required to pay an indemnity of £200m (H. H. O'Farrell, *The Franco-German War Indemnity and Its Economic Results*, 1913, pp. 1–3).

[3] Neither figure included a claim for pensions and allowances. Keynes, *A Revision of the Treaty* (1922), p. 115.

[4] A. L. Bowley, *Some Economic Consequences of the Great War* (1930), pp. 87–90. The fullest examination of the financial consequences of the war seems to be E. Victor Morgan, *Studies in British Financial Policy, 1914–25* (1952). Cf. also E. Mantoux, *The Carthaginian Peace or the Economic Consequences of Mr. Keynes* (1946), particularly chaps. V, VI.

meant that in many cases the normal replacement and improvement of plant and machinery had to be postponed, although in other cases the reverse happened—there was new building and modernization of plant for the wartime industries which were a contribution to postwar expansion. The war had added £7,000 million in round figures to the National Debt. Yet Britain's resources, except in shipping, were on the whole intact, and the great industrial effort of the war had demonstrated the strength and flexibility of her economy; indeed, it had given many grounds for confidence in the future.[1]

Nor did her standing in international finance, although weakened, suggest permanent decline; on the contrary, her readiness in supplying substantial reconstruction loans in the early postwar years to her continental neighbours showed an over-confident belief in her ability to restore her position as the world's money market. Yet she had lost about a quarter of her overseas investments, money, that is, invested by British firms or private citizens in businesses in foreign countries, or lent to foreign governments. These investments had amounted to about £4,000 million before the war, and the interest payments on them came in as a normal and important part of the country's imports. The British government took over during the war about a quarter of them; the stock was sold abroad and the proceeds used to buy munitions and other supplies, particularly in the United States. In this process the owners were given war stock at home in exchange. The United States became a great creditor country, and an important element in maintaining the British balance of payments was reduced. The United Kingdom's rôle in financing purchases for herself and her allies could not have continued at the same pace after the spring of 1917, and the United States entered the war to become the financier of the coalition, although in no spirit of openhandedness; her assistance took the form of loans and not of subsidies or gifts. Great Britain was granted loans for the purchase of munitions and supplies, which were passed on, with British loans, to her European allies; thus she accumulated a vast debt on behalf of her allies rather than of herself. In round figures she owed £842 million to the United States, and was owed £1,740 million by her allies:[2] virtually

---

[1] F. W. Hirst, *The Consequences of the War to Great Britain* (1934), pp. 246–57.
[2] i.e. (in £ million), France, 508; Italy, 467; Russia, 568; Belgium, 98; Serbia-Yugoslavia, 20; other allies, 79. Keynes, pp. 254–8.

the whole of British indebtedness to the United States had been so incurred. This applied even to Russia after the revolution of March 1917; the British Treasury continued to finance the bulk of Russia's expenditure in the United States, and the whole of her other foreign expenditure.

When we contemplate this catalogue of losses and debts, it is easy to assume that the rather depressing course of the country's economic and domestic affairs in the nineteen-twenties, a period of declining markets in the traditional export trades and much labour unrest and frustration at home, was due to some failure of national energy and enthusiasm. 'England is not interested in anything at all', wrote C. F. G. Masterman in 1922. 'It cares nothing about local, municipal, or Parliamentary politics. It is like a sick man resting after a great outletting of blood.'[1] And yet there are many signs that belie this view. The mood immediately following the war was much rather one of an over-confident, almost vindictive, determination to exploit the victory, at home and abroad, and contemporary accounts do not suggest any particular sense of tiredness. Certainly not in the case of Lloyd George and his entourage, the 'Garden Suburb', and among his leading ministerial supporters, whose domestic programme and ideas about the future of Europe were being canvassed and argued with great vehemence.[2] The visible aspect of the House of Commons, according to Keynes's well-known anecdote, was of hard-faced men who had done very well out of the war; and Stanley Baldwin, who made this observation, might have noted some hard-faced men on the Labour benches who meant to do well out of the peace.[3] The phase of militant trade unionism which followed the armistice meant a determination to fight out the battle with the domestic capitalist now that the Germans had ceased to confuse the issue. If the brave new world failed to realize these expectations it was not necessarily through any failure of will on the part of the men concerned, but rather because military victory had given a delusive sense of opportunity.[4]

Nor would it be correct to assume that the pacifist trends of the

[1] A. J. Youngson, *The British Economy, 1920–1957* (1960), pp. 56–7. C. F. G. Masterman, *England After War* (1922), pp. 6–11, 23–4.

[2] Joseph Davies, *The Prime Minister's Secretariat* (Newport, Mon., 1951), chaps. 4, 5; J. R. M. Butler, *Lord Lothian*, pp. 61–6.

[3] Keynes, p. 133; Harrod, p. 266; cf. G. M. Young, *Stanley Baldwin* (1952), pp. 28–9.

[4] 'Innovation, freedom, and scepticism were the characteristics of British society in the twenties': A. Marwick, *The Explosion of British Society, 1914–62* (1963), p. 47.

next twenty years were the product of a genuine defeatism or loss of nerve which would make effective fighting in a future war impossible. The starting point even of the more widespread and maddeningly oversimplified view of the peacemongers was realistic. The war was seen as one in which mass slaughter had profited no one; surely no one would want to start it all again? Foreign assertiveness would probably not lead to war unless it were challenged by some intolerable provocation. There was thus a real and widespread difficulty among Englishmen in believing that the totalitarian governments of the thirties wanted war for its own sake, but when belatedly their real character was revealed the country entered a new war with the old resolution, and it was the civilians who now stood firm under fire.

There is another sense, however, in which the first world war losses are thought to have been a setback to the efficiency of the nation. There was soon to be talk of the lost generation. The war had killed off three-quarters of a million men, some of whom had already made a mark in life, and had obviously removed many others who would have done so in due course. But, after all, over 6 million were recruited, and the majority survived; so too did 1,130,657 men who were granted temporary or permanent tribunal exemptions and about 3 million in protected trades and occupations, including John Maynard Keynes and his pacifist friends. The country was not drained of talent, and for the survivors there were greater opportunities.

Was there a lost generation in politics? It has sometimes been argued that many of those who survived the war disliked what they saw of the postwar world and turned away from it, leaving politics for too long in the hands of the ageing representatives of the pre-war generation. It is true that Bonar Law, Stanley Baldwin, Ramsay MacDonald, and Neville Chamberlain were a somewhat uninspiring quartet of prime ministers, particularly by contrast with the two supermen who preceded and followed them. But in fact the warriors soon began to enter politics. For them and for many civilians, parliamentary service retained its attractiveness, if we can judge by the numbers who were ready to stand and be defeated. As ministerial office does not usually come to M.P.s before middle age, and as the ex-officers who went into Parliament were in the nature of things fairly young men, there is nothing surprising in the fact that high office was held in the twenties by those who had begun to make a mark in political life before the war.[1] Nor is there reason to think that the country wanted other types of leader. By 1922 the country was indeed somewhat disillusioned, bored with international crises and in an escapist mood; the energetic men lost their attraction as the result of a growing conviction that their dynamic personalities and spirited reactions were perpetuating the very crises that they sought so strenuously to solve. The Lloyd Georges, Birkenheads, Churchills, Geddes, and Curzons went suddenly out of fashion; Bonar Law ('tranquillity') and Stanley Baldwin ('safety first') were rather comforting to a sceptical electorate which had temporarily lost its appetite for robust foreign politics.[2]

2. THE PATTERN OF SOCIAL LIFE

The war had shaken the authority of the dominant élites in almost every sphere, political and industrial as well as intellectual and social. Men wore lounge suits to hear Melba at Covent Garden and proposed to dispossess the coal owners. The young Mayor of Hackney received Queen Mary in a brown Harris tweed suit and red tie. Queen Victoria was as dead as Queen Anne, and the fact was reiterated with almost monotonous brilliance by almost too many writers. Lytton Strachey's *Eminent Victorians* was published in 1918. In their desire to repudiate the past the new school of biographers was patronizing to the point of distortion.[3] There was a sense of release with some revolutionary undertones; nothing appeared quite so inevitable and unshakeable as it had before the

---

[1] In all general and by-elections between 1918 and 1955 there were 18,000 candidatures: P. W. Buck, *Amateurs and Professionals in British Politics, 1918–1959* (1963), pp. 4–11. Among those who entered Parliament after war service and later held office were: 1918—T. Inskip, Walter Elliot, Archibald Boyd Carpenter, D. H. Hacking; 1922— C. R. Attlee, A. V. Alexander, G. Lloyd George, D. E. Wallace, D. Margesson; 1923—R. A. Eden, V. Warrender, L. Hore Belisha, Ernest Brown; 1924—H. Dalton, Oliver Stanley, H. Crookshank, Frank Merriman, A. Duff Cooper, and Harold Macmillan. The list is not exhaustive.

[2] On the lost generation, E. L. Woodward, *Short Journey* (1942), p. 116; Mowat, p. 9; and an article by L. B. Namier, in *Conflicts* (1942). He remarks that 'it is not a generation which seems to have perished in the last war, but an atmosphere, an inspiration, *un élan vital*' (pp. 74–5).

[3] Much later Philip Guedalla, one of the two most prominent exponents of this 'new biography', genially dismissed it as 'rude biography'. He is almost unreadable today. Lytton Strachey is not, partly because his malice was deeper and therefore more sincere. J. M. Keynes's biographical sketches in the *Economic Consequences of the Peace* helped to set the fashion. 'About 1922 the world suddenly got very full of arrogant and languid young people of uncertain sex engaged in the new Bloomsbury sport of expressing their bored yet intolerant confidence that art and brains ended with them and Maynard Keynes', is the comment of one irritated onlooker (Douglas Jerrold, *Georgian Adventure* (1938), p. 240).

upheaval of war, and after the victory nothing perhaps seemed, for a time, impossible. The mood was one of impatient expectation.

Why was expectation so frequently disappointed? The most evident and mundane reason is that many aspirations which appeared reasonable and easily realizable to their advocates were linked to the country's economic health, and this was stubbornly retarded by a great complex of external problems which were not finding solutions. The isolationism of the times, which really meant just a great boredom with foreign affairs, extended to the economic field, for people did not want to be reminded of such dull and depressing things; they felt a positive sense of betrayal when after being promised tranquillity in 1922 they were asked to do some hard thinking about protection in 1923. It was easier to become angry at the obtuseness and ineptitude of authority, and to seek refuge in panaceas. The nineteen-twenties is the heyday of these forms of escapism: almost any ism except jingoism had its followers, and the cult of pacifism, socialism, communism, and even of fascism, capitalism, spiritualism, and vegetarianism, gave hope to bored, idealistic, or frustrated minds.

The effect on social life seems to have been to arouse a taste or hope for change but mainly as an improvement on the existing deeply settled habits of family life and class structure as they had emerged from the war. This desire for the *status quo amelioré* in no way differed from the normal aspiration of classes in a settled industrialized community for some progress within their existing walks of life, except for the somewhat false hopes of dramatic improvement inspired by wartime talk of homes for heroes and a better world generally. The depression of the twenties and thirties heightened the contrast between aspirations and reality, but it was never very clear how fundamental was the citizen's wish to change, as distinct from improving, his lot, even though he continually grumbled about it.

It was a lugubrious age, and the English visitor during these years could be astonished at the deep and unabashed satisfaction with which his American hosts viewed their own, not dissimilar, way of life. The year 1914 is roughly the point at which it ceased to be fun to be an Englishman. The racy types, the cheerful Cockneys, the brassy music hall dames, the superb, imperturbable policemen, professors and schoolmasters of an awful, Olympian authority, the great hostesses, the proud clerics: all these people, so self-assured and so dissimilar, had in common during the prewar generations an unreflective belief in themselves as Englishmen or women. It had long been familiar; Charles Dickens had rightly castigated its more arrogant and Podsnappery forms.[1] It had a late flowering among the golden youth of Edwardian England; it went overseas and was buried for ever with the best of Kitchener's army.

After the war there was no cult of self-assurance. The working classes were taught to be sorry for themselves. Returning to Bermondsey in 1947 to write a sequel to *Liza of Lambeth* Somerset Maugham remarked on the contrast with the men and women that he had known there in the nineties. 'The people were well-off; most earned £10 a week, and many possessed motor cycles. But they were pale-faced and bitter, and I could not recognize them any more.' By the nineteen-thirties self-conscious anti-patriotism had reached Oxford, where the Union Society resolved in February 1933 that it would not fight for King and country. The robustly self-confident men were now tending to look a little foreign or eccentric, like Hilaire Belloc or Bernard Shaw, or to be survivors of an older, more positive generation, like Robert Blatchford or Winston Churchill. The national or patriotic style however had been only one and perhaps not the most typical of such positive attitudes; the robust and indeed cheerful bearing seemed to have departed from every walk of life. Acting was reduced to a technique of clipped diction and restrained gestures, and it was said that a wave of self-consciousness had killed the remarkable histrionic qualities of Welsh pulpit oratory.

But as the country settled down once again to the normal routine of peacetime work and living the day-to-day problems of food, housing, work, transport, schooling and growing up, marriage and old age filled most people's conscious thoughts. The political struggle at Westminster, in which there was a great deal more talk than in the past of social improvement, had not yet made much impression on men's minds.[2] It was still not really believed that the state could substantially improve men's lives. In subsequent chapters the not unsuccessful labours of governments in these fields will be

---

[1] 'There is in the Englishman,' said Mr. Podsnap, 'a combination of qualities, a modesty, an independence, a responsibility, a repose, combined with an absence of everything calculated to call a blush into the cheek of a young person, which one would seek in vain among the Nations of the Earth.' *Our Mutual Friend*, chap. xi, book I.

[2] Cf. R. Graves and A. Hodge, *The Long Week-End, A Social History of Great Britain 1918–1939* (1940), pp. 64–8; Douglas Jerrold, pp. 255–8.

described, but it will be convenient here to note some of the broader social needs of the country, which were dependent for their remedy on varying degrees of official action.

Everything had a run down look after the war; and although a few coats of paint brightened shop fronts and suburban windows the basic housing problem called for more heroic remedies. The country was now predominantly urban, with half the population living in the greater towns and cities, those with over 100,000 population. The coming of the rural omnibus services was rapidly ending the isolation of villages which even in 1914 might have had no more than a horse bus twice a week to bring them into a neighbouring country town. This and the private motor car soon turned many villages into outer suburbs, and at a rough estimate it could perhaps be said that not more than 10 or 15 per cent of the population now lived in genuine rural isolation. One of the greater mysteries of our economic life is the fact that in spite of vast building programmes, the constant subdivision of larger houses, and an almost stationary population there always seems to be a housing shortage. The loss of three-quarters of a million lives and the absence of any appreciable damage by enemy action (only a few houses here and there in the London suburbs had been destroyed by German bombs) did not lessen the housing crisis of the early twenties. A suburban house which might have changed hands at £450 in 1915 could be sold for £2,000 in 1920, and for a time rented accommodation was almost unprocurable. Slum clearance was not the cause of the immediate post-war congestion, for it was not until the nineteen-thirties that this problem was systematically tackled.

The shortages were due in the main to three causes. The first was the natural mobility of the population, which was continually creating new areas of congestion, either in the more attractive suburbs or in overcrowded working-class districts. The drift of country people into the towns, and the drift of the townsmen away from the congested heart of even the smaller towns and cities into the more accessible demi-rural suburbs, had been pushing up the demand in housing before the war. The second cause was a search for flats or smaller houses, as a result of the wave of postwar marriages, the small families which were partly a cause and partly a result of smaller accommodation, the damping down of social ambition as a result of the prevailing sense of depression, the difficulty of getting servants, and the like. But the main reason was

undoubtedly the virtual cessation of house building for at least ten
years. A great boom in cheap houses, which had led to a wide and
beneficial draining of slum population from inner and outer suburbs
of London and the great towns, had stopped almost completely in
1910.[1] Nothing was done during the war years, and the restrictive
practices of the building trade unions, which had contributed to the
slowdown before the war, were followed by the further running
down of the building trade and of the building materials industry.
A serious attempt was made after the war to get houses built with
public aid, but contracts gave too little incentive to economy.
Accordingly the government's attempts to assist the citizen with
subsidies merely sent the costs higher, without producing many
houses. The luckless Minister of Health, Addison, was blamed and
sacked by Lloyd George. It was not until 1923 and 1924 that
Neville Chamberlain and John Wheatley shared honours with a
more intelligent subsidy policy, and the situation began to ease.[2]

So there was still an 'awful slum' and not necessarily because of the
poverty of the occupiers of badly built or deteriorating property.
But as unemployment stayed obstinately well over the million mark
all through the twenties after the short post-war boom, 'the Poor'
remained. There were certain differences, however, between their
position and that of the prewar generation. They had become the
unemployed; and no one now cared to assert that their lot was
inevitable because of the inscrutable workings of divine providence
or their own incapacity. Officials and sociologists were aware of a
hard core of unemployables, but the social contract had now been
reformulated as an obligation on the part of industry and the state
to provide work. A vision of the promised land of full employment
had been momentarily glimpsed during the war, and trade union
membership had reached 8·3 million in 1920.[3] It proved to have
been a mirage during the succeeding years, but now the assumption
that man by taking thought could solve this problem was publicly
accepted (with whatever secret reservations) by all political parties.
This left the unemployed hopeful or impatient rather than hopeless
and resigned.[4]

---

[1] The main cause is generally thought to have been the 1909 budget, which threatened
the increment on land values which the builders of cheap houses relied on for their
profits after cutting their profit on bricks and mortar to zero: R. C. K. Ensor, *England,
1870–1914* (1936), p. 510.
[2] M. Bowley, *Housing and the State, 1919–1944* (1945), pp. 15–35.
[3] It had fallen to 4·4 million by 1933. S. Pollard, *The Development of the British Economy,
1914–1950* (1962), pp. 267, 242–8.
[4] W. H. Beveridge, *Full Employment in a Free Society* (1944), pp. 90–9.

Moreover, after the interim payments from 1918 to 1920, various forms of unemployment relief, all conveniently but somewhat ungraciously labelled 'the dole' (insurance benefit, transitional benefit with a needs test, public assistance) prevented actual destitution, and with differing attitudes among the men themselves and their families. Some settled down to life and even to love on the dole; sometimes the unskilled labourer with a large family might get along almost as well with his 'benefit' and the yield of family allowances as he would with a job. A working girl after experiencing the rigours of domestic service might take a short blind-alley job such as door-to-door canvassing and then receive as much in unemployment pay as she could possibly earn scrubbing floors. On the other hand there were craftsmen who hated to take inferior jobs, and the dignified, respectable families who kept up appearances before the world. 'A terrible story was told me here', wrote a *Times* correspondent at a by-election in Durham in January 1929. 'Scores of the miners' cottages present to the world the usual clean curtained windows and carefully scrubbed doorsteps, but if you get a peep inside there is no furniture.'[1] On the other hand the more gregarious Welsh families in the Rhondda, according to a report by the Pilgrim Trust in 1938, were only too eager to exaggerate and dramatize their distress.[2] In spite of these contrasting attitudes the shock of unemployment was extreme because of its extent and suddenness. Before the war it had been slighter and more diffused, and generally greater in the south and the London area than in the north and Midlands. Now the position was largely reversed, and it was the catastrophic fall in demand in some of the great staple industries in the north after the prewar and wartime prosperity that demanded attention. One effect on the trade unions of the extension of unemployment relief was to make the wage structure more rigid. As they had less responsibility for their unemployed members they tended to concentrate stubbornly on maintaining existing wage levels.[3]

For the majority of the population, made up of the regularly and more highly paid workers, technicians and distributive agents, and the traditional middle class engaged primarily in clerical work and

[1] *The Times*, 23 Jan. 1927; cf. Hugh Dalton, *Call Back Yesterday* (1953), p. 207.
[2] *Men Without Work* (Cambridge, 1938), reports on six urban areas, quoted Pollard, p. 247.
[3] See below, pp. 249–50.

the professions, conditions were not greatly different from what they were before the war. But higher taxation, housing shortages, the 'new poverty' resulting from an inelastic income structure in a period of considerable inflation, and the now slightly defiant acceptance of the middle-class virtues of a good appearance, seemly behaviour, and identification with traditional patriotic attitudes, all combined to strengthen the sense of lurking adversity.[1] This, as the class which had saved for its old age, felt the full impact of cost-of-living increases on the retired, old, and small rentier members who relied on fixed (or in the case of house property, frozen) income. On this stratum of the population fell the main extra tax burden for public assistance, housing subsidies, and the other forms of welfare state expenditure which were to make the country fit for heroes to live in, and more technically to transfer part of the national wealth, probably 5 or 6 per cent, to the lower income groups. In 1925 the working class received £55 million more in social services than it paid in taxes, and in 1935 £91 million more, contributing 85 per cent of the cost in the first case, and 79 per cent in the second.[2]

Although the middle class aired its grievances occasionally in letters to the press it tended to feel itself at once exploited and forgotten, while rich and poor, upper and lower classes, got most of the attention in the nagging social-political-economic debates of the times. The 'rich' were presumably the numerically small high income groups, which could make substantial contributions of death duties to the Exchequer and which comprised on the one hand the older landed aristocracy with country houses and estates to maintain and on the other the wealthier 'big business' men who satisfied the Labour conception of what capitalists were really like. The Labour party's dilemma was that the punitive taxation of the rich, in the form for example of the super-tax payers, would not greatly help the economy, and the punitive taxation of the middle class would destroy Labour politically. Lloyd George had grasped this point as early as 1915. After Philip Snowden, in a speech in the Commons on 12 May 1915, had proposed to pay for the war by taxing everyone over a certain figure at the rate of 15 shillings in the

[1] Roy Lewis and Angus Maude, *The English Middle Classes* (1950), pp. 74–80; Masterman, pp. 24, 56–80.

[2] The position had been the reverse before the war. A. M. Carr-Saunders and D. C. Jones, *A Survey of the Social Structure of England and Wales* (1937), pp. 147–53. In terms of real wages, wage earners' position had improved by 15½ per cent in 1934 as compared with 1914. Mowat, p. 492.

pound, Lloyd George pointed out that this would bring in only £165 million, whereas the country needed £1,000 million a year.[1]

The issue was further confused by great indecision among Labour propagandists about the 'bourgeoisie'. Should they follow orthodox Marxist doctrine by sweepingly denouncing all the middle class as class enemies, or should they remember Karl Marx's narrower definition of the capitalist, the controller of capital, 'personified capital endowed with will and consciousness'?[2] It was never very clear. Omnibus denunciations, although they included such late examples as Aneurin Bevan's 'vermin',[3] became fewer as time went on; the denunciations began to have a stereotyped air, like newspaper battle cries and politicians' slogans generally, and the British working man did not feel in his bones the requisite sense of antagonism. An alternative course was to lump the middle classes with the unprivileged. On the whole the middle classes stayed Conservative.

3. EDUCATION AND HEALTH

The tendency for every aspect of politics to be judged on class or ideological lines was strongly marked in such matters as the mental and physical welfare of the masses. The ministers in charge of these problems during most of the interwar period were Conservatives, who with their conscientious civil servants undoubtedly represented socially favoured elements of the community; their well-intentioned paternalism could easily be derided as either patronizing or unsympathetic.

After 1945 this produced its crop of myths. It was, for example, frequently asserted that only the 'rich' had enjoyed such social benefits as a university education before the war.[4] We can dispose

---

[1] *Who is to Pay for the War?* (1915, National Labour Press pamphlet); cf. Pollard, pp. 63–6.

[2] 'Thus use-value is never to be regarded as the direct aim of the capitalist . . . a miser is only a capitalist gone mad, a capitalist is a miser who has come to his senses.' Karl Marx, *Capital* (London, Dent, 1933), pp. 138–9. Conservatism was the fig leaf of capitalism, therefore concerned with profit and not use-value for the benefit of the community. George Lansbury in particular always seemed very worried about use-value; cf. Lewis and Maude, pp. 65–74.

[3] See below, p. 507.

[4] A writer in *The Times* of 19 May 1960 referred to 'the rare grammar school boy at the university' in the thirties. Even if the writer were assuming that the only universities in England were those of Oxford and Cambridge the statement is statistically questionable, and the further assertion that only these rare grammar school birds among university students read the 'Pelican' paperback series is very odd. Even so careful a writer as Dr. Sidney Pollard said in 1962 that in the interwar period, 'higher education was still mainly for the rich, rather than for those best able to profit from it' (*op. cit.*, p. 266).

of this particular legend at once by saying that as early as 1920–21 2,888 students entered the universities of England and Wales from the grant-aided secondary schools; of these 62·2 per cent were of elementary school origin. This meant that some 38 per cent of the total university entrants in England and 87 per cent in Wales came from the elementary schools. In the autumn of 1938, 4,225 students from the grant-aided secondary schools went to English and Welsh universities; 437 out of 798 open entrance scholarships and exhibitions awarded at Oxford and Cambridge in 1938 were won by pupils at grant-aided secondary schools; and of the 437, 67·7 per cent were won by pupils who had paid no fees in their schools and 65·4 per cent by those who had been previously educated in public elementary schools.[1] These and similar figures are sufficient to show that the universities were not mere finishing schools for the idle rich. It remained true, however, that the numbers of boys and girls going on to the universities from any class of society was small as compared, for example, with those of the United States.

It has been said that the guiding principle of the British parent with regard to education is not the continental conception of a career open to talents but a less rationally based solicitude to afford his child a better chance in life than he himself enjoyed.[2] This was certainly the drive behind the varied educational advances before 1914. The Education Act of 1870 had promised elementary education for all; and the first generation was concerned with the provision of schools and teachers, and the minimum achievement of the '3 R's' for some 3 million children. The English public schools, with their emphasis on moral earnestness and organized games, were largely the result of Dr. Arnold's civilizing work at Rugby, which was widely copied; most of the schools on the present Headmasters List are modern creations, usually of the boarding school type. The non-public secondary schools, today called county or grammar schools, were also being greatly extended and developed from the eighteen-seventies onwards, and were usually confined to day boys. There were a few girls' schools of the public school type, and a wide range of girls' high schools similar to the boys secondary grammar schools. But between the elementary and secondary school worlds there were few links until 1907, when the 'scholarship' provisions

---

[1] Board of Education annual reports for 1924–25 (Cmd 2443), p. 27; 1924–25 (Cmd 2695), pp. 103–6; 1938 (Cmd 6013), p. 148; K. Lindsay, *Social Progress and Educational Waste* (1926), pp. 35–48; G. A. N. Lowndes, *The Silent Social Revolution* (1937).

[2] Lowndes, p. 125.

began. Special Board of Education grants were made available for such secondary schools as would accept a triennial inspection and admit one-quarter of their entry each year from the elementary schools by examination. This was in turn a result of the 1902 Education Act, which had encouraged the new local education authorities to build secondary schools. A University Grants Committee was set up in 1911. All was ready for a big advance after the war, on lines laid down in H. A. L. Fisher's Education Act of 1918.

It is true that economy campaigns in 1921 and 1931 prevented the full development of the plans visualized by Fisher, but they did not weaken the basic educational structure of the country, or prevent the realization of his essential proposals.[1] The act abolished all exemptions from school-leaving before fourteen, gave local authorities permission to raise the school-leaving age to fifteen, provided for the establishment of day continuation schools for youths between fourteen and sixteen, and made increased financial provision for every type of school from the nursery stage onwards. In 1920 the provision of 200 state scholarships (in addition to the existing system of L.E.A. grants and university awards) allowed increased numbers of students to enter the universities. The Geddes axe proposed to cut £18 million from the education estimates in 1922, but this cut was quickly reduced to one-third. The result was a slowing down of school building, the deferment of the raising of the leaving age by local authorities, and the decline of the continuation schools, which usually ceased to be compulsory. It was, broadly speaking, the official attempt to educate those over fourteen who hated the very idea that was abandoned in the name of economy. For those who sought education, facilities continued to expand.

The state scholarships, after being briefly discontinued, were restored in 1924 and increased to 300 by the Labour government in 1930. The numbers of secondary schools in the country increased by 50 per cent between 1920 and 1931, and the number of free places in these schools rose to 43 per cent in 1930.[2] The Hadow Report of 1926 led to a further major advance by the provision of separate schools after the age of eleven for those who did not go to

---

[1] 'Expansion did not suffer any marked set-back when the industrial activity of the war years gave way to the economic difficulties of 1921' (Lowndes, p. 115).

[2] In 1929 the total number of scholars in the grant list schools was 386,993; to this has to be added those at the public schools. The total of French secondary school scholars in 1927–8 was 286,690 (Lowndes, pp. 119–20).

the grammar schools. New university colleges were founded.[1] The universities were assisted by an annual Treasury grant through the University Grants Committee, although it did not bridge the gap between income and adequate expenditure in departments and colleges which failed to interest the private benefactor. In these cases, which included the arts side of most of the provincial universities, research grants of any sort were virtually non-existent, staffs were small, salary scales for most of the lecturing staff less attractive than the Burnham scale for teachers; but in stressing the wide differences between the various institutions we must not lose sight of the net advance which the existence of the newer creations made possible.

The main purpose of higher education was still considered to be the provision of professional training for gifted individuals for entry into the establishments of church and state, including teaching and the civil service. Stress was laid on the argument that popular government was doomed unless it could call to its aid men of professional training to handle the problems of the postwar world.[2] The two greatest of the British universities, in spite of their wealth and resources, continued to regard their splendid undergraduate schools rather than postgraduate research as their most useful and typical activity. It was only gradually (and not it would seem before 1939) that the American (and in some measure Welsh) conception of the university as a finishing school for all citizens of average ability was widely canvassed. There is no evidence that this was particularly attractive to parents at this time. The large percentage of boys and girls who reached the universities from elementary schools, and often therefore from working-class homes, shows that 'the rich' did not have a virtual monopoly; the small actual numbers of the children of well-to-do parents at the universities (where the total numbers were not above 30,000 a year) show on the other hand that a university career was not the main objective of school leavers.[3] The Ministry of Education was evidently satisfied that it was providing higher education for those who were capable of benefiting from it and benefiting the community in the process. Where some

---

[1] Swansea 1920, Leicester 1921, Exeter 1922, Hull 1928; the last three were external colleges of the University of London, the first a constituent college of the University of Wales.

[2] Cf. A. M. Carr-Saunders and P. A. Wilson, *The Professions* (Oxford, 1933), pp. 499–503.

[3] Mowat, pp. 206–11, for a good sketch although the figures on p. 207 are difficult to follow.

new popular demand for educational expenditure appeared the government did its best to win credit by generous support. Thus the adult education movement led to the development of extra-mural departments of the universities, with relatively generous fees to lecturers which sometimes supplemented the relatively meagre regular salaries of the university staffs.

While educational advance meant in the main the orderly development of plans which had been laid in the generation before 1914, health was a field for some new discoveries and innovations in policy. When the Ministry of Health was set up in 1919 with health and housing as its two specific functions it took over the work of the old Local Government Board and the National Health Insurance Commission. We have already referred to housing, and there was to be a systematic extension of governmental activity over the whole field of public assistance, local government organization, medical care and the like which earned for Neville Chamberlain both a high reputation and surprisingly acrimonious relations with the Opposition between 1924 and 1929. In food and living conditions there was a notable advance, leading to the successful administration of food supplies in the second world war. The discovery of the vitamins by Dutch scientists, confirmed by Professor Frederick Gowland Hopkins in 1912, played a dramatic part in this, in spite of the stubborn faith of the British working man in the life-giving qualities of beer and chips, fried fish and vinegar, white bread and tea.

British scientists were beginning to apply the new data on nutritional matters during the first world war, well ahead of Germany in this respect. Two lessons learned were that malnutrition was not confined to the poorer sections of the population and that science could in time provide an adequate diet at prices within the reach of all. The first point was driven home by the poor quality of many recruits during the war (the same depressing discovery was made in the United States and other countries), and to some extent the demands of war forced investigation which confirmed hopes of the second. The ravages of scurvy among troops in the East was not effectively met by the traditional use of lime juice, and it was not until late in 1916 that lemon juice was established as the really powerful antiscorbutic, and then supplied in large quantities. The residual lemon pulp supplied depressingly insipid marmalade for the home front. Scientists and officials clashed when Lord Devonport appealed in 1917 for voluntary rationing in bread, meat, and sugar, and later for a 'Meatless Day', for the effect would be to transfer consumption to imported supplies or to lower energy and even the patriotic impulses dangerously. Expert advice, largely followed by his successor, Lord Rhondda, was to concentrate on ample supplies of bread and flour as the best and cheapest form of energy. In 1919 a team working under Dr. Harriette Chick among starving children in Vienna confirmed Sir Edward Mellanby's discovery that rickets was essentially a vitamin-deficiency condition, and after the war, although rationing soon ended, experimental research of this type was undertaken systematically, although it was not until after 1945 that the man in the street finally became vitamin-conscious.[1]

4. Exports and Unemployment

During the twenties the aspirations of Labour and the plans of the government were upset by the unexpectedly heavy unemployment figures, which never sank below a million. This disconcerted the trade unions, whose postwar programme had been to consolidate and improve on their wartime gains; instead of prosperous and expanding markets which would provide the best conditions for successful wage battles for their regularly employed members they had to face such problems as dilution, the call for a general lowering of wages to reduce prices, demands for longer working hours, the defection of unemployed members, and the competition of the Communist party.[2] The governments of the twenties, whatever their party colour, were also disconcerted by the failure of the country to get back to prewar levels of industrial activity. While following, with great stubbornness and consistency, deflationary fiscal policies which they hoped would achieve this end, they were forced to listen to proposals for many drastic alternatives—from protection and currency manipulation to nationalization and state-supported programmes of public works. The broad issue was whether to hang on and try to restore the old prosperity or whether to seek more or less drastic changes in the national economy. The unemployment figures were high, but looking at the matter from another angle, 90 per cent of the country was at work.

Unemployment, the root cause of industrial unrest and symbol of

[1] W. H. Beveridge, *British Food Control* (1928), pp. 333–44; John Boyd Orr, *Food, Health and Income* (1936), pp. 23–8; J. C. Drummond and Anne Wilbraham, *The Englishman's Food* (1957 edn.), pp. 431–47; Asa Briggs, *Seebohm Rowntree* (1961), pp. 150, 152.
[2] Pollard, pp. 88–9; W. Arthur Lewis, *Economic Survey, 1919–1939* (1949), pp. 74–89.

the unsolved problems, was due primarily to the failure to maintain the prewar level of exports. How far was the setback the result of transitory causes? Even before the war the annual rate of increase of British exports was falling, and there had been a substantial decline of the British share of the world exports of manufactures. The most important cause of this, although not the only one, had been the industrialization of certain foreign countries, which had led to increased competition with British goods in traditional markets. The process had been strengthened by tariffs in the great new industrial states such as Germany and the United States, but this was a minor factor in the decline, for these two countries and France had taken less than one-fifth of the world imports of manufactures in the early eighteen-eighties. During the first two years of war the export trade had shown remarkably little change from that of 1913, although later the growing shipping shortage and the increasing allocation of essential raw materials to munitions production and the direct war services had been bound to hit it adversely. The process then became a double one: on the one hand the United States and other countries less directly affected by the war than the United Kingdom were encouraged to develop their own production further and to replace the British in some of their traditional markets; on the other, the British export industry not only lost touch with some of its customers but had of necessity to suspend the usual continuing process of adaptation to new tastes and to new challenges of foreign competition. The German market, Britain's best customer in 1913, was closed entirely.[1]

The crisis did not become apparent until the end of the short replacement boom which followed the war. The war ended as it had begun with fears of slump and unemployment, which in both cases proved to be unfounded. For a little over a year, from about March 1919 to April 1920, there was an astonishing demand for goods at home and abroad, due on the one hand to the fact that the world had money to spend, and on the other to the fact that for so long it had been unable to buy. Up to a point this had a beneficial effect in cushioning the dislocation of manpower resulting from demobilization and the closing down of war industries, and it naturally strengthened the belief that a return to prewar levels of output would be soon achieved. But the development was too

[1] J. H. Clapham, *An Economic History of England* (Cambridge, 1938), vol. III, pp. 521–34; on the prewar position, pp. 21–68; Bowley, pp. 207–20.

brief and fierce; the boom tended to become a bubble, the demand forced prices up, and the government was still maintaining its own expenditure at a high level and thereby creating additional purchasing power. One result of the boom was heavy speculation taking the form on the one hand of new company flotations and on the other of amalgamations; the textile, shipping, shipbuilding, and engineering industries were all affected, and while in some cases the creation of larger units was a necessary step towards greater efficiency, in others the effect was to nullify the advantages of experienced personal management without providing any compensating advantage.[1]

The collapse came when the more urgent tasks of restoring and reconditioning the country's industry had been completed, when the worst shortages had been removed, and when, with the release of shipping, food and raw materials began to arrive more plentifully in Europe from overseas. There was a general collapse of prices in 1920, and widespread unemployment. In the depression which followed it was perhaps inevitable that dislocations due to the war should continue to monopolize attention. The essential thing seemed to be to cure the inflation by lowering prices and wages and to restore the London money market as a means, among other things, of providing the credit which would restore the purchasing power of former customers abroad. Certainly by this stage victory no longer appeared to possess a magic quality which would carry the world triumphantly through the problem of reconstruction. The conviction that wars never pay, much proclaimed by the pacifists, began to find gloomy endorsement in many business circles. Hopes of great reparations payments which would cover the cost of the war and finance the peace were rapidly fading, and the restoration of central European purchasing power became a more urgent and certainly more respectable objective.[2]

All the same the depression in the export industries did not suggest that the basic purpose was wrong—in other words that the country was trying to export the wrong things—but rather that the dislocation caused by the war was more intractable than had been anticipated. The causes were felt to lie primarily in the financial field. The result was a great but partly frustrated effort during the nineteen-twenties to restore the country's traditional export domin-

---

[1] Youngson, pp. 24-6.
[2] Lewis, pp. 41-5.

ance and the rôle of the City of London in financing a great part of the world's business. The alternative would have been the development of new classes of exports. This was happening in some cases, such as the growth of the rayon and motor car and motor cycle industries which were bringing prosperity to the south and the Midlands, although on a small scale as compared with the United States.[1] It has also been argued that a bolder attempt should have been made to encourage sales of producer goods as compared with consumer goods. This had, in fact, been the tendency for the half century before 1914; consumer goods (mainly textiles) which had formed 77 per cent of British exports in 1857–59 had fallen to 61·8 per cent in 1911–13, while the export of producer goods had risen from 21·8 per cent in 1857–59 to 33·7 per cent in 1911–13. The respective figures for 1927–29 were 56·4 and 37·5 per cent—a perceptible but very limited move in the same direction, at a time when both Germany and the United States were expanding rapidly and capturing a large share in the world market for such goods.[2] Such arguments tended at the time to be dismissed as counsels of despair, but it can be argued now that it was the failure to direct more energy into the newer trades rather than the decline of the old which was disquieting. The worst of the depression seemed, however, to have spent itself by 1922, and a great effort throughout the world to stabilize international finances, in which Great Britain and the United States played the main part, led to a general re-establishment of the gold standard by 1925.[3]

Of the great export industries on which so much depended, cotton illustrates most clearly the difficulty of distinguishing between long-term trends and the results of the war.[4] The tendency has perhaps been to minimize the adverse effects of the latter. While there was a relatively small decline before the war there was nothing at that time to suggest to the shrewd leaders of the industry any serious upheavals or decay. Textile manufactures had supplied 58·7 per cent of the total British exports in 1890–92; the figure had certainly

[1] G. C. Allen, *British Industries and their Organization* (1959), pp. 21–2, 30–2; Pollard, pp. 99–110, in a good account of new and growing industries, points out that 'fundamentally, unlike the old staples, they were based on a buoyant home market'.
[2] Cf. the discussion of this point in Lewis, pp. 77–9, quoting figures of Dr. W. Schlote, *Entwicklung und Strukturwandlungen des englischen Aussenhandels von 1700 bis zur Gegenwart.*
[3] Youngson, pp. 22–5; A. C. Pigou, *Aspects of British Economic History, 1918–1925*, pp. 42–59.
[4] Clapham, p. 126, citing Cd 9070; Allen, pp. 218–25; B. Bowker, *Lancashire Under the Hammer* (1928), pp. 27–55.

fallen to 51·2 per cent in the period 1911–13. After the war, how-ever, the average total export of cotton piece goods between 1920 and 1923 was only about 4,000 million linear yards as compared with 7,075 million in 1913. Exports of cotton yarns also dropped by some 13 per cent after the war, largely because of the development of weaving in India. The decline was mainly in the cheaper classes of cloth and yarn. The views of representatives of the industry show that as late as 1916–17 they were confident that the strength of the cotton trade in the competitive markets of the world was 'practically unimpaired' and that the machinery and plant were on the whole highly efficient. They recognized that Japan was destined to become 'Lancashire's principal competitor in years to come', but evidently did not anticipate a setback comparable with that which in fact took place in the nineteen-twenties.

It does seem that we must look on the whole to war and postwar developments for the explanation. One important influence for example was the serious disorganization resulting from the inflation and speculation of 1919 and 1920, when a large number of mills, representing over 40 per cent of the productive capacity of the industry, changed hands.[1] Another was the development, stimu-lated by the war in a number of countries, of manufacture for their own use, usually with a surplus for export; the most notable example was Japan, whose percentage increase in the world's export of cotton piece goods between 1913 and 1924 was roughly equal to the British decline. India too was steadily increasing her domestic manufacture, at Britain's expense. It is also important not to ex-aggerate the extent of the decline in the immediate postwar years, when the industry was trying to find its bearings, and there were some compensations. The finer goods, using chiefly Egyptian cotton, continued to do well, and the makers of 'finished threads', such as J. and P. Coats, more than held their own. Sales of cotton piece goods increased in Europe and the United States, and more or less held their position in the Near East and the Dominions. The catastrophic drop was in exports to the Far East, which took 62 per cent of these exports in 1913, and only 44·6 in 1924–25. Yet in 1924 exports of cotton yarns and cloths still provided, as in 1913, a quarter of the country's exports. It is in the second half of the nineteen-twenties that the value falls relative to the country's total exports; in 1929 it was 18·5 per cent only.

[1] Mowat, p. 26; Clapham, p. 537.

The woollen and worsted industries also had their postwar difficulties, which were due, however, less to foreign competitors than to changes in taste and supply. The heavy wool stocks which had accumulated in Australia owing to the war and immediate postwar shipping shortages led to great fluctuations in price, and there were the usual (and perhaps a little more than the usual) fluctuations in fashion. But for the first postwar years it seemed that Yorkshire goods would continue to be in much more steady demand than those of Lancashire.[1]

In shipbuilding the wartime losses, enormous though they were, had been made good in a vast building effort during the war itself and the months following the armistice. In 1920 the world's tonnage of sea-going steam and motor ships was 53·9 million gross tons, as compared with 47·9 million in 1919 and 45·4 million in 1914. Britain's share was 18·1, 16·3, and 18·9 million tons in the corresponding years. The 1919–20 boom and the anticipation of its continuance seemed to justify further extensive building. This was one of the industries in which Britain had for long been the world's chief supplier; 22 per cent of launchings had been on foreign order before 1914, and the figure rose to 41 per cent in 1920. Shipyard capacity, already greatly expanded during the war, was further increased in 1919 and 1920. Then the slump hit the industry badly and the tonnage under construction in British yards had fallen by the end of 1922 to one-third of the figure for April 1921. The depression was due mainly to the fact that the world had all the shipping it needed for the time being, but also to the partial discontinuance of building for the Royal Navy. However, about a million tons of shipping continued for some years to be produced by the British yards, mainly as replacement for old, sunk, or obsolete vessels.

Restrictions on international trade during the interwar years also reduced the demand for the services of British merchant navy. The 16·3 million tons of British shipping of 1919 represented 34 per cent of the world's total. The comparable figures for British shipping for 1930 and 1939 were 20·4 million tons in 1930, and 18 million tons in 1939; this meant 29·9 and 26·1 per cent of the world's total respectively. Thus British merchant shipping was a little less in 1939 than it had been in 1914, whereas it had been greater in 1930 than in 1914 or 1939. The economic nationalism of the thirties

[1] Clapham, p. 530; Allen, p. 226.

was partly to blame. Mounting tariffs, exchange restrictions, and subsidies to new shipping fleets curtailed business for Britain and other traditional specialists in the carrying trade. The trend even before 1914 was for Britain's share of world shipping to drop; the figure of 26·1 per cent in 1939 represents, however, a bigger percentage decline than the continuance of the pre-1914 trend should have produced.[1]

In the case of iron and steel the most notable fact is that pig-iron production in the United Kingdom fell from 10·3 million tons in 1913 to 7·4 million in 1924 and to 6·3 million in 1925, and that the British share in the world's production of pig-iron continued to fall after 1925. German output, which had been much the same as the British in 1913, had reached 10·177 million tons in 1925, and United States production had increased from 31·462 million tons in 1913 to 37·288 million in 1925. In the immediate postwar years the reason for the decline in home consumption and export was partly the ample supplies of scrap steel left over from the war, but the main explanation seems to have been the replacing of wrought and cast iron by steel, both at home and abroad. Steel held its own, although the export figures are complicated by the fact that crude steel was imported, and the bulk of the output was absorbed by home production.[2]

It is, however, in the coal industry that the loss of exports was most obvious and most painfully reflected in labour conditions. Although exports had reached 98 million out of a total output of 287 million tons in the peak year of 1913 there were basic difficulties which must have become apparent in the near future, even without the interruption of war conditions. In the years before 1914 rising costs, due primarily to the inevitable exhaustion of the more easily worked and easily accessible coal seams, had been more than balanced for a time by the expanding foreign demand, which had enabled the coal exporters to pass on the increased costs to the consumer. The demand for British coal had been due to its quality, to the absence as yet of satisfactory substitutes, to the proximity of many British coalfields to the sea, and in turn to the proximity to the

[1] The reasons for this, and the figures in these two paragraphs, are discussed in S. G. Sturmey, *British Shipping and World Competition* (1962), pp. 37 and 52, and chaps. 3 and 4 generally. See also C. E. Fayle, *The War and the Shipping Industry* (1927), pp. 378–9.

[2] D. L. Burn, *The Economic History of Steelmaking* (1940), chaps. XIV, XV; Allen, pp. 106–10, 130–32; Pollard, pp. 115–16.

sea of many foreign industrial areas, where it proved cheaper to import from Britain than to bring the coal overland from continental mines. Baltic, North Sea, French, and Mediterranean ports thus took over 80 per cent of the British exports; most of the rest, mainly South Welsh anthracite, went to South America. These favourable conditions were not likely to last, but timely adjustment might have been made if peace had continued. The war, however, accelerated changes, most of them to the disadvantage of the British industry. The export trade to Europe largely ceased, with a resultant stimulus to coal production in continental countries and the search for substitutes; at home, it was natural that production should be concentrated on the more easily worked mines and that modernization of equipment and increased mechanization should have been postponed. The world output in the early twenties was less than that of the prewar average; even so, in the short postwar boom the British industry exported less than half the prewar quantity. This was partly due to the restrictions resulting from the continuance of the wartime governmental controls; exports were limited, and the price of coal in the home market was fixed at a low figure. When these restrictions were removed after the collapse of the boom there was some improvement; by 1928 exports had reached about two-thirds (72 million tons) of the prewar figure. But this was not a real recovery. Competition had been reduced and exports helped by an American strike in 1922 and by the disorganization of the Ruhr in 1923; a government subsidy in 1925–26 gave further assistance.

The real truth of the matter was that with a general increase in productive capacity in coal mining throughout the world there had been no corresponding increase in demand because of the spectacular increase in substitutes. Electricity from hydroelectric or coal-consuming power stations, and the ever growing use of oil for shipping and road transport, reduced the demand for coal from both British and foreign mines; and even where industry had not succumbed to the use of oil as fuel, economies in the shape of more efficient heat conservation further reduced demand. Thus although the consumption of coal remained high, the export market was becoming increasingly competitive; and the British owners were wedded for far too long to the belief that harder work, longer hours, and lower wages were an adequate substitute for the many alternative plans of reorganization, mechanization, closing of un-

economic pits, and other devices urged by their critics. The failure
of the miners' strike in 1926 meant the postponement of drastic
change for another twenty years.[1]

The measure of economic difficulty was coming to be the unemployment figures, and the intractable million. The slump in
exports accounted for the greater part of this; production for the
home market had not changed greatly in the aggregate, but exports
were never more than 80 per cent of their prewar volume. The
broad nature of the problem was soon evident to those who could
read the figures; but what was the remedy? We can sum up the
policies of the two leading parties (although with some over-
simplification) by saying that while Labour with its more or less
urgent demands for socialization looked for action by the state it
had as yet no real programme for applying state action in the field
of foreign trade; the Conservatives on the other hand, while they
were not without expedients, were unable to secure the country's
consent to the use of the directive power of the state in the form
that they desired. They put forward protection of the home market
as a cure for unemployment in 1923, but this plan, while it united the
party, divided the country, and from 1925 onwards Winston
Churchill as Chancellor of the Exchequer kept the party loyal to
free trade and the gold standard. The leaders of the Labour party
were also kept to free trade and after 1925 to the gold standard by
Philip Snowden, another fierce supporter of former Liberal orthodoxies, who succeeded in preventing any positive action by his
party throughout the two periods of Labour rule. His left-wing
critics inside the party regarded unemployment as incurable under
the capitalist system, although they never succeeded in convincing
the party that the abolition of capitalism would abolish unemployment. When MacDonald and Snowden left the party in 1931 they
took its only economic policy with them.

We put our finger on the most specific cause of England's difficulties in the nineteen-twenties when we emphasize the failure to
recover the prewar export position. The problem was tackled with
more drastic expedients and with a greater sense of urgency—
although not on the whole with greater success—during the thirties.
Why were these expedients not used in the twenties? For, perhaps,
three reasons, which were largely interrelated. The first was the con-

[1] A. M. de Neuman, *Economic Organization of the British Coal Industry* (1934), pp.
14–32.

servative impulse, worldwide and affecting all walks of life, of the period; the second was that the stultifying effects of economic nationalism on the world economy were not yet fully realized; the third was that the obstacle to recovery in the external world and even to some extent in domestic affairs was felt to lie far more in political or social than in strictly economic conditions. It was, after all, not unreasonable to ask in 1919 whether the foundations on which the 'fragile, precarious, and soaring fabric of western civilization' had been built were not dangerously undermined.

The most urgent task thus became one of restoration: the clearing of channels of trade, the repairing of vast shortages of food and raw materials, and the establishment of a stable medium of exchange, together with the solution of problems created by the death of millions of workers, by revolution and starvation, by new political grievances, and by new outlooks and desires. Appalled at the reckless devastation of the war, amazed that the will and strength of the belligerents should have carried them on for so long, the economists of the nineteen-twenties were surprised and relieved at the degree of recovery that was in fact achieved. We misunderstand the nineteen-twenties in the field of economic policy if we think of it as a decade of drift and of defeatism: it was rather one of self-congratulation on a remarkable achievement. Sir Arthur Salter, looking back in 1932 over the preceding three years of depression, recalled that in 1929 'the world as a whole was well above all earlier standards and seemed to be advancing at an unprecedented pace to levels of prosperity never before thought possible'.[1]

5. THE POLITICAL PARTIES

Into this mood of cautious optimism the Labour party could scarcely enter, but it had as yet no really convincing alternative programmes to offer. By far the most important fact in British domestic politics after the first world war was, nevertheless, the establishment of this new amalgam of men, ideas, and policies as the second party in the state, a position formally achieved at the 1922 general election. The Liberals were pushed permanently into the third place. On the other hand the electorate was not prepared to give this new party a clear majority between 1918 and 1945, and

[1] Sir Arthur Salter, *Recovery: the Second Effort* (1932), pp. 3, 4, 22–3; A. J. Youngson, pp. 50–57; K. Polanyi, *Origins of Our Time, the Great Transformation* (1945), pp. 32–40; Gustav Stolper, *This Age of Fable* (New York, 1942), chap. 11.

it is evident that the Conservatives received a regular bonus in votes from cautious members of the public who could not make up their minds about the Labourites even when they had no traditional love of Tories.

It will be useful to note briefly the characteristics of the two main parties at this point of departure in the twenties, as an introduction to the more detailed story of their love-hate relationships during the forty years that follow. The historian has to remind himself repeatedly that in the subtle functioning of the two-party system the ends and in large measure the means followed by rival parties may not differ, and, on the other hand, that success in the party struggle depends on the concealment of this fact. The paradox of continuity in policy is that it forces the parties to stage their greatest battles where differences are least likely to upset the ship of state. It is obviously best to claim office on the mere ground of superior ability to the existing set of rulers, thus avoiding the need to change policies at all. But this is difficult for a new party with leaders still untried. In this sense the Labour party had a double problem: it had to decide how far to go in a radical direction in order to capture all potential adherents, and how far to bar the extremists who might capture the party or frighten the uncommitted electorate.

It was not in origin a socialist party. Its solid basis was the trade union membership, reinforced by a small but disproportionately influential group of non-working class idealists and intellectuals. The organization of the Labour Representation Committee, set up in 1900, had provided for an Executive Committee of twelve members, made up of seven from the trade unions, one from the Fabian Society, and two each from the I.L.P. and the S.D.F. This was absurdly unrepresentative of trade union strength, which made up about 93 per cent of the total membership, but officially the L.R.C., and the Labour party after 1906, continued for some years to have no political platform, and trade union influence was exerted to prevent the adoption of a socialist programme. The most important of the socialist societies was the I.L.P., whose total membership, however, never reached 50,000. They were the Girondists of the movement, and although ready on all occasions to expound their views, were careful not to shake the unity of the party by forcing these views on their trade union brethren. The more forthright socialists tended to hive off into the smaller S.D.F. (which withdrew from the L.R.C. in 1901) or the Communist ranks after 1917. Accordingly, Henderson's reorganization of the party in 1918 gave it a programme rather as an indispensable basis for concerted action than as an ideological conversion; the speeches of some trade unionist delegates showed a continued uneasiness at its socialistic implications.

The constitution adopted in 1918 referred to five party objects, one of which was 'to secure for the producers by hand or by brain the full fruits of their industry, and the most equitable distribution thereof that may be possible, upon the basis of the common ownership of the means of production and the best obtainable system of popular administration and control of each industry and service'. Another said more generally that the aim was the emancipation of the people, 'and more particularly of those who depend directly upon their own exertions by hand or by brain for the means of life'. The uneasy trade unionists consoled themselves with the reflexion that their overwhelming influence in the party under the new constitution would enable them to prevent the socialistic implications of these phrases from being rapidly applied.[1] The essential point of the new arrangements was the decision to encourage the formation of constituency organizations (a local Labour party in each constituency) and to create a nationally organized party in the place of the federal structure of 1900. The socialist societies lost their separate representation, and the decision to place voting for seats on the executive in the hands of the whole party conference gave the ultimate control of all elections to the unions. Nevertheless, although the situation seemed ultimately fatal to the I.L.P., it shared in the growth of the years from 1918 to 1922; and in the 1922 election over 100 I.L.P. members, including the Scottish contingent, were elected to Parliament. This element secured MacDonald's election as leader in place of J. R. Clynes.[2]

But there was no real future in the party for the genuine extremist. The affiliation of the Communist party continued to be refused. In Parliament the party whip was withheld from Communist M.P.s. The position of individual Communists inside the party or the trade unions was more difficult; a new rule excluding those who did not 'individually accept the Constitution and principles of the Labour party' was endorsed by the Edinburgh conference in 1922,

[1] The confused historical background of these decisions is described in E. Eldon Barry, *Nationalization in British Politics* (1965), chaps. 1–3.
[2] W. L. Guttsman, *The British Political Elite* (1963), pp. 228–42; Fenner Brockway *Inside the Left* (1922), pp. 138–9.

but raised problems of identification.[1] Moreover, the growth of constituency parties based on individual membership made it desirable to cast the net as widely as possible, for outside Parliament the party as such, like the Conservative National Union, was primarily a vote-getting agency.[2]

The recruits to the Labour party from outside the trade union ranks came mainly from the Liberal party and they were able to give a decisive lead towards a somewhat circumspect acceptance of evolutionary socialism and a foreign policy based on disarmament, collective guarantees, and democratic control. We shall look further at the second of these developments in the next section. Sidney and Beatrice Webb formed close links with the Labour party only during the war, but Sidney became a member of the party executive in 1916, and powerfully reinforced I.L.P. influence in favour of giving some socialist flavour to the new party constitution. Sir Leo Chiozza Money, also a Fabian, had written persuasively on a socialist theme in *Riches and Poverty* in 1905, and in *The Triumph of Nationalization* in 1920. Dr. Addison after his break with Lloyd George joined Labour and published his *Practical Socialism* in 1926. There were many others, writers and parliamentary candidates; an interesting recent survey of the careers of some seventy prominent recruits shows that only two appear to have had previous official connexions with the Conservative party, and most of them were upper or upper-middle class products of the public schools and older universities. Karl Marx would doubtless have seen this as a proof that as the class war nears the decisive hour a portion of the middle-class ideologists joins the revolutionary class.[3]

Liberalism did not decline through any repudiation by the country of its well-tried and respectable political principles: it was rather that these seemed likely to find a more practical application through the medium of the two rival parties. The Labour party had captured radicalism and promised to go far beyond Asquithian reformism, given half a chance: while for those who wanted as little as possible of either radicalism or reformism the Conservative party seemed to offer a better prospect than the Liberal party of

---

[1] G. D. H. Cole, *History of the Labour Party from 1914*, pp. 144–9; H. Pelling, *The British Communist Party* (1958), pp. 8–27; C. F. Brand, *British Labour's Rise to Power* chap. 8.

[2] R. T. McKenzie, *British Political Parties* (1955), p. 455.

[3] Catherine Ann Cline, *Recruits to Labour, the British Labour Party, 1914–1931* (1963), pp. 5–7, 24, 30–31.

tranquillity and good government. Liberalism thus faced a painful dilemma.[1] Should it try to outbid Labour with bold Hobhousian schemes of public planning for social and economic progress? Or should it vie with the Tories as the party of stability? A profound and underrated element in British public life is the continuing respect of vast numbers of the electorate for the old ruling classes, the squire in the village (or his contemporary counterpart), and the public-spirited aristocrat in national affairs. It was believed as late as the early nineteen-sixties that a third of the working-class vote was still given to the Conservative party for approximately this reason. The Liberal party in the early twenties could point to its own hierarchy of revered aristocrats, headed by Earl Grey. But the fortunes of war had given the Tories their decisive lead just at the moment when the anti-socialist front was being formed; the glory had departed from Liberalism in the years before 1914, and the glory that attached itself to Lloyd George after 1916 benefited only him or his Tory allies. When he rejoined the Opposition Liberals after 1922 his star had faded and he was on balance an electoral liability to them. The dilemma was never resolved. It is important, however, not to exaggerate the extent of the Liberal decline. The British voting system operates unjustly for the smaller parties: the Liberals still polled some three million votes in 1924, although with only forty-one seats.

But it was certainly the case that renegade Liberals reinforced the ranks and hopes of the Tories as well as of Labour. If England abhors coalition it abides its Conservatives, who were as firmly in office in 1960 as they had been in 1900. If one seeks for a pattern broad enough to incorporate the main strands of modern British politics one might find it in lengthy periods of Conservative rule, each broken by a short weak phase of reformism and each followed by a powerful reformist type of government which exhausts itself in the exuberance of its triumph.[2] Thus in 1922, when Labour was hopefully taking up the challenge from an exhausted Liberalism, the Conservative party, with the confusion of coalition behind it, also began to look to its new image. How far should it adopt any of the expedients of the Left? The Tories had their own brand

[1] K. Minogue, *The Liberal Mind* (1963), pp. 141–6.
[2] Conservative-Unionist governments in office, 1886–1905, with a weak Liberal interlude (1892–95) followed by a strong one (1906–15); after the coalition had collapsed, Conservatives in office 1922–40, with two weak Labour interludes (1924, 1929–31), followed by a strong Labour government (1945–51).

of reformism, which they regarded as more realistic and therefore less vote-absorbing than the Labourite panaceas. They comforted themselves with the hope that while the middle and upper classes were unlikely to be driven to the support of Labour, the working classes would be kept below the revolution mark by the reasonable level of prosperity which it was confidently believed would return to the country as a result of the government's fiscal and monetary policy, together with the well-tried genius of the British manufacturer.

'What is my party?' asked Stanley Baldwin of his biographer. 'Diamond Jubilee die-hards and Tory Democrats pulling me two ways at once.' Had he forgotten the hard-faced business men whose appearance so irked him in 1919?[1] It was certainly the party of the business men: what else was there for them? With the country gentlemen, the lawyers, and the other professional men they made up its largest and now most characteristic section. The extrusion of the landed aristocracy from its place of dominance had been registered by Bonar Law's election in 1911, and the preference for Baldwin instead of Curzon as Prime Minister in 1923 was to confirm it. Far to the right there were still perhaps a hundred members who represented the old Toryism in creed and outlook, not primarily concerned with the party as a mass party but rather with its traditional responsibilities—'individualism, the white man's hard won burden, armed neutrality, and the land'.[2] On the other wing, however, there were those who in later Coalition days were ready for the fusion of Unionist and Liberal, and those who, while distrusting fusion, were ready to outstrip the Liberals in social reform.

As the Liberal party withered, Liberal policies could be adopted in social legislation to save the Tory conscience from enslavement to plutocracy. In a little book entitled *Tory Democracy*, published in 1918 just before the end of the war, Lord Henry Bentinck warned the party to beware lest Plugson of Undershot,[3] having conquered shells and cellulose, should capture the country's political life: 'that way lies . . .damnation for the Tory party; for it will inevitably lose its national character and sink into a tariff-mongering faction'. He turned hopefully to the encouraging record of the 'Young Tories' of the immediate prewar years. The war had killed some of

---

[1] G. M. Young, *Stanley Baldwin* (1952), p. 55; see p. 76 above; Guttsman, pp. 289–98.
[2] Feiling, p. 94.
[3] Thomas Carlyle's Captain of Industry: *Past and Present*, Book III, chap. 10.

their proposals; but the government had adopted others. Neville Chamberlain, who had given much thought to housing and local government problems, wished to make this field his own. In February 1923 when the 'young Tory', Sir Arthur Griffith-Boscawen, failed to find a seat, Bonar Law sent Neville Chamberlain to the Ministry of Health (which had replaced the Local Government Board in Addison's day). In these hands Tory Democracy, looking back to *Sanitas omnia sanitas* and forward to the welfare state, advanced its plans to save the soul of Conservatism.[1]

6. Foreign Policy

The slump in foreign trade was an aspect of the general problem of external policy which had many new and puzzling features. What rôle must the country now play in world affairs? How far had the prewar assumptions ceased to apply? For that matter, what were the prewar assumptions?

These were not easy questions to answer. Not only had the war left many uncertain and transitory features but there had been a curious imprecision about these matters even before the war; no country was less given to the writing down of rules of conduct or the explicit formulation of aims and programmes of foreign policy.[2] Indeed, public and even cabinet discussion might put dangerous ideas into people's heads, leading to injudicious activity. Lloyd George has commented on Grey's habitual reticence in the 1906–14 cabinet on foreign issues. 'There was in the Cabinet an air of "hush hush" about every reference to our relations with France, Russia and Germany.'[3] But Lloyd George was a social and political parvenu.

---

[1] Lord Henry Bentinck, *Tory Democracy* (1918), pp. 2–4, 79–87. Lord Hugh Cecil, in *Conservatism* (1912) and *Conservative Ideals* (1926), thought that the only essential element was 'to oppose revolutionary change', but that the 'balanced principles' of Toryism combined with natural conservatism incidentally provided 'the most secure political guide for a social reformer'. Pierse Loftus, *The Creed of a Tory* (1926), Walter Elliot, *Toryism and the Twentieth Century* (1927, advocating Tory leadership of a scientific revolution), and similar works, all affirm responsibility for social reform without displaying any detailed interest in programmes. Reginald Northam, *Conservatism—The Only Way* (1939), can be quoted as an example of more polemical works in which an enunciation of Conservative merits and principles is essentially a defiant answer to Socialist propaganda. R. T. McKenzie, *British Political Parties*, an authoritative study of party organization in the twentieth century, throws only incidental light on the formulation of party doctrine.

[2] Short outlines of British foreign policy covering a large part of the period are M. R. D. Foot, *British Foreign Policy since 1898* (1956), P. A. Reynolds, *British Foreign Policy in the Inter-War Years* (1954), and the present writer's *British Foreign Policy since Versailles* (1968).

[3] LlGM, vol. I, pp. 46–51.

Before his day British politicians and diplomatists had been drawn from closely linked social and family circles, in which prolonged discussion of policy was unnecessary—everyone knew in a general way what everyone else was or ought to be thinking and doing. The numbers in the foreign service had always been very small; the members were largely drawn from the same upper social classes, with a financial qualification; informality, an ease of manner, and perhaps some absence of original thought, were sufficient among people who understood each other so well.[1] The highest diplomatic art consisted in the smooth handling of each problem as it arose, without much regard to theory.

The continent never ceased to puzzle about this strange nonchalance. How explain the combination of worldly success and apparent simplicity? Did it conceal great cunning, or even some unusual biological superiority? 'The whole nation, as such, has an unconquerable prejudice against thinking', wrote Count Keyserling ironically in 1928. 'It is not intelligence but instinct—rising at its highest to intuition—which determines the course of their lives.'[2] This might have been adequate in the past, but in the nineteen-twenties the world was acquiring strange and less kindly aspects, and it was doubtful whether the effortless non-intellectualism would suffice much longer. Grey, however, thought it would. Towards the end of his life, in 1925, he could still argue that the British Empire had been well served by these methods. 'It has, at any rate, been saved from capital and disastrous mistakes; such mistakes as are made by a great thinker, calculating far ahead, who thinks or calculates wrongly.'[3]

Britain's relative power and influence in the world were not lessened by the war, and it is misleading to think of her as having been substantially weakened.[4] Victory had removed the German threat, it had made England the predominant power in the Middle East and Africa, it had created a powerful Anglo-French military alliance and brought all the self-governing Dominions into active partnership with the Mother country, it had aligned the United

[1] T. H. S. Escott, *National and International Links* (1922), pp. 112–31.

[2] Count Hermann Keyserling, *Europe* (1928, Eng. translation), p. 19. This view was faithfully echoed by Englishmen themselves: cf. R. H. Tawney, *The Acquisitive Society* (1921), p. 1.

[3] Viscount Grey, *Twenty-Five Years 1892–1916* (1925; Peoples' Library edn., 1928), vol. I, p. 50.

[4] Cf. the comments on this point of P. A. Reynolds, pp. 1–6; Lord Strang, *Britain in World Affairs* (1961), pp. 289–301.

States decisively with the European allies, and it had created in the League of Nations an international organization which, if it guaranteed peace as it was meant to do, would perpetuate the favourable position of the victors. Against this had to be set the weakening of the country's economic ascendancy, the anti-war reaction which gave a derisory character to all plans for military preparations in the twenties and still prevented thoroughgoing rearmament in the late thirties, the weakening of British influence in China, the disruptive force of nationalism in India and Egypt and other parts of the Empire, the greater vulnerability of the British Isles as a result of the air and underwater weapons perfected in the war, the enigma of Soviet policy, and the flare-up of new political animosities as the ostensible victors squabbled over the often illusory spoils. There were clearly two sides to the balance sheet, but it is misleading to count only the costs. A great enemy had after all been beaten, his power of offence destroyed.

The essential change in Britain's foreign relations after 1918 was one, not of strength, but of function. She had to a remarkable degree, and to the exquisite annoyance of potential allies, managed down to 1914 to keep herself almost entirely free from binding commitments to other governments. Her centuries-old abandonment of territorial ambitions on the continent, the first and greatest fact in the history of British foreign policy, received no credit; it was, like free trade, taken for granted at home and abroad as an irrevocable product of British domestic politics. But its corollary was that apart from a desire to keep the great powers away from certain vital coastlines—the entrance to the Baltic, the English Channel, and the Mediterranean—and occasional attempts to seize or hold strategically placed footholds—Calais, Gibraltar, Malta, Cyprus—on the periphery of the continent, she had followed for generations a cautious, watchful policy, never indifferent to the possible appearance of another conqueror who might dominate Europe or threaten her shores but always slower than her continental neighbours to take alarm. Outside Europe she was prepared to defend any portion of the Empire from attack, and she had allied with Japan in 1902; but this and the simultaneous adjustment of differences with the United States in the Caribbean and elsewhere (1901–3) were designed to free her hands rather than to prepare for joint action.

Lord Salisbury had been the typical exponent of this realist and empirical approach, and the commitments to France, starting with Lansdowne's offer of support in the spring of 1905, marked the beginning of a new phase. In the same year the treaty with Japan was revised. But Britain's formal commitments remained at a minimum, her aim was peace and her pose isolationist, and public opinion moreover raised no objection.[1] Nor did the claims of humanitarianism involve automatic commitments; while eloquent voices periodically demanded that the government should do something to aid victims of atrocity from Naples and Armenia to Kiev and the Congo, others including Gladstone in his more circumspect moods deprecated knight errantry. The net result was rather frequent diplomatic intervention which lost the country some potential allies (including Turkey but not Belgium), and which established a popular assumption that only liberal parliamentary states were Britain's natural allies. This was not very good politics. Nevertheless, international altruism had not yet been institutionalized. All this changes after 1918. Britain had been conscripted for international service in the war, and thereafter was never granted a discharge.

For this there were a number of reasons. The most fundamental was that the circumstances of the war had made her, with France, the leading opponent of certain potentially aggressive powers, whereas before 1914 (and after 1947) she was a supporter, the protagonists being France and Russia in the first case and the United States in the second. She and France had borne the main burden of the war against Germany after 1917; Russia had moved into an orbit of her own under Lenin, and the United States after a cometlike intervention in European affairs had gone flashing off into space after 1919, although always threatening to return. Italy was of less magnitude, and under Mussolini was soon to resume the balancing rôle which on the whole she played very clumsily. This left France and Britain as the two powers which were primarily responsible for handling defeated Germany. Lloyd George and a succession of French ministers had been jockeying for the leadership of the wartime coalition and the immediate postwar Europe, and were too intimately involved in the peculiar shape of the Versailles treaty and its sequel to be able to wash their hands of it, as the

---

[1] L. M. Penson, 'Obligations by Treaty: their place in British Foreign Policy, 1898–1914', in *Studies in Diplomatic History and Historiography in Honour of G. P. Gooch*, ed. A. O. Sarkissian (1961), pp. 88–9.

Americans had done. Although British governments after 1922 were anxious to disentangle themselves from the Franco-German quarrel and to resume the mediatory rôle which they had tried to play before 1914, they never succeeded in persuading either British or foreign opinion, or indeed themselves, that Germany was not their concern. Later Soviet Russia, Italy, and Japan each chose to regard Great Britain as on balance a greater or more direct threat to its ambitions than France. Thus the Commonwealth, in addition to the danger of internal collapse, was threatened by much more powerful external dangers than in the past.

But a second reason for the embarrassing prominence now thrust upon Great Britain was the miscarriage of the attempt, so laudable in itself, to formalize and institutionalize the work of preserving world peace. It was hoped to do this either by providing a forum which would apply the solvent of benign objective publicity to stubborn interstate differences, or by mobilizing an irresistible weight of world power, economic and military, against an aggressor. Public opinion and the prominent rôle of the British delegation in the drafting of the League of Nations Covenant on these lines made it impossible for Great Britain to withdraw from the League, but the withdrawal of other powers, starting with the defection of the United States in 1920, made it impossible to carry out the League's essential purpose. So Britain and France were left as the embarrassed nursemaids of a rather endearing spastic infant, the product of some injudicious international love making. At no time in the interwar years could British ministers free themselves from the popular assumption that on them rested the initial responsibility for defending victims of aggression in any part of the world. And yet their belated, but specific, refusals to accept these unlimited obligations were frequent from 1924 onwards, starting with the rejection of the Geneva protocol and the exclusion of German frontiers east of the Rhine from the Locarno guarantee in 1925. The issue was further confused by the fact that aggression, as viewed by League supporters, usually offered in this period only an indirect threat to immediate British interests, whatever the ultimate danger. The real handicap was the loss of manoeuvring power and freedom to bargain.[1]

[1] The analysis of 'traditionalist' and 'collectivist' British schools of thought on foreign policy in A. Wolfers, *Britain and France between Two Wars* (New York, 1940), pp. 212–28, does not emphasize sufficiently the inhibiting effects of this loss of manoeuvring power.

Popular interest in foreign policy was a third complication. There
is a great difference of course between what is wanted by the vast
mass of ordinary men and women, going about the rather worrying
daily business of earning a living, and what is advocated by the
articulate publicists, ranging from pressmen, advertising agencies,
philanthropic and pacifist societies, contemporary historians,
military critics, economists, and other writers, to the established
political parties. The former certainly wanted peace, they wanted
to be left alone and not to be bothered by foreigners and foreign
crises; in this sense we can say that the general current was pacific
and even isolationist for many years. But the effective pressures in
foreign policy-making were due to more complicated, strident,
and dogmatic programmes which gave precision, and some deliberate or unconscious misdirection, to this vague escapist urge. The
masses remained patriotic, that is, they were always prepared,
throughout the interwar years, to rally to the government if they
were assured of a national danger, whether military or even, as in
1931, economic. Short of this, however, the flexibility of British
diplomacy was hampered by the elaborately formulated doubts of
the publicists as to how far the small group of specialists who had
conducted British foreign policy before the war could any longer be
trusted.

This distrust of professionalism in diplomacy inspired the Union
of Democratic Control, which had been founded on the outbreak of
war with E. D. Morel, Norman Angell, Charles Trevelyan, Arthur
Ponsonby, and Ramsay MacDonald as its more prominent members.
Along with varying degrees of scepticism as to whether the charges
against Germany were justified they held the belief that faulty
diplomacy had precipitated the war both by the ineffectiveness of
the conciliatory machinery and by giving the maximum of advantage
to sinister elements who desired war for their own advantage.
Open diplomacy would be a guarantee of peace because it would
put the control of foreign affairs into the hands of the people, peace-
loving henceforth for the best of reasons; and international negotiations must be conducted by an organization of states in which the
majority would also, in their own interests, favour peace.[1]

This reasoning had its roots in nineteenth-century Liberal
thought, Cobdenite-pacifist and anti-imperialist, 'pro-Boer' in some

[1] G. R. Crosby, pp. 16–20, 29–30; A. J. P. Taylor, *The Trouble Makers* (1957), also
stresses the escapist element in these views: pp. 169–170.

cases with suspicions of the humanitarian backwardness of the Foreign Office aroused by its stonewalling of the demands of the Macedonian and Congo committees. It was also strongly attractive to elements in the Labour party with the same Liberal background, combined with more specific Marxist assumptions as to where Tory-inspired, big-business, capitalist-imperialist elements would lead the country if the opportunity arose.[1] They had been rather vaguely bound to the Stuttgart resolution of the Second International of 1907 which had called for the exerting of every effort to avoid war and to achieve the social revolution if war broke out; and although after a brief hesitation in August 1914 the bulk of the party had supported the war, the tendency to blame all international troubles on the machinations of the class enemy was revived by the Russian revolution. In face of all the evidence the belief that 'the capitalist' was the essential warmaker in modern industrial states was to have a vigorous life throughout the twenties and thirties; he was thought to be hesitating only over the choice between Soviet Communism and rival imperialists for priority in attack. Linked with this, but with curious, nostalgic echoes of Gladstone on his high horse, was the condemnation of all national interests as by definition selfish.[2]

The practical effect of this vigorous range of challenges to the traditional methods of conducting the country's foreign policy was undoubtedly an increase in 'democratic control'; in particular, day to day dealings with foreign countries were subject to much greater publicity, sometimes with devastating effects on difficult and delicate negotiations.[3] It was also necessary for the government of the day to keep within the framework of certain fixed conceptions and procedures. Adherence to the League of Nations Covenant, which embodied many of these, was a guarantee of international respectability, and it was dutifully supported by the parties in the Lloyd George coalition from the start; but, as the party normally in power during the interwar years, the Conservatives were more

[1] H. M. Swanwick, *Builders of Peace* (1924), pp. 23–37; G. P. Gooch, *Under Six Reigns* (1958), pp. 171–4; E. Windrich, *British Labour's Foreign Policy* (1952), pp. 11–21, a useful summary which tends to over-stress continuity in Labour's foreign policy.

[2] See below, pp. 325–7, 343, and cf. Stafford Cripps's comment in November 1937: 'The difficulties, doubts, and hesitations which now apparently beset our once bold imperialists are due to their inability to agree as to whether the threat of working-class power or of rival imperialisms is the greater in the world today.' To counter this there were realists who believed in the possibility of national danger (Sexton, Dalton, Bevin).

[3] H. Nicolson, *Curzon: The Last Phase* (1934) gives one of the rare contemporary expositions of the dangers of democratic control (pp. 389–403).

keenly aware than their critics of the practical restrictions which it imposed on the government's powers of initiative. It could only be hoped that influence, in the form of past reputation and the goodwill earned by ideological respectability, would compensate for deficiencies in armed strength resulting from disarmament. In commending the League Covenant to the House of Commons on 21 July 1919 Lord Robert Cecil disclaimed on behalf of the government any intention to rely upon force to carry out a decision of the Council or the Assembly of the League. 'This is almost impracticable as things stand now. What we rely upon is public opinion. I myself think that is right.'[1] But this view was not accepted by the world generally, or by League advocates who were unable to recognize the incompatibility of aims.

The power of the faithful League states was constantly being reduced by disarmament in the cause of risk-taking for peace, but the corollary to this was to take the alternative risk of allowing substantial treaty revision, a course which was greeted with horrified protests in the thirties by many of those who had demanded, and indeed were still demanding, disarmament. This is perhaps all that need be said on these general issues for the moment; we shall be able to follow some of their consequences later, and view with whatever sympathy they deserve the embarrassed contortions of British diplomats and their political chiefs, as they strove to square many political circles in the twenties and thirties.

We may, however, note that the strenuous domestic opposition on foreign affairs gave direct and sometimes powerful encouragement to British critics abroad; for the bipartisanship of the prewar years largely disappeared from British politics after 1919. Essentially the problem of foreign policy was that of handling three distinct but interlocking problems, which we can call the Atlantic, the Franco-German, and the Communist.

The first was that of putting Anglo-American relations on a basis of complete friendship, trust, and cooperation, an aim which supplied the most positive objective of British foreign policy right down to 1964, and which never received in America the almost unqualified approval which was given it by British politicians of all parties down to 1945 (and with some reservations thereafter). The belief that the English and Americans were, if not brothers, at least cousins, and anyway Anglo-Saxons, and thus had a species of

[1] P.D., 5 Ser., HC, vol. 118, 21 July 1919, col. 990.

family relationship similar to that existing between Britain and her self-governing dominions, gave an idealist and sentimental note to the relationship among certain groups and individuals in both countries. To this could be added a widespread acceptance by the British of America's sense of her own uniqueness as a land of freedom, opportunity, and superiority to the political standards and base ambitions of the old world.[1] There was thirdly the realist view, expounded by the British Admiralty from the beginning of the century, that with her commitments in Europe Great Britain could not afford a quarrel with America over either Atlantic or Pacific affairs.

American policy towards the blockade and the idea of a negotiated peace with Germany had disillusioned many British officials and politicians by 1916, and after his entry into the war Wilson's curiously offensive manner in keeping the contaminating contacts with his European co-belligerents, associates but never allies, to a minimum disillusioned many more.[2] Wilson's genuine sense of moral superiority expressed isolationism in terms of leadership, and to achieve his self-imposed mission he looked for support, but also for stimulus, to the potential radical opposition in England, just as his Republican opponents sought to discredit the Wilsonian entanglement with Britain by patronizing the cause of the southern Irish.[3] After 1920 the American determination to lead Europe ideologically while avoiding any military, political, economic, or even emotional commitment, left a sense of helplessness in the Foreign Office, although it remained axiomatic that the two countries must not quarrel.[4] There continued to be a remarkable affinity between the broader lines of American and British pacifist-socialist criticisms of Conservative foreign policy throughout the twenties and thirties.

[1] 'American ideas were incompatible with the exercise of power, but not with a sense of power . . . Britain was undoubtedly taking the brunt of the new American energy and interest in foreign affairs.' A. E. Campbell, *Great Britain and the United States 1895–1903* (1960), pp. 206–7, and chap. 7 generally, on the pre-1914 position.

[2] D. C. Watt discusses official and right-wing reactions to United States policies in *Personalities and Policies* (1965), essay 2. He gives (p. 211) ringmastership in the Pacific, continentalism, and leadership in Europe as the three themes of U.S. thinking on foreign policy. Professor R. W. Van Alstyne says the leading concepts were security, expansion, and neutrality, expansion of influence replacing expansion of territory after 1898. *American Diplomacy in Action* (1944), p. 5.

[3] L. W. Martin, *Peace without Victory, Woodrow Wilson and the British Liberals* (Yale, 1959).

[4] 'Of course Anglo-American relations were "paramount" and all that, but Mac-Donald was exceptional in meaning it' (R. Vansittart, *The Mist Procession*, 1958, p. 318).

One reading of modern British history would make the tension between the expanding land empires of the United States and Russia and the imperial British possessions on their periphery the dominating factor in foreign policy for the half-century after 1815,[1] and it is certainly the case that the two constituted the chief threat to the British empire in that period. But while the idea of war with the United States became 'unthinkable' in England during the next generation, it remained familiar and even popular with regard to Russia; Liberal ideology condemned Tsarist rule at home while gradually abandoning the Gladstonian half-belief in its liberating rôle abroad. The period of circumspect cooperation between the two countries from 1907 to 1917 was followed by some awkward readjustments of attitude after the Communist victory, for while British Labourites felt that they must extol the proletarian triumph they were as hostile as the other two parties to the forcible Bolshevik liberation of surrounding states, and completely opposed to the spread of Communism at home. The Conservative political and big-business spokesmen saw no need to pretend any respect or liking for the domestic procedures or revolutionary propaganda abroad of the Soviet government or the Comintern, but had accepted by 1922 the need to try the experiment of peaceful co-existence with them. The New Economic Policy, followed by Stalin's concentration on domestic progress after 1927, the Litvinov advocacy in successive stages of disarmament, the League, rearmament, and resistance to Germany, also did nothing to remove the deep Conservative conviction that the immediate advantage of cooperation could not remove the ultimate incompatibility. The Communist penetration of bourgeois circles in both England and the United States in the thirties did not imply any lessening of this sense of incompatibility; it was simply that some intellectuals decided that they liked Communism, or their own idealised image of it. The same was true of a larger number of working-class sympathizers who were readily convinced that adverse comments on Soviet collectivism were capitalistic lies. It was the Labour party which failed to make up its mind about Communism, and in opposition repeatedly gave open political support to the Soviet government

---

[1] Geoffrey Barraclough, 'Europe and the Wider World in the Nineteenth and Twentieth Centuries' in *Studies in Diplomatic History* . . . ed. A. O. Sarkissian, pp. 364–82.

without making much headway towards agreement with it when in office.[1]

Russia and the United States were felt to be potential super-powers, temporarily inactive through domestic distractions which seemed unlikely to change very speedily. As a result it was the traditional continental problem, essentially the problem of Germany's future, which dominated international politics. The bipolar Soviet-American world politics of the post-1945 era were not seriously visualized by any active politician in Britain, although Hitler had thought a lot about the Russian half of the problem, even if he could not fit the other half, America, into his dreams.[2] The British government's attitude towards the Franco-German problem was remarkably consistent in its basic assumption, which had not been finally abandoned in September 1939, that Germany could be brought into a peaceful relationship with the western European states by the removal of specific grievances. This view was compatible with the belief that there were a great many fanatics and troublemakers who wished to exploit the grievances, but it was also compatible with the flickering hope that behind and beneath the wild men there was a peaceable Germany waiting to emerge. It followed that France's more consistently pessimistic views of Germany's conduct were usually questioned, although never rejected outright.

On this issue in particular popular reactions were almost invariably embarrassing to successive British governments. Lloyd George was warned by 203 Conservative members[3] against leniency towards Germany in April 1919, but the general trend of Labour and pacifist criticism was to reinforce the German case uncritically, with regard both to the terms of the Versailles treaty and to the stigma of inequality through enforced disarmament. To add to the

---

[1] The Council of Action opposing aid to Poland (1920) and the vociferous support of the Soviet viewpoint in the Anglo-French-Soviet negotiations in the summer of 1939, helped by the ready acceptance of information from the Soviet embassy, are cases in point. The Labour party did not accept the guarantee of Poland in March 1939 until they had consulted Mr. Maisky (see p. 402 below).

[2] Nor could he make up his mind about the Russian. 'Ripe for dissolution' (*Mein Kampf*, 1927); 'In five or ten years . . . Russia would be the World Power with the greatest military weight of all' (*Documents on German Foreign Policy 1918–1945*, ser. C, vol. III, p. 1051; comment to Simon and Eden, April 1935).

[3] Including Sir Samuel Hoare and Mr. Edward Wood (later Lord Halifax): R. B. McCallum, *Public Opinion and the Last Peace* (1944), p. 118. He remarks that the younger Conservatives 'learned to see the German point of view far in arrears of their Radical contemporaries, with the melancholy result that they began to repeat the Radical ideas on the subject at the time when these could be proved wrong not merely by speculation but by experience'.

mental confusion of Tory politicians was the uncompromising anti-German tradition among some of the permanent officials and ambassadors, with Sir Robert Vansittart and Sir Warren Fisher as the principal exponents in the thirties.

While it can always be argued that abler or more ruthless politicians will do better than the men actually in office it has equally to be remembered that under a liberal-democratic system of government public opinion is a powerful limiting factor in certain issues, while almost completely indifferent to others. The embarrassments and frustrations of British foreign policy in the interwar years were due to the fact that public opinion and her own vast inherited obligations had for a moment of time imposed on the country a function beyond her strength. It is largely correct to say that she was expected to become the policeman (or woman) of the world. The nearest we can get towards defining the uneasy, instinctive counter-programme of successive governments is to say that it aimed at peace, the military defence of the Commonwealth and maintenance of the country's formal treaty commitments, and beyond that the position of mediator—honest broker or court missionary rather than policeman—in all other international issues.

3

PEACE WITHOUT TRANQUILLITY

1. COUPON ELECTION

WHEN the sirens announced the good news on 11 November 1918 there was much aimless, happy running about for the rest of the day by crowds who knew that this was something to celebrate, although there was no very obvious way of doing so. In London thousands stood outside Buckingham Palace and in a long roar of jubilation and goodwill drowned the King's attempt to speak. For a few weeks the country was relaxed and satisfied with its leaders, with itself, with its wonderful, swift victory. The mood lasted long enough to carry Lloyd George and his followers to victory at the polls.

His decision to fight an immediate general election was sensible and indeed inevitable; the alternatives are not convincing. In reply to the King's objections he argued that no ministry could carry out the difficult tasks of reconstruction without a genuinely representative parliament behind it. This was the compelling reason for an early election: the government dared not allow its critics to accuse it of hanging on to office when the case for doing so no longer existed.[1] But no doubt he was thinking too of his own position. It is true that Bonar Law, in a rare display of enthusiasm, had said that he could be 'Prime Minister for life if he likes', but others might not think so. All his instincts prompted an immediate attempt to get together, from the confusion of party loyalties that made up the wartime coalition, a more compact team and a safer majority.

Although he had been ready for an election since the spring, and knew that this would probably throw his critics among Asquith's

[1] D. Lloyd George, *The Truth about the Peace Treaties* (1938), vol. I, p. 157; H. Nicolson, *King George V* (1952), pp. 328–30. On 5 November Lloyd George, after discussion with Bonar Law, had asked the King for an early dissolution.

followers into open electoral defiance of the government, he does not seem to have regarded the breach in the Liberal party as irrevocable. Little had been done to build up a coalition Liberal organization, and when two Liberal deputations called on him in November to urge agreement with Asquith he seemed quite willing, after consultation with Bonar Law, to accept their suggestion that Asquith, with some of his supporters, should enter the government as Lord Chancellor. This makes Asquith, who refused to fill what could not have been more than the third place in the government, the essential obstacle to Liberal reunion at this point.[1] It is true, however, that although the lines of Liberal cleavage thus remained indistinct until the armistice, the two leaders, Bonar Law and Lloyd George, had agreed in October to appeal to the country as a coalition, with the Conservatives supporting about 150 Lloyd George candidates. This decision was confirmed at a meeting of Conservative M.P.s on 12 November. The Labour party decided to withdraw from the coalition, although members of the National Democratic party, a group acting independently of the Labour party, received the letter of endorsement sent by the two leaders to their supporters. The conclusion must be that Lloyd George anticipated, but did not seek, the final break with the Asquithians.

The letter was labelled 'the coupon' by Asquith; it hardly deserves the criticism or the importance that is usually attached to it. Nor is it quite the case that the vote in the Maurice debate was the acid test. Only 71 of the 106 Liberals who voted against the government on that occasion were standing again, and seventeen of these received the letter. A recent analysis shows that, in all, 541 coupons were issued for 602 constituencies. There were no coupons in the remaining 61 and none was issued for any Irish constituency. The letter was sent to 364 Conservative, 159 Liberal, and 18 National Democratic party candidates.[2] As a means of identifying supporters the letter was a perfectly legitimate political device, and Asquith could clearly not have it both ways. The distribution of letters between the two main coalition parties looks at first somewhat unfair to Lloyd George's followers, for the proportion does not correspond very closely to the state of parties at the dissolution. Even with the exclusion of the 106 of the Maurice debate there

[1] Jenkins, *Asquith*, pp. 476–7; Lloyd George, *The Truth about the Peace Treaties*, vol. I, pp. 173–5; R. Blake, *The Unknown Prime Minister*, pp. 386–7.
[2] Trevor Wilson, 'The Coupon and the British General Election of 1918', *Journal of Modern History*, March 1964, pp. 29–35.

would remain 154 Coalition Liberals and 281 Conservatives. It seems, however, that there was no sharp practice on the part of the Conservative party organization in the allocation of coupons; Lloyd George could simply not find candidates for more than about 150 seats.[1] Nevertheless, as his name and the emotions of the day had guaranteed a coalition victory it may well be argued that the real Unionist victory was gained in this obscure interparty bargaining over seats, and that the pendulum had been swung in their favour before a single vote had been registered. Remembering Winston Churchill's fate in 1945 and the trend of voting in favour of the Conservatives in 1910 we may well speculate as to what the result would have been if Lloyd George had endeavoured to lead (if he had been allowed to lead) a reunited Liberal party against the Conservatives in 1918. As it was, the majority of voters had no great problem of choice; Lloyd George's prestige facilitated the natural swing towards Conservatism.

His dependence on Tory support, eased though it was by Bonar Law's friendship and loyalty, made the defection of Labour the more regrettable. The Labour Party Emergency Conference resolved to withdraw its members from the government on 14 November, a decision which was endorsed at the Albert Hall the same evening, when J. H. Clynes's plea for a continuance of the Coalition was shouted down, Bob Williams and William Gallacher talked about revolution, and the party went into the electoral battle on an anti-conscription and reformist platform based on Sidney Webb's charter, *Labour and the New Social Order*, which had formed the basis of the party's political programme since the previous summer. The Labour M.P.s who stayed in the coalition included G. N. Barnes, G. J. Wardle, James Parker, and G. H. Roberts.

The course of the election showed a remarkable transition in Lloyd George's public statements. On 12 November he appealed to the coalition Liberals to initiate the reign on earth of the Prince of Peace. They must not allow themselves any sense of revenge, any spirit of greed, any grasping desire to override the fundamental principles of righteousness.[2] On 11 December, the eve of the election, he summed up the issues as the prosecution of the Kaiser,

---

[1] The state of parties after the second 1910 election was: Liberals 272, Unionists 272, Irish 84, Labour 42. D. Butler and J. Freeman, *British Political Facts, 1900–1960* (1963), p. 98; I have used this useful work throughout this book for similar statistics. Cf. also Blake, p. 393.

[2] T. Jones, *Lloyd George* (1951), pp. 160–1.

punishment for those guilty of atrocities, the payment of indemnities by the Central powers up to the limit of their capacity, expulsion of enemy aliens from Britain, the rehabilitation of those
broken in the war, and widespread domestic reforms. He would
probably have denied any inconsistency. The coalition election
manifesto, issued on 22 November, had contained provision for a
respectable list of domestic reforms, a measure of imperial preference, Home Rule (outside Ulster) for Ireland, and steps towards
Indian self-government, but it would seem that as the campaign
went on the party organizers pressed for something stronger than
the earlier reasonable tone. If so the electorate got the slogans
they deserved. It may also be doubted whether there was any need
for the more dramatic utterances. G. D. H. Cole reflected in later
years that although audiences listened in good part to his demonstration of the absurdity of the popular cries for hanging the Kaiser,
making Germany pay everything and the like, they nevertheless
voted for the Coalition.[1] The low total poll (only about 52 per cent
of the electorate) and the numerous reports of quiet and orderly
meetings seem to show that the country took the government's
success for granted.

Lloyd George may not at this stage have fully mastered the
conflicting arguments of the experts as to Germany's capacity to
pay, but in his Bristol speech of 11 December he quoted the
grandiose and absurd figures put forward by a specially appointed
committee under W. M. Hughes, the Australian Prime Minister,
in preference to the relatively sober estimates of the Treasury.[2]
However, he did explain in general terms the difficulties of enforcing
payment, and insisted in after years that he had not committed the
government to anything specific, which was certainly true. There
was, at any rate, no doubt about the government's mandate. In the
new House of Commons, which met early in 1919, it was supported by 383 Conservative-Unionist M.P.s, 133 Coalition Liberals,
and 10 Coalition Labourites. The main opposition groups were
63 Labour M.P.s, 28 Asquithian Liberals, and 7 Irish Nationalists.
73 Sinn Feiners refused to take their seats.

2. Labour Claims its Reward

Lloyd George now entered on his second and longer term of

---

[1] Cole, p. 35; Mowat, pp. 2-8.
[2] See p. 143 below.

office as Prime Minister. It was to last until the revolt of the Conservative rank and file in October 1922. Although the Tory leaders
were, for the most part, loyal to him throughout, his position
depended too much on his own exceptional qualities in exceptional
situations; in the end he seemed an obstacle to normality, perpetuating the very storms which he continued so triumphantly to
ride.

Amid a great deal of nonsense that has been written about the
Welsh there is J. M. Keynes's description of Lloyd George as the
goat-footed bard, the 'half-human visitor to our age from the hag-
ridden magic and enchanted woods of Celtic antiquity', who was
'rooted in nothing', 'void and without content', 'a vampire and a
medium in one'.[1] The Celts are a language group, biologically
indistinguishable from other western European populations, and
Lloyd George, far from being rooted in nothing, was always
fortified by the habits and standards of his Welsh homeland.
'Throughout his career, his values were Welsh values', writes a
perceptive recent commentator. 'His animosities and prejudices
were shaped fundamentally by his earliest Welsh experiences, and
the crucial decisions of his life were invariably tested against the
touchstone of the reaction of Liberals in Wales.'[2] But if, as he
argues, the devotion of Lloyd George to Wales formed his one
fixed principle in political life, we can hardly be surprised if those
who know little about Wales failed to detect in him the more
traditional standards. He was a product on the one hand of the
radical-nationalist upsurge among the small professional and middle
class of the principality between 1868 and 1892, and on the other
of the social adventurism of men who move far away from a predominantly rural background to conquer the world of business or
politics in the big cities. From among these backwoodsmen have
emerged a few political geniuses, such as Bismarck and Abraham
Lincoln, who have made similar conquests with much the same
accusations of treachery, opportunism, and folly by outraged
loyalists of the establishment.[3]

---

[1] These epithets, written in 1919, were first published in 1933 in Keynes's *Essays in Biography* (1951 edn.), pp. 32–3.

[2] Kenneth O. Morgan, *David Lloyd George* (1963), p. 11; cf. Malcolm Thomson, *David Lloyd George, The Official Biography* (1949), pp. 35–45.

[3] Lincoln was sanctified only after his death. To his contemporaries he was the baboon, the imbecile, the wet rag, the Kentucky mule. J. G. Randall, *Lincoln, the Liberal Statesman* (1947), p. 65.

.The willingness to sacrifice the lives, careers, and interests of his fellow countrymen in pursuit of victory is a brutally necessary responsibility of the great war minister. Lloyd George's absence of old school and other ties with the English governing classes facilitated some ruthlessness; he was less conspicuously loyal to associates than Winston Churchill in World War II. In an illuminating comparison of the two Mr. John Ehrman suggests that both were eminent in three essential fields. The first was the ability to inspire or at least sustain the morale of the nation. The second was the ability to direct strategy and to secure its acceptance by colleagues and allies. The third was the ability to harness, or cause to be harnessed, to such a strategy the national economy and administrative system.[1] Churchill had a better technical grasp of military matters and got on better with the military chiefs; Lloyd George was a superb negotiator, particularly adroit and persuasive in handling allies. Both were excellent administrators, and they combined tremendous dynamism and will-power with an intellectual grasp of the technical complexities of central wartime administration. Both were allowed extraordinary power as a condition of victory. But after December 1918, Lloyd George had to adapt his methods and personality to the needs of peacetime administration. All the characteristic gifts of charm, energy, great flexibility of method combined with basic seriousness of purpose, and the indefatigable pursuit of results, remained. It was simply that the public taste for dynamism declined as the need for it became less obvious.

Strains began to appear in Tory loyalty after Bonar Law's retirement from the government through ill-health in March 1921. 'Fusion' was seriously discussed during 1920, and had periodic airings in the press from February onward, but without success.[2] Balfour (Foreign Secretary), Austen Chamberlain (Chancellor of the Exchequer), and Birkenhead (Lord Chancellor) supported the Prime Minister well—too well in some respects, for they ultimately found themselves out of touch with the party rank and file. The Coalition Liberals included Winston Churchill, well to the fore again as Minister of War, the equal of Lloyd George and Birkenhead in his astonishing self-confidence, drive, and courage; his fortunes seemed bound up with those of the Prime Minister, although the difference

[1] John Ehrman, 'Lloyd George and Churchill as War Ministers', *Transactions of the Royal Historical Society*, 1961, pp. 105–114.
[2] Stanley Salvidge, *Salvidge of Liverpool* (1934), pp. 180–8.

of eleven years in their ages meant that he still had precious time at forty-six for a reknotting of party ties. In spite of his vast charm and persuasiveness, Lloyd George could be a difficult leader. The process of dominating his colleagues and getting things done led him to dress them down on some occasions, and to ignore them on others. Milner and Curzon found it less easy than some of their colleagues to take these things in their stride.[1] But because he knew in some cases, and suspected in others, that the civil servants, like the generals, distrusted him he was more inclined to rely on a widening circle of amateur aides than to appeal to the permanent officials over the heads of their ministers.[2] All these things sapped in time the foundations of coalition.

Although the peace settlement was probably Lloyd George's first preoccupation throughout 1919 it was labour unrest and the general impatience of the country with the aftermath of wartime restriction which dominated domestic politics. There was no great readiness to accept the view that recovery at home must await tranquillization abroad. Demobilization provided the first shock, and only the first of a long series of official improvisations.

An orderly programme for releasing men from the armed forces had been prepared by the Ministry of Reconstruction, based broadly on the assumption that it was desirable to start by returning to industry those who were most urgently needed. In mid-December 1918 priority of release was granted not only to men with jobs awaiting them in certain trades but also to men on leave who could produce written offers of employment. This obviously meant that many short-service men would get out first. Even without this tangible grievance it would have been difficult to keep the men under arms. President Wilson had also to send his civilian army home as fast as he could find shipping for them, and French troops rioted in Paris. There was trouble among British service men even before the end of 1918, and Lloyd George, following his usual practice of blaming the minister in charge, angered Milner on 6 December by accusing him before a considerable number of people of dilatoriness and neglect in connexion with the discharge of miners from the army. Several thousand British troops in rest camps at Dover and

[1] Cf. letters by Milner, 7 December 1918 (Frank Owen, *Tempestuous Journey*, p. 504) and Curzon, 8 January 1918 (Beaverbrook, *Men and Power*, pp. 396–7 and other examples, pp. 328–36).
[2] Cf. L. Mosley, *Curzon, the End of an Epoch* (1960), pp. 207–11; R. Vansittart, *Mist Procession*, pp. 243–4.

Folkestone refused to embark for France on 3 January 1919. Other startling incidents included the burning of Luton Town Hall.

Peace was not yet signed, and whatever the process of demobilization, large forces must still be maintained until a satisfactory settlement had been reached. So serious was the situation at home, however, that Sir William Robertson thought he might have to give the order to fire on the mutineers, and thought also that even the more quiescent troops might not be depended on to quell the disturbances. Preferential treatment to men on leave was stopped on 7 January 1919. Lloyd George was sure that Milner, so indispensable a colleague only a few months earlier, was now, as an administrator, 'limp, flabby and ineffective'. So Winston Churchill went to the War Office, and acted swiftly; on 29 January fresh orders were issued which based release squarely on length of service.[1]

This eased the situation, and demobilization proceeded steadily from this point at the rate of some 10,000 a day; by the end of the year most of the wartime service men had been released, although not without some further disturbances in some of the camps. Lloyd George issued an appeal to the armed forces to remain at the 'strength of safety' until a satisfactory peace settlement had been made, and a large force was indeed imperative for Plumer's army of occupation in the Rhineland. However, young soldier battalions were used as far as possible for this purpose. The escapism of the war-weary men had no revolutionary intent; rather the reverse, for it appears that most of them when they got back home wanted only a quiet life. The soldiers' 'revolt' remained spontaneous and undirected; it was no doubt symptomatic that one group turned for guidance to Horatio Bottomley and not to any working class body. Nevertheless, the trouble coincided with widespread industrial strikes, and some socialist writers since have argued that the co-ordination of the two movements could have brought about the downfall of the régime.[2] But this is guesswork, and improbable. Although there was some revolutionary language among local leaders and shop stewards, the tendencies were self-destructive; their syndicalist ideas prevented any coordinated revolutionary

[1] Lloyd George, *The Truth about the Peace Treaties*, vol. I, p. 157; T. Wintringham, *Mutiny* (1936), pp. 305–26, on post-armistice disturbances; S. R. Graubard, 'Military demobilization in Great Britain following the first world war', *Journal of Modern History* (1947), vol. XIX, pp. 297–311; Mowat, pp. 22–3.
[2] Allen Hutt, *The Post-War History of the British Working-Class* (1937), p. 16; cf. Pollard, p. 90.

programme. The national executives of the trade unions had no stomach for anything of the sort.[1] They had, however, every determination to consolidate Labour's wartime gains, and to use for their own purposes the uneasiness of many working men as to the future.

Thus a complicated situation arose in which the union leaders had sometimes to face both ways, pressing the government on the one hand for concessions, and on the other repudiating local strike action and violence which had the same ostensible ends. The two lines of action were quite distinct. Official union action was seen when the Miners' Federation at its Southport conference resolved on 14 January 1919 to demand a 30 per cent wage increase, a six-hour working day, nationalization, and workers' control to the extent of half the membership of a Mining Council which would control the industry. When these demands were rejected the Federation decided on 12 February to ballot its members, who agreed to strike action by a majority of six to one. Meanwhile the miners were forming with the railwaymen and transport workers the 'Triple Industrial Alliance', whose completion was announced on 25 February. All three unions, as well as the engineers and others, had their demands, and the alarming prospect of something approaching a general strike was looming before the government at the end of February. In contrast to this formidable, nationwide initiative (which looked more resolute than in fact it was) the Clyde shop stewards, continuing the agitations which had so often hampered production during the war, were trying to get their way by strictly local action. Supported on this occasion by local union officials, they called a general strike for 27 January which was well and even violently supported in the area, and lasted until 11 February.

The situation early in February, with rioting soldiers, syndicalist activities in the north (where the Glasgow movement had repercussions in Belfast and Edinburgh), and the threat of a national labour stoppage, was alarming enough to the government, which rightly assumed however that the root cause was working class uncertainty as to the immediate future. Too many people, deprived of both the impelling purpose and the compulsory hard work of wartime activity, worried about finding new jobs, irked by the meagre poor food, and hardly able to keep warm, were grumbling. It was the beginning of postwar disillusionment. The government's

[1] Pribićević, pp. 131–43.

policy in these circumstances was one of sensible procrastination, tiding over the immediate difficulties until the peace was signed, the soldiers demobilized, and the more manageable labour claims settled. However, the Clyde workers, whose ostensible aim was a forty-hour week as a means of absorbing some of the unemployed, forced the authorities to take more drastic action. Vast masses of workers continued to assemble in the streets of Glasgow in the last days of January; there were plenty of violent speeches, and on the 27th the Red Flag was hoisted on the municipal flagstaff. After fighting between the police and rioters on the 31st the troops marched in. The national officials of the unions concerned condemned the strike, which was over by 11 February. Of the leaders William Gallacher and Emanuel Shinwell received brief prison sentences in April. Here the government, presumably fearing a genuinely revolutionary movement, had reacted forcefully. For the most part, however, it was content to mark time.[1]

Parliament had already made provision in November 1918 for the maintenance for six months of at least the minimum wage level prevailing at the time of the armistice. This act was twice renewed, and was not finally dropped until September 1920. Another temporary measure, which prepared the way for a permanent system of unemployment insurance, was the payment of out-of-work donations to both ex-service men and unemployed civilian workers. Although at first the scheme seems to have been intended to apply only to civilians in firms working for the Ministry of Munitions it was soon decided that as almost every industry in Great Britain was dependent in some measure on the war effort the relief must be made available for a limited period to all the civilian unemployed.[2] In dealing with the miners the government tried to mix firmness with conciliation. Although they were warned that the full powers of the State would be used to break a miners' strike they were offered a Coal Commission which would study not only wages and hours but also nationalization. After some haggling the offer was accepted on the Federation's terms. The Commission was to consist of three direct representatives each of the miners and coalowners, and three further representatives appointed by each side; twelve in all, with Mr. Justice Sankey as chairman. Another plan for talking

[1] D. Kirkwood, *My Life of Revolt* (1935), pp. 171–4; W. Gallacher, *Revolt on the Clyde* (1936), pp. 223–40; Mowat, pp. 24–5.
[2] A. C. Pigou, *Aspects of British Economic History*, pp. 28–9.

out labour difficulties was the summoning by Lloyd George for 27 February 1919 of a national industrial conference of representatives of the employers, trade unions, and Whitley Councils. With the Sankey commission and the National Industrial Conference in urgent discussion during the next few weeks the industrial situation was a little quieter, but it was clear that trouble might flare up again at any moment. For one thing, the triple alliance and the engineers were boycotting the conference, busy with plans of their own.[1]

No doubt it was the government's plan to play for time and to prevent trouble by holding out the prospect of good things in the near future; and as these often did not materialize it was easy to say that it had bluffed and broken its word. It must be remembered however that at this stage of our history the control or regulation of industry had still not been accepted as a normal function of the state; it is reading back later conceptions to suggest otherwise. Labour wished to believe, and perhaps did half believe, that the government had pledged itself to continue the use of the wartime controls in a socialist direction. In fact, all it had done was to urge employers and workers to get together and solve their own problems; it had its own programme of domestic reforms, set out in the coalition election manifesto of 22 November, but these did not include any form of nationalization.

Certainly, however, it was easy for the Labour leaders to read more into the government's statements than this. The Sankey Commission quickly produced an interim report on 20 March, and on the same day Bonar Law told Parliament that the government was prepared to carry out the recommendations of the Sankey report in the spirit and in the letter. But as there were three groups of recommendations it was that of Sankey and the three industrialists that the government accepted. Their report steered a course between the proposals of the miners' and of the coal owners' representatives. It recommended a 2s a day wage increase for adults, a seven-hour, and if practicable in due course a six-hour, day, a levy of 1d per ton to improve housing conditions, a voice for colliery workers in the direction of the mines, and either nationalization or some other system of unification 'by national purchase and/or joint control'. The miners' delegate conference on 26 March also accepted the interim report; after a ballot the strike notices were withdrawn

---

[1] R. Page Arnot, *The Miners: Years of Struggle* (1953).

and the commission then settled down to the second stage of its deliberations, which continued until the following June. Had the government accepted nationalization? The miners thought so.

All this time the government was having trouble with its coalition supporters, who were uneasy about its social programme and the newspaper accusations of undue leniency towards Germany. Lloyd George spent much of his time in Paris from 11 January until 28 June 1919, interspersed with visits to London. He was in London during the critical month from 8 February to 5 March. There was some plausibility in his later assertion that Lord Northcliffe and the papers that he controlled deliberately distorted everything said or done at the peace conference; but something more than this is necessary to explain the fact that as many as 233 Conservative M.P.s supported a telegram of protest to the Prime Minister on 8 April against the reported plans to whittle down the German reparations payments. The fact is that many of them had read too much into the speeches of their leaders during the general election; less skilled in the subtleties of verbal reservation, they had stated roundly that Germany would pay the whole cost of the war. There was, therefore, an anxious appeal to the Prime Minister to fulfil his pledges to the country. Kennedy Jones, Northcliffe's chief henchman in the Commons, had assiduously worked up the discontent, but he had not created it. Bonar Law hurried over to Paris. Lloyd George proposed a reply saying that the government meant to stand faithfully by its election pledges in respect both of the peace terms and of the social programme; this was sent off after the reference to the pledges on social problems had been struck out on Bonar Law's objection that it would be unnecessarily provocative in the state of the party's mind at the moment.

The peace conference was at its final point of crisis, and Lloyd George could not leave Paris for the moment. But a week later, on 16 April, in one of his masterly and dominating speeches in the Commons, he reviewed the whole course of the negotiations, told the House that he would as soon rely on a grasshopper as on the 'reliable source' of Kennedy Jones's information, and after appealing for a peace of right and not passion, asked whether he had the House's fullest confidence. The result was the complete collapse of the critics, without any surrender of the government's position. Lloyd George insisted, like Bonar Law, that reparations must be governed by Germany's capacity to pay; on the other hand, he was quite willing to reaffirm his pledge that the Kaiser should be tried and punished.[1]

We shall examine the peace conference and its aftermath in the next section. The signature of the peace treaty in June meant the end of one source of uncertainty about the future, and at home the country was showing distinct signs of settling down by the autumn without much satisfaction of the Labour demands. The National Industrial Conference continued to make recommendations without much response from the government until the trade union members got tired of it and withdrew in 1921. A more urgent problem was that of coal, for on 23 June 1919 there appeared the final Report of the Coal Commission.

Once again—not surprisingly perhaps—each section of the commissioners had its own views, and this diversity was fatal to the success of any one of them. They agreed on one point of importance —the nationalization of the coal measures. Otherwise Sankey recommended state ownership of the mines; the six miners representatives wanted both state ownership and workers control; the three coal-owners and two of the industrialists condemned nationalization, but proposed joint committees at the pit, district, and national levels for the discussion of matters relating to the industry; the remaining industrialist, Sir Arthur Duckham, sent in a one-man report proposing the amalgamation of collieries into district companies, with a minority of workers' representatives and a limit on profits. It was the last plan, which retained the principle of private ownership and promised to eliminate inefficiency resulting from a multitude of small pits and companies, which attracted the government. On 18 August Lloyd George rejected nationalization outright, arguing that there was no majority in the commission in favour of anything, but agreed to the essentials of the Duckham plan. When the Miners' Federation rejected the Duckham solution, the government could say with some justification that there was no general support for any change. If this was true of the industry it was also true of the country at large, for nationalization was something which needed getting used to, and it was still rather frightening and foreign to the masses with their deep, instinctive desire to be left alone.

The successful ending of the peace negotiations in June 1919 momentarily increased the government's reputation but it made more difficult the postponement of domestic issues. Labour unrest

[1] Lloyd George, *The Truth about the Peace Treaties*, vol. I, p. 563.

and the threat of a general strike wave continued; perhaps there is some truth in the view that the absence of a state of emergency was the one emergency for which the world was not prepared. The government, assuming in domestic as in foreign affairs a subconscious desire to maintain the old tensions, looked for signs that the country was slipping back into the old grooves. From this point of view it seemed to some observers that the war ended only with the collapse of the railway strike in October 1919.[1] But in September, when the government's temerity in rejecting the nationalization of the mines had led the Miners' Federation to ominous discussions about direct action, it was the railwaymen's claim that temporarily captured attention.

The personalities of the Geddes brothers, who had both played a part in the earlier negotiations, and the undoubted desire of the government to delay the railway crisis until the danger point in the miners' negotiations had passed, gave support to the view that the cabinet was seeking a showdown on this issue. The strike began at midnight on 26 September. It was true that the government's final definite offer (which seemed very much more sinister to the Labour representatives when Sir Auckland Geddes called it 'definitive') involved a reduction of wages for some grades, as compared with the current rate. The demands of the locomotive men, however, were met in full, and many anomalies in the scales of men doing the same work in different companies were removed. The minimum fell to 40*s* a week as compared with the current 51*s*, although the prewar rate on the other hand had been only 18*s*. The terms were conditional on a fall in the cost of living which no one anticipated, and the Labour extremists seem to have assumed that Lloyd George was deliberately provoking a strike because he did not explain this fact to them in sufficiently clear language.[2] The government certainly feared the political implications of a normal trade dispute in an industry which could so easily paralyse the community; so too did some of the trade union leaders. The dispute was remarkable for the well-organized publicity on both sides. In the end the government on 5 October 1919 postponed the issue by agreeing to maintain the existing system for another year.

This was not the end of the government's labour difficulties, but it had become apparent by the end of 1919 that the agitation had

---

[1] Douglas Jerrold, *Georgian Adventure*, p. 227.
[2] Hutt, p. 26; V. L. Allen, *Trade Unions and the Government*, pp. 171–84.

lost its revolutionary edge. The government's contribution to this was perhaps no more than tactical: by general promises and limited concessions discontent was kept to an uneasy simmering, although the cooling-off process was not complete. The real beneficiaries were the established leaders of the unions and the reconstituted Labour party. They eliminated many of the wilder men while impressing themselves on the country as the real opposition, a process which was helped by the industrial transformation of the year 1919, for the cessation of war contracts and the return of service men to civilian employment allowed many employers to get rid of their more militant shop stewards, with the consequent collapse of the shop stewards' committees.[1] At the same time the postwar boom, although it lasted for little more than a year, kept up wages and kept down unemployment, and tilted the balance in favour of more persuasive methods. Employment continued to improve until the summer of 1920, and in the process the reabsorption of demobilized men in industry was largely completed; in any case ex-service men continued to receive the out-of-work donations until March 1921. The railway strike was regarded as something of a triumph for the Labour Research Department, an offshoot of the Fabian Society, which by skilfully directed publicity was considered to have routed the government's propaganda offensive.

But the miners also found it necessary at this stage to substitute propaganda for more militant action. After a final refusal by Lloyd George in October 1919 to agree to nationalize the mines a special Trades Union Congress was called, but when this met in December it decided to explain to the public the case for 'Mines for the Nation' instead of striking. The campaign did nothing but confirm the lack of public support; complaints that the national leaders had given no help to it merely revealed the fact that the doubts of the government and general public were not absent from trade union circles as well. In March 1920, after the Miners' Federation had voted by 524,000 to 346,000 in favour of a general strike to enforce nationalization, a special Trades Union Congress voted by a substantial majority (3,732 to 1,050) against this course and in favour of 'political action in the form of intensive political propaganda'. A few days later, on 29 March, the government granted a wage increase to offset increases in the cost of living.

[1] Pribićević, pp. 102–7; Cole, p. 96.

3. PEACEMAKING AT PARIS

The peace negotiations with Germany had certain distinctive features. They were rather speedier than comparable general settlements in the past; they excluded the representatives of the defeated from the main discussions; they produced, unlike their successors after the second world war, a definitive peace treaty; they included the United States; and they excluded Russia. Great Britain's rôle too had its distinctive character; it recalled in some ways the part she had played in the 1815 settlement, but there were vital differences, and not only in the measure in which Lloyd George differed from Castlereagh.

The most noticeable is the influence, in various forms, of British opinion; the fact that it was making itself heard in highly dramatized and often contradictory forms, ranging from the extremes of a quite impracticable pacifism to an equally impracticable vindictiveness, did not ease for Lloyd George the problem of making up his own mind. While the main body of his parliamentary supporters demanded severity, the Radical in him (and perhaps his hope of working his passage back to Liberal respectability) inclined him towards leniency. The reconciliation in his own mind is perhaps to be found in the fact that he distinguished between the German leaders and the German people (much as the 1815 peace-makers had distinguished between France and Napoleon). He was always ready with promises to destroy German militarism and make an example of the Kaiser and the 'war criminals'. But he was conscious of the unwisdom of perpetuating national grievances by creating fresh 'Alsace-Lorraine questions' or by impossibly onerous financial terms. He wanted a punitive peace as a basis for appeasement. This distinction had already been made in the statement of Allied peace terms sent to Wilson on 10 January 1917; it was not so much contradictory as naïve in its assumption that the conquered would accept territorial and other sacrifices with a good grace merely because these appeared just to the victors.[1]

Lloyd George in fact came to the peace conference with very much the same outlook as President Wilson on the broader character of the peace settlement, and with a far more realistic approach to detailed issues. The President's reputation was at its height at the time of the armistice. But it depended on an aloofness and geo-

[1] Lloyd George, *The Truth about the Peace Treaties*, vol. I, p. 58; H. I. Nelson, *Land and Power*, pp. 15–16, 47–51 (the best academic study of the peace settlement).

graphical remoteness which had hitherto enabled him to affirm general principles without having to go too closely into the problems of his European associates. Would he be able to retain a basis of principle in the intricate compromises that such a peace settlement would demand? On the whole he failed to do so: he was defeated not so much by the wickedness of Europe as by the technical complexity of the issues that he had to discuss, and his own lack of conversational dexterity.

There is much to be said for the view that the rôle which Wilson had designed for himself was played by Lloyd George. As a European state that had been heavily involved in the war and had yet retained something of her traditional peripheral aloofness, Great Britain was more closely concerned than the United States with such matters as the territorial settlements on the continent, while having no claims of her own. Great Britain, again, had at least as close an interest as the United States in a League of Nations, and a deeper emotional commitment; the early discussions at the peace conference showed that her plans for it had been more thoroughly worked out than those of the Americans. Moreover, as Keynes remarked, English interests—the destruction of the German fleet, the expropriation of the marine, the surrender of the colonies, the suzerainty of Mesopotamia—did not conflict with the Fourteen Points as vitally as did those of France: there was not much for the President to strain at, especially as the British were ready to concede in point of form whatever might be asked.[1] Lloyd George, so quick and buoyant, the skilled debater who always seemed master of his brief, could not only dominate many discussions by greater mastery of detail, but often found himself in a natural mediatory position between the President and some of the governments whose ambitions shocked him. Thus it was Lloyd George, far more than Wilson, who had the final word and the restraining voice on many issues.

When fighting stopped on 11 November 1918 the Western allies and the United States had before them a variety of plans and suggestions, but there had hitherto been little attempt by the heads of government to reach agreement between themselves. This was partly because search for agreement might have ended in disagreement which it was best to avoid while the fighting lasted. However, there was at least a machinery for consultation. The Supreme War Council became the directing body of the peace conference; during

[1] J. M. Keynes, *Essays in Biography* (1951 edn.), p. 33.

the greater part of the proceedings it took the form of the Council
of Ten (the Prime Ministers and foreign secretaries of the five main
Allies and Associated powers). This directing body was well supported by a businesslike secretariat and a flexible procedure which
owed much to British models and to the personal contribution of
Sir Maurice Hankey. When the conference opened on 12 January
1919 two months had already elapsed since the signing of the
armistice agreement, and during this period many decisions had
been taken or tacitly accepted which vitally affected the subsequent
course of developments. One was that the conference should meet
at Versailles, which implied Clemenceau's chairmanship; the
British and American governments had at first favoured a Swiss
town, but Wilson had unexpectedly decided in favour of the French
capital in order to ensure his own safety. Another was the abandonment of the idea of a preliminary peace, much talked about in
November 1918. The Allies had agreed to accept the Fourteen
Points, subject to the reservations of 4 November; and Germany
had accepted the armistice after receiving those details from Wilson.
But at Rethondes on 11 November Germany had made a purely
military agreement to suspend hostilities; moreover it had asked
for no elucidation of the Fourteen Points, apparently not wishing
to resolve their ambiguities. Wilson could have gone far towards
securing a peace with the maximum emphasis on American conceptions if he had insisted on peace preliminaries being promptly
signed with the Points and the Cobb-Lippmann interpretation as a
basis; with American troops still in Europe his position would have
been at its strongest. He showed no sense of urgency about the
matter however, and his decision to attend the peace conference in
person meant delay until his arrival. The French rather welcomed
this, for they were already hoping that the armistice negotiations,
dominated by Foch, would consolidate the arrangement that they
thought essential to their security. The British government, awaiting
the result of the general election, were also not inclined to hurry
matters.[1]

In the discussions about the enforcement of the armistice terms
some of the basic American attitudes were taken up, with certain far-
reaching results. There can be no doubt that in the economic field

[1] F. S. Marston, *The Peace Conference of 1919* (1944), pp. 29–35, 230; Lord Hankey,
The Supreme Council at the Paris Peace Conference 1919 (1963), pp. 11–13; Rudin, pp.
388–91.

the Americans felt that they had an opportunity to play a part comparable with that of the British in naval, and the French in land, warfare. But the blockade, enforced by the British navy, dominated the world movements of supplies through the Inter-Allied Maritime Transport Council, and to have fallen in with its continuance would have left the British government as the directing force in the economic situation too. A plan which went far beyond the immediate needs of the armistice period had indeed been put before the War Cabinet by the Foreign Office in August 1918. It visualized the continuance of the controls during the period until the conclusion of the final peace treaty; neutral cooperation should be secured, and as rapidly as possible an international administration set up which would supersede the blockade. Some such organization was considered essential in order to ensure a fair distribution of supplies and the limited available shipping. But it was also claimed that so peaceful and beneficent an example of international co-operation would be 'the inevitable corollary of the whole idea of a League of Nations', and would give practical meaning to its some-what visionary political aspirations. With the cabinet's approval the proposal was put to the State Department on 15 October, but was bluntly rejected by Herbert Hoover, with Wilson's agreement, on 7 November. 'For the buyers of these supplies to sit in majority in dictation to us as to prices and distribution is wholly inconceivable.' He added on the 13th that no arrangement should be made for feeding Germany until his arrival in Europe.[1]

The result of Hoover's refusal was the break-up of the Allied economic organization, and three months were to elapse before a new body, the Supreme Economic Council, was set up with himself in the dominant rôle, and with the functions, general organization, and some of the personnel of the body proposed in November. The delay had already prevented the inclusion in the armistice of provision for the handing over of the German ships, and frustrated a plan which Churchill had urged on Lloyd George on armistice night to rush 'a dozen great ships crammed with provisions' into Hamburg. The new body meant a waste of three months, and even so, with its hastily improvised arrangements and partly inexperi-enced staff, compared unfavourably with the organization that

---

[1] Alfred Zimmern, *The League of Nations and the Rule of Law* (1936), pp. 151-9; S. L. Bane and R. H. Lutz, *The Blockade of Germany After the Armistice* (Stanford, 1942), Hoover to Wilson, 11 November 1918, pp. 11-12; cf. pp. 8, 15.

could have been set up in November. Hoover's good intentions were not in doubt; but he had to deal with American business interests who were eager for the resumption of exports to central Europe.[1]

The continuance of the blockade was necessary in order to prevent the flow of contraband into Germany before the signing of the peace treaty; but it did not exclude the provisioning of Germany, which had been promised in the armistice discussions. The tendency, however, was to assume that the blockade was merely a 'food blockade'. British trade interests were also believed, even by United States officials, to be receiving private commercial information from the censorship to the detriment of foreign firms; repeated and explicit denials of this apparently made no impression. Another obstacle was the problem of paying for the supplies which America was anxious to export. The United States government had no power or intention to do so itself, either for Germany or the smaller enemy countries. Food production in the United States had been stimulated to meet the needs of the war, with the promise of high prices; in November 1918, Hoover estimated the surplus at some 18 million to 20 million tons, and he continued to receive pressing messages from American farmers and business men urging him to arrange for exports. In February 1919 Congress appropriated 100 million dollars to provide for the relief of European populations other than the ex-enemy countries, and in the same month Great Britain provided £12,250,000 for food relief in other parts of Europe than Germany, including the smaller ex-enemy countries. But who was to pay for the supplies to Germany? Yet another problem was to decide how serious or urgent the shortages really were. Dr Alonzo Taylor, one of the American experts, believed that the German government could cope with the situation until the beginning of May 1919. In the Danube basin the essential problem was the sudden growth of economic nationalism among the new states; it was hard to find a single potato in Vienna, whereas millions of bushels of them were to be obtained in Hungary.[2]

In this particular crisis it was the French who ultimately concentrated on themselves the main weight of American pressure, with

[1] J. A. Salter, *Allied Shipping Control* (Oxford, 1921), pp. 220–22; W. S. Churchill, *The World Crisis* (1929), vol. V, pp. 20–21.
[2] Bane and Lutz, pp. 112–5; Zimmern, p. 159, quoting Palmer, *Bliss: Peacemaker*, p. 367; F. M. Surface, *American Pork Production in the World War* (Stanford, 1926), pp. 120–22.

Lloyd George dexterously intervening on the United States side in the last stages. Germany had been sinking the world's tonnage as fast as possible until the armistice, and it was physically impossible for the Allies to supply at once both Germany's needs and their own. When the armistice was renewed on 16 January 1919 it was accordingly stipulated that the whole German mercantile marine should be at the disposal of the Allies and the United States for the duration of the armistice 'in order to ensure the re-victualling of Germany and the rest of Europe'. On the following day she was promised a first importation of 200,000 tons of bread-stuffs and 70,000 tons of pork products (Hoover was under pressure to dispose of the large and perishable American surplus of pork products at this point).[1] Long negotiations followed, for the Germans made difficulties, some more reasonable than others. The gold reserve in the Reichsbank of about £120 million was her most tangible asset, but not sufficient to cover the whole of the food that she wished to import; and while British experts were uneasy at the effect of a depletion of her gold reserve on her currency, the French had their eye on her gold and securities as reparation payments. Ultimately the solution would be the revival of her export trade as a means of obtaining foreign exchange, but it was a question whether this could be achieved in time to meet the immediate situation.

Aiding the Germans were the beginnings of an agitation in England against the 'hunger blockade' and the growing conviction among the British experts that somehow the food must be delivered. The President and the Prime Minister, Keynes tells us, were firmly supporting this view, but it was not always possible to hold their attention. By February the issue was approaching deadlock; the Germans were insisting that food supply should be definitely assured and financed by British or American credits before they surrendered their ships; the French and the British naval and shipping authorities were arguing that this piece of typical German intransigence, not justified by anything in the armistice agreements, prevented all progress. The French wanted the blockade to continue undiminished: Foch said that of the Allied weapons, *le canon et le blocus*, only blockade remained. M. Klotz, the French minister of finance, and the French financiers were equally firm in their view that German gold, the only immediately available asset, must be preserved for French rehabilitation, and not be allowed to

---

[1] Bane and Lutz, p. 28; W. E. Arnold-Forster, *The Economic Blockade, 1914–1919* (1920: Naval Staff Monograph), pp. 94–5, a short authoritative account.

pass into the pocket of the Chicago packers. Keynes claims a substantial part in breaking the deadlock. Lloyd George was primed with the facts, and the issue thrashed out at a meeting of the Supreme War Council on 8 March. In the opening stages of the discussion the French raised their objections, and the matter seemed to be making no real progress. Lloyd George's intervention transformed the debate. 'He can be amazing when one agrees with him', wrote Keynes later. 'Never have I more admired his extraordinary powers than in the next half-hour of this conference.' Clemenceau retreated, although he questioned the reality of German famine and the Bolshevik danger, which he believed was being used as a bogey to frighten the Allies.[1]

The necessary arrangements were completed at a conference at Brussels on 13–14 March, after a hint had been given by Keynes to the German delegate, Dr. Melchior, that Germany must open the proceedings by giving a firm assurance about the ships. Food supplies then started to flow into Germany, and there is no truth in the assertion that she was starved by the Allies until the signature of the peace treaty, although on the other hand there were still difficulties over payments, particularly in connexion with the revival of her export trade.

The tendency for the British and Americans to draw together, and then for the British delegates to draw ahead with more precise or more farreaching proposals than their American colleagues, was seen in other aspects of the settlement. While the French and Italians were, of necessity, dominated by their territorial interests and fears of a revival of central European power, the Americans were wary of commitments which ran counter to their own *laissez-faire* tendencies in both foreign and domestic politics. Plans for the drawing up of the League of Nations Covenant illustrated these tendencies clearly enough. There was first of all a clash over procedure. Wilson had intended that at least the general principles should be decided in early debate in the Council of Ten. The French, perhaps thinking in terms of practical urgency, drew up an agenda which put it last. Lloyd George on 21 January proposed an international committee. Clemenceau and Lloyd George, who had objected successfully to the participation of the smaller states in the vital discussions on the peace settlement, now insisted that they should be represented on the League of Nations committee. The

[1] J.M. Keynes, *Two Memoirs* (1949), pp. 52–62; Arnold-Forster, pp. 97–8.

distinction might be defended on the ground that the great powers had won the war, whereas the small powers would be vital to the success of a League that would keep the peace; Clemenceau probably thought it a good way to keep them quiet by giving them something to do, but the American delegates suspected a plot to make the committee as unwieldy as possible. Lloyd George proposed Smuts and Lord Robert Cecil as the British representatives, a plain hint that he wished the committee to exclude heads of delegations; Clemenceau's intention was the same. Wilson, however, decided to attend, and thus became the inevitable chairman.[1]

There is no doubt some truth in the view that if the British and French Prime Ministers with their civil and military advisers had taken part in the discussions a less ambitious, more down to earth plan would have emerged. Wilson's interest was not primarily in organization, but in the broader causes of international struggle, which he wished to see identified, defined, and denounced. These had been set out in the Fourteen Points, and were again mentioned, in an even more generalized form, as objects of the League in the draft covenant; the British with one exception (freedom of the seas) were prepared to accept the analysis, but obviously felt that analysis was not enough. What was the limit of safety in concession and example? What political machinery would bring the governments together in the systematic consultation from which law-abiding habits would emerge?

The British aim was essentially an improved Concert of Europe; as the official British commentary said later in 1919, 'to establish an organization which may make peaceful cooperation easy and hence customary and to trust in the influence of custom to mould opinion'.[2] British plans were first worked out by the Phillimore Committee between January and March 1918; after submission to the cabinet and subsequent modification they were sent to President Wilson, and other schemes, including a French plan drawn up by M. Bourgeois with a somewhat bolder treatment of sanctions than the British, were being circulated. A revised edition of the British programme had been submitted to the cabinet by Lord Robert Cecil on 17 December 1918; it was then taken to Paris and formed the basis of the so-called Hurst-Miller draft, which emerged from a

[1] R. S. Baker, *Woodrow Wilson and World Settlement* (1932), vol. I, chap. 14; Zimmern, pp. 237–40; F. P. Walters, *A History of the League of Nations* (1952), vol. I, pp. 25–39.
[2] Cmd 151 (1919). Lloyd George, *The Truth about the Peace Treaties*, vol. I, pp. 605–37.

meeting of British and American legal advisers on 1 February. In turn it provided the essential parts of the League structure; the machinery of the 'improved Concert' would function through the Council, the permanent members of which were to be the Principal Allied and Associated Powers (the United States, the British Empire, France, Italy, and Japan).[1]

Some of the sweeping commitments which Wilson had hoped would be adopted by the member states had to be modified, mainly as a result of British criticism. According to the 14th Point the purpose of the League would be to afford, under special covenants, 'mutual guarantees of political independence and territorial integrity to great and small alike'. This might exclude peaceful change and the British Foreign Office had been very chary since the days of Castlereagh about treaties of guarantee. Owing to Lord Robert Cecil's opposition the guarantee ceased to apply automatically; in the case of aggression the Executive Council would advise upon the plan and the means by which this obligation would be fulfilled. But while the English text said 'advise upon' the French text said 'look to' (*aviser*) which left the gate of misinterpretation even more widely open. Shortly after this, as a concession to domestic pressure, Wilson agreed to exclude any matter which by international law was solely within the jurisdiction of a party to a dispute. Thus war had not been excluded from international society; the most that the members were compelled to do was to discuss the problem. This might or might not lead them to take action. It certainly left them with a moral obligation to refrain from war. But the force of the moral sanction was in the British view primarily a matter of domestic public opinion on which peace must wait.

Wilson's hands were tied throughout by his own instinctive isolationism and that of his advisers. In April, French plans for an international General Staff and a permanent commission to watch over armaments and armament industries were rejected by the President as an interference with national sovereignty, just as decisively as Hoover had rejected economic controls on the same grounds six months before. In essentials, it was the British conception of the League which triumphed, although the ambiguities of the guarantee clauses left the French convinced that they had a League pledged to maintain the security of its members.[2]

---

[1] Zimmern, chaps. 6–10; Walters, vol. I, chap. 5.

[2] Zimmern, pp. 240–55; R. Lansing, *The Peace Negotiations* (1931), pp. 72–82, 109–12, on his differences with Wilson over the guarantee and other provisions.

This was of double importance to them, for not only had they to maintain on the continent a preponderance disproportionate to their real strength, but they had also to live alongside a new Germany which by no stretch of faith could be expected to be satisfied with the terms of peace. Although Wilson and Lloyd George opposed the more extreme territorial plans of Clemenceau and the French soldiers, they were both victims of the type of moral isolationism which assumed that what seemed good to them would seem reasonable to their enemies. This is the explanation of the curious paradox under which the territorial settlement was at first praised in England and America as a triumph for self-determination, with juster frontiers than before the war, and later condemned as the symbol of a Carthaginian peace. The triumphs of self-determination were at Germany's expense; she was in no mood to proclaim their justice. It is important, however, to remember that Lloyd George believed that he had prevented abuse. It is also well to remember Clemenceau's comment at a critical stage in the negotiations, that the Germans did not necessarily have the same conception of justice as the Council of Four.[1]

The two great fights were over Poland and the Rhine. In both cases Wilson, after some show of reluctance, accepted the French proposals, and Lloyd George opposed them. The Polish state was recognized when its representatives were summoned to appear before the conference on 18 January, and there was no disagreement as to the broad lines of Wilson's 13th Point: the new state should include all indisputably Polish populations, and should have free and secure access to the sea. But when the report of the Polish committee came before the Council of Ten on 19 March Lloyd George made a vehement protest against some of its proposals, pointing out that the number of Germans that it included in the new Polish state was not less than 2,132,000, including 412,000 in the Danzig district alone. Wilson argued, sensibly but not idealistically, that the new state would be threatened by Germany on two sides, and that the strictly ethnological line advocated by Lloyd George would not give it security. Balfour agreed with Wilson. However, Lloyd George insisted that the matter should be returned to the committee for reconsideration.[2]

---

[1] Cmd 2169 (1924), pp. 90–1; P. Mantoux, *Les délibérations du Conseil des Quatre* (Paris, 1958), vol. I, p. 43.
[2] Nelson, pp. 166–75; T. Komarnicki, *Rebirth of the Polish Republic* (1957), pp. 318–25.

The Rhine frontier had produced an even more serious deadlock. Following emphatic recommendations by Foch, André Tardieu on behalf of the French government proposed on 25 February that the western frontier of Germany should be fixed at the Rhine, and the Rhine bridges occupied by an inter-allied force. This meant that the area on the left bank would form some sort of independent German state. It also meant a permanent occupation of the Rhine frontier, with token British and American forces. The French disclaimed any territorial ambitions. Nevertheless, both Lloyd George and Wilson were adamant in opposing the separate Rhineland state, although they found it less easy to agree on alternatives. On 14 March they accepted, apparently on Lloyd George's initiative, a joint military guarantee by America and Britain to France against future German aggression, but Wilson, shamefully bullied by the French press, eventually agreed to a much longer occupation of German territory than Lloyd George considered wise.[1] When the deadlock was reached Lloyd George, after two or three days retreat in the Forest of Fontainebleau, set out the British objections to the more extreme French proposals, and his own suggested terms, in a forthright memorandum of 25 March 1919. A direct result was that the decisive discussions took place henceforth in the Council of Four.[2]

In the end, the necessary compromises were made; the Anglo-American guarantee, a long occupation of the Rhineland, Danzig (a Free City under the League umbrella) as the port of Poland, and plebiscites in disputed Polish frontier areas. Lloyd George's demand for the exclusion of strategic or transportation considerations in the delimitation of the Polish corridor could not be maintained.[3] The remaining issue of major controversy was the fixing and apportionment of German reparations payments.

There is some truth in Lloyd George's later assertion that as far as Britain was concerned, it was the politicians, relying on departmental advice, who were persistently doubtful as to the possibility of extracting payments on a huge scale, and that it was the financial and business experts who were exultantly confident. But it was, nevertheless, Eric Geddes, who for this purpose must be counted a politician, who wanted to make the pips squeak, and Lloyd George's

[1] Lloyd George, *The Truth about the Peace Treaties*, vol. I, p. 403; Nelson, pp. 219–48.
[2] Hankey, pp. 99–103, 104–14; Lloyd George, *op. cit.*, vol. I, pp. 214, 404–16.
[3] Cf. Seth P. Tillman, *Anglo-American Relations at the Paris Peace Conference* (1961), pp. 184–93.

own nominees on the Reparations Committee, W. M. Hughes, Lord Cunliffe, and Lord Sumner, put forward some of the most fantastic estimates of German ability and liability to pay. These three had been members of a committee appointed by the cabinet which reported in December 1918 that the Germans could and should pay something like £24,000 million in a generation, so Lloyd George was not unaware of their uncompromising stand. The Board of Trade on the other hand had put Germany's capacity at £2,000 million; the Treasury put it at £3,000 million, a sum which satisfied Bonar Law. Lloyd George's critics blame him less for any misunderstanding of the figures than for his action in appointing such extremists as Lords Cunliffe and Sumner, the 'Heavenly Twins', to the Reparations Commission. However, by mid-March 1919 he was becoming openly critical of their proposals, and asked the Treasury expert, J. M. Keynes, to work out a scale of payments which would yield a much lower figure—£5,000 million—although this was still higher than the Treasury believed to be practicable.[1] In his memorandum of 25 March Lloyd George insisted that the full amount chargeable greatly exceeded Germany's capacity to pay, and that what she did pay should if possible be completed with the generation which made the war. A compromise which suited the British government as much as any other was the decision on 28 March to omit the total reparations figure from the peace treaty; this was to be determined subsequently by a Reparations Commission. So there was time for political passions on the issue to cool; on the other hand, as long as the uncertainty lasted, Germany's credit, and with it her capacity to attract loans from abroad, would be weak. Another decision was to include pensions and allowances in the reparations bill; although this was difficult to justify under the armistice terms it was accepted by Wilson as a result of Smuts's argument that Germany would never be able to pay in full and the inclusion of these items would merely alter the distribution among the recipients in Great Britain's favour.[2]

The treaty of peace with Germany was signed at Versailles on 28 June 1919. A final intervention by the British delegation had led to a more prolonged discussion of the German counter-proposals than the French and Americans had intended; after meetings with

[1] R. F. Harrod, *The Life of John Maynard Keynes*, pp. 236–7, 242–3; D. Lloyd George, *The Truth about Reparations and War-Debts* (1932), pp. 11–19.

[2] On the capacity-to-pay controversy, Keynes, *The Economic Consequences of the Peace*, pp. 186–91, etc., and the reply by E. Mantoux, *The Carthaginian Peace*, pp. 111–132.

the British cabinet colleagues and the Empire representatives Lloyd George demanded reconsideration of the German–Polish frontier, shortening of the Allied occupation of Germany, and the fixing of a definite figure for reparations. When Clemenceau grumbled that he was proposing concessions to the Germans only in matters that affected France, Lloyd George replied briskly that if the Germans asked for colonial concessions he would be prepared to give them back East Africa, providing that France would return the Cameroons. The British had enough colonies already.[1] In the end he secured a plebiscite for Upper Silesia (which in due course gave an overwhelming majority for restoration to Germany), but the reparations clauses, after much discussion, remained substantially unchanged.

So peace was made with the main enemy. Lloyd George had judged British public opinion shrewdly when he told Clemenceau on 2 June that the only question on which he was likely to be seriously attacked was reparations. The treaty was ratified by the Commons without serious criticism. Clynes for Labour referred to blemishes, but thought that the authors of the treaty had acted with the highest and noblest considerations for human government; Sir Donald Maclean for the Liberals intended a compliment when he said that Democracy had won the war and Democracy had signed the treaty. Horatio Bottomley, who recorded his opinion that a sufficient indemnity had not been exacted, found only one supporter. Opposing trends of criticism were uneasily balanced, and the real issues dodged, in a general agreement that the treaty was 'severe but just'.[2]

Settlements with Austria, Hungary, Bulgaria, and Turkey followed, but already by 1920 the troubled state of the world was a depressing reminder of the fact that it is usually easier to make a peace treaty than to make a peace. The British rôle continued to be prominent and influential; and if as time went on Lloyd George showed more pertinacity than perspicacity in his untiring search

---

[1] Lloyd George, *The Truth about the Peace Treaties*, vol. II, pp. 718–9; P. Mantoux, vol. II, p. 271.

[2] Lloyd George, *The Truth about the Peace Treaties*, vol. II, pp. 729–35; cf. Lord Elton, *The Life of James Ramsay Macdonald* (1939), pp. 348–58. The Labour Party's published views were, however, much more violently critical than Clynes's: cf the two major pamphlets, *The Peace Terms* (1919) by Arthur Henderson, and *Labour and the Peace Treaty* (1919), which denounced France, reparations, the unilateral disarmament of Germany, and the League as it had emerged from the conference. H. R. Winkler, 'The Emergence of a Labor Foreign Policy in Great Britain, 1918–1929' (*J.M.H.*, September 1956, pp. 248–9).

for solutions he could at least claim that the issues were not being shirked. In the end this contributed to his undoing: as the country became tired of the problems that he handled so energetically it inevitably became a little tired of him. And in any case there were problems enough at home to worry about after the signature of the German treaty had finally put the possibility of war aside.

4. SLUMP AND DEFLATION

There was general agreement that the first essential was to restore Britain's position as a great financial centre and with it at least her prewar position in the world's export market. With this went a growing uneasiness as to the effect of high wages and taxation on industry. The problem was to decide how the government's influence should be used and how far a *laissez-faire* policy would do more good than harm, or at any rate avoid some embarrassing challenges without disaster to the community. Lloyd George, the constructive radical with a genius for getting things done, found in the programmes of the later war period, developed by Christopher Addison at the Ministry of Reconstruction, a natural expression of his desire to take charge and do good over a wide field of social and industrial activity. In fact, however, the urge to use the state machinery, which had grown so enormously during the war, to direct society and industry during the peace ran counter to the more powerful urge of almost everyone outside Labour circles to be free of state control, although the government was still held responsible for whatever was amiss in the national economy.[1]

Lloyd George had clearly lost no popularity in resisting the nationalization of the mines and other proposals, more or less disguised, for the continued state direction of industry. Recognition by the trade union leaders before the end of 1919 of the need to educate opinion on this matter meant their acceptance for the time being—sometimes without great reluctance—of the traditional labour–employer relationship, with the main emphasis on wage claims rather than on control. They still looked to the state as an ally, willing or otherwise, against the unsatisfactory employer, but

---

[1] ' "Back to 1914" became a common cry.' R. H. Tawney, 'The Abolition of Economic Controls, 1918–1921', *The Economic History Review*, 1943, vol. XIII, pp. 1–23. A. T. Lauterbach, 'Economic Demobilization in Great Britain after the First World War' (*Political Science Quarterly*, September 1942, p. 393), finds it hard to determine how far the economic setbacks of the nineteen-twenties 'were a specific result of the British methods of economic demobilization'.

while on the one hand this pointed to the need to capture power through the ballot box it left them on the other still uncommitted—and often undecided—on many problems of national economic policy, particularly in the export field. The immediate task was to consolidate the war gains in wages and conditions and to extend them where possible. Consequently during 1919 2,600,000 work-people were directly involved in wage disputes, with a loss of 34 million working days; in 1920 the comparable figures were 2 million and 27 million. The 1919 figures were the highest since those of 1912.[1] Although the miners had postponed action a strike of iron founders directly involving 50,000 men began in September and continued unsuccessfully until it was called off at the end of January 1920. There had been a successful police strike in London in August 1918, but when renewed on 1 August 1919 with a demand for the right of trade union membership, the new Commissioner of the Metropolitan Police, Sir Nevil Macready, refused all concessions on this vital issue, and the strike collapsed quickly. The strikers were dismissed. There were other strikes, of varying success and magnitude. More persuasive methods were employed with conspicuous success by Mr. Ernest Bevin, who became the 'Dockers' K.C.' after justifying before the Industrial Court and public opinion the dockers' case for decasualization and higher wages.[2]

With labour relations returning to their prewar basis, and with employers clamouring for the ending of all administrative controls, the government was willing enough, up to a point, to divest itself of responsibility. This was not solely a matter of political expediency. It was in a different position from that of its postwar successor in 1945, for it could look back on a very much more flourishing prewar economy which could still be glorified as a triumph of *laissez-faire*. In spite of the efficiency of nationally-managed enterprise during the war the case for planned economy had not been proved; nor did anything like the adversities of the nineteen-thirties seem likely.[3]

In the circumstances the new responsibilities assumed by the state were not inconsiderable. In fiscal policy, although there was in principle a return to private activity in foreign trade, there was also a growing body of regulation designed to meet temporary

[1] Pigou, p. 164.
[2] A. Bullock, *The Life and Times of Ernest Bevin* (1960), pp. 116–32.
[3] Pollard, pp. 89–91.

postwar conditions, and these tended to remain as the beginning of protection. The McKenna duties of 1915 on motor-cars, clocks, watches, and other goods of a luxury character whose importation might have made undesirable demands on shipping and foreign exchange in wartime, were renewed annually until Snowden abolished them in 1924, amid cries that the motor-car industry would be ruined. The main body of wartime import restrictions was removed in September 1919 but a number of key products were excluded; in 1920 the importation of dye-stuffs was forbidden except under licence, and in 1921 the Safeguarding of Industries Act imposed an import duty of $33\frac{1}{3}$ per cent on synthetic dye-stuffs and other articles. These were goods, claimed to be essential to the country's industry in peace or war, whose production it was thought desirable to foster. The act also provided for a duty of $33\frac{1}{3}$ per cent to prevent 'exchange dumping' of goods imported from a foreign country at low prices owing to depreciated currency, and a further $33\frac{1}{3}$ per cent duty to meet the dumping of goods at prices below the cost of production. The government also began a scheme of export credits in 1919 to enable temporarily embarrassed foreign customers to buy British exports, and these arrangements were modified and extended in subsequent years. It was decided in 1921 to guarantee bills drawn by traders instead of making advances. After being applied in the first instance to states of central and south-eastern Europe it was extended to all countries with certain exceptions which included, for the time being, Russia. This also was a temporary arrangement which tended to become permanent. Frowned on by the orthodox free traders of the Labour party, it commended itself for both business and political reasons to the Tories.[1]

A policy of *laissez-faire* in a self-regulating world market thus remained the country's ostensible trade objective, modified on a relatively minor scale to safeguard the country's economy in the abnormal postwar years. In monetary policy the Treasury and the Bank of England were experimenting with innovations which it was hoped would make possible a return to the prewar position, that is to say, the establishment of the country on a gold basis at the prewar parity as soon as possible. It became necessary, on 20 March 1919, to discontinue the pegging of the American exchange by means of loans and the sale of securities in the United States; as

[1] Youngson, pp. 58–64; Pigou, pp. 139–41.

a result the rate of exchange fell from the pegged level of 4·76½ dollars to the pound sterling. On 31 March an Order in Council prohibited the export of gold coin and bullion. These arrangements had to be made because the pegging of the exchange by the means followed in wartime was no longer practicable, and there was an obvious danger that the fall in the exchange resulting from un-pegging would lead to a large sale of gold at high profit abroad. The alternative means of maintaining the gold reserve would have been the imposition of a high discount rate, which would have restricted credit and probably produced an immediate trade depres-sion. However, parity and a return to the gold standard seemed the path of wisdom. On 15 December 1919 a Treasury minute laid down that in future the maximum fiduciary issue of currency notes in any year should not exceed the issue of the previous year. This was a policy declaration which made possible the withdrawal of over £70 million worth of currency notes during the next four years,[1] one aspect of a process of deflation which was accompanied in due course by an improvement in the exchange rate. By the end of 1922 the pound had already largely recovered its prewar parity with the dollar.[2]

There were already signs by the summer of 1920 that the boom was not going to last much longer, and in the last two years of the Lloyd George administration economic depression had the effect of accelerating the government's plans for decontrol. Although the main cause of the depression is to be found in the declining demand for British exports, official monetary policy, resulting from the austere connivance of the Bank of England and the Treasury, was a contributing factor. The raising of the bank rate to 6 per cent in November 1919, the restriction of the note issue in December, and some efforts by bankers to ration credit during the following weeks did not check the monetary boom and accordingly on 15 April 1920 the Treasury bill rate was raised to 6½ per cent and the Bank rate to 7 per cent, the highest peacetime rate since 1907 and until 1957. This time-honoured device had the desired effect of chilling the optimism of business men by a warning—which is what the increase in the bank rate was intended to convey—that the authorities

[1] The Treasury fixed a maximum of £320m for the note issue for 1920, and announced that this would be reduced to £248m by 1924. Pigou, p. 189.
[2] For general assessments of postwar monetary policy see E. V. Morgan, *Studies in British Financial Policy* (1952), chap. 6; Pigou, Part v, chap. 1, etc.; L. Robbins, *The Great Depression* (1934), p. 76 *et seq.* Youngson, pp. 33–5.

meant business on their own behalf and were determined to use their powers to check the rise in prices and profits. Unfortunately the effect, at first salutary, was ultimately harmful; other conditions combined with it to produce, not an even level of restrained prosperity, but a severe depression, undoubtedly increased by the fact that the 7 per cent rate was maintained for nearly a year. But it appears that this result was not due to any lack of understanding; it was deliberately done with an eye on the American exchange in pursuit of the goal of prewar gold parity.[1]

However, the full effects of the slump did not become obvious until the beginning of 1921. Prices were falling steadily, orders were falling off, but the completion of old orders kept work going in most of the export industries until the end of the year. British postwar exports reached their maximum in July 1920, and in November were still greater than in the previous February. Organized labour, which had been showing a declining enthusiasm for strike action at the beginning of the year, was in no great hurry to start a new phase of militancy as the unemployment figures mounted, and during the greater part of the year 1920 it displayed decidedly more zest in attacking the government on political issues. Of these the treatment of Soviet Russia was the most dramatic.

The Labour leaders had no more confidence in the Soviet régime than had members of the Coalition government, but they were agreed on one point: Russian Communism should be left alone, as long as it stayed at home. On this point they were more singleminded than the government, which had involved itself in 1918 in a half-hearted policy of intervention, designed to help the Czechoslovak forces in Siberia, to prevent stores and munitions at Archangel from falling into Soviet hands, and generally to frustrate Soviet attempts to help the Central Powers. In 1919 help to the Germans was no longer an issue, but while Lloyd George, firmly supported by Balfour and Bonar Law, was consistent in his determination not to be drawn into open war with the Bolsheviks he accepted the view in February 1919 that material aid should be supplied to the various White governments. The great proponent of intervention plans was Churchill, the determined War Secretary; Lloyd George said that he had 'Bolshevism on the brain'. Lloyd

[1] 'Once that decision was taken, with American prices moving as they did, to allow the monetary slump here to become profound, in spite of the damage thereby done to industry and employment, was a necessary means to an accepted end.' Pigou, p. 197; pp. 186–96 on the general causes of the slump. Also Morgan, pp. 202–10.

George himself, however, took the initiative in the Supreme Council in May 1919 in proposing aid in munitions, supplies, and food to Kolchak's régime at Omsk, to enable it to become the 'Government of all Russia'.[1] This led to the Allied note of 26 May which Kolchak accepted, only to find himself in retreat after July, and Lloyd George soon found that the course of events confirmed his earlier and less sanguine views. British forces began to withdraw from Archangel in August 1919, and Kolchak was captured and killed in January 1920.

The Labour party condemned intervention, taking more or less sincerely the view that it represented a capitalist attack on working men who were seeking to lay the foundations of Socialism, but at first many of the leaders also condemned Bolshevism, or at any rate the conduct of the Bolshevik leaders. During the first half of 1919, however, the rank and file opposition to intervention gathered strength, and at the Labour Party conference in June 1919 the more right wing leaders such as Brace, Clynes, and Sexton were not well received when they condemned a proposal for direct action. Robert Smillie denounced the Executive Committee of the Labour Party for taking up 'exactly the position of every exploiter and capitalist and politician in this country at the present time' and young Herbert Morrison said that intervention was 'a war against the organisation of the Trade Union movement itself, and as such should be resisted with the full political and industrial power of the whole Trade Union movement'. A 'Hands off Russia' committee, on which young Harry Pollitt was prominent, was formed on 7 November 1919.[2]

Nevertheless the problem seemed to have solved itself with the collapse of White resistance, and the demand for a general strike, which as we have seen was also put forward by the miners in March 1920, was not accepted by the T.U.C. But the Russian problem flared up again in the spring, when the Poles captured Kiev on 7 May in a successful offensive. Having put themselves in the wrong they seemed in the next few weeks to be about to collapse before a vigorous Soviet counter-attack. The most curious feature of the situation which followed was that although Lloyd George and his Labour critics took defiant attitudes towards each other

---

[1] Mantoux, vol. II, pp. 195–204, leaves no doubt as to Lloyd George's initiative; but cf. Hankey, pp. 67–73, 167, 183–4, on Churchill's rôle throughout.

[2] T. Komarnicki, *The Rebirth of the Polish Republic*, Part II, is the fullest account of both the labour and diplomatic reactions; also Hutt, pp. 34–5; Bullock, pp. 133–42.

they differed little in their ultimate aims and fears; neither wanted a Communist victory which would spread Bolshevism throughout Central Europe and neither trusted the Poles. The Labour leaders dodged the issue by assuring themselves—as J. H. Thomas put it in a Commons debate on 21 July—that the Bolsheviks had neither said nor done anything to indicate that they desired anything else than the independence of Poland: in short, that there was no reason to worry about a Polish defeat or to do anything to stop it. Having thus accepted Soviet assurances of peaceful intention at their face value it was an easy step to the conclusion that the British government wanted a fresh war, first to save the Poles and secondly to achieve imperialist, capitalist aims against Russia. This certainly seemed a reasonable assumption to the London dockers when at the moment of Poland's greatest triumph on 10 May they refused to load the *Jolly George* with munitions for the Polish forces.

However—and in spite of some displays of official satisfaction at the early Polish successes—the truth of the matter is that neither the British government nor the Labour movement had any real influence on the swiftly moving Soviet–Polish drama. After the tide had turned in June Curzon in a note of 11 July proposed an immediate armistice, with the withdrawal of Polish forces to the line provisionally fixed as a suitable Polish frontier at the peace conference. The Poles also asked for an armistice, and the Russians agreed to open discussions; these were soon seen to be merely delaying tactics, and as the Soviet forces rapidly approached Warsaw a further note by Curzon on 3 August was virtually an ultimatum, warning the Soviet government that if the advance continued help would be given to the Poles. This led Henderson on the following day to call for immediate 'Citizen Demonstrations' against war with Russia, and on the 9th a Council of Action was set up to mobilize 'the whole industrial power of the organized workers' to defeat this war. But before either the Council or the government could act or react the 'eighteenth decisive battle of the world' had been fought on 16 August; Pilsudski's counter-stroke with five divisions against the extended Soviet lines of communication was completely successful, and it was Russia's turn for a vast retreat. Both sides now had the sense to make peace. Negotiations began at Riga on 21 September, and after much haggling were concluded on 18 March 1921.[1]

The issue was settled by the Warsaw victory; munitions, even if

[1] Komarnicki, p. 738.

the British government had persisted in sending them, would not have arrived in time to affect the result.[1] But what led to the springing up of 350 Councils of Action throughout the country was the desire to avoid war; any war. As one of Labour's franker spokesmen, James Sexton, said in the Commons on 16 August, the British workers were not concerned about Russia or Poland; all they were concerned about was that 'under no circumstances shall this or any other Government compel them to go to war with any country'. The Polish episode was the first clear manifestation of a new anti-war self-interest transcending party lines; the Chanak crisis two years later was the next. Meanwhile, the Labour party had no intention of allowing its opposition to 'capitalist, imperialist' policies to drive it into collaboration with the Communists. At the beginning of August 1920 a British Communist party was formed by the fusion of the British Socialist party and two other groups. Unlike the Communist parties of other European countries it was formed by the joining together of existing revolutionary groups instead of by splitting a section of the established party. Under Lenin's direct instructions its members were told to accept the risk that association with their compromising Labour brethren would corrupt the purity of their own standards,[2] and they applied for affiliation to the Labour party on 10 August. The first of many refusals followed.[3]

But the general or near general strike, fended off in 1920 by the caution of the T.U.C. and the circumspection of the government, again seemed possible in the spring of 1921, when Labour contemplated the slump and the unpalatable antidotes to it. With the unemployment figure standing at 857,840 in December 1920 it was evident that the boom period was at an end, but worse was to follow: in January it rose to 1,213,386, and with very occasional exceptions it was to remain over a million throughout the twenties. The government met the situation with palliatives in the form of unemployment pay, but as a long term solution it could see no

---

[1] By omitting all reference to the Polish victory some left wing writers give the impression that the Council of Action was decisive in bringing the war to an end with a satisfactory peace. Cf. Hutt, pp. 37–40; G. D. H. Cole, *A History of the Labour Party from 1914*, p. 107.

[2] H. Pelling, 'The early history of the Communist Party of Great Britain, 1920–9', R. Hist. Soc. *Transactions*, 1958, pp. 41–6; William Gallacher, *The Rolling of the Thunder* (1947), pp. 7–17.

[3] This decision by the Labour Party Executive was endorsed at the party's annual conference in June 1921 by 4,115,000 votes to 224,000: Cole, pp. 113–14.

alternative to a general lowering of costs of production to offset the collapse of export prices. This was achieved in the main by bringing to an end government control of industry and agriculture, and with it the need to maintain minimum wages, sometimes by subsidies. The mines were decontrolled in April 1921; in June state help was withdrawn from the housing programme; in August the railways passed out of direct government control into the hands of four companies, formed by amalgamations which extinguished many smaller ones; in September the Corn Production Act of 1920 was repealed, and with it went the Agricultural Wages Board and the minimum wage for farm workers.

This deflationary policy, which seemed to many to carry the best hope of a return to the vanished and partly mythical prewar prosperity, was not solely an attack on wages; but wage reduction was its most painful and obvious feature. However, in spite of further hints at direct action over unemployment the Labour party and the T.U.C. showed no desire for anything beyond a political campaign which would make a big issue of unemployment at the next election. The general line was to demand work or a reasonable standard of maintenance while vigorously attacking the government for its mismanagement of foreign policy and consequent perpetuation of adverse economic conditions abroad.

The miners were hit too hard and too abruptly by the new turn in government policy to be able to accept their lot unprotestingly.[1] Until the end of 1920 they had still been negotiating to consolidate their wartime gains, although they had given up for the time being the demand for nationalization. They had begun another strike for wage increases on 16 October 1920, although their allies in the Triple Alliance were unwilling to join in without full powers being given to them to settle the dispute. A temporary settlement, whereby a wage increase was related to future output, had been reached with the government on 28 October 1920, but this agreement was to last only until 31 March 1921, and the Miners' Federation lost no time in putting forward its plans for a permanent wage settlement, including a national pool of profits and a national wage scale which would consolidate recent gains and ensure a satisfactory wage level even in the less profitable districts. It was at this point that the rapidly worsening export position made it clear that the abnormally high export prices, on which the existing wage structure depended,

[1] R. Page Arnot, *The Miners: Years of Struggle*, chaps. vii–ix; V. L. Allen, pp. 185–90.

could not be maintained. The government saw no reason why it should bear the worry and the cost of running a hard hit industry, and on 15 February 1921 it announced that its control of the mines would end on 31 March, when the temporary agreement expired. The owners, who had hoped that the government would bear the brunt of wage cuts, accordingly had to act for themselves. New wage rates announced for 1 April involved general and often very large reductions, and ignored all the plans for a national scale and pool. The miners struck throughout the country on 1 April, and after an appeal to the Triple Alliance, notices went out to the railwaymen and transport workers to strike on Tuesday, 12 April.

It was a moment of sharp apprehension for the government, which looked on the prospect of a general strike with the greatest dismay. To meet such a situation an Emergency Powers Act had been passed in the previous October, 1920; under it a 'state of emergency' was declared on 31 March. Large preparations to maintain food supplies, transport, and even public order were quickly and perhaps rather ostentatiously set on foot. The threat passed on what came to be known as 'Black Friday'. To the miners and many others in the Labour movement this term was an accusation of betrayal by the railwaymen and the transport workers and even by Frank Hodges, the miners' secretary. When it came to the point the miners' two partners in the Triple Alliance could look only with alarm at a movement of such vague and farreaching political possibilities, and their doubts were strengthened by their limited control of the miners' plans. They did their best to get the negotiations going again; and when they succeeded (on the 12th), postponed their own strike until Friday, the 15th. Then on the Thursday evening Frank Hodges, replying to questions put to him at a meeting of Coalition M.P.s in the House of Commons, seemed to show willingness for some temporary wage settlement, without prejudice to the ultimate solution of the problem of a national pool. On the following morning Lloyd George invited the miners' leaders to an immediate meeting on this basis. When the miners' executive rejected this offer by a majority of one, and repeated the refusal in spite of urgings from Unity House, the railwaymen and transport workers called off their own strike, due to begin that evening.

This was Black Friday; it killed the Triple Alliance, although the ghost made one or two lifelike appearances later.[1] While the

[1] Page Arnot, pp. 312–24.

other two unions were attempting to discuss the government's offer with Herbert Smith, the acting president of the miners, he expected them first to demonstrate their good faith, exclaiming, 'Get on t'field—that's t'place'. The significance of this much quoted answer seems to be that he knew that discussion meant surrender— there was very little else to discuss. Ernest Bevin of the transport workers, a rising figure in the trade union world, was among those who believed that a stoppage on so confused a basis of alliance would be disastrous.[1] The miners therefore struck alone; at the end of June they had to give in and accept the employers' terms. The miners' case was defeated by the facts of the economic situation; with the disastrous shrinking of the overseas markets it was not easy to prove that the industry could meet wage demands based on the boom conditions, or that reorganization, however desirable for other reasons, would greatly help the sale of British coal abroad.

The industry, nevertheless, was able with the help of a government subsidy to cushion the impact of wage reductions in some degree. A new standard for wage rates was fixed at a figure over 20 per cent higher than the prewar level; the owners' profit was fixed at 17 per cent of the standard wage rate, and profits beyond this figure were to be divided in the proportion 17 to 83 between the owners and the miners. The system of district settlement was continued; as a result there was wide difference in the wages for shifts between one district and another. A new agreement in May 1924 raised the minimum addition to the standard wages to $33\frac{1}{3}$ per cent and reduced the owners' standard profit to 15 per cent, improvements for the miners which were made possible by the temporary increase in exports resulting from the Ruhr occupation.

With the frustration of the Triple Alliance, the lessening demand for labour, and the growing hopes of political success in the Labour party, the phase of postwar labour militancy came for the time being to an end. The party was attacking with more and more confidence the government's record in foreign affairs, convinced that it had both a good platform and a good cause in its demand for better relations with Russia and a drastic amelioration of the economic burdens which were hampering the recovery of Central Europe.

---

[1] 'I fail to find the lionlike conduct inside the Triple Alliance that is on the platform': Bullock, p. 178.

5. The Irish Treaty

The summer of 1921 also saw a decisive change in the government's Irish policy.[1] Immediately after Bonar Law's withdrawal from the government in March the idea of a negotiated peace with the rebels began to make headway in the cabinet. There are those who argue that in agreeing to this Lloyd George threw away the substance of victory.[2] This may have been true in a military sense. But the battle was essentially a psychological one, for the control of minds at home and abroad whose animosity was too potent to ignore. In this latter process Sinn Fein had won a propaganda victory which can be measured by the extent to which the British government's willingness for extensive concessions was forgotten. When Congress in the United States in 1919 passed resolutions in favour of sympathy with 'the claims of Ireland to self-determination' and the 'aspirations of the Irish people for a government of their own choice' it ignored the fact that a Home Rule Act was already on the Statute Book and that the Catholic majority was still opposed to self-determination for the Protestant minority. The picture of a wronged and repressed Ireland, goaded into revolt by an alien government that savagely rejected all concession, was by now generally accepted. The historian must note that the area of difference, although real, was narrower than this, and that the government played into the hands of its opponents with remarkable consistency. How easy to be wise after the event! The executions after the Easter rising, the threat of conscription, and the failure of the Convention in 1917 and 1918 to reach agreement on a form of home rule within the Empire, meant that England had finally lost touch with the large body of Irish opinion which had hitherto, if only because of the habit of long association, been prepared to acquiesce in the English connexion. In this sense the 1918 election was a disaster. If legislation establishing some form of Irish parliament had been on the statute book before the election, the Nationalist party would have had something to show, and a greater chance of holding its seats. As it was, Redmond's followers were almost completely replaced by Sinn Feiners, the final figures showing 73 Sinn Feiners, 26 Unionists, and only 6 Redmondites. Sinn Fein could say that it had made no secret of its aim of an independent republic,

---

[1] Frank Pakenham, *Peace by Ordeal* (1935), is the fullest account.
[2] L. S. Amery, *My Political Life*, vol. II, p. 230.

and that its programme had been decisively endorsed by 80 per cent of the Irish voters.

The policy of the Republicans was now to set up a completely independent government for all Ireland and so to harry all representatives of the English connexion as to make the continuance of the Union in any form impossible. On 21 January 1919 thirty-seven of the 106 Irish M.P.s met in Dublin and announced in English and Irish the establishment of the Irish Republic.[1] They demanded the evacuation of the 'English Garrison' and asked for the blessing of Almighty God in the last stage of the struggle. Thus their declaration of independence was also a declaration of war. The opening skirmish took place on the same day when nine Volunteers at Soloheadbeag in County Tipperary shot dead two policemen escorting a load of gelignite needed for quarrying.

This was merely one of an endless series of such incidents, which now multiplied; the police and troops did their best to defend themselves and to hit back, but for over a year they made little headway, and they were indeed being steadily driven out of villages and small towns into large, well-fortified barracks. One purpose of these attacks was to secure arms and explosives for the inadequately equipped Republican forces. Another was to terrorize civilians who helped the government, whether as paid agents, spies, or informers, or merely from the habit of cooperation with the established authorities. A third was to shake the morale of the police and the troops and to destroy the loyalty and cohesion of the Royal Irish Constabulary. By these means it was hoped to prove that British rule had broken down, or alternatively that Ireland was the victim of military aggression. Arthur Griffith told the Dail with some complacency on 27 October 1919 that the British counter-measures 'are of the greatest assistance to our efforts in the United States, and it is there that the centre of gravity of the political situation is for the present fixed'.[2]

After escaping from Lincoln jail on 3 February 1919, De Valera had gone to the United States in June, and spent the next eighteen months there in publicizing the Irish case. He had a somewhat mixed reception, for although there were any number of enthusiastic crowds and excited meetings to cheer the American-born Irishman, the Irish–American politicians who followed John Devoy

---

[1] De Valera, Arthur Griffith, and thirty-four other Republican M.P.s were in jail.
[2] D. Macardle, *The Irish Republic* (1937), p. 327.

and D. F. Cohalan were too uncompromising in their hostility to Great Britain and to Woodrow Wilson to forward De Valera's plans. Their policy was one of aggressive isolationism which did not exclude the possibility of an Anglo-American war arising from such issues as the freedom of the seas. In such a war Ireland would presumably be an advanced American base. De Valera on the other hand was willing enough, after Irish independence had been secured, to give the British government all the assurance it needed that Ireland would never become a hostile base; but his suggestion to this effect in February 1920 to the New York correspondent of the *Westminster Gazette* was angrily attacked as a surrender of Ireland's control over her foreign policy. The difference on this issue was so serious that Cohalan refused to support resolutions at the Democratic and Republican Conventions in 1920 demanding recognition of the government of the Irish Republic, and De Valera had to be content with expressions of sympathy.[1] But all this publicity for the Irish cause had its effect in London.

The fundamental objection to Irish independence was political, and indeed strategic: if the Irish had long memories, so had the English. Ireland had been a hostile base in the past, even the recent past. *Raison d'état* ruled out any abdication which would recreate this situation in the future. A good deal of rather dubious history was quoted in the long controversy. The British government's assumption was that an established state had the right to defend itself against a minority seeking to disrupt it. 'Any attempt at secession', Lloyd George declared in December 1919, 'will be fought with the same determination, with the same resources, with the same resolve as the Northern States of America put into the fight against the Southern States.' A reply to this 'heroic defiance of the weak by the strong' came from Erskine Childers, who said that nations cannot secede from a rule they have never accepted. 'We have never accepted yours' (this was not true) 'and never will. Lincoln's reputation is safe from your comparison. He fought to abolish slavery, you fight to maintain it.' He might have added that Abraham Lincoln, unlike Lloyd George, had found a great ideological issue to justify his fight against secession; but now self-determination, which appealed to much uncommitted British and American opinion, was the reigning ideology, and it had been

[1] Patrick McCartan, *With De Valera in America* (Dublin, 1932); D. Ryan, *Unique Dictator* (1936), pp. 101–42; Macardle, pp. 380–5.

captured, without a struggle, by the secessionists. So the Irish usually came well out of these dialectics, but still the cabinet in London regarded the concession of the ultimate demand of the rebels as unthinkable. It was forced in the circumstances to try to fight out the issue on the spot, while going as far as safety seemed to allow towards self-rule.[1]

In terms of the 1914 situation they were, indeed, able to make a considerable advance; the Liberals had already agreed in 1914 to the repeal of the Act of Union, and now the Conservatives were also brought to agree, and to abandon the intransigent Ulster Unionists. So too were the southern Irish Unionists, who by now had reconciled themselves to something approaching Dominion Home Rule.[2] After his return from the peace conference Lloyd George decided to introduce a new Home Rule Bill, superseding the 1914 measure which had been in suspense during the war. The 1914 Act had provided self-government through an Irish parliament, while an imperial parliament at Westminster with forty-two Irish members would continue to control foreign relations, the armed forces, war and peace, foreign trade, taxation, customs and excise, and the external relations of Ireland generally. The new bill, introduced in December 1919, set up two Irish parliaments, one at Dublin and one at Belfast; the constitution of each was essentially the same as that of the 1914 model. There was also provision for a Council of Ireland, composed of representatives of the two parliaments, to deal with affairs of common interest: evidence that the government did not believe that the partition of geographical Ireland need be permanent.

The history of the northern Irish constitution since 1921 gives a good indication as to how Home Rule would have worked if Redmond had been able to bring it into operation in 1914.[3] The Republicans of 1920 scorned this attempt to reconcile Irish aspirations and British interests, but it had at least found a place in the scheme of things for Ulster. Hitherto the Ulster Unionists had assumed that whatever happened elsewhere in Ireland, Ulster would continue to be governed from Westminster. The idea that they should govern themselves was not greatly welcome, but the northern parliament would at least guarantee their position in whatever

---

[1] T. Jones, *Lloyd George*, pp. 186–90.
[2] D. Gwynn, *The History of Partition*, pp. 176–82.
[3] N. Mansergh, *The Government of Northern Ireland* (1936), especially Part III.

settlement was finally reached in the rest of Ireland. But this led to a new point of view about the boundaries. Hitherto the Ulster Unionists had demanded the existing nine counties of Ulster. The bill limited Ulster to six of these—Antrim, Armagh, Down, Fermanagh, Londonderry, and Tyrone. Even in these six counties there would be a considerable Nationalist minority, with Nationalist majorities in two—Tyrone and Fermanagh: but an Ulster limited to the six would have a safe overall Unionist predominance, whereas if it attempted to rule the nine counties the northern parliament would find the Nationalist minority far too large to manage (700,000 Nationalists to 900,000 Unionists).[1] After difficult discussions the Ulster Unionist Council accepted the government's proposal, not without deep regret at the abandonment of such staunch Unionists as Lord Farnham and his supporters in the counties of Donegal, Cavan, and Monaghan.

Accompanying the leisurely negotiations over the new bill (which did not become law until December 1920) there was an attempt to fight out the issue with the rebels. It was a type of warfare that was to become ever more familiar to the British government during the next forty years, with a small army of self-appointed, civilian-clad, intangible gunmen fighting no pitched battles, but justifying their fitness for self rule by the assassination of unwary individuals, the burning down of offices and barracks, wrecking, ambushes, and the 'execution' of civilians who collaborated with the authorities. The declared object was to make the 'alien' rule impossible. The government forces consisted of some 40,000 soldiers and police, whose main problem was to identify their assailants. The numbers of the latter were exaggerated; while Lord French claimed in April 1920 that they numbered 100,000, Dorothy Macardle doubts whether the whole Republican army at this point can have numbered more than 15,000 men, and believes that during the greater part of the campaign those in active service were probably about ten thousand. But an enemy whose nearest approach to military uniform was a soft hat and a trench coat, whose base was a private house and whose lines of communication were maintained by girls and women, could only be fought by the constant search of houses for weapons and suspects, and this became the main form of counter-action. During the course of 1920, when the struggle was at its

---

[1] In the three excluded counties there were 70,000 Protestants and 260,000 Roman Catholics. Macardle, p. 353, etc.

height, the numbers of the Republican army were being considerably reduced by arrests, casualties, and lack of arms and ammunition. But the ultimate aim of the rebels was to force the British government to a decision, and the activities of the government forces provided a propagandist target which largely compensated for the actual losses. While the Republican soldiers regarded the shooting of unarmed civilians as an act of warfare and claimed under arrest the rights of prisoners of war, the shooting of individuals by the police or soldiers was denounced as civil murder; Erskine Childers and other writers, including English journalists, kept the English press supplied with colourful and harrowing stories of the sufferings of the Irish population from midnight raids and other activities of the British forces.[1] Later in 1920 the character of the supplementary British forces supplied a convenient target.

A new Irish Secretary, Hamar Greenwood (L. S. Amery's brother-in-law), was appointed in April 1920. A resolute and competent Canadian[2] he recognized the futility of military operations against the evanescent terrorist forces and the numerical inadequacy of the R.I.C., which could no longer recruit its numbers in Ireland. He arranged for the enlisting of recruits in England, mainly ex-service men, who came to be known as the 'Black and Tans' from their diversified uniforms; there was also a force of a thousand ex-officers known as the Auxiliary Division of the R.I.C., or 'Auxies'. Thus strengthened, the government forces gradually got the upper hand of the rebels during the next twelve months. By the summer of 1921 their ammunition was growing short; the Republican flying columns were being fiercely harried and by now very large numbers were imprisoned or interned. Volunteers were often insufficiently armed to defend themselves against capture, and desperate attempts were being made to improvise with home-made bombs, refilled cartridge cases and the like. It would seem that the Republican attacks on individuals, whether on the ground of spying, informing, collaborating, or merely serving in the government forces, became more widespread and ferocious in this period, in an attempt perhaps to force a decision and certainly to prove that the Republican Army was operating with undiminished effective-

---

[1] Macardle, pp. 345, 358; Pakenham, pp. 34–42.
[2] 'Hamar was a man of quick clear-cut decision and of unflinching moral and physical courage' (Amery, vol. II, p. 228). '. . . a Canadian adventurer, Sir Hamar Greenwood, was appointed as a tough-skinned careerist who introduced rougher methods' (Denis Gwynn, p. 192).

ness. The murder of fourteen officers in their beds in Dublin on 21 November 1920, regarded in England as a 'dastardly murder', 'the most desperate of all the actions of the Republican murder gang', was greeted by Michael Collins as a triumph for his Counter-Intelligence Service. Hitherto the Republicans had usually refrained from killing women, but on 17 April 1921 they murdered a poor woman who lived six miles from the town of Monaghan; after being put through the farce of a trial, she was shot through the head and her body left by the roadside. Another woman, Mrs. Lindsay of Coachford in County Cork, was executed after giving British military authorities information of an intended ambush which had led to the capture and execution of five rebels. Women were also shot at and sometimes killed when accompanying British officers to social functions.[1]

The long succession of incidents, large and small, were plentifully reported in the British press. They caused shock and indignation, but as time went on the effect was more than counterbalanced by the campaign against the forces of the Crown, comprehensively and inaccurately labelled the 'Black and Tans'. The accusation against them was of excessive and indiscriminate violence in reprisals. It is, of course, difficult to know in this type of warfare what is legitimate and what is not. Three things however are clear. One is that the rebels, who had chosen to shoot it out with the authorities, were getting the worse of the exchanges. The second is that 'reprisals' (an emotive word useful for reprobating any governmental counter-measures) did cover some unauthorized violence by the police, usually after their own officers had been killed. The third is that the activities of the Black and Tans were greatly exaggerated: an obvious point indeed as soon as we remember how late they appeared on the scene. Whoever killed Thomas MacCurtain, Lord Mayor of Cork, on 20 March 1920 (and there is some evidence that he was killed as a moderate by the I.R.A.) it was not the Black and Tans, who were not in existence at the time.[2] The government maintained that the new constables soon justified themselves both by their efficiency and, on the whole, by their discipline.[3]

[1] P. Beaslai, *Michael Collins* (Dublin, 1937), pp. 182–4; Macardle, pp. 413, 458–9, 477; Amery, vol. II, p. 229. *Annual Register 1920*, pp. 120–2, 132–6; *1921*, pp. 4–8, 19, 38–9, gives a representative selection of some of the more gruesome details.

[2] Mowat, p. 68, ascribes it to the Black and Tans; cf. Beaslai, pp. 168, 178.

[3] The arguments for and against are well summarized by Mowat, pp. 70–2; Pakenham, pp. 53–61; cf. Sir N. Macready, *Annals of an Active Life* (1924), vol. II, pp. 281–3, 452–5.

Since 1916 Lloyd George had been involved in efforts to find a satisfactory compromise between all those interested in Ireland's fate; he made ingenious proposals, and when they were rejected tried something else, and there were the familiar accusations of opportunism.[1] But as usual his basic intentions—the limits of concession—were firm. On 16 August 1920 he told parliament that he would be pleased to discuss a settlement with anyone, including Sinn Fein. The essential conditions were: separate treatment for the six counties; no secession; nothing that would impair the security of the United Kingdom and its safety in time of war. At this stage he thought Dominion Home Rule tantamount to independence in its practical effect on security; 'Dominion Home Rule would mean that Ireland could organize its own army and navy', he said in a speech at Cærnarvon on 9 October. 'Dangerous weapons like armies and navies I think we had better not trust them with. It would hurt them to grasp weapons of that kind.' However, Dominion Home Rule was being increasingly advocated by all those who disliked the Irish war, or Lloyd George, or both; Asquith and the Liberal newspapers, Northcliffe and his press, and some prominent Tories outside the cabinet. By the end of 1920 the prospect of a settlement more generous than the Partition Act but with greater guarantees for military security than that suggested by the term 'Dominion Home Rule' must already have been in his mind. He professed himself ready in December, as a result of approaches from Dr. Clune, the Archbishop of Perth, and from Father O'Flanagan, Vice-President of Sinn Fein, for a truce, but the Republican cabinet was not ready to accept.[2]

Unofficial peace moves continued during the first half of 1921, conducted on the British side through A. W. Cope, the Assistant Under-Secretary for Ireland, and it appears that a truce would have come sooner than it did if De Valera, now back in Ireland, and Michael Collins had been ready for it. By the summer of 1921 the I.R.A. was so short of ammunition that it had to make the burning and destruction of property on a large scale its chief method of attack. The Dublin Customs House was destroyed by the Dublin Brigade of the I.R.A. on 25 May. Then on 22 June, at the opening of the Northern Parliament, King George V, prompted by General

---

[1] 'His record in relation to Ireland had been almost incredibly opportunist.' Gwynn, p. 197.
[2] Beaslai, chap. 11.

Smuts and with the agreement of the British cabinet, called on all Irishmen to make peace, and three days later De Valera received and accepted an invitation from Lloyd George to a conference to discuss a final settlement.[1]

This was the decisive turn in the struggle, and it is well to remind ourselves that both sides had surrendered to force. Without the rebellion, Southern Ireland would have got no more than the original Home Rule Act, although it would not necessarily have been the worse off for that; the possibility of a reconciliation with the north would at any rate have been stronger, and time and judicious nagging would no doubt have wrung further concessions from Westminster, without the bitterness and strife which accompanied and followed the struggle. The British would not have secured the guarantees of their military interests and of Ulster if they had meekly accepted the verdict of the Dail and Soloheadbeag on 21 January 1919. What followed was a settlement which might be said to correspond to the realities of the situation, although Hamar Greenwood was convinced that it was a surrender by the British government at the moment of victory.[2] The negotiations were protracted, but the substance of the original British terms—Dominion status, including complete autonomy in all domestic affairs, and the safeguarding of various British strategical and economic interests—was embodied in the final agreement.

The Irish haggled, at first in the obvious hope of securing formal independence or a formula nearer to it than Dominion Home Rule, later it would seem because many who were willing to accept the British terms were unwilling to admit the fact publicly. Partly at least for the same reason De Valera, Cathal Bruga, and Austin Stack stayed in Ireland while more moderate men were sent to London. The leader of these was Arthur Griffith. It is probably true that on balance the truce had weakened the Irish forces more than those of the government; the relief throughout Ireland was obvious and widespread, and made it difficult to start the war again without a better excuse than Lloyd George's terms had provided. On the English side too a renewal of the struggle would have been highly distasteful, but Lloyd George, the master negotiator, did not allow the Irish to believe that this would influence him. All contemporaries

[1] Pakenham, pp. 70–91; Beaverbrook, *The Decline and Fall of Lloyd George* (1963), pp. 82–93.
[2] Cf. also Macready, vol. II, p. 562.

seem to agree that this was his supreme achievement as a peace-maker. Shrewd, tenacious, adroit as ever in turning phrases and corners in complicated discussions, he was also on this occasion studiously conciliatory in manner, and he and the other British delegates were determined to see the best side of the Irish delegates, a sentiment which was reciprocated.

The two main problems were the future of Ulster and the oath. Early in November Griffith agreed to a proposal by Tom Jones, the assistant secretary to the cabinet, that a commission should be set up to delimit the boundaries of Ulster. There has been in subsequent years much argument as to what Griffith understood by this proposal: it certainly implied that Ulster would at first stay out of the southern Dominion, but there was a reasonable assumption that without the Catholic areas of Tyrone, Fermanagh, Armagh, and Down, Ulster would not be a viable state. On the question of the oath the delegates' instruction seemed specific: all that they could agree to was that an oath of loyalty to a treaty of association which would recognize the King as head of the Association. Even on this point their final instructions were verbal and ambiguous. On the morning of 5 December it appeared that the negotiations would break down, but a final impressive warning from Lloyd George that failure to sign would produce war in three days secured the agreement of Griffith, Collins, and the other delegates just after midnight on the 6th.

What they had agreed to was Dominion status similar to that of Canada, an oath of allegiance which included a pledge to be faithful to King George V and his heirs and successors, a share (subject to negotiation) of the national debt, naval and coastal defence in British hands for five years (after which Ireland might undertake a share of coastal defence) and the use of certain harbours and other facilities. These were to be limited in peace time to Berehaven, Cobh, Lough Swilly, and Belfast Lough, although they would be extended to such other places as the British government might require in times of crisis. If after the ratification of the treaty the Northern Parliament expressed a wish for exclusion from the Irish Free State, a commission would determine the boundaries of Northern Ireland 'in accordance with the wishes of the inhabitants so far as may be compatible with economic or geographic conditions'.[1]

---

[1] The negotiations are described by Pakenham, Parts III, IV; Macardle, pp. 545–70; P. Beaslai, *Michael Collins*, vol. II, pp. 293–323; W. S. Churchill, *The Aftermath* (1929), pp. 302–6.

The treaty[1] was approved, promptly in England, grudgingly in Dublin, where most people were satisfied and no one wished to show the fact too openly.

6. THE COALITION: DECLINE AND FALL

The Irish settlement brought the government a momentary popularity, but the treaty was not easily swallowed by the Conservative party. The same, however, could be said of many of the ambiguous achievements of the government since the war. Discontent among Tory under-secretaries and junior ministers had led to a series of meetings between them in August and September 1921, and on 31 October a group of forty-three Tory M.P.s had supported a die-hard motion in the Commons criticizing the government for negotiating with the Irish rebels at all. On 17 November at a meeting of the National Union of Conservative Associations a breakaway from the coalition had been prevented only by heroic efforts; there was a secret dash to Liverpool by Birkenhead to brief Sir Archibald Salvidge, who made a powerful speech, supported by Worthington-Evans and others. The Irish treaty did nothing to dispel the discontent.

Here was one of the ablest cabinets in British history, with the prestige of military victory still around it, once more endeavouring to present retreat as statesmanlike compromise. For those who still wanted a constructive policy the record was disappointing, whether it concerned the home front and unemployment, or the Empire, or the failure to pacify Europe. For those, the majority now of the party, who just wanted to end the coalition because of a vague escapist hunch that public life would be simpler, purer, and easier without it, a return to normal party politics, 'the in and out system', made a growing appeal. On 13 January 1922 an influential correspondent, J. C. Davidson, urged Bonar Law to lead an independent Conservative party on a programme of 'Honest Government, Drastic Economy, National Security and No Adventures abroad or at home'.[2]

Lloyd George was sufficiently aware of this restlessness and of the uncertainties of the future to be anxious for a general election immediately after the Irish settlement. But Austen Chamberlain,

---

[1] Cmd 1560 (1921); N. Mansergh, *The Irish Free State, Its Government and Politics* (1934), pp. 26–49.
[2] Blake, pp. 436–8; Beaverbrook, pp. 124–36; Salvidge, pp. 222–9.

Birkenhead, and Churchill were lukewarm, and it was decided to postpone a decision until after the meeting of the Supreme Council at Cannes in January 1922; then the idea had to be dropped after the Conservative party chairman, Sir George Younger, had publicly denounced it. Bonar Law was still a passive supporter of the government, but declined in January Lloyd George's offer of the Foreign Secretaryship. In February Lloyd George offered to resign in favour of Chamberlain, who loyally scouted the idea.

The moment for a dissolution passed in January, and Beaverbrook attributed the missed opportunity to the fault of indecision on Lloyd George's part, 'an early sign of declining powers'.[1] But it was political power that was declining, and the first months of 1922 did nothing to strengthen the government with any notable success.

The Washington naval conference (November 1921 to February 1922) had on the whole a good press in England. It marked the end of British naval supremacy, the dissolution of the Anglo-Japanese alliance, and the dismantling of all fortifications in Hong Kong and other British insular possessions in the Pacific. British (including Dominion) capital ships were not to exceed fifteen. It was put to the public as a gesture of Anglo-American friendship, but this scarcely concealed the fact that the United States press without much amiability accepted parity as no more than the country's due and in some cases even treated it as less than its due, in view of the American ability to outbuild any other power. For those who could see a little below the surface there were some very disquieting features. The dissolution of the old relationship with Japan, for which a new British–American–French–Japanese four-power treaty of 13 December 1921 was rightly looked on as little more than a face-saving substitute, worried City interests and some diplomatic circles. Worrying too from another point of view was the fact that Canada strongly, and Australia and New Zealand with more concern as to future relations with Japan, felt it necessary to fall in with American views on the need to abandon the old alliance. Again, the degree of naval disarmament achieved, although ideologically respectable, was not in the form which best suited British defensive interests; the limitation on the numbers of capital ships for all purposes made a Far Eastern fleet impossible, but there was no guarantee of United States support there, and on the other hand the limitation or abolition of submarines was prevented, mainly

[1] Beaverbrook, p. 137.

because of French hostility. Having abandoned all pretensions to great power status with her army and airforce, she was reduced to a one-power standard at sea, with American strength as the yardstick, but with Japan privately visualized as the most likely potential enemy. All that could be said was that the Washington agreements and the Irish settlement had removed some causes of friction with the United States; there was no adequate *quid pro quo*, nothing really beyond a hope (which did not get any brighter during the twenties) that more positive cooperation would follow.[1]

Lloyd George had greater hopes of a settlement of outstanding European difficulties, but here too French hostility was unyielding, and Russian and German suspicions insuperable. If there is no sign of failing energy or resolution in his pursuit of this goal, there is surely evidence of some decline in his judgment of realities. Knowing what we do now about the intricate Soviet–German reactions we can also say that there was a lamentable deficiency of information about the details of continental politics, partly but not entirely the fault of the Foreign Office. And yet the conception was rather a splendid one. To arrest the economic decay of Europe, to normalize political relations by bringing Russia into the Concert of Europe again, and to solve the Western European problem by a give-and-take settlement of Franco-German differences—all this was worth striving for. The programme failed as far as Britain was concerned because she had too little to offer. A trade delegation under Krassin had come to London in May 1920, and an Anglo-Russian trade agreement had been signed in May 1921. But it did not involve either *de jure* recognition and the restoration of British credits, or Russia's payment of debts and compensation for seized foreign property. The opponents of any shaking of the blood-stained hands, fiercely led by Churchill with American approval, made it impossible for Lloyd George to offer the one without securing the other. During 1921 Germany and Russia, the two outcasts, were planning economic exchanges fairly openly, and the chances of military collaboration were being secretly explored. Meanwhile France's rigid insistence on full reparations benefits had culminated in a serious fall in the mark in November 1921. On the assumption that security was the key to French intransigence the British government responded favourably to a proposal by Briand in December for some Anglo-French security pact to replace the abortive treaty of guarantee, but

---

[1] See also pp. 300–2 below.

neither Curzon nor Lloyd George was prepared to guarantee more than France's eastern frontier.

In this situation Briand's agreement at Cannes on 6 January 1922 to the summoning of a world economic conference in April was virtually repudiated when he was replaced by Poincaré on the 13th. It had been agreed that the Russians should be invited and be offered recognition in return for guarantees against subversive propaganda and of respect for private property. All other matters paralysing the European system were to be discussed. But from now on Poincaré was adamant in his refusal to discuss the peace treaties, reparations, or general disarmament at the conference; Russia would have to agree to special international stipulations regarding private property, and a non-aggression pact, if concluded, would have to exclude French measures of coercion against Germany. Lenin had at first believed that the meeting would enable Soviet Russia to make profitable bargains with western capitalists; when he discovered in February that onerous conditions, including the payment of Tsarist debts, would be pressed he ceased to take the conference seriously, although he was not going to forgo his government's first opportunity to take part as a recognized government in the counsels of Europe. His main objective was to break the united economic front of the 'capitalist' states against Soviet Russia. Great pressure was put on the German government to conclude a Soviet–German alliance. Rathenau, the German foreign minister, was not prepared to wreck the conference in advance, but he took the unsigned draft with him to Genoa.

Faulty tactics ruined what little chance there was of any real achievement. Lloyd George, with a threat of resignation, had forced the cabinet to agree to recognize Russia, and after the conference had assembled at Genoa on 10 April with leading representatives of thirty-four countries he threw himself during the first week into close secret discussions with the Soviet delegates. These made no progress, but Rathenau, uninformed and inclined to panic, did not know this, and was stampeded by the Russians into signing the Soviet–German treaty at Rapallo on 16 April.[1] The sensation was

---

[1] Russia received *de jure* recognition and a promise of closer economic relations; both countries agreed to abandon all claims for debts and damage against each other, with the proviso on Germany's part that Russia should not compensate other claimants. Each granted the other most-favoured-nation treatment. H. Kessler, *Walter Rathenau* (1929), pp. 326–52, supplemented by Gerald Freund, *Unholy Alliance* (1957), pp. 92–124. Negotiations for a secret military agreement quickly followed. These were unknown and for many years English writers continued to dismiss the treaty as a mere sign of Rathenau's vanity: cf. H. Nicolson, *Curzon*, p. 244.

immense, but as the western powers had nothing to offer Germany or Russia in rivalry with it there was nothing much more to do at the moment. Lloyd George's neglect of the Germans was a decisive tactical blunder. His zeal and resilience survived the shock, however, and the conference continued for six weeks, with detailed discussions in four commissions on political, commercial, financial, and transport problems. All observers agreed that he had never shown greater patience, tact, determination, and good humour. The results can only be described as inconclusive. The real failure was masked by an agreement to continue at the Hague the discussion on the question of nationalized private property in Russia.

In later life Lloyd George looked back on the conference with pride as the outstanding effort of his last period of office; evidently the grand scale of the project and his own unflagging leadership convinced him that any failure could be attributed to the limited vision of others. At home he justified his efforts mainly as a counter to unemployment. Churchill and Curzon had been strongly opposed, and the latter was evidently glad to have been kept away from Genoa by a timely attack of phlebitis. There was also no enthusiasm among other high-ranking Tories such as Chamberlain and Bonar Law. The temptation to fasten all blame on the Prime Minister was almost irresistible after his five full years of office. There was continued talk of a general election, talk of fusion (of the Tories and Lloyd George Liberals), talk also of Liberal reunion and of other combinations; but the plain fact was that a dominant element in every party was beginning to dream of life without Lloyd George.

Meanwhile the government continued its unlucky or unpopular course. The Geddes Report, in response to the demand for governmental economies, was published on 10 February 1922 and proposed cuts amounting to £86 million; no one minded that the service departments should give up £46 million, but the proposed £18 million cut in education brought violent protests from the Opposition, followed by a hasty promise from Sir Robert Horne on 1 March that there would be no reduction of teachers' salaries and that the cuts would amount to not more than a third of the sum suggested. In southern Ireland the treaty was followed by civil war between the new government and the Sinn Fein extremists, and on 13 April a certain Rory O'Connor—a 'grand name for a rogue'[1]—dug himself in in the centre of Dublin, proclaimed a Republican government for

[1] Lord Vansittart, *The Mist Procession*, p. 284.

all Ireland, and conducted terrorist attacks in both Ulster and the south. On 22 June Sir Henry Wilson was murdered by two Irish ex-service men in broad daylight on the steps of his house in Eaton Square. The cabinet was openly attacked for 'shaking hands with murder', and Churchill in the Commons on 26 June warned the Irish government that the terrorist campaign must end. Bonar Law's guarded but explicit criticism of the Irish settlement in the ensuing debate was followed by stronger language behind the scenes.[1] Michael Collins captured O'Connor's position on 30 June, but fighting continued throughout Ireland. A further embarrassment for Lloyd George was an unsavoury 'honours scandal' with allegations of the virtual sale of titles and peerages for contributions to Coalition Liberal funds; the names of criticized recipients were bandied about in both houses of Parliament for some weeks after 22 June.[2]

It was a crisis in Turkey which brought down the government in October, for it led to a Tory revolt against war, recalling Labour's revolt over the Polish crisis in 1920. It is important, however, to remember how far the rebels had gone before the final crisis arose. From the beginning of 1922 the criticisms of Lloyd George were being vigorously canvassed, although the leaders, Austen Chamberlain, Birkenhead, Balfour, and for a time Curzon, firmly defended him. Stanley Baldwin, a dim and silent newcomer to the cabinet as President of the Board of Trade since March 1921, was listening to the hard, cynical, brilliant talk of the great figures with quiet distaste, and this distrust was shared by Sir Arthur Griffith-Boscawen and Lord Peel. The case for ending the coalition was urged on Chamberlain by a group of Tory under-secretaries at the end of July, and they were irritated rather than subdued by a hectoring lecture on loyalty from Birkenhead. The occasion for a break alone was wanting.

The Chanak crisis was due simply to the commendable refusal of Lloyd George, Churchill, and Birkenhead to panic; but the background of events is long and complicated, and it is possible to suggest a number of errors of judgment in British policy towards Turkey after the war. The most serious was a misjudgment of local strengths. The severe treaty of Sèvres of 1920 had set up a neutral

[1] Blake, pp. 440–2.
[2] Owen, pp. 622–8; Gerald Macmillan, *Honours for Sale* (1954), pp. 14–36; William B. Gwyn, *Democracy and the Cost of Politics* (1962), pp. 236–40.

zone around Chanak on the Asiatic side of the Straits, and the
Greeks had been encouraged to use their army to crush the revolt
of Mustafa Kemal against the Sultan. The Greek adventure was
disastrously crushed in August 1922 when their army was thrown
into the sea at Smyrna, and it seemed for a moment that the victorious Kemalist forces would surge across the Straits and carry war
into the Balkans. They were warned by the Allied High Commissioners in Constantinople on 11 September not to invade the
neutral zone, and on the 15th a British appeal was telegraphed to
Greece, Yugoslavia, Rumania, and the British Dominions to help
in defending the Straits. News of this appeal was published on the
16th before the telegrams had been deciphered, much to the
embarrassment of the Dominion prime ministers. But it was a bold
gesture which succeeded, in spite of the fact that Poincaré on the
19th withdrew all French troops from the area. On the 25th Kemal
demanded the withdrawal of British troops; General Harington
refused, and on the 29th Lloyd George, supported by Churchill
and Birkenhead, sent Harington orders to deliver another ultimatum to Kemal. Harington judged the situation differently
however, and after more talking the Turks accepted an armistice
on 10 October.

It is generally agreed that Harington's caution may have prevented a war, and that the ultimatum might have started one.
Nevertheless, the basic complaints, that Lloyd George was fanati-
cally pro-Greek, or that he wanted to start a great war in the East to
bolster his régime, show that his critics were running away from the
real issue. This was to decide where British interests really lay.
Although the Australian and New Zealand governments both
promised support in reply to the telegram of 15 September, Hughes
in a speech drew a distinction between 'the vital interests of the
Empire' and a 'filibustering expedition' in support of Greek
interests; they were prepared to support only the former, which
included the inviolability of the Gallipoli peninsula. On 6 October
Bonar Law wrote a letter to *The Times* and *Daily Express* which
supported British action at Chanak, but asserted that the retention
of the freedom of the Straits and prevention of war and massacre
in the Balkans were not specially British interests. France was
rumoured to have encouraged the Kemalist forces.

The course of action for our Government seems to me clear. We
cannot alone act as the policemen of the world. The financial and social

condition of this country makes that impossible. It seems to me, therefore, that our duty is to say plainly to our French Allies that the position in Constantinople and the Straits is as essential a part of the Peace settlement as the arrangement with Germany, and that if they are not prepared to support us there, we shall not be able to bear the burden alone, but shall have no alternative except to imitate the Government of the United States and to restrict our attention to the safeguarding of the more immediate interests of the Empire.

Clearly these did not include 'the freedom of the Straits'. In spite of the opening reservation, the letter was the most extreme statement of isolationism that the country had heard since Salisbury was in his prime.

It convinced the Tory malcontents that they now had a leader. When Austen Chamberlain sought to persuade the Tory M.P.s at the famous Carlton Club meeting on 19 October 1922 that they should maintain the coalition as a united front against Labour, Bonar Law's reply, preceded by an effective attack on Lloyd George by Baldwin, was decisive. The motion against the continuance of the coalition was carried by 187 to 87. But it was much more than a vote for change for its own sake. It was the final surrender of a rôle which may not have been beyond the country's strength, but was certainly beyond its emotional capabilities.

4

THREE FAILURES

1. TRANQUILLITY ELUDES BONAR LAW

THE coalition had been overthrown by a revolt of the Tory under-secretaries, who looked to Bonar Law to lead the Conservative party out of the coalition and into a general election on its own programme. The plot succeeded all too well: it took the party some years to recover from the victory.

The three short ministries that followed the coalition under three new Prime Ministers (Bonar Law, November 1922 to May 1923; Baldwin, May 1923 to January 1924; Ramsay MacDonald, January to October 1924) each left somewhat the same impression of personal inadequacy among the leaders. No doubt leadership, after a surfeit of achievement, was at a discount; the country wanted to be left alone. The Tories neatly unloaded on Lloyd George all the unpopularity of the predominantly Conservative coalition government: the Goat had become a scapegoat. In the general election on 15 November 1922 Bonar Law achieved a handsome victory for national escapism when he promised 'tranquillity and freedom from adventures and commitments both at home and abroad'. Henceforth he neither did nor said anything memorable; after his resignation on 19 May 1923 Baldwin successfully concealed for a time any pretensions to ideas or originality, but he was hastily repudiated when he asked the country to do some hurried hard thinking about protection in the general election of 6 December 1923. Ramsay MacDonald in the Labour government that followed took a more positive line, although mainly in the field of foreign affairs; this merely confirmed the widespread and quite erroneous suspicion that he was a dangerous man, and Baldwin was returned to office with a splendid majority at the first opportunity (29 October 1924), although only after protection had been dropped. Thenceforward the standard of unobtrusive leadership was faithfully maintained, for although Churchill was to provide a memorable exception in the Second World War there was no sign that the country or the parties desired anything so robust in the years that preceded and followed it.

It is thus not enough to say that the Prime Ministers of the period were rather unimpressive men. They were tough and adroit enough to reach the top of the greasy pole and to maintain themselves there. They did so because they were the types of men that the two parties, on balance, preferred; or at any rate clung to because it was believed that the country preferred them. It was, as a Liberal critic remarked a few months after the fall of the coalition, the political stock-in-trade of quite a number of living gentlemen that they were not Mr. Lloyd George.[1] After a chance conversation with Lloyd George in June 1921 Neville Chamberlain remarked that he 'thought the little beast showed his usual astuteness', and later he thought that it would be useful if the Unionists had some ideas of their own: 'that is where both L.G. and Winston have the pull'.[2] But to him as to many others it was, for the moment, enough that Bonar Law was not Lloyd George.

In its escapist mood the country looked indulgently on the Conservative cabinet which Bonar Law formed immediately after his election to the leadership of the party on 23 October 1922. Curzon (Foreign Secretary) and Derby (Secretary for War), together with Bonar Law himself, were the only prominent survivors of the coalition government. Balfour, Birkenhead, Austen Chamberlain, Sir Robert Horne, Worthington-Evans, and other prominent coalitionists refused to join. The under-secretaries had their reward: Amery as First Lord of the Admiralty, E. F. L. Wood as President of the Board of Education, Sir Philip Lloyd-Greame as President of the Board of Trade. Stanley Baldwin, who had been at the Board of Trade since April 1921, became Chancellor of the Exchequer. Apart from Ireland, where it was agreed that the new position must be loyally accepted, only protection remained of the traditional Unionist problems; but there was no disposition to raise the fiscal question at the election, which was therefore fought on the simple issue of a change of government. Grateful for this easy choice, the

[1] Philip Guedalla, *Collected Essays: II, Men of Affairs* (n.d.), pp. 82, 144.
[2] Keith Feiling, *Life of Neville Chamberlain* (1946), pp. 90-1, 96-7.

electorate gave Bonar Law a decisive victory, with 345 Conservative seats, as against 142 Labour and 116 Liberal.[1]

The most significant fact of the election was that the Liberals, even with Lloyd George and his following in opposition, could not impress themselves on the country as an alternative government. Asquithians and Lloyd Georgeites were further weakened by having to fight as separate groups, but the fact remained that the Labour party had, by a small but decisive lead, finally established itself as one of the two main parties of the state. Tory and Socialist were in future to build up each other's reputation by reciprocal attack; neither paid the Liberal party the same compliment.[2] The Tory majority, as it happened, was deceptive: the party had been favoured by the distribution of seats, and had polled a minority of the total votes.[3]

For the time being the party was not looking for adventure. 'Tranquillity' was not so much a policy as a call for a change of mood: goodwill and hard work at home, good offices in liquidating some stubborn issues abroad, with a due spirit of abnegation as Britain's contribution. Bonar Law soon showed that, behind a diffident manner, he was a more expeditious chairman than his predecessor; but if the cabinet got through its business more quickly, there was little opportunity for the old, expansive debates on general policy, and indeed little in the way of general policy to debate.[4]

There were signs after the end of 1922 that the worst of the slump was over, although beyond a certain point unemployment figures obstinately refused to fall, or exports to rise. There had been some improvement in the unemployment figures between July 1921 (16·7 per cent) and December 1922 (12·8 per cent); in January 1923 the percentage was 13·3 and in June 1924, 9·3. They began to rise again after that, reaching 10·9 in April 1925.[5] In broad terms 'the intractable million' of regularly unemployed remained. There was still too little evidence to say whether this could be attributed to the continued dislocations following the war, or to more fundamental causes. The government preferred on the whole to blame the

---

[1] L. S. Amery, *My Political Life*, vol. II, p. 241; Blake, *The Unknown Prime Minister*, pp. 459–75.
[2] Feiling, p. 101.
[3] Conservative, 5,500,382; Labour, 4,241,383; Liberal, 4,189,527; Others, 462,340.
[4] Amery, vol. II, p. 246.
[5] Pigou, pp. 40–2; A. J. Youngson, *The British Economy 1920–1957*, pp. 28–30.

war. It saw the best hopes of recovery in its monetary policy and in tranquillization abroad, with the continuation of the policies of deflation and decontrol at home. But in the meantime recovery might be delayed, and would have to be paid for. There are signs that the attempt to restore London as the financial centre of the world by acting as if it were still the financial centre of the world was causing some misgiving in the cabinet. But as Chancellor of the Exchequer Baldwin followed loyally the advice of the Treasury officials, merely noting the reservations of J. M. Keynes as evidence of the ultimate indecision of the 'pure finance people'.[1] The debt settlement with America was a focus for some uneasiness which he did not appear to share.

President Wilson had been adamant in refusing to consider cancellation of the debts, and Congress had set up a War Debts Commission in February 1922, with instructions to collect the debts in twenty-five years at a rate of at least $4\frac{1}{4}$ per cent interest. In an ingenious attempt to justify the British position Balfour as acting Foreign Secretary had sent a note[2] (drafted by Lloyd George) to the French government on 1 August 1922. After reminding it that Great Britain was owed altogether four times as much as she owed the United States he said that she was prepared to remit all debts due to her from her Allies in respect of loans or from Germany in respect of reparations, as part of a general settlement; but as America's insistence on payment made any such all-round cancellation impossible, she would collect from her European debtors only enough to pay her American creditors. This sweet reasonableness, which Mr. E. H. Carr has called 'too-clever-by-half diplomacy', put everyone else in the wrong; all the same, it was perhaps no bad thing that the idea of all-round cancellation, which Lloyd George had proposed to Wilson in 1919, had been boldly adumbrated. The Americans, however, wanted the money, or at any rate to be asked to remit it, as Keynes suggested in 1921, in humbler and more emotional terms.[3]

It was difficult for the Treasury and the Bank of England, anxious above all to demonstrate British solvency, to plead poverty. Their inclination was all in favour of the best bargain attainable between equals. Baldwin went to the States in January 1923 with a formidable

[1] G. M. Young, *Stanley Baldwin*, p. 46.
[2] Published as Cmd 1737.
[3] J. M. Keynes, *Essays in Biography*, p. 61.

upholder of orthodoxy in Montagu Norman, the Governor of the
Bank of England. The British embassy urged that a settlement
before Congress rose on 4 March was imperative for political
reasons. Baldwin was convinced that he must get the best settlement he could, and quickly. He rejected the first American offer;
the second, slightly better, Bonar Law firmly refused to consider.
The third offer was a settlement spread over sixty-one years, with
3 per cent for the first ten years, 3½ per cent thereafter, and arrears
carrying 4½ instead of 5 per cent interest (Bonar Law had objected
to anything more than 2½ per cent for the arrears, and thought that
they should be remitted altogether). Baldwin accepted *ad referendum*,
knowing that the Prime Minister was unconvinced, and came home
to state his case.

Many of the dilemmas of Anglo-American relations were involved in the discussion. To all English statesmen, American
goodwill was basic, a permanent quarrel on any issue unthinkable;
but it did not seem to be entirely unthinkable or even undesired in
some American quarters. The debt settlement, like the agreement to
naval parity, the dropping of the Anglo-Japanese alliance, and the
Irish treaty, was a contribution to the building up of an Anglo-
American friendship which, in this phase of intense isolationism,
offered no tangible reward. To many Americans, Britain was still a
formidable and sophisticated competitor, and this element of competition was shared by British governments who were determined to
maintain, while they were forced to concede, parity in many fields—
in finance as well as in naval armaments. But there was also the hospi-
table face of America, and Baldwin's name can be added to the list of
those envoys who were thought to have strengthened goodwill by
the frankness and tact of their language, which was received with
good humour in Washington. Baldwin spoke clearly about the
difficulties of payment for a debtor frustrated by the creditor's unwillingness to accept payment in direct delivery of goods or to see
the sale of her own products to the debtor country interrupted,
and he was assured by correspondents after his return that his plain
speaking had advanced good feeling and paved the way for a better
understanding. He somewhat marred the good impression by com-
menting rather less flatteringly on American attitudes to some
journalists at Southampton, although he may have been unfairly
reported. Bonar Law looked glumly at the terms, and at first talked
about resignation; he even wrote an anonymous letter to *The Times*

on 27 January 1923 criticizing the proposals. But the rest of the cabinet were favourable. In the end he agreed.[1]

All would have been so much simpler if Britain's European debtors had been prepared to pay up. It was clear that the French objected to paying anything at all. They were as unwilling as the Americans, although for different reasons, to link reparation and debt payments; from this point of view the Balfour note was particularly ill-timed. After half-hearted efforts to pay some reparations the German government had been granted a partial moratorium in May 1922; in June, Rathenau was assassinated, the mark continued to fall, and there was then a request for a total moratorium until the end of 1924. At this point the French decided to take what they were entitled to by force: in short to secure 'productive guarantees'. Only a week after the Balfour note Poincaré elaborated his plans, which included the exploitation of the Ruhr, the collection of custom duties along Germany's eastern frontier, and the appropriation of 25 per cent of the value of German exports. In a letter of 1 September he made disparaging remarks about the British war effort and said flatly that there could be no question of settling war debts until the reparation payments due to France had been completed. Convinced that he had been abandoned by England in the European settlement, he had no scruple about abandoning her in the Middle East. When Bonar Law took office the two countries were as near to a complete breach as they had ever been since the formation of the *entente cordiale* in 1904.

Bonar Law felt no zest for a fight, and although he liked the prospect of the French coercion of Germany even less his instinct was to assume a mediatory rather than a directing position. He did not interfere with Curzon's handling of the Near Eastern settlement, although at the end of December 1922 he seemed 'willing to give up everything and anything rather than have a row'. When the reparations problem reached crisis point in December, Bonar Law told Poincaré that British public opinion would never condone an advance into the Ruhr, and Sir John Bradbury, the British delegate to the Reparations Commission, emphatically dissented from the decision of the French, Italian, and Belgian delegates to declare

---

[1] A. W. Baldwin, *My Father, the True Story* (1956), pp. 118–19; G. M. Young, pp. 44–7; Sir Evelyn Wrench, *Geoffrey Dawson and Our Times* (1955), p. 215; Sir James Grigg, *Prejudice and Judgment* (1948), pp. 98–103: cf. R. Blake, *The Unknown Prime Minister*, pp. 491–2, and the same author's second thoughts in 'Baldwin and the Right', in *The Baldwin Age* (1960), pp. 39–40.

Germany in default. But when the French occupied the Ruhr basin all the same on 11 January 1923 the British government, while doing nothing to forward the French designs, was not prepared to help the Germans by obstructing the French lines of communication, invoking the League machinery, suggesting compromises, or even publicly condemning French and Belgian action.

The general tendency of British foreign policy in 1923 was to emphasize the rôle of self-appointed mediator in continental affairs. The Turkish settlement removed the last of the outstanding issues of the peace settlement in which the country's direct interests were involved. In the Ruhr struggle there seemed every reason to deplore the continuance of the quarrel and equally to avoid taking sides. On the other hand there was a general cry for the government to do something. Here is the real point of transition to the policy of 'appeasement', in the correct dictionary sense of the word, which the British government was to follow until March 1939. It meant—it always meant to the Conservatives—the achievement of a state of tranquillity in European affairs by some positive action on Britain's part, in questions which were more directly the concern of other powers than herself. Such a mediatory policy, involving some interference in the intimate affairs of near neighbours, is seldom disinterested, generally suspect, and almost always ineffectual. In the Franco-German disputes which formed the main subject of British efforts at tranquillization for the next fifteen years the Germans believed, rightly, that in the last resort Britain would side with France; France, that Britain was not giving her the support that she had a right to expect. But as both hoped to benefit from the mediator's somewhat awkwardly contrived efforts to appear fair to both sides they could not afford to be too rude to her, however exasperating her conduct. This in turn might lead her to exaggerate the progress of her efforts and the extent of her own objectivity.

Bonar Law's inactivity in the Ruhr crisis was doing the government's reputation no good, and Curzon's skill in handling the Turkish negotiations was not sufficiently understood to provide an antidote. Immediately after the general election he had travelled to Lausanne, where in conference with the Turks, French, Italians, and Greeks he had secured by 4 February 1923 all the essential British requirements. If some of these concerned points on which Turkish and British interests did not really conflict, others were more difficult, for the Turks had been arrogantly self-confident in the opening phase of the conference at the end of November 1922. With some justification, indeed, for they had won their victories, and in the general election the British cabinet's Turkish policy, whatever it was, had been repudiated. It was thus, as Sir Harold Nicolson has shown in his classic study of the conference, a personal triumph of expert diplomacy that Curzon achieved at Lausanne.[1] At the beginning the situation appeared unpromising. The Anglo-French alliance had almost collapsed, and although the French defection before Chanak had shocked French opinion sufficiently to force Poincaré to stop short of an open breach there was no prospect of genuine cooperation. It seemed all too probable that he hoped to avoid a Franco-Turkish breach by leaving Curzon in a position in which, deserted as usual by France and Italy, he would be forced to agree either to a humiliating peace or to the break-up of the conference. Yet he could not threaten war; the British press loudly told the world so, and the cabinet confirmed it. 'The feet of the Prime Minister were glacial', Curzon commented sadly to a secretary after seeing Bonar Law in Paris on 31 December.

His own hands, nevertheless, were now free; freer at any rate than any Foreign Secretary's could have been under Lloyd George. Before entering the conference he insisted on securing from Poincaré and Mussolini a public affirmation of their complete accord, and at the opening meeting he used the prominence which everyone was willing to thrust upon him to secure for himself the chairmanship of the decisive meetings. Thenceforward he skilfully guided the discussions; by choosing Turkish demands in western Thrace, where the Turkish case was weakest, as the first item he effectively isolated Ismet Pasha, and when subsequently the debate turned to the question of the Straits he was quick to detect and exploit a reservation on the Turkish side towards the Russian plan, which would have excluded the interest of all but the littoral powers. The Turks preferred the British plan which, while recognizing Turkish sovereignty in Constantinople and the Straits, provided freedom of transit in times of peace for ships of war of all nations (subject to limitation of numbers and length of stay), and in war to the warships of all nations except belligerents. Even on the question of Mosul, which the British government was determined to secure for Iraq, Curzon shattered the Turkish case so thoroughly in debate with a

---

[1] Harold Nicolson, *Curzon: The Last Phase* (1934), chaps. x, xi; cf. *King George V*, pp. 372–4.

threat to invoke Article 11 of the League Covenant, as to make it impossible for Turkey to break up the conference on this issue; she agreed to settle it by direct negotiations with Great Britain.

Thus by 1 January 1923 all the main points in the treaty which had been the special concern of the British delegation had been settled; there remained outstanding only the problems of finance, economy, and status of foreigners with which France and Italy were more directly concerned, and which had been referred to committees under French and Italian chairmanship. Many of these were settled during the following week, although Ismet Pasha chose to be obstinate on a few points. A draft treaty was presented to the Turks on 31 January. On the 30th Poincaré, through the Havas agency, issued a statement that the French government regarded the draft as merely a basis for further discussion; but he had second thoughts and hastily repudiated this act of sabotage, apparently realizing the danger of a separate Anglo-Turkish treaty, which Ismet Pasha indeed virtually offered on 4 February. Curzon wisely resisted the temptation to score this personal triumph. He was not prepared to sign until his French and Italian colleagues were fully satisfied. So the conference was adjourned, and the teasing and technical issues on which the Turks had chosen to haggle were settled at a more leisurely pace when it was resumed in the following summer (24 April to 24 July) with Sir Horace Rumbold as the British representative.

The British government had every reason to be satisfied with the settlement. A thoroughly quiescent Turkey was an essential basis of stability in the Middle East; it was of the highest possible advantage to the British at a time when public opinion at home ruled out any dramatic or adventurous action in defence of Britain's still vast interests and responsibilities in the area. By 1922 it was already abundantly clear that Arab nationalism was not prepared to accept British tutelage with much enthusiasm and in Iraq, Palestine, and Egypt the British authorities were already embarked on the long struggle to justify British control by local concessions and good government, with the promise of self-government in the not too remote future. To the dour, suspicious, but unadventurous Turkey to the north was to be added shortly the stable although chauvinistic régimes of Ibn Saud in Arabia to the south and of Riza Khan in Persia in the east. Riza Khan, after seizing power in February 1921, had promptly repudiated the Anglo-Persian agreement, but his relations with Great Britain after becoming Shah of Persia in 1925 were not unfriendly, and provided a further strong barrier against Russian expansion towards either Mesopotamia or India. Curzon, moreover, had achieved a personal ascendancy with the Turks which defeated the attempts of French and Italian agents to reduce British influence. This does not mean, however, that the Turks agreed very readily over Mosul. It was not until Turkey had been discredited by suppression of the Kurdish revolt in 1925 and a League of Nations enquiry had awarded the area to Iraq, that Turkey finally acquiesced in this solution in a treaty between herself, Iraq, and Great Britain in June 1926.[1]

Curzon's refusal to separate himself from his two allies on 4 February 1923 was an earnest of his desire to restore British influence and credit in Europe, and he turned to this task on his return to England. He had no illusions at all as to the difficulty of any working agreement with Poincaré: but perhaps he expected too much from his own colleagues.[2]

2. BALDWIN AND PROTECTION

To most Englishmen the promise of tranquillity meant an end to foreign crises and, somehow or other, the removal of postwar difficulties at home. There were no doubt links between the two: almost any activity cost money, and economy in government expenditure was a widely proclaimed palliative; exports needed stable markets. Nevertheless, the situation was much over-simplified. No one really knew what to do about unemployment, and what was being tried was undramatic and experimental; in the meantime the parties vied with one another in proclaiming their constructive contributions to peace. Although Ramsay MacDonald and the near-pacifist Labour spokesmen did this more resoundingly and perhaps with more conviction than the Tories, Stanley Baldwin was beginning to catch the public ear with a note of vague goodwill peculiarly his own; it embraced moreover industrial as well as foreign peace.

In the debate on the address on 16 February 1923 he spoke after MacDonald, who on this occasion was in anything but a conciliatory mood towards France, and insisted that it was impossible for the country to undertake to manage all the affairs of the world single-handed. Nevertheless, the government was striving for peace, at

[1] Amery, vol. II, pp. 325–34.
[2] Nicolson, *Curzon*, p. 344.

Paris and Lausanne. Then after telling the Communist member for
Motherwell that the country would never have a Communist
government, for 'no gospel founded on hate will ever seize the
hearts of our people', he went on to the passage which was soon to
echo far beyond the House.

> It is no good trying to cure the world by repeating that pentasyllabic
> French derivative 'Proletariat'. The English language is the richest in
> the world in monosyllables. Four words, of one syllable each, are
> words which contain salvation for this country and for the whole
> world, and they are 'Faith', 'Hope', 'Love', and 'Work'. No govern-
> ment in this country today which has not faith in the people, hope in
> the future, love for its fellow-men, and which will not work and work
> and work, will ever bring this country through into better days and
> better times, or will ever bring Europe through, or the world through.[1]

The man was to go on talking in this way, and the people and the
politicians liked him; he always seemed to stand for something
friendly and decent and rather reasonable. The trouble was that so
little in the way of professionally articulated policies ever seemed
to follow. His closer associates soon discovered his boredom with
the technical details of government, whether in finance or foreign
affairs or any of the more complicated matters of cabinet discussion.
Yet with all his mental indolence he was not inactive; he did not
lack courage, and he did not shirk responsibility. There was a
certain inability to think out the consequences of his own programmes; Amery soon noticed the 'curious incoherence between
Baldwin's political ideas and his actions and appointments'. But he
had a genuine political flair, and he was neither frightened nor subdued by the more experienced or aggressive members of his cabinet.
Nobody thought him a great prime minister. But something about
him satisfied his party and the country for many years: they doubtless got the leader they deserved.

So this likable man, playing by ear, expounding his bewilder-
ments more readily than his theories, happy (as it was thought)
with his pigs and England and Mary Webb, was rather a comfort
after ten years of greatness. Curzon was the last of the dominating
coalition figures, surviving into a new era, with outmoded expertise.
His intellectual mastery, eloquence, argumentative skill and fine
draftsmanship, his sense of his own importance and that of his
country, his calculated arrogance, the aristocratic geniality which

[1] P.D., 5 Ser., HC, vol. 160, 16 Feb. 1923, cols 561–2; cf. A. W. Baldwin, p. 126.

he mistook for tact—these were the qualities, almost indeed a caricature of the qualities, of the superior Victorian person. Neither the manner nor the approach to politics suited the times. Baldwin and Curzon represented the two eras, and in spite of their anxiety to avoid any appearance of rivalry the difference is sufficiently pronounced.

When Bonar Law's unsuccessful search for health in the early months of 1923 made his resignation probable, both Curzon and Baldwin looked forward to the succession. Curzon had acted as Prime Minister in Bonar Law's absence, and does not seem to have visualized Baldwin as a rival. When the diagnosis of cancer in the throat finally compelled his retirement on 19 May 1923 Bonar Law was greatly troubled as to what recommendation he should make and greatly relieved to find that constitutional practice did not compel him to make a recommendation at all.[1] On this occasion, as in 1894, the monarch had to choose. Although King George V's personal view was that the Prime Minister must be a member of the House of Commons he recognized Curzon's vast claims, and consulted some Privy Councillors before deciding. Balfour gave a tepid support to Baldwin, as a Commons man, although he was 'without any signs of special gifts or exceptional ability'. Salisbury, the Lord President, supported Curzon. Amery and Bridgeman pressed the case for Baldwin, but their views, if we can judge from Sir Harold Nicolson's account, did not really affect the King's choice, which was made on Balfour's advice.[2] Baldwin took the gratifying news modestly. Some of the more dramatic accounts of Curzon's chagrin seem to be apocryphal, but he made no secret to the King's private secretary of his mortification, and determination to retire at once from public life.[3] The new Prime Minister had no difficulty in persuading him to remain; but between them there was no fundamental accord.

Baldwin's first government held office for only six months. It did little to advance Tory reunification. It did not attract Austen Chamberlain and his supporters. Embarrassed apparently by the opposition to Chamberlain's return by some of those who had 'stuck by the ship in difficult times', Baldwin offered him the Wash-

---

[1] Blake, pp. 514–15.
[2] H. Nicolson, *King George V*, p. 376.
[3] *Ibid*, pp. 377–8; Amery, vol. II, pp. 259–60; Young, pp. 49–51; Blake, p. 527. The last (chap. 32) is the best and fullest account, with details of the important rôle of Colonel Ronald Waterhouse.

ington embassy on 26 May, and mentioned McKenna as the probable Chancellor of the Exchequer. This strange preference for a Liberal Free Trader was enough to alienate so easily ruffled a man as Austen, whose disinclination to join was increased by Birkenhead's argument that it was better to wait until Baldwin's inferior team had discredited itself. The offer to McKenna was presumably a desperate attempt to add a distinguished name; but he had been ill, and his pre-condition of a safe seat could not be met. After holding the Chancellorship himself for some weeks, Baldwin appointed Neville Chamberlain in August. The cabinet in general remained much what it had been under Bonar Law.

Foreign and domestic policy were more closely linked than usual perhaps in the government's discussions during the summer, for the continued dislocation of foreign trade was widely attributed to the highly dramatized events in the Ruhr and to the fall in the French exchange, and these in turn were taken to explain the unemployment figures. Anything therefore that would manœuvre Poincaré out of his untenable position and provide some Franco-German compromise would be welcome, but clearly this was not the whole of the story. Curzon's approach was combative rather than persuasive, and there were soon signs that Baldwin did not think that the country could afford the luxury of fresh quarrels. Moreover, there were the more permanent lines of economic policy to be considered.

Baldwin at the Treasury had seemed to be thoroughly satisfied with the official deflationary policy. His budget, opened on 17 April, had won general praise not only for its point and brevity but also for its refusal to give anything much away. He found himself with an unexpectedly large surplus, but he devoted practically the whole of it to debt reduction, although there was a somewhat grudging reduction of income tax from 5s to 4s 6d. This 'sound money' policy was warmly endorsed by both Ramsay MacDonald and Asquith, and what faint criticism there was came from critics on the Conservative benches, including his predecessor, Sir Robert Horne, who had not hesitated to suspend the Sinking Fund. It must be remembered that from the point of view of the Treasury and Bank of England the deflationary policy seemed to be justifying itself, to the extent at least that prices and money wage rates were fairly stable between January 1923 and June 1924. The cost of living index moved down by 4 per cent, and the retail price of food by 6 per cent; the money rate of wages moved up by 1 per cent. The goal of a restored gold standard also seemed in sight; by March 1923 the dollar exchange had reached the high level of 4·70 to the pound, although it fell to 4·61 in June.[1]

But if the economic crisis was no worse, it was also no better: there was still the intractable million. The bankers offered cold and academic comfort to Amery and the tariff reformers, who were irked by Bonar Law's pledge not to raise the matter of protection in the present Parliament. Although the arguments against the evils of deflation were less familiar than those against inflation, which were being dramatically advertised by the German crisis, J. M. Keynes was arguing that of the two deflation was perhaps the worse, 'because it is worse, in an impoverished world, to provoke unemployment than to disappoint the rentier'.[2] Labour spokesmen continued to thunder against the inefficiency of capitalism in failing to utilize the country's resources adequately or to conquer poverty, but they were kept sternly by Philip Snowden to free trade and *laissez-faire* standards as far as overseas markets were concerned.

While he was well enough aware of the economic aspects of the Franco-German crisis, Curzon was thinking far more in political terms; he wanted to restore England's standing in Europe. He handled Poincaré, as he thought, with circumspection, avoiding an open breach; the conduct of the Soviet government was publicly trounced, that of the Italian government openly condoned.

Curzon had never liked Lloyd George's commercial negotiations with Russia. He passionately resented the anti-British Soviet propaganda in India and the Middle East. He protested sharply against the recurrent ill-treatment of British subjects. He had received the shrill and thin-skinned Russian commissar for foreign affairs, M. Chicherin, at Lausanne, with expansive bonhomie which the Russian evidently interpreted as patronizing banter. Worsted at Lausanne, the Narkomindel was in no mood to receive meekly a note from the British chargé d'affaires in Moscow, Hodgson, of 30 March 1923, protesting against the death sentence passed on a certain Monsignor Butkevic, a Soviet citizen and Roman Catholic priest accused of espionage by the Ogpu. This intervention in Soviet domestic affairs was rejected next day in a note signed by an official named Vainshtein with rude comments on British conduct in

[1] Pigou, pp. 150–1, 168.
[2] Amery, vol. II, p. 279; J. M. Keynes, *Essays in Persuasion*, p. 103.

Ireland and India. So on 8 May a formidable indictment of Soviet conduct in the form of a memorandum in twenty-six paragraphs was sent to Hodgson for delivery to the Soviet government. It surveyed all the causes of Anglo-Soviet difference since 1920 and made demands for prompt redress within ten days, failing which Hodgson would be withdrawn from Moscow. The demands included compensation for the death or imprisonment of two British agents, and for the recent seizure of two British trawlers; unequivocal withdrawal of the Vainshtein correspondence; abandonment with apologies of the anti-British activities of the Soviet agents in Teheran and Kabul. The Soviet government was appalled at the prospect of a breach with England at a moment when the French advance into the Ruhr had conjured up the alarming prospect of a general war; by a curious coincidence, Foch had arrived in Poland with great publicity on 2 May, and the British C.I.G.S. had followed a week later. On 11 May a reply signed by Litvinov accepted all the specific British demands, although on the question of propaganda there were familiar evasions.

Very well pleased with this success, Curzon nevertheless put aside the bludgeon in his bout with Poincaré. His aim, following the advice of the British ambassador in Berlin, Lord D'Abernon, was to bring the French occupation of the Ruhr to an end with an agreement based on an expert assessment of Germany's capacity to pay. During the first weeks of the occupation British policy had been almost entirely negative, although the refusal to allow the British zone to be welded into the single Franco-Belgian administration was both a practical and a moral challenge to the French plans. Now, after a good deal of British prompting, the German government promised on 7 June to accept the decision of an impartial body with regard both to the mode of payment and the amount involved. The advantage of this procedure was that it reminded the French of the interests of the United States and of other powers with reparations claims, thereby avoiding in some measure an exclusive Anglo-French clash and providing a possible basis for compromise. However, Poincaré insisted that before negotiations began passive resistance must be abandoned. Curzon replied to this on 11 August with a long and forceful note which reviewed the whole history of the problem, and followed the Balfour Note in stressing the burden imposed on the country by the dislocation of foreign trade which French action had caused, or accentuated. Up to this point Curzon had kept British policy firmly in his own hands, although he knew that Bonar Law and after him Baldwin were uneasy at the continued Anglo-French tension. After Poincaré's latest rebuff in July the cabinet would have preferred to suspend the argument for the time being but it finally agreed to the despatch of the new note. Its qualms can easily be understood. Curzon had done something to rally world opinion, and something to encourage the Germans. He had not convinced Poincaré, who continued to demand unconditional surrender.

The fact is that although Curzon could be challenging and reproachful, he had no real control over French policy, which ran its course and came to its own unrewarding conclusion. Curzon's own concentration relaxed after the *tour de force* of his note of 11 August; suffering again from phlebitis, he spent ten days at Bagnolles, and then retired at the beginning of September to Kedleston, where rapid communication was difficult save through the telephone in the butler's pantry. Greece had appealed to the League of Nations after Mussolini's brutal attack on Corfu, and Curzon agreed on 2 September that the League authority must be upheld; Lord Robert Cecil was instructed accordingly, and made a very determined speech on the 5th. But five days later, when Mussolini had repudiated the authority of the League, Poincaré had made it clear that he was prepared to accept the unsatisfactory compromise proposed by the ambassadors' conference in Paris. Curzon gave in and did the same.

There followed another apparent retreat when, on 20 September, Baldwin, travelling home from Aix-les-Bains, talked to Poincaré in Paris. A communiqué after the meeting announced their discovery that on no question was there any divergence of views or purpose between the two countries. Had Curzon been abandoned by Baldwin as he had himself abandoned Cecil and the League Council? He evidently thought so, and believed that he had been tricked by the French ambassador and one of his own officials. The inside story of this episode has still to be revealed. It appears that Baldwin had told Curzon all about the forthcoming interview, and had said that its purpose was to impress on Poincaré the unity of British policy; moreover, he did not see the communiqué before it was published. What is certain is that he had been thoroughly outmanœuvred. He was strengthened in his dislike of contacts with foreigners. It seemed that with Curzon out of town British acquiescence in French policy was complete. Germany surrendered four days later. But she would probably have been forced to do so anyway, and there is no reason to think that further dialectical triumphs by Curzon could have saved her. He did her one further service, however, in the following weeks, for his emphatic opposition did much to kill the separatist movement that Poincaré was favouring in the Rhineland.[1]

Baldwin told Curzon that he wished to impress on the French that there were no longer two foreign policies in London, and the statement rings true: his thoughts were much on Tory unity at the time. Shortly after his return to London he told Amery (on 8 October) that he was convinced that nothing but protection could solve the unemployment problem. On the 10th Neville Chamberlain found that he was thinking of an immediate dissolution. In later years he even claimed that he wanted an election because a defeat would pull the party together.[2] It is against all common sense that a Prime Minister with an assured majority should throw it away for so chancy a result, but he may well have believed that there would be a victory that would unite the party. Baldwin, however, subsequently gave conflicting explanations of his decision. He told Dr. Tom Jones in September 1935 that he had become convinced that unemployment could not be dealt with without a tariff, and that the chances of securing this had improved since the war; 'it was a long calculated and not a sudden decision' on his part. But he added, 'the Goat . . . was on the water . . . I had information that he was going protectionist, and I had to get in quick'. Was this a long-matured plan to end unemployment, or a device to reunite the Tory party, or a sudden decision to anticipate Lloyd George? Amery was convinced that it was the return of Lloyd George, 'full of ideas of a bold Empire policy with Imperial preference well to the foreground' which really prompted Baldwin's sudden decision on 8 October, and Neville Chamberlain evidently accepted this in subsequent years as an adequate explanation of Baldwin's decision.[3] We have little evidence as to the economic arguments which had so suddenly converted Baldwin, and no reason to think that they differed from those with

[1] Nicolson, p. 372, and fn. 1, gives some details of Baldwin's activity. Young, p. 62.
[2] Feiling, p. 108; A. W. Baldwin, p. 123.
[3] Amery, vol. II, p. 280; Feiling, p. 108, fn. 1. R. T. McKenzie, *British Political Parties*, p. 111, fn. 1, thinks that this explanation is implausible. He is in error in stating that Amery's statement is unsupported. Baldwin himself said later that his aim was political: T. Jones, *Lloyd George*, p. 208.

which he had been familiar since his entry into Parliament in 1908. On balance it seems that it was the politician's sense of expediency which decided the matter: this was the one cause which would dish the Liberals, bring together the Tory dissidents, consolidate his own position as party leader, and after all do no harm to the country if it succeeded. Two things are remarkable about the election. One is the lack of serious preparation. The other is the consolidation of Baldwin's position in spite of his defeat.

The cabinet agreed that Baldwin should announce the decision to the National Unionist Association at Plymouth on the 26th as his personal view. His speech was well received, the pronouncement of an honest man thinking things out for himself. The electoral programme included plans for the protection of special industries, with complete fiscal freedom except for a pledge to place no further taxes on essential foods. Austen Chamberlain regretted this piece of timidity. But he supported Baldwin's view that an immediate dissolution was the wisest course, and the party was thus compelled to take the plunge with the minimum of preparation. Henderson's defiant and expeditious defence of free trade at a luncheon on 2 November may have hurried things on.[1] The dissolution was on 16 November; polling on 6 December. The unfortunate Tory candidates were for the most part inadequately briefed; they had to refurbish the arguments that had failed to win the 1906 election, and their Labour and Liberal opponents did the same with the counter-arguments, more effectively. To an electorate which, in the absence of thought, needs to be habituated by constant re-iteration to any new idea, the simple statement that Baldwin had changed his mind was not enough. The Harmsworth press backed Lloyd George and free trade. So Baldwin lost the election; yet such are the peculiarities of the British electoral system that while losing 88 seats the party increased its total votes.[2] The losses were in marginal seats for the most part; of these Labour gained 47 and the Liberals 41. The Conservatives with 258 members, as compared with the 191 Labourites and 159 Liberals, were still the largest party in the Commons, but they no longer had a clear majority.

This might have been the end of Baldwin. The elder statesmen

---

[1] Mary Hamilton, *Arthur Henderson*, pp. 232–3.

[2] From 5,500,352 in 1922 to 5,538,824 in 1923, according to Butler and Freeman. Amery says, a drop of 75,000. The percentage of the total vote was 38·2 in 1922 and 38·1 in 1923. The electorate had not changed its basic attitude towards the three parties; it was unconvinced of the need for change. The chief Labour gains were in Greater London, the Liberals in Lancashire. Amery, vol. II, p. 285.

of the party deplored his tactics; while Balfour contented himself with throwing up his hands and casting his eyes to the ceiling, Curzon was more outspoken.[1] But it soon became evident that there was no one to take his place. Lord Long of Wraxall suggested an Asquith government with Tory support. The only alternative seriously considered was an anti-Socialist coalition led by Balfour or Asquith, but neither would agree; Asquith preferred to put Labour in office, satisfied that in its mediatory position his party would thrive. Baldwin himself soon recovered from any depression that the defeat had caused him; he began to argue that it was a blessing to the party, and it was soon discovered that the election had remarkably increased his popularity and the affection felt for him in the country. A gathering of Conservative peers, M.P.s, and candidates acclaimed his leadership and sang 'He's a Jolly Good Fellow' at a special meeting on 11 February 1924.

3. First Labour Government

The advent of a Labour government was an act of domestic appeasement on the part of those who believed that the wild men would be tamed by office. Baldwin resigned after the defeat by the combined Liberal-Labour votes in the Commons on 21 January. MacDonald was sworn in as a Privy Councillor at 12.15 on the 22nd, and the King invited him immediately afterwards to form a government. The wild men limited their wildness to a respectful refusal to wear knee-breeches. Lord Stamfordham kindly sent them the address of Messrs. Moss Brothers.[2]

Office imposed a severe test on so young a party, handicapped as it was by a vast inexperience of the routine of government and also by the suddenness of the call, the lack of a popular issue, and a minority of votes in the House of Commons.[3] It had come to office because the country was unconvinced by the protectionist programme, not because it had become enthusiastic for any Labourite panacea. With the Liberals obstinately determined to keep their identity there was no prospect of a long-term Lib.-Lab. programme. There was a further handicap in the party's uncertainty (partly

---

[1] Dugdale, vol. II, p. 362; Amery, vol. II, p. 289; Kenneth Young, *op. cit.*, p. 435.

[2] Nicolson, *King George V*, pp. 384, 391. Sartorial conservatism was felt to be a sad departure from the 'spirit of Hardie': 'miners and dockers were deliberately trained to behave as though they were stockbrokers or landed gentry'. J. Scanlon, *Decline and Fall of the Labour Party* (1932), p. 15.

[3] Cf. R. W. Lyman, *The First Labour Government* (1957), pp. 89–93; the book is a judicious and fairly detailed study. Cf. R. K. Middlemas, *The Clydesiders*.

concealed from the world) as to its own objectives, for while there were obvious divergences between, for instance, the Glasgow extremism of John Wheatley and the inevitable gradualness of Sidney Webb, no one had as yet plumbed the depths of circumspection of which the Prime Minister himself was capable. As things had turned out the need for Liberal support suited MacDonald very well; he could resist the extremists, and familiarize the country with the picture of Labour ministers carrying out with the utmost respectability the ordinary functions of government. There was no need for him to reveal how cautiously he would have applied a Socialist programme even with a safe majority.

A word must be said here about MacDonald's character and reputation. The war had established him as a political nonconformist, some sort of rebel (usually the precise nature of his protest was misunderstood), and a speaker and writer of persistent but always very generalized critical temper. His fine presence, his somewhat melancholy eloquence, and the constant suggestion of a superior nature saddened by the selfishness of a predatory world, appealed widely to the mood of the early nineteen-twenties. Even the Clydesiders mistook the rolling of the r's for the rolling of the thunder. MacDonald more than any other politician of the day was the voice of conscience, chiding selfish individualism, deploring the lust for battle and profits and empire of his unregenerate fellow countrymen, but not condemning the country, or the empire, or even the industrial system itself. In his writings he had expounded over the years a very evolutionary form of socialism which would lead in time to 'the management of those economic instruments such as land and industrial capital that cannot be left safely in the hands of individuals' but as 'the condition, not the antithesis, of individual liberty'.

> The state today is anarchistic. We have gone well through our epoch of exploitation by individuals and classes, and the diastole and systole of history goes on. Or, to use a more familiar simile, the pendulum swings backwards—but not along the path of its forward swing. It has moved onwards.[1]

This was written in 1911. The onward-moving, backward-swinging pendulum of progress continued to absorb his attention, while possibly puzzling his readers. There was no sense of urgency; and still no sign in 1923 that he felt strongly the need for immediate

[1] J. Ramsay MacDonald, *The Socialist Movement* (1911), pp. 247–8.

action except in the field of foreign affairs. But it was possible for both his critics and his extremist followers to read into his pronouncements a revolutionary programme soothingly presented in order not to upset the bourgeoisie too much. There were therefore still hopes or fears, according to the quarter, that he was after all a wild man.

This he was not: but the difference was a tribute to his good sense rather than a sign of timidity. He accepted as profoundly as Balfour the view that the whole essence of British parliamentary government lies in the intention to make the thing work. This lesson the Labour party too had, in his view, to learn if it wished to be accepted by the electorate and allowed to carry out in office its own brand of evolutionary reformism. It must be prepared to work the system according to accepted forms and still more with an appearance of conformity with middle class modes of thought and social experience.[1] MacDonald was embarrassed when the *Marseillaise* and *Red Flag* were sung at an Albert Hall rally over which he was presiding, and when George Lansbury on 5 January tactlessly referred to the fate of King Charles I.[2] The problem was one that Labour politicians had to examine frequently during the next thirty years: would the language of class hostility achieve a sufficient gain in working-class support to balance the alienation of sympathetic fringes of the bourgeoisie? As the working-class vote was assumed to be secure anyway they concluded for the most part that it would not.

So MacDonald was content in his first administration to show that Labour could man a national government and that he could make some personal contribution himself to the improvement of European affairs.[3] He chose his cabinet carefully, and the decisions were for the most part his own; some were surprising, and many difficult to make. Only two I.L.P. extremists were included: John

[1] Thus the Fabians came into their own. M. P. McCarran, *Fabianism in the Political Life of Britain, 1919–1931* (Washington, 1952), pp. 312–26, and chaps. 8, 9 generally.

[2] When King George V referred to these episodes MacDonald 'spoke very openly' about his 'difficult position': H. Nicolson, *King George V*, p. 386. But the King was said to have worn a red tie when he received MacDonald: R. Postgate, *The Life of George Lansbury* (1951), p. 225. Dugdale, vol. II, p. 364.

[3] He was handicapped, he told an American correspondent, by his small income and previous lack of good assistants and secretarial help. Also of course by the fact that he had not previously held office. Cf. H. Pelling, *A Short History of the Labour Party* (1961), p. 53. He was well aware of the limited range of talent and ability at his disposal: Philip, Viscount Snowden, *An Autobiography* (1934), vol. II, pp. 594–600; H. Morrison, *An Autobiography* (1960), p. 99.

Wheatley, the ablest of the Glasgow M.P.s, as Minister of Health,
and F. W. Jowett as First Commissioner of Works. They were
more than balanced by a number of appointees from outside the
party, and all to the right of it although moving towards it. Lord
Haldane became Lord Chancellor; Lord Parmoor, ex-Tory and
present pacifist, married to Beatrice Webb's sister, Lord President;
Lord Chelmsford, a non-party man, First Lord of the Admiralty;
and Lord Thomson, Secretary for Air. The remaining offices were
filled mainly by trade unionists and one or two Fabians who were
already established as the leaders or schoolmasters of the party. After
considering J. H. Thomas for the Foreign Secretaryship and ignoring E. D. Morel and Arthur Henderson he decided that he alone
could fill the office. Philip Snowden, the stern free trader, was an
obvious choice for the Exchequer, but MacDonald seemed absurdly
reluctant to find a place for Henderson, who finally went to the
Home Office. Clynes became Lord Privy Seal and Deputy Leader
of the House; J. H. Thomas, Colonial Secretary; Thomas Shaw, a
textile worker, Minister of Labour. The War Office, first offered to
Henderson, went to Stephen Walsh, a miner. The Fabians were
represented by Sidney Webb (President of the Board of Trade)
and Sir Sydney Olivier (India), both of whom were sent to the
House of Lords. Among the under-secretaries there was some
promising talent: C. R. Attlee, A. V. Alexander, William Graham,
Emanuel Shinwell, and Margaret Bondfield.

In its nine months of office, with the Opposition ready and alert
to vote down any piece of obnoxious legislation, the opportunities
of doing anything distinctive in home policy were limited indeed,
and the story can soon be told. Its most important piece of legislation was Wheatley's Housing Act; its most popular, Snowden's
budget. Wheatley showed enterprise and adaptability in his unaccustomed position; he was the first to discover that the Liberals
would sometimes acquiesce in administrative decisions which they
disliked, even when legislation on the same subjects would provoke
a storm. Thus he successfully revoked the regulations imposed by
the previous government on the Poplar Board of Guardians, in
spite of Asquith's protests. The distinctive feature of Wheatley's
Housing Bill was that it attempted to provide houses for letting at
'reasonable' rents. The subsidy of £6 a year for twenty years of the
1923 act was increased to £9 a year for forty years for houses with
satisfactory conditions of letting. Neville Chamberlain made some

objections in debate, but he was willing to recognize that the matter was an immensely difficult one, subject to trial and error; he was open to conviction. The bill passed. An earlier measure, designed to prevent evictions for non-payment of rent—in effect to allow the unemployed to live rent free—failed through lack of Liberal support, much to Ramsay MacDonald's relief.

Snowden's budget, almost aggressively anti-protectionist, thoroughly pleased the Liberals; the McKenna duties were swept away, duties on foodstuffs reduced, and the undertakings with regard to imperial preference given by the previous government at the Economic Conference repudiated.[1] The last point was submitted to a free vote of the House and carried by only a narrow majority. Snowden also had something for the Tory worshippers of deflation; he went even further than Baldwin by increasing the Sinking Fund. He pleased other sections of the community by reducing the entertainment duty, repealing the inhabited house duty, lowering telephone charges and the tax on motor cars, and abolishing the special tax on corporation profits.[2]

But in all this there was little consolation for the unemployed. Nor did a succession of strikes and stoppages by the railwaymen (January), dockers (February), and miners (March) suggest that they expected much from the government.[3] Later there was discussion whether the government would have done better to put their Liberal sponsors on the defensive with a bold socialist programme; but so far as concerned the immediate problem of providing work there was no solution in the portfolio of socialist panaceas. Nor did Snowden's budget help; the Conservatives claimed that the repeal of the McKenna duties led to immediate serious unemployment in the motor-car, piano, and clock trades, and although it soon became clear that no particular disaster had befallen them it was hardly possible to argue that this was the way to create more jobs. A not very ambitious scheme for expenditure up to £28 million for road-building and other public works was announced in July. MacDonald pinned his hopes much more on an improvement of British trade through the tranquillization of the continent, and for once Snowden agreed with him. So too indeed did the Tories.[4]

---

[1] G. M. Young, p. 78.
[2] Snowden, vol. II, chap. 46; Cole, p. 163.
[3] Cf. Bullock, pp. 236–40.
[4] Complaints of the 'betrayal of the workers' by the first Labour government are

It is usual to contrast the meagre results of the domestic policy of the first Labour government with its achievements abroad. But to do this is in some measure to confuse goodwill with negotiating skill. Ramsay MacDonald came into office at a moment when France and Germany were ready for a mediator, and when the two opposition parties at home were ready to welcome any reasonable compromise. Where goodwill was not enough, as in the government's contacts with the difficult and demanding politicians of Egypt, India, Soviet Russia, and Mexico, the results were less happy.[1]

Nevertheless, the achievement itself should not be minimized. This was one of the relatively few occasions when the rôle of mediator, satisfying the Foreign Office's uneasy urge to control events without commitments, was readily acceptable to, and not secretly resented by, the continental powers concerned. Even in this case there was the usual half-concealed expectation that the result would be to involve Great Britain more closely in continental affairs, through some form of guarantee of the settlement. This was encouraged by the fact that the British government was now actively canvassing plans for strengthening the security functions of the League. Lord Robert Cecil had put forward proposals at Geneva in February 1923 for a treaty on these lines which limited the obligations of members to the continent in which aggression had occurred. After amendments in the light of an alternative French draft prepared by Colonel Requin, there emerged in September 1923 a draft Treaty of Mutual Assistance, which was sent by the Assembly to the governments for their comments. It had added to Cecil's basic proposal provision for the drawing up of voluntary agreements between groups of states to maintain peace in their own areas. This plan, with its heavy responsibilities for Great Britain, which would have had the major task of applying economic sanctions and of

---

voiced by John Scanlon, a political journalist and part-time secretary to John Wheatley: *Decline and Fall of the Labour Party* (1932), pp. 13–83; *Pillars of Cloud* (1936), chap. 1–8.

[1] On MacDonald at the Foreign Office: George Glasgow, *MacDonald as Diplomatist* (1924); cf. W. P. Maddon, *Foreign Relations in British Labour Politics* (1934), mainly an acute study of the formation of Labour party attitudes to foreign affairs before 1924. R. Vansittart: 'a good Foreign Secretary . . . It has long been the fashion to deride him, but he played well in his first innings. The scoreboard speaks.' *op. cit.*, p. 323. H. R. Winkler, 'The Emergence of a Labor Foreign Policy in Great Britain, 1918–1929' (*J.M.H.*, Sept. 1956), argues that Clynes rather than MacDonald converted the party to the more sober line followed by MacDonald in 1924 and Henderson after 1929 (pp. 249–51).

supplying the naval forces needed by the League against any aggressive power in Europe, was still under consideration when Labour came into office on 22 January 1924, and it did not give its final decision until July. There was therefore a possibility during these six critical months that by accepting the draft treaty or its substance Great Britain would powerfully reinforce the French security system.

The essential steps towards the patching up of some form of Franco-German agreement had, however, already been taken by the Baldwin government, and MacDonald made little headway as long as Poincaré remained in office. Baldwin on 12 October 1923 had invited American participation in an international commission on Germany's capacity to pay, and Poincaré had given a rather surly promise of French participation at the end of November. The Dawes committee, with Sir Josiah Stamp and Sir Robert Kindersley as the British representatives, was already sitting when the Baldwin government fell. After the publication of the Dawes report on 9 April 1924 Poincaré seemed determined to insist on full British support for France in any future military and economic sanctions against Germany as a condition of French evacuation of the Ruhr. In short, both governments were calling for the abandonment of the policy which the other had followed in the Ruhr question in 1923. It was only after the decisive victory of the Left in the French elections in May 1924, and the accession to office of the Radical-Socialist Edouard Herriot on 2 June, that MacDonald's achievement as a peacemaker became possible.

The Dawes report (mainly written by Sir Joseph Stamp) had been accepted by the French experts, who had agreed to regard its proposals as an indivisible whole. It provided for the evacuation of the Ruhr and insisted on the need for a balanced budget and stabilized currency on a gold basis. Reparations payments were to rise from £50 million to £125 million in five years; payment was to be guaranteed by the ear-marking of various domestic sources of revenue and by a foreign loan of £40 million. There was provision for the appointment of a foreigner as agent-general for reparations; this was intended to safeguard the arrangements, but the French press at once began to demand additional guarantees. The decisive turn in the discussions did not come in fact until 21 and 22 June, when Herriot and MacDonald met at Chequers. The two readily agreed that the Dawes plan must be carried out, and that an inter-

national Allied conference to work out the details should meet in
London in July. Over this conference MacDonald presided with
tact and a certain magnificence. It was the most successful and
perhaps the happiest episode in his career. Stresemann accepted the
Allies' proposals under protest on 16 August, and the international
loan was floated successfully in October.

On 18 July the government announced its rejection of the draft
Treaty of Mutual Assistance: there seems no doubt that the Baldwin
government, if it had remained in office, would have done the same.
But already on 21 June at Chequers MacDonald and Herriot had
agreed that the problem of security should be the second objective
in their joint programme, and after the more or less happy solution
of the Ruhr-reparations problem in London the scene shifted to
Geneva. This was regarded at the time as another triumph for
MacDonald's leadership and even showmanship; he did much to
put the League in the centre of the political stage, without committing his country to anything in particular in the process.

All the dangerous ambiguities of the cult of the League, the
idealism, self-righteousness, and political futility which seemed
inseparable from its operation, begin to play their confusing part
in the formulation of British opinion from this stage. There was
agreement between the British political parties on the need to
support the League. If they differed it was because the Labour
leaders professed a greater faith in the salutary effects of public
discussion in discrediting selfish and dangerous policies. Such
pressure, it was also tempting to argue, would be more effective if
the potential aggressor had obligingly divested himself in advance
of the armaments which might otherwise tempt him to be defiant.
The objections, both theoretical and practical, to these views were
more frequently canvassed in Paris than in London. In England the
mystique of Geneva and the League was growing; the material and
moral resources of the League powers were both exaggerated. The
League was a symbol of power to those who argued, with apparent
hard-headedness, that no aggressor would dare to resist the combined
strength of fifty League members. It was a symbol of hope to those
who saw it shining as a peak of Alpine purity amid the necessarily
selfish interests of nation states.[1]

British governments were tacitly agreed in playing up the usefulness of the League as a convenient forum for international dis-

[1] See below, pp. 327–8.

cussion, while remaining hostile to the French conception of the League as a guarantee of the security of the League powers. Accordingly, while MacDonald and Herriot were readily agreed in raising the prestige of the League by their presence at the fifth Assembly, they were at once involved in a public debate over their rival interpretations of its functions. In a speech to the Assembly on 5 September MacDonald expounded his plans for an improved League, strengthened by the inclusion of Germany and even Russia; strengthened further by disarmament. Among the government's reasons for rejecting the draft treaty had been the unsatisfactory nature of the regional guarantees that it had provided; these, it was thought, might very easily develop into the older type of military alliance, and be more likely to prevent than to promote disarmament. MacDonald turned to arbitration as the solution, and although Herriot stated the French thesis with equal emphasis he accepted the principle of arbitration, albeit with formidable reservations.

Committees then set to work to draw up a new instrument which was presented to the Assembly on 1 October as a draft Protocol 'for the pacific settlement of international disputes'. The essential provision was for the acceptance by all the member states of the obligation to submit disputes to arbitration, after which, if all means of conciliation failed, the League Council might call on them to apply sanctions under Article 16 against the aggressor. A disarmament conference was to meet on 15 June 1925, and the Protocol was not to come into force until this conference had adopted a disarmament plan which the Council was to prepare and communicate to the government not later than 15 March 1925. Its authors could claim that after five years of hard thought and work they had provided the essential links between security, disarmament, and arbitration. But the Protocol was severely handicapped by what Professor Zimmern called the 'almost Byzantine subtlety' of its clauses. The articles included several definitions of aggression, and the arbitration machinery, although very elaborate, was not complete.[1] Hitherto arbitration had been regarded as essentially a judicial process, but the new machinery on the one hand attempted to deal with disputes which involved the 'reserved' issues of prestige and national interest, and on the other hand still omitted those which would involve the

---

[1] A. Zimmern, *The League of Nations and the Rule of Law*, pp. 350–7; 364. George Glasgow, a strictly contemporary observer, wrote, 'Much cry and little wool is perhaps its best epitaph . . . its meaning being mostly negative and atrophied with reservations'. *op. cit.*, p. 207.

revision of existing treaties or existing state boundaries. There was a certain anxiety in England during the discussions as to what the cabinet representatives might be doing with the British fleet; but the published text of the Protocol showed that the Admiralty retained complete control. The possibility that a failure of compulsory arbitration might involve the country in sanctions efforts beyond its strength remained; but as everything had been made to depend on a satisfactory disarmament programme the country was as yet committed to nothing beyond the terms of the original covenant. The Labour government had fallen before any decision had been taken about ratification.[1]

Meanwhile it was making little real progress in its bargaining over other outstanding problems. Curzon had refused to recognize the Obregon government in Mexico and the chief sufferers from his action were a Mrs. Evans, who owned a property of some 2,700 acres, and other British subjects. General Obregon on 6 June promptly gave Cummins, the British diplomatic representative, four days to leave Mexico. Mrs. Evans was murdered on 2 August. Egypt had been unilaterally declared an independent kingdom by the British government in 1922, but there were important points outstanding including the future of the Suez Canal and of the Sudan, and MacDonald invited the Egyptian Prime Minister, the elderly rebel Zaghlul Pasha, to London to discuss them. Zaghlul was strangely hesitant, evidently fearing that almost any contact with the British government would compromise him in the eyes of his nationalist followers, but after delaying all the summer he unexpectedly announced that he would pay a private visit to London and be at MacDonald's disposal on 25 September. He stayed at Claridge's, visited the Wembley Exhibition but avoided the Sudan pavilion, and in his talks with MacDonald patiently refused all concessions. MacDonald on his side had nothing more to concede.

The Anglo-Soviet negotiations did lead to a draft treaty, but its essential clauses were, like those of the Geneva Protocol, contingent on conditions which the Tories were not prepared to accept. Lloyd George was soon denouncing it as a fake, although it was no more than an attempt to complete the process of Anglo-Russian reconciliation which he had followed in the Anglo-Soviet trade agreement and the Genoa conference. On 1 February MacDonald announced the government's recognition of the Soviet government

[1] Mary Hamilton, *Arthur Henderson*, pp. 242–50.

as the *de jure* ruler of Russia, a great triumph and a most striking landmark in Soviet eyes.[1] A conference, with Arthur Ponsonby and K. Rakovsky as the principal delegates, met in London in April. The stumbling block throughout was the problem of the pre-war Russian debts. At a meeting on 20 May the British representatives tried to force Rakovsky's hand by refusing any official guarantee of a British loan. This meant that Rakovsky would have to seek the loan which he hoped for in the City, where any approach to British capitalists was likely to meet with a refusal unless the Soviet authorities were prepared to pay their existing debts as a means of re-establishing Russian credit. Rakovsky did not therefore try his luck in the City, but continued instead to ask for a British government loan large enough to enable them to cover the pre-war debts and to purchase in Great Britain machinery and other material needed for the restoration of Russian industry and agriculture. All the time, following the usual Russian technique of negotiation, there were persistent press attacks on the British government both in Russia and from Soviet sympathizers in England. Deadlock was reached by 4 August. MacDonald was also facing at this point the crisis in the reparations conference; but he got up at 5 o'clock on the morning of 6 August, and sent personal letters to all the British and Russian delegates appealing for reconsideration. By teatime, rather dramatically, agreement had been reached.

On the whole it meant a British surrender. Russia was promised a loan guaranteed by the British government, which MacDonald had hitherto refused, and only in return for this did Rakovsky agree to negotiate with the bondholders. However, Russia had admitted its liability to the bondholders, and the British government was not prepared to recommend the loan to Parliament until the claims had been investigated and lump sums fixed for the payment of miscellaneous claims. There were two treaties, a general and a commercial, both signed on 7 August. Russia gained admission to the Export Credits scheme, in return for which British goods received unconditional most-favoured-nation treatment in Russia. There were promises of amity and of the cessation of propaganda. Nothing in the bearing of the Russians or the tone of the Soviet press offered the slightest hope of any genuine amity; all the while the Comintern was elaborating its plans to overthrow the Labour party and capture the mass of the British workers. The treaty, said a contemporary,

[1] E. H. Carr, *The Interregnum, 1923-1924* (1954), pp. 244-53.

was merely an agreement to agree if and when the parties could agree to agree. But for the Labour government there still seemed merit in any bridge of goodwill, however insubstantial.[1]

It was too insubstantial to bear the weight of Opposition censure. Labour had now been just long enough in office for a further general election to be practicable, and MacDonald himself did not seem averse to a trial of strength.[2] Although the immediate cause of the government's downfall was the trivial issue of the Campbell case, there loomed ahead a probable defeat when the Commons were asked to ratify the Russian treaty. It was essentially the party's alleged susceptibility to Communist pressure which supplied the election issue. J. R. Campbell was the acting editor of the Communist *Workers' Weekly*. He had been arrested on 5 August on a charge of inciting mutiny; a week later the case was withdrawn. The two opposition parties were determined to see something sinister in this action of Sir Patrick Hastings, the Attorney General; it was attributed to the efforts of the same left-wing pressure group which was supposed to have brought about a resumption of the Anglo-Soviet negotiations on 6 August. A Conservative motion of censure on 8 October produced a defiant if somewhat embarrassed response from MacDonald. He flatly rejected a Liberal offer of a Select Committee, thus making the matter a question of confidence. Liberals at last decided to combine with Conservatives to defeat the government, and Parliament was at once dissolved (October 1924).[3]

Whether the Liberals chose wisely is difficult to say in the absence of any evidence that they would have fared better in any other circumstances; their most fateful step had been taken when they put Labour in. The Conservatives on the other hand had chosen the time well. Nine months in Opposition had brought about a remarkable revival in Baldwin's standing in his party and the country. He refused as leader of the opposition to harry MacDonald unduly. Lethargy, magnanimity, tactical shrewdness, but also a sharp awareness of the danger of throwing moderate Labour into the arms of the extremists, shaped this policy; in the meantime MacDonald sent him the more important Foreign Office papers and there was no

[1] E. H. Carr, *Socialism in One Country 1924–1926* (1964), vol. III, pp. 21–8; W. P. and Z. Coates, *A History of Anglo-Soviet Relations* (1945), chap. 7, detailed and pro-Soviet.

[2] The growing tension with the I.L.P. members also predisposed him to welcome a change: cf. Fenner Brockway, p. 152.

[3] Amery, vol. II, p. 395.

bitterness between them.[1] During the summer Baldwin in a number of speeches had sketched rather vaguely a new Conservative programme, and talked much about the need for industrial peace, while Labour had had ample opportunity to show the world that it had no solution to the problem of unemployment or of foreign markets. A heavy defeat for Labour was already in sight when the publication of the 'Zinoviev letter' on 25 October gave the electorate a final anti-Red scare four days before polling.

The letter probably made no substantial difference to the overall result of the election. Any marginal voter (who was so often merely an absentee voter) who hurried to the polling booth to vote against Labour because of its alleged pandering to Communism would have had sufficient to alarm him in the broader controversy over the Anglo-Russian treaty. The very heavy poll (80 per cent of the total electorate as compared with 74 per cent in 1923) favoured the Conservatives, whose supporters increased by over two million; even so, Labour gained over a million votes, and the Liberals lost more than that number. Thus the party that lost the election in a much truer sense than Labour was the Liberal party; for if many preferred Conservatism as the bulwark against socialism so did many others prefer Labour as the bulwark against Conservatism. In spite of all his difficulties with a minority government and an awkward and inexperienced team MacDonald's courage and political sense in taking office had been vindicated. The first Labour government had proved that Labour could govern. When the pendulum swung against Toryism five years later it was seen that Labour not Liberalism was finally established as the country's alternative.

This is the broad lesson of the 1924 election, although the distribution of seats was as usual not very accurately related to the voting strength of the parties. The Conservatives had 419 seats and 8,039,598 votes, as compared with 258 seats and 5,538,824 votes in 1923. Labour had 151 seats as compared with 191 in 1923, but an increase of votes from 4·3 to 5·5 million; it fought 512 seats as against 422 in 1923. The Liberal seats fell catastrophically from 159 to 41; Asquith was defeated at Paisley by his Labour opponent, but the party still polled about three million votes as compared with 4·3 million in 1923. One only of the seven Communist candidates, S. Saklatvala, was elected, regaining the North Battersea seat that he had lost in 1923.

[1] G. M. Young, p. 76.

The authenticity of the Zinoviev or 'Red' letter cannot be proved, for only copies of it reached the Foreign Office and the press. They came from a 'well-known business man' who claimed to have received the letter from a friend in touch with Communist circles. However, the letter corresponds so closely in style, contents, and context with Cominform pronouncements of the time as to leave no doubt that if Zinoviev did not write this letter he might well have written another exactly like it.[1] Dated 15 September 1924, and signed by himself and by O. Kuusinen (a Finnish member of the secretariat of the Executive Committee of the International) and A. MacManus (the most prominent British member of that body), it urged the British Communist party to stir up the British masses and bring in the unemployed in order to secure the ratification of the Anglo-Soviet treaty, and went on to give urgent general advice as to the preparation of British labour for the ultimate class struggle. Labour foreign policy was an inferior copy of that of the 'Curzon Government'.

The letter has been dismissed by some as a forgery on the ground that it was all too pat—with everything that the professional anti-bolshevik could want, at just this moment.[2] But this really only means that it was relevant to the occasion. There are plenty of authentic examples of the same style, at just this time. Instructions dated 10 October 1924 from the Executive Committee of the Communist International called on the British Communist Party, in the forthcoming general election, to criticize sharply in principle the MacDonald government, to unmask its imperialist character, and to carry on a bitter fight against its policy in China, India, and Egypt. Slogans were to include 'for the Anglo-Russian treaty', 'not His Majesty's Government but a real workers' government', 'the fraternization of soldiers and workers', 'soldiers should not shoot upon workers on strike', and the like. Earlier examples of instructions on similar lines go back to 6 February 1924. There is really nothing surprising in the government's discovery in October 1924

[1] In which case the letter could have been a forgery in the sense that it was put together from authentic documents. The only internal evidence for forgery appears to be that the signatures and one or two phrases used were not in the accustomed form. Cf. W. P. and Z. K. Coates, chap. 8, especially pp. 183–4; Carr, pp. 29–32.

[2] Professor Mowat writes: 'It doesn't miss a bet. If it was not a forgery, it might just as well have been, for all the credence such a puerile concoction was worth' (*op. cit.*, p. 194). Vansittart: 'the letter was probably genuine' (*op. cit.*, pp. 330–1). Subsequent discussions of the problem, including that revealed by the case of J. D. Gregory in 1928, are summarized in Lyman, Appendix B (pp. 286–9).

that the Russians could be such embarrassing neighbours. What is surprising is that it expected anything else.[1]

[1] The 'Instructions' of 10 October was among the documents seized on the arrest of Communist leaders in October 1925, and published in Cmd 2682. Coates, pp. 218–93, does not mention the seized documents. This and other documents referred to above are printed in *The Communist International 1919–1943* (1960), vol. II, pp. 82–172, edited by Jane Degras. The text of the 'Zinoviev letter' is printed in the *Survey of International Affairs, 1924* (1928), pp. 492–3. The most recent study is that of Lewis Chester, Stephen Fay and Hugo Young, *The Zinoviev Letter* (1967). Following statements made to a London newspaper by Mme Irinee Bellegarde in December 1966 they elaborated the story of the forgery of the letter in Berlin by two young anti-Bolsheviks, Alexis Bellegarde and Alexander Gumansky.

5

THE SEARCH FOR TRANQUILLITY
1924–1930

1. TORY REUNION

Of one thing Stanley Baldwin, amid all the uncertainties of the future, was convinced; his victory in 1924 was a proof of popular support that transcended party boundaries. 'Rightly or wrongly,' he said in a speech in March 1925, 'we succeeded in creating the impression that we stood for stable Government and for peace in the country between all classes of the community.'[1] For many, the times were hard, but they would be harder still if men were not prepared, at home and abroad, to make the best of things. There was little that the government could do to change the basic pattern, and much that it might do to find a way to happier and more prosperous days by encouraging peace, co-operation, and hard work.

Those who look back to the second Baldwin administration as an era of lost opportunity must recognize this first impulse of fairness and constructive goodwill. The majority and the security that it gave him seem to have come as a surprise. With his natural indolence it may have inclined him rather too readily to the side of those who argued, with more or less passion, in favour of allowing time to solve the problems of industry, war, unemployment, Commonwealth relations, and even the gold standard. In 1925 he was capable of a courageous call for 'peace in our time'. In 1929 he was content to appeal to the country on a platform of 'safety first'. The ministry did not lack men of brains and vigour. For the most part he left them to run their departments as they saw fit. Thus he failed to give a decisive impulse towards the solution of what we have now come to regard as the country's deeper problems; at the most

[1] G. M. Young, p. 93.

he felt a certain vague pessimism, but no imperative anxiety, about the future. 'Baldwin was increasingly comforting himself', wrote L. S. Amery later, 'with the view that a Prime Minister's business was, not to shape or impose policies, but to prevent the mischievous policies of others by carrying on in office.'[1]

Accordingly his cabinet-making in 1924 fully consolidated the favourable position of the Conservative party, without giving it any very distinctive objectives. Reunion was completed. At the cost of another disappointment for Curzon, Austen Chamberlain was given the Foreign Office; Birkenhead and Worthington-Evans came in as Secretaries of State for India and War; when Curzon, who had been made Lord President, died in March 1925, Balfour succeeded him. The 1922 under-secretaries continued to enjoy the fruits of their successful rebellion. The most surprising appointment was that of Winston Churchill as Chancellor of the Exchequer;[2] it dished the Liberals by capturing Lloyd George's greatest potential ally, but it also dished the Tories by bringing in an uncompromising Free Trader who could be relied on to oppose backsliding on the tariff question. It has been argued that it probably never occurred to Baldwin, with his curiously inconsequential mind, that Churchill in his key position would be likely to throw his whole weight against this policy, but in fact Baldwin himself—without apparently waiting for any lead from Churchill—quickly reassured the free traders by promising that the Safeguarding Duties would not be used as a back door to protection.[3] Neville Chamberlain, who could have had the Exchequer, preferred to undertake important work at the Ministry of Health, and Amery was happy in his appointment to the Colonial Office. 'A capable, sedate Government', was Churchill's own verdict in after years. 'The state of the nation and of the world was easier and more fertile by the end of our term than at its beginning.'[4]

---

[1] Amery, vol. II, p. 299.

[2] After losing his seat at Dundee in 1922 Churchill stood as an 'Independent anti-Socialist' candidate (although still nominally a Liberal) for election in the Abbey division of Westminster in March 1924. He received much help from ex-coalition Conservatives, and was defeated by the official Conservative candidate by only 43 votes out of 20,000 cast. In the general election he stood for the Epping Division of Essex as a 'Constitutionalist', and won by a 10,000 majority. He represented Epping until 1945, and then Woodford from 1945 to 1964.

[3] *Ibid*, vol. II, p. 478; cf. R. Blake, in *The Baldwin Age*, pp. 47–8.

[4] W. S. Churchill, *The Gathering Storm*, p. 21; cf. R. W. Thompson, *The Yankee Marlborough* (1963): 'as dreary a Government as Britain ever suffered', p. 244, and a 'dreary Chancellor', p. 240.

2. LOCARNO AND TRANQUILLITY

Its biggest and earliest success was the Locarno agreement, which seemed to be amply justified by the tranquillity of Europe in the years that followed. Like many another postwar agreement it failed to fulfil its promise, and came to be condemned both for creating an exaggerated notion of the goodwill of its participants and for the dodging of awkward related problems. But to the many who looked so ardently in 1925 for the ending of postwar tensions its basic achievement of Franco-German reconciliation seemed weighty.

The foreign field, as the new government surveyed it after the election, was disturbed at many points. There was a new crisis in Egypt following the assassination of the Sirdar, Sir Lee Stack, on 19 November 1924. Relations with the Soviet Union could hardly be worse; the recognition accorded by the Labour government was not withdrawn, but the Anglo-Russian agreement was not ratified, Comintern propaganda continued, raids on the Communist party headquarters in October 1925 and on Arcos House in May 1927 produced disturbing but not unexpected evidence of subversion, and the Russian trade delegation and diplomatic staff were then asked to leave the country. With Britain now firmly fixed in the minds of the Soviet leaders as the spearhead of capitalistic-imperialistic aggression there was a very real danger that a continuance of the Franco-German quarrel would drive Germany and Russia, the two outcasts, closer together.[1] But the Ruhr occupation, in its economic if not in its military consequences, had shown France that she could not carry out a coercive enforcement of the Versailles treaty singlehanded. She was looking to Britain for increased guarantees of security, and this meant her ultimate acceptance of the established British policy of conciliating Germany, which had the added recommendation that it might prevent a further drawing together of Germany and Russia.

Outside Europe communist hostility was widespread, and sometimes effective. In China the Kuomintang or People's Party held together during the lifetime of its leader, Sun Yat-sen, but with growing tension between the communist faction under Borodin and the right-wingers under General Chiang Kai-shek. It was convenient to develop an ideological front by denouncing the privileges of the British and other foreigners, just as it was convenient for the

[1] E. H. Carr, pp. 33–4.

other foreigners to remind themselves that the British, with the greatest stake, might well be expected to bear the brunt of nationalist provocations.

Austen Chamberlain suited the times; no one could claim for him unusual gifts of imagination or political flair, but he had a certain splendour, good nature and good manners, friendship for France at the time when it was greatly needed, and firmness in pursuing cautious policies up to their practicable limits. Balfour thought him a bore. Vansittart affirms that he did not bore the Foreign Office, which 'found in him more modesty than is usual on high'.[1] He did all that could be reasonably asked of a statesman who did not happen to be faced with the dilemmas of British foreign policy in their acutest form.

Egypt had first to be dealt with. An ultimatum following Stack's murder demanded an indemnity of £500,000 and the evacuation of Egyptian troops from the Sudan. This brought to an end for the time being the curiously elusive negotiations in which MacDonald had patiently awaited Zaghlul Pasha's appearance in London. George Lloyd, a man of magnificent if perhaps somewhat misplaced energy, replaced Allenby.

Egyptian and Russian affairs prevented attention to continental problems for some weeks. In the meantime, discussions with the Dominions revealed general distaste for the Geneva Protocol. Australia, Canada, and South Africa objected to the strengthened obligation to intervene in matters of remote interest to themselves; the Canadian delegate to the League complacently described his country as a fireproof house, far from inflammable materials. India visualized a heavy burden of sanctions falling on herself in the event of crisis in Asia. Australia and New Zealand objected also to the idea of the compulsory authority of the Permanent Court in matters which might affect their own domestic interests (they were thinking of Asiatic immigration). The British government had its own objections. Balfour killed the scheme in an urbane memorandum which airily dismissed preoccupation with the prevention of aggression as pathological: 'it is not wholesome for the ordinary man to be always brooding over the possibility of some severe surgical operation: nor is it wise for societies to pursue a similar course'. Austen Chamberlain fathered the memorandum at Geneva on 12 March 1925, but he told the disappointed Council that his government would favour the supplementing of the Covenant by 'special arrangements in order to meet special needs'. It is sometimes forgotten that the Protocol was dependent on the acceptance of an agreed plan for disarmament, and this was still being argued about in 1934. Would Labour have accepted the Protocol? The well formulated objections of the British and Dominion governments had certainly been accepted by some members of the Labour government, including Haldane and apparently MacDonald. Vansittart claims that MacDonald continued to mourn the decision: 'I knew we were done when the Protocol failed.'[1]

Chamberlain's offer opened the way for a new alignment in western Europe. Stresemann saw its possibilities more clearly than his right-wing opponents and some of his cabinet colleagues; more clearly perhaps than Chamberlain. He aimed at a position of balance and therefore of freedom between east and west, and his success owed much to the bogey of a Russo-German alignment which had already been proved to be something more than a bogey at Rapallo. The general tendency in England was in line with the Lloyd George-Wilson assumption that the change of régime in Germany in 1918 meant a change of heart; as a reformed character, she was likely to settle down to a permanent career of peace and good works if she were not goaded into violence by the French. 'What made the old Germany formidable,' remarked Sir James Headlam-Morley in a memorandum written for the perusal of the Foreign Office in February 1925, 'was the strength which came from loyalty and discipline, the overwhelming confidence in her own national mission, the long subservience to her rulers, the immense pride in her army. All this is now gone. The moral basis of the empire has been overthrown and not even the French have really been able to restore it.' He saw no need to be alarmed at German ambitions 'so long as we see to it that Germany is confined within her present limits'.[2] This Germany herself seemed ready to guarantee, as far at least as her western frontiers were concerned. In proposals which she had been making since 1922 she offered to join with the other powers interested in the Rhine in pledges to maintain peace for a generation, with a disinterested neighbour acting as a trustee.[3]

---

[1] 'Any notion of pooling resources according to situation and power was rejected by [MacDonald's] successor at the Foreign Office for "practical reasons". All negative reasons are practical.' Vansittart, p. 332. Zimmern, pp. 365-7.
[2] Sir James Headlam-Morley, *Studies in Diplomatic History* (1930), p. 189.
[3] Gustav Stresemann, *Vermächtnis* (Berlin, 1932), Vol. II, pp. 22-36.

It was not over this proposal so much as over the related problem of Germany's entry into the League that complications arose. Mac-Donald had proposed her admission in September 1924 and Herriot had agreed, but the German acceptance in principle had been coupled with certain conditions, of which the most important was that she should be exempted from any obligations under Article 16 of the Covenant. This France was not prepared to accept, and Germany's first application for membership was rejected on 14 March 1925 on the ground that her acceptance of the Covenant must be unconditional. The result was something of a crisis in Russo-German relations, although it was largely concealed from western eyes.[1] In the League without reservations, Germany would be liable to take part in sanctions against Russia and to give facilities and a base for attack, and the news that negotiations had commenced for a Rhineland security agreement added to Soviet foreboding. Stresemann assured the Russians that he would not join in any action against them, but they were not convinced. He also had to overcome formidable opposition at home; the Reichswehr, including von Seeckt, were strongly hostile to his 'western orientation', as was the able but troublesome ambassador in Moscow, Brockdorff-Rantzau. The Russians made as much fuss as possible; in fact they overplayed their hand.

On the eve of the decisive conference at Locarno on 5 October Chicherin arrived in Berlin and made a press attack on the League, Article 16, the western powers, and particularly Great Britain. This greatly helped the German plans, for the other Locarno powers felt it expedient to agree to a formula which left each state member of the League to cooperate to the extent of its military situation and geographical location. Stresemann also secured the final abandonment of Briand's attempt to reaffirm Germany's eastern frontiers by the incorporation of France's alliance with Poland and Czechoslovakia in the Locarno agreements. The agreements were initialled on 15 October; everyone had some cause for satisfaction including even the absent Russians, who were relieved to find that Stresemann had really made Article 16 innocuous.[2] The basic document was that of the treaty of mutual guarantee of the Franco-German and Belgo-German frontiers between Germany, France, Great Britain,

---

[1] G. Freund, *Unholy Alliance* (1957), chap. 10; L. Kochan, *Russia and the Weimar Republic*, (1952), pp. 102, 120.
[2] Stresemann, vol. II, pp. 163–204; Freund, pp. 234–5.

Belgium, and Italy. Arbitration was provided for in individual treaties or conventions between Germany and Belgium, France, Poland, and Czechoslovakia. France signed separate treaties for mutual assistance with Poland and Czechoslovakia to meet the case of aggression by Germany.

To the British cabinet this seemed an admirable and constructive settlement. The risk was that Germany would be helped to recover strength which she would misuse. Chamberlain was aware of this problem. He hoped to make Germany's position too tolerable to be jeopardized on a gambler's throw. 'I am working not for today or tomorrow, but for some date like 1950 or 1960 when Germany's strength will have returned', he told the King in February.[1] This was appeasement (in its non-pejorative sense), and with it came the appeaser's problem.[2] But Stresemann was the answer to the appeasers' prayer, a new type of German politician who was to be rewarded and kept in office because he accepted peace on the conquerors' terms. German disarmament and the demilitarization of the Rhineland remained; reparations would continue to be paid. If France had abandoned the Ruhr type of intervention Germany had accepted the loss of Alsace-Lorraine. The ingenuity of the double guarantee of the western frontier meant that the British government had found on the French side a substitute for the guarantee treaty abandoned after America's defection in 1920, and on the German side a means of ensuring the preservation of her sovereignty, and self-respect. Really, as the bargain stood in October 1925, it was a blessed and profitable liquidation of postwar difficulties for all concerned. But could Germany be trusted to accept these terms of quiescence indefinitely?[3]

The dilemma was implicit in Stresemann's well-deployed arguments as to the need for concessions to popularize his policy of fulfilment. The ratification of the Locarno agreement was carried in the Reichstag only after substantial opposition; and he had made abundantly clear his inability to accept the Polish frontier as final,

---

[1] Nicolson, p. 407. Austen Chamberlain in *Down the Years* (1935) pp. 172–8, was still optimistic.

[2] It may be said here, once and for all, that this word is used throughout this volume, unless specifically stated otherwise, with its contemporary meaning of tranquillization, or constructive peacemaking. It did not involve any notion of surrender to threats, or the placating of aggressors, for it was thought of as the policy of victors. In this context the opposite of an 'appeaser' was a 'war monger', not a 'resister'.

[3] G. A. Grün, 'Locarno, Idea and Reality', *International Affairs*, Oct. 1955, pp. 468–9.

or to abandon close links with Russia. The Reichswehr was neither silent nor acquiescent. Enough of these things was known in London to cause uneasiness, but Stresemann must clearly be helped, and after him Brüning. The enigma of Stresemann's ultimate aim is unsolved. He saw the advantages of collaboration with the western powers as a means of bringing occupation to an end; he saw the need for a period of peace and economic recovery for his country. Did he also dream of the day, as von Seeckt certainly did, when a restored Reichswehr would take back all that the country had lost, particularly to the Poles? He found it best to show every sympathy with such plans, and he knew enough about the secret rearmament for us to know that he did nothing to stop it. But he died in 1929; how he would have handled the future is guesswork.[1]

In the meantime the three foreign ministers, whose terms of office largely coincided, worked through the League, raised its standing by regular meetings at Geneva, and maintained the Locarno spirit as a symbol of goodwill in a nervous world. In fact, however, goodwill was soon wilting through lack of nourishment. France had agreed to evacuate not only the Ruhr but also the first zone of the Rhineland, and the Allied evacuation of this area was completed by 1 February 1926. But in March 1926 Germany's entry into the League with a permanent seat on the Council was blocked by the counter claims of Spain, Brazil, Poland, and China. Stresemann, his position at home weakened by this rebuff, could not delay longer the conclusion of the treaty of Berlin with Soviet Russia on 24 April. The treaty, which was published on the 27th, reaffirmed Rapallo and provided that if either power were attacked the other would remain neutral and not join in any economic or financial boycott. After an initial press storm the text was accepted without much fuss in Paris; the British press and government seem to have been more reserved and perhaps more uneasy. But Britain and France worked harder still to secure Germany's seat at Geneva in the autumn. Even when a final inspection of German armaments by British, French, and Belgian representatives had produced a long and startling report denying that Germany had disarmed, or had any intention of disarming, and insisting that she had bamboozled the

---

[1] On his attitude to the illegal rearmament in Germany and Russia, cf. J. W. Wheeler-Bennett, *The Nemesis of Power* (1953), p. 141 fn. 2; Freund, pp. 245–7; G. Hilger and A. G. Meyer, *The Incompatible Allies* (1953), chap. VII; and H. W. Gatzke, *Stresemann and the Rearmament of Germany* (1954).

Control Commission in every way possible, nothing happened. Perhaps the indictment defeated itself by its frankness and created a picture of Allied blimpishness. The report was ignored, and in a statement of 13 December 1926 the powers concerned gave Germany a clean bill of health and agreed to the withdrawal of the Commission of Control on 31 January 1927.[1]

This did not mean that the French general staff were reassured, and French politicians were equally unready to agree voluntarily to any further reduction of reparations or evacuation of occupied territory. When Briand, with the approval of Chamberlain, sought in an intimate afternoon conversation with Stresemann at Thoiry in September 1926 to make plans for a comprehensive settlement of Franco-German problems—based on the total liberation of the occupied territory including the Saar, and a massive financial operation by an economically-restored Germany to assist the franc, with corresponding reparations and debt settlements—he was repudiated by the French cabinet, and ought perhaps to have resigned. France henceforth made concessions more and more grudgingly, and linked political or economic assistance with guarantees of good conduct in terms of fulfilment. Briand was left with little but his charm of manner to offer in support of the Franco-German rapprochement.

Chamberlain's policy, seen against this background, was friendly, but he too had little to bargain with. Appeasement—the word was coming into general use—seemed peculiarly the mission of Great Britain, and it was at once her pride and her weakness that she did not expect others to appease her; rather she found a surprising number of countries to whom she must offer solace and concessions, cash and other consolations. It was made clear to her that in a number of cases they might turn rather nasty if she did not. She had ceased to be an expansive power, but she still had influence and possessions and wealth; might she not contribute to tranquillity by handing some of them to others? At home, pacifist and socialist propaganda encouraged the view that the anguished cries of the have-nots were proof of the selfishness of the haves, dominated by the hard-faced men, capitalist and nationalist, blimpish and imperialistic. Baldwin was a man of peace but an active tranquillizer at home rather than abroad; Austen Chamberlain found more foreigners to like and

[1] J. W. Wheeler-Bennett, pp. 185–6; J. H. Morgan, *Assize of Arms* (1945), vol. I, p. 240; Kochan, pp. 112–19.

trust than Baldwin had ever succeeded in doing, but he was not disposed to give much away.

As a result, the later years of the ministry did not show any notable triumphs abroad. There were indeed no notable objectives. The breach with Russia in 1927 was not due to any desire to overthrow the Soviet régime or to organize a major offensive against it, and in China and elsewhere it was usually British business that stood at bay. Sun Yat-sen's death in 1925 had been followed by an open breach between General Chiang Kai-shek and the Communist wing of the Kuomintang. When in December 1926 the British government announced its sympathy with the new Nationalist government under Chiang and its willingness to negotiate the revision of the 'unequal treaties' the Communists replied by launching a violent anti-foreign campaign, evidently with the hope of weakening Chiang's position by associating him with foreign interests. There was an attack, initiated by the Russian agent Borodin, on the British concession at Hankow. Chamberlain showed great restraint. Chiang's government was recognized; the Hankow concession was surrendered; but as quickly as possible the British forces in the vital centre of Shanghai were strengthened by three brigades of troops under Sir John Duncan. Negotiations over the revision of the treaties then followed under the able British minister, Sir Miles Lampson, and in the meantime Chiang's forces defeated their former Communist allies and in July 1927 Borodin and his mission were expelled.

In Europe, although the Soviet government professed to fear the worst, Chamberlain pursued no more than the limited objective of making Communist propaganda unprofitable. He found no support in Germany, one proof that the Locarno spirit had led to no progressive cooperation between Stresemann and the western powers. German credits to Russia after the breach made further funds available to her for propaganda, and Stresemann was unmoved by Chamberlain's complaints on this point in March 1927. Stresemann was anxious to reduce Anglo-Russian tension, but only while avoiding commitments to either side.[1] Gradually the Berlin-Moscow link began to loosen, as the German Foreign Office came to see it as an obstacle to the further exploitation of the westward trend. This did not begin to happen until the time came for a

---

[1] Stresemann, *Vermächtnis*, vol. III, pp. 150–66; cf. Kochan, *The Struggle for Germany, 1914–1945* (1963), pp. 52–3.

further round of concessions in 1929–30, although it had been implicit in Chamberlain's policy from the start. His conviction that the defence of Germany's eastern frontier was not worth the bones of a British grenadier was not a direct invitation to Germany to pursue an anti-Russian policy; if it gave her a free hand it was against Poland. But it forced Germany to look to London for an understanding, a tendency which was not discouraged later by Arthur Henderson, and which continued under various guises until the *volte-face* of the Anglo-Polish guarantee of 31 March 1939. The Soviet government's powers of manœuvre were limited by its unique capacity for terrifying all its bourgeois neighbours, but as German friendship cooled into anti-Comintern violence, France and Russia began to draw together, a tendency already noticeable in 1930. Anglo-Soviet distrust was too strong for the corresponding reconciliation to make much headway.[1]

Relations with the United States were cordial, with reservations. They tended to be viewed in isolation; when tensions appeared it was often forgotten in England how much they were due to continental reactions, and particularly those of France. While Chamberlain aroused American suspicions by his close accord with Briand, Briand aroused American suspicions by his search for a closer accord with the United States. Recent studies in the documentary origins of Coolidge's diplomacy have tended to emphasize the escapist quality of every aspect of United States diplomacy at this time.[2] American isolationism was no longer absolute: the dominant assumption, held sincerely but with increasing sophistication as it encountered the higher levels of professional experience, was that the Republic had unique responsibilities as the 'great moral reserve', in Hoover's words, of the postwar world. This meant 'leadership', with the necessary consultative, emotional, and intellectual admixture in European affairs, although with a careful avoidance of the slightest responsibility for the carrying out of decisions. In the State Department the view was not so much that American interests could never be involved in European disturbances as that Britain and France were strong enough to look after the continent, occasionally restrained by American interventions from undue heavyhandedness. At the same time, the United States' new consciousness of

[1] Kochan, pp. 54–61; E. H. Carr, *German-Soviet Relations* (1952), chap. 5.
[2] Particularly R. H. Ferrell, *Peace in Their Time, the Origins of the Kellogg-Briand Pact* (Yale, 1952), an exhaustive treatment, and the same author's *American Diplomacy in the Great Depression* (Yale, 1957), chap. 2.

great power status and the need to defend her shores and her economy made her a hard bargainer over anything touching her own interests. A constant nervous interest was thus accompanied by great concern to avoid entanglements. Briand's dramatic proposal of 6 April 1927 for a Franco-American pact of perpetual friendship, far from creating simple joy in the State Department, was regarded as an ingenious attempt to inveigle the United States into a 'negative military alliance'.[1]

This suspicion was strengthened by the fact that at just this moment France was holding up her debt settlement with the United States and was not prepared to accept Coolidge's invitation to a naval conference at Geneva. Coolidge was subject to domestic pressure to resume the building of auxiliary vessels, which had not been regulated by the decisions of the Washington conference. Briand's refusal was believed to be due to his continued irritation over the Washington quotas. The British government accepted the invitation and the conference between the two powers and Japan opened on 20 June 1927, but the absence of France and Italy made any general agreement for limitation impossible. In any case the British Admiralty and cabinet were not prepared to reduce their cruiser strength below what seemed the limit of safety. The conference adjourned without result, leaving the Americans convinced that although the British had conceded parity in principle they were really aiming at superiority by insisting on a larger number of small cruisers than the United States wished or needed to build. The British suspected that the American preference for a smaller number of larger cruisers was due to dislike of British blockade practices.[2]

As a means of making the proposed Briand treaty innocuous the State Department hit on the ingenious plan of making it universal. But then, just when the moment was drawing near for a great ceremony of signature by the nations in Paris, Chamberlain announced in Parliament on 30 July 1928 a tentative Anglo-French agreement to limit the building of capital ships, aircraft carriers, surface vessels of or below 10,000 tons, and submarines over 600 tons. This caused great exasperation in Washington, for it proposed

---

[1] This was emphatically denied by, among others, Professor J. T. Shotwell, who wrote the message for Briand. Ferrell, *Peace in Their Time*, pp. 70–83; cf. Shotwell's *War as an Instrument of National Policy* (New York, 1929).

[2] The conference is discussed more fully below, p. 302. Cf. Ferrell, *Peace in Their Time*, p. 110.

to ban the large cruisers and large submarines which the United States wished to build. For governments which were supposed to desire American cooperation so ardently this move seems surprisingly inept, but we know little as yet of its diplomatic background. Coolidge was so irritated that for the remaining months of his term of office he could scarcely bear to hear the word 'disarmament'.

There was some truth in Chamberlain's private complaint that at this period the United States had no real foreign policy: but she achieved the alternative of leadership status through the Briand-Kellogg pact of 27 August 1928.[1] While this enabled opposition critics in England to compare American idealism with Chamberlain's rather unproductive realism, it did not remove his doubts. American spokesmen were careful to insist that the pact did not bind their government to any forcible action against disturbers of the peace; nor did it preclude rearmament in self-defence. A new cruiser-building programme was accepted by the U.S. Senate on 5 February 1929. A more convincing American contribution to progress was the appointment of the banker Owen D. Young as chairman of a committee of experts which began meetings in January 1929. Its task was to complete the reparations settlement and provide a final liquidation of all economic problems arising from the war.[2]

The glory of Locarno was already fading, and loyalty to France had created more problems than it solved. Austen had played his part with modesty and dignity, and not without success. But he had done little to advance Anglo-American cooperation: when American admirals and politicians showed themselves to be quite impervious to the argument that no rivalry need exist between two naval powers equally dedicated to the maintenance of peace, he had no soothing alternative to offer.[3] Soviet relations were, it seemed, incapable of improvement, and perhaps a better reason for some caution in disarmament. He could say that he had at least helped to give the League its finest hours, and Europe some years of much desired repose.

[1] Fetrell, *American Diplomacy in the Great Depression*, pp. 72–3; Petrie, vol. II, p. 324.
[2] Cmd 3343; A. J. Toynbee, *Survey of International Affairs* 1929 (1930), pp. 111–66; H. Schacht, *The End of Reparations* (1932).
[3] H. C. Allen, *Great Britain and the United States* (1954), pp. 744–50.

3. GOLD AND COAL

A stable Europe and restored markets remained the indispensable basis of economic recovery. Unemployment had been increasing again since the summer of 1924; the percentage of unemployed in industry rose from 10·3 in 1924 to 11·3 in 1925, with the highest figures in ship-building and ship-repairing (33·8), dock, harbour, and river services (29·9), steel and iron (24·5), and shipping (20·8). In the textiles the percentage rose from 7·0 in 1924 to 14·6 in 1925 in the woollen and worsted industry, although it fell from 13·7 to 8·3 in cotton. But it was coal which continued to dramatize the employment problem. Coal had a good year in 1924, owing to the drop in German output from the Ruhr occupation, but the percentage of unemployment in the industry rose from 5·7 in 1924 to 15·8 in 1925.[1] Thus it had become one of the worst hit of the exporting industries. Its large numbers and the approaching end of the subsidy, together with the stubbornness and, many said, mental limitations of both miners and owners, made it the subject of the final head-on clash between Labour and the government, a clash which had been so often threatened and so often postponed since 1919.

Baldwin's concern at the continued depression in the export industries was due in the main to the prospect of further industrial strife. He showed no awareness of any contribution that his government could make to a permanent solution, apart from the completion of the Treasury's quest for monetary stability by a return to the gold standard, and of political tranquillization abroad with its general stimulus to trade. The return to the gold standard was to be the last step in the deflationary policy which the Treasury had been pursuing, with the approval of successive Chancellors, since the war. It was taken for granted that the triumphant restoration of parity with the dollar would re-establish the former dominance of the London money market and be to the general benefit of the country's economy. That the more immediate effects would be detrimental to the country's export trade, particularly in coal, was scarcely mentioned in public discussion, although there were a few critics from the start, and the possible industrial consequences were understood by Churchill's advisers. A committee of experts appointed by Snowden in June 1924 had reported in favour of the

[1] Figures from Pigou, p. 50, and the *Ministry of Labour Gazette*.

return without much reference to the broader consequences. J. M. Keynes was already expounding the case for a managed currency on lines favoured also by R. G. Hawtrey, Reginald McKenna, and others, although even they were not inclined to regard this manipulation as incompatible with the gold standard. Keynes was almost alone among the experts in his belief that the country should not return to the gold standard at all.

Churchill listened to all the arguments, and although he accepted for the most part the orthodox view of the Treasury his speeches were ample and effective, and show a full grasp of his brief. Keynes' followers, he suggested, wanted to establish a quicksilver standard.[1] So his first budget, presented on 28 April 1925, followed the deflationary trend of its immediate predecessors and was generally well received. It embodied plans to help industry and reduce unemployment by reducing direct taxation; to this end income tax and supertax were lowered, while provision was made for a new pensions scheme as a corresponding gesture to the workers. It also restored the McKenna duties and the preferences on wine, sugar, and tobacco abolished by Snowden, and it announced the return to the gold standard at $4·86 to the pound. The Gold Standard Act was passed early in May. Opponents of deflation had additional cause for pessimism in the allocation of £50 million to the Sinking Fund.[2]

All this provided little comfort to Baldwin, whose anticipation of further labour trouble betrayed itself in appeals for forbearance and nostalgic references to the good old times. Speaking on 6 March 1925 on Mr. F. Macquisten's private bill to free trade unionists from compulsory contributions to the funds of the Labour party he recalled the old family business where nobody got the sack and where 'a number of old gentlemen used to spend their days sitting on the handles of wheelbarrows smoking their pipes'. But times, he said sadly, had changed; there was no alternative to the growth of two enormously strong forces, business and labour, each tending to amalgamation, and on both sides there were 'many men with good heads and no hearts, and many men with good hearts and no heads'. The speech contained a warning that the government must resist any of these associations which might directly injure the

---

[1] Apart from the debt settlement Churchill has nothing to say about these Treasury activities in his memoirs (cf. *The Gathering Storm*, pp. 19–20). P. J. Grigg, *Prejudice and Judgment* (1948), pp. 180–86; Harrod, p. 357.

[2] Grigg, pp. 195–6; Pigou, p. 151.

state, called on the Tory party to make a gesture to the country by withdrawing support from the bill, and ended with what was apparently a defiance of Communists and other left-wing trouble-makers. 'Although I know that there are those who work for different ends from most of us in this House, yet there are many in all ranks and all parties who will re-echo my prayer: "Give peace in our time, O Lord".'[1]

If the speech made a good impression for the moment it did little or nothing to check the turn in the Labour movement towards more militant industrial action which followed the political set-back of the 1924 general election. This may have been inevitable in the circumstances, and it did not imply any abandonment by the dominant figures in the trade unions and Labour party of the con-viction that only the conquest of political power would fully satisfy their demands. The party indeed had settled down to the business of opposition with every intention of doing better next time. Plans were laid during 1925 to strengthen the finances of local Labour parties by the enrolling of larger numbers of individual members making small regular contributions, and by gradually transferring to the local parties the expenses of full-time local agents. The local parties were also asked to contribute to a central by-elections fund. These were moves intended both to strengthen the party's finances, which had been gravely weakened by three elections, and to eman-cipate it in some measure from dependence on the unions, which were in any case not prepared to finance many candidates. It was also a challenge to the I.L.P., whose own organization in the constituencies was running a membership drive, with the I.L.P. Guild of Youth directly challenging the Youth Sections of the local Labour parties.[2]

There were some criticisms of the party leadership and some recriminations; this, however, was little more than a continuance of the harrying of MacDonald which had constituted the sole contribution of the left-wingers to the progress of the first Labour government. The party conference which opened in Liverpool on 29 September 1925 turned down a proposal by Bevin that the party should never again take office without a majority; and it again turned down the Communists. The more militant phase of industrial action that was being prepared was thus a supplement to, and not an

---

[1] Stanley Baldwin, *On England* (1926), pp. 41–52.
[2] G. D. H. Cole, *A History of the Labour Party from 1914*, pp. 173–8.

abandonment of, political action, by men concerned with the short term objectives of wage claims; the ultimate line of cleavage within the Labour ranks was between those who were prepared to push the challenge to its immediate end and those who saw the ultimate end in terms of a national disaster.

4. GENERAL STRIKE

Although the general strike of 1926 was interpreted by most Labour writers and publicists as a defence of hour and wage standards against capitalist attack it had its origin in different considerations. It will be remembered that the miners' wage settlement of 1921 had been somewhat improved by a new agreement made between owners and miners in June 1924 for twelve months. During the early weeks of 1925 the miners' leaders had hoped to raise the relatively favourable wage level of 1924, and do not appear to have anticipated the slump. Plans were also being discussed early in the year, on Bevin's initiative, for the revival of some substitute for the triple alliance which would mobilize the main sections of industry—railwaymen, miners, transport workers, and engineers—for concerted action.[1] It was only when they met the owners in March 1925 that the miners' leaders, whose plans for further concessions included a national minimum wage of 12s a shift, found that the owners were, on the contrary, convinced of the need for lower wages and longer hours. The miners were thus thrown on the defensive, and three months of abortive negotiations made it clear that no subsidy was likely to come from the government, wedded as it was to the conviction that sterling wages and the cost of living were too high in comparison with other European countries. Without a government subsidy, with the foreign demand for coal dropping disastrously (a process accentuated by the increase of 10 per cent in cost resulting from the return to parity), and with the evidence of vanishing profits in almost all districts, the owners could see no alternative to a return to the 1921 wage structure and the eight-hour day. The miners' reply was essentially that their present wages were below living standard already. More efficient production and the cutting away of 'the waste and parasitic growth of profits' would meet the short term needs of the industry; the ultimate solution could only come from the elimination of under-

[1] A. Bullock, *The Life and Times of Ernest Bevin*, vol. I, pp. 270–72; Cole, pp. 179–80; J. H. Jones, G. Cartwright, and P. H. Guénhault, *The Coal Mining Industry* (1939).

consumption which was part of the general crisis of the capitalist world. As the owners wished to maintain this world and the miners did not, it was for the owners to find a solution. 'Nowt doin' ' was the reply of the massive, laconic, unyielding miners' President, Herbert Smith, to requests for concessions. Or, as the more talkative miners' Secretary, A. J. Cook, put it, 'not a penny off the pay, not a second on the day'.[1]

On 30 June 1925 the owners issued notices ending the 1924 agreement within a month. The government appointed another court of inquiry, this time under Mr. H. P. Macmillan, and the miners appealed to the General Council of the T.U.C., which promised wholehearted support. On the 28th the court of inquiry reported largely in the miners' favour, and after Baldwin had failed to find any compromise (although the owners showed more flexibility in the discussions than the miners) the General Council on Friday the 31st came decisively into action by issuing an embargo on the movements of coal to take effect at midnight. This was 'Red Friday', labour's day (or night) of victory; the government gave in, at least to the extent of promising a subsidy to enable the industry to carry on without change of hours and wages for some nine months. In the meantime, another inquiry; and, more important, time for the testing of nerves, and for the final preparations for industrial battle if none of the four main parties sounded the retreat.

Of these, the miners were not prepared to budge, and the owners were not prepared to budge very far. The new commission of enquiry with Sir Herbert Samuel in the chair did its work with great thoroughness and after holding public sittings and hearing witnesses presented a report on 19 March 1926 which gave the miners, as A. J. Cook admitted, 80 per cent of what they had demanded. This referred, however, to the commission's long term proposals, which included the nationalization of coal royalties, reorganization of the industry through the amalgamation of smaller mines and other devices to eliminate unprofitable working, better facilities in the shape of improved housing, pithead baths, and holidays with pay, as well as better remuneration in the shape of family allowances and profit-sharing schemes. On the other hand,

---

[1] Much has been written about the strike: W. H. Crook, *The General Strike* (Chapel Hill, 1931), and J. Symons, *The General Strike* (1957), are detailed and fair enough to all parties. There is also a full and interesting study in Mowat, pp. 284–331, with valuable bibliographical comments. The miners' story is given by Page Arnot, *The Miners: Years of Struggle*, chap. XIV.

the commission rejected nationalization and any continuance of the government subsidy, and accepted the owners' contention that the immediate crisis facing the industry could be met only by a reduction of working costs through a temporary reduction of wages. This the miners steadily refused to accept. No one at the time seems to have had a favourable impression of the owners' representatives. Neville Chamberlain found them 'not a prepossessing crowd' which presumably means that they struck him as hard-faced and unadaptable men.[1] But they do not appear to have rejected the commission's long-term plans outright, and both Samuel and the government accepted their argument for wage reductions. The miners wanted reorganization first, stolidly impervious to the argument that it would 'take years'. What is quite clear is that the government, the third major element involved in the struggle, was determined not to give way before the threat of the general strike. It was the fourth party to the dispute, the T.U.C., which was not prepared for a fight to a finish.

The government had no doubt that British and international Communist organizations were eager to take advantage of any major strike or national stoppage of work. Harry Pollitt, J. R. Campbell, and other members of the party were arrested on 14 and 21 October 1925 and sentenced to short terms of imprisonment for sedition and incitement to mutiny. Documents seized at the time were published by the Home Office in June 1926.[2] They included the Comintern's instructions of October 1924 for the general election, and suggestions from the same source in April 1925 on the eve of the British Communist party congress. The Comintern, while not exaggerating the party's influence, spoke hopefully of the prospects of the Minority Movement, the rise of a revolutionary spirit among the British workers, and the need to extend the Minority Movement from the metal, mining, and transport unions to cover the textile and seamen's industries. A. J. Cook was one of a line of Labour leaders—it seems to have ended with Harold Laski—who brought the hint of revolutionary violence into their speech-making, quite against the familiar line of the Labour party and the T.U.C. Beatrice Webb dismissed him as an 'inspired idiot' but his dark threats were alarming enough to those who chose to take

[1] Feiling, p. 156.
[2] *Communist Papers. Documents selected from those obtained on the arrest of the communist leaders on the 14th and 21st October 1925.* Cmd. 2682. (London, H.M.S.O., 1926). Pelling, *The British Communist Party* (1958), pp. 32-9.

them seriously. The police and armed services, drawn mainly from the working classes would not, he said, 'shoot against their kith and kin when the order comes', and for this and many other reasons a strike of the miners would mean the end of capitalism. The Communist-inspired Minority Movement, active among the miners and supported by Cook, held a delegate meeting in March 1926 and claimed a million members.

There were those in the government who hoped for a compromise solution, and others who set great store on the maintenance of its conciliatory and neutral rôle; but all were agreed that the Red Friday situation—one in which the government was forced to give way before the peremptory threat of a national industrial stoppage—must not recur. Strike action on anything approaching a national scale was bound to be political in its effect, whatever the immediate industrial aim; and in time, if allowed to continue, its aim was bound to become political too. And this was a prospect which attracted the leaders of the Parliamentary Labour party and many of the T.U.C. leaders as little as it did the government.

Nevertheless there was widespread sympathy with the miners, particularly as the owners seemed to be stiffening their terms at every opportunity; when the lock-out notices expired on Friday, 30 April, a special conference of trade union executives approved of whatever strike action might be necessary to give the miners effective backing. The T.U.C. General Council did its best in the last stages to argue the government into a temporary renewal of the subsidy and the miners into an understanding to 'consider' wage reductions when schemes of reorganization had been 'initiated'. But there was to be no Red Saturday (or Monday). Late on the Sunday night, when the cabinet, the T.U.C. Industrial Committee, and the miners' delegates were assembled in different parts of 10 and 11 Downing Street searching for a formula, the cabinet decided to discontinue the negotiations on the ground that the Labour leaders were trying to force the government's hands with 'overt acts'[1]. Baldwin gave them a curious letter which said 'Good-bye. This is the end', but also said that the government had been ready to

---

[1] The specific 'overt act' was the refusal of the *Daily Mail* printers ('Natsopa' members) to print the Monday issue because they disliked the editorial, which had been written by the editor himself, Thomas Marlowe. Labour sympathizers view the incident as an excuse which the Tory extremists seized on to ensure a stoppage (cf. Cole, p. 185), Conservatives as a 'last straw' (cf. Feiling, p. 157). Citrine says he discovered later that 'Churchill had been to the *Daily Mail* office': W. Citrine, *Men and Work* (1964), p. 172.

continue discussions and the subsidy for a fortnight and could not resume negotiations without the repudiation of the overt act and the immediate and unconditional withdrawal of the instructions for a general strike. When two T.U.C. delegates arrived with a reply about 1.30 a.m. they were told that the Prime Minister had gone to bed.[1] The significance of this particular incident has been greatly exaggerated. What was important from the government's point of view was that on the following day the strike notices had not been withdrawn. The general strike had begun.

It ended on 12 May, a nine-days' wonder, which was of no help to the miners but which settled some other issues. At first the opposing forces seemed well matched in resources and resolution. The General Council called out the workers in a number of key industries —transport, iron and steel, building, and printing—and in these there was an almost universal cessation of work. There were occasional but not widespread acts of violence and no sign of a revolutionary mood; throughout, the mass of workers treated the affair as a wage dispute of rather dramatic proportions, but nothing more. The government on its side was well prepared with measures to keep the essential services going, it had made preparations— sometimes a little too ostentatiously—to deal with violence, and it had the spontaneous support and help of many middleclass people in the improvizations that kept the civilian life of the country going. Churchill and the group allegedly favouring dramatic action were diverted by useful jobs: Churchill edited the *British Gazette*.[2] While on the one side local strike committees, organized by groups of trade unions, showed energy, enthusiasm, and organizing ability, on the other the government found abundant volunteers for such emergency tasks as driving buses, lorries, and trains, unloading ships at the docks, acting as special constables, serving in canteens, and the like. Among the unions which did not take part were the National Sailors' and Firemen's Union, still led by the right-

---

[1] The two delegates then said that they would send a letter. According to A. W. Baldwin, four private secretaries were available (*My Father: The True Story*, p. 136), but the delegates did not show any desire to get the Prime Minister out of bed. Cf. A. Hutt (p. 134): '... they were coolly told by an attendant that Mr. Baldwin had gone to bed and given to understand that their continued presence was entirely superfluous'. Cole, p. 185: 'The Trade Union negotiators ... found the Cabinet dispersed and the door banged in their faces'. Other versions: Grigg, p. 188; Fenner Brockway, *Inside the Left*, p. 187; Citrine, pp. 171–2.

[2] To the annoyance of *The Times*: J. E. Wrench, *Geoffrey Dawson and Our Times* (1955), pp. 248–54: cf. Grigg, pp. 188–9. *The British Worker* was produced in reply: Fenner Brockway, pp. 190–93.

wing Havelock Wilson, and the Electrical Power Engineers Association. It was in Plymouth that the much publicized football match between police and strikers took place.

The speedy collapse of the strike is the essential problem for the historian. It was due to the intolerable dilemma that faced the T.U.C. When the first days had brought no collapse of the government's resistance their gamble had failed: they faced the alternatives of increasingly stern measures to disrupt the country's economy or a partial acquiescence in the government's effort to keep it going.[1] The first was distasteful to them, the second futile; and both might lead to the capture of the movement by extremists. The vast, idle labour force could not indefinitely do nothing; there would be either a drift back to work or increasing violence. As a result, the T.U.C.'s moves were contradictory. There had been no previous planning, no working out of the precise rules of this unfamiliar game. The transport workers had been called out, but the people—including the strikers—had to be fed. The printers' strike stopped not only the capitalistic press but also the *Daily Herald*. Permits were therefore granted for the movement of essential transport and other work. But the strikers' own measures made communication difficult; the granting of permits thus fell largely to the local strike committees, with much consequent confusion and abuse. Ernest Bevin, as secretary of the Strike Organization Committee, established communication with the local centres by despatch riders, but these were more useful in bringing reports to headquarters than in bringing clear directives away from it.

On 7 May all the permits which the T.U.C. or local committees had been issuing for transport were revoked. This at once threatened the movement of food supplies and there were protests from the co-operative societies. The government was bound to take the new challenge very seriously, for the forceful picketing by the London dockers was now preventing all movements of food supplies from the docks. Accordingly on the following day it used substantial military forces to convoy food lorries from the London docks, opened recruiting for a Constabulary Reserve, and printed in the *British Gazette* an announcement that any action by the armed forces in aiding the civil power would receive the government's full support. This might, as some Labour supporters professed to

---

[1] Citrine's diary of the general strike (*op.cit.*, chap II) admirably records the day-to-day reactions of the General Council of the T.U.C.

believe, mean that the government was seeking to provoke a revolution; but to the government it meant resolute action to prevent it. While it is true that Churchill favoured a show of force, it is also the case that only by a display of force could the dockers' boycott be broken. On the same evening, 8 May, Baldwin made a conciliatory broadcast speech, and this gave a slight opening to J. H. Thomas, who had been in touch with Sir Herbert Samuel since the 6th. Baldwin would do no more than suggest that the Labour leaders should trust him; he was not prepared to make any promises until the general strike had been called off unconditionally. On Tuesday, 11 May, the Negotiating Committee of the T.U.C. decided to do this, and a deputation consisting of J. H. Thomas, Arthur Pugh, and Ernest Bevin told Baldwin at 10 Downing Street on the 12th that it would be 'terminated forthwith'.

The general strike took place because it had been the chief nostrum of the unions for many years; it failed because the government refused (in contrast to 1925) to give way to the mere threat, and the trade union leaders were not prepared to face the consequences. Walter Citrine, the acting secretary of the T.U.C., thought it 'a sympathetic strike on a national scale' but concluded that 'the machinery of the trade unions was unfortunately not adapted to it'.[1] It did not fail through any lack of resolution on the part of the strikers, although there is some evidence that J. H. Thomas, C. T. Cramp, Ben Turner, and others had convinced themselves that in a few days it would have collapsed through a general return to work. Figures subsequently available do not appear to confirm this, and the strikers and local committees were astonished at an unconditional surrender which had at first been assumed to be a resounding victory.[2] The alternative cause of apprehension was that the strike would get into the hands of extremists, and Thomas told the Commons on 13 May that this was what he had dreaded most. This is not incompatible with the view that the strike was collapsing: the extremists might have argued that the time had come for desperate measures. The absence of conditions meant that there was a danger of further trouble through 'victimization' by employers, although some blunt words from Baldwin in the House of Commons scotched the worst of this. It also meant that the miners' problem was unsolved.

[1] Citrine, pp. 216–17; cf. Bullock, pp. 332–42; V. L. Allen, pp. 197–200.
[2] Symons, pp. 207–11, discusses the figures; cf. Fenner Brockway, p. 192.

Yet in spite of continued widespread sympathy for them and continued depression in many industries, there was to be no repetition of anything resembling a general strike; and as there appears to have been no unwillingness for it on the part of the rank and file of the Labour movement we must attribute this result primarily to the leaders. What is clear, however, is that the general strike of 1926 produced little or no sign of the revolutionary impulse which had perhaps existed in the same quarters in the early nineteen-twenties. The strike weapon itself lost much of its attractiveness from this point. In the period 1919–26 about 44,600,000 working days were lost annually, on an average, through strikes; from 1927 to 1939, the annual average was only a little over 3 million.[1] If the postwar strike wave can be regarded as a continuance of the tendency to civil violence which had troubled Asquithian England, it had exhausted itself by 1926.

The fact that the political leaders of the three great parties all set their faces against general strikes did not mean only that they saw the danger of power passing into the wrong hands. It also meant that each party was still engaged in an inconclusive debate as to what its economic policy should be. If one successful general strike had led to another the industrial result would have been the forcing up of wages and the cost of living with inflationary results and further depression in the exporting industries through the necessarily increased cost of exports; as this would have horrified the Conservative administration and its advisers it would no doubt have led to a dissolution and a general election from which a Labour government might have emerged. But if so the Labour leaders would still have had to decide what to do with their victory. On this there was much debate, with less clear-cut ideas than those of either the Conservative or Liberal theorists.

5. Safety First

The result of the strike was a victory that the government failed to turn to real advantage. Labour supporters and much uncommitted opinion in the country, while rejecting the strike weapon as inexpedient, also deplored the fate of the miners and the continued unemployment; and on this issue the government had little to say. Baldwin's inability to give his cabinet any intellectual lead became

[1] *Statistical Abstract of U.K. 1930*; cf. Cole, *op.cit.*, pp. 191–2, for further comments and figures. In 1927 and 1928 the number of days lost was 1,174,000 and 1,388,000 as compared with 162,233,000 in 1926.

more noticeable amid the general debating on economic policy that took place in the later years of his ministry both inside and outside the government. The appearance of leadership was certainly lacking, but it would also seem that he remained unconvinced as to either the political expediency or the practical utility of many of the plans that were being put forward.

'Cannot you trust me to ensure a square deal for the parties—to secure even justice between man and man?' he had exclaimed in his broadcast speech of 8 May. But when the Minister of Labour, Arthur Steel-Maitland, urged him to propound the terms of a genuine industrial peace at this moment when his reputation was so high he was unresponsive. Steel-Maitland put forward a plan for consultations to this end with Philip Snowden and Montague Norman, to be followed by the drawing in of Pugh and Bevin to represent the trade unions, and some representative of the employers. Baldwin's biographer could trace no response whatever to this appeal.[1] Nervous exhaustion following the tensions of the crisis left him without energy for fresh experiments. The punitive elements in the post-strike arrangements thus had no antidote, and seemed to justify the charge that he had surrendered to the extremists of his own party. This is obviously true to some extent, although he had no doubt about the need for most of the decisions taken.

The miners' strike continued for some months, and ended with a drift back to work on the owners' terms. The government, while accepting the need for longer hours, did what it could to ensure the carrying out of the long-term proposals of the Samuel Report. These arrangements were embodied in the Eight Hours and the Mining Industry Bills, the first of which came before the Commons in June. The cabinet maintained its refusal to grant any subsidy or loan, and insisted that miners and owners must settle the dispute between themselves, although it was willing enough to act as a go-between. The only effect of its intervention was to give the owners further opportunities to demonstrate their rocklike refusal to consider any form of national settlement, for which the miners' leaders were still pressing. In September Churchill and Baldwin both condemned this stubbornness and shortsightedness, but government proposals for a settlement on a district basis were put forward on 7 October.[2] For some weeks more the Miners' Federation held out,

[1] G. M. Young, p. 121.
[2] Churchill's remarks are quoted by Mowat, p. 334; cf. Grigg, p. 192.

and early in November the General Council of the T.U.C. promised to help with a general levy. But with the end of its funds in sight, and with the knowledge of a large scale return to work, the miners' delegate conference called off the strike on 26 November, leaving the district associations to make what terms they could with the owners.[1]

The stubbornness of both parties gives the dispute its unusual prominence (for other hard-hit industries were not driven to such lengths), and both groups of leaders were condemned. Baldwin on 27 September called the owners' representatives 'discourteous and stupid', and in October at the Labour Party conference Robert Williams said that the miners' leaders 'may be likened to the sightless Samson feeling for a grip of the pillars of the Temple, the crashing of which may engulf this thing we call British civilization'.[2] Friends who cried that the miners had been starved into submission presumably hoped that the grim struggle, which had already cut coal exports by half, would continue until the owners had been driven to surrender by the imminent ruin of their business, for there could be no other outcome in an industry in which costs consisted so largely of wages and in which sales were dependent on an increasingly unstable market. The struggle was between the financial resources of the mine owners and of the Miners' Federation; it was the latter, rather than the miners, which was starved into submission. Neville Chamberlain wrote on 20 June that the miners 'are not within sight of starvation, hardly of under-nutrition, so well are they looked after by the guardians'. Baldwin also denied in August that there was serious want in the British coalfields, and the N.S.P.C.C. issued a report which stated that there was no urgent need among miners' children. No doubt strike pay, and the poor relief that was available for wives and children (although not for the strikers themselves), together with contributions from the other unions, from Russia, and from the general public, did prevent actual starvation, although on a more meagre standard than that of the normal wage scale, which was low enough in many districts.[3] Of the owners it must be said that their adamantine lack of tact in resisting suggestions of reorganization must not be taken to prove that the various expedi-

[1] Page Arnot, pp. 457–523.
[2] A. Hutt, *The Post-War History of the British Working Class*, pp. 171–2.
[3] Left-wing accounts of voluntary aid to the miners from many sources confirm this conclusion, without of course giving any thanks to the government: cf. Hutt, pp. 168–9; Feiling, p. 158.

ents under this head would really have meant the salvation of the industry. The problem was that of a severe drop in demand largely outside the industry's control.

In the post-mortem in the Labour ranks on these unhappy events there was an increasing tendency to blame the government for the general strike, on the argument that Winston Churchill and others of like outlook had deliberately ignored the conciliatory inclinations of the trade union leaders on Sunday, 2 May. This is an over-simplification of the position from the Tory point of view. Churchill showed zest for any fight, and it was doubtless considered that the bold course was best; many Tories thought that they could see the sinister influence of extremists behind the Labour party's facade of constitutional respectability. But if the general strike had been called off at any point there is no doubt that Baldwin could have carried the cabinet with him in accepting the situation.

The Trade Unions Act of 1927 also seemed to the Opposition a triumph of Tory reaction, a device intended not only to curb national strikes and left-wing extremism but to hamstring the Labour party itself. The bill, introduced in May 1927, had two main features. It attacked 'general' strikes by declaring illegal those with any object other than or in addition to the furtherance of a trade dispute; and it laid down—reversing on this point the Trade Union Act of 1913—that trade union members need not contribute to their union's political funds unless they gave written notice of their willingness to do so. It also defined intimidation and declared it illegal, and sought to prevent local authorities from forcing trade unionism on their employees. Most of the Labour and T.U.C. leaders had condemned the general strike with more or less frank-ness, and as there were Tory trade unionists it could be argued that 'contracting in' for the political levy was fairer than 'contracting out'. The hard fact nevertheless was that a great many trade unionists would not bother to contract in, and that the clause was a serious—and no doubt deliberate—attack on the Labour party's finances. Neville Chamberlain had not liked the provision which he thought was 'merely aimed at popularity', and had proposed to the cabinet the provision of statutory machinery for discussion before a strike could begin. But this was rejected, and Lloyd George was able to say that the bill was nothing but an attack, without constructive proposals. However, it became law, after fierce criticism and the elimination of some of the more obnoxious earlier clauses. During the next two years the Labour party's affiliated membership fell from 3,388,000 to 2,077,000, mainly it was believed because of the 'contracting in' provision.[1]

Contrasting with, and to some extent hampered by, this bitter class and party struggle was the constructive work of Neville Chamberlain at the Ministry of Health. In this contribution of an experienced administrator to what was not yet known as the welfare state the Conservative party had the one unqualified achievement of the Baldwin ministry, and Chamberlain the one unquestioned achievement of his career. The remarkable success of John Burns in fending off attempts to reform the Local Government Board between 1906 and 1914 had left a big task of modernization to the postwar generation. The first step had been the creation of the Ministry of Health in 1919, but with a wide and somewhat confusing range of duties. It was concerned not only with health in the more familiar and medical sense of the word, but also with such matters as old-age pensions, poor law, and housing, and with almost any aspect of life that could involve disease. 'Its officials must watch and measure the water supply and grading of milk, boric acid in confectionery, or phosphoric acid in raspberry cordial. They wrote in equal volume about plague-infected rats and activated sludge, vigilantly inspected shellfish of the Menai Straits or cockle-beds of Pegwell Bay.'[2]

Chamberlain, looking forward to a few years of continuous administration, laid before the cabinet on 19 November 1924 a provisional programme of twenty-five bills which was largely completed by 1929. Much of it was controversial. The Widows, Orphans, and Old Age Pensions Bill, for which provision had been made in the 1925 budget, was introduced speedily and attacked by the Labour members because it was contributory. It was tied to the national health insurance, the normal weekly contribution of workers and employers being increased for the purpose; pensions were to be payable at sixty-five, and the widows and orphans of insured persons were to receive pensions as of right. The bill also had its critics among the businessmen in the House, but it was successfully passed, as was also the more complicated Rating and Valuation Bill. This was a measure of rationalization and moderni-

---

[1] Because of the party's financial dependence on the trade unions it suffered after this 'nearly two decades of pecuniary distress'. W. B. Gwyn, *Democracy and the Cost of Politics*, pp. 232–6.
[2] Feiling, p. 127.

zation which concentrated rating powers in the hands of county, borough, and district councils and standardized the basis of valuation and assessment. The opposition came from a variety of interested parties including both the Lansburyites who foresaw the abolition of the guardians, and the Tory squires and business men who foresaw ruin at the hands of Socialist councils. With Baldwin's strong support and after various concessions, including the omission of London, the bill passed its third reading in December 1925.

The guardians had to be dealt with, rather sooner than Chamberlain had intended, when the general strike brought 'Poplarism' to a fresh crisis. An earlier brush between the Poplar Guardians and the government in 1921 had led to the setting up of the Metropolitan Common Poor Fund, whereby the greater part of the cost of outdoor relief was shared by London as a whole. The situation worsened again as Poplar's example was followed in other East End areas. Here relief was on an increasingly generous scale, no longer concerned only with the needs of the destitute. The ratepayers paid, and the government made loans. When West Ham, with an accumulated debt of about £2 million, applied for a further loan, Chamberlain introduced in July 1926 the Guardians (Default) Act which enabled the Minister of Health to appoint his own nominees where he considered necessary. This he did in the cases of West Ham in 1926 and of Bedwellty (Mon.) and Chester-le-Street (Durham) in 1927. He had again to face bitter attacks from some of his Labour critics.

He also had to fight some battles in the cabinet, where the formidable personality and political flair of the Chancellor of the Exchequer were directed towards objectives similar to his own. Churchill was becoming aware of the inadequacy of the government's financial programme to remedy the continued economic depression. If unemployment was no worse it was showing no sign of improvement in the great exporting industries, which were suffering not only from loss of markets but in some cases, as the protectionists argued, from competition by foreign importers at home. 'No wonder that the home market is being increasingly eaten into, till today we import some £350 million of foreign manufactures', wrote Amery to Baldwin in April 1927. At this point he was convinced that the Chancellor, on whom in a peculiar sense the responsibility fell, 'does not even realize that the problem exists'. 'The one thing on which the Treasury, poor dears, pin all their hopes is debt conversion, for the sake of which they are trying to stifle every scheme that might improve Empire trade or get industry out of the rut.'[1]

In fact, Churchill, loyal to the free trade and deflationary policies on which he had based his régime at the Exchequer, was not so much ignorant of, as robustly hostile to, either safeguarding or any manipulation of the gold standard; but he was looking round for a popular alternative. This he found in a plan for reducing the burden of rates on industry and agriculture by means of substantial Exchequer subsidies. Neville Chamberlain, whose ambitious plans for poor law and local government reform were now being elaborated, agreed as to derating, but not to the way in which the block grants were to be used. He wanted to limit them to health alone. His plans and their probable unpopularity filled Baldwin and many members of the cabinet with alarm, and Churchill although an ally was not prepared to accept 'a purely departmental solution'. The arguments went round for a year or more, and Chamberlain was talking of resignation in March 1928. In the end there were compromises whereby industry received less than the total exemption to which Chamberlain had objected and the rate-aid to the railways was to be used to reduce freight charges. Churchill presented his scheme in the 1928 budget, with persuasive eloquence. £17 million would be used to reduce rates on industry by three-quarters; £4¾ million to relieve agricultural land and houses of all rate charges; £4 million to reduce railway freight transport by three-quarters; and £3 million to launch Chamberlain's local government legislation.[2]

As it happened this ambitious programme was of little political help to the Conservatives, and did not even still the criticisms of the rank and file of the party. The relief to industry was not sufficient to make much difference to the exporters. The protectionists were not mollified. Amery noted ruefully that while Churchill could produce his 'mass of manœuvre' of £29 million for derating, the Treasury stubbornly refused to find a mere half million or less to support the Empire Marketing Board. The complicated rating and valuation bill which Chamberlain had to introduce after the budget led to many disappointments for firms which were not classifiable as industrial, and it soon became clear that rates would go up in some areas. Nor did Chamberlain's crowning achievement, the vast

[1] Amery, vol. II, pp. 486–9.
[2] Grigg, pp. 199–201.

Local Government Bill of 1929 to which he had dedicated himself, prove in any way an electioneering asset for the party.

It did bring about, however, a profound reorganization of English local government, generally with the effect of concentrating authority into the hands of the county councils, while strengthening the control of the Ministry of Health. Its starting point has been said to be his father's position that the poor law was a limb of the body of social services, and not merely the code of a depressed order. To the county or county borough councils were transferred the powers of the Boards of Guardians (which thus disappeared after nearly a hundred years of Benthamite inspiration), and to the county councils the highway functions of rural areas. The derating provisions, anticipated in the budget, carried further the revolution in local government finance which had been in progress since 1888, and they were used to give much greater control to the central government, in return for its greatly increased contribution to the cost of local services. The Ministry of Health could now reduce the grant to any local authority if its expenditure, public health activities, or road maintenance were considered unsatisfactory. Poor law and health were the most important of the ministry's functions in supervising the work of the local authorities but its responsibility for both the structure and finance of local government made it, in Professor Smellie's phrase, 'a Ministry of the Interior with a sanitary bias'.[1]

The Commons could still rise above politics and economics on occasion. Many believed that the two debates on the revised Prayer Book were the finest of their generation. It was the wish of the hierachy of the Church of England to introduce a Prayer Book which would make allowance for presentday needs and for those who inclined to a High Church, but not a Romish, position. But the acts of the Church could not become law without the approval of both Houses of Parliament, and the revised Prayer Book, so carefully prepared, was debated in the Commons on 15 December 1927. The debate, which was not on party lines, reached a high level and a disappointing one for the Church. A speech by Mr. Rosslyn Mitchell aroused echoes of 'No Popery', and with the emphatic support of the nonconformist members the proposal was rejected by 230 to 205. After this shock the Church put forward a modified version six months later, but this was also rejected, after

[1] K. B. Smellie, *A Hundred Years of English Government* (1937 edn.), pp. 381–9.

another excellent debate which did not, however, perhaps reach quite the heights of the first. There had been memorable speeches by Baldwin, Hugh Cecil, and Bridgeman; prominent among the opponents of the measures were Joynson-Hicks, Simon, Douglas Hogg, and Inskip. The extent and spontaneity of Conservative feeling on the subject was as much a surprise as the intellectual quality of the discussion. The Church had to accept the lay verdict.[1]

But somehow the busy and useful activities of government and parliament were failing to hold the interest of the country. Unemployment was always tending to increase, derating had failed to arouse any wide enthusiasm, and Baldwin showed no desire to enliven the scene, even by a modest reshuffle of ministerial offices. There was a continued sense of uneasiness at the state of the economy, even though a certain measure of recovery was undeniable. There is evidence of considerable controversy inside the cabinet, and Amery, back in England in February 1928 after an Empire tour of seven months, pressed the case for imperial preference, with little response.[2] Baldwin and Churchill seem to have convinced themselves that the country's existing fiscal policies were on the right lines and provided the best hopes of a long-term solution. In an unemployment debate on the Address in 1928 Baldwin doubted whether the depressed basic industries would ever recover, but argued that the country was righting itself by its own efforts; 90 per cent of the working population were, after all, at work. This qualified pessimism was not to the liking of the rank and file of the Conservative party, and Churchill's aggressive free trade speeches infuriated them. At the end of July the whips reported the party to be in a state of open mutiny. On 2 August the cabinet, considerably shaken, agreed to a workable scheme for safeguarding from which no industries would be excluded. It seems that Baldwin had no doubt as to the advantages of some form of protection. But his fear of accusations that he was going back on his election pledges and no doubt the Chancellor's robust opposition to any form of safeguarding resulted in the whittling away of even this limited undertaking during the following months. Derating was reaffirmed as the party's main industrial panacea.

The Labour party suffered from much the same paralysis of initiative and ideas. There were proposals in plenty from the I.L.P.

[1] G. K. A. Bell, *Randall Davidson* (1935), vol. II, pp. 1325–60; cf. Grigg, pp. 216–17.
[2] Amery, vol. II, p. 491.

and the Communists but MacDonald and his closer supporters did not wish to lose the next election by frightening the electorate and were following as carefully as Baldwin a policy of safety first. In this the party was supported by the trade unions, which were conscious of having lost ground and membership as a result of the 1926 *débâcle* and the continued unemployment. Militant industrial action was at a discount and at the same time there were, as it seemed, good prospects of a Labour government in the near future. The I.L.P. on the other hand, true to its rôle as the propagandist of Socialism within the party, put forward in 1925 a programme which would produce 'Socialism in Our Time' and to which the Labour party would be committed even in a minority government.[1] The practical result of two years of discussion was, however, that MacDonald succeeded in dodging any commitment to the party at all. At the 1927 Labour party conference he condemned the programme of *Socialism in Our Time* as likely to ensure an electoral defeat, and he proposed that the Labour party should get to work on its own programme for the next election. He was supported by Bevin, who wanted 'a short programme of immediate objectives'. It was in this spirit rather than that of the I.L.P. that the programme called *Labour and the Nation*, drafted by R. H. Tawney, was submitted to the party conference at Birmingham in 1928, although it was criticized by I.L.P. speakers such as Wheatley for being neither an immediate programme for the election nor a statement of genuine Socialist objectives. This MacDonald accepted, and he agreed to various proposals for greater precision; but still the document remained a statement of long-term objectives rather than an election programme. This was produced when the time came by MacDonald and the party executive.

It was from the Liberal party, whose leader after Asquith's death in February 1928 was Lloyd George, that there came a programme which seemed at once bold and practical, foreshadowing wide schemes of public works which were to conquer unemployment and indeed solve the country's longer term economic problems. It owed much to J. M. Keynes, who was now able to gain publicity and backing for his programme of economic expansion based on an adroit use of deficit-financing at home and currency management

---

[1] It was not, in fact, a very bold programme: its most prominent feature was a demand for a national minimum wage. R. K. Middlemas, *The Clydesiders*, pp. 180–5; R. E. Dowse, 'The Left Wing Opposition during the first two Labour Governments', *Parliamentary Affairs*, vol. XIV(i), p. 89.

abroad. Unemployment was to be relieved by a great public works programme including housing and above all great road building plans. The Liberals had little hope of a future based on 'safety first'; for them boldness was their sole chance of capturing the approval of the electorate. But they also had in Lloyd George a great and restless leader who at sixty-five knew that his chances too would probably end if he suffered defeat in the next election. He was prepared to use much of the 'Lloyd George fund'—the Coalition-Liberal campaign residue—to finance the election programme and the election itself.[1] Much preparatory study during 1927 produced in January 1928 the Liberal 'Yellow Book', under the title, *Britain's Industrial Future*. This set out the new programme, incorporating the results also of earlier reports on coal, agriculture, and town planning. After a year of public debate a statement of the proposals in their final form was put forward in March 1929 as the Liberal election programme in the 'Orange Book', a pamphlet entitled, *We Can Conquer Unemployment*.[2]

But all in vain. The bold plans on which so much thought and money had been lavished, and which were to be so largely incorporated into British policy during the next twenty years, were either derided as unworkable by the Tories or calmly annexed by the Labour party, which once again demonstrated its capture of the Radical tradition. Its election programme promised immediate measures to deal with unemployment, including housing and slum clearance, electrification, new roads and bridges, afforestation, and assisted emigration; insisted on the need to restore the depressed industries and increase working-class purchasing power; and also promised a foreign policy based on the League, disarmament, and peace. Socialism was neither mentioned nor implied; even with a clear majority the party would not promise any measure of nationalization except in the case of the mines.

Baldwin, who had been deftly dodging the safeguarding demands of his back-benchers, firmly rejected heroic remedies of the Lloyd George type, and insisted that the unemployment problem would solve itself in the end. His government had done its best for five

---

[1] The greater part of the fund was spent in supporting the 512 candidates. What remained after the 1929 election was reduced by losses on investments resulting from the economic crisis. The Lloyd George family group broke away from the party in 1931 and again withdrew the financial support of the fund. W. B. Gwyn, pp. 238–9.

[2] Asa Briggs, *Seebohm Rowntree*, pp. 197–211; Frank Owen, *Tempestuous Journey*, pp. 707–12; T. Jones, *Lloyd George*, pp. 225–31; Harrod, pp. 374–6.

years. Could it not be trusted to do as well in future? The country did not altogether disagree with him. The general election took place on 30 May 1929, after dissolution on the 10th; and in spite of the tremendous effort of Lloyd George and the Liberals the Conservatives polled the greatest number of votes—8,664,000 as compared with eight million in 1924. The Liberals indeed added over 2 million to their total votes (polling 5,301,000) but it was the Labour party with a total poll of 8,365,000 which did best in practice. As usual the seats did not correspond very accurately to the voting figures. The final result was 289 Labour, 260 Conservative, and 58 Liberal seats.

There is much to be said for the view that by their onslaught the Liberals weakened the Tories without helping themselves; the electors who wanted a change preferred in the main to turn to Labour. Defeat again seemed to have made no difference to Baldwin's hold on his colleagues. Amery remarked ironically in his diary, after the cabinet had agreed to immediate resignation, 'We all parted very happily, voting ourselves the best government there has ever been, and full of genuine affection for S.B.'[1]

6. SECOND LABOUR GOVERNMENT

It was the custom in after years to say that the second Labour government's minority position prevented the adoption of any bold left-wing measures. But in fact Labour's election programme had not promised any bold left-wing measures. And although its extensive plans for public works and economic expansion had echoed the Lloyd Georgeite objectives, its activities in office fell far short even of the point at which the Liberals would have objected to its boldness. MacDonald agreed to form a government on 5 June 1929. Apart from George Lansbury, he chose his cabinet colleagues from the right wing of the party, and he was as anxious as he had been in 1924 to show that they were able and willing to undertake the full responsibilities of a national government.[2] The principle of continuity in policy was fully accepted, with the desire to achieve the same broad ends as their predecessors, if with better judgment and vision. The dependence of domestic recovery on tranquillity abroad remained axiomatic.

[1] Amery, vol. II, p. 501.
[2] Lansbury was sure that 'they—that is, the Nabobs' did not want him; 'if they were really sensible they would send me to Russia'. R. Postgate, *The Life of George Lansbury*, p. 245.

The domestic scene soon worsened, but there was noticeably more competition for the Foreign Office than for the home departments. MacDonald told Lord Stamfordham on 4 June that he had offered to go to the Foreign Office himself and give up the premiership, but his colleagues were not agreeable. He was still determined, however, to play an active part in the shaping of foreign policy and for that reason would have liked to send his good friend J. H. Thomas, with whom he could work easily, to the Foreign Office. This was prevented by Arthur Henderson's flat refusal to take any office than that of Foreign Secretary, with a resulting legacy of ill-feeling between him and Thomas.[1] The Conservatives shared MacDonald's doubts as to Henderson's ability and application; Thomas, in spite of his rôle of professional wag and rough diamond, was thought to be sounder and more adroit. The office which Henderson firmly refused was that of Lord Privy Seal with responsibility for employment policy. At MacDonald's request Thomas accepted this rather thankless task.

The government's short term of office came to be so thoroughly associated in the public mind with its abortive attempts to handle the economic crisis in 1931 that its earlier record tends to be forgotten. It had, however, a fair record of achievement in foreign affairs before things began to change so radically in 1930. MacDonald was concerned about the tensions in Anglo-American relations, which he was determined to handle himself. British stubbornness in the 1927 naval discussions was dismissed by many left-wing critics as proof of deficient responsiveness to the moral leadership of the United States, which they still firmly believed in in spite of its obvious combination with extreme forms of isolationism. The naval issues are discussed elsewhere, in their Commonwealth setting.[2] There was not the slightest doubt that only the acceptance of the substance of the American conditions would remove the strain, and a fresh start was facilitated by President Hoover's election and the change of government in Britain.[3] There was soon talk of a visit by MacDonald to meet the new President in person. The Americans preferred to delay the visit until a basis of compromise had been worked out, but it took place, after

[1] Nicolson, p. 435; Snowden, *Autobiography,* vol. II, pp. 763–7.
[2] See pp. 301–3 below.
[3] On 22 April 1929 Hugh Gibson, the U.S. delegate to the preparatory disarmament conference, said that a yardstick formula 'was ready in the President's safe': *Documents on British Foreign Policy 1919–1939* (B.D.), 2nd ser., I, no. 6.

MacDonald had been left to invite himself, in October 1929. It was a great personal triumph for him, although on the technical plane he and Hoover were each mainly concerned in their talks at Rapidan on 6 October and elsewhere with evading fresh concessions to the other. MacDonald made several public speeches, nearly all extempore, and was much praised for tact, vigour, and manly diplomacy. This favourable opinion was confirmed by his conciliatory and effective chairmanship of the London naval conference in 1930.[1] In the same year another imperial conference, and the first of the Indian Round Table Conferences, enabled him to shine in a similar rôle.[2]

In other spheres of external policy too the government had some early successes. The new Chancellor of the Exchequer, Philip Snowden, astonished the world and perhaps himself in August 1929 by the undiplomatic vigour with which he demanded a fairer distribution of annuities under the Young Plan. There was no doubt that the British were worse off to the extent of over £4 million as compared with the allocations under the Spa percentages, but as usual a graceful concession on her part was expected to sweeten the ungraciousness of others. By the end of August he had secured about 83 per cent of the amount that he was demanding, although mainly as the result of German, rather than French or Italian, concessions. But as Dr. Schacht remarked in 1931, it was not of decisive importance to Germany whether it was 40 billion or 40·4 billion marks that she was unable to pay.[3]

In these matters Henderson as Foreign Secretary had shown some diffidence in asserting his own views, although he accepted more wholeheartedly, and perhaps more uncritically, than MacDonald the three cardinal postulates of Labour foreign policy: disarmament, the eschewing of nationalist advantage against the common good, and the strengthening of the 'constructive machinery of peace' through the League of Nations.[4] He was a capable administrator, shrewd and reliable and down-to-earth in his hand-

[1] R. H. Ferrell, *American Diplomacy in the Great Depression* (New Haven, 1957), pp. 73–83; M. I. Cole, ed., *Beatrice Webb's Diaries, 1924–1932* (1956), p. 223; R. Bassett, *1931, Political Crisis* (1958), pp. 36–7.
[2] See p. 317 below.
[3] Hjalmar Schacht, *The End of Reparations* (1931), p. 100. Cf. Snowden, *Autobiography*, vol. II, pp. 779–91.
[4] Cf. the comments of H. R. Winkler, J.M.H., *op.cit.*, pp. 253–8, and his essay on 'Arthur Henderson' in *The Diplomats, 1919–1939* (ed. G. A. Craig and F. Gilbert, Princeton, 1953), pp. 311–37.

ling of business; as long as the basic postulates did not conflict too noticeably with his approach to immediate issues he was always sure of his ground. He undertook the resumption of relations with Russia, although without any great enthusiasm, and the Soviet government was inclined to haggle over details, probably relying on the more left-wing elements in the Labour party to force Henderson's hand. But by the end of September 1929 the Soviet negotiator, Dovgalevsky, had given the indispensable undertaking against propaganda, although nothing else; an exchange of ambassadors followed. The rest was anti-climax; as the British government was not prepared to grant a loan to the U.S.S.R., the Soviet authorities in the circumstances showed little interest in the development of Anglo-Soviet trade. A commercial agreement on a most-favoured-nation basis was, however, signed on 16 April 1930.[1]

Henderson also handled the personal issue of Lord Lloyd's dismissal in July 1929 with some adroitness. As High Commissioner of Egypt Lloyd had proved himself almost the last of the great proconsular agents, and there was a long record of differences between him and Chamberlain and the Foreign Office which made protest on his behalf in the Commons difficult, although Churchill gallantly attempted it. Henderson scored something of a parliamentary triumph in defending his action, and embarked hopefully on the negotiation of a new treaty with Egypt. He was prepared, against MacDonald's wishes, to give Egypt a limited foothold in the Sudan, but a draft treaty on these lines negotiated with Mohammed Mahmud Pasha was rejected by the Wafd under Nahas Pasha, who won a clear victory in an election on this issue in December 1929. After this there were further negotiations in London which were broken off in May 1930, primarily over the issue of an independent Sudan.[2]

So on the whole the new government had not made too bad a start in the foreign field, and it had retained Liberal support. Moreover it had found time, in spite of its preoccupation with unemployment, for one or two useful pieces of domestic legislation. One was the 1930 Housing Act, which encouraged slum-clearing projects. Another was the Coal Mines Act of 1930, which introduced successful plans for restricting output and stabilizing wages, and

[1] D. N. Lammers, 'The Second Labour Government and the Restoration of Relations with Soviet Russia, 1929', *Bulletin*, Institute of Historical Research, May 1964.
[2] C. F. Adam, *Life of Lord Lloyd* (1948), pp. 218–22; cf. Lloyd's *Egypt since Cromer* 1934), vol. II.

abortive plans for increasing efficiency by amalgamation.[1] On this occasion Lloyd George decided to lead his Liberal followers into the opposition lobby, and was given a dressing-down, as effective as it was unexpected, by the young Welsh phenomenon, Aneurin Bevan. The stubborn conservatism of the mineowners over amalgamation was partially relieved by further legislation in 1936 and 1938, but not in time to make much difference before the war. The Agricultural Marketing Act of 1931 showed a somewhat similar predilection for monopolistic, price-raising schemes and was effective only in the case of hops; but it was followed by more ambitious plans for potatoes, milk, and pigs in 1933.[2] We shall discuss some of these developments in section 5 of chapter 6. These bills did nothing to compensate for complete failure over unemployment.

The manifold effects of the world economic crisis, inaugurated or at least symbolized by the collapse of the New York stock market in October 1929 and the elaboration of the high Hawley-Smoot tariff system between May 1929 and June 1930, were followed by a wave of tariff increases and bank failures round the world, and were reflected in the further decline of British exports and ever rising unemployment.[3] The out-of-work increased from just over a million in June 1929 to double that figure a year later. The restoration of stable political conditions abroad as the indispensable condition of a flourishing world economy remained the objective of Mac-Donald's government as it had been of Baldwin's. But the party had promised a rapid reduction in unemployment figures in its election manifesto, and the two opposition parties as well as the left wing of Labour demanded quick results. To achieve this end J. H. Thomas had been given the assistance of George Lansbury, the First Commissioner of Works, Tom Johnston, Under-Secretary of State for Scotland, and Sir Oswald Mosley, the new Chancellor of the Duchy of Lancaster. Thomas after some rather light-hearted bravado and promises of a 'complete cure' worked hard at the task, but with no success.

The cabinet felt that it must endorse the Treasury view that public works' schemes should be undertaken only if they were

[1] W. H. B. Court, 'Problems of the British Coal Industry between the Wars', *The Economic History Review*, 1945, vol. XV, pp. 13–18.
[2] Youngson, pp. 98–100, 116; J. H. Jones, G. Cartwright, and P. H. Guénault, *The Coal Mining Industry*, chap. 6.
[3] J. K. Galbraith, *The Great Crash, 1929* (1955).

financially self-supporting. This led to the breach with Mosley, who put before the cabinet early in 1930 plans for a bolder programme ignoring financial restraints, and echoing the Lloyd George panaceas. It was rejected in May, and Mosley resigned. He had much sympathy and support among the rank and file, and at the Llandudno conference of the party in October 1930 James Maxton in a motion regretted the government's failure to apply the bold unemployment policy outlined in *Labour and the Nation*. MacDonald's eloquence ensured its defeat: but the problem remained unsolved.

6

CRISIS AND RECOVERY

1. LABOUR ABDICATES

WITH the beginning of the nineteen-thirties we enter a period of great change throughout the world, and for Great Britain a period of constant and controversial improvisations in policy. The world economic crisis and its political repercussions saw the collapse of widespread hopes of a return, even if in an improved and somewhat disguised form, to the older stability. The new age meant not only the discarding throughout the world of many political inhibitions with sweeping programmes of political expansion, state planning, and revolutionary ideology. It also meant, even for states which had no desire at all for innovation, the failure of the self-regulating market and monetary systems which in the past had given them a deceptive sense of security and self-sufficiency. They showed their disillusionment with a policy of high and often ill-judged economic nationalism and protectionism which in itself contributed much to the shaping of this unwelcome new era.

In Great Britain at any rate there was no adventurous mood. The conservative impulse of the nineteen-twenties had failed in policy but not in public appeal. If the masses were prepared to give support to a strong government, it was in the hope that with a 'doctor's mandate' it would end the crisis, rather than create new ones. This perhaps explains why the National government in Britain after the autumn of 1931 was to be assailed so continuously, so violently, and yet on the whole so unsuccessfully by its critics at home and abroad.

By the end of 1930, if not earlier, it had become clear to Snowden and MacDonald that the economic depression had developed into a world crisis of such intensity as to rule out the usual palliatives. They were thus faced with a double problem: that of carrying out whatever drastic steps were needed at home, and of making the contribution which Britain was traditionally expected to make to the amelioration of conditions abroad. Henderson and the Foreign Office were already concerned at the threat to the position of the German Chancellor, Heinrich Brüning, and anxious to save his government from supersession by one of the extremist parties—the National Socialists, the People's Party, the Stahlhelm or the Communists—who had little loyalty to the Weimar régime and its international obligations. The need for economic aid to Germany and Austria, French reluctance to do anything for Germany without political guarantees which would have meant political suicide for Brüning, the lack of progress in Franco-Italian naval discussions, chilly relations with Moscow, deadlock in the Indian and dis-armament discussions, and forebodings of financial disaster in a dozen foreign capitals—these were all problems that called for effective British initiative at a moment when the Labour govern-ment's shaky domestic position made any initiative problematical.[1] At home the continued steep rise in the unemployment figures meant that a symptom of depression was becoming a major factor.

The severity of the world economic crisis is not to be ascribed to any one cause. It was a cumulative process resulting from the dramatic collapse of a great inflationary boom in a world which lacked the reserves—political, economic, and emotional—to take such a crisis in its stride. Under more normal (or at least pre-1914) conditions the downward movement of a business cycle would be expected to continue until the delicate processes of supply and demand had produced a more or less automatic recovery. Over-production as a result of decreasing demand would be followed by a lowering of prices to meet competition, by restriction of output and of raw material purchases, by unemployment, a fall in wages and profits, and a tendency for investors to hold back and for manu-facturers to use up stocks. Then there would be a revival as the fall in price began to tempt the consumer again and the fall in interest rates offered cheap capital for new enterprises. But this was a cyclone rather than a cycle. By June 1931, perhaps earlier, it had become brutally obvious that the corrective effects and traditional expedients for meeting a slump were not operating. When contemporaries

[1] B.D., II (ii), nos. 51, 158, 205, etc.

began to seek explanations they differed, and they differed even more as to remedies. The United Kingdom, although not the worst hit country, was in many respects the one most gravely concerned with this diagnosis because of her vital involvement with the structure of world finance and trade.

It was generally conceded that there was no longer a self-adjusting process of revival. Economic nationalism and a strong tendency in most countries to multiply state controls were both a symptom and a cause of this inelasticity. There was no longer, as in pre-war days, an essentially free market in which capitalist and business forces could, painfully but on their own initiative, work out their own salvation or damnation. But this did not mean that a planned and internationally-controlled economy was as yet accepted as being either practicable or inevitable or desirable. On the one hand it could be argued that wholly abnormal political conditions resulting from the war were inhibiting the natural flow of capital, on the other that much of the trouble was due to the increased economic activity of states in supporting, more or less willingly, the mono-polistic influence of international cartels and labour organizations. At the time it did not seem necessary to believe that these rigidities of the labour market and cartel prices were the inevitable outcome of modern technical conditions, and it was recognized that they could not survive without the direct or indirect assistance of the state.[1]

The political repercussions of the crisis in the United Kingdom turned largely on this issue. By the end of 1930 the numbers of registered unemployed in Great Britain had risen to 2,660,000, with a correspondingly onerous burden on the Exchequer. But the slump had had practically no effect on wage rates, which had hardly fallen at all since 1924 in spite of the decline in the demand for labour. Industrial profits indeed fell by 16 per cent in 1930, as compared with a fall of only one-half per cent in wages.[2] Wage rates were maintained at this level partly because the trade unions refused to accept the economist's bleak proposition that the price of labour should vary with the demand, partly because, with the postwar development of unemployment insurance, the unions were no longer concerned, as they had been before 1914, with the main-

---

[1] L. Robbins, *The Great Depression* (1934), pp. 59–61; Sir A. Salter, *Recovery* (1932), pp. 22–31; for later views, A. J. Youngson, *The British Economy 1920–1957*, chap. III; S. Pollard, *The Development of the British Economy, 1914–1950*, chap. IV (6).
[2] H. V. Hodson, *Slump and Recovery, 1929–1937* (1938), p. 57; cf. Robbins, p. 82.

tenance of their own unemployed.[1] On the contrary they had every reason to press the government for more. Keynes's theory had not yet provided an escape from this impasse. On coming into office Labour had increased the rates of benefit payable to the unemployed and transferred the cost of transitional benefit from the Insurance Fund to the Exchequer. These increases had not satisfied the trade unions and left-wing elements of the party, but they had reached a figure which, with the increase of unemployment, made a heavy budget deficit inevitable.

The 'disequilibrium' of the labour market was accompanied by a parallel disequilibrium in the money market. Here too the causes were in some dispute, the remedies a matter of sometimes quite passionate controversy. Since 1925 and the return to the gold standard the attempt to reestablish London's position as a centre of world finance had had a precarious success, but always with the fear that its resources would prove inadequate to meet a major drain. Between 1925 and 1929 Britain's monetary gold reserve showed a net increase of only £7 million (to £719m.), as compared with an increase of £565 million in France (to £1,631m.); it has been shown that of the six European countries which had stabilized their currencies at the pre-war level in the 1920s she alone was unable to regain an export level at least as high as that prevailing before the return to the old parity.[2] Even during the period of prosperity from 1925 to 1929 there was much cause for uneasiness, which increased when the withdrawal of American funds after 1928 threw on London the main responsibility for financing Europe. There were a number of reasons for the uncertainties of the British position. The most obvious perhaps was that her share of world trade had been falling since 1925 and her income from exports, visible and invisible, was no longer sufficient to give her the ample surpluses for foreign investment which had been the basis of her financial strength before the war. There was also a serious drop in the net income from investment overseas as the world slump after 1929 led to the falling off of dividend payments, to governmental defaults and the like. But the importance of London as a great financial centre remained in the sense that large balances were held there,

---

[1] 'It is one of the consequences of unemployment insurance in the form in which it existed during that period that it increased the rigidity of wages. In a period when the equilibrium of wages tends to fall this means disequilibrium in the labour market.' Robbins, p. 84.

[2] A. Loveday, *Britain and World Trade* (1931), p. 158.

and were coming and going all the time in the normal course of international business, yielding in the process a useful profit. Unfortunately a dangerously high proportion of these deposits were of a short-term character and liable to be withdrawn at any moment; this preference of the foreign investor for short-term deposits was a phenomenon which appears to have been, in part at least, a direct result of political instability in the post-war world. In these circumstances a run on sterling could after a certain point leave the City unable to meet its obligations.[1]

The Labour government, although it showed no taste for adventurous solutions of these problems, was anxiously aware of their existence, and only too ready to give the experts the chance to talk. On 4 November 1929, Snowden announced the setting-up of a Committee of Enquiry into Finance and Industry, with Lord Macmillan as chairman; on 22 January 1930, MacDonald announced the setting-up of an Economic Advisory Council under his own chairmanship; in June 1930, following a suggestion (which the Conservatives rejected) by MacDonald in May that a three-party committee should examine the unemployment problem, Labour and Liberal met on a two-party basis, and in December 1930 this was replaced by a Royal Commission under Judge Holman Gregory. Later there came the May committee. One reason for all this consultation was that a minority government must somehow reinforce its authority with either all-party support or with some form of independent advice; unfortunately these extended discussions did not even produce agreement within the Labour party itself. Nor was there unanimity outside Labour circles.

Snowden remained grimly loyal to the existing orthodoxies, with faith in free trade, hope for sterling and a statutory limit to charity: Bevin and Citrine, who represented the trade unions on the Economic Advisory Committee, supported with increasing confidence the case for state sponsored schemes of economic expansion, in general accord with the ideas of G. D. H. Cole, J. M. Keynes, and R. H. Tawney. MacDonald as chairman and J. H. Thomas, who was often present, supported Snowden, and the industrialists' representatives, Sir Arthur Balfour, Sir John Cadman, and Sir Andrew Duncan, similarly set their face against anything but the traditional virtues of state economy, cost cutting, and wage reduction in the effort to restore the export trade. In July 1930 MacDonald appointed

[1] Hodson, pp. 24–8.

a small committee of economists (Keynes, Hubert Henderson, Professors Pigou and Robbins, and Sir Josiah Stamp) to review the economic condition of the country and make recommendations; it also could not agree, for while three members favoured a revenue tariff and protection for the iron and steel trade, Pigou and Robbins were opposed, and Robbins put in a spirited minority report of one against the proposal. The Macmillan committee, which was holding more searching discussions on much the same problems and at much the same time, found Keynes active in expounding his views on the monetary crisis and its possible solutions, although in the committee's report, which he played a large part in drafting, the abandonment of the gold standard was not given much attention. There was, nevertheless, sufficient to persuade Bevin, who followed the discussions closely, that abandonment was inevitable.[1]

But all this expert talk did nothing to help Snowden in the problem of a heavy budget deficit that was looming before him at the beginning of 1931. A Treasury representative, Sir Richard Hopkins, warned the royal commission on unemployment insurance that continued state borrowing on the existing vast scale for this 'unproductive' purpose and without adequate provision for repayment by the Unemployment Insurance Fund would speedily damage belief abroad as to the stability of the British financial system.[2]

With the opposition in its own ranks to any economies in unemployment pay or the social services, the government could hope only for all-party agreement on an economy programme, for which the Conservatives, although helpful enough in some directions, were not yet ready. The Tory leadership had chosen to campaign for imperial preference in the previous summer, but reservations as to duties on food precluded any genuine deal with the Dominions. For this reason the press lords, Beaverbrook and Rothermere, decided that Baldwin must go; and they said so sufficiently loudly to rally the party to his support. But the criticism continued, and when Baldwin found himself in political agreement with Mac-Donald's conciliatory attitude towards the Indian nationalists, Churchill gave open expression to another strand of criticism by resigning from the shadow cabinet on 27 January 1931. By the

[1] Harrod, p. 427; Bullock, pp. 436–7.
[2] He gave similar testimony to the Macmillan committee. P. Snowden, *Autobiography*, vol. II, pp. 890–1; R. Bassett, *Nineteen Thirty One, Political Crisis* (1958), pp. 43–4.

beginning of March 1931 Baldwin had been convinced by his most trusted lieutenants that the party had turned against him; but he was persuaded to stay on pending the results of a by-election in St. George's, Westminster. He bestirred himself and denounced the press lords on 17 March; and the Baldwin candidate, Duff Cooper, decisively beat his Tory opponent a few days later. Baldwin owed much to Neville Chamberlain's support; and Chamberlain owed his own succession to the leadership six years later to this domestic crisis. But in the meantime the party had little to offer in the way of constructive opposition.[1]

Nor was the Liberal voice unequivocal; it was by no means certain, in spite of Lloyd George's insistence, that there was a majority for the carrying out of an agreed programme. Agreement on what? Asquith's former supporters distrusted the Lloyd George-ites, and some prominent members of the party, including Sir John Simon, were more in sympathy with Tory plans for a tariff than with the traditional Liberal panacea of free trade. Simon, Ernest Brown, and Sir Robert Hutchinson repudiated the party whip in June 1931.[2] However, a Liberal proposal of 11 February 1931 for the setting up of a small and independent committee to advise on reductions in the national expenditure was accepted by all three parties, although twenty-one Labour back-benchers voted against it. This was the origin of the May committee. It consisted of two representatives of each of the three major parties, with a chairman, Sir George May, recently secretary of the Prudential Assurance Company. Snowden fell ill early in March, and after a severe operation was not able to present his budget until 27 April. But this turned out to be an interim affair without substantial extra taxation. It seemed good sense to wait in the hope that the reports of the Gregory and May committees would solve his essential problem by giving him the indispensable minimum of all-party tolerance. A second budget would then follow.[3]

Unhappily, things worked out the other way. If Snowden's interim budget in April had contained some anticipations of austerity to come there might have been greater confidence abroad in the government's ability to cope. But there was no such sign. During

[1] The best account is Feiling's, pp. 177–87; cf. Duff Cooper, *Old Men Forget*, pp. 170–76; Churchill, *The Gathering Storm*, pp. 26–8; G. M. Young, *Stanley Baldwin*, pp. 142–63.
[2] T. Jones, *Lloyd George*, pp. 232–4.
[3] Snowden, vol. II, pp. 900–16.

the early summer the general wave of alarm as to the safety of foreign investments which followed the banking collapses in Austria, Germany, and Hungary, and which in any case would have led to withdrawals from London, was heightened by doubts as to the stability of the British system itself.

After the Credit-Anstalt's inability to meet its liabilities became known early in May 1931 there were attempts by the Austrian government, the Austrian National Bank, and the house of Roth-schild to supply it with funds, and a credit was granted by the Bank for International Settlement on 29 May. But this checked only tem-porarily a drain which had now been transferred to the Austrian government itself; and it at once had repercussions on German finances, heavily involved in the Austrian collapse. Foreign creditors, particularly French and American, renewed their withdrawal of balances from Berlin; this process accelerated until by 20 June the Reichsbank, in spite of having raised its discount rate to 7 per cent, lost Rm. 150 million in little over twenty-four hours. President Hoover's proposal at this point of a moratorium for one year on all inter-governmental debts, including reparations, would have had greater chance of success if its practical details had been worked out in advance; for it was impossible for any French government to survive the hostility of the Chamber to an unqualified surrender of even the 'unconditional' reparations. The British government accepted the proposal at once, but the French found it necessary to make conditions, and while the bargaining went on the psycho-logical effect of the proposal was largely lost. So the drain, still in the main due to the action of foreign creditors who needed their funds for other purposes, or who were coming to distrust its safety in Germany, recommenced, and was followed in July by an even more alarming development—a collapse of public confidence inside Germany, and the beginning of a flight from the mark. When on 13 July the failure of the Danatbank, one of the most important in Germany, precipitated a panic-stricken run on other German houses the German government closed all Berlin banks except the Reichs-bank, and German assets were frozen.[1]

It would seem that MacDonald and his advisers were rather more concerned with the German position than with their own during the second half of July 1931; partly perhaps because the dangerous

[1] Hodson, p. 68; E. W. Bennett, *Germany and the Diplomacy of the Financial Crisis, 1931* 1963), chaps. 7, 8; B.D. II (ii), nos. 3, 55, 62, 69, 187, etc.

political implications of the German crisis were more obvious than the monetary storm that was gathering over London, partly because confidence in the capacity of the British money market to take any situation in its stride was still unshaken. It is true that there had been no very great cause for satisfaction at the state of Britain's external economic relations for many years, but this had bred a certain familiarity with adversity and had left the British much less prone to despair than the buoyant Americans, facing in bewilderment the unbelievable end to perpetual prosperity. So it is primarily of the continental crisis that we hear during July. And it was serious enough. There were first of all the anxious discussions over the terms of the Hoover Moratorium, in which Henderson and Stimson drew together in their impatience with French policy. On 16 June the Bank of England, without informing Henderson, advanced £4,300,000 to provide the Austrian government with funds for guaranteeing the foreign liabilities of the Credit-Anstalt; Henderson was not opposed to this move in principle but felt that he had been deprived of a useful bargaining weapon in negotiations with the French over the unwelcome plans for an Austro-German customs union. A week later the Bank contributed a quarter share of a $100 million dollar credit to the German Reichsbank; this was due to expire on 16 July, but by this stage withdrawal had become impossible. Dr. Luther, the Reichsbank president, desperately seeking help in foreign capitals, had to be told on 9 July that Great Britain could not provide a long-term credit; the possibility of a loan in Paris was made to depend on an undertaking to refrain from demands for treaty revision, and a telegram from the Nazi leaders on 21 July made it clear that they would not recognize such terms. Brüning came to a conference with a remarkable array of distinguished foreigners in London (20–23 July) to appeal to the other powers for help, but without success. On 27 July Henderson and MacDonald visited Berlin: they were well received, they did their best to counter the chilly disapproval of Paris, there were conferences and an impressive speech by MacDonald, but no loan.[1]

Even now the sense of really urgent crisis was lacking in London. When the May committee's report was published on 31 July, a few hours after the House of Commons had adjourned for the summer recess, a monetary crisis had been added to the problem of domestic

[1] B.D. *ibid.*, nos. 221–31.

economies.[1] A run on sterling had begun; withdrawals had been heavy, at the average rate of nearly £2½ millions a day, throughout the second half of the month. But the situation did not appear quite sufficiently desperate to necessitate the curtailment of summer holidays. On 31 July Snowden warned the Commons that the report of the May committee would come as a shock to public opinion both at home and abroad, and on the same day MacDonald appointed a 'Cabinet Economy Committee' including himself, Snowden, J. H. Thomas, Henderson, and William Graham. Its task was to consider how far the May committee proposals for meeting an anticipated deficit of some £120 millions could be carried out, but it was not intended at first that it should meet before 25 August. Then the holidays began—MacDonald went to Lossiemouth, Neville Chamberlain also to Scotland, Hoare to Cromer, Baldwin to Aix-les-Bains. But all were within call. Snowden stayed in London, where the officials were watching the situation anxiously.

The crisis finally became a matter of dramatic urgency when the two aspects, domestic and foreign, were fused, and it became generally understood that the financial landslide could be arrested only by a speedy balancing of the budget. But this did not happen (although the possibility had been obvious for some time to such knowledgeable people as Neville Chamberlain and the civil servants) until the second week of August. During July the withdrawal of money by foreign creditors could still be regarded as due primarily to need abroad rather than to doubt as to its safety in London. One of the main causes was seasonal: the Paris market was short of funds every summer as a result of French Treasury and sinking fund operations and tended to draw on its foreign balances.[2] Other factors of course were already operating—including precautionary withdrawals by nervous creditors who realized that London was seriously embarrassed by the central European drain and freezing arrangements, and this naturally increased the likelihood of the event which it was intended to anticipate. Nevertheless, although the loss of some £34 million between 13 and 30 July had not been checked by the increase of the bank rate to 4½ per cent, it was hoped that the storm could be weathered with the help of credits from the

---

[1] The Report of the Macmillan committee, published on 13 July, and the Interim Report of the Insurance and Unemployment committee of 4 July, had already spread gloom.

[2] The Bank of England lost £33 million in 1929 (June–September), and £11 million in 1930 (May–July) for this reason. Hodson, p. 71.

Bank of France and the Federal Reserve Bank of New York of £25 million each. The arrangement was announced on 1 August, and seemed to have had the desired effect; for the moment the drain checked, and the Bank actually gained gold during the next few days. But the withdrawals started again. Drastic measures to restore confidence were now imperative. As the Bank of England's own credit in Paris and New York was exhausted, soundings were taken in New York with a view to the raising of a government loan and it was made clear that a substantial sum would be forthcoming only in return for satisfactory assurances about the country's financial position.

So the budget must be balanced. A warning to MacDonald, apparently on 8 August, of the gravity of the situation brought him to London on the night of 10–11 August; he had been delayed before this by talks in Scotland with Mr. Stimson. Baldwin was called back from his journey to Aix-les-Bains, Chamberlain from Scotland, and Sir Herbert Samuel, in Lloyd George's absence through illness, was called in to speak for the Liberals. The problem now was to settle the painful details of drastic economies, and to find a government which could carry the programme in Parliament and the country. Twelve days of frustrating discussion made it clear that this task would not be carried out by the Labour party.

August 1931 was one of those turning points of our recent history—along with July 1914, September 1938, and November 1956—in which the reputations of British ministers seem to depend to an extraordinary degree on a meticulous examination of every facet of their activity. The personal records and recollections of most of the leading actors and many minor ones are available.[1] In fact, the course of events is not really in question; motive, ultimately a matter of subjective judgment, provides what basis there is for controversy. Briefly it can be said that the crisis at the cabinet level went through three stages. First, the cabinet economy committee held several meetings between 12 and 18 August, and at the same time (on 13 August) MacDonald and Snowden explained to Chamberlain, Baldwin, and Samuel that a comprehensive list of economies, based on, but not identical with, those suggested in the

---

[1] They include those of Snowden, Henderson, Addison, Dalton, Samuel, Neville Chamberlain, Hoare, Amery, Bevin, and King George V. They were analysed in some detail by the late Reginald Bassett, whose extreme accuracy has baffled but apparently not convinced MacDonald's surviving critics. His book, *Nineteen Thirty-One, Political Crisis*, is the fullest available account of the negotiations.

May report, was being urgently prepared. Secondly, MacDonald
failed on the five critical days, 19–23 August, to find a programme
of economies which would satisfy the Labour ministers, the T.U.C.,
and the opposition leaders. Finally, on 23 and 24 August, after the
King had returned to London from Scotland early on the 23rd,
a series of discussions and meetings between him, MacDonald, and
the leaders of the two opposition parties led to the public announcement on the evening of the 24th of the formation of a National
government headed by MacDonald.

It was a courageous step, even if it was not taken without some
characteristic touches of self-pity and self-dramatization. He was
sixty-five. Perhaps the decision, which he obviously weighed with
the knowledge that it might be politically suicidal, was not unaffected by the consideration that he had not many more years of
active life before him. His critics among his former Labour
colleagues have consistently attributed his decision to vanity and
selfishness. G. D. H. Cole, who was by no means the most vitriolic,
could see no explanation of his conduct other than a growing
contempt for his own followers, a determination to keep them in
subordination, an inability to make up his mind on any question of
policy, and a set purpose of retaining office at any price.[1] Finally
reduced to the reiterated assertion that MacDonald betrayed the
party, these views are very much what we can always expect from a
party that had lost a leading figure; we can compare them with the
Conservative hostility to Churchill between 1906 and 1915 and
between 1931 and 1939, or the Liberal distrust of Lloyd George
after 1916. A party cannot commit suicide by admitting that the
rebel is right. Rebellion in the nature of things is a personal gesture;
personal ambition alone can explain the heinous sin of separation
from the party.

But these recriminations, by concentrating attention on Mac-
Donald's rôle, divert attention from the decisive event, which was
the collapse of the Labour ministers' resolution to cut the pay of the
unemployed. It is important to realize how near the cabinet came to
doing this. The cabinet economy committee put to the cabinet on
19 August provisional figures to meet the deficit (which was now
estimated, for the year April 1932–April 1933, at £170 million).

---

[1] G. D. H. Cole, *A History of the Labour Party from 1914*, pp. 254–8. Among strictly
contemporary works, that by L. Macneill Weir, *Tragedy of Ramsay MacDonald* (1938),
by MacDonald's parliamentary private secretary, is one of the most severe.

£78,575,000 was to be met by economies, and £88½ million by taxation. Among the economies, those in unemployment benefit were to produce a saving of £48½ million, made up of £28½ million on unemployment insurance and £20 million on transitional benefit; the rest were to come from reduction in teachers, service, and police pay amounting to £20,900,000, and other items amounting to £13,150,000. Harold Nicolson remarks that the news of the willingness of the committee to accept the odious necessity of a cut in unemployment benefit filled the hearts of Treasury officials with 'sweet, short-lived joy'.[1] The majority of the cabinet, after unhappy debate for nine hours on the 19th, accepted, 'provisionally' of course, all the proposed economies except that on transitional benefit, a problem which was referred to a sub-committee. Other expedients: debt conversion, reduction of allocations to the sinking fund, a revenue tariff, were discussed, and Snowden found that he had only five supporters in his uncompromising opposition to the last course. The impossibility of securing Liberal support for a tariff seems, however, to have prevented any further advocacy of this solution. Nevertheless, amid much that is tentative and uncertain, the acceptance by the majority of the cabinet of at least the £28 million cut in unemployment insurance is established, together with that of the other pay cuts for teachers and the rest.

Their nerve seems then to have been shaken by the General Council of the T.U.C., which after listening to MacDonald and Snowden on the afternoon of the 20th decided that they could not accept a single one of the Chancellor's proposals.[2] When the cabinet again discussed the problem on the 21st there was agreement that to accept dictation by an outside body such as the T.U.C. was impossible; nevertheless the minimum economy programme had now become the maximum, and the cabinet was not prepared to go substantially beyond what had been provisionally accepted on the 19th. This meant £56,375,000, leaving £133,635,000 to be raised by taxation, and although after a forceful intervention by Snowden they reluctantly agreed to ask the opposition leaders whether their support would be given if the figure were raised to £76 million (including some £12½ million from a 10 per cent cut in unemployment pay), they were finally, on the 23rd, unable to agree even when the opposition said yes.

[1] Nicolson, pp. 456–7.
[2] Citrine, pp. 281–6; Bullock, p. 483.

Thus it was that the second Labour government came to its rather sorry end. It put party before country, but only because it was able to persuade itself that the issue was a party one after all. The conviction that the economies would impose an unfair measure of sacrifice on these sections of the community that the party represented was never absent; it had been asserted explicitly in the minority report of the two Labour representatives on the May committee, and was no doubt shared by many of the Labour ministers. Given this assumption, it was an easy step to the conclusion that bankers, big business men, Tories, and even the Liberals were shrewdly creating or exaggerating a situation for their own class or party advantage. Snowden remarked impatiently in the spring that most of the Labour members had no ideas beyond soaking the super-tax payers. In his quarterly report to the Executive of the T.U.C. in August, Bevin said that the crisis was due to the City's practice of borrowing abroad on 'short term' and lending on 'long term'; and 'the City must not be saved at the expense of the working class and the poorest of our people'. The T.U.C.'s position was clear enough; as Citrine put it a fortnight later, 'for years we have been operating on the principle that the policy which has been followed since 1925 in this country, of contraction, contraction, contraction, deflation, deflation, deflation, must lead us all, if carried to its logical conclusion, to economic disaster'. Having taken a theoretical position as strongly defined as this they felt justified in disclaiming responsibility for the existing crisis.[1] The Labour ministers, while they seem to have accepted MacDonald's complaint that the General Council's views did nothing to meet the actual crisis, were not prepared to sponsor the economy programme if it meant a split in the party. This was probably the essential issue, although the conviction in the party that the infuriated electors would throw out the authors of the cuts no doubt helped.[2] They were still prepared to accept a £22 million cut in unemployment pay; even the proposed further 10 per cent cut was accepted by eleven members on the 23rd and opposed by only eight.[3] But they preferred to resign and to leave the Conservatives to take office rather than accept a breach in the cabinet and the party.

[1] Bullock, pp. 480–4; cf. V. L. Allen, pp. 250–8.
[2] R. D. Denman, *Political Sketches* (1948), pp. 4–6.
[3] These were the figures given by MacDonald to the King on the evening of 23 August: Nicolson, p. 464. Other versions give a minority of nine. Bassett thinks that twelve (including MacDonald) against nine is the soundest conclusion: *op. cit.*, pp. 139–40, for a full discussion.

They also preferred to stand together and fall together as an independent party rather than to enter a coalition. It was on these issues, and not on that of the 10 per cent cut, that MacDonald was in a minority. His most sympathetic biographer argues convincingly that he was moved primarily by a sense of duty, and was convinced that both the nature of the economic crisis and the reputation of the Labour party demanded a brief participation by Labour representatives in a National government. But the majority of the party, comforting themselves with the view that it was not a genuine national crisis at all, soon began to say that MacDonald had gone over to 'the enemy'. 'This was dirty, poisonous', wrote Henderson's biographer, paraphrasing the critics; 'he now proposed to head a Government composed of their bitter and lifelong political opponents.'[1]

2. NATIONAL GOVERNMENT AND THE DOCTOR'S MANDATE

Did the formation of the National government end a crisis, or create a new one? In fact it did both, and it is important to remember that nothing had been decided up to this point other than that the Labour cabinet was not prepared to accept the MacDonald–Snowden proposals. It does not follow that these proposals, even if they had been accepted by the government and by Parliament, would have met even the immediate difficulties of the gold drain; almost certainly they would not. Their purpose was to secure American and French credits of £80 million to meet the continuing withdrawal of funds from London. There was no certainty that it would prevent further withdrawals. Confidence in sterling was not re-established by the formation of the new government, even although it proceeded to put through the essentials of the Snowden programme, so there seems no reason why it should have been achieved by the old.

There were probably two basic, and partly contradictory, reasons for this continued lack of confidence. One was a spreading doubt abroad as to whether the country could any longer adapt itself to modern conditions. This was indeed to make a caricature of some of the virtues of the British economic system, whose managers were not devoid of new ideas in spite of an imperturbability which could easily be mistaken for mental ossification. Even continued adherence to the gold standard was not due to unawareness of the

[1] Bassett, pp. 344–51; Mary Hamilton, *Arthur Henderson*, pp. 384–6.

arguments for its abandonment; but Keynes himself, its principal critic in the past, held that, having retained, the country had better maintain it, since it involved the worldwide reputation of the London market and an obligation of honour to redeem at par in gold the large deposits accepted from foreigners.[1] Nor was the general unflappability of the Bank of England and the Treasury a sign of unawareness; it was admittedly a different matter with the chairmen of the joint stock banks and other practical banking experts who had seemed to the Macmillan committee to be totally unfamiliar with the most elementary textbook knowledge of economics.[2] But more specific was a doubt during these weeks as to whether, with the high expenditure on unemployment relief, static industries, the rigid wage level, and the permanent sense of strain in maintaining the traditional monetary policy, any British government could keep on the gold standard much longer. The publication of the reports of the Macmillan and May committees in July widely advertised the problems of the country rather than its ability to handle them boldly. The numerous signs of political resistance to economies, the general crisis talk in the press, and in September the Invergordon episode, all combined into a picture of a country sinking under burdens that it had not the courage or the strength to bear. Was England finished? At any rate, was gold? The foreign investor was taking no risks. The drain continued.

In these circumstances the National government acted on the assumption that its mission was to do whatever was necessary, without being tied to any stereotyped course. In practice, this meant that the Conservatives, being the dominant partners, took advantage of the situation to push through policies which were as bold as their ways of thinking allowed. The cabinet announced on 24 August did not indeed reveal the extent of their predominance for it included only four Conservatives (Baldwin, Neville Chamberlain, Cunliffe-Lister, and Hoare) together with four Labour members (MacDonald, Sankey, Snowden, and Thomas), and two Liberals (Samuel and Reading). But the extreme smallness of the National Labour contingent (fifteen members of Parliament, including the four ministers and Lord Amulree) and the relative smallness of the Liberal group, made them junior partners from the start, and critics did not fail to ask how far such a coalition could

---

[1] J. M. Keynes, *Essays in Persuasion* (1952), pp. 288–94.
[2] Harrod, pp. 414–5.

truly be called 'National'. Nevertheless, the term continued to be used by this essentially Tory administration; it probably conferred a certain vague additional authority, and under four successive prime ministers coalitions continued to lead the country through trials and tribulations until the electorate chose a new model in 1945. Liberals were all of the Lloyd George group, although he himself was too ill to join.[1] Of the eighteen ministerial appointments outside the cabinet, eight went to Conservatives, six to Liberals, and three to Labour. The Solicitor-General for Scotland, J. C. Watson, was described as 'non-party'. On 27 August the three directing bodies of the Labour movement—the National Executive of the Labour party, the Consultative Committee of the Parliamentary Labour party, and the General Council of the T.U.C.—issued a joint manifesto which finally repudiated all responsibility for, and connexion with, the new government. However, on the 28th the Treasury was able to announce that it had secured credits in Paris and New York, and it appeared that with the prospect of a balanced budget and a strong government prepared to put the finances of the country in order the movement of sterling might return to something like normal.

Snowden presented his emergency budget in the Commons on 10 September. To meet the estimated deficits (£74,679,000 on 31 March 1932; £170,000,000 a year later) income tax was to be raised from 4s 6d to 5s in the pound, surtax payments increased by 10 per cent, allocations for the sinking fund reduced from £52 million to £32·5 million, and indirect taxation increased by higher duties on beer, tobacco, petrol, and entertainment. This would leave some £70 million to be covered by economies in national expenditure, and these were set out in a National Economy Bill on which MacDonald opened the debate on the 11th. The economies followed closely the proposals put to the Labour cabinet. £56 million was to come from the promised cuts in service and police pay and teachers' salaries together with unemployment reductions, to which was added the much debated 10 per cent cut which would bring in the further £14 million. The new government had received a vote of confidence on 8 September by 309 votes to 249, and there was no doubt as to the passing of its financial programme; but before this could be done a fresh wave of foreign panic, reflected in further shocks to

[1] After a major operation late in July. His son Gwilym accepted the parliamentary secretaryship of the Board of Trade.

the London money market, pushed the government several stages towards a revised and more embracing conception of its responsibilities.[1]

When the National government was formed all the leaders, with varying degrees of finality, had insisted on its temporary character. On 28 August Baldwin had told a Conservative party meeting that its sole purpose was to pass legislation necessary to effect economy and balance the budget. MacDonald and Baldwin both visualized an early election, with the parties fighting independently. But this was on the assumption that after the passing of the legislation the immediate crisis would be over. Suppose it were not? Should the National government continue in office without an election to handle further phases of the 'emergency'? Should it, as a coalition government, fight an early election asking for a mandate to deal with the continuing crisis? The Liberals strongly urged the first course. They knew that with the Conservatives in the ascendant an election programme, on a coalition basis or not, would include a full tariff and result in divisions, isolation, or even extinction for the Liberal party. Many Conservatives wanted from the start to consolidate their position with an early election, and, party interests apart, could argue that without popular endorsement the economy programme could never be successfully enforced. Then came the renewed run on sterling. Withdrawals had been comparatively small in the first days of September. Trouble began again in Germany with the reopening of the Berlin stock exchange on 3 September; this soon affected the Amsterdam and Swiss markets, which had both invested heavily in Germany, and in the Netherlands also there were heavy falls in many long-term securities as a result of the operation of international speculators. The Dutch banks and other continental houses began to draw heavily on their balances in London, and on 15 September, just at the point when this new trend was becoming clear, there came the news of 'unrest' among the ratings at Invergordon.[2]

This was mainly a matter of bad publicity. The reductions in the pay of the armed services were real enough, but were accepted elsewhere without resistance, although no doubt with ample grumbling. At Plymouth, where the sailors were also dissatisfied, MacDonald himself went among them and explained the reasons

---

[1] Mowat, pp. 402–3; Bassett, pp. 222–46.
[2] Hodson, pp. 77–8.

for the cuts, with complete success. What happened at Invergordon was that on 13 and 14 September the men on shore leave were persuaded by agitators, who included some recognized Communists, to refuse to fall in for duty on the morning of the 15th. This passive resistance ended when the men complied with Admiralty instructions to sail the ships back to their home ports.[1] Some modifications of the pay cuts (none was to exceed 10 per cent) and the absence of disciplinary actions ended the naval crisis; but contemporary authorities seem to be agreed that foreign financiers were genuinely alarmed and in three days, from 15 to 18 September, a further £33 million were withdrawn. So, on Monday, 21 September, Great Britain went off the gold standard. The Treasury announced the suspension of that section of the Gold Standard Act of 1925 which required the Bank of England to sell gold at a fixed price. The necessary legislation was put through on the same day. The stock exchange closed for two days, and the bank rate was raised to 6 per cent.

If it had to be done, this was the best way to do it. Keynes, who on 19 September had gloomily denounced the budget and the economy bill as replete with folly and injustice, was now jubilant. Every possible effort, he wrote, to the limits of quixotry, had been made to maintain the value of money in the interest of foreign depositors, even at the risk of driving British trade almost to a standstill. In the course of a few weeks the Bank of England had paid out £200 million in gold or its equivalent at a time when the money which London had lent abroad was largely frozen. Now it was possible to plan the future realistically; the dry bones of industry were stirred; 'there are few Englishmen who do not rejoice at the breaking of our gold fetters'.[2] Englishmen, in reality, seemed singularly unconcerned, and there was bewilderment and considerable consternation abroad, even if, as Keynes believed, 'the claims of honour have been, in the judgment of the whole world, satisfied to the utmost'. The decision brought to an end the most urgent phase of the crisis, for it was at last possible to settle the domestic future of the country without the fear of immediate financial disaster. There were now two main issues before the country and the politicians: should there be an election, and should there be a tariff?

[1] Kenneth Edwards, *The Mutiny at Invergordon* (1937), pp. 180–5.
[2] J. M. Keynes, *Essays in Persuasion*, pp. 162, 288–9.

The crisis which led to the abandonment of the gold standard had, at the most, confirmed the case for an immediate general election; the argument that the government needed a clear mandate had already been widely canvassed. The fact that some Labour speakers, after rejecting the economies, also advocated an election shows their confidence that the electors would throw out the government programme; some were anticipating immense majorities.[1] The only obstacle (but at first a formidable one) was the unwillingness of both MacDonald and Samuel to go to the country on an agreed programme, which would inevitably be a Tory programme. In the course of negotiations inside the cabinet it began to dawn upon the Conservative leaders that MacDonald, far from being their camp follower, was still their master; a skilfully worded statement to the press on his behalf on 28 September, saying that he would not lend himself to the plans of any one party and wanted a 'doctor's mandate' giving 'a big united central block' authority to deal with the country's difficulties, ruled out controversial planks such as tariffs, raised him in some measure above all the parties, and made it impossible to displace him except by abandoning the 'National' platform altogether. His expulsion from the Labour party followed immediately. He was obviously intensely unhappy at the whole position, believing in his mission but disliking the prospect of a fight to smash the Labour party; but he accepted the need for the election and when after a week's deadlock it was agreed late on 5 October that each of the three parties in the National government should issue its own programme the way was clear for an immediate dissolution.[2]

There followed a remarkable victory for the National government. Polling day was on 27 October. It was a relatively quiet election, perhaps because the electorate had made up its mind well in advance. Perhaps for the same reason the total poll was less than in 1929. Labour lost nearly two million votes; their total (including 284,462 I.L.P. supporters) was 6,649,630. This compared with 11,978,745

[1] Mowat speaks of uneasiness abroad 'caused by Conservative efforts to work up an early general election' (p. 403). Bassett calls attention to 'the nature of the Opposition campaign and fears of its success at the polls' (p. 239). The latter would clearly be the disquieting factor to foreigners. Cf. A. Marwick, 'Middle Opinion in the Thirties', *E.H.R.*, April 1964, p. 289.

[2] Lloyd George refused on 8 October to support the Liberal party's decision to fight the election. Major Gwilym Lloyd George resigned on the same day. On the other hand, Simon announced on 3 October that he and fellow-thinking Liberal M.P.s were forming an organization in support of the government. Bassett, pp. 276–82; 290. Frank Owen, *Lloyd George*, pp. 712–20.

Conservatives, 1,403,102 Liberals, and 341,370 National Labour; a total of over 13,500,000 for the National government. The government secured 554 seats, including 473 Conservative; the Opposition 56 (Labour 46, Independent Labour 6, Independent Liberals 4).[1] The result had a tremendous effect abroad. Conscious of their own troubles, the Americans had been greatly impressed by the increase of the income tax to 5*s*, wrongly interpreting this as meaning that patriotic Englishmen had been asked to contribute 25 per cent of their entire incomes to national survival. The events of September, culminating in the Invergordon 'mutiny', had left doubts as to whether the people would accept this crushing burden. The overwhelming response seemed proof of the utmost patriotism and courage. No doubt many Englishmen thought the same.

3. THE BEGINNING OF RECOVERY

However, the honourable burial of the gold standard and meritorious acceptance of economies (which were opposed, it would seem, mainly by the Labour party stalwarts who as employed workers were least affected by them) left the central problem of the country's economic recovery untouched. This was the state of industry and in particular the continued depression in the basic export trades, which found its expression in the unemployment figures. These rose to the record level of 2,843,000 in the third quarter of 1932; it was only after this that a slow improvement began, and even in 1937 unemployment was still higher than it had been in 1929.

Thus the new government had no heaven-sent solution of the economic problem. What it did provide was confidence. With its powerful parliamentary position it could act; and if its actions were not so efficacious as had been hoped and expected they at least supplied tangible proof that something was being done. Although without the drama of Roosevelt's first moves in 1933 they satisfied the same uneasy popular thirst for activity. The ministry benefited from the contrast with the enforced inactivity of its predecessor, just as, in the later thirties, when the international situation and its desire for peace predisposed it to a waiting policy, it lost ground

[1] There were 72 Liberal M.P.s all told; but they were hopelessly divided into three groups, Samuelites and Simonites supporting the government, and four members of the Lloyd George family group, which controlled the Lloyd George fund. Ramsay Muir, chairman of the National Liberal Federation, explained in *The Times* on 10 October that the sudden withdrawing of funds immediately before the election had made it difficult to contest any but safe seats. W. B. Gwyn, pp. 239–40.

before robust critics demanding action. The new government was also involved in its first year in a range of external problems—India, Manchuria, the German situation and the disarmament conference, the Statute of Westminster, Ottawa conference, and Irish land annuities—which helped to divert attention from the pressing domestic scene. So the process of economic recovery, which we shall sketch briefly in the remainder of this chapter, could proceed without undue political controversy.

When Parliament opened on 10 November 1931 the small Labour opposition, noisy in conscious self-encouragement, greeted Mac-Donald's vague and woolly opening with ribald laughter, and it was deduced that the government was not very clear as to what it intended to do next. But Churchill reminded the house with gusto that the election had given an overwhelming vote against free trade (a change which he frankly accepted) and British importers were evidently drawing the conclusion that they must hastily build up stocks in anticipation of protective duties. In the cabinet a majority certainly wanted protection; the size of the cabinet had been increased to twenty, and with eleven Conservatives and protectionist converts alongside the four Labour and five Liberal members it only remained to be seen how painlessly and expeditiously a tariff programme would be introduced. But time was needed to talk round the minority. Accordingly an Abnormal Importations Bill, hastily presented on 16 November, gave the Board of Trade powers for six months to impose duties up to 100 per cent on a wide range of manufactured goods which were considered to be entering the country in abnormal quantities. A similar interim measure enabled the Ministry of Agriculture to protect the British market against out-of-season imports of fresh fruit and vegetables.

This legislation gave a little time for negotiations. Snowden remained in the cabinet, but as Lord Privy Seal with a viscountcy; the key positions at the Exchequer and Board of Trade went to Neville Chamberlain and Runciman, and the latter, although Snowden's choice, was a convert. Samuel became Home Secretary and Simon Foreign Secretary. Sir Donald Maclean (Education) and Sir Archibald Sinclair (Scotland) were Liberals who remained free traders. For a time the free traders found it hard to say yes or no. Then on 22 January 1932 the 'agreement to differ' formula, which had been so useful in averting a cabinet split before the election, was accepted again. Samuel, Sinclair, Maclean, and Snowden remained unconvinced, but they remained in the government, free to vote and speak as they liked. Samuel told the Eighty Club on 7 December that 'in stopping the flood of abnormal importations from abroad we seem to be letting loose a flood of abnormal importunities at home' and openly advised those whose welfare was injured by the restrictions to make their voices heard. In anticipation of British tariffs foreign countries were already threatening, or actually imposing, retaliatory measures. A French decree published on 14 November imposed a surtax of 15 per cent *ad valorem* on nearly all British imports, and cancelled the most-favoured-nation treatment of British coal which had existed for two generations. All this, however, if it foreshadowed years of bargaining and counter-retaliation, did not convince the protectionists that on balance the country would be weakened by giving itself the tariff weapon.[1]

On the contrary: the need for action, the day-to-day conviction, accumulating over the years, that foreigners were no longer playing the fiscal game according to the Victorian rules, the absence of any obvious alternative, and the hard fact of a surplus of £409 million imports over exports, all confirmed belief in the need for the experiment. Was there no alternative? For the most part the government's critics did not attack its belief in tariffs so much as its belief in their all sufficiency. The T.U.C. and several of the Labour ministers had been prepared for a revenue tariff before the crash, and Keynes, who had become a convert to protection as a temporary expedient as early as February 1930, saw increasing advantages in its retention.[2] To those who had advocated a tariff only as an alternative to national economies or the abandonment of the gold standard it seemed unnecessary and even unethical to adopt all three expedients. But having secured these weapons the government's quest for innovation stopped. While Keynes continued to advocate large public works' programmes based on borrowing at home and concerted capital expenditure abroad with some form of international bank or agency to relieve governments of anxiety concerning their external balance of payments, the Labour party for a time reverted from the misty qualifications of the MacDonald era to demands for full-blooded Socialism, with control or public

[1] D. R. E. Abel, *A History of British Tariffs, 1923–1942* (1945), pp. 89–90.

[2] However, as Benham pointed out in 1941, the great majority of economists, both in Great Britain and elsewhere, 'were and are in favour of free trade'. F. C. Benham, *Great Britain under Protection* (New York, 1941), p. 24. Harrod, pp. 424, 431, 446.

ownership of the banks and major industries. The government, well briefed by its cautious Treasury advisers, saw little practical sense in these bold schemes.[1]

Soon, however, the Labour party began to draw new lessons from the 1931 crisis. At first there had been a search for scapegoats—the duchesses who had captured MacDonald, the bankers whose alleged ramp was so loudly denounced by Hugh Dalton, who as a Doctor of Science in Economics was supposed to know about these things. But it was all too obvious that a lamentable vagueness had hitherto characterized the party's policy statements, and that little precise study had ever been devoted to the detailed application of programmes. The party executive appointed a policy committee in December 1931 which began to work through a number of sub-committees and gradually fashioned between 1932 and 1939 a series of programmes which were to form the basis of its great ministry after 1945. This evolution of programmes was probably helped on balance by the disintegration of the I.L.P. group after 1931.[2]

It was also becoming evident that the new trend even of Conservative policy was towards a greater degree of management of the economy than had seemed decent in the twenties. Thus both the major parties, behind the usual public show of exasperated disagreement, were moving towards a planned economy, although neither wished to go the whole way: trade union influence favoured the regimentation of the employer but not the worker, and the Tory ministers still preferred, no doubt, to save themselves the trouble of coercing either. A large groundwork of social and political agreement, 'Butskellism in all but name', was nevertheless being established in this way by elements in both parties in the thirties. From it arose the ideological structure on which the mixed economy of the forties and fifties was based.[3] This search for 'agreement', to which we shall refer again later in this chapter, was the natural aim of a number of M.P.s in the National government, including Harold Macmillan among the Tories and the National Labour group led by MacDonald.

Meanwhile there were signs of recovery already in 1932, and much

---

[1] Harrod, pp. 442–3; Cole, p. 273; *Britain in Depression* (essays sponsored by the British Association, 1935), pp. 31–51.

[2] See below, p. 333.

[3] Cf. A. Marwick, 'Middle opinion in the thirties', *E.H.R.*, April 1964, pp. 285–98; also Cole, pp. 278–9.

activity within the prescribed limits. The great day came for Neville Chamberlain on 4 February 1932 when he moved the financial resolution of the Import Duties Bill. The proposals embodied some compromises, mainly to persuade Runciman that he had not agreed to full-blooded protection. There were to be 10 per cent customs duties on nearly all imports (this was supposed to be justified for purposes of revenue and the trade balance) and it was left to an Import Duties Advisory Committee to recommend additional duties to the Treasury. There were certain exemptions, including the more important foodstuffs and Empire products, pending an imperial economic conference at Ottawa. Chamberlain referred with some emotion to his father's efforts, and Amery reminded the House that Disraeli had warned his free trade opponents, 'in the spring tide of their economic frenzy' that a 'dark and inevitable hour would arrive'. Samuel also echoed earlier controversies by hurling at his Treasury bench colleagues a full-scale vindication of free-trade principles. Snowden did much the same in the Lords. However, the bill became law with the full support of the Conservatives, although 32 Liberals voted with the opposition.

In April Chamberlain produced his first budget; the Governor of the Bank of England called it the first honest budget since the war, although Amery thought it a dry, unimaginative performance, conforming strictly to the Treasury type of finance. Both were, perhaps, right: Chamberlain was determined that the nation should not suppose that the crisis was over. He called for hard work, strict economy, firm courage, unfailing patience. With the anticipated yield from the new tariff the budget was more or less balanced; there was no tax relief. The outstanding innovation was the securing of power to borrow up to £150 million (later increased to £350 million) to set up an exchange equalization account, so that liquid resources, accumulated when circumstances were favourable, could be used to protect the exchanges against speculative operations and seasonal fluctuations. Immediately after this, on 21 April, the Import Duties Advisory Committee made its first recommendations; these included the raising of duties to between 20 and 33⅓ per cent *ad valorem*.

The 1932 budget, for all its caution, took its place in an experimental policy. The call for austerity and the deflationary nature of the economies partly concealed this. But there were a number of innovations, none of which was a failure, although the extent to which any one of them directly helped recovery is debatable. One problem, successfully tackled, was that of the bank rate and the cheap money policy. Might not recovery be assisted by making money available for investment at low rates of interest? When the Wall Street collapse had led to a flow of funds to London the bank rate had been lowered by stages to 2½ per cent in the spring of 1931 but in this case the tremendous impact of the foreign monetary crisis created the run on sterling and the rate had to be raised, although not beyond 4½ per cent. After going off the gold standard the authorities put the rate up to 6 per cent for a time, but in 1932 the cheap money policy was tried again, this time successfully. The rate was lowered to 5 per cent in February and then by stages to 2 per cent in June, and it remained at that figure until 1939.[1]

The immediate purpose of this move was to help the Treasury to lower the rate of interest on a vast mass of government securities. The £2,000 million of the War Loan, about one-third of the internal debt of the country, with its high rate of 5 per cent, was, as Chamberlain remarked, 'hanging like a cloud over the capital market'. Conversion had been contemplated by Snowden, and it was expected at 4 per cent; Chamberlain's personal decision brought it down to 3½ per cent, and at this figure the conversion was announced at the end of June. At the time the Lausanne conference was seeking a solution of the reparations problem, and he was travelling a good deal and badly handicapped by gout; but a formula which meant virtually the end of reparations was found on 7 July, 1932, and on the 13th he sailed with an impressive British delegation under Baldwin's leadership to Canada to bargain over preferences at Ottawa.[2] Of all these developments, the conversion was the most completely and obviously profitable. There was a risk in bringing the rate down to 3½ per cent; but better terms were not really available and 92 per cent of the War Loan was converted at the new rate.

4. THE OTTAWA CONFERENCE

The Ottawa conference also did something to help recovery, although it was a disillusioning experience for those who sought, in Baldwin's words at the opening session, 'to clear out the channels of trade'. It soon became clear that if the Dominions brought any

[1] Cf. Benham, pp. 227, etc.; Robbins, pp. 104–5.
[2] K. Feiling, *The Life of Neville Chamberlain*, pp. 219–20; Sir Henry Clay, *Lord Norman* (1957), p. 457.

sentiment into the imperial economic relationship it was to congratulate themselves on the generous way in which they had treated the Mother Country in the past. Mr. S. M. Bruce spoke of the Import Duties Act as a tardy response for the benefits which British industry had long enjoyed in the Australian market![1]

In fact, while none of the four major Dominions allowed any United Kingdom imports to enter duty free, over 80 per cent of Empire imports were still being admitted duty free into Britain under the Import Duties Act. At this point Australia had in the Scullin tariff one of the most ruthless examples of high protection in the world; as a result of the depression her exports had fallen by nearly 45 per cent in value, and to the already high tariff had been added a general tax, called a 'primage' duty, of 10 per cent on all imports, and a surcharge of 50 per cent on certain goods. Canada also had a high protective tariff, which under Mr. R. B. Bennett, the Conservative Prime Minister, had been increasing during the crisis by various measures, including a general surcharge of 3 per cent on all imports. South Africa and New Zealand had more moderate tariffs, the latter with valuable preferences for British goods; but India gave few preferences to Great Britain, and Newfoundland none. The preferences, where they existed, gave British goods lower rates in Empire markets than those of foreign importers; they did not allow competition on equal terms with local manufacturing industries, which indeed often regarded British exporting firms as their chief competitors. On the other hand they looked for increased preference in the British home market for their exports of foodstuffs and raw materials, the price of which had been nearly halved in foreign markets since 1929.[2]

From this situation could emerge little hope of a removal or lowering of barriers to trade. In general, the Dominions asked the United Kingdom to help them by maintaining or increasing its restriction on competing foreign imports, while they tended to increase their duties on foreign goods rather than to lower them on British goods. The essence of the situation was that while British goods were directly in competition with many Empire goods in Empire markets, Empire goods were mainly in competition with foreign, rather than with British, goods in the United Kingdom market.

[1] Hodson, p. 165.
[2] Benham, p. 94; Abel, p. 156.

In this somewhat baffling situation relations were not improved by the negotiating methods of both sides. The Empire delegates, and particularly the Canadians, were fierce, direct, and at times almost insulting in their horse trading; the British delegation tended (so it was said) to avoid giving a lead and to rely on the meticulous scrutiny of the Dominions' proposals by their team of civil servants. The British representatives, partly from conviction and partly to placate the free traders whom they had left behind them in the cabinet in London and the converted free-trader—Mr. Runciman—whom they had with them in Ottawa, undoubtedly shied away from the full measure of inter-Empire trade which Australia, Canada, and New Zealand were demanding both for practical and in some measure perhaps sentimental reasons. In this process plans for a common agricultural policy and still more for a coordinated policy of industrial production made no headway. The embarrassment of the British delegates was increased by Amery's presence; he heartily supported the Dominions' plans, and although only a private visitor was soon in intimate relations with the many unofficial groups of agricultural and business experts who had flocked to Ottawa. He records in his diary that on 17 August Chamberlain accused him of wrecking the conference by inciting the Dominions to make impossible requests, a charge which he demurely denied.[1]

One of the most awkward issues was that of a British duty on meat, which Australia and New Zealand keenly desired and which the British delegates did not finally refuse until the third week of the conference, by which stage Runciman was 'threatening to sing his *nunc dimittis* over meat restriction'.[2] Bennett pressed for a total prohibition of Russian imports, primarily in the interests of Canadian fish and lumber, but this also was rejected. Baldwin told Bennett bluntly on 8 August that the Canadian concessions were not an adequate return for what the British were offering, and the haggling continued, with a further strong attack by Canadian industrialists on Russia's alleged dumping. Finally, on the night of 19–20 August, the Canadian delegates attacked so violently a series of resolutions affirming freer Empire trade as the object of the conference that Chamberlain, their author, withdrew from the discussions, although he was persuaded later to put his signature to the Anglo-Canadian agreement in memory of his father.

[1] Amery, vol. III, p. 86.
[2] Feiling, p. 214.

But in fact something was achieved. Great Britain made her concessions, and signed separate agreements with each Dominion, with some advantages to herself. She agreed to increase certain preferences, to continue to give free admission to over 80 per cent of Empire products, to impose or increase duties on foreign imports of certain goods including wheat, to maintain her 10 per cent duties on foreign goods for five years, and to restrict imports of foreign meat, although in the interest of her own farmers she reserved the right to place a quantitative limit on imports of Dominion meat as well. Among the separate agreements that with Canada included a clause which, by safeguarding Canadian timber from undercutting by the Soviet government, made it necessary for the British government to denounce the Anglo-Soviet trade agreement of 1930. Canada, Australia, and New Zealand undertook to protect only those industries which were reasonably capable of survival; and they promised that protective duties against British products should be kept to a level which would give British producers full opportunity of reasonable competition. Although these two provisions seemed important they were difficult to apply, and of more immediate usefulness to British exporters was the promise of the three governments to abolish the surcharges imposed during the crisis; moreover, all the Empire governments gave increased preference to British goods, sometimes reducing the existing duties, sometimes raising them on foreign goods, sometimes following both processes.[1]

By this stage the country was beginning to understand the use that the doctors were making of their mandate. Eschewing a whole-hearted acceptance of any of the panaceas that were being advertised, they were trying to extract modest profits from each at a minimum risk. They supported imperial preference just sufficiently to gain some additional sales in Dominion markets, without prejudicing their plans for trade agreements with foreign countries. They disliked the expense and the Liberal-Labour flavour of public works programmes, and were convinced that they would draw too few unemployed from the dole to justify the ruinous cost. But they were prepared to encourage or finance during the next few years a wide range of specific projects from the building of the *Queen Mary* to the Swansea main drainage scheme. In the cheap money policy and other developments they were encouraging an

[1] J. H. Richardson, *British Economic Foreign Policy* (1936), p. 142; Benham, p. 94 *et seq.*

inflationary trend without openly abandoning the call for austerity
and economy and its deflationary effects. They gained a little more
elbow room and lost a little more of their national flavour when the
Liberal free-traders, Samuel and Sinclair, resigned, with Snowden,
on 28 September 1932; MacDonald's pleas were unavailing, but he
could not accept the view that the Ottawa conference as a fulfilment
of Tory desires had destroyed the government's national character.
So the tariff policy could be developed, although it was still viewed
primarily as a bargaining weapon. Recovery, as measured by rising
employment figures and indices of industrial output, was definitely
beginning in 1933 and the improvement continued, accelerated by
the rearmament programme after 1937, until the beginning of the
second world war.

5. INDUSTRY: THE UNSOLVED PROBLEMS

It was, nevertheless, a sobering fact that unemployment among
insured workers was still higher in July 1939 than it had been in
July 1929, and that this was due mainly to the continued depression
in the export industries. In exports, the 1929, and still more the
1913, level of prosperity had not been regained.[1] What was new
was the recognition that it probably never would be in its traditional
forms. It might be attained by new methods and new industries; the
shape and extent, but not the need, for these innovations was now
the subject of debate.

The great staple industries, even if depressed, were still a major
and vital part of the country's economy, and could not yet be
written off. In so far as markets were still available—if on more
stringent competitive terms than before the war—the right course
was to assist their development. But this was bound in some measure
to hamper the change over to new products and customers, and the
difficulty was to decide, in cases where there were alternative
opportunities for capital investment, tariff bargaining, the employment of skilled personnel, the use of raw materials and the like,
which sector of the economy to favour. This was essentially a

---

[1] In the peak year, 1937, industrial production in general was about a quarter greater
than in 1929; exports were only 83 per cent of the 1929 volume. G. C. Allen, *British
Industries and Their Organization* (1959 edn), pp. 25-6. The map on p. 277, kindly prepared by Mrs. E. Wilson of the Geography Department of the London School of
Economics, shows the percentage of unemployment of insured workers by regions in
1937, adapted from Ministry of Labour statistics. At this point the worst effects of the
world economic crisis were over but the improvement due to the rearmament programme was not being substantially felt.

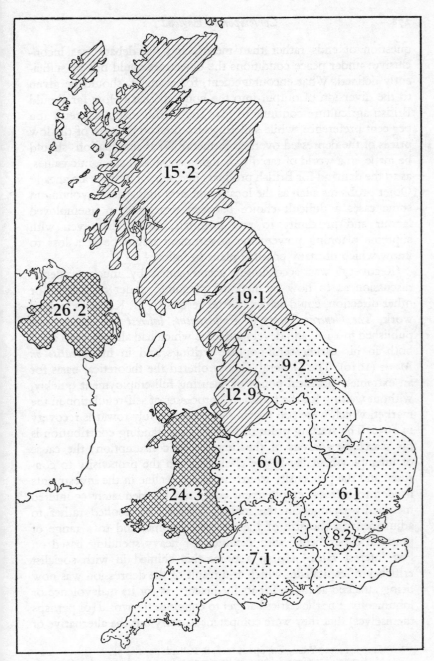

UNITED KINGDOM: DISTRIBUTION OF UNEMPLOYMENT, 1937

question of ends rather than means, and the debate was inconclusive: under peace conditions the objectives could not be sufficiently defined. What encouragement, for example, should be given
to the diversion of output into the home market? How far should
British agriculture continue to give the British manufacturer a 100
per cent preference, while suffering also the competition of the low
prices of the depressed overseas farmers? What anticipations should
be made, in a world of rapidly changing social and economic values,
as to the demand for British products five, ten, or more years ahead?
Other problems such as the location of new industries, involving in
some cases a difficult choice between proximity to unemployed
labour and proximity to raw materials, meant that even with
supreme planning powers the government might be at a loss to
know which of many possible plans to follow.[1]

'Recovery' was accordingly accompanied by much academic
discussion as to how far national planning, under capitalistic or
other direction, could achieve better results. J. M. Keynes's famous
work, *The General Theory of Employment, Interest and Money*, was
published in 1936, and developed ideas which had already been aired
both in his earlier semi-popular writings and in his *Treatise on
Money* (1930). The General Theory offered the theoretical basis for
an extremely practical policy of ensuring full employment quickly,
without waiting for the traditional processes of self-regulation in the
market, which were still moving so imperceptibly towards recovery
in 1936. The starting point of Keynes's outstanding contribution is
his searching analysis of the function of consumption; the cause
of unemployment lay in the clash between the propensity to con-
sume and the propensity to invest, and a decline in the investments
needed to increase employment could not be adequately countered
merely by changes in the rate of interest. He looked rather to
adjustment in the size of the national income, and to a range of
practical experiments with facilities for heavy spending based on
low interest rates.[2] Up to a point this chimed in with socialist
criticism of capitalism, which as a result of the depression was now
being attacked as much for its inefficiency as for its malevolence or
inhumanity. But the critics had yet to convince the world (or perhaps
themselves) that they were competent to carry out the alternative of

---

[1] Allen, pp. 24–32; Youngson, pp. 96–111; S. Pollard, pp. 184–92.
[2] J. M. Keynes, *The General Theory of Employment, Interest and Money* (1936), chaps.
8, 9, and 18.

complete socialist planning or that it was a practicable alternative. Dr. Karl Mannheim asked in 1935, 'who will plan the planner?' and although the Webbs showed ample confidence in Soviet abilities in this direction they were by no means so starry-eyed when they contemplated their English colleagues.[1]

Keynes was not an advocate of state socialism; his book ended by insisting that it should be possible to cure unemployment by a 'right analysis' while preserving 'efficiency and freedom'. It was welcomed by those of the younger generation of both Socialist and Conservative writers and politicians who felt it possible to reconcile planning with the maintenance of a free society.[2] The need for a greater measure of state control of the economy had been urged by Mr. Robert Boothby, Mr. Harold Macmillan, and other young Conservatives as early as 1927.[3] The world economic crisis had reinforced the argument and brought into existence a number of groups for the systematic study of planning programmes; the most successful of these was P.E.P. (Political and Economic Planning), formed in March 1931. It poured out a long series of reports on British economic life, housing, social services and the like, while the National Labour Committee (composed of Labour supporters of the National government) offered in the columns of its *News-Letter* a forum for radicals of all parties. These inter-party planners were increasingly concerned with the international situation,[4] but on the economic side the call was clear. *The Next Five Years, an Essay in Political Agreement*,[5] published by Macmillans on 26 July 1935, advocated deliberate economic planning 'in broad outline', with nationalization of public services and mining royalties, together with public control of the joint-stock banks and the Bank

---

[1] Karl Mannheim, *Mensch und Gesellschaft im Zeitalter des Umbaus* (1935); revised as *Man and Society in an Age of Reconstruction* (1940), p. 74; S. and B. Webb, *Soviet Communism—A New Civilisation?* (1935); 2nd edn., without the question-mark, 1937. All-out planners included Stafford Cripps in *Why This Socialism?* (1934), and G. D. H. Cole, *Principles of Economic Planning* (1935), etc.

[2] Douglas Jay, *The Socialist Case* (?1938), states the case for planning in a free society, accepting Keynes's approach at many points.

[3] R. Boothby and others, *Industry and the State* (1927).

[4] See p. 359 below.

[5] It sold 8,000 copies, and had 153 signatures of many prominent political and literary figures. The 'Next Five Year Plan' group soon began to disintegrate owing to the competition of Lloyd George's 'Councils of Action for Peace and Reconstruction' and Macmillan's launching of a radical political movement in 1936, using 'The New Outlook'. Interesting correspondence on these developments is given in M. Gilbert's *Plough My Own Furrow* (1965), chaps. 20 and 21. A. Marwick's important article, 'Middle opinion in the thirties' (*E.H.R.*, April 1964), is the best general account. Cf. Lord Salter, *Memoirs of a Public Servant* (1961), p. 241.

of England; the sponsoring group included Mr. Harold Macmillan as a joint treasurer, with Lord Allen of Hurtwood as chairman of the executive committee. Keynes's system was to come into its own during the war; the planning groups of central progressive elements prepared the way, less dramatically and conspicuously than in the field of international relations, but perhaps more effectively in the progress towards inter-party agreement.

During the thirties the government's activities did in practice satisfy some of the Keynesian requirements: there was cheap money, slum clearance, and some public-works plans, and in due course more work in the armaments industry. But these were essentially palliatives relevant to the older tradition. There seemed no solution at the moment of the problem of reviving foreign markets. In the meantime the waste, muddle, and popular hostility which accompanied some of Roosevelt's government-sponsored public works schemes confirmed the official doubts on these matters in Whitehall.[1]

The relatively poor progress of the newer industries was in some ways more disquieting than the stagnation of the older ones, which were thought to be doing as much as could be expected. Among the latter, cotton and coal-mining were looked on as the worst sufferers. Others included agriculture, shipbuilding and ship-repairing, and the woollen and worsted industry, to which could be added the railways and water-transport. In terms of employment there had been a drop from a total of 3,505,000 for these industries in 1929, to 2,916,000 in 1932; the 'recovery' of the next few years brought the figure up to only 3 million. However, there was some improvement in the employment figures for both cotton and coal between 1929 and 1937; in agriculture alone was there a further decline.[2]

This as it happened was not so depressing as it sounds, for by 1937 agricultural prices were generally higher, and output about one-sixth greater, than they had been in 1931. This in spite of a continued fall in the total acreage of arable land. English farming has to be highly efficient to survive. In this period there was continued improvement in the techniques of production and in mechanization, the latter hastened by the reintroduction of minimum wage

---

[1] Youngson, pp. 252–60; S. E. Harris, ed. *The New Economics: Keynes' Influence on Theory and Public Policy* (1947), pp. 26, 135 etc.

[2] Employed workers: 925,000 (1925), 888,000 (1929), 809,000 (1932), 708,000 (1939).

scales for agricultural workers in 1924. Labour-saving took the form of greatly increased use of agricultural machinery, particularly tractors. Ultimately, however, the prosperity of British agriculture was dependent on state policy. To the competition of cheap food from overseas, which had chronically hampered the British farmer since the eighteen-seventies, had been added the further fall in the price of such produce since 1929 resulting from the high tariff protection of western European countries; as the *Statist* said at the time, the world's agricultural surplus was being offered the country in a series of bankrupt sales.[1]

After some interim protection in the winter of 1931–32 the government's first major step was the Wheat Act of May 1932, which guaranteed to registered growers a standard price of 10*s* per cwt. This measure fulfilled its purpose; it provided wheat growers in the United Kingdom with a secure market without taxing imports of Empire wheat and it avoided the accusation that a staple article of food was being protected. The cost was met by a tax on flour, paid by the consumer. As a result of the act, the acreage under wheat rose rapidly from its low crisis level of 1,200,000 acres in 1931 to 1,760,000 in 1934; and although this was a record year the figure was more or less maintained. Sugar beet production, created and subsidized for ten years under an act of 1924, had expanded to an acreage of over 400,000, but had no independent life; its main value was as a relief measure. The subsidy was continued in 1936 with a limit on production but not on time.[2]

Another device, extensively used, was to help the farmer by standardizing the grading and pricing of his produce. For this purpose marketing boards were set up. The Milk Marketing Board, created in 1933, was the most important of these, but its activities were typical. A statutory and rather high minimum price was fixed for milk that was to be swallowed fresh in its liquid state, and a low price for milk used to manufacture something else—such as cheese, butter, and plastics. The Board took charge of all payments between farmers and distributors; the effect was to subsidize the producers of 'manufactured' milk out of the relatively high prices paid by the consumers of 'liquid' milk. Was this expedient? It had obvious advantages. The price of milk for manufacture could be

---

[1] *Statist*, 3 June 1933, quoted A. W. Rather, *Planning under Capitalism* (1935), p. 136.
[2] Pollard, pp. 138–44; C. S. Orwin in *Britain in Recovery* (essays sponsored by the British Association, 1938), pp. 169–71.

kept low to meet the competition of low priced imports, while the supply of 'liquid' milk, which commanded a good retail price owing to the absence of foreign competition, could be adjusted to the demand. There was an opportunity for the welfare state to dramatize milk, and attempts were made to distribute supplies at low prices in the depressed areas, although without much success at this stage. There were also marketing boards for bacon, hops, and potatoes. So agriculture recovered; but the limitations remained. As long as Dominion products could come in freely the industry could not expand far; but the balance of national interest, even in anticipation of war, seemed to favour the existing compromise.[1]

On the other hand, the stagnation of coal and cotton, where expanding industry had been the compensation for the tribulations of agriculture in earlier generations, could only be deplored. The output of coal dropped from 258 million tons in 1929 to 207 million in 1933, and increased to 241 million in 1937; exports dropped from 60·3 million in 1929 to 38·9 million in 1932, and had risen only to 40·4 million in 1937. Thus the 1929 export position was not regained. Bilateral agreements with Norway, Sweden, and Denmark in 1933 and 1934 resulted in increased sales to Baltic markets; but some of the Polish coal which was thus driven out found new markets at Britain's expense in other European countries. There was also some discrimination against British coal in France, Germany, Italy, and Belgium. Nevertheless the basic cause of decline was probably the more difficult conditions underground—exhaustion of accessible seams and so on—at a time when world demand was static; the expanding continental industry was thus bound to provide serious competition, usually in more favourable technical circumstances. Mechanization in the British pits was increasing, but not sufficiently to prevent this relative decline in competitive strength. Output was more or less maintained in the home market; that it did not increase in the interwar years with the rise in population and of industrial production was because of the growing use of such substitutes as oil and electricity and the more economical production of gas, and perhaps there is some truth in the view that a bolder process of amalgamation and of central planning would have increased efficiency and selling power. This was the argument for nationalization, but it can at any rate be said that under private enterprise the industry still managed to sell 38 million tons abroad in

[1] A. W. Rather, chap. xi; A. W. Ashley in *Britain in Recovery*, pp. 175–96.

1938, whereas twenty years later it was exporting less than 7 million tons annually.[1]

In the cotton industry also recovery was confined on balance to the home market. By the late thirties the home demand had regained the 1929 level, whereas the quantity of exports was down by half. The most serious loss was that of the Indian market, protected by high tariffs; in all, two-thirds of the export losses were due to the development of domestic industries by Britain's former customers. The remaining losses were due to Japanese competition. Heavily favoured by low production costs, the Japanese industry largely captured the international market for cheap textiles that was opening up with the beginnings of recovery in various countries. The Ottawa agreements were not a great help; the small preference in the Indian market was not sufficient to offset the cheapness of the Japanese product, although the agreements were more helpful after the middle thirties in the Dominions. In the Crown Colonies a quota system, introduced in 1934, saved British cotton imports from virtual extinction by Japanese competitors, and trade agreements led to increased sales to the Scandinavian countries. The position in the wool textile industry was much the same—a net loss of export markets, and a recovery in home sales which was not sufficient to restore the pre-slump position.[2]

But there was still life in the British textile industry, and a promising growth in rayon production, even though this was not sufficient to balance the export losses on cotton and wool. Indeed, this also was in one sense a story of relative decline, for from being one of the world's two largest producers in 1913 she was outstripped in 1939 by the United States, Germany, Italy, and Japan. She exported very little by comparison with Japan and Italy. Nevertheless, the actual growth of output, particularly in continuous filament yarn, was impressive.[3]

This point illustrates the difficulty of arriving at a satisfactory estimate of the extent of Britain's economic recovery. On the one hand it could be argued that whereas before the great depression Great Britain was lagging behind her rivals, after it the position was almost reversed. While the volume of industrial production was

---

[1] *Britain in Recovery*, p. 56, shows that the annual output per person employed increased from 253 tons in 1931 to 298 in 1936. See also pp. 233–50; Allen, pp. 56–9; A. de M. Neuman, *Economic Organization of the British Coal Industry* (1934).

[2] Allen, pp. 220–25.

[3] Allen, pp. 280–94; Pollard, pp. 103–4, 107.

well below the pre-slump level almost throughout the thirties in both the United States and France, in Britain the volume of industrial output in 1937 was over 20 per cent greater than it had been in 1929. A less favourable picture appeared if one looked at the export field, where her sales of the newer products such as rayon and motor vehicles were not sufficient to replace her losses on the traditional staples nor to give her—proportionately—as large a share of the world market in these goods as the United States. The number of insured persons employed had increased from 10,200,000 to 11,500,000 between 1929 and 1937; wages and industrial profits were higher in spite of a 5 per cent fall in the cost of living.[1] But the benefits of this increased activity were found mainly in the home market.

This, however, was a necessary and from some points of view even a desirable result of the isolationist policy followed by the Treasury. The conversion scheme for War Loan, announced on 30 June 1932, was accompanied by a temporary ban on foreign lending, and although this was somewhat relaxed in October it remained substantially true that down to the war all investment in foreign countries was prohibited, except for certain transactions of immediate benefit to the country. While on the one hand this meant that British capital was not helping the recovery of foreign countries where recovery might have helped British exports, on the other it provided funds for investment in home industries where recovery had its most manifest advantages.

Housing in particular benefited from this state of affairs; there was a remarkable building boom throughout the country which was already under way in 1932 and in turn helped related industries supplying materials, power, and furniture.[2] In these trades unemployment dropped, although it remained high elsewhere.[3]

---

[1] Benham, p. 218, writing in 1941.

[2] Although it has been argued that a building boom was overdue, and would probably have come about even if interest rates had not fallen. Lewis, p. 86; Pollard, pp. 238–40, 258–6; M. Bowley, *Housing and the State*, pp. 48–73.

[3] The attempt to take unemployment relief out of politics by setting up a central Unemployment Assistance Board in 1934 with a full-time professional staff was a well-intentioned effort by Chamberlain to provide a humane settlement during the continuance of the slump. Although it provided for considerable latitude in meeting claims it was violently attacked because many of the rates to be paid were found to be less than those previously provided under the transitional scheme. After a standstill act in February 1935 the old arrangements continued more or less unchanged until April 1937.

6. ANGLO-AMERICAN FRUSTRATIONS

Recovery had been achieved at a cost. It was incomplete, and in certain directions it had created new problems for the British economy. The government's policy contributed to the contemporary growth of economic nationalism, not only by its own bilateral commercial policy, but also because the abdication of the rôle of financial leadership in 1931 left the world without a generally-accepted international monetary standard. This is not to say that there was any real alternative. Although Britain was the first to depreciate her currency and thus could be said to have set the example in unilateral action, she had been driven to this decision by the nervous preference of the foreign investor for short term deposits and by the freezing of British assets abroad; she could no longer in 1931 command the confidence and therefore the resources needed by the world's banker. But as a result the countries remaining on gold were in due course driven off it, and the growth of restrictive currency systems in country after country severely hampered the revival of world trade, which it was Britain's interest to foster.

A further consequence was a habit of competitiveness in financial policy with the United States, which was to have repercussions far into the future. Late in 1932 the low value of sterling, which may have been deliberately maintained at approximately 70 per cent of the previous gold parity by the operations of the Exchange Equalization Account, certainly had a deflationary effect on United States export prices, which were still linked to gold. The U.S. Treasury suspected that the Fund was being used to depreciate sterling in the interests of British trade, although many authorities, including the Harvard expert, Professor Sprague, maintained that the British aim was stability rather than profits. However that may be, no ground of agreement in these matters could be found between the two governments during 1933. While the British government accepted the desirability of an early return to the gold standard, although with devalued sterling, Roosevelt was coming to the conclusion that to keep the dollar on gold would frustrate his plans for raising the internal price level. MacDonald visited Washington in April 1933 as chairman of the forthcoming World Monetary and Economic Conference and there were discussions about the whole range of Anglo-American financial contacts, including war debts; but all that emerged was a vague statement that monetary stability and a rise in prices was desirable. A 'token' instalment of $10 million in silver (purchased in India at the market price) in acknowledgement of the debt was made by the British government in June, and was accepted by the President as not constituting a default. But this, and the offer of a further token payment later in the year in United States currency (when U.S. regulations made it impossible to accept silver) merely strengthened those patriotic elements in America which felt that Uncle Sam was being out-smarted by his over-clever Transatlantic creditors, a sentiment that was perhaps not entirely absent from government circles in Washington too.

The collapse of the world economic conference was the direct result of Roosevelt's dramatic message of 3 July 1933 rejecting international monetary stabilization in the interest of domestic advantage. Then between October 1933 and January 1934 the United States Treasury, by a process of gold purchases with continually raised prices, drove down the exchange value of the dollar, which fell on 15 November to the lowly figure of $5·50 to the pound. In January 1934 U.S. gold stocks were revalued after the price of gold had been fixed at $35 per fine ounce. The gold content of the dollar was fixed at 59·06 per cent of its old parity value on 31 January. The practical result of these highly technical transactions was that the British Treasury lost the initiative in monetary matters which it had been able to use at the expense of the dollar in 1932. Under regulations issued by the Secretary to the U.S. Treasury in February 1934 the British and other authorities could not purchase gold from the United States unless they were prepared to sell it at the American price. In short, they could not operate at all in the dollar market except on American terms.[1]

As one contemporary authority put it, the Americans had shown their teeth and proceeded to beat the British at their own game; acting on the assumption that the Exchange Equalization Account had been used by the British to keep the pound undervalued they set up their own stabilization fund to maintain the already devalued dollar, and a struggle between the two funds in pursuit of rival monetary objectives was clearly visualized.[2] The effect on American prices was to strengthen American competitive power in foreign

[1] N. F. Hall in *Britain in Recovery*; Hodson, p. 194; Clay, *Lord Norman*, pp. 454–5.
[2] N. F. Hall, p. 150. The *Economist* remarked gloomily on 17 November 1934 that the United States was smashing the post-crisis gold standard before it had been set up.

markets and to raise still higher the barriers against imports into the United States. Figures issued by the U.S. Department of Commerce for the first six months of 1934 showed that there was an excess of U.S. exports over imports of 173 million dollars, and an inflow of long and short-dated capital amounting to 560 million dollars. These and other substantial items were paid for in the main by the import of 920 million dollars of gold—roughly equivalent to half the gold reserve of the Bank of England. America's fiscal isolationism was at its height during Roosevelt's first term of office, and represented a conscious retreat from the abundant although abortive efforts of Hoover and Stimson to help Europe in its difficulties. Fortunately the desire of both governments for stable exchanges prevented the disastrous competition in depreciation of the currencies for temporary trade advantages which at one time seemed likely to develop. The growing influence of Henry Morgenthau at the Treasury helped to modify Roosevelt's thorough distrust of British financial practices, although he did not tell the President that in his view the British had 'acted peculiarly' in their stabilization policy because they were convinced that Roosevelt had double-crossed them in London in 1933.[1]

The United States acquiesced without enthusiasm but without official recrimination in the cessation of British war debt payments. Morgenthau did not find it difficult to establish amicable relations with Chamberlain, and perhaps did not share Roosevelt's belief that as Chancellor of the Exchequer 'he thoroughly dislikes Americans'. The next monetary crisis, which the United States Treasury anticipated in good time, was in Paris. The working of the exchange equalization system depended on there being a free market in gold in which the two funds could operate, and the weakening of the franc was partly the result of their operations. In the autumn of 1935 Morgenthau had urged the importance of a monetary agreement between France, Great Britain, and the United States, but could make no headway with Laval. A renewed flight from the franc started with the German occupation of the Rhineland in March 1936, and continued after the accession to office of Léon Blum's coalition government in June. With some reluctance Blum and Vincent Auriol, his Minister of Finance, were brought to accept the need for devaluation, and set a good example to the other two by agreeing to concert action with them; the practical result

[1] J. M. Blum, *From the Morgenthau Diaries* (1959), pp. 138–82.

was that the three governments in simultaneous declarations promised to cooperate in monetary matters and repudiated any intention of manipulating their currencies to secure export advantages. This was the so-called Tripartite Agreement of 25 September 1936, which the Russians immediately attempted to shake on Saturday the 26th by selling £1,200,000 in order to drive down the price of sterling. Prompt buying by the U.S. Treasury prevented what was regarded in Washington as a Communist assault on Blum's position.[1]

We know from his published diaries that Morgenthau was strongly influenced by his desire to use American financial policy to bolster the confidence of the democracies against the totalitarian powers, although this political goodwill did not have many concrete results. While the Treasury was developing an international conscience the State Department under Cordell Hull was conducting its own brand of economic diplomacy against discriminatory practices hampering international trade. Hull had persuaded himself that fierce trade rivalry had caused the First World War; he was a firm advocate of that form of appeasement which argued that the conclusion of trade agreements with the Axis powers would help to avert a second one.[2] This concern for the improvement of world economic conditions was genuine and new, but it was difficult to commend to American opinion except in terms of direct advantage to the economy of the United States. To embarrassed British officials the moral undertones of the Cordell Hull programme seemed mainly designed for their discomfiture. The situation between the two countries remained advantageous to the American economy; Great Britain was never allowed to sell in the United States as much as she bought there.[3] So strong, however, was the hope of greater cooperation with the coy Transatlantic giant that British governments were usually prepared in the last resort to accept United States policy on its own terms.

At this stage the only concrete result was a British–Canadian–American reciprocal trade agreement. Hull had frequent talks with the British ambassador, Sir Ronald Lindsay, during 1936 in which he reproached the British for their preferential tariffs and dis-

[1] Clay, pp. 422–9.
[2] *The Memoirs of Cordell Hull* (1948), vol. I, pp. 363–5; R. N. Gardner, *Sterling–Dollar Diplomacy* (1956), pp. 5–12.
[3] U.S.A. was the chief supplier of the United Kingdom with £87·5 million imports in 1935; she took £22·9 million of British exports. The only country with which the British balance of trade was more unfavourable was the U.S.S.R. Richardson, p. 126.

criminatory practices and contrasted them with the United States policy of seeking trading agreements for the purpose of lowering tariffs and so easing international trade. According to this view of the problem preferences (and particularly the Ottawa agreements) were reprehensible, protection was not.[1] Traditional American hostility to the British Empire had been dramatically reinforced during the depression by the Ottawa decisions, which came at a time when American manufacturers were looking desperately abroad for markets. But the American exporter wanted to sell more to foreigners, not to encourage foreign sales at home; and Congress was interested in Hull's trade treaties only in so far as American exports benefited by them. Hull did not explain, and perhaps did not really understand, that in view of the strong balance of payments position of his country American exports could not be greatly increased without either a substantial granting of credit abroad or a drastic lowering of the high tariffs to allow the influx of dollar-earning imports. In these circumstances, Britain had little to gain from the negotiations, but it was considered essential for political reasons that they should take place. They dragged on for a year. While seeking a yet larger share of the British market, Hull was unable to offer much in return.[2] The agreement, which included Canada, was finally signed in Washington on 17 November 1938.

While the problems of economic recession and recovery were probably the first preoccupation of British cabinets between 1930 and 1937, the political situation abroad was only a little less worrying. In the next two chapters we must therefore examine the two spheres, that of the Commonwealth and of Western European defence, which provided most of the issues of external policy in this period. We shall see that in both cases ministers were harassed by mounting demands for the assumption of greater responsibilities in face of an actual or relative decline in resources; and in the case of the Commonwealth there was the persistent pressure for devolution of authority which it was necessary always to handle with patience and goodwill.

[1] e.g. W S. Culbertson, *International Economic Policies* (1925): the object of protection 'is to diversify a nation's economic life and to afford varied opportunities for the application of the genius of a people. It is in no sense aggressive. . . . Preference, on the other hand, is an expression of modern imperialism. In contrast with the policy of protection it is aggressive . . .' Quoted Gardner, p. 18.

[2] 'Because Britain was our major customer, the variety of products to be considered was wide. Because Britain was a large exporter of manufactured products, many of which competed with ours, we had to be doubly careful in granting concessions on such items.' Hull, *Memoirs*, vol. I, p. 529.

7

THE COMMONWEALTH IN TRANSITION

1. WHAT HAD THE COMMONWEALTH IN COMMON?

THE three political parties in Great Britain can each be said to have accepted complete self-government as the ultimate destiny of every part of the Commonwealth and Empire. But it was hoped that this would not result in the ending of the special ties between them, but rather that they would continue to be linked in a free and mutually beneficial association, infused with the ideals of parliamentary liberalism, administrative efficiency and honesty, racial tolerance, and broadly similar interests in foreign policy which were the objectives of liberal-minded imperialists at the beginning of the century. This combination of free association with a special relationship characterizes the Commonwealth in its final stage of evolution. It resulted from the growth of responsible government during the nineteenth century in forms which had made it unnecessary for the second Empire to go the way of the first. Englishmen, both in political circles and among wide classes of the general public, were familiarizing themselves from the beginning of our period with the concept of evolution towards the free association Commonwealth, and the consummation of this process after 1945 became a matter for general congratulation at home, often to the bewilderment of both friends and critics abroad.[1]

The achievement of this positive relationship was the conscious aim of some loosely linked groups mainly working in Great Britain, but with associates, disciples, and critics elsewhere. In his reconstruction administration in South Africa after the Boer War Milner recruited the remarkable group of young men known as the 'Kinder-

[1] P. Knaplund, *Britain Commonwealth and Empire, 1901–1955* (1956), chaps. 11, x and generally: a full textbook treatment. On the economic effects of the transition: M. B. Brown, *After Imperialism* (1963), pp. 447–54.

garten' who were to be active in many rôles in later life but who remained advocates of the new imperial ties. They included L. S. Amery, Robert Brand, Lionel Curtis, F. S. Oliver, Philip Kerr (later Lord Lothian), John Buchan who became Governor-General of Canada, and others. They were an able and vocal pressure group, and did much to air new conceptions by their speeches and writing. *The Round Table*, founded in 1910 by Kerr and edited by him for many years, was an academic journal of good quality and a medium for the whole group.[1] Their earlier ideas, inspired by Milner, pointed to a Commonwealth superstate which was in many ways impracticable. They were greatly influenced by the plans of Joseph Chamberlain for an imperial tariff, and the search for a closer economic relationship between all parts of the Empire, based on the privileged market of the United Kingdom, was to remain a live theme until the Common Market discussions of the early nineteen-sixties. It was to have a formidable partisan in Lord Beaverbrook. Imperial federation was a more contentious issue, for its various assumptions as to a central direction for the Empire were incompatible with the centrifugal tendencies of the Dominions. But it had Milner's blessing and Lionel Curtis took up the theme with strong convictions in his book, *The Problem of the Commonwealth*, published in March 1916. There were varying degrees of scepticism about this programme, however, even in the *Round Table* group, and the discussions at the 1917 imperial conference virtually killed it. Yet the urgent need to bring the Dominions into a working relationship with the government in London remained, and already before 1914 the problem was being studied by a growing number of civil servants and ministers who were seeking a practical basis for imperial defence and foreign policy. The Committee of Imperial Defence, established by Balfour in December 1902, and guided for many years by its secretary, Major Hankey, was always prepared to consult with Dominion representatives. It made plans for a combined and coordinated system of imperial defence, although the essential burden continued to rest on the mother country.[2]

For those parts of the Commonwealth which had not attained

---

[1] J. R. M. Butler, *Lord Lothian* (1960), pp. 11–59; S. C. Y. Cheng, *Schemes for the Federation of the British Empire* (1931), p. 126; J. E. Tyler, *The Struggle for Imperial Unity* (1938).

[2] The outstanding source is Lord Hankey, *The Supreme Command*. F. A. Johnson, *Defence by Committee*, (1960), pp. 11–162, is useful, but misses important points. See also Lord Hankey, *Government Control in Wartime* (1945) and *Diplomacy by Conference* (1946). He became assistant secretary in 1908, secretary in 1912.

self-government British rule continued with varying degrees of native administration, provided either by the recruitment of a westernized civil service or through delegated authority. It was generally although rather vaguely assumed in Britain that a beneficent but essentially economical paternalism characterized these efforts. The lone district officer or trader or missionary, bearing the white man's burden to some tropical white man's grave, a Sanders of the River or Livingstone of the Zambesi, was still the respected popular stereotype. The Empire has been well described as the apotheosis of the do-it-yourself movement. As in the field of defence, people and politicians were ready enough to forget the magnitude of their problems. It seemed reasonable to assume that in many areas, such as those of the tribal African colonies, fitness for self-rule could not be achieved in the foreseeable future; this view was hardly questioned in the case of Africa, and indeed some of the African leaders were themselves to be caught unawares by the wind of change in the nineteen-fifties. On the other hand it had reluctantly to be recognized that these evolutionary methods were being violently and passionately challenged by Indian Nationalists. Their demands thus provided the great central problem of the Empire's future in the twenties and thirties.

To understand the complexities of the Indian issue for the British cabinet we must recognize that it embodied a number of problems, only one of which was exhaustively debated in public. This was in essentials a question with strong moral undertones: was the devolution of authority by the British authorities keeping pace with the progress of India's capacity for self-rule? What could not be publicly discussed to any extent was the problem of imperial defence and the rôle of each part of the Commonwealth in the formulation of a common defence policy; even more difficult as a subject for frank discussion was the nature and future of the Commonwealth itself. If the process of Dominion Home Rule were carried to completion in every vital region of the Empire, with a right of association so free as to allow neutrality towards the rest in a future war, would there be any 'Commonwealth' or 'Empire' left as an effective force or entity in world politics?

India was the essential element in this problem. Owing to its vast size and population, its wealth and commercial importance, its geographical position as an Asiatic sub-continent commanding the sea routes from the British Isles and Africa to south-east Asia,

Australia, and New Zealand, its manpower resources, its considerable military strength in a future war, and its fortress position against strong northern invaders, it occupied so central a position in the Empire as to leave some doubts as to whether there could be an Empire in any real sense without it. This, of course, was even more true of the United Kingdom; the Commonwealth could scarcely exist without her, and the individual members were vitally interested in her survival of any attack from Europe. Thus England and India, because of their vulnerable situations and extensive resources, were together the two vital positions in the defensive system of the Commonwealth. Although there was a sincere desire to prepare India for self-government by training leaders and officials and by composing communal differences there was an inevitable if largely unconscious tendency to retard the abandonment of control over Indian resources until at least the outbreak of war, which began to seem a possibility after 1931.

The First World War had magnificently vindicated those who placed full trust in Dominion loyalty. It was natural to assume that continued and increased aid during the war and collaboration thereafter could best be secured by closer consultation, so that the Dominion governments could feel their responsibility for decisions and also be satisfied as to their own freedom of choice. But this involved an equal freedom of dissent. Lloyd George's decision in December 1916 to summon 'an imperial conference' was governed by these general political considerations as well as by the urgent need for further imperial aid. The form of the invitation was designed to allow the inclusion of Indian representatives, and to this the Dominions made no objection, although membership of the imperial conferences had been designed only for 'self-governing Dominions'. The dilemma that loomed largest before the Dominion governments was not so much that of reconciling distance with prior consultation as of combining the freedom of initiative which had to be left to London with the maintenance of the Dominions' fully independent status.

In pursuit of the last aim there were continuous discussions which led finally to the Statute of Westminster of 1931.[1] Apart from

[1] The best and most up-to-date treatment of these developments is the forthcoming authoritative study by H. Duncan Hall, *A History of the British Commonwealth of Nations, 1900–1953*, of which I have been able to read the first part, to 1926. Gwendolen M. Carter, *The British Commonwealth and International Security, the Role of the Dominions, 1919–1939* (Toronto, 1947), chaps. I–III, remains useful.

uneasiness in some quarters lest the decentralizing tendencies would end by refining away all meaning from the Commonwealth link there was no tension in these negotiations. There is a good case for the view that the Commonwealth in its modern form dates from the imperial conference of 1911, and the feeling that the word 'Empire' was no longer adequate led some members to talk for a time of their 'family of nations'. The word 'Commonwealth' was first officially used in this connexion by the 1917 conference. Smuts preferred the fuller term, 'The British Commonwealth of Nations', which had been in occasional use since the eighteen-eighties, and he gave it wide currency in his speeches from 1917 onwards. Sir Robert Borden spoke of 'an Imperial Commonwealth of United Nations'. The Irish insisted on using it in the Anglo-Irish treaty of 1921, because of its association with the fullest degree of Dominion autonomy. Sidney Webb and the Fabian Society and the evolutionary wing of the Labour party also favoured the title and the approach to imperial relations that it implied, or was believed to imply.[1] There seemed, however, to be need for a clearer definition of the constitutional position, and it was proposed that a constitutional conference should be called after the war to discuss the matter. Although London in 1923 felt this to be unnecessary in view of the recognition of the status of the Dominions in the Imperial War Cabinet and the League Covenant, talks proceeded less formally, following warnings from Smuts that unless there was 'the most generous satisfaction for the Dominion sense of nationhood and statehood' in these young nations, there would be separatist movements in the Commonwealth.

While these discussions had been going on during the war and the peace conference, contact was successfully maintained because there was unity of command and full agreement as to the immediate aim —victory and the consolidation of victory. This culminated at Versailles, where Commonwealth statesmen, including Smuts, Borden, and Hughes, were active in such fields as the drafting of the League Covenant, the financial discussions, and the settlement in the Pacific, and were supporters of Lloyd George's stand on the future

[1] It was also the title of an early work by H. Duncan Hall (1920), which was widely read and referred to in Smuts's important memorandum on Dominion status in 1921; this was in turn the basis of proposals by General Hertzog, L. S. Amery and the Dominions office at the Imperial Conference of 1926. See H. Duncan Hall, 'The Genesis of the Balfour Declaration of 1926' (*Journal of Commonwealth Political Studies*, Nov. 1962), pp. 171–6, and fn. 6. Also W. K. Hancock, *Survey of British Commonwealth Affairs* (1937), vol. I, p. 1.

of the Rhine provinces and Poland. Following the imperial conference of 1921, agreement was secured in the negotiations leading to the Washington conference and the dissolution of the Anglo-Japanese alliance, but only after much argument. The issues were complicated both by differing views as to the need to follow the lead of the United States and also by divergences of policy among the Dominions themselves. Canada opposed the continuance of the alliance for both isolationist and pan-American reasons, while Australia and New Zealand agreed with the United Kingdom in favouring renewal in some form which would ensure friendly relations with both Japan and the United States.

But in India and Ireland the government's authority was fiercely challenged, and the Chanak crisis in 1922 raised the whole problem of its right to assume Dominion cooperation without prior consultation.[1] It does not appear that Lloyd George's message to the Dominions just before midnight on 15 September 1921, asking whether they wished to be represented by a contingent in the event of war with Turkey, justifies the weight of constitutional criticism that has sometimes been placed on it. The acute phase of the crisis developed rather suddenly, and the Dominion governments had undoubtedly left the initiative in the Turkish question to the British government, just as they had done in other aspects of the peace settlement in Europe and the Middle East. Insofar as the issue was one of procedure it was possible to say that the particular difficulty would not be repeated, but the broader result was to limit more sharply the independent initiative of the United Kingdom in the making of imperial foreign policy without any reciprocal increase of voluntary commitments by the Dominions.[2]

A further result was the increasing emphasis placed in all the Dominions on the need for parliamentary approval of any decision to go to war. Even in New Zealand, where the government had immediately promised full support, the Labour party condemned the absence of parliamentary consent. In Australia, which promised support but in slightly more qualified terms than New Zealand, there were similar criticisms from the Opposition, while Smuts and Mackenzie King both said that their governments could not commit themselves to war before consulting parliament. This was not followed, however, as might have been expected, by any general

[1] See pp. 171-3.
[2] Carter, pp. 84-9

move to improve liaison with the government departments or the cabinet in London; and in Canada's case at least this was because the closer identification with British policy would run counter to the current isolationist trend, while her subordinate rôle in the professional relationship might detract from complete Dominion autonomy. The British cabinet had thus been reminded that it should speak in foreign affairs for Britain alone, although it was taken for granted that in doing so it would continue to comprehend the interests of the whole Commonwealth. The Dominion governments were kept fully informed; following a decision of the 1921 conference they received an ample flow of telegrams and despatches on which they seldom commented. Their small and rudimentary departments of external affairs were not, indeed, capable of coping with so much information until after World War II. In another sphere the position was even more anomalous. The Committee of Imperial Defence continued to be concerned with the defence of the Commonwealth as a whole, but without an agreed foreign policy could not plan either armaments or defence policy on an imperial scale.

The tendency of the twenties in all the Dominions was predominantly isolationist, at three levels—at home because of the thriving sense of national self-sufficiency, in imperial relations because of the urge to assert full constitutional freedom, and in international relations because of the reaction (accelerated by the American example) from the onerous requirements of fully active League membership. It was still the case that for an adequate reason and in particular an armed attack on any part of the Commonwealth, all might, and most certainly would, go to war. The survival of Great Britain was in the interest of all, and the Dominions could not be indifferent to or opposed to whatever steps she chose to take to defend herself against attack in Europe. The Chanak crisis had shown, however, that no automatic acceptance of the British lead in a matter of peace and war could be assumed. Australia and New Zealand, conscious of the neighbourhood of the Asiatic masses and of United States isolationism, were keenly interested in maintaining their links with the United Kingdom and the lines of communication through the Middle East and Singapore; they welcomed the development of the Singapore base after 1922, and Bruce was moved by the Chanak episode to appoint a liaison officer, attached to the staff of the High Commissioner in London, to improve the confidential relations between himself and the Foreign Office. Canada, like South Africa, preferred to keep its hands as free as possible, for the facts of geography guaranteed its immunity from any of the world's crises and it was unlikely to call on Great Britain for help in its relations with its great neighbour. In 1923 an important precedent was created when the Halibut Fisheries agreement between Canada and the United States was signed by a Canadian representative and not by the British ambassador.

Commonwealth representatives were not invited to take part in the negotiations of the treaty of Lausanne, and Mackenzie King was not prepared for some time to acquiesce in its ratification on behalf of Canada. At the 1923 conference his attitude helped it establish the principle that each part of the Commonwealth should be free to conclude its own international agreements.[1] In the negotiations for the Draft Treaty and the Geneva Protocol the Foreign Office did its best to keep in close touch with the Dominion governments, and the rejection of both plans was influenced by knowledge of Dominion reluctance to participate. Smuts's criticism was that this would turn the League into an 'armed alliance to maintain the *status quo*'. While the Labour government failed to consult the Dominions before formally recognizing the Soviet government, the Conservatives were careful to keep them closely informed about the Locarno negotiations. But these were conducted in the name of Great Britain and not of the Empire, and neither Canada, South Africa, nor Ireland was willing to adhere to the Locarno treaties, although Australia and New Zealand would have done so readily if pressed. All subsequently expressed their approval of British action in concluding the treaties. At Geneva, British and Dominion representatives were usually in accord, but again the latter were not unwilling to emphasize their independent status, and to discourage attempts to make the League anything more than a centre of free discussion.

All this left the Commonwealth and Empire singularly unprepared to meet the series of rapid, savage, interlocking challenges which assailed it throughout the world during the nineteen-thirties. But

---

[1] The British government continued to maintain the view that neither the Covenant of the League nor any conventions concluded under its auspices were 'intended to govern the relations *inter se* of the various parts of the British Commonwealth'. The Irish Free State challenged this view when it sought in 1924 to register the Anglo-Irish agreement of 6 December 1921 with the League. The dispute was never resolved. J. E. S. Fawcett, *The* Inter Se *Doctrine of Commonwealth Relations* (1958), pp. 16–20.

during the optimistic twenties war talk still had no immediacy and Commonwealth goodwill was a gentle tranquillizer mixing well with such other opiates as the Geneva spirit.[1] The amicable elaboration of constitutional safeguards against undue maternal solicitude appeared to be a beneficial exercise for both the mother country and the family. The Balfour Declaration of 1926 and the Statute of Westminster of 1931 were the result.

When Dominion representatives met under Balfour's chairmanship on 27 October 1926 there was little criticism (except on grounds of wordiness) of the terms in which the South African Prime Minister, General J. B. M. Hertzog, asked for complete positive affirmation of the international standing and independence of the Dominions. He agreed, however, to drop the word 'independence' because of Mackenzie King's objection that in North America it meant secession, and he agreed, on British and Australian pressure, to the use of the term 'British Empire' in the formula.[2] Balfour's draft of the key sentence, which referred to Great Britain and the Dominions of Canada, Australia, New Zealand, South Africa, Newfoundland, and the Irish Free State, reads as follows:

> They are autonomous Communities within the British Empire, equal in status, in no way subordinate one to another in any aspect of their domestic or external affairs, though united by a common allegiance to the Crown, and freely associated as members of the British Commonwealth of Nations.

As Amery pointed out later, the word 'Empire' was the only one which covered all the types of community involved, from colonies and mandated territories to autonomous states and allies.[3] The Balfour Report, however, was not enough; both the 1926 and 1930 imperial conferences sought an act of Parliament which would give the force of law to their various resolutions. This was done in the Statute of Westminster of 1931, in a text agreed between all the governments. The Crown was defined as the symbol of free association, and it was recognized that no law of the United Kingdom Parliament would be binding on any Dominion except with its request and consent.

[1] But contemporaries were not unaware of the anomalies: cf. A. B. Keith, *Dominion Autonomy in Practice* (1929), pp. 56–66.

[2] H. Duncan Hall, 'The Genesis of the Balfour Declaration', p. 189; cf. Van den Heever, *Life of Hertzog* (Johannesburg, 1946), pp. 212–18; R. Macgregor Dawson, *Mackenzie King* (1958), vol. I, chap. 15.

[3] L. S. Amery, *My Political Life*, vol. II, pp. 384–93.

These developments were disquieting for those who wished to apply the weight of Commonwealth influence effectively in matters of defence and foreign policy. Owing to the possibility that attempts to tie the Dominions down might lead to open disagreements or formal severing of the attenuated constitutional link, the United Kingdom government hesitated to push consultation too far. The agreement of 1926 was that as regards 'the conduct of foreign affairs generally . . . as in the sphere of defence, the major share of responsibility rests now, and must for some time continue to rest' with the United Kingdom. Its duty was to inform first and then to act as it believed the Dominions would wish it to act. Some misunderstandings were inevitable in the circumstances, but they were surprisingly few. There was no doubt after 1930 that Ireland was interested only in the reduction of her last legal connexion with the United Kingdom to vanishing point, although she had apparently no desire to see England and France overthrown by a continental rival. In Canada and South Africa isolationism was widespread; among the non-Anglo-Saxon stock it had a self-assertive as well as an escapist quality. Nor were New Zealand and Australia at all willing to believe that there was any need for them to be drawn into European politics, although their support of the mother country in a defensive war was axiomatic. For them the Pacific was the main anxiety, whereas for Great Britain it was necessarily a sphere which could be neither ignored nor given priority. They both viewed the decentralizing tendency of the Statute of Westminster without enthusiasm, and it was some years before either took steps to ratify it.[1]

In general, in spite of the emphasis on the right of the Dominions to their own foreign policies which had been established at the Paris peace conference and during the following four years, they were in no hurry to develop offices of external affairs, to appoint large numbers of diplomatic representatives, or to acquire the continuous experience that an independent foreign policy demands. It was accepted that the United Kingdom continued to have the main responsibility for the defence and interests of the Commonwealth as a whole. This state of things might well be transitional, it was in a sense flattering, but it was detrimental to a vigorous foreign policy. It was also true, of course, that as the home government was left

[1] N. Mansergh, *Survey of British Commonwealth Affairs, Problems of External Policy, 1931–1939* (1952), pp. 16–18; J. E. S. Fawcett, *op.cit.*, pp. 46–8.

with the responsibility it was also left with the blame when things went wrong. However, when the great crisis arose in 1939 all the Dominions outside Europe followed the United Kingdom into war.

2. THE DEADLOCK IN IMPERIAL DEFENCE

The responsibility and the disparity were greatest in imperial defence. The Admiralty replied to a request from the Imperial War Cabinet in March 1917 for a postwar naval defence scheme by proposing a single imperial navy, which the Dominions rejected as impracticable; instead, Lord Jellicoe on their invitation spent over a year (February 1919 to March 1920) in visit and report. Assuming an ultimate Japanese offensive in the Pacific he proposed a permanent British Far Eastern fleet of twenty capital ships (including four carriers) based on Singapore, with light cruisers, destroyers (43) and submarines (36). His report is remarkable for its strong emphasis on the importance of aircraft and on adequate anti-aircraft defence. It would have cost £20 million a year, with a British contribution of 71 per cent of the cost, the others paying in proportion. It is significant as a yardstick for measuring the subsequent meagre provision. The Admiralty's own plan in 1919 was to maintain thirty capital ships in the postwar era.[1]

All this was swept aside by the Washington conference in 1922. The Jellicoe plan was sunk without trace. Japan was alienated by the dropping of the Anglo-Japanese alliance, and granted immunity from attack by the demilitarization of the western Pacific islands (not including those of the Japanese mainland). Britain was limited to a total of fifteen capital ships, and the convention was accepted that this overall figure had to include the Dominion navies. The decisions prevented a naval armaments race, but it was against Britain's peculiar interests to make quantitative reduction in capital ships alone. She could not secure the abolition of submarines. Her economy, based on long supply routes in times of war, her major offensive weapon of blockade, and her obligation to provide forces to meet the possible simultaneous attack of major powers in European, Mediterranean, and Far Eastern waters, called for much more varied forces than were needed to defend the largely self-supporting island empire of the United States, even with a two-

---

[1] Bacon, *Jellicoe*, chaps. 24, 25; Robin Higham, *Armed Forces in Peacetime* (1962), pp. 106–9.

ocean navy. Moreover, the British navy would provide the first line of defence against an aggressor in Europe and probably in the Far East who might, or might not, ultimately assail the United States and the Dominions. So during the remainder of the twenties the British government, although powerfully swayed by economy plans and disarmament pressure, could never view the naval scene with equanimity. But its views found little response elsewhere.

All that survived the torpedoing of Jellicoe's programme was the idea of a Singapore base. But the base made little sense without a powerful fleet to use it. Failing this, friendship with Japan could alone guarantee the safety of Hong Kong and the Straits Settlements. The C.I.D. in 1921 accepted the view that the Mediterranean was the most convenient central position for the fleet, and that a base in Singapore (or perhaps Sydney) should be prepared to receive the fleet if it were sent eastwards in a hurry. Hong Kong, owing to its forward position, had to be regarded as expendable. This strategy was explained by Amery to the 1923 imperial conference, and the construction of a great Singapore base was accepted, although only after initial objections from Canada. When the Labour government decided in 1924 to stop work on the base, the proposal was welcomed by Canada and South Africa. However, as a result of Beatty's representations the Conservatives on their return to office revived the project, which was always ardently supported by the Australian and New Zealand governments, and the stage of serious planning of the site began. Not much had been completed when the Labour government again stopped work on the base in 1929; but it was started again by the National government after 1931.

By 1926 the plans which had been continuously under review since 1909 for the standardization of equipment and training and the exchange of ships and officers between the United Kingdom and the Dominions were in satisfactory working order, and the obligation of the latter to make themselves responsible for local defence had been accepted. The Admiralty hoped that in time the growth of these local forces would enable them to take an increasing share in the work of the main fleet. But within the overall figures little could be done in this direction before 1936, and it is correct to say that it was at sea that the tradition of imperial unity remained strongest, because here the preponderance of the United Kingdom was most pronounced.[1] There was a corresponding financial burden:

[1] Mansergh, p. 77.

the United Kingdom naval estimates reached £57,300,000 for 1928–29.[1]

All this the United States viewed with little sympathy. The Geneva naval conference ended in deadlock in August 1927 when the British representatives insisted on a minimum of fifteen large cruisers (10,000 tons) and fifty-five smaller (7,500 tons), or 562,000 tons. The conference had been called for the purpose of applying the Washington categories, combined with the 5–5–3 ratio, to non-capital ships. Japan took part, but officially France and Italy did not. The Americans preferred twenty-five large and twenty smaller cruisers. The ostensible reason for the difference was that the larger cruisers seemed more suitable to the Americans for coastal defence purposes; but it was believed in British naval circles that the aim was also to cut down the large numbers of smaller British warships which were needed to enforce a blockade. The Americans certainly wanted larger cruisers to match the Japanese building programme. Blockade or not, the Admiralty was undoubtedly right (as the experience of World War II was to show) in insisting that its varied needs, including convoy protection, called for a greater number of smaller vessels than the Americans favoured. On the other hand the British debating position was weakened in two ways. To reach the tonnage figure desired by the Admiralty, the United States would have to embark on a considerable additional new building programme; and in any case the cabinet soon decided that 'mathematical parity' was not enough, and that some equality 'in strength, in offensive power', was needed. The second decision, which led to Viscount Cecil's resignation, suggested direct competitiveness; the first, expansion not limitation.[2]

The breakdown, followed by the Anglo-French disarmament deal in 1928, was an embarrassment to Anglo-American relations for the next three years. The mutual suspicions aroused were to a large extent pointless, for neither government wanted to pay the bill. In London the peace-loving and even parsimonious Chancellor of the Exchequer, Winston Churchill, managed to limit the cruiser building programme to one only in both 1927 and 1928. He also got the cabinet to agree in 1928 to place the ten-year rule on a

---

[1] Or 25s 1d per head of the population, as compared with Australia, 10s 9d; New Zealand, 9s 9d; South Africa, 1s 2d, and Canada 29 cents. A. B. Keith, *Dominion Autonomy in Practice*, p. 70.

[2] M. Tate, *The United States and Armaments* (1948), pp. 150–94; Viscount Cecil, *A Great Experiment* (1941), pp. 185–9; R. H. Ferrell, *Peace in Their Time*, pp. 110–11.

moving basis, which effectively removed all sense of urgency. The plan to build three cruisers in 1929 was dropped. Then Ramsay MacDonald in 1930 gave in to the Americans and accepted fifty cruisers, and President Hoover openly pressed for the abandonment of some of the British blockade practices. But on Henderson's insistence it was decided to maintain belligerent rights of contraband control to the fullest extent.[1]

Economy also hit the R.A.F. Trenchard and Hoare had saved it from destruction by Bonar Law, and a home defence force of fifty-two squadrons had been sanctioned in June 1923. But after Locarno a committee under Birkenhead decided that its completion could be delayed from 1928 to 1930. The date of completion was later postponed until 1936, and then by the Labour government to 1938.[2] In this atmosphere of economy, studied affability, and short-term planning the British, Commonwealth, and United States governments were psychologically quite unprepared to meet the great crisis of Japanese conquest in Manchuria after September 1931.

3. MEDIATION IN MANCHURIA

The Sino-Japanese imbroglio was the moment of truth for the makers of British foreign policy, for although the immediate consequences were not disastrous the new and permanent limitations to British power and influence in the postwar world were revealed. The policy-makers in Whitehall understood the lesson far better than the general public. Even in the Foreign Office, however, no drastic changes of policy appear to have suggested themselves. The best course seemed to be to carry on as soothingly as possible, hoping that the felicities of a vanishing world could be restored. The method preferred was nearer to mediation than to leadership.[3]

For this there were two practical reasons. One was the virtual impossibility of halting the progress of the Japanese armies in Manchuria by a long range economic boycott or other form of economic sanction and still less by naval action (military sanctions under the League) without United States cooperation, or even with

---

[1] B.D., II (i), nos. 77, 79 etc; W. N. Medlicott, *The Economic Blockade* (1952), vol. I, pp. 11–12; R. G. O'Connor, *Perilous Equilibrium: The United States and the London Naval Conference of 1930* (Kansas, 1962).

[2] Higham, pp. 129, 162–3.

[3] I. S. Friedman, *British Relations with China: 1931–1939* (1940), is a useful general survey.

it. The other reason was the impact of Chinese nationalism on all the interested foreign powers. For the British authorities the preceding years had seen a long series of negotiations over extra-territorial rights in the Chinese treaty ports. After Chiang Kai-shek's expulsion of the Communists from the Kuomintang in 1927 and his capture of Peiping in June 1928 the prestige of his government called for successes at the expense of foreign interests, with a marked reluctance to give them precise guarantees in return for the surrender of extraterritorial rights. All such privileges were unilaterally abrogated by the Nanking government as from 1 January 1930, although negotiations continued. So exasperated was the State Department that at one point in February 1931 H. L. Stimson, the Secretary of State, proposed Anglo-American financial sanctions and the seizure of the Shanghai customs. Henderson replied that for many reasons, including the Kellogg Pact, the British government really could not contemplate the seizure of customs houses.[1] In Manchuria itself the unstable régime of Marshal Chang Hsueh-liang (son of Chang Tso-lin) had led to attacks on Soviet railway interests in the north in July 1929; the Russian authorities bided their time, and then at exactly the right moment in November 1929 sent in troops and secured a complete Chinese collapse and the withdrawal of the offending measures. In many ways this was a remarkable forerunner of the Japanese intervention, which differed from it mainly in poor presentation of the Japanese grievances to the world. No one denounced the Soviet action at Geneva. In fact, no one seemed to have heard about it.[2]

The Japanese treaty rights allowed them to station troops on the South Manchurian Railway and to live and work in Southern Manchuria. The Chinese rightly believed that they would lose control of Manchuria altogether to the Soviet and Japanese empires unless they resisted. They were known to be planning a new railway system which would ruin the South Manchurian Railway. Probably, too, there was some truth in the Japanese military view that the Minseito government, which had been in office since 1929 in Tokyo and had the support of many of the heavy industrialists in opposing foreign adventures, had encouraged Chinese monkey

[1] B.D., II (viii), no. 366.
[2] The British minister, Sir Miles Lampson, commented, perhaps a trifle wistfully, on this episode: ' . . . the Soviet technique, combined of ruthless realism and semi-Asiatic subtlety, has proved itself admirably suited for dealing with the Chinese race' (B.D., *ibid.*, p. 1028).

tricks by a studiously conciliatory policy. Thus when an explosion on the railway track near Mukden on 18 September 1931 led the Japanese army to put into immediate operation plans to seize strategical control of the railway zone the reaction of British experts and business interests in Shanghai and London was scarcely one of surprise, or even of disapproval. It was not until the end of the year, by which time the Japanese army had taken control of the whole of southern Manchuria, that the affair had begun to take the character of empire building by an act of conquest.

As soon as this point was established an acute dilemma faced the Pacific Dominions, Australia and New Zealand. The menace of an expanding Japanese empire had never been entirely out of their thoughts since the Russo-Japanese war of 1904-5. Neither Anglo-Japanese friendship nor empire defence had been sufficient to solve the problem of their security. Their territories, with those of the Dutch East Indies and the Chinese seaboard with its vast British commercial interests, would be among the possible victims of Japanese maritime expansion. In view of the unstable balance in Japan of army versus navy, expansionist versus non-expansionist forces in heavy industry, liberal versus conservative politics, and the rival attractions of expansion on the mainland sponsored by the army and overseas by the navy, it was natural for some elements in the two Dominions to be reluctant to court an open breach which would canalize in their direction the energies of their difficult Pacific neighbour. Economic considerations were also involved. Both had been, like Canada and other primary producers, badly hit by the slump, and the increase of export outlets was the main preoccupation of their governments in the autumn and winter of 1931. Japan happened to be among the few hopeful prospects, for she was buying 25 per cent of Australian raw wool and 40 per cent of Australian wheat in 1931-32, as compared with some 7 per cent of each in the twenties. There was also a small but growing New Zealand export of wool to Japan.[1]

Balancing these inducements to a conciliatory policy was the recognition that the smaller powers must stand by the League as a means of collective security and keep in step with the United States, and that Chinese provocation, however real, could not justify the later developments of Japanese expansion. The influence of Dominions further away from the Far East, such as South Africa

---

[1] Carter, p. 136, and fn. 3.

and the Irish Free State, tended to favour resolute League action. On balance, however, Great Britain, New Zealand, and Australia were joined in awareness of danger, and separated by the fact that while the main British defence problems were still in Europe, the other two found their main danger in the Pacific.

The complexity of local tensions and antagonisms in Manchuria was largely concealed from pro-League supporters in the west, and the case was debated in somewhat general terms as a glaring example of the one-sided aggression which the Covenant existed to handle. Under the British lead, during Lord Reading's short tenure of the Foreign Secretaryship, the Council proposed to follow the precedent of the Graeco-Bulgarian dispute of 1925 by seeking first to stop hostilities and then to offer a fair settlement based on a consideration of the merits of the dispute. The issue was confused almost at once by a deceptively forthcoming move on the part of the State Department. Mr. Stimson publicly welcomed the League's first steps but declined to join in the immediate despatch of a commission of enquiry in accordance with the Graeco-Bulgarian precedent, as suggested by the Chinese delegate on 28 September. It has been argued that this revelation of a divergence among Japan's potential critics, which was known to the Japanese delegation as early as 23 September, may have been decisive in encouraging the Japanese government at a moment when it might still have been overawed by world opinion. Stimson's subsequent course is difficult to follow, partly because of the State Department's aversion to the appearance of collaboration with other powers, partly because at this period, in the heyday of isolationism and the depths of the depression, an adventurous policy was as impossible for him as it was for the government in London.[1] The U.S. consul in Geneva took a seat at the Council meeting on 16 October, but the precedent was not repeated. General Dawes, however, took part in its proceedings behind the scenes after 16 November, although he told Briand that the United States would not join in the consideration or the enforcing of sanctions.[2]

Sir John Simon, who did not take office as Foreign Secretary

---

[1] President Hoover states in his memoirs that Stimson desired economic sanctions throughout the crisis, but also that he and the rest of the cabinet agreed during October 1931 not to go beyond moral pressure (*The Memoirs of Herbert Hoover*, vol. II, pp. 366–70); H. L. Stimson and McG. Bundy, *On Active Service in Peace and War* (1948), pp. 78–9; R. L. Wilbur and A. M. Hyde, *The Hoover Policies* (1937), p. 601.

[2] C. G. Dawes, *Journal as Ambassador to Great Britain* (New York, 1939), p. 416.

until 9 November 1931, told Stimson through the British embassy on the following day that Great Britain was also not contemplating anything of the sort, but apparently failed to elicit any very clear comment from Stimson in reply. It even seemed to some observers that the main purpose of United States policy was to ensure or forward its own economic interests in Manchuria, an 'economic imperialist' argument which provided the theme of a well-known book by Charles Beard in 1946.[1] Whatever Stimson's real inclination (and he evidently felt strongly the need for some decisive gesture) he was finally warned by Hoover at the end of December 1931 that the United States could not participate in any form of sanctions. In the meantime Japan refused to consider the League's proposals for mutual evacuation of forces as a preliminary to negotiation, and the Council adopted (on a Japanese proposal of 21 November 1931) the alternative of a commission of enquiry on the spot. This sailed for the Far East early in February 1932 with Lord Lytton as chairman, and with four other members representing the United States, France, Germany, and Italy.

The later misunderstanding between Simon and Stimson is implicit in these proceedings. The American felt that he must do *something*. Sanctions were ruled out. Moral leadership, so flatteringly accepted by the world as a substitute for American action in the days of Kellogg and Wilson, remained. There is no need today to emphasize the fact that it is among the myths of history to say that the United States offered and Great Britain refused to apply any form of economic pressure against Japan in this crisis. Nevertheless, something happened in January and February 1932 which gave the myth a very wide circulation and it did not begin to be challenged seriously until after the Second World War.[2] Some confusion arose from the fact that Simon accepted but saw no great merit in two new moves by Stimson. The first was a note, sent on 7 January 1932 to Japan, China, and the other signatories of the Nine-Power

---

[1] B.D. II (viii), nos. 714, 717, 748; C. A. Beard, *American Foreign Policy in the Making* (Yale, 1946), pp. 111–4, 134–41.

[2] H. L. Stimson's story, as given in *The Far Eastern Crisis* (New York, 1936), laments his impotence in terms which seem to blame his British opposite number. Sir John Pratt, with inside knowledge as a British official, criticized Stimson's account in a letter to *The Times* of 30 November, 1938. This is amplified in his *War and Politics in China* (1943), chap. 13. B.D. II, vols. viii and ix give the full British documentation. The first extensive American correction of the earlier legends was by Miss S. R. Smith, *The Manchurian Crisis, 1931–32* (New York, 1948). A recent American survey is R. H. Ferrell, *American Diplomacy in the Great Depression* (1957), chaps. 8–11. R. Bassett, *Democracy and Foreign Policy* (1952), deals fully with British reactions.

Treaty of 1922, saying that the United States would not recognize any impairment of American rights in China or any situation contrary to the Kellogg Pact of 1928. The Foreign Office at first thought that the United States was merely reserving its legal rights, and that there was no need to issue a similar declaration since Japan had recently given assurances to the League that it would maintain the open door. The second step was a proposal, discussed with Simon on the transatlantic telephone between 11 and 15 February, for the 'invoking' of the Nine-Power Treaty. This apparently meant joint diplomatic representations by the remainder of the nine powers in Tokyo, threatening non-recognition of Japanese conquests, but nothing more. Stimson believed Simon to be unenthusiastic. Simon was a shy, accomplished, subtle lawyer, who was suave and peace-loving and high-principled and incapable of sounding angry or enthusiastic about anything. He showed little power of decision outside the law and home politics. But he appears to have made no objection in principle to Stimson's proposal, although he thought it better to limit the protest to Shanghai, and he felt it unwise to give the impression that the League was to be put aside. Accordingly he got the Council to accept a clause about non-recognition, which covered the Manchurian situation, on 16 February, and the Assembly on 11 March. This was in no sense a rejection of Stimson's Nine-Power proposal.[1]

The crisis in Shanghai followed an incident on 18 January 1932 when five Japanese, including two priests, were assaulted by a Chinese mob, but the real cause was Japanese exasperation at the Chinese boycott which was hitting Japanese trade hard, strengthened by the inclination of the Japanese Admiral to give the navy a share of the international limelight. Although a Japanese ultimatum to the Mayor of Shanghai demanding apologies, punishments, compensation, and suppression of anti-Japanese organizations was fully accepted on 28 January, Japanese forces were landed, and the suburb of Chapei was bombarded on the 29th. The Chinese troops put up an unexpectedly good resistance. It is now evident that the Japanese government did not wish to extend the war to China proper, but it was not until 3 March that the first corner was turned in an armistice agreement concluded under Admiral Sir H. Kelly's mediation on the man-of-war *Kent*. During the preceding weeks there were vigorous protests from London and Washington, and

[1] B.D. II (ix), nos. 431, 432, 455, 458, 469.

the British and American forces in the international settlement were reinforced, but in London the government and Chiefs of Staff had been brought to a stark realization of the defencelessness of all British interests in China if the Japanese really chose to attack them. The Treasury added the emphatic warning that the country was in no better position financially or economically to engage in a Far Eastern war.[1]

In these circumstances the Shanghai situation called for firm, tactful, in short, highly adroit handling by British diplomats. The outcome was one of the outstanding minor successes of British diplomacy in the interwar years. The small strengthening of British forces in Shanghai was not a threat to Japan, but a precautionary measure against an attack by the local Chinese on the international settlement, following the 1927 precedent. As soon as it became evident that the Japanese government desired to back out of the Shanghai involvement, British mediation became invaluable to both the contestants. Neither could sign anything which gave the slightest appearance of advantage to the other. In spite of this, and largely as a result of skilful and patient interventions by the British minister, Sir Miles Lampson, during two months of negotiations in Shanghai, the phrases and sentences were gradually put together to form the cease-fire agreement, which both sides managed to sign on 5 May 1932.

And in the meantime, while there was a prospect of settling and localizing the Shanghai crisis, it seemed a mistake to link it with the much more intractable Manchurian problem; this was the main reason for Simon's doubts about the Stimson proposal in February.[2] Subject to this tactical modification Simon was prepared to co-operate, but instead of approaching the remaining signatories of the Nine-Power treaty Stimson abandoned his plan and set out his theories about non-recognition in a letter to Senator Borah. He wrote later that the British 'nonjoinder' had killed his *démarche*.[3]

---

[1] B.D. II (ix), no. 660, fn. 8, no. 636, summarizes the C.O.S.'s conclusion on 3 March that if Japan attacked, the British forces at Shanghai would be able only with difficulty to reach the open sea; Hong Kong, Singapore, and Trincomali might well fall before the main fleet could reach Singapore. A Japanese book by Shinsaku Hirata, *The Navy Reader*, published in Tokyo in April 1932, presumably under the auspices of the Japanese Naval Department, deployed precisely the same arguments, and was known in London. The cabinet accepted the conclusion that the ten-year rule must be abandoned (see p. 335). S. W. Kirby, *The War Against Japan* (1957), vol. I, pp. 11, 12; Basil Collier, *The Defence of the United Kingdom* (1957), p. 24.

[2] B.D. II (ix), no. 469.

[3] Stimson, *The Far Eastern Crisis*, pp. 97–8.

If we put aside the unworthy assumption that Stimson was merely playing politics and making sure that Simon and not himself should be the scapegoat for the inaction of all the powers, we must ask why he regarded the invoking of the Nine-Power treaty as of such importance. The answer no doubt is that at this period the enunciation of principles of international conduct with moral undertones still satisfied the American sense of mission without challenging isolationist sentiment and without creating any danger of retaliation. The powers with vulnerable positions in the Far East could not trail their coats so easily. 'Refusal of recognition costs nothing and to a sanctimonious government it might well appear a very handy sort of chloroform wherewith to stifle the outcries of unintelligent idealists', wrote Sir Ronald Lindsay tartly on 21 January.[1]

All through the early months of 1932 there was an uneasy feeling among British diplomats that the United States government would somehow manage to push the British into more forceful action, and then leave them in the lurch. Yet there could be no breach. 'America always leaves us to do the difficult work *vis-à-vis* Japan', Simon told the cabinet on 29 January. But, he added, 'we cannot afford to upset the United States of America over this, and I do not mean to do so'. The British ambassador in Washington stressed the same point more irritably on 3 March.[2]

> I know that the Americans are dreadful people to deal with—they cannot make firm promises, but they jolly you along with fair prospects and when you are committed they let you down. Taking the short view it is hard to remember a bargain with them that has been really satisfactory to us in itself; but on the long view there has never been a case when we were not right to have made the bargain. And never since 1812 have we ever come down on the non-American side of any fence.

Stimson's aim was simple but inadequate. Although the threat of sanctions was ruled out, he hoped that his statements of principle would still have some deterrent effect. Hoover, however, was so incapable of what Stimson called 'even the fairest kind of bluff' that he was little help; he was even incubating from February onward a public statement that the United States would always employ peaceful means in international affairs. This statement was made,

---

[1] B.D., *op.cit.*, no. 102.
[2] *Ibid.*, nos. 153, 665.

indeed, in May on his behalf by Under-Secretary of State William R. Castle, when Stimson was in Europe.[1]

As the League power with the greatest stake in the non-European world, Great Britain could have assumed the rôle of moral leadership with resounding condemnation of Japanese conduct, to the satisfaction of a great many people throughout the world, and even in the MacDonald government. Sheer expediency, the determination to avoid the slippery slope of descent to a disastrous direct quarrel with Japan, was no doubt the decisive reason why she did not.[2] There were others, including the need to keep her hands as free as possible to deal with events in Europe, and perhaps something of the century-old diplomatic tradition of the concert system, which bound the powers together in a network of constantly changing relations on a theoretically equal footing. This sense of membership of a grouping of mutually dependent powers was not shared by the United States, whose traditional position of uniqueness had been accentuated by refusal to join the League. It meant that Britain's part in the solution of family squabbles in the international society which did not directly affect her interests was still that of a court missionary rather than a judge or jury, still less a prosecuting counsel. It was one possible interpretation of the Covenant. Her predominant approach to foreign policy was that of a mediator even as late as the winter of 1938–39.

The Lytton Report, published on 1 October 1932, did not deny faults on both sides, but proposed that Manchuria should be largely an autonomous state under Chinese sovereignty, with a local gendarmerie set up after the withdrawal of foreign troops. The Japanese, who had arranged for the establishment of an independent state called 'Manchukuo' in February 1932, made it clear in discussions in the League Council in November 1932 that they did not intend to withdraw their forces or influence. In the meeting of the Special Assembly on 6 December the Irish delegate had considerable support when he asked for an uncompromising stand based on the full acceptance of the Lytton Report and the doctrine of 'non-recognition'; but a speech by Simon on the 7th, stressing

[1] R. H. Ferrell, *American Diplomacy in the Great Depression*, pp. 186–7; Stimson, *On Active Service*, p. 87; S. R. Smith, p. 152.

[2] Cf. Vansittart's remarkable minute of 1 February, 1932: ' . . . (7) The Japanese are more afraid of the U.S. than of us, and for obvious reasons. At present, however, they share our low view of American fighting spirit. (8) By ourselves we must eventually swallow any and every humiliation in the Far East. If there is some limit to American submissiveness, this is not necessarily so . . .' (B.D. II(ix), p. 283).

the complicated nature of the evidence and the desirability of further efforts at conciliation, swung the debate against measures of moral condemnation unsupported by means of enforcement. Simon quoted specific criticisms of China from the Report, such as the virulence of the anti-foreign propaganda, the economic boycott, and China's failure to follow 'the road of international cooperation' since 1922. On the other hand he virtually limited direct reference to Japan's misdeeds to quoting the Report's statement that the Manchurian situation was not 'a simple case of the violation of the frontier of one country by the armed forces of a neighbouring country'. Three English newspapers on the following day reported M. Matsuoka as saying to a friend that Simon had said in half an hour what the Japanese delegation had been trying to say in ten days.[1]

There is some evidence of argument behind the scenes among the Commonwealth representatives, but Canada, Australia, and New Zealand followed Simon's lead. Only after this further attempt at conciliation had failed did the Assembly on 24 February 1933 reaffirm the Lytton Report's conclusion and the doctrine of 'non-recognition', while avoiding language which would point directly to sanctions. Japan announced her withdrawal from the League on 27 March.[2] The British Foreign Secretary throughout the crisis had sedulously played the part of a distressed neutral seeking a constructive compromise. If in his speech of 7 December 1932 he had shown his determination to avoid a breach with Japan a little too openly, he had given no more than a glimpse of the underlying realism of British policy. No rapid effective action against Japan was possible without the full support of the United States and the Soviet Union. There was no prospect of this at this stage. British policy was shaped accordingly.

4. THE GOVERNMENT OF INDIA ACT

Something of this mediatory impulse can also be detected in the government's handling of Indian constitutional reforms, which were under continuous discussion with the antipathetic communal

[1] None of the correspondents claimed to have heard Matsuoka's remark. Why 'ten days'? The Assembly was only in its second day. These quotations, and the whole history of the subsequent controversies as to Simon's attitude, including Stimson's interpretation, are recounted by Bassett, *op.cit.*, pp. 280–321.

[2] Carter, pp. 153–63; F. P. Walters, *A History of the League of Nations*, vol. I, pp. 490–99.

leaders from 1930 to 1935. India was still the brightest jewel in the imperial crown, but with problems vast and embarrassing to all concerned. The Congress party, which during the first thirty years of its existence before the death of G. K. Gokhale in 1915 had maintained friendly relations with the British Raj and been fully conscious of the practical difficulties of representative government, was now revolutionary, emotional, and provocative, denouncing gradualness as obstruction and energetically appealing to the world for immediate release from bondage. This transition had taken place quickly during the later war years; B. G. Tilak and Mohandas K. Gandhi emerged as leaders after Gokhale's death, and Gandhi had undisputed control for a time after Tilak's own death in 1921. Discontent and disillusionment of varied origin had accumulated during the war, the cost of living was rising, Muslims were irked by the fate of the Caliphate, three-sevenths of the population went down with influenza in 1918–19, the course of the war with its reverses shook British prestige, and sporadic violence led to police counter-measures. The result was the launching of the first campaign of so-called passive resistance under Gandhi's direction on 24 February 1919.

This was undoubtedly on the theory that Britain's difficulties were India's opportunity, for the Punjab on the eve of the third Afghan war was chosen as the main scene of revolutionary action. Mob violence, attacks on individual Britons, and the destruction of buildings connected with the British seemed to be well organized. It culminated in General Dyer's shooting of hundreds of Indians who had assembled for a meeting at Amritsar on 13 April. Dyer was thanked afterwards by local deputations and the heads of the Sikh community for restoring order. But after being at first officially approved his conduct was officially condemned; he was dismissed, and the vast publicity of the event and its sequel meant on the one hand that the Congress could proclaim the brutality of British imperialism, and on the other could privately assure itself that the British would hesitate to use force in future. Later in the year the Congress party rejected the Montagu-Chelmsford reform plan as quite inadequate, and demanded full responsible government within fifteen years. In 1920 it set itself to gain self-rule or *swaraj* in one year by means of non-violent non-cooperation.

In this way the revolutionary phase of nationalist action was launched, and during the twenties continued with no particular profit to anyone. British governments and political parties were pledged in the historic announcement of 20 August 1917 to the 'increasing association of Indians in every branch of the administration and the gradual development of self-governing institutions with a view to the progressive realization of responsible government in India as an integral part of the British Empire'.[1] Nevertheless, Indian divisions, communal and political, and political inexperience were felt to provide obstacles to any rapid advance of India towards Dominion status. The system of dyarchy introduced in 1919 for an experimental period of ten years was intended to provide political experience at the ministerial level to Indians in the provinces in certain 'transferred' subjects, and at the centre the existing Legislative Council was converted into an elected bicameral legislature for British India, but with the executive still responsible to the British Parliament and the Secretary of State for India. That dyarchy was not completely a failure was due in the main to moderate nationalists who formed the National Liberal Federation and heartily supported the Montagu-Chelmsford proposals. They supplied ministers to take charge of most of the transferred subjects, and did their best to make the system work in order to justify Indian claims to fitness for further responsibility. But with the Congress boycott of the provincial elections and their own limited numbers the Liberals could not develop sufficient public backing to bring into existence a two-party system, the necessary foundation for effective representative government.

It was considered to be good revolutionary tactics to keep harrying and harassing the imperial power, but it probably did the movement more harm than good. A saint with political ambitions, Gandhi had perfected his exasperating technique during a twenty-year leadership of Indians in South Africa, and no one has ever been able to decide whether the blatant contradictions between his stated aims and their practical application were due to confused thinking or to a rather whimsical opportunism. He had supported British policy during the Boer War and made speeches in support of recruiting early in the Great War. But at that time, having just returned from South Africa, he knew little at first hand about Indian conditions, and it was on the advice of the older Congress

[1] R. Coupland, *The Indian Problem, 1833–1935* (London, 1942), p. 52ff. The effect of the announcement was reduced by faulty presentation in the form of a reply to a parliamentary question. Lionel Curtis endeavoured to repair the damage in his *Letters to the People of India on Responsible Government* (1918).

leaders that he refrained from active politics for a year and spent the time visiting Indian villages, with the result that he became the only Indian leader who was widely known to the masses. The anarchic element in the Congress programme was largely his contribution, and a more constructive quality appears when his influence was reduced, as it was during his comfortable imprisonment from 1922 to 1924. But the contradictions remained. Relying heavily on funds supplied by Hindu big business interests the movement nevertheless paraded every variety of radical belief from socialism and communism to the all-sufficiency of village economy and the spinning wheel.

The denunciation of British rule did not prevent many of the leaders, including Gandhi himself, from visualizing their future as part of the Commonwealth.[1] They remained remarkably loyal to the idea of responsible government on the British model instead of the American or other parliamentary systems. Nor could the view that the practical obstacles to *swaraj* would disappear with independence altogether disguise the fact that no workable system of Indian government had been put forward apart from the parliamentary dictatorship of the Hindu majority, which the Muslims, the princes, and the smaller minority groups rejected. Gandhi had supported the Caliphate movement in 1920 as an excellent basis for Hindu-Muslim unity, but this was too opportunistic a gesture to carry real conviction, and the limits of reconciliation were illustrated when the Moplahs, fanatical Muslim peasantry of south-west India, were inspired by the movement to subject their Hindu neighbours to wholesale slaughter as a preliminary to forcible conversion. The number of Hindu-Muslim riots increased each year after 1921; there was a fortnight's rioting in Calcutta in 1926 with arson, looting, and nearly 500 casualties.

The Muslim League, led by Mohammed Ali Jinnah, supported the demand for *swaraj*, but put forward more and more prominently the need for safeguards for the Muslim position, including separate electorates, a federal system leaving full and complete autonomy to the provinces, veto rights for substantial minorities (the three-fourths rule), and the maintenance of the Muslim majority in the Punjab, Bengal, and the North-West Frontier under any system of boundary revision. An attempt by an all-party (but predominantly

[1] Dr. S. R. Mehrotra, *India and the Commonwealth, 1855–1929* (1965), p. 132 and chap. III generally; 'Imperial Federation and India, 1868–1917', *J. of Comm. Pol. Studies* (1963).

Congress) committee under Pandit Motilal Nehru to draw up an agreed constitution in 1928 resulted in general assurances to the Muslims against harassment or exploitation, but rejected separate electorates, made it clear that the Indian states must accept democratic reforms inside their own territories, and dealt very vaguely with such fundamental problems as the future of British troops and service chiefs in the armed forces, federation, the conduct of foreign policy, and India's place in the Commonwealth. By making Dominion status its goal the committee did nevertheless assume continued Commonwealth membership. On this ground Pandit Jawaharlal Nehru and his friends were not prepared to vote for it. The Hindu Mahasabha, representing the most extreme and uncompromising wing of Hinduism, went further. The Muslims, on the other hand, drew their various parties together, and on 1 January 1929 reaffirmed their demands for a federal system with complete provincial autonomy, separate electorates, and a guaranteed share in central and provincial cabinets.[1]

If in spite of this communal deadlock and the virtual failure of dyarchy the British political parties were well prepared to go much further towards self-government the reason was not that they were blind to the difficulties, but that world disarmament and a great Indian settlement were the two major pace-setting policies which might bring laurels to MacDonald's hard-pressed minority government. In accordance with the promise in 1919 of reconsideration after ten years the Simon commission had been appointed in 1927 to examine the possibilities. It included two Labour members, Clement Attlee and Stephen Walsh (replaced shortly by Vernon Hartshorn), together with Viscount Burnham, Lord Strathcona, the Hon. Edward Cadogan, and Colonel Lane Fox, and it recommended responsible government for the provinces and a federal basis for the central legislature, but with no change in the central executive.[2] After being boycotted and condemned by nationalist opinion in India it was quietly buried by the British government. Attlee tells us that MacDonald in 1930 did not give even five minutes to ascertain the views of his two emissaries,[3] and a fresh start was made with Round Table conferences in 1930, 1931, and 1932. Churchill found, as he says, that Baldwin considered the time to be too far

[1] Coupland, pp. 68–96.
[2] Cmd 3568, 3569.
[3] C. R. Attlee, *As It Happened* (1954), p. 66.

gone 'for any robust assertion of British imperial greatness'. Baldwin felt that the hope of the Conservatives lay in not being outpaced by the Labour and Liberal parties on this issue. This view Churchill did not accept, and he accordingly resigned from the Conservative shadow cabinet on 27 January 1931. When the new government took office in the autumn it at once asked for a vote of confidence in its Indian policy; an amendment by Churchill providing that the House should not be committed 'to the establishment in India of a Dominion Constitution as defined by the Statute of Westminster' mustered only a little over forty votes in the division lobby.[1]

Although Churchill chose to stress political expedience as a reason for the government's Indian policy it was the conscience of liberal-progressive elements in all parties which was the driving force in the discussions leading to the Government of India Act of 1935. And it was the failure of the Congress party to prove that it had the capacity or the forbearance to provide a viable government for all India which satisfied these elements that enough had been done for the moment. When Lord Irwin in the autumn of 1929 affirmed that Dominion Status for India was the goal of British policy and announced that the Simon report should be followed by conferences with Indian representatives, Congress replied by demanding in effect the immediate setting up of a Dominion constitution for India. The preliminary difficulties were waved aside as irrelevant, and after a demand for immediate complete independence a fresh campaign of 'non-violent' civil disobedience with the usual terrorist incidents was launched in April 1930. It was promptly denounced by the Muslims as a move to subject their 70 millions to the Hindu Mahasabha.

The first Round Table conference, with representatives of the three British parties and all the Indian groups except the non-cooperative Congress party, met in London on 12 November 1930 and agreed in principle to the setting up of an all-India federation in which the states would participate, with responsibility in Indian hands apart from certain safeguards regarding defence, external relations, and finance. No solution of the communal question could be found. The second conference (September-December 1931) was notable for the presence of Gandhi as the sole Congress representative, following a truce negotiated between him and Lord Irwin and his acceptance of the general conclusions of the first

[1] W. S. Churchill, *The Gathering Storm* (1948), pp. 26-7, 53.

conference. His voluminous robes, sojourn in the East End of London, reception at Buckingham Palace, eating habits and days of silence impressed the British public but were no compensation for his inability or unwillingness to offer practical suggestions or to compromise. Lord Irwin, who seems to have felt a certain affinity for Gandhi's fox-terrier shrewdness, thought that 'intentionally he was completely sincere, yet in some matters he was the victim of unconscious self-deception'.[1] In the minorities committee he busied himself for a week with informal meetings, over which he presided, in an attempt to find a solution of the communal problem, but he had to report complete failure. He then recommended the completion of the constitution without a prior communal agreement. This the minorities (Muslims, Hindu Depressed Classes, Indian Christians, Anglo-Indians, and the resident British community) rejected. Gandhi for his part rejected dyarchy at the centre and any delay in the setting up of responsible government at the centre or in the provinces. So the second conference failed; he returned to India and yet another civil disobedience campaign began.[2]

By now, however, the broader lines of a new constitutional structure had been defined, and the government went ahead with the preparation of a bill embodying detailed provisions for presentation to Parliament. A third Round Table conference (November-December 1932), meeting without representatives of Congress or of the British Labour party, gave further consideration to the central organization in connexion with the franchise, federal finance, and the participation of the Indian states. In view of the absence of agreement between the communities the Prime Minister announced the government's own proposal for minority representation in August 1932, on lines broadly similar to the existing system, but with separate electorates for the Depressed Classes; this produced a 'fast unto death' by Gandhi and provision in the 'Poona pact' for a system of indirect election of 'outcast' representatives (thus preserving the principle of the indivisibility of the Hindu community). Then the government's proposals were embodied in a White Paper which was subjected to searching scrutiny by a joint select committee of both Houses of Parliament, sitting almost continuously for eighteen months. Indian delegates took part in

[1] H. Nicolson, *King George V*, pp. 507–8; Birkenhead, *Halifax* (1965), chap. 16.
[2] Coupland, pp. 113–27.

the cross-examination of experts and witnesses. Lord Salisbury, hostile to federation and convinced that the proposals had not been properly thought out, led the onslaught on the Secretary of State for India, Sir Samuel Hoare, who himself became a witness. He had to deal with 10,000 leading and supplementary questions, and discharged the task with a sound technical grasp and good temper. The Report, with some amendments to the original plans, was carried in the committee by 19 votes to 9, the minority including 4 Labour members who considered the proposals inadequate.[1] In the Commons, after long barrages of denunciation of the proposals from Churchill ('a monstrous monument of shame built by pigmies') and other critics, the second reading was carried on 11 February 1935 by 404 votes to 133; the bill finally reached the Statute Book on 24 July 1935.[2]

The furious assaults of the diehards, together with the complaints of Labour and Congress spokesmen that the act did not go far enough, diminished both the credit due to the British government for its boldly constructive policy and the chances of a cooperative effort in India to make the new arrangements work. The Act was an invitation to Congress to make British rule superfluous by proving India's fitness to replace it; it was a declaration of faith in a democratic solution which needed, however, some time and some experimentation and much goodwill to establish the vast network of political conventions and administrative machinery needed for an entire subcontinent. Congressmen did not believe, or professed not to believe, in the British willingness to make the final surrender of authority. Gandhi, and perhaps other leaders, do not even seem to have properly grasped what the act contained.[3] Congress had no desire and no intention to hamper its future freedom of action to suit the reservations of the minorities, although to everyone else a federal type of government seemed indispensable in view of the country's diversities. Above all, however, its popular objective was freedom from foreign rule rather than the goodwill of a 'foreign' power earned through collaboration. Even so, the innate Indian tendency to strike attitudes while others acted had a lot to do with

---

[1] *Joint Committee on Indian Constitutional Reforms, Report and Proceedings* (H.M.S.O., 1934).

[2] Coupland, pp. 127-33; Viscount Templewood, *Nine Troubled Years* (1954), pp. 42-103. On Labour's attitude: Vera Brittain, *Pethick-Lawrence* (1963), pp. 130-33.

[3] He left it unread for many years: W. K. Hancock, *Studies in War and Peace in this Century* (1961), p. 74, quoting Lord Linlithgow.

the continued crying for *Purna Swaraj* without any serious attempt to define its practical meaning since the Nehru discussions of 1928.

The 1935 Act established complete responsible government and autonomy in the eleven provinces, subject to certain 'safeguards' enabling the Governor to act in defence of minorities, the maintenance of law and order, and the like. It brought the states and the provinces into a federal central government and legislature for the management of central affairs with indirect election from the provinces to the lower house, and it established dyarchy at the centre, which meant that ministers would be in control of all subjects except foreign affairs and defence, although again with 'safeguards'. Gandhi had not seemed to object in 1932 to the continued reservation of these two subjects for a time. Thus Indian ministers could have taken over virtually the whole internal administration of India, and could have seen to it that no need to apply the safeguards ever appeared. The Muslim League followed Congress in rejecting the experiment; Mr. Jinnah spoke of 98 per cent of safeguards and 2 per cent of responsibility. The Labour party at Westminster also worked hard to discredit the act, saying that its keynote was mistrust; 'restrictions of every kind all the time', said Mr. Attlee in January 1935, forgetting that the act went far beyond the Simon commission recommendations which he had signed so readily a few years before. Whether the government should have done more or less is a matter now for academic debate among the specialists; to the present writer it seems a courageous step and a risky one from the point of view of British interests, but one which failed to capture the imagination of the world through a certain inability on the part of this government to give a noble ring to any of its actions.[1]

Anyway, the result was frustration for all concerned. The federal scheme was rejected by the Muslims and Congress, but could not

[1] One can but speculate as to what Gladstone, Woodrow Wilson, or Franklin D. Roosevelt would have made of the opportunity. Professor Mansergh rightly points out that the banality of the opening description, 'an Act to make further provision for the government of India' suggests a lack of vision. Where was the rousing affirmation of early Dominion status which Indian opinion eagerly awaited? Mansergh also thinks that the fundamental trouble was the slowness of Britain's fulfilment of its declared policy of self-government. Coupland thinks the process swift; 'the British system of government had been developed up to almost its final stage in a fraction of the time it had taken in Britain itself or in the Colonies'. Mansergh, pp. 348, 350, and chap. IX passim; Coupland, *The Indian Problem, 1833–1935*, pp. 141–8; C. R. Attlee, *As It Happened*, gives his approval of the Simon commission's proposals (pp. 66–8), but is silent about his criticisms of the 1935 Act (cf. p. 79).

have been established in any case owing to the decision of the Princes not to join. Congress fought the provincial elections, and after some parleying, their members took office in seven provinces in July 1937 and gained valuable experience until they all resigned at the end of 1939. Non-Congress ministries took office in Bengal, the Punjab, and Sind. The central executive remained virtually that of the 1919 Act; thus the Simon commission's proposals, Attlee's first love, provided the basis of Indian rule until Attlee himself gave India independence in 1947. At home, as one of Churchill's later supporters has remarked, the young Conservatives who deeply admired him were tortured by the spectacle of this brilliant, inimitable personage daily alienating his friends, his party, and the House of Commons, with disastrous consequences for himself, India, and his country. He really knew extremely little about the subject, but helped to throw doubt on the sincerity of those in the Conservative party who did. In so doing he also threw doubt on his own motives and credibility in the long feud which he was fighting with the leaders of the party over defence.[1]

[1] The Earl of Kilmuir, *Political Adventure* (1964), p. 45.

8

FOREIGN POLICY AND DEFENCE

1. Divergent Views of Foreign Policy

ALONG with the problems of economic crisis and partial recovery at home there went a deterioration in the political situation abroad which the government sought to handle by the same patient and rather hand-to-mouth methods. Political and economic issues were clearly linked; economic distress might lead governments of a certain nationalistic type to a blustering or warlike policy, either in direct pursuit of economic advantage (as in the Japanese conquest of Manchuria in 1931–33 and the Italian conquest of Abyssinia in 1935–36), or in rough and angry diplomatic gestures, which on the whole seemed to satisfy the needs of Hitler's foreign policy down to 1937. Britain's only major ally was France, but she too was shaken by the economic crisis and little disposed to action outside Western Europe. The Soviet government opted for quiescence abroad pending economic reform at home, but without amiability towards any foreign state and with a terrorist régime justified by allegations of capitalistic hostility. The United States, amiable to the last, took refuge in extremes of atavistic isolationism. The assumption that economic recovery might prove a solvent of foreign aggressiveness was false but not unreasonable, and with it went a parallel tendency to underrate the military potential of economically weakened totalitarian states.

There was continued disappointment throughout the nineteen-thirties at the British government's failure to solve all the world's problems, political and economic. The critics asked too much. There was a double source of error in criticisms which were persistently and naggingly hostile to attempts to strengthen the apparatus of national power, while deploring the government's failure to act with compelling authority in every international crisis. Critics of all political hues underrated the forces (which sometimes included themselves) impeding stronger action, and repeatedly misunderstood what the government was trying to do. Whether it was very clear itself is of course another matter. The disparity between the country's worldwide commitments and its capacity for meeting them did not lessen the peculiar determination of ministers and their advisers to play a prominent part in every international crisis as it arose.

But if the handling of policy was mediocre, the difficulties were real. Later when the issue narrowed itself to that of stopping Hitler at all costs the failure to prevent war was taken as the sole criterion of statesmanship, and attributed to a weakness of will, rather than of resources. The really savage and persistent polemics which then assailed the government all stemmed from the basic argument, majestically propagated by Sir Winston Churchill, that the Second World War could easily have been prevented. 'It was a simple policy to keep Germany disarmed and the victors adequately armed for thirty years', he wrote in 1948. 'But this modest requirement the might, civilisation, learning, knowledge, science, of the victors were unable to supply.'[1] Generalizations about the origins of the war in these and similar passages do sometimes start with references to the behaviour of all the victorious powers of 1918 but they usually end by attributing responsibility to British ministers alone. To see these problems in the right perspective we must, however, keep in mind the conditions which were impeding a robust foreign policy of any sort in the early thirties.

First of all there was, of course, the economic situation. The developments described in chapter 6 meant that the majority of people in Great Britain were far too worried about their own troubles and the problem of making ends meet in a period of wage cuts, mass unemployment, and rising taxation, to have any zest for foreign adventures. In this sense the country was, for some years from 1930, thoroughly depressed by the depression, shivery and

[1] W. S. Churchill, *The Gathering Storm*, vol. I, pp. 14–15. But in a conversation with Liddell Hart and others in February 1936 he argued that 'nothing could have stopped [the danger from Germany] except splitting her up after the War'. On the same occasion Duff Cooper 'chided Winston as being the author of the rule of "No war for 10 years"'. B. H. Liddell Hart, *Memoirs* (1965), vol. I, pp. 303–5. A study of Churchill's parliamentary speeches between 1935 and 1938 shows that he was by no means as unqualified a critic of a conciliatory policy towards Germany and Japan as is suggested in *The Gathering Storm*: cf. R. H. Powers, 'Winston Churchill's Parliamentary Commentary on British Foreign Policy, 1935–1938' (*J.M.H.*, June 1954, pp. 179–82).

disillusioned and keeping its fingers crossed in the hope that nothing worse was to come. For politicians and economists who had to think of the more technical problems of mobilizing the country's resources for war the times also seemed highly unpropitious, even although a big rearmament programme might have short-term advantages in reducing unemployment and stimulating some parts of industry. But economic recovery was being sought along different lines, in the knowledge that Britain had not recovered, and probably never would recover, the vast financial strength which had enabled her in the past to support her own prolonged war efforts and subsidize those of her allies. She would have to look to the United States for financial aid in another war of the 1914–18 type. There was no prospect at this stage of any such support; the dominant isolationist and pacifist thinking of the United States was still in the phase of arguing that foreign countries should reduce their armaments in order to find means to pay off existing war debts. The general feeling of a need for husbanding existing resources was also fatal to any serious consideration of widespread economic sanctions in a League crisis, and here too the United States' support would be as essential as it would be improbable.

But this sense of economic vulnerability was only a special aspect of the almost universal refusal to consider the problem of war seriously in any form. It is generally believed that the pacifist movement in Great Britain as an influence on political action (including votes at by-elections) was at its height in 1933. General A. C. Temperley, British delegate to the disarmament conference which opened in February 1932, refers with evident embarrassment in his memoirs to the thousands of telegrams from well-wishers that poured into the delegation's office in Geneva. 'One felt almost a sense of shame that one was taking part in a colossal make-believe, that the people had not been told the truth, for nothing but a miracle could bring success.'[1] Integral pacifism of the George Lansbury type was, however, professed by relatively few. Even fewer were self-confessed militarists, who accepted war with equanimity as something normal, necessary, and inevitable in modern life. The vast majority were isolationist in their double conviction that war could be avoided and should be avoided. The habit of peace would make men peaceful; the peace-making

[1] A. C. Temperley, *The Whispering Gallery of Europe* (1939), pp. 168–9. Viscount Cecil, *A Great Experiment* (1941), pp. 191–3, 238.

machinery of the League of Nations, made irresistible if need be by 'collective security' (a term curiously misused to describe the means rather than the end of collective action) would do the trick without special effort on anyone's part, providing one had faith in its potentialities. Sir Harold Nicolson recalls the fact that he was asked in 1935 in a public debate whether he supported the policy of collective security and no political entanglements in Europe. The audience saw no inconsistency in the question.[1] This attitude was escapist even more than isolationist; very few men of fighting age seriously contemplated becoming 'conscientious objectors' in a future war, but they were prone to the view that there need be no such war. The leaders of all three political parties confirmed this view by continually affirming their belief in the possibilities of further disarmament and in the genuineness of many foreign grievances.

The basic blimpishness of all militarists thus became a commonplace of discussion. This was the case even with Winston Churchill; although his return to the forefront of politics in the mid-twenties was accompanied by affirmations of the need for peace, he remained an old-style warrior and therefore 'detestable' in many young eyes. In a letter describing a visit with her friend Vera Brittain to a meeting during the Abbey election campaign in March 1924 Winifrid Holtby wrote,

> He really and truly points an accusatory finger at the crowd, and cries in sepulchral tones, 'I say, that if another war is fought, civilization will perish' (Laughter. A sweeping gesture). 'A man laughs,' (Out goes the finger.) 'That man dares to laugh. He dares to think the destruction of civilization a matter for humour!' . . . Indeed, he is such a preposterous little fellow, with his folded arms and tufted forelock and his Lyceum Theatre voice, that if one did not detest him one might love him from sheer perversity.[2]

The refusal to believe that anyone who spoke realistically about the problem of war could be both honest and intelligent inhibited the frank examination of rearmament problems until 1939.

The case for peace was lovingly and uncritically rehearsed in numerous meetings of peace societies, the League of Nations Union, students' debates, Labour party conferences and constituency meetings, and in books which were usually more notable for

1. Quoted by D. C. Watt, *Britain Looks at Germany* (1965), p. 21.
2 Winifrid Holtby, *Letters to a Friend* (1937), p. 246.

sincerity than for penetration. Forty societies were affiliated to the National Peace Council, and its president from 1933 to 1936, Dr. G. P. Gooch, remarks that interminable debates took place without agreement, and without altering anybody's views.[1] The horrors of a future war were duly stressed (and indeed exaggerated) and a variety of arguments were developed all tending to deprecate the unilateral accumulation of arms by Great Britain. The most obvious of these was that she should take 'risks for peace' and reduce her diminished forces still further in order to deprive the disarmed of any excuse to build up their strength.[2] Another, very much hammered in by left-wing critics of the government but not confined to them, was that conservative elements in society—business men, arms manufacturers, Tory capitalist imperialists, all professional soldiers above the rank of captain, members of the House of Lords with nephews in Kenya—would if given half a chance use the national forces for their own selfish ends. It was presumably on the assumption that any national issue concealed unworthy aims that the Oxford Union was asked on 9 February 1933 to debate the motion that 'this House will in no circumstances fight for its king and country'. The use of a phrase which recalled traditional and some would say old-fashioned patriotic attitudes caused some misunderstanding, and also helped to give the debate its wide publicity.[3] The motion could be supported by those who were determined not to fight anyone and those who were careful to say that they would fight only for an international cause. Were there no worthy *national* causes—self-defence in fact? Many, including Mr. Beverley Nichols, the author of a cocksure little book

[1] 'One section, to which I belonged, believed in resisting naked aggression; . . . the other, represented by Quakers and pacifists, refused to contemplate even an economic boycott which might lead to serious trouble.' G. P. Gooch, *Under Six Reigns* (1958), p. 292. Cf. A. Marwick, *Clifford Allen* (1964), pp. 153–9.

[2] In his book on *The Private Manufacture of Armaments* (October, 1936), vol. I, Mr. P. J. Noel Baker argued that the example of their 'actual abolition in Great Britain might well prove decisive in securing the adoption of a new policy by the world at large' (p. 559).

[3] Many years later Dr. C. E. M. Joad, one of the six opening speakers, told the present writer that as he and one of the proposers of the motion were walking home after the meeting they congratulated themselves on the result, and one of them said, 'this is something that ought to reverberate round the world; but of course it will be forgotten by tomorrow morning'. A third leader in *The Times* on 13 Feb. under the title, 'The Children's Hour' played down the importance of the debate, ascribing it to a 'little clique of cranks'. Winston Churchill disagreed when speaking at the anniversary meeting of the Anti-Socialist and Anti-Communist Union a week later; they had all seen 'with a sense of nausea the abject, squalid, shameless avowal' made by 'callow ill-tutored youths'.

decrying the stupidity or sinfulness of non-pacifists, did not think that such situations would ever arise. 'These pictures are silly little bogy pictures, which are not worthy of the serious consideration of an intelligent scullery-maid.'[1] The book, which sold well, is a good example of the tendency to shirk the basic dilemmas. By this stage Hitler was in office and the Japanese conquest of Manchuria was complete.

The assumption that 'the League', in the shape of those powers which continued to support it, had moral authority which would enable it, even with shrunken resources, to coerce any aggressor, was wrong not only on technical grounds but also in its reliance on the League's control of public opinion. Austen Chamberlain remarked to Mussolini that the League was excellent when sparrows quarrelled, but would not avail when eagles fought. To succeed peacefully the League would have to rally effective support against war, not by preaching to the converted, but inside an aggressor state. It failed to do this in the case of Japan in 1931-2, Germany in 1933 and after, Italy in the Abyssinian crisis, Russia during the Soviet-Finnish war in 1939-40, and probably the same is true of Soviet opinion during the Hungarian crisis in 1956 in face of United Nations criticism. The only states which seemed capable of such guilty reactions were, by a curious but inevitable paradox, the more faithful League powers themselves. There was often public criticism of the motives of a government that sought to mobilize League support, and constant suspicion between the two leading powers, France and Britain. America's isolationism always had moral undertones of disapproval of the actions of all other governments, and reinforced the continued British suspicion of French attempts to organize the League as a security system for the maintenance of the Versailles settlement. The case for an international police force, expounded in a persuasive and learned book by Lord (David) Davies and his collaborators in 1930, failed to carry conviction for the same reason.[2] When André Tardieu put forward a French plan for such a force in February 1932,[3] at the beginning of the disarmament conference, Litvinov put the point bluntly by asking

---

[1] Beverley Nichols, *Cry Havoc!* (1933), p. 247. Some very distinguished soldiers, including the new C.I.G.S., thought the same in 1933. Liddell Hart, vol. I, p. 228.

[2] David Davies, *The Problem of the Twentieth Century* (1930); the gist of the argument for the force is in chaps x, xi. The technical details of the carefully worked out plans for quotas, etc. are still of value.

[3] David Davies supported the French plan in a pamphlet published in April 1932, entitled *Suicide or Sanity?*

what guarantee there would be that such an army 'would not be exploited in the interests of some state which has won for itself a leading part in the international organization'?

Finally in the most important of the specific problems, that of dealing with Nazi Germany, there was no clear lead from opinion. Although the influence of the U.D.C. in organizing sympathy for Germany has probably been overrated, its influence had been decisive in the early twenties, and reinforced the attempt of the Conservative government during Austen Chamberlain's foreign secretaryship after 1924 to persuade itself that Germany was a reformed character. If E. D. Morel as editor of *Foreign Affairs* from 1919 until his death in 1924 chose to dwell on the injustice of the Versailles settlement[1] he was in full accord with the views of Keynes, Norman Angell, and others as to its economic inexpediency, and in succeeding years Germany's economic crisis continued to be almost universally attributed to the treaty (reparations and lost territory) rather than to the blunders of her wartime economic policy.[2] Historical scholarship, taking this almost for granted, developed a new and almost world wide passion for diplomatic history with an emotional preference for the view that most international conflagrations are the product of spontaneous combustion; this worked powerfully in Germany's favour in the great controversy over war guilt. The Weimar régime mobilized its historians for this academic battle. After a preliminary publication of documents by Karl Kautsky in 1919 a majestic series of forty-four volumes of pre-war German diplomatic documents was published between 1922 and 1929, and interpreted in numerous explicit and insistent monographs, heavy with references, by major German historians such as Erich Brandenburg and by a vast number of younger scholars who combined a Ph.D. thesis with the defence of the Fatherland. The documentation was not complete,[3] and although the general trend was always to represent German action as defensive the essential achievement was to implicate all the European powers in the prevailing international anarchy.

Much of the reluctance after 1933 to rush into a fresh campaign

---

[1] C. A. Cline, *Recruits to Labour, The British Labour Party, 1914–1931*, pp. 71–6.
[2] A view that was not seriously challenged until the publication of J. T. Shotwell's book, *What Germany Forgot* (1940), chaps. I, II, VIII.
[3] The Bismarck period (1871–90), was sketchily treated with strange gaps, and the documents for the origins of the 1870 war were withheld. The series after 1890 was weak on the Balkans and the Far East. Military advice and influence was not dealt with.

of denunciation of German aggressiveness was due to the profound impression that this interesting and widely-read exploration of recent history had made on the educated public of every western country. It was not merely that everything distasteful to Germany in the Versailles treaty could be represented as an unjust projection of the war-guilt clause. It was also because the accidentally appalling consequences of the normal political bickering and struggle between governments seemed to have been proved and seemed to point, in this sceptical and nervous generation, to a solution. The two best-known studies of pre-1914 diplomacy in Britain were by eminent and representative members of the U.D.C.; G. P. Gooch in *History of Modern Europe, 1878–1919* (1923) attributed the war to 'international anarchy' and G. Lowes Dickinson chose this term as a title for his own book, published in 1926. Nearly all British and American historians in this field were 'revisionists' by the late twenties.[1] When the book of the American professor, S. B. Fay, *The Origins of the War*, was published in two volumes in 1929 the final word appeared to have been said on the subject.[2] The British Foreign Office's reply was to publish between 1926 and 1936 its own series of diplomatic correspondence for the period 1898 to 1914, but this tended to confirm the 'six of one, half a dozen of the other' argument.[3] In a sense all this was irrelevant. What mattered were the future intentions of Germany. The widespread belief that her sense of grievance under the Versailles treaty, whether justified or not, had weakened the Weimar régime, that it was the real basis of Hitler's popularity and the real explanation of his intransigent foreign policy, nevertheless made violent measures (which from other points of view seemed imperative) quite impracticable for some years.[4]

[1] A distinguished exception was R. W. Seton-Watson, who wrote one of the best of the earlier works on war origins, *Serajevo, A Study in the Origins of the Great War* (1926); cf. pp. 286–91. Cline, pp. 73–6.

[2] B. E. Schmitt's *The Coming of the War*, 2 vols., published in 1930, was more critical of Germany and a work of equal authority to Fay's. But Fay told people what they wanted to believe, and had a greater vogue. Albertini's authoritative work (1941–44) is in line with Schmitt's. There is a German translation of Fay, but not of Schmitt or Albertini.

[3] G. P. Gooch and H. W. V. Temperley, eds., *British Documents on the Origins of the War, 1898–1914* (London, H.M.S.O.). A corresponding French series, covering the years 1871 to 1914, began publication in 1929 and was completed after the second world war. Polemically, both series largely missed the bus. The decisive impression had been made on the minds of historians by the German series, the first in the field.

[4] The problem was to decide whether the brutalities of the Nazi domestic revolution, and even such anti-Versailles gestures as the reoccupation of the Rhineland, foreshadowed the intention to launch a general war. G. P. Gooch in *Under Six Reigns*

With these economic and emotional obstacles to a vigorous foreign policy in Europe there went two others. The first was the preoccupation with the defence and development of the Commonwealth, which was accepted as having first claim (after the defence of the United Kingdom) on the home country's loyalty and resources. The second was the weak state of British armaments. The need for rearmament was accepted by the cabinet after 1933, but time, money, political opposition, international limitation agreements, and the technical wastage of the nineteen-twenties were handicaps to rapid advance, and foreign policy suffered accordingly. We shall be dealing mainly with this aspect in the subsequent sections of this chapter.

2. The Beginnings of Rearmament

The developments outlined in chapter 7 were bound to discourage any vigorous action in European affairs. War in the Far East or the collapse of the British position in India resulting perhaps from disaffection in the armed forces were possibilities; they were by no means remote, and there were vulnerable points along the whole line of imperial communications from the English Channel through the Mediterranean and Red Sea to Singapore. The Dominions expected much, and offered little beyond goodwill, and the Navy had been too diminished by age and disarmament to handle major crises in more than one part of the world at a time. It is equally true, however, that the situation in Europe was too lowering to encourage any vigorous programme *outside* Europe. Cautious, apprehensive, and conciliatory, the National government from 1931 onwards strove continually to make itself helpful as a mediator between the continental powers.

Until at least the end of 1938 the attempt to secure by these means the tranquillization or appeasement of the continent was the proclaimed aim of the British government and its foreign secretaries. The mediatory rôle satisfied their uneasy desire to influence events while postponing a final commitment to enforce their political preferences in Europe. There were, no doubt, occasions when these interventions were helpful to the parties in dispute. But by sponsor-

(p. 304) remarks of the Rhineland occupation, 'a few shrewd observers sensed that it was the first step towards German domination of Europe, as we now know it to have been, but I was not among them'. On the other hand he had severed all links with official Germany in 1934. The dilemma of those genuinely seeking a fair solution of the German problem is poignantly described in chap. 19 of these memoirs.

ing abortive solutions Great Britain sometimes became the scape-goat for the failure of other powers who might be more directly involved and were certainly no more active than herself. In seeking to cling to these shreds and tatters of her former isolationism she was deceiving herself in two ways. She was taking too rosy a view of the survival of her political influence (still exceptionally and perhaps irrationally strong and pervasive under Lloyd George). And she was in some measure (this was true of the reactions of the general public as well as the government) shutting her eyes to the extent to which the strategical shrinking of the world, with the revolution in communications which had its most dramatic effects in warfare, had combined with the iconoclastic element in the new ideological systems to create conditions directly dangerous to herself. There was rather too optimistic an assumption that the old Europe, as modified by the Versailles treaty, could be restored if sufficient tact, negotiating skill, give-and-take, and good manners were used by the British Foreign Office.

As each attempt to get the dissatisfied powers back to a life of mutual forbearance failed, to the accompaniment of the drums and marching of totalitarian hordes, the streams of refugees, and the agonized megalomania of dictatorial oratory, the British cabinet's reaction was one of puzzled disbelief, a state of mind encouraged by its total inability to adjust itself to the political ethos of the new systems. Anything so bizarre and flamboyant and basically ridiculous as the earlier antics of Fascist and Nazi tubthumpers seemed un-likely to last; did not all revolutions—and all revolutionary leaders—become respectable in time?

To strengthen the country's armaments was however essential in the circumstances, although the political atmosphere, both at home and abroad, made rapid progress impossible. Hitler had secured his domestic position by the end of March 1933, and the British govern-ment and Foreign Office had already shown alarm in 1931 and 1932 at the prospect of a Nazi success leading to a German military revival. On the other hand there was still the hope that the dis-armament conference could pull off an agreement, perhaps freezing the position for some years. Hitler virtually offered, in a speech of 17 May 1933, to postpone rearmament for a period of years in return for a recognition of equality of rights. The British therefore hope-fully put forward with Italian support a plan for a five-year period of preliminary disarmament. France proposed more bluntly a system

of supervision leaving the existing size of armies virtually unchanged
for four years. Germany's reply, on 14 October 1933, was to walk
out of the disarmament conference and the League. Still, this move
might be merely tactical. There was a confused reaction to the new
Germany in Labour and 'liberal-progressive' circles in Britain, for
while the Fascist, anti-semitic, anti-communist domestic features of
the régime aroused instant distrust it was still an article of faith that
she had genuine grievances under the Versailles treaty, and that they
were genuinely felt. At just this moment on 26 October 1933
Labour won the East Fulham by-election with a turnover of 10,000
votes and a reaffirmation of the extreme brand of Labour's pacifism,
evidently with the approval of the electors. Members of the government were also widely denounced as warmongers in the municipal
elections in which Labour gained over 200 seats on 1 November.
So the cabinet felt that it too must talk peace. There was general
agreement when Baldwin on 27 November 1933 deplored the
prospects of an arms race.[1]

The antipathy to war preparations was too universal to be a
party issue; but the members of the National government were well
aware that the Labour party, weak in electoral support for the
moment, might capture it in a comeback fight. In fact, the issue
muddled rather than strengthened the Labour party for a time.
The official opposition line was to assume that there were practicable and decent solutions of all foreign difficulties just round the
corner which the government was persistently rejecting owing to
personal weakness or selfish, class, pro-Fascist, or other reactionary
impulses. This, however, scarcely concealed differences inside the
party. At the Hastings conference in 1933, for example, the chairman,
Joseph Compton, roasted the government in the usual unqualified
terms for the Manchurian disaster, while avoiding any admission
that force—military sanctions—was a legitimate or essential weapon
in such a crisis. The League powers had wriggled out of their
responsibilities, instead of 'mobilizing all the vast economic and
moral resources at the disposal of the League', and in this 'tragic
and ignoble surrender of Right to Might' the 'British Government
—the "National" Government—played the chief guiding part'.[2]
While the pacifists dominated the party the assumption had to be

[1] Baron von Neurath 'expressed particular satisfaction' with the speech: B.D.II(vi),
p. 150.
[2] Yet they must not make Japanese aggression 'a pretext for the sabotage of disarmament'. E. Windrich, *British Labour Foreign Policy*, pp. 105–6.

that moral pressure (a sufficiency of League resolutions in sufficiently rousing terms) with at most the threat of economic sanctions (the reality of a ruthless food blockade for example was never visualized) would suffice. This trend had been strengthened when George Lansbury succeeded Arthur Henderson as leader of the Labour party in 1932.

In the meantime it had broken its link with the I.L.P. There had been differences throughout 1930 and 1931 over the question of party discipline, and the I.L.P. had appeared in the 1931 election as a separate party. In the summer of 1932 the majority, led by James Maxton, decided to disaffiliate from the Labour party, and those who rejected this decision under Frank Wise formed a new group inside the Labour party called the Socialist League, and were reinforced by Stafford Cripps and friends who had made Easton Lodge their spiritual home.[1] After Wise's death in 1933 Cripps led and largely financed the group. More than any other Labour leader he took quite literally all that he had heard about the intentions of capitalists: nothing they did could be approved, for everything was detrimental to the workers.[2]

So although Dalton and Bevin were moving towards the view that Britain must acquire arms and use them, they were ahead of the majority of the party. Dalton, however, vigorously propagated the view that the disarmament conference was failing because of the British government's action in not backing proposals for wholesale disarmament in 1932; if it had done so Hitler, it was argued without any evidence, would not have dared or wished to rearm. The reason for this supine attitude was believed to be MacDonald's jealousy of Arthur Henderson, the president of the conference. And yet Dalton had no patience with many of the views of Stafford Cripps, who was arguing in May 1933 that Churchill would defeat the government over India in the following spring, form a government, introduce Fascist measures, and abolish further general

[1] With E. F. Wise as the first chairman the executive committee included C. P. Trevelyan, Harold Laski, William Mellor (ex-editor of the *Daily Herald*), H. N. Brailsford, G. D. H. Cole, R. H. Tawney, Aneurin Bevan, Ellen Wilkinson, D. N. Pritt, etc. E. Estorick, *Stafford Cripps* (1949), pp. 116–7; Colin Coote, *The Life of Richard Stafford Cripps* (1957), p. 150.

[2] e.g., 'if war comes before the workers in Great Britain have won power, that war will be an imperialist war' (addressing the Socialist League conference, 1934; Estorick, p. 140). 'It was not possible for any group of capitalists to submit themselves to regulation by their rivals and abandon all hope of political support for their own Government' (hence, the impossibility of cooperation in an effective League policy). S. Cripps, *The Struggle for Peace*, 1936, pp. 53–4, 57.

elections. Laski and others outside Parliament professed similar views at this time.[1] Of the other two prominent Labour leaders, Lansbury remained a thorough-going pacifist; Attlee faithfully reproduced the party line, whatever it was at the moment. On 4 October 1933 the party's annual conference passed two international resolutions unanimously. One called for total disarmament and an international police force. The other called on the party to conduct anti-war propaganda and to take all steps including a general strike to stop any action by the government leading to war. The proposers of this resolution were thinking of Soviet Russia, not of Hitler. Attlee said in the Commons on 7 November 1933,

> We must be prepared to take risks for peace. We on this side propose entire disarmament. We believe in an international police force . . . I want to see air forces abolished and an international air service. I should like to see all the armies of separate states abolished . . . Of course, there must be a police force which is loyal to the ideals. But I suggest that, without that, we may get a useful breathing space by qualitative disarmament.[2]

A little faith: some risks for peace: action only through the League. All the Labour spokesmen for more than the next three years tried to persuade themselves that this was a practicable and honourable alternative to the government's own courses.[3]

During the twelve months after Hitler's withdrawal from the League Labour continued to vote against the service estimates, and the government continued to hope that something could be salvaged from the disarmament conference. Later views that British ministers were deaf to warnings about Germany are the reverse of the facts; but the experts themselves were not unanimous. Sir Eric Phipps, the ambassador in Berlin, thought that there was a chance that Germany would settle down if her claims were met. He was quite sure that if they were not she would passionately insist on territorial revision even to the point of war.[4] Sir Robert Vansittart did not accept this qualification, and wrote strong minutes in the Foreign Office insisting on Germany's determination on war for its own sake. An

---

[1] Hugh Dalton, *The Fateful Years* (1957), pp. 36, 42–3, 48–9. Dalton thought that Laski didn't understand the English; cf. Colin Coote, *The Life of Richard Stafford Cripps*, pp. 151–4.

[2] P.D., 5 Ser., HC, vol. 281, 7 Nov. 1933, col. 149.

[3] Proposals on the lines of Attlee's speech were elaborated in the first resolution of he Labour party conference. Dalton, pp. 44–5.

[4] B.D. II(v), no. 492.

equally powerful critic was Sir Warren Fisher,[1] the Permanent Secretary to the Treasury and head of the Civil Service, who took the view for a time that agreement with Japan was imperative, even at the risk of a breach with the United States. He believed with Vansittart in the basic aggressiveness of Germany and not merely in the viciousness of Nazi policy. Neville Chamberlain shared his views on the Germans. But Eden, who met Hitler in February 1934, came to the unexpected conclusion that the foreign minister, von Neurath, was the more dangerous character of the two; and he told Mussolini that he thought Hitler to be sincere in desiring a disarmament convention.[2] A Foreign Office minute of 21 March 1934 argued that the disarmament obligations of the Versailles treaty were dead; it would be better to arrange for the funeral while Hitler was still in a mood to pay the undertakers for their service. The French thoroughly disliked this type of argument, but as they were not prepared to use force or to bury disarmament themselves they could only strengthen their position and await events. In April 1934 Louis Barthou, French foreign minister, rejected the British proposals and set to work to stiffen Polish and Czech hostility to Germany and bring about an agreement with Russia. British policy on the other hand led to the Anglo-German naval agreement of 1935.

The Chiefs of Staff had been hammering away with objections to the Ten-Year Rule since 1928 and had called in February 1932 for the re-equipment of the armed forces and the end of the Rule. The cabinet had agreed to the second in principle.[3] During 1933 the political situation prevented any great progress with the first, although paper work went on, including the beginning of the systematic studies under the direction of Major Desmond Morton of Germany's vulnerability to blockade. Two papers discussing this problem were before the C.I.D. in October 1933 and January 1934.[4]

[1] Sir (Norman Fenwick) Warren Fisher, K.C.B., 1919, G.C.B., 1923, G.C.V.O., 1928; born 22 Sept. 1879; died 25 Sept. 1948. Entered Inland Revenue Department 1903. He was private secretary to Sir Robert Chalmers for two years, and the driving force in the I.R. Department during the war. He was the Permanent Secretary of the Treasury and head of the Civil Service, 1919 to 1939. This formidable figure was a strong believer in cooperation with the Services. See the article by H. P. Hamilton in the *Dictionary of National Biography, 1941–1950.*

[2] B.D. II(vi), nos. 302, 303, 322; Vansittart, *The Mist Procession*, pp. 487–8; Earl of Avon, *The Eden Memoirs, Facing the Dictators* (1962), pp. 60–79.

[3] M. M. Postan, *British War Production* (1952), pp. 1, 9; W. K. Hancock and M. M. Gowing, *British War Economy* (1949), pp. 62–3; R. Higham, *Armed Forces in Peacetime, Britain 1918–1939*, p. 174.

[4] W. N. Medlicott, *The Economic Blockade* (1950), vol. I, pp. 12–14.

In October 1933 the cabinet set up a Defence Requirements Committee under Sir Maurice Hankey and including Fisher, Vansittart, and the Chiefs of Staff, to examine deficiencies; and although Japan was visualized as the main problem in the first instance the committee agreed in February 1934 that Germany was the 'ultimate potential enemy'. This view left little room for action against Italy, for example, and the committee also urged the revival of the old friendly cooperation with Japan. Its specific proposals were intended to remove deficiencies in the existing categories of armaments and not to provide an expansive programme of rearmament to keep pace with foreign powers. The cabinet accepted the substance of the technical recommendations of the Hankey Committee on 18 July 1934, and also the estimate that 1939 was the earliest date at which the defence preparations would be completed.[1] It was inevitable that certain priorities should be imposed by the state of public opinion and of the country's finances. It was for example possible to make out a case for 'defensive' re-equipment in the shape of fighter aircraft, anti-aircraft precautions, and a modernized navy, at a time when it was still politically impossible to advocate conscription, heavy bombers, and big guns. The Royal Navy, however, was still too powerful (together with the French) to have much cause for alarm at German naval building for some years, although it was not capable of taking on the full strength of the Japanese and Italian navies as well.

The 1934 discussions were merely the beginnings of a long debate between the services, forced to think seriously of German problems again after being mainly preoccupied with the possibility of a Russian threat to India or trouble with Japan in the Far East. The theories advanced by the Air Staff, following the teaching of Sir Hugh Trenchard in the twenties, placed an emphasis on the priority of the air weapon which the other two services had never accepted. Nor did they entirely accept it now, particularly as the financial result would be the partial starvation of their own efforts. During the next five years the two Chancellors of the Exchequer, Neville Chamberlain and his successor Sir John Simon, made funds available for rearmament which were certainly large although always inadequate to meet all service demands. The Army suffered most, for until 1938 the theory was that its purpose was limited in Europe to repelling or forestalling invasion and to defence operations outside

[1] Hancock and Gowing, pp. 63–4.

Europe, and that anything more would constitute preparation for aggressive war.[1]

The cabinet continued to be depressed, not to say overwhelmed, by advice as to the devastating consequences of German bombing. The Hankey Committee believed that Germany might be in a position to deliver a knockout blow on London by or even before 1938. Working on the ratio of casualties to bombs dropped on London in the first world war, the experts produced some horrifying figures. Damage was estimated almost on the later nuclear bomb scale. In 1937 for example a C.I.D. report to the cabinet assumed that on the outbreak of war Germany would be able to carry out an immediate sixty-day attack on British towns, with 1,800,000 casualties. Seasoned coffin timber for the dead would cost £300,000 a month. Five per cent of the country's property, valued at £550 million, might be destroyed during the first three weeks of war.[2] It was believed that the bomber could be checked only by the deterrent effect of counter-bombing, including the destruction of enemy air bases. Baldwin echoed this view when he said in 1932 that the bomber would always get through. Both the effectiveness of the Luftwaffe and the ineffectiveness of possible defences were in fact vastly exaggerated, with profound effects on politics during the next six years. With visions of London in ruins the Hankey Committee proposed the immediate creation of twenty-five new fighter squadrons for defence and plans for an expeditionary force to occupy and prevent the use of bases in the Low Countries. The cabinet accepted the plan in principle but on grounds of economy could make available only half the amount required.[3] On 19 July 1934 Baldwin announced rearmament in the air,[4] and later remarked that the frontier of England lay no longer on the chalk cliffs of Dover but the Rhine.

The policy that emerged, in a rather troubled and hand-to-mouth fashion, was, then, to build up the country's defences but to seek an agreement with Germany which would enable her to settle down to peaceful ways. This was essentially Sir John Simon's approach and the opposition continued to insist that Germany had legitimate grievances. The policy was accepted with varying degrees of con-

[1] Webster and Frankland, pp. 86–91.
[2] R. M. Titmuss, *Problems of Social Policy* (1950), pp. 12–22; P. K. Kemp, *Key to Victory; The Triumph of British Sea Power in World War II* (Boston, 1957), pp. 18–27.
[3] Higham, pp. 175–6.
[4] With consequent Labour and Liberal votes of censure.

viction by the rest of the cabinet, as they studied with varying degrees of scepticism Hitler's periodical assurances of peaceful intentions. We know now that he was determined to rearm as quickly as possible, but probably did not finally decide that he must ultimately fight England until the summer of 1937. His policy in 1934 and 1935 was one of bloodcurdling warnings interspersed with conciliatory gestures, and an avoidance of direct crises with his neighbours; he ignored the opinion of the German Foreign Office in making a non-aggression pact for ten years with Poland in January 1934, and in February decided to postpone indefinitely the use of force against Austria. When the Austrian Nazis assassinated Dollfuss in July they were repudiated. This, and foreign criticism following the purge of 30 June 1934, may have decided him to postpone the public announcement of German rearmament, which to the alarm of the German Foreign Office had been planned for October. Herr von Ribbentrop, the ambulant and compromising windbag (as Phipps described him) continued to hint that Hitler might rejoin the League, on terms. It was also unwise to do anything to impede the peaceful acquisition of the Saar, which was achieved by plebiscite in January 1935. Hitler welcomed the proposal, made by the British and French ministers on 3 February, for an Air Pact, which was based on the Locarno principle of an agreement by the signatories on non-aggression against each other. But he was less forthcoming to the invitation to collaborate in Eastern and Danubian pacts. And when a British white paper on 4 March referred to the illegal rearmament of Germany as the main reason for increases in the British estimates there was a show of indignation in Germany, and he took the opportunity to make the announcement. Complete freedom in providing for defence was to be resumed, with a conscript army of thirty-six divisions. The Luftwaffe had, he announced, come into existence again on 1 March.[1]

While Churchill continued to give wonderful, graphic warnings —'our enormous metropolis here, the greatest target in the world, a kind of tremendous, fat, valuable cow tied up to attract the beast of prey'—and Attlee to move his votes of censure on every rearmament proposal, the government's search for agreement with Germany went on. According to the German ambassador's report on 23 March 1935 the majority in the cabinet still supported Simon, who would leave no stone unturned 'to bring Germany into a

[1] D.G.F.P., Ser. C(III), nos. 12, 105, 115, 116, 119, 123, 138, 503; Avon, pp. 123-5.

system for safeguarding peace'. Only Hailsham and Neville Chamberlain took the opposite view, while Baldwin was vexed and undecided.[1] Baldwin allowed himself to be panicked by Churchill and the Foreign Office into a greatly exaggerated estimate of German strength in the air.[2] But the result was an urgent re-examination of the air expansion programme, and the adoption by the cabinet in due course of Scheme C, designed to produce 1,512 first-line aircraft, fighters and bombers, by 1937, and later of Scheme F, to be completed in 1939. The new programme was announced to Parliament by Lord Londonderry on 22 May 1935. He was succeeded by Sir Philip Cunliffe-Lister as Secretary of State for Air on 7 June 1935. He promoted 'shadow factories' which facili-tated expansion later, and the production of the splendid Hurricane and Spitfire fighters.

There seemed no practical means of preventing the arms race which Germany had launched, but the itch to do something and to demonstrate continued zeal for disarmament led to further attempts to negotiate. Late in March 1935 Simon and Eden paid Hitler the visit which had been postponed by the earlier coolness. He was profuse in his assurances of peaceful intent, although equally insistent on his need for arms—a matter of security and self-respect. His offer of a naval agreement was accepted, and it was signed in London on 18 June 1935, with repeated exclamations by Ribbentrop as to the high statesmanship and historic character of the Führer's action in accepting a 35 per cent ratio (with equality in submarines). We now know that as early as 7 May 1935 Hitler was rehearsing arguments to justify the occupation of the Rhineland; in the mean-time, as Italy developed her plans against Abyssinia, the Germans continued to receive friendly and sometimes indiscreet expressions

---

[1] D.G.F.P., *ibid*, no. 552.

[2] Hitler's announcement about the Luftwaffe created no surprise; nor did his sub-sequent statement to Eden and Simon that Germany had already reached parity in the air with Britain. But since 1933 the Air Ministry and Foreign Office had differed widely as to the size of the German air force, the former maintaining that British aircraft were still far more numerous than the German, the Foreign Office insisting that Germany had caught up in strength. Baldwin's figures of air strength in the Com-mons on 28 Nov. 1934 gave Britain a fifty per cent margin for the next two years. Churchill challenged these, evidently relying on the F.O. figures, in this debate and in March 1935. On 10 April Simon wrote to MacDonald accepting Hitler's claim to parity, and Baldwin on 22 May made one of his famous confessions to the effect that he had been completely wrong on 28 Nov. In fact, he had been right. Post-war figures show that Germany had only half the British total of operational planes in March 1935, and that the Air Ministry's estimate giving the same figures in April 1935 was substantially correct. See Churchill, vol. I, pp. 93–8; Webster and Frankland, vol. I, pp. 69–70; Avon, pp. 182–6.

of goodwill from many highly placed persons in London, including Eden, Duff Cooper, the Prince of Wales, and others. Neville Chamberlain was as usual less forthcoming.[1]

What was so conspicuously lacking from the conduct of British foreign policy at this period was any sense of authority. The ministers faced a genuine dilemma, and are not to be condemned for their anxious search for peace by negotiation, even if they sometimes misread the intentions of other powers. But there was nothing magisterial in their bearing, and no one could really feel that there was anything bold or passionate or even resolutely pacific about these men. And although Neville Chamberlain after becoming Prime Minister in 1937 introduced more positive and direct methods his personality remained unimpressive. In an age of great publicists abroad, England was curiously deficient in leaders of commanding stature, able to put things forcibly and win respect for their toughness and political judgment. This situation did not change until the arrival of Winston Churchill at 10 Downing Street in 1940.

3. The Abyssinian Crisis

The cabinet were agreed in 1935 that Germany was the greatest ultimate danger to Great Britain, that the danger might become a reality within a few years, that Britain's defences should be improved, and that the state of public opinion precluded rapid or total rearmament. There also seems to have been a general acceptance of the Treasury view, firmly adumbrated by Neville Chamberlain, that the country's economic health would not allow it to finance both complete economic recovery and a complete rearmament programme. Nor apparently was there dissent from the general proposition that in the circumstances it was not desirable that relations with Soviet Russia, Japan, or Italy should deteriorate. The statesmanlike courses before the government seemed therefore to be, at home the launching, in spite of its cost and unpopularity, of rearmament, and the use of Britain's influence abroad to steer into innocuous channels the passions and ambitions to which foreigners seemed so prone.

This would probably be a fair statement of the broader reaction of the cabinet to the complex and puzzling range of foreign problems which were continually impinging on the discussion of department business. When it came to more detailed discussions there can

[2] D.G.F.P., Ser. C(III), nos. 555, 560; Ser. C(IV), nos. 72, 131-2, 141, 156, 531.

hardly have been full agreement about anything. Almost every member of the cabinet seems to have had a foreign policy of his own, and to have fancied himself in Simon's shoes. There were widely differing views as to how far the difficult foreigners were capable of restraint, whether Germany, in particular, would know when to stop, how to handle the United States, what to do about Russia, when to change from the rôle of mediator to that of protagonist. Distrusting foreigners in general, Baldwin, unlike MacDonald, gave no clear lead. The differences of viewpoint in the cabinet are really no more than evidence of this lack of decisive intellectual leadership among complex, worrying, deteriorating problems. The three foreign secretaries, Simon, Hoare, and Eden, were each, for different reasons, incapable of imposing a bold, simple policy. The cabinet rallied loyally to Neville Chamberlain after the summer of 1937, mainly because he had made up his mind about priorities.

What is certainly clear is that with Germany beginning to emerge in 1935 as the overriding problem the tendency to look for accommodation elsewhere was strengthened. But this did not meet with much response. The Soviet government found it hard to believe that Great Britain had not replaced France as the instigator of anti-Soviet movements in Europe, and that the British reluctance to quarrel with Japan was not an expression of anti-Soviet policy. These views were systematically aired in the Moscow press, and if Eden's conversation with Stalin in April 1935 cleared the air for the moment it did not change the propaganda line.[1]

Moreover the rumours of Anglo-Japanese conversations upset Washington as well as Moscow. The Defence Requirements Committee in February 1934, by naming Germany as potential public enemy no. 1, had implied the need for a rapprochement with Japan, since it was not considered possible to quarrel successfully with both. This idea had the support in the cabinet of Neville Chamberlain, who urged it as a corollary to preparations against Germany. MacDonald, Simon, and the majority of the cabinet were not attracted by this course if it meant tension with the United States. But the latter, while hostile to any concessions to Japan, was unhelpful; she would neither promise support to the British in the Far East nor approve any strengthening of the Royal Navy. Indeed, at Anglo-American talks in the summer of 1934 the American

[1] Avon, pp. 152-65.

delegates, on Roosevelt's instructions, actually proposed a further reduction of naval armament by one-third, while the British pressed for their old target of seventy cruisers.[1] When the talks were resumed in October the American attitude was unchanged; they were not prepared for any concessions to Japan, although a continued insistence on the 5–5–3 ratio was certain to strengthen intransigent elements in Tokyo. The British hopefully sounded the Japanese for counter-concessions, but they were as unyielding as the Americans. In November opposition to an Anglo-Japanese agreement was appearing in the London press and was stimulated by the Round Table group, and in a blunt speech at a Chatham House dinner on 13 November General Smuts threw his weight against any such agreement at the expense of Anglo-American relations. Nothing could be done, and in December Japan gave notice that she intended to denounce the Washington naval agreements.[2]

But the main distraction from concentration on the German problem was Mussolini's quarrel with Abyssinia. The probability that he was planning the conquest or domination of the whole state had been obvious since the Wal-Wal episode in November 1934. There was just sufficient ambiguity in Britain's earlier attitude for him to hope that she would accept his conquest of a great East African empire without too much fuss. Italy had been vigorously pressing her claims in this area since the eighteen-eighties, and as recently as 1925 an Anglo-Italian agreement had conceded an exclusive Italian sphere of economic influence in western Abyssinia, subject to the consent of the Abyssinian government, for whose backward and obstructive régime London had, however, no great enthusiasm. Mussolini's main reliance was on the unwillingness of France and Britain to weaken the front against Germany. The Franco-Italian agreement of January 1935 could well be taken to mean that Laval had given him *carte blanche* in east Africa, although not in so many words, and at the Stresa conference (11–14 April 1935) the three powers had condemned Germany's repudiation of her obligations under the treaty of Versailles, without any mention of Abyssinia by the British representatives, Simon and MacDonald. France further revealed her apprehension over Germany by signing a Franco-Soviet pact of mutual assistance on 2 May. On the other hand Mussolini had had sufficient warning through diplomatic

---

[1] Feiling, pp. 253–4; D. C. Watt, *Personalities and Policies* (1965), pp. 87–99.
[2] *The Times*, 14 Nov. 1934: cf. *International Affairs*, Jan. 1935.

channels that public opinion in England might prevent acquiescence in blatant Italian aggression. During the summer the Foreign Office fell back onto its favourite rôle of mediation, trying to find some relatively small territorial adjustments as a basis for an Italian-Ethiopian compromise. Nothing was achieved. The Italian attack began on 3 October.

One cannot read through the numerous memoirs of ministers involved in this crisis without realizing once again how baffling was the dilemma that faced them. No local British interests were involved in the dispute—this was formally established by a Foreign Office commission under Sir John Maffey, appointed in February, which reported in June. But to the League supporters this very fact supplied the best of reasons for her intervention. The Labour leaders, while continuing their routine condemnation of rearmament, faced the issue at the party conference at Brighton (27 September–4 October), to the extent of accepting by an overwhelming majority a resolution, moved by Dalton, in support of sanctions against Italy. Thus the conference rejected Lansbury's pacifism, after Ernest Bevin's brutal gibe about 'hawking your conscience from body to body asking to be told what you ought to do with it', and also the academic Leninism of Stafford Cripps, who saw the issue in the most abstract terms as a clash of rival imperialisms which in the workers' interest should be left severely alone. There was massive support for the motion from Bevin, John Marchbank, and other T.U.C. figures. But it begged the question in its assumption that economic sanctions ought to be sufficient to prevent war, and if not that Britain's lead would bring the forces of 'the United League of Nations' effectively into action.[1]

There was no certainty that economic pressure would be effective if Mussolini chose to brazen things out, and even less that the French would ever allow a unanimous decision at Geneva in favour of military sanctions, in other words of war. And although both the cabinet and its advisers appear to have accepted the view that in the long run Italy was bound to lose such a war there was no disposition to regard it lightly. The imbroglio would leave Japan

---

[1] Following Bevin, Cripps said: 'whether you call it military sanctions or war matters not; it is the same thing. That means the use by our Government of the workers for military action against the workers, in this case, of Italy'. (Estorick, pp. 142–3). Attlee, who had acclaimed the 1933 resolution for a general strike against war, now abandoned Cripps, although he did not think that sanctions would lead to war against Mussolini. Attlee, *As It Happened*, pp. 79–80; Dalton, pp. 66–9.

and Germany with a free hand, and it appeared that the Admiralty, with its long tradition of Anglo-Italian friendship, had absolutely no plans in its pigeon-holes for an Anglo-Italian conflict. The Royal Navy was reinforced in the Mediterranean, but its only major operation was to move the fleet from Malta to Alexandria because of its vulnerability to Italian dive bombing from Sicily. Malta had no anti-aircraft defences.

So a mediated settlement had great attractions. But the lesson of the Manchurian crisis seemed to be that even if one could do nothing effectual one should give moral leadership in condemnation of aggressors: this was where Stimson seemed to have done better than Simon in 1932. The results of the Peace Ballot, announced on 27 June 1935, showed that out of 11,559,165 voters the great majority (over 10 million in each case) favoured all-round reduction in armaments, all-round abolition of national armaments, the prohibition of the private manufacture of armaments, and continued membership of the League. The same majority favoured economic and non-military sanctions against an aggressor, but only 6,784,368 supported 'if necessary, military measures'. There was a largish minority—2,351,981—against military measures. What did these figures mean? That disarmament was theoretically desirable, but not to be carried out unilaterally; that the League was respected and accepted; and that there was complete confusion over the issue of military sanctions. It was assumed, perhaps by all the voters, that economic sanctions could be made effective without an ultimate willingness to use force; it was not stated starkly that military sanctions meant war; and even so, a large minority was opposed to its use in any circumstances. It was reasonable to assume that those who voted started by being supporters of the League, and that the non-voters included many who were not.[1] The rôle which the cabinet assigned to itself in the Abyssinian dispute was that of moral leadership at Geneva combined only with such measures of conciliation and of coercion as would command the unanimous support of the League powers.

The government had been reconstructed early in June. Baldwin replaced MacDonald as Prime Minister, Simon went to the Home Office, and after Eden had been tipped in the innermost circles as his successor the appointment went to Sir Samuel Hoare, on the

---

[1] Cecil, *A Great Experiment*, pp. 254–63, 276, and the comments of G. M.·Gathorne-Hardy, *A Short History of International Affairs* (1938), pp. 405–7.

grounds of seniority, good work for the India Bill, and a reputation for shrewdness. He was supported by Neville Chamberlain. Eden joined the cabinet as Minister for League of Nations Affairs, after making a not unreasonable objection to the duality of authority at cabinet level. The division of functions between them does not in fact seem to have been at all clearly defined during the Italian negotiations of the next six months.[1] While the conciliatory machinery of the League was going ineffectually through the prescribed stages the search for a compromise continued. Eden was sent to Rome at the end of June to propose an arrangement whereby Britain would cede to Abyssinia access to the sea at Zeila, and Abyssinia would cede Italy some territory in Ogaden province. There was a polite discussion between him and Mussolini, but no progress; it was now clear that while the Duce was prepared to leave in nominal independence (but under Italian control) an Abyssinian state consisting of the central provinces of Tigre, Amhara, Gojjam, and Shoa, he wished to annex outright the surrounding provinces, which had been conquered by Abyssinia during the last fifty years.[2] In spite of this uncompromising answer, the negotiations, in which Vansittart was the driving force on the British side, continued. Mr. (later Sir) Maurice Peterson was sent to continue the search for a plan in Paris in October. With Laval and Vansittart both determined to satisfy the mounting Italian appetite the concessions expected of the Emperor of Abyssinia mounted too.[3]

There was nothing in the speech which Sir Samuel Hoare made to the Assembly on 12 September which conflicted formally with these negotiations. By now a great many decent people in the world wanted to see something unpleasant happen to Mussolini, and when the British Foreign Secretary, crippled by arthritis, limped to the microphone to say that his country stood for the collective maintenance of the Covenant he was merely repeating what he had recently said, without arousing any emotions anywhere, in the House of Commons. In his memoirs he lists the many phrases in which he insisted in the speech that Britain's obligation was collective, that she could not act alone.[4] He professes to wonder what had

---

[1] Avon, pp. 217–20; Templewood, *Nine Troubled Years* (1954), p. 136.
[2] Avon, p. 226; M. Toscano, 'Eden's Mission to Rome on the Eve of the Italo-Ethiopian Conflict', *Studies in Diplomatic History*, ed. A. O. Sarkissian (1961), pp. 126–52.
[3] M. Peterson, *Both Sides of the Curtain* (1950), pp. 115–6.
[4] 'If risks for peace are to be run, they must be run by all. The security of the many cannot be ensured solely by the efforts of the few, however powerful they may be,' etc. Templewood, pp. 169–71.

so greatly excited his audience. This is too modest. As he tells us himself a few pages earlier, he had drafted the speech, with Vansittart's invaluable help, as a revivalist appeal to the Assembly. But although it might deter Mussolini with a display of League fervour, its ultimate purpose (as one might expect from Vansittart's participation) was anti-German. It was thus part of a wider policy, which Laval had approved in discussions on 10 and 11 September. While there should be cautious negotiation to keep Mussolini on the Allied side there should also be created at Geneva a united front as a necessary deterrent against *German* aggression. Britain needed French support in negotiations for an Air Pact with Germany, as a first step towards wider armament agreements. Both agreed that the idea of war with Italy must be excluded as too dangerous and double-edged for the future of Europe.[1]

No one has equalled this government in the gentle art of putting itself in the wrong. The speech revived belief in the League on the part of everyone except Hoare and Laval and Mussolini. The general election on 14 November 1935 was taken by Labour to prove that the Tories had stolen Labour's clothes. The government promised to uphold the Covenant, fill gaps in the national defence, but also work for the general limitation of armaments.[2] However, Labour gained a hundred seats, and now had 154 M.P.s, while the Liberals had twenty; but the government retained a powerful though reduced majority of 432, which continued to support National governments until the next election in 1945. Lansbury had resigned the Labour party leadership on 8 October. The choice of his successor seemed to be governed by reciprocal antipathies which ruled out Dalton, Cripps, and Morrison; Attlee, who had offended the least and impressed the least, was elected, but the choice was regarded as provisional. It lasted for twenty years.

Events now moved quickly in the Abyssinian affair. Into the details and the anxieties of the ensuing crisis it is unprofitable to go very far, for it is evident that as soon as Mussolini had made up his mind to risk seeing his adventure through, Laval's veto on war would be decisive. By 10 October 1935 fifty nations had agreed to apply sanctions to Italy. During the coming months a Committee of

---

[1] *Ibid.*, pp. 166–8; *Misc. No. 3 (1936)*, Cmd. 5143, nos. 36, 50.
[2] Before the election Baldwin had endeavoured on 13 September to explain the need for rearmament to the T.U.C. through Sir Walter Citrine, believing that it was 'useless to speak to George Lansbury, a sincere and avowed pacifist'. Lord Citrine, *Men and Work* (1964), p. 353.

Eighteen was responsible, through its subcommittee on economic measures, for the practical details. But the League had also appointed a Committee of Five to seek a compromise solution, and it continued to do so even after the beginning of the Italian attack. The technical difficulties of an effective sanctions policy were enormous, and in fact it would seem that Italy's stocks were such that no embargoes, however complete, could have halted the war (in view of its relatively short duration) before her victory.[1] Much depended of course on the length of Abyssinian resistance and the extent to which the economic distress which would ultimately descend on Italy would be a deterrent. The first League sanctions list, not including oil, was due on 18 November, and on 15 November Cordell Hull produced a 'moral embargo' in the shape of an appeal to American exporters not to export abnormal quantities of oil, copper, trucks, tractors, scrap iron and scrap steel to the belligerents. *Normal* quantities, however, could still be exported, and on 5 December Hull admitted to the British ambassador that his government could not prevent increased oil shipments. This made the oil sanction rather pointless, although Mussolini appeared to threaten, without saying so in as many words, that he would make it a *casus belli*. The British were prepared to apply it; Laval was not, and he and his successor postponed a decision by repeated devices. What no one seemed to understand was the extent to which the Italians had been stocking up in East Africa before the war began. Total American exports direct to Italian possessions in Africa had been valued at only $20,000 in January 1935; they were worth $1,704,000 in August, $508,000 in September, $363,000 in October, $590,000 in November, and $374,000 in December. These figures included $828,000 worth of petroleum and petroleum products which were sent direct to Italian Africa during the last three months of 1935. In short, the Italians had prepared themselves against an oil sanction before there was any chance of its being imposed.[2] The chief

---

[1] Apart from stockpiling, economic sanctions could be frustrated by (*a*) absence of accurate statistical information and market information as to supplies, shortages, etc.; (*b*) the impossibility of exercising traditional belligerent rights of interception, search, and seizure when war had not been declared; (*c*) the existence of strong non-League powers, such as Japan, Germany, Brazil, U.S.A.; (*d*) absence of machinery for checking smuggling by nationals of the League powers and others; (*e*) position of seized cargoes under Prize Law. It seemed clear that seizure of cargoes would have caused strong resentment in the U.S.A.

[2] The American story is told authoritatively by H. Feis, in *Seen From E.A. Three International Episodes* (New York, 1947), part 3, 'Oil for Italy: a Study in the Decay of International Trust', from which the above figures are drawn. Imports into Italian

practical result of the sanctions episode was to give the British experts in blockade a thorough shaking up, with valuable results after 1939.[1]

Sanctions were effectively applied in the end only by the House of Commons towards the unhappy Foreign Secretary, Sir Samuel Hoare. The 'Hoare-Laval pact' was not a demoniacal aberration, with Mr. Hyde suppressing the beneficent Dr. Jekyll of 12 September. It was simply a further version of the Zeila-Ogaden plans for a compromise settlement first sketched by Eden to Mussolini in June, and approved in principle by the Committee of Five in September. Peterson's negotiations in Paris with a French expert, St. Quentin, followed in October, with the British representatives seeking to limit the concessions which the French demanded of the Abyssinians as the only means of satisfying Mussolini's appetite. It was accepted that Abyssinia should have a port, preferably in territory ceded by Italy at Assab, and Italy should have in exchange parts of the Tigre province conquered by her troops, together with a large zone for economic exploitation in the south.[2]

On his way to a much needed holiday in Switzerland Hoare was persuaded to stop in Paris on 7 and 8 December for urgent talks with Laval to put this provisional plan into final shape. He was supported at different stages by Peterson, Vansittart, and the British ambassador, Sir George Clark. What was finally agreed was an elaboration of the previous plans, although Hoare had been pushed to concede some points by Laval's insistence that nothing less would satisfy Mussolini. Peterson said later that he could have got better terms. Vansittart seemed satisfied that a good job had been done. What the public never understood was that neither the cabinet nor Eden nor any of the permanent officials had previously questioned the need for, or the basic lines of, the plan. When it was published prematurely as a result of a deliberate French indiscretion

---

Africa dropped to \$22,000 worth in January 1936, proof that the moral embargo was effective in this area. U.S. exports to Italy still totalled \$5,420,000 dollars in January 1936 (pp. 302–8).

[1] The Advisory Committee on Trade Questions in Time of War (A.T.B. Committee) produced a paper in June 1935 on the possibility of exerting economic pressure on Germany with Russian assistance. It was then mainly concerned for the next twelve months with problems of economic pressure on Italy. In its annual report for 1936 the Committee drew the conclusion, after a full examination of the Abyssinian crisis, that effective League sanctions against Italy within a limited period would have been possible only with the exercise of belligerent rights. Medlicott, *The Economic Blockade*, vol. II, pp. 13, 14.

[2] Peterson, pp. 116–19.

it had a most hostile press, and was generally regarded as a sudden and complete reversal of the sanctions policy. After an embarrassed attempt to stand by Hoare the cabinet decided that it must abandon the proposals, and he resigned without recanting on 19 December. Eden succeeded.[1]

Ostensibly Hoare had fallen because the Paris terms did not carry the League's approval. Lord Halifax remarked ironically a week later that the proposals were not so different from those put forward by the Committee of Five. 'But the latter were of respectable parentage; and the Paris ones were too much like the off-the-stage arrangements of nineteenth century diplomacy.'[2] This largely shirked the main issue. There had been a confused call for stronger measures than the country, in the government's opinion, was in a position to undertake. The League's endorsement might have sanctified proposals which would reward the victor, while at the same time leaving the weaker party with more than he would retain after defeat; more probably it would have further discredited the League. Eden was a paladin of the League, he represented the youth and conscience of the Conservative party under Baldwin, and a certain reserve and habit of deploring the nastier facts of international life strengthened an impression that he was not always in tune with the rest of his colleagues. His interesting and valuable memoirs certainly show him to be rather frequently irked and ruffled, and during the next two years he was to grumble at both Baldwin's indifference and Neville Chamberlain's all too close attention to foreign affairs.

Nevertheless the main decisions of 1936, a year in which nearly all aspects of British foreign policy were under constant criticism, do not show him to be any more adventurous, or able to make any greater use of the League machinery, than his predecessors. Flandin, who had replaced Laval, could not be persuaded to abandon French objections to the oil sanction, although the British government favoured its early imposition. In January 1936 Eden recommended to the cabinet the Foreign Office's plan for a *modus vivendi* with Germany pending the completion of Britain's rearmament; a few weeks later he elaborated the proposal, arguing that as Germany's deteriorating economic position might drive her to war, Britain

---

[1] Vansittart, *The Mist Procession*, pp. 536–45, and *Lessons of My Life* (?1943), pp. 49–56 ('I should have liked to resign'). Peterson, pp. 120–3; Avon, pp. 288–304; Templewood, pp. 177–82.
[2] Feiling, p. 275.

would be well-advised to do everything possible to assist her
economic recovery. It was true that she might use such help for her
own rearmament, and that France and Soviet Russia might be
resentful, but he was prepared to risk it. To achieve results, concessions to Germany would have to be of value to her, although
they 'must only be offered as part of a final settlement which includes some further arms limitation and Germany's return to the
League'. On 12 February Ralph Wigram of the Foreign Office
hinted to a German diplomat that a 'working agreement' between
Britain, Germany, and France might include an air pact and exclude
'certain things' in the treaty of Locarno. Hitler was interested, but
mainly in the evidence that Britain, like Italy, was unlikely to react
violently to the occupation of the Rhineland.[1]

Certainly Eden was not prepared to reply by any threat of force
or sanctions when the German reoccupation did take place on
7 March 1936.[2] He rightly believed that it would be impossible to
commend forcible action to the country, and that the French were
not prepared to move. The only positive result was the Anglo-
French reaffirmation on 19 March of their obligations under the
Locarno treaty. The plan for a 'working agreement' is the obvious
basis of the 'appeasement' policy pursued by the Chamberlain
government in 1937 and 1938.[3]

Eden also thought it right to end sanctions against Italy as soon
as the fighting was over, and he was a firm and consistent supporter
of non-intervention in Spain when this issue became the dominant
one in British foreign policy after July 1936. In his resignation speech
in February 1938 he was to say that his aim had been the appeasement of Europe, but as the term was then used the same claim
had been made by all his immediate predecessors, to signify their
active devotion to the cause of peace. The prudential as distinct from
the altruistic aspects of this policy were always present: all were
forced to act within the limitations of national power that we have
examined in its many facets in this chapter.

In any case the existing national commitments were very much
more extensive than the government's critics, then or later, would
allow. In a speech to his constituents in Leamington on 20 Novem-

---

[1] Avon, pp. 323–4; D.G.F.P., Ser. C(IV), nos. 562, 568, 594; E. M. Robertson,
Hitler's Pre-War Policy and Military Plans (1963), pp. 70–79.
[2] He discusses his reasons at length: *Avon*, pp. 330–67. Churchill supported the
government: R. H. Power, p. 181.
[3] See pp. 364–8 below.

ber 1936, Eden said that the country must have strength if its ideals were to prevail in a rearming world; after rearming its strength would never be used in a war of aggression, or for a purpose inconsistent with the Covenant or the Pact of Paris. But after these entirely edifying affirmations he went on to show how wide were the obligations for which the country must, if the occasion arose, fight. They were her own defence, the defence of all the territories of the British Commonwealth throughout the world, the defence of France and Belgium against unprovoked aggression in accordance with existing obligations, and the defence of Iraq and Egypt according to the treaties; to this he added the curious assurance that her arms 'may, and, if a new Western European settlement can be reached, they would, be used in defence of Germany were she the victim of unprovoked aggression by any of the other signatories of such a settlement'.

The speech reminds us that Chamberlain was not alone in voicing his hopes of a bargain with Hitler. It also reminds us that Britain's obligations were already much greater than before 1914. Its main significance lies, however, in Eden's insistence that the country had no automatic obligation under the Covenant to help a victim of aggression.[1]

4. THE BALDWIN SUNSET

Those who see in the popularity of Baldwin's last ministry (June 1935 to May 1937) little more than the successful manipulation of an abdication crisis, no doubt over-simplify the issues; nevertheless, his handling of this unusual type of public embarrassment satisfied and absorbed the country, which clearly was not greatly worried as yet by events abroad. One irritated commentator remarked at the time that his capacity for hiding his incapacity had grown from one premiership to another. He was sixty-eight in August 1935, frequently complaining now of tiredness. 'In these moods', wrote a close acquaintance in February 1936, 'he naturally reflects upon his latter end, the danger of repeating Ramsay's example and outstaying your ability and welcome.' He was already looking forward to the happy day of release, when 'Neville will take over'. He was not idle: he assiduously attended his many committees, and indeed it was these that made him tired.[2] His essential

---

[1] Avon, pp. 477–8; cf. A. Wolfers, pp. 373–9.
[2] Thomas Jones, *A Diary with Letters, 1931–1950* (1954), pp. 171–5.

failure continued to lie in his inability to give a decisive lead on recurrent issues of general policy about which, however, he might feel strongly in a rather vague way.

He agreed with friends who insisted on the unwisdom of ostracizing Germany. There was talk in May 1936 of a meeting with Hitler. Tom Jones, who tried to arrange this, told Hitler that Baldwin had said recently that 'among the objects which he hoped to pursue were the following: to launch the young king, to get alongside Germany, and to hand over his party united and in good heart to his successor'. Three days later Baldwin himself told Eden that England must get nearer to Germany, but when asked 'how' retorted 'I have no idea, that is your job'.[1] The meeting with Hitler did not take place. The gesture was one of insurance rather than confidence, and did not lessen the urgency of the defence programme in Baldwin's eyes. Looking for a deputy to take charge of it, he turned in February 1936 to Neville Chamberlain, and after his refusal thought at first of Hoare, a decision which, it was remarked, would disappoint those who desired Churchill and please those who dreaded Eustace Percy.[2] In the end Sir Thomas Inskip was appointed in March to the new office of Minister for the Co-ordination of Defence. Churchill would certainly have been a more dramatic choice, but it could well be argued that the problem at this stage was one of patient planning in committee rather than of offensive strategy. The exclusion, which he resented, served him well in the end.

Inskip's appointment heralded a vital new phase in British re-armament. The programme agreed on in 1934 had been intended mainly to repair deficiencies, that is, to bring the armed forces up to their existing paper strength. The new programme, presented to the Commons by Baldwin on 9 March 1936 after some months of expert and ministerial debate, was essentially a programme of expansion, although its full implications could not be revealed. But they included a new Two-Power standard of strength for the Royal Navy, and dominance in the air to be achieved by 1939. Chamberlain allotted £1,500 million to the defence budget, to be spent over five years.

Neville Chamberlain's reputation was firmly established in Parliament and in government circles, where he was accepted as the

---

[1] *Ibid.*, p. 199; Avon, p. 374.
[2] Feiling, chap. 19; Jones, p. 175.

ablest figure in the cabinet, and the next Prime Minister if Baldwin resigned fairly soon. He was only nineteen months younger than Baldwin, however, and, although energetic and wiry, had his own troubles, including prolonged attacks of gout. His shyness and irritability at all forms of flippancy and humbug in public life (but particularly those to which his political opponents seemed so prone) deprived him both of the public appeal and private tolerance which Baldwin had earned over the years. His patriotism, sense of responsibility, loyalty to friends, and willingness to take blame for unpopular decisions earned him on the other hand the trust of close colleagues who relied increasingly on his drive and technical mastery in many spheres of government outside, but dependent on, the Treasury. He was the real controller of economic policy; he could take credit for the degree of recovery which had been achieved by 1936. He continued to supervise the application of revised regulations for the Unemployment Assistance Board, following the storms which had accompanied its birth, and in November 1936 the new scales were finally put into effect.[1] He had also, while balancing the cost of substantial rearmament against the financial requirements of continuing recovery, given a strong impetus to the defence programme. He worked very hard, he knew his own files as well as his civil servants knew them, and he had the business of most of his cabinet colleagues at his fingertips as well. He knew how to make up his mind. Perhaps he knew less well how to change it.

Although defence and public assistance were being given a good airing by the government's die-hard and Labour critics respectively, they were hardly sufficient to shake it seriously during the winter of 1936–7, although Churchill was to write later that only the abdication crisis saved Baldwin after his 'Fulham election' speech of 12 November.[2] Everyone agreed that Baldwin handled the crisis with deftness and dignity, and that he had the ear of the Commons and the country. Wider issues were for a time forgotten. Yet it might be asked whether the affair ever involved the catastrophic possibilities that some agitated observers appeared to foresee.

King George V, who possessed, as his biographer rightly remarks, no demagogic graces, had passed from a respected to a venerated figure in his last years. It may well be that the change followed his Christmas broadcasts, which began on 25 December

---

[1] See pp. 284, fn. 3, above.
[2] Churchill, *The Gathering Storm*, p. 168; see p. 361 below.

1932. 'His was a wonderful voice—strong, emphatic, vibrant, with undertones of sentiment, devoid of all condescension, artifice or pose. The effect was wide and deep.'[1] His Silver Jubilee celebrations in May 1935 brought great demonstration of affection and loyalty throughout the country; it was observed, and not only in London, that the poorer the streets, the more flags that were displayed. After receiving addresses of welcome on 9 May in Westminster Hall, he drove with Queen Mary on the following days through many of the working-class suburbs of London, amid much popular hilarity and cheering, and afterwards said simply, 'I'd no idea they felt like that about me'. This was perhaps due, not so much to any expectation of unpopularity, as to a tacit assumption shared by many others that the drift of political sentiment was increasingly indifferent to the monarchical idea. Could it be that there was a more positive rôle still to be played by royalty under the constitution? The question remained after the King's death on 20 January 1936.

For this very reason the gifts, charm, and genuine popularity of the Prince of Wales, who now succeeded as King Edward VIII, caused stirrings of uneasiness in some quarters. Professor Laski, who in a pamphlet of January 1932 had described the formation of the National government as a palace revolution which left the real balance of power dependent upon the will of the King, was alarmed at the 'fuss' over the King's death and the accession, evidently anticipating disasters for socialism.[2] A few people may have agreed with him. Some were worried by reports of the new King's sympathy for Fascism. Others simply feared that, with lively impulses and ideas of his own, he would be tempted to overstep the bounds of constitutional restraint. It does not appear that Baldwin and his colleagues had any anxieties under these heads. Edward VIII welcomed his high office and took his responsibilities seriously; he had been trained for it, he was irked by what he regarded as the failure of his parents to bring the monarchy fully into the twentieth century, he proposed to modernize its image. Red tape would be reduced, court etiquette simplified. He was soon giving considerable time and thought to economies at Sandringham and Balmoral. His desire to marry an American, Mrs. Simpson, whose undefended petition for a second divorce was filed in October 1936, was something which he hoped could be reconciled with his public duties,

---

[1] H. Nicolson, *King George V*, p. 526.
[2] Kingsley Martin, *Harold Laski* (1953), pp. 84–5, 106–7.

not an excuse for escape from them. He always insisted in after life that he had wished to be King and to remain King.[1]

The essential point, which Baldwin judged correctly, was that the British public would not have been prepared to accept Mrs. Simpson either as Queen or as a morganatic wife. This issue was made clear to the King between his first discussion with Baldwin on the point on 16 November 1936 and the final speech which Baldwin made to the House of Commons on 10 December. Although the delay had led to some anxieties as to whether the King would attempt an appeal to the country over the heads of his ministers, it had in fact served its purpose by assuring Baldwin of the overwhelming support of the Labour party, his own party, and the Dominions. A chivalrous plea by Churchill for delay merely emphasized his normal isolation in the Commons. It seems clear that the King himself had realized from the start that marriage probably meant abdication.

The institution of monarchy did not suffer from the crisis. It strengthened a widespread opinion that the burden of royal duty is a grievous one, and the harshest thing said about Edward VIII was the remark of a Labour M.P. that he was a weakling who had failed to measure up to the demands of his office. The obvious sense of inadequacy and almost of panic with which his successor, the Duke of York, became the new King as George VI could not but confirm the belief in onerous burdens dutifully borne. Meanwhile it was observed that on Coronation Day, 12 May 1937, Baldwin almost divided the cheering with the royal pair.[2]

---

[1] As Duke of Windsor he gave his own account in *A King's Story* (1951); cf. J. W. Wheeler-Bennett, *King George VI* (1958), pp. 268–74.

[2] G. M. Young, *Stanley Baldwin*, chap. 24; Wheeler-Bennett, pp. 293–301.

9

THE COMING OF WAR

· 1. THE SEARCH FOR APPEASEMENT

IT is impossible to think of Neville Chamberlain's premiership (28 May 1937–10 May 1940) except in terms of the international situation, which led with a frightening inevitability to exactly the results that he sought to avoid—war and defeat. And while the country was moving towards war in Europe in alliance with Poland and France, it had two major, and easily forgotten, defensive distractions elsewhere. The outbreak of open war in Nationalist China in July 1937 was followed by a rapid advance of Japanese armies and the continued threat of either an open Japanese attack on the isolated British possessions and concessions or, more probably, incidents leading to war as the headstrong and trigger-happy Japanese generals threw their weight about with scant regard for the politicians in Tokyo.[1] In the eastern Mediterranean there was a double threat from Italian expansionists and Muslim national-ists, although the two tended to some extent to neutralize each other. While Turkey watched Italian moves in the Dodecanese apprehensively, Egypt in July 1936 signed a treaty of close alliance with Britain with provision for Egyptian independence, un-restricted immigration of Egyptian nationals into the Sudan, and the continuance of a British force in the neighbourhood of Alex-andria for eight years. In Palestine the White Paper of 1930 had annoyed the Jews through its limitation of agricultural develop-ment, and the counter-efforts to mollify them had angered the Arabs, who were further enraged when the Peel commission[2]

---

[1] The government's preoccupation with Japan has been largely ignored by writers on the period. Birkenhead, *Halifax*, in dealing with the period 1937–39, omits all reference to the Far East.

[2] Cmd 3692 (1930); Cmd 5479 (1937).

recommended partition in July 1937. The Arab revolt, mounting in intensity from September 1937 to April 1938, was dealt with by mobile forces from the Canal area in July, but these had to return to face a possible Italian attack in September. Concentration of resources in the European zone was both paramount and impracticable, as Hitler counted on Italy and Japan to distract Britain's attention.

When Chamberlain succeeded the weary and exhausted Stanley Baldwin he had, like the opposition leaders, great confidence in his own plans and panaceas. His colleagues welcomed the brisker and more systematic leadership that he offered. Simon alone had had a longer record of public service. The lack of an obvious successor or even an outstanding second in command in the Commons no doubt increased his combative sense of responsibility. He felt reasonably at home with all classes of public business, including foreign affairs.[1] He had been a member of the cabinet almost continuously since 1922, hearing and often taking part in discussions on foreign policy; as Chancellor since 1931 he had been constantly involved in negotiations with foreign governments, and he had established a close working contact with Eden in the process. It is said that in his youth he and Austen, as the sons of Joseph Chamberlain, had been virtually brought up on foreign affairs.[2] In the controversies of the next three years, he was sometimes assailed as a novice in diplomacy, but in fact this is one of the less sensible of criticisms: his political education compares favourably enough with that of other statesmen whose competence has never been in question.

The accusation does, however, remind us of the rule that a Prime Minister may share his successes but must take sole responsibility for failures: and Chamberlain's busy, conscientious, determined initiative in directing extremely unpalatable policies could not fail to make him everybody's scapegoat. Much of the criticism was undoubtedly unfair, if only because it exaggerated his control of events. Nor can it be shown that he took the conduct of foreign affairs into his own hands or peregrinated abroad to anything like the same

[1] Feiling, p. 305.
[2] This, according to Neville's son, in a letter to *The Times* of 26 Nov. 1962, was Austen's comment when dismissing as a flippancy his remark to Neville Chamberlain in front of Eden, 'you must remember that you do not know anything of foreign affairs'; cf. Lord Avon, *Facing the Dictators*, p. 445, where the remark is evidently taken at its face value.

extent as Lloyd George or Churchill, or even Disraeli or Mac-
Donald or Macmillan on occasion. There is evidence of frequent and
regular consultation with colleagues and officials about the difficult
problems of the times. Lord Templewood tells us that the foreign
policy committee of the cabinet, a body of some nine or ten
ministers which had had only an intermittent existence under Baldwin,
now met regularly under his chairmanship, in close consultation
with the Chiefs of Staff, although according to Duff Cooper it did
not include the defence ministers. It held over fifty meetings between
1937 and 1939. Eden, who was asked to continue in office, appears
like the others to have welcomed the new Prime Minister's interest
in foreign affairs, although he did not much relish the attentions of
the foreign policy committee. Nor did the Foreign Office much like
Chamberlain's continued reliance on Sir Horace Wilson, an able
civil servant with whom he had worked closely for many years.[1]

The real basis of criticism must be sought far more in Chamberlain's faults of manner and tactics than in the broader aims and
planning of policy. In the post-1947 era it was possible to admit
that Britain did not have the strength to police or the authority to
lead the world. The same was true of 1937, but it was political
suicide to say so. There may well have been no real alternative to the
unpopular decisions for which Chamberlain so readily took
responsibility.[2] But it is by no means certain that an abler or more
resourceful politician could not have put a different face on a very
similar policy to his. And if his critics were inclined to forget that
the individual even in the highest places is the tool of impersonal
forces, so was he. While he had great determination and a stubborn
resolve to think matters through and act realistically he often failed
to convince others of the fact. He was a first-rate debater in Parliament but a poor publicist for his own policies outside it, at a time
when political effects of a quite outstanding importance were being
produced by the resounding, flamboyant propaganda technique of
the dictators (which Roosevelt and some day perhaps Winston
Churchill alone seemed likely to match on the other side). The still,
small voice and badly phrased, off-the-cuff speeches of the Prime

---

[1] Sir Horace John Wilson, born 1882; K.C.B., 1924, G.C.M.G., 1933; Permanent
Under-Secretary, Ministry of Labour, 1921–30; chief industrial adviser to the govern-
ment, 1930–39; seconded to the Treasury for service with the Prime Minister, 1935;
Permanent Under-Secretary, Treasury, and head of the Civil Service, 1939–42.

[2] This however is something that even his most perceptive critics seem unwilling to
admit. Francis Williams, *A Pattern of Rulers* (1965), pp. 135–94, comes near to doing so
at times.

Minister, mournful and moderate, carefully denuded of any note of menace or anger, were a poor reply. Furthermore it is a not un-important consideration that he had handicapped himself in carrying through a contentious national policy by the acerbities of his ex-changes over many years with the Opposition leaders, a difficulty that was increased when he became the government's main spokes-man on foreign policy in the Commons after Eden's resignation. It was not so much his belief in peace as his belief in himself that irked them.

Nevertheless it must be remembered that dissatisfaction with the government's foreign policy was essentially a product of the Baldwin era, and had already taken shape before Chamberlain came to office: indeed, his own policy was in some measure an expression of the same dissatisfaction. The movement for inter-party agreement outside the predominantly Conservative ranks of the National government could be seen in 1936 in Harold Macmillan's 'Next Five Years' and 'New Outlook' groups, and in Churchill's 'Arms and the Covenant' demonstration at the Albert Hall in December, with the T.U.C. secretary, Walter Citrine, in the chair. Similarly there were plans and much talk of the united front against Fascism and war among the left-wing groups during 1936, antedating both Chamberlain's accession and the Spanish civil war.

In the Labour movement pacifist sentiment of varying shades was stronger in the constituency parties, and particularly the women's sections, than in the trade unions, but the union leaders, while preparing mentally to square up to the Fascists, were still sure that they must do nothing to approve the rearmament programme of 'reactionary' Conservatives. The Edinburgh conference of the Labour party in October 1936 had accordingly paraded the old jumble of paradoxes and ambiguities: a strong League, no com-petitive armaments, collective security, automatic sanctions, dis-armament by international agreement. It had given no clear lead to Labour M.P.s who at last decided for themselves in July 1937 not to vote in future against the estimates for the fighting services. But while the Labourites distrusted Tories and Fascists they also distrusted their would-be Communist allies. The Popular Front movement was launched in January 1937 in a joint manifesto by the Socialist League, I.L.P., and the Communist party, demanding unity of all sections of the working class to oppose Fascism, reaction, war, and the National government. Its spiritual home was the Left Book

Club, founded in March 1936.[1] The Labour party, while agreeing readily enough with the programme, had no intention of allowing Communist infiltration in the name of the Popular Front movement. The Socialist League was promptly expelled from the party. The lesson was reiterated in the May (1938) manifesto of the party executive.[2]

Chamberlain's views on foreign affairs just before taking office are set out in a letter to Morgenthau of 26 March 1937, in reply to a secret verbal enquiry (with Roosevelt's knowledge) as to the prospects of world disarmament. Chamberlain replied that England was rearming, to the gratification of many nations, and that the main source of fear was Germany. Germany was determined to make herself so strong that no one would attempt to resist her demands, whether for European or colonial territories, and with this intention in her heart was 'not likely to agree to any disarmament which would defeat her purposes'. Only the belief that her efforts would be countered by superior force would deter her. Japan, too, had 'far-reaching ambitions'; the recent German–Japanese agreement was a warning that if Britain were seriously involved in Europe she could not count on Japanese neutrality. So he deprecated any fresh disarmament campaign and suggested that America's greatest single contribution to world peace would be the amendment of the existing neutrality legislation. We know that the passage in this letter referring to Germany's ambitions was written by Chamberlain himself into a Foreign Office draft.[3] It reveals his aim as essentially that of 'appeasement through strength', in the political jargon of 1939, rather than the peace-at-any-price policy attributed to him by some of his critics. It meant that bolder lines might have to await the attainment of the safety limit of rearmament, but that he had no illusions about the menace of the 'bandit nations'.

Diplomacy was closely linked to the rearmament plans. Here, as

---

[1] Organized and directed throughout by Victor Gollancz and his firm, with Professor Laski and John Strachey as co-selectors, the Club gave members monthly a 'Left Book of the Month' for half-a-crown, and organized clubs throughout the country for their discussion. Although professing to welcome all left-wing enthusiasts it took for granted the dedicated anti-fascism of the Soviet government and the unqualified virtues of the communist movement: all other political forces, including the Labour party, were found wanting in varying degrees by this yardstick. The club's membership reached 57,000 in April 1939. Its *raison d'être* was largely destroyed by the Soviet-German pact of August 1939. It was dissolved in 1948.

[2] E. Windrich, pp. 138–58; she is silent about the ambiguities in outlook. G. D. H. Cole, *A History of the Labour Party from 1914*, pp. 318–35, faces them.

[3] J. M. Blum, *From the Morgenthau Diaries* (1959), pp. 458–67; Avon, p. 527.

in other spheres, Chamberlain as Prime Minister brought greater urgency but no essential new ideas to an existing programme. He was critical of Baldwin's 'appallingly frank' confession on 12 November 1936 that the state of public opinion alone prevented in 1934 and 1935 the launching of a big rearmament programme, for he felt that Baldwin might justifiably have drawn attention to the necessary delays and work done in these years in drawing up the new programme.[1] He claims, and this has never been contradicted, that he was mainly responsible for the impetus and revisions which made the programme a reality. In the budget of April 1936 he provided £158 million for the defence estimates for 1936-7, and an increase in income tax from 4s 6d to 4s 9d in the pound; in April 1937 income tax was increased to 5s, and he proposed a new tax on business profits, the National Defence Contribution. This, however, proved violently unpopular in the City, and had to be modified later after a stubborn stand by Chamberlain in the early days of his premiership.

Two considerations still prevented full rearmament. The first was the decision that the programme must be compatible with normal trade. The second was that, within the budgetary allocations available, the guiding principle must be defensive safety. The first consideration was the result partly of contemporary economic theory, partly of political thinking. The Treasury's time-honoured or dishonoured task of curbing military extravagance was reinforced by the conclusion that the 1931 crisis, still so fresh in men's minds, was itself the result of reckless governmental expenditure, which must be righted by austerity, belt-tightening, and taxation.[2] In any case a sound economy, adequate foreign exchange resources and a flourishing state of external trade, were necessary to support a rearmament programme and still more a future war. It was in this sense that finance was called 'the fourth arm'. But the political situation also was still thought of in terms of peacetime diplomacy. The purpose of this phase of rearmament was not so much to win a major war, as to be able to threaten and warn, and to deter Hitler (or other opponents) with the prospect of a long and unprofitable struggle.

[1] See pp. 332-4 above; and on Baldwin's gaffe, Feiling, pp. 312-3; Young, pp. 227-31. The incident is put in its right setting by R. Bassett, in the *Cambridge Journal*, Nov. 1948, pp. 84-95.

[2] Cf. M. M. Postan, *British War Production* (H.M.S.O., 1952), p. 13, and chap. 11, 'Early rearmament, 1934-1938', the best available account. There is a useful sketch in P. K. Kemp, *Victory at Sea, 1939-1945* (1957), pp. 17-31, and W. K. Hancock and M. M. Gowing, *British War Economy* (H.M.S.O., 1949), pp. 62-72.

The second consideration, combined with the financial limit, led to a fairly satisfactory programme of expansion for the Royal Navy, a lavish development of the Air Force, and an almost complete standstill for the Army. Excessive fears of a German knockout blow remained. Sir Edmund Ironside remarked in his diary on 29 December 1937 that the cabinet were terrified of a war in which Great Britain might be annihilated in a few weeks by attack from the air.[1] As late as July 1939 Captain Liddell Hart, an expert much respected in ministerial circles, mentioned a quarter of a million casualties and £100 million-worth of damage as likely results of a week of enemy bombing.[2] Parity in the air with Germany was not achieved before 1939, but the inhibiting factor now was not finance but the necessarily slow process of design and experiment needed to equip the R.A.F. with the splendid new types—the Spitfires, Hurricanes, Battles, Blenheims, Whitleys, Hampdens, Wellingtons, and others—which would make it technically dominant when the time came. The Air Staff rejected the alternative of a hasty output of largely obsolescent types; it was this 'rearmament in width', as the German expert, General Thomas called it, which partly explained the German lead at this time. The cabinet in February 1936 had sanctioned the more ambitious programme, Scheme F, based on these new types. It was designed to provide 8,000 new aircraft by 1939, doubling the current programme, and with adequate reserves and a greater emphasis on offensive power. Plans on these lines went steadily ahead, aided by the successful expansion—after some crises—of the indispensable factory capacity.[3]

By comparison the Army seems at first sight to have been extra-ordinarily neglected. But as long as the purpose of rearmament was to bolster diplomacy with the appearance of an impregnable defence rather than to build a war economy, air and sea were bound to have priority, and this necessarily meant (if the Treasury's financial ceiling was to be maintained) that the Army came last on the list. This became known as the policy of limited liability. It must be remembered that of all forms of rearmament a large army with the shadow of conscription would be the least acceptable to public opinion, and that the case for disarmament was still being actively pressed in Labour circles and in America. There was also a theory

[1] *The Ironside Diaries* (1963), pp. 42–3.
[2] B. H. Liddell Hart, *The Defence of Britain* (1939), p. 154.
[3] See p. 339 above. Postan, pp. 18–20; Webster and Frankland, vol. I, pp. 70–73.

that the French army, as long as it stayed behind its fortifications, was the finest in the world, but that British divisions might encourage a suicidal urge to attack.

Essentially, however, the assumption was that the transition to a full war economy could be made only after war began, or when it was imminent. The argument was put in various forms that the armed forces had four main objectives: home defence, the maintenance of lines of communication to Great Britain, defence and internal security of imperial territories, and the defence of allied countries. For these ends five Regular divisions, one mechanized, had to suffice. The Imperial Conference of May 1937 heard a masterly statement by Eden as to Britain's inability to defy Germany, Italy, and Japan simultaneously, the consequent need for a *modus vivendi* with them pending the completion of the costly rearmament programme, and the desirability of greater help from the Dominions. But Dominion opinion was divided and rather unresponsive,[1] and in general willing to leave the British government to its policy of appeasement in so far as Germany's next round of continental demands was concerned. General Hertzog in particular was profoundly convinced that Hitlerite intransigence was due to the treaty of Versailles.[2]

If in these circumstances priority was to continue to be given to imperial defence it was more than likely that the fourth objective could not be met. Hore-Belisha, the Secretary of State for War, very much influenced by Captain Liddell Hart at this period, was determined to make the best of his limited opportunities. The most dramatic evidence of this was the replacement on 1 December 1937 of Field-Marshal Sir Cyril Deverell, the C.I.G.S., and Lt. General Sir Harry Knox, the Adjutant General, by Viscount Gort and Major-General C. G. Liddell, younger and apparently livelier men. There were other efforts at modernization, but nothing approaching the high level of mechanization pressed by Liddell Hart.[3] Hore-Belisha felt it necessary to warn the General Staff in February 1938

[1] H. Duncan Hall, 'The Commonwealth in War and Peace', in *The British Commonwealth at War* (1943), p. 13; N. Mansergh, *Survey of British Commonwealth Affairs, Problems of External Policy, 1931–1939* (1952), pp. 82–92; D. C. Watt, *Personalities and Politics*, pp. 162–6.

[2] On the other hand the Canadian Prime Minister, Mr. Mackenzie King, so far departed from his habitual attitude of studied non-commitment as to tell Hitler at the end of June 1937 that in the event of an attack on the United Kingdom all the Dominions would come to her aid. He repeated this publicly in Paris on 2 July. H. Duncan Hall, *North Atlantic Supply* (1955), p. 6; G. M. Carter, *op.cit.*, p. 278.

[3] B. H. Liddell Hart, *Memoirs*, vol. II, pp. 63–113.

that it was unlikely that an expeditionary force could be provided for use on the continent for the time being. Until 1936 it had been assumed that twelve Territorial divisions would also be available for a field army, but subsequently it came to be accepted that their duties would be mainly confined to manning the anti-aircraft defences. Nevertheless, expenditure on the Army rose from £8·5 million in 1935 to £44·3 million in 1938.[1]

Altogether there was no great novelty in the government's external programme in the summer of 1937, apart from a new determination to get things done. Its origin is to be found in the rearmament discussions and the plans for a working agreement with Germany which Hoare and Eden had favoured in the winter of 1935–6.[2] The differences that were to develop between Chamberlain and Eden did not turn on these appreciations, but essentially on Eden's tendency to play by ear and his consequent distaste for negotiations with Italy (but not apparently with Germany). His inclination to rely too greatly on early American action was also an issue between them. But both recognized that American help was vital in dealing with Japan. Both seem to have believed—with Hertzog and Roosevelt and many others—that German grievances (Central Europe, Danzig, the colonies) might be genuinely felt and be of a more respectable moral character than the purely predatory imperialism of Mussolini in the Red Sea and the Mediterranean. The solution of these German problems by peaceful change might ease tensions. Eden, indeed, seems to have been more ready than Hitler for a colonial settlement in the last weeks of 1937.[3] Many later critics conveniently forgot how widespread was the belief even in 1938 that Hitler knew when to stop while Mussolini probably did not.[4] The two agreed also about Moscow: Eden warned his cabinet colleagues in December 1937 not to rule out the possibility of a Berlin–Moscow axis, and to make in the circumstances every

---

[1] R. J. Minney, *The Private Papers of Hore-Belisha* (1960), pp. 87–98; Postan, pp. 27–34; R. Higham, *Armed Forces in Peacetime*, a critical account (pp. 233–42).

[2] See pp. 349–50 above.

[3] M. Gilbert and R. Gott, *The Appeasers* (1963), pp. 101–4. Churchill also, in December 1937, advocated a restoration of 'war conquests' to Germany, and colonial concessions: R. H. Powers, p. 181.

[4] R. W. Seton-Watson, the outstanding academic critic of Hitler in 1939, wrote in *Britain and the Dictators* (completed 25 March 1938): 'With Russia under Stalin our interests need not collide: with Germany under Hitler a compromise is difficult but by no means impossible: with Italy under Mussolini there can be nothing better than armed neutrality and perpetual vigilance' (pp. 189–90). 'The convenient thesis of Germany's unfitness to administer colonies' was 'as untrue as it is insulting' (p. 79). The book hardly mentions Japan.

possible effort to 'come to terms with each or all of our potential enemies, but not by conduct which would lose us our friends, actual or potential'.[1]

There is no justification for the view that armament questions were ignored in the negotiations with Hitler; if anything, the diplomatic proceedings were linked too slavishly to the rearmament programme, which since 1934 had been based on the avoidance of war before 1939.[2] France, too, with her obsolete air force, her jittery right-wing politics, her financial shakiness and stagnant armaments industry, was considered an economic liability; there was as yet no prospect of American aid on the 1917–18 scale, or indeed on any scale. Chamberlain was also a man of peace; he was genuinely horrified at the prospect of war. So indeed were most politicians of his generation. But he seems to have had a profound belief in his mission and his aptitude as a peacemaker. The good man and conscientious statesman must leave no stone unturned, explore every avenue, try and try and try again. But preparation for war, postponement of war, and avoidance of war were difficult ends to pursue simultaneously and convincingly.

Immediately after taking office he followed up his letter to Morgenthau with another which again emphasized German aggressiveness and asked for some Anglo-American collaboration, particularly in relation to Japan. The State Department, evidently startled by the spectre of entangling alliances, gave a wordy but quite negative answer on 1 June 1937. In order to explore the possibilities of an agreement with Germany an invitation was also sent to von Neurath to visit London; it was accepted, and then cancelled on 20 June. Ribbentrop, the German ambassador in London since October 1936, was still sourly contemplating the unsympathetic British from behind the vast windows of the German embassy, and was probably the real obstacle. Approaches to Hull and von Neurath having led nowhere, Chamberlain thought it best to sound Mussolini; it could be argued that with her precarious resources Italy might genuinely welcome a *détente*, and it would be useful to separate her from her Axis partner. After some preliminary contacts

---

[1] Avon, p. 520.

[2] Cf. B. Celovsky, *Das Münchener Abkommen von 1938* (1958), p. 171, n.5, who can see only a policy of 'peace at any price'. Halifax told Phipps on 23 March 1938: 'Our effort in rearmament has been considerable, but we are only approaching the stage where production will give us a return on the expenditure on which we have embarked. Quite frankly, the moment is unfavourable, and our plans, both for offence and defence, are not sufficiently advanced' (B.D., III(i), no. 107).

Mussolini offered peaceful assurances through Grandi on 24 July, and on the 27th Chamberlain sent a letter to Mussolini (without showing it to Eden, who however made no subsequent objection), offering to begin negotiations at any time to remove misunderstanding or suspicion. Mussolini reciprocated on 2 August.

However, the Duce, with a showy toughness which was becoming increasingly a substitute for the mystique of dangerous living, continued to infuriate Eden by mixing talk of agreement with provocations in all directions: anti-British propaganda from the Bari station, from time to time an outrageous speech on the bleating democracies or some such theme, intrigues among the Arabs, and a continued evasion of attempts to end international intervention in Spain. Submarine attacks, undoubtedly of Italian origin, on Mediterranean shipping in August led to effective Anglo-French action; at the Nyon conference in September agreement was reached (aided by Italy's injudicious absence) for the patrolling of the shipping routes. In the meantime the opening of talks was put off.

At this point Hitler and Mussolini were both preoccupied with their plans for self-assertion—the one in central Europe, the other in the Mediterranean—and each wished to embroil Britain with the other. The real importance of the reoccupation of the Rhineland had lain in the fact that it allowed a great armaments industry to be safely developed there; and in August and September 1936 plans had been launched by Hitler for the Four Year Plan which was to make Germany ready for a major war not later than 1940.[1] Eden's proposal for a 'working agreement' in February 1936 and the advice of the then anglophil Ribbentrop seems to have encouraged Hitler's hopes of some profitable agreement with England, probably on the basis of the anti-communist crusade. Mussolini had been alarmed since the beginning of the sanctions crisis at this prospect, which would leave him without support in his Mediterranean adventures, and he worked hard to disrupt it. Among the major triumphs of Italian diplomacy at this period was its purloining of diplomatic correspondence, particularly from the files and cupboards of the British embassy in Rome. In October 1936 Mussolini was able to lay before Hitler a copy of the paper entitled 'The German Peril' which Eden had presented to the cabinet in January 1936, and which advised an agreement with Germany pending the completion of British rearmament, after which Germany's search for pre-

[1] A. S. Milward, *The German Economy at War* (1965), pp. 15–27.

dominance in Europe could be resisted. Hitler was apparently genuinely shocked, but convinced that as Germany was rearming faster she would keep her lead.[1] The German–Italian axis was announced in November 1936. A year later Ribbentrop had lost hope of making progress with the British, and Mussolini had consolidated his position: his visit to Germany late in September 1937 seems to have strengthened Hitler's animosity towards Britain, and with it Mussolini's own freedom of action. On 6 November Italy joined the anti-Comintern pact (originally concluded between Germany and Japan on 21 November 1936) which was far more an anti-British pact. On the 5th Hitler, as we know today, expounded his programme for war to the heads of the armed forces at the 'Hossbach' meeting, an exposition which is as remarkable for its underlying lust for battle as for its shrewd insistence on the practical advantages of carefully timed early action.

There was thus no chance of a lasting pacification, or appeasement, of Europe, in the not ignoble form which Chamberlain may have genuinely believed possible: but while he and Eden were sufficiently realistic to be sceptical about ever achieving this consummation they were well aware that the invitation to talks might at least serve to buy time.[2] When a second opportunity to open intimate conversations with Germany was offered by an invitation to Goering's hunting exhibition, Halifax was at first inclined to reject it, and Chamberlain and Eden thought it worth while to accept.[3] Hitler on 19 November spoke at length to Halifax and with apparent sincerity about his devotion to peace, and Halifax specifically referred to Great Britain's willingness to recognize Germany's legitimate demands in central Europe, always, however, in terms of 'peaceful procedure'.[4] But it soon became evident that Hitler had not responded to the implied British terms. The bargain, pointing ultimately to disarmament, was an absurd one from his point of view: the first phase of expansion which he was planning was necessary to con-

---

[1] E. M. Robertson, *Hitler's Pre-War Policy and Military Plans 1933–1939* (1963), pp. 87–92, 96–7; see p. 350 above.

[2] Avon, p. 324; Robertson, p. 96. Cf. Chamberlain's comment: ' . . . until our armaments are completed, we must adjust our foreign policy to our circumstances, and even bear with patience and good humour actions which we should like to treat in very different fashion' (to Mrs. Morton Prince, 16 Jan. 1938, Feiling, p. 322).

[3] So Templewood, pp. 281–2; Halifax, *Fulness of Days* (1959), p. 184; Birkenhead, chap. 20. Cf. Avon, pp. 508–16; Iain Macleod, *Neville Chamberlain* (1961), p. 210.

[4] D.G.F.P., ser.D., vol. I, nos. 31, 33; Paul Schmidt, *Statist auf Diplomatischer Bühne, 1923–45* (1949), pp. 377–9.

solidate his bases for further advance, to make possible the fulfilment of military strength, not to destroy it.

Anglo-French discussions in London on 29 and 30 November did nothing to encourage speedier action. The French Prime Minister, Camille Chautemps, admitted that France would not fight if Germany annexed Austria, although Delbos, the Foreign Minister, countered this by insisting that she must fight if her ally, Czechoslovakia, were attacked. Chamberlain believed that British opinion would not approve of war to maintain Czechoslovakia in its existing form, but he promised that his government would work for a satisfactory settlement on a basis of greater local liberties for the Sudeten Germans, and for a comprehensive solution of the German problem by peaceful change. He also promised never to agree to a separate Anglo-German understanding. Colonies were discussed; here too the French were ready for some concessions, but as Chamberlain showed himself hostile to the surrender of any British colonies it was decided to drop this point.[1] What emerged very clearly was the desperate French need to avoid a major crisis, their tendency to pin all hopes on Britain, and their hostility to, and lack of enthusiasm for, any negotiations with Italy. After this, talks between Eden and Grandi in December made little progress. Eden wanted a cessation of propaganda and other signs of repentance from the Italians, while Chamberlain saw a deadlock which could only lead to further Italian intransigence. Neither found much cause for optimism in all this. Nor did Chamberlain share Eden's hopes of American action, although he approved of his efforts to foster it.

The United States did agree to take part in a meeting of the Nine Powers at Brussels over the Sino-Japanese dispute in November. Eden put to Hull on 19 October a suggestion for a combination of aid to China and economic pressure on Japan, and on the eve of the conference he offered that Britain would stand shoulder to shoulder with the United States in whatever form of positive action was necessary, including a substantial force of ships. But the chief American delegate, Norman Davis, could promise nothing, and the conference achieved nothing. Eden followed up his proposal by offering staff conversations and eight or nine capital ships for a joint demonstration. The United States government remained

[1] Feiling, pp. 333–4; Avon, pp. 516–8; A. H. Furnia, *The Diplomacy of Appeasement* (1960), pp. 270–2; F.R.U.S., 1937, vol. I, pp. 180–3, 186–8.

vaguely encouraging, with hints of large forthcoming gestures even if precise commitments were firmly avoided.[1] The Japanese bombed the British ambassador, Sir Hughe Knatchbull-Hugessen, in August, and apologized tardily; when they sank an American gunboat, the *Panay*, and attacked H.M.S. *Ladybird* on 12 December it seemed that the United States might react violently, although rejecting Eden's offer of a joint protest. Roosevelt was momentarily interested in a U.S. Treasury plan for the freezing of Japanese assets, and Morgenthau promptly sounded Sir John Simon on the transatlantic telephone. At the same time Roosevelt sent Captain R. E. Ingersoll of the U.S. Navy to London to open discussions with the British Admiralty for joint action in the event of war with Japan. Simon passed the economic proposal on to Chamberlain and Eden; the British economic warfare experts were instructed to get to work at once on plans for an economic blockade of Japan, and continued to work on them until the following March 1938. But Japan apologized; Roosevelt had lost interest in Morgenthau's plan by 21 December; and Ingersoll was soon recalled. In January 1938 three U.S. cruisers were, however, sent to visit Singapore, and the date of the American manoeuvres in the Pacific was advanced.[2]

After his momentary contemplation of violent action Roosevelt fell back on the safer policy of the 'eternal question mark',[3] under which the State Department maintained a universal doubt as to how the United States would behave in any given situation. While this did not exclude the possibility of action against aggressor states or 'bandit nations', it did exclude any firm commitment to support British or French policies. It was well in tune with American opinion, critical of aggressors but not at all warlike. Roosevelt now proposed to revert to moral leadership and revived a plan for an international conference on disarmament and similar questions. Cordell Hull had with difficulty secured the abandonment of a dramatic appeal to the world on these lines on armistice day, 11 November 1937. He argued that it was unrealistic, when the Axis powers were furiously rearming, to turn public opinion in the democratic countries away from self-defence and to try to revive the completely

---

[1] Avon, pp. 533–40; Cordell Hull, *Memoirs* (1948), vol. I, pp. 550–8; H. Feis, *The Road to Pearl Harbor* (1950), pp. 8–16.

[2] J. M. Blum, *From the Morgenthau Diaries*, pp. 485–93; W. N. Medlicott, *The Economic Blockade*, vol. I, pp. 14, 383–5.

[3] Nancy H. Hooker, ed., *The Moffat Papers, 1919–1943* (1956), p. 194; cf. E. L. Henson, 'Britain, America, and the month of Munich', *International Relations*, Apr. 1962, p. 291.

collapsed disarmament movement.[1] But Roosevelt continued to
brood over the idea, and he put a modified version of it to Chamberlain in a personal message on 11 January 1938. The Prime Minister,
who may well have had the same objections as Hull, suggested in
reply a reconsideration of the timing of the plan which otherwise
might cut across his own plans for negotiations with Germany and
Italy.

There is no doubt that this incident has been given altogether
disproportionate attention, mainly because of Churchill's tendency
to overstate the case against Chamberlain and Baldwin. He gave
wide publicity to an incorrect version of the facts in the first volume
of his memoirs in 1948, and others have faithfully echoed the assertion that but for Chamberlain's mild suggestion of delay, Roosevelt
would have saved the world from war.[2] Roosevelt did not offer to
call any of the leading powers to the conference: to have done so
might well have 'put the dictators on the spot' as Professor Mowat
has suggested (although they would have been more likely to put
Roosevelt on the spot with resounding declamation about their
grievances and aspirations).[3] What was proposed was a conference
in Washington of the United States and nine small powers, namely
two Latin American states, Sweden, Holland, Belgium, Switzerland,
Hungary, Yugoslavia, and Turkey, to discuss quite general issues
such as disarmament, raw materials, belligerent and neutral rights,
and the principles of international conduct. It was hoped that this
discussion would favour the Prime Minister's effort to reach agreement with Germany and Italy. It was not, however, proposed to
discuss any of the specific disputes between the major powers, and
Roosevelt's draft invitation was careful to say that the United

[1] Cordell Hull, vol. I, pp. 546–8.
[2] W. S. Churchill, *The Gathering Storm* (1948), p. 199. Duff Cooper writes: ' . . . the
offer by the President of the United States of direct intervention in European affairs
presented an immense opportunity which, if it had been seized upon, might have
proved one of the turning-points in European history and would probably have
averted the coming war' (*Old Men Forget* (1953), p. 210). Boris Celovsky: Roosevelt's
'Kampf gegen den amerikanischen Isolationismus erlitt damit einen schweren
Rückschlag. Er brauchte mehr als drei Jahre, um diesen Kampf zum siegreichen Ende
zu bringen' (p. 245; cf. pp. 34–6).
[3] Churchill says that Roosevelt proposed to bring together 'the leading European
Powers to discuss the chances of a general settlement, this of course involving however
tentatively the mighty power of the United States'. He has simply got his facts wrong.
So have others. Mowat calls it 'a conference of the leading powers', p. 596. Similarly
Wheeler-Bennett, *Munich*, p. 270; A. H. Furnia, *The Diplomacy of Appeasement*, p. 275;
A. J. P. Taylor, *The Origins of the Second World War*, p. 144; Amery, *My Political Life*,
vol. III, p. 231; *Survey of International Affairs*, 1938, vol. II, p. 7; A. L. Rowse, *All
Souls and Appeasement*, p. 64.

States could not depart from its traditional policy of freedom from political involvement. In the circumstances it cannot be described as anything but an innocuous gesture which satisfied Roosevelt's urge to do something rather dramatic without committing his country to anything in particular.

When Eden, who had been on leave, returned and insisted on the enormity of any rebuff to the President, Chamberlain agreed rather irritably to a further telegram to Washington on 21 January saying that the British government now felt that there was no need to defer the President's statement, and would support it. A further message to the same effect was sent on 12 February.[1] But in the meantime Roosevelt had blown cold, it may be that he was not sufficiently enamoured of the plan to be ready to push it through in face of Hull's disapproval, but it is more probable that Hitler's assumption of the supreme military command in Germany, the elimination of Generals Blomberg and Fritsch, and the replacement of von Neurath by Ribbentrop, caused alarm. Roosevelt replied to each British message that he was postponing the plan for the time being, and in fact it was soon dropped for good.

Both Chamberlain and Eden had been uneasy, although for different reasons,[2] over the possible repercussions of Roosevelt's proposal to announce the plan to the assembled diplomatic corps at the White House on 22 January, throwing in references to the decline of international standards, the world's frantic rearmament, and the inequities of the postwar settlements. Eden rightly deplored the sketchy reference in Chamberlain's reply of 13 January (drafted apparently by Cadogan) to the forthcoming negotiations with Italy, which seemed to foreshadow *de jure* recognition of the conquest of Abyssinia without an adequate *quid pro quo*. As was so usual at this time, the Americans were more critical of Mussolini than of Hitler, and believed that it was with Germany that British negotiations were pending; Roosevelt hoped that his plan would facilitate British attempts to remove German 'injustices' created by the peace treaties. However, the telegram to Washington on 21 January explained that *de jure* recognition would be granted only as part of a general settlement.

Our tentative conclusion must be that far too much has been

---

[1] Macleod, pp. 212–3, for Chamberlain's view of these events.
[2] Avon, p. 555.

made of this episode.[1] The differences between Eden and Chamberlain over Italy were more serious, although it was Mussolini's frame of mind, rather than the case for an Anglo-Italian *détente*, that Eden distrusted. He evidently did not believe that Mussolini's recent conduct was compatible with desire for a genuine reconciliation, and thought that Mussolini might well desire it in order to offset the blow to his prestige from a successful German assault on Austria. Yet there was surely a case for making the attempt: the Italians might yet have the sense to know that they would have a safer and more prosperous future as a much-courted neutral than as the junior partner of the Nazis. It is difficult, however, to see how Eden could have remained in office after Chamberlain's clumsy attempt to hurry on the discussions.

As Eden seemed determined to delay matters until Italy gave demonstrations of goodwill it was on Chamberlain's invitation that Grandi opened the talks at 10 Downing Street on 18 February 1938, Eden being present. Grandi's account of this three-hour conversation makes the most of the obvious difference of opinion between the two Englishmen, and at a number of points he claims to have widened the breach between them. However that may be, Eden resigned on the following day, and the cabinet accepted Chamberlain's decision to go on with the conversations.[2] Halifax, the new Foreign Secretary, suggested a Mediterranean pact to Ciano on 7 March, and although the Italians rejected this scheme, continued talks in Rome, conducted by Lord Perth, the British ambassador, resulted in the Anglo-Italian agreement of 16 April, which made British recognition of the Italian empire in Abyssinia dependent on the withdrawal of the Italian volunteers from Spain. In his resignation speech on 21 February Eden was reticent about details, but described his policy several times as a search for appeasement.[3]

It soon became evident that Mussolini's interest in discussions with Britain did not mean that he intended to oppose a Nazi coup in Austria. If Hitler imagined that his proceedings up to this point

[1] This is the view of the State Department's historians, W. L. Langer and S. E. Gleason, *The Challenge to Isolation, 1937–1940* (1952), p. 31; pp. 21–32 deals fully with the question, while pointing out gaps in the State Department's documentation. In these cases the authors rely on Churchill's account. The British Foreign Office documents are not yet available. Cf. Sumner Welles, *The Time for Decision* (1944), pp. 61–8. Hull's *Memoirs* do not mention the episode. Templewood, pp. 262–75, is sympathetic to Chamberlain; Avon, pp. 548–60, is not.
[2] *Ciano's Diplomatic Papers* (1948), pp. 164–99; Avon, pp. 571–96; Macleod, pp. 212–7.
[3] P.D., 5 Ser., HC, vol. 332, 21 Feb. 1938, cols. 45–50.

had satisfied Chamberlain's standard of peaceful change he was mistaken; in his diary Chamberlain called Hitler's reception of the Austrian Chancellor, Dr. Schuschnigg, at their meeting on 12 February 1938 'outrageous bullying'. Sir Nevile Henderson, the British ambassador, had been instructed late in January to make another attempt to reach an understanding, and Hitler was not ready for him until 3 March. In a ten-minute speech to the scowling Führer (the longest he ever managed to make) Henderson affirmed the British offer of agreement based on the limitation of armaments, a peaceful solution of the Czech and Austrian problems, and colonial adjustments. Hitler replied with a half-hour harangue and a warning that if Britain opposed a just settlement in Central Europe he would have to fight. As usual treaty revision was demanded as a right; any attempt at a bargain was evaded; and Germany was presented as a proud and self-confident community, ready to respond to reasonable treatment, but prepared to strike like lightning if she were thwarted.[1]

2. AUSTRIA AND CZECHOSLOVAKIA

Hitler had been seeking in his own rough (and quite unconvincing) way to deal with Austria by 'evolutionary' methods.[2] A gesture of defiance by Schuschnigg on 9 March reversed these plans, and after an ultimatum Schuschnigg resigned, Seyss-Inquart, Hitler's tool, was installed as Chancellor on the 11th, and German troops marched in. Chamberlain publicly condemned the treatment of Austria on the 14th and abandoned for the time being the 'peace talks' with Germany; it was obvious that the first great crisis of Nazi expansion, with probable repercussions on Czechoslovakia, had begun.[3] It coincided with, and accelerated, a considerable strengthening of the rearmament programme. The Committee of Imperial Defence on 10 February 1938 had confirmed that until the spring of 1939 the army would not be in a position to take part in anything but 'colonial warfare in operations in an Eastern theatre', and on the

[1] Feiling, pp. 337–42; Sir Nevile Henderson, *Failure of a Mission* (1940), p. 115. D.G.F.P., ser. D(i), nos. 131, 135–46.

[2] U. Eichstädt, *Geschichte des Anschlusses Österreichs, 1933–1938* (1955); J. Gehl, *Austria, Germany, and the Anschluss* (1963), pp. 166–95; G. Brook-Shepherd, *Anschluss, The Rape of Austria* (1963), pp. 42–63; G.D.F.P., ser. D(i), no. 282–98.

[3] The best study of the crisis is perhaps the Chatham House volume, *Survey of International Affairs, 1938* (1951), by R. G. D. Laffan and others. B. Celovsky, *Das Münchener Abkommen von 1938* (1958), is wider than its title; it over-simplifies Chamberlain's rôle. J. W. Wheeler-Bennett, *Munich, Prologue to Tragedy* (1948), is a summary of exasperations; it appeared before the British documents, but is still useful.

same day Hore-Belisha sent a memorandum to the cabinet with plans for making the army as efficient as possible within these depressing limits. But on 7 March, in introducing the fourth White Paper on defence, Chamberlain announced that the overall figure of £1,500 million would have to be greatly exceeded, and as a result of Hitler's Austrian coup the Chiefs of Staff pressed for the rescinding of the rule that rearmament must not impede the course of normal trade. When Chamberlain asked for their views on a proposal, made by Churchill in the Commons on 14 March, for a 'grand alliance' of states for mutual defence against aggression[1] they replied emphatically that the country was not ready for war in 1938, that nothing could be done to help Czechoslovakia, and that war with Germany at this stage might well lead to ultimate defeat. On 22 March the cabinet agreed to abandon the normal-trade prerequisite, and on 27 April Scheme L, providing for a total of 12,000 aircraft within two years, replaced Scheme F: a big effort to cover what seemed (wrongly) to be the one vulnerable point in the country's defences.[2]

This was in fact the real end of Chamberlain's appeasement policy, properly so-called. Hitler had repudiated the method, 'peaceful change', but as Chamberlain's original plan had made no provision for resistance to Germany before the safety point in rearmament had been reached sometime in 1939, there remained a gap which had to be filled with an uneasy and not very well thought out use of the old stand-by, mediation. There seems no doubt that the whole cabinet was accustoming itself to the prospect of war, although all its members recoiled from the thought of a war whose proclaimed purpose would merely be to keep the great majority of the Sudeten Germans, and possibly the majority of the German Austrians, under governments that they disliked. To this extent the policy followed, apart from expediency, was considered right in itself.[3] They were equally convinced that Britain's treaty obligation to France, which would be involved if her frontiers were threatened in a war with Germany, must be honoured, but that as there was no treaty commitment on Britain's part to defend Austria or

---

[1] 'There is still a good company of powerful countries, united very powerful, that share our dangers and aspirations.' He did not name them. Cf. Feiling, pp. 347–8.

[2] Postan, pp. 16–19; Kemp, pp. 24–28; Webster and Frankland, pp. 74–9; Minney, pp. 87–98; Feiling, pp. 340–42; Hancock and Gowing, pp. 68–70; *The Ironside Diaries*, pp. 109–55.

[3] Cf. C. K. Webster, 'Munich reconsidered: a survey of British policy', *International Affairs*, April 1961, p. 149.

Czechoslovakia there could be no automatic support of France in a war arising from the Franco-Czech alliance. Britain could therefore offer herself as a go-between. On the other hand there must be warnings to Germany. It is difficult to imagine a more remarkable series of potential false positions for any government, and difficult to think offhand of any two statesmen less endowed by Providence than Chamberlain and Halifax with the dexterity to manoeuvre around them.

The cabinet discussions following the Austrian coup show signs of the old dilemma of Anglo-French relations: a blunt refusal to go beyond existing commitments might be regarded as wounding, a sympathetic statement might be twisted by the clever Frenchmen into a moral commitment. Duff Cooper tells us that he fought hard for a friendly gesture to France, and he seems to have been satisfied with the result. This took the form of a note to the French government of 22 March in which Halifax reaffirmed the determination to fulfil all the British obligations to France under the London agreement of 19 March 1936, but repeated the warning that had been given to Chautemps on 29 November 1937 that they could not undertake in advance obligations beyond the Locarno commitment.[1] On 24 March Chamberlain spoke to the same effect in the Commons. The British government could not give automatic promises of support in a war arising over an area 'where their vital interests are not concerned in the same degree as they are in the case of France and Belgium'.

> But while plainly stating that decision I would add this. Where peace and war are concerned, legal obligations are not alone involved, and, if war broke out, it would be unlikely to be confined to those who have assumed such obligations. It would be quite impossible to say where it would end and what governments might become involved. The inexorable pressure of facts might well prove more powerful than formal pronouncements, and in that event it would be well within the bounds of probability that other countries, besides those which were parties to the original dispute, would almost immediately become involved. This is especially true in the case of two countries like Great Britain and France, with long association of friendship, with interests closely interwoven, devoted to the same ideals of democratic liberty, and determined to uphold them.[2]

But behind these carefully worded pronouncements, which had

[1] Duff Cooper, *Old Men Forget*, p. 218; B.D., III(i), no. 106.
[2] B.D., III(i), no. 114; P.D., 5 Ser., HC, vol. 333, 24 March 1938, cols 1405–6.

to serve the purpose of maintaining relations with the French, of preventing Czech intransigence or Hitlerite brainstorms, preserving some freedom of manoeuvre, and preparing British public opinion for a possible war, there were intimate and at times blunt arguments with the French about what could really be done. Great emphasis was laid on the argument that, whatever the French government's intentions, it would be impossible to save the Czechs from military defeat or economic strangulation by Germany. In the meantime a war 'to keep the Sudeten Germans under Czech rule' would be a poor rallying cry for the entente forces, it would be difficult to mobilize Dominion support, and it would bring Germany into the fight with all the self-confidence of a just cause. These arguments were pressed on Léon Blum and Paul-Boncour and had to be deployed again when Edouard Daladier succeeded as Prime Minister, and Georges Bonnet as Foreign Minister, on 10 April.

In these discussions of relative military power there was, as we now know, a serious exaggeration of Germany's strength, especially in the case of the *Luftwaffe*. But doubts as to France's ability to sustain a major war at this stage were also growing; her armament and aircraft production were still lagging, and the French economy in general was shaken at this point by a wide wave of strikes which had brought almost the whole metallurgical industry in the Paris region to a standstill. The flight from the franc continued, and placed the tripartite agreement in jeopardy. In pursuit of compulsory holidays, with the forty-hour and five-day week, the workers, as Reynaud bitterly commented in the French Chamber, were preferring butter to guns. Daladier received emergency powers, brought the strikes to an end, and called for a new armaments effort without which 'France would be at the mercy of an invader'. But although the drift was halted, the domestic situation did not greatly improve. Morgenthau thought France should adopt exchange control to save the melting away of her gold assets, but only the Communists favoured this; the Daladier government preferred the alternative of a substantial depreciation of the value of the franc to 175 to the pound sterling.[1] Although this was a serious blow to the tripartite agreement and distasteful to the U.S. Treasury, Morgenthau agreed to it as a result of strong representations from the British government on 3 May. The depreciation would probably hurt England more than the United States but Chamber-

[1] J. M. Blum, pp. 502–3.

lain felt that for political reasons it was imperative to preserve the tripartite understanding.

Daladier, like Chautemps, was not convinced that the traditionalist policy of France in central and eastern Europe could be maintained, and he had chosen Georges Bonnet instead of Paul-Boncour as his foreign minister when the latter refused to abandon the eastern alliance.[1] On 28 and 29 April, Daladier and Bonnet conferred with Chamberlain and Halifax in London, and in long and rambling discussions tried to define the precise degree of help that each power could afford the other. The British ministers, basing themselves on the views of the military attachés in Berlin and Prague, again insisted that it would be impossible to prevent an immediate success for a German attack on Czechoslovakia, and that as, on the British side, 'the political situation was considered to be dependent upon the military angle', it would not be safe to rely on the use of force at this stage, i.e. before 1939. A doubt remained, however, whether the present French ministers were not secretly preparing their minds for a permanent withdrawal from central European commitments rather than a tactical postponement of the crisis. The U.S. ambassador, Bullitt, was convinced after long conversations in May that Daladier had decided that the ultimate dissolution of Czechoslovakia was inevitable.[2]

In the meantime, the government had made a gesture of appeasement or goodwill towards Ireland on 25 April 1938 in three agreements. These brought the trade war over the annuities to an end, accepted the new constitution of 29 December 1937 whereby the 'sovereign independent democratic state of Eire' replaced the Irish Free State, and abandoned the treaty ports which Britain had maintained since 1921. Churchill attacked the settlement in a speech of great exasperation on 5 May.[3]

As it happened the Germans were in no hurry to precipitate a crisis with the Czechs. Austria had to be assimilated, and a prolonged political offensive, in which Konrad Henlein, the leader of the *Sudetendeutsche Partei*, received his orders from the German

---

[1] J. Paul-Boncour, *Entre Deux Guerres* (1946), vol. III, pp. 96–100.

[2] B.D., III(i), no. 164; F.R.U.S., vol. I, pp. 494–5.

[3] See p. 268. Britain received a lump sum of £10 million and abandoned claims to about £100 million. The sums withheld by the Free State since 1932 were about £4,800,000 annually. The duties imposed by the British government had made good this amount. W. K. Hancock, *Survey of British Commonwealth Affairs*, vol. I, pp. 320–44; N. Mansergh, *Survey of British Commonwealth Affairs*, pp. 306–20; Churchill, vol. I, pp. 215–7; cf. p. 335.

ambassador in Prague, was launched. In the 'Karlsbad programme' of 24 April Henlein made eight demands which if granted by the Czechoslovak government would have created a completely autonomous Nazi state within Czechoslovakia; in rejecting the programme on the 25th, M. Hodža, the Czech Prime Minister, promised a nationality statute which would meet the requirements of the minorities.

On this basis the British government did its best during the next three months to steer the powers towards a peaceful solution. The Czechs were urged to make all reasonable concessions to Sudeten demands, while at the same time the German government was reminded in the terms of the Prime Minister's speech of 24 March, that a war could not easily be localized. Ribbentrop appeared to welcome an Anglo-French démarche on these lines on 11 May.[1] Henlein, who had in the meantime shown no disposition to concede anything, was sent to London by Hitler in the second week of May, and endeavoured to persuade some distinguished listeners that the Karlsbad programme was not an ultimatum. These signs that Hitler was for the moment in a quiescent mood seemed to be abruptly dispelled in the crisis of 21 May, but it now appears that for once his astonished protestations of innocence were justified.

Rumours of German troop movements led to Beneš's decision to call up a class of reservists; two Sudeten German farmers on a motor bicycle were accidentally shot by a Czech policeman; there were some scuffles between Sudeten Germans and the police in Komotau; the German press let itself go on the theme of 'bestial murder'; and with remarkable promptitude British, French, and Soviet warnings against an attack on Czechoslovakia were sent to Berlin. The British warning, which Henderson on Halifax's instructions gave Ribbentrop on the evening of the 21st, was in terms of the speech of 24 March: if France supported Czechoslovakia, 'His Majesty's Government could not guarantee that they would not be forced by circumstances to become involved also'.[2] However, on the 22nd, Phipps was instructed by Halifax to remind Bonnet that while prepared to give full aid if France became a victim of German aggression, Great Britain still could not undertake to join in immediately with France if Czechoslovakia became a victim of German aggression. This scrupulous effort to leave the French under

---

[1] B.D. III(i), no. 208.
[2] *Ibid.*, nos. 250, 254.

no illusion as to Britain's exact position does not seem to have told Bonnet anything new, although he was later to use these secret warnings as a partial justification of his own negative policy.[1] Hitler continued to protest his unaggressive attitude although he had secretly taken the decision, after brooding over the 'humiliation' of 21 May, to 'smash Czechoslovakia by military action in the near future', in the words of his directive to the Wehrmacht of 30 May. 1 October 1938 was to be the deadline for this 'Operation Green'.[2]

Then for two months the initiative lay with Beneš and Henlein, while London and Paris urged the Czechs to be conciliatory, and the Sudeten representatives asked continually for more. By the last week in June Henlein's demand for the establishment of a virtually independent Nazi state inside Czechoslovakia had been accepted by the Czechs as a basis of discussions, their own concessions being embodied in a draft statute of national minorities. The negotiations were suspended on 9 July when Henlein was called to Berchtesgaden. On 10 June Bonnet had suggested mediation, and on 18 July Lord Runciman was proposed to the Czech government as an independent arbitrator. Halifax went to Paris on the 19th for the visit of the King and Queen, and pressed the Runciman plan on the French ministers, who agreed reluctantly, stipulating that in order not to compromise Czechoslovakia's sovereignty, he should be a 'mediator and adviser' and not an arbitrator. Beneš agreed even more reluctantly. Runciman had no special knowledge of the problem, but British statesmen are prepared to make pronouncements on anything providing that they have their experts to brief them.[3]

The justification for the Runciman mission was that there seemed very little else to do, and the fatal itch to do *something*, to try, try again, continued. It kept the contestants sulkily in touch for a few weeks longer. A menacing silence by Britain might have been more effective and less compromising. Beneš, as a result of his own tactical sense and of Runciman's prodding, rather skilfully put the Sudeten German negotiators in the wrong by progressively accepting their demands, and Henderson still believed on 27 August that if the Czechs agreed to 'the grant of genuine autonomy to the

---

[1] B.D., *ibid.*, nos. 271, 285, 286, 502; B.D., III(ii) no. 855. A. H. Furnia, in *The Diplomacy of Appeasement* (1959), calls this Chamberlain's 'astonishing duplicity' (p. 315). Who was deceived? Certainly not Bonnet. Sir Eric Phipps had been transferred from Berlin to Paris on 24 April 1937.

[2] D.G.F.P., D(ii), no. 221.

[3] B.D., III(i), nos. 508, 516, 523, 526.

Sudeten' Hitler would 'probably cooperate'. On the other hand, while estimates as to Germany's strength and desire to fight were somewhat conflicting, information reaching the Foreign Office from the beginning of July anticipated a German march on Prague in the autumn; the danger period would be between the gathering of the harvest and the coming of winter. A partial mobilization was called for September, after the harvest. Colonel Mason-Macfarlane, the military attaché, was satisfied that this information should be taken seriously.[1] The German military manifestations might of course be merely a war of nerves. But the message that they were designed to convey was obvious enough: peace depended on a suitably complete Czech surrender before an irrevocable decision to fight had been made by the Führer.

Hitler might well be carried away and commit himself irrevocably in his forthcoming speech at the Nuremberg congress on 12 September. The belief in his irritability and impulsiveness was still dominant: would a warning restrain or goad him? The risk had to be taken, and after a visit to London by the military attaché, Halifax sent a message to Hitler through Henderson on 11 August expatiating on the 'grave and incalculable risks' to peace involved in the German military preparations. Hitler did not reply. Sir John Simon reaffirmed the declaration of 24 March in a speech at Lanark on 27 August; war, he said, was like a fire in a high wind limited perhaps at the start, but who could say how far it would spread? In spite of the holidays a meeting of the available cabinet ministers was called for the morning of 30 August; Henderson was summoned from Berlin to report on the situation, and Duff Cooper, who had been yachting in the Baltic and talking rather mysteriously to Colonel Beck, arrived just in time after hurrying back through the Kiel Canal. 'Is it not positively horrible to think that the fate of hundreds of millions depends on one man, and he is half mad?' wrote Chamberlain on 3 September.[2]

The issue between Chamberlain and Duff Cooper, his one open critic in the cabinet a month later, was narrower than contemporaries imagined, but real enough. Neither wanted a war to prevent autonomy for the Sudeten Germans; neither believed that England could stay out if France fought. But the one hoped and expected

---

[1] B.D., III(i), no. 530, ii, nos. 562–4, 575–80, 658; accurate reports also came from Mr. Ian Colvin, *News Chronicle* Central European correspondent: *Vansittart in Office* (1965), pp. 216–22. Henderson, pp. 143–4.

[2] Feiling, p. 357.

that France would fight; the other hoped and expected that she would not.[1] It misses the point to say that Chamberlain and his supporters trusted Hitler or had any confidence in him. It is rather the reverse: they had heard so much about his paranoidal imbalance that they underrated the element of long-term calculation in his programme.

In these discussions the idea of a personal visit by Chamberlain to Hitler was first raised. On 31 August the Service ministers under Inskip's chairmanship examined plans for war preparations. The result was not encouraging. Beneš was warned once again that time was running out, and on 4 September he made his supreme gesture: according to the dramatic story which he told in 1945 he summoned Kundt and Sebekovsky, the two leaders of the Sudeten party, to the Hradshin Palace and promised to accept whatever they demanded for the German minority. The result was the origins of 'Plan No. 4', dictated by the two leaders, written down by Beneš, and accepting the essentials of the Karlsbad programme.[2] The British activities also included plans for a blunt warning to Hitler before the Nuremberg congress, and urgent messages to the French to ascertain where they stood. At the beginning of September French troops were ordered to man the Maginot Line, and Daladier on the 8th declared stoutly to Phipps that if German troops crossed the Czechoslovak frontier, the French would march to a man. But it could not be said that the French had done anything up to this point to convince the Germans of their determination. Nor had there been any serious attempt to mobilize and parade Soviet support; Bonnet seems to have been convinced from the start that Stalin had neither the power nor the will to fight. Without denying its contingent treaty obligations to assist Czechoslovakia under the Czechoslovak-Soviet treaty of 16 May 1935 the Soviet government through Litvinov had pointed out in May that its help depended on the right to traverse Polish and Rumanian territory, and Litvinov reaffirmed this position in September, although he argued that Rumanian consent at least could be obtained through the League of Nations. This was certainly not true; and in any case the French, like the British and

---

[1] Duff Cooper wrote later, 'at that time much confusion of thought was caused by people asking whether we should or should not fight for Czecho-Slovakia. But that was not the issue. Nobody wanted to fight for Czecho-Slovakia. The question was— could we or could we not keep out of a European war in which France was engaged'? (Duff Cooper, pp. 224–5.)

[2] Celovsky, pp. 286–97.

German governments, had little belief in the military power of
Russia after the purges. Their pessimistic views were confirmed by
the military attachés' reports from the embassy in Moscow.[1]
Poland, while professedly faithful to her obligations to aid France
if attacked, made no secret of her utterly unsympathetic attitude
towards Czechoslovakia's problems.

The various British warnings may have persuaded Hitler of
Britain's contingent commitment to support France, but even this
is by no means certain; the stern warning that Nevile Henderson
was to have delivered was abandoned owing to the ambassador's
insistence that in the emotional preliminaries of the Nuremberg
congress it might have exactly the opposite effect from that intended.
He claimed to have made the British position as clear as daylight to
the people who counted. Chamberlain tried to make it even clearer
by assuring British journalists on the 11th that 'Germany cannot
with impunity carry out a rapid and successful military campaign
against Czechoslovakia without fear of intervention by France and
by Great Britain'. Doubts were certainly not lessened when The
Times, with elephantine helpfulness, asked on 7 September whether
it might not be worth while for Czechoslovakia to cede its 'fringe
of alien population'.[2] No newspaper of any importance supported
The Times and the Foreign Office promptly published a denial that
the query represented the views of the British government. As it
happened the New Statesman had said much the same on 29 August
and another influential paper, La République, published a similar
suggestion in Paris on the 6th from the pen of Émile Roche, known
as a close collaborator of Bonnet and Flandin.[3]

Looking ahead we must say that the war which ultimately came
to Europe on 1 September 1939 became inevitable on 12 September
1938. Hitler had said in a directive of 18 June that he would not take
action against Czechoslovakia unless firmly convinced that France
would not march and therefore that Britain would not intervene
either.[4] His intuitions now told him that this would be the case,
and his speech to the assembled legions on the 12th, with its venom
and vituperation against the Czechs, meant that he had taken the risk

---

[1] G. Bonnet, Quai d'Orsay (1965), pp. 178–80; B.D., III(i), nos. 148, 202, 210, 270, 355.
[2] 'A mild suggestion, often made before', was the editor's own comment: Sir Evelyn
Wrench, Geoffrey Dawson and Our Times, p. 372. The full story is given in History of The
Times, 1921–1948 (1952), vol. II, pp. 927–36.
[3] B.D., III(ii), no. 808; Wheeler-Bennett, pp. 95–7.
[4] D.G.F.P., ser. D(ii), no. 282.

of the violent solution. The Fourth Plan had conceded autonomy; he now demanded the right of self-determination. He had already confirmed the order for 'Operation Green' to begin on 30 September, and arranged for a Sudeten German revolt on the 13th.

If 12 September set Hitler on one decisive path, the 13th set Chamberlain on another. The French did not meet the challenge of the Nuremberg speech by a swift and unequivocal reaction; instead, the cabinet argued all day and disagreed. Bonnet seemed to Phipps to have lost his nerve; he told the British ambassador that peace must be preserved at any price. Astonished at Bonnet's collapse, 'so sudden and so extraordinary', Phipps went to Daladier, who seemed to have forgotten his sturdy attitude on the 8th; he now said that at all costs something must be settled to prevent the entry of German troops, for otherwise France would have to face her treaty obligations. He urged either that Runciman should bring the two parties together or that a three power conference (Britain, France, and Germany) should work out a pacific settlement.[1] Chamberlain, faced with these desperate appeals to patch up any solution that would save the peace, telegraphed an offer to visit Hitler by air immediately.

The result was the two meetings at Berchtesgaden (15–16 September) and Godesberg (23–24 September). The visits were a diplomatic blunder of the first magnitude. We must remember that Chamberlain was still, in his own view, a mediator; yet no one believed in his impartiality, although many believed in his dedication to peace. Hitler, who had been given repeated warnings that Britain would in certain circumstances fight with France, certainly believed in neither. By the act of stepping forward as a mediator Chamberlain ceased to be a mediator, for he was bound to become in the process the spokesman of Anglo-French policy, interested in the desired end and the scapegoat for its unpopular features. In eleven days he passed from mediation to a direct threat of war. Roosevelt at one point was eager to mediate, but drew back when his advisers warned him that he would be bound to be blamed for any unpleasant consequences.[2] Chamberlain too should have stayed at home, protesting his loyalty to France, and leaving Daladier to handle a problem which was largely of France's own creation.

However, he flew with determination and almost eagerly to the

[1] B.D., III(ii), nos. 855, 857.
[2] Hull, *Memoirs*, vol. I, pp. 590–1; Langer and Gleason, p. 33; *Moffat Papers*, p. 211.

strange encounter. Although he thought Hitler the 'commonest little dog' he had ever seen, without one sign of distinction, he could not detect during their first meeting any trace of the insanity which he had been led to expect. Somehow the Führer's emphatic talk, occasionally indistinct through anger and excitement, gave the impression that he could be relied on to keep his word—perhaps because he seemed to have no inhibitions about demanding everything he wanted. The essential point, soon reached, was the 'return to Germany' (to which they had never belonged) of the 3½ million Germans in Czechoslovakia. Would this be the end? Chamberlain asked. Did Germany not aim at the disintegration of the Czechoslovak state? Hitler said that as he was out for racial unity he didn't want a lot of Czechs. But his reference to the probable secession of the Polish, Slovak, and Hungarian minorities was fair warning that the complete disintegration of the state was in the programme, and it was not on this point that Chamberlain made his stand. This happened when Hitler said that 300 Germans had just been killed and that he was determined to stop it at the risk of a world war. When he refused to consider a joint appeal to both sides 'to keep quiet while we have time to converse' Chamberlain retorted that in that case no further progress was possible, and Hitler replied that if the British government would accept the idea of secession there might be a chance of further talks. Everything seems to have been discussed in very general language, and there was no promise on the German side to follow any particular procedure for the secession. All the same, Chamberlain had been firm, according to his own views; he had reacted sharply when Hitler had threatened violence, and secured a promise of restraint.[1]

There is evidence, derived mainly from Duff Cooper's memoirs, of prolonged argument in the cabinet on 17 September about the Berchtesgaden terms, but Duff Cooper himself, 'impressed by the fearful responsibility of incurring a war that might possibly be avoided', was prepared to postpone it in the faint hope of a domestic revolution in Germany, and to agree to secession, providing that Hitler behaved himself.[2] In short, *all* the cabinet accepted the

---

[1] He also secured the definite and repeated assertion that this was Hitler's last major problem to be solved: a lie, but this had yet to be proved. Hitler specifically denied that in his case 'appetite grew with eating and that after the attainment of one objective he would always proceed to new demands' (B.D., III(ii), p. 344; cf. D.G.F.P., *loc. cit.*, no. 500).

[2] Duff Cooper, p. 230. It is worth noting that he had no doubt about Germany's strength: she was probably the most formidable Power that had ever dominated Europe,

Berchtesgaden terms.[1] The French, after long conversations with Chamberlain, Halifax, Simon, and Hoare at 10 Downing Street on the 18th, did the same. Their determination to prevent a situation which would formally involve their treaty obligations to fight left them no alternative. 'Self-determination' was accepted, but with two conditions: there should be a cession of territory by Czechoslovakia, and not a plebiscite; and Britain should give a guarantee of Czechoslovak neutrality after the Sudeten settlement. Plebiscites were dangerous expedients: they might be demanded elsewhere, even in Alsace-Lorraine. When Chamberlain hedged at first on the question of a guarantee, Daladier explained that French military plans still depended on the use by French air squadrons of Czech airfields to attack Berlin and industrial areas in Silesia. Thus he disagreed with Chamberlain's suggestion that the guarantee would help Czechoslovakia rather than France: Hitler was a Napoleon with the religious authority of Mahomet and a British guarantee for Czechoslovakia would help France 'in the sense that it would help to stop the German march to the East'. After an adjournment Chamberlain announced that the British delegates agreed to the guarantee.[2]

The Anglo-French terms were rejected by the Czechoslovak government on 20 September, and then accepted after further pressure and a warning from Bonnet that France would not support Czechoslovakia in a war resulting from a rejection. Face-saving played its part in the formulation of the precise demands. French cabinet ministers salved their consciences by stipulating that there should be no forceful language; Bonnet, who desperately wanted Czech compliance, allowed an official spokesman to tell the French press that he and Daladier had been forced to agree to the 'British Proposals' because of the refusal of their British colleagues to commit themselves to the military support of France unless her integrity were threatened. He also showed reluctance to put his demands in writing, but was forced to do so by Hodža and the French minister, de Lacroix. Hodža in turn wished to have it clearly on record that

etc., and he remarked: 'We certainly shouldn't catch up the Germans in rearmament. On the contrary, they would increase their lead.'

[1] Chamberlain, with Halifax, gave a full account of the Berchtesgaden discussions to a Labour delegation (Citrine, Dalton, and Morrison), on the evening of the 17th, and said that 'he was satisfied that Hitler now knew that if France came in Great Britain would also come in'. Lord Citrine, *Men and Work*, p. 365.

[2] B.D., *ibid.*, no. 928.

he was submitting to the inevitable. The British minister, Newton, because of his more straightforward instructions, seems to have been more prominent in making representations.

But what Hitler sought was the Sudeten areas delivered to him by the Reichswehr and not by M. Beneš. After listening at the Godesberg meeting to a long statement by Chamberlain of proposals for the orderly transfer of populations, indemnification of the Czechoslovak government for property to be taken over, and the substitution of international guarantees for the Czech fortifications, he rejected this programme on the grounds of urgency and the unstable condition of Czechoslovakia. He talked at length about the Slovak, Hungarian, and Polish claims. What seems evident is that he was determined not to be involved in complicated discussions in which Beneš, given half a chance and with any form of international mediation, would be able to salvage areas and populations on the ground of economic interest, national security, mixture of populations, and the like. Hitler favoured plebiscites for the same reason that the French wished to avoid them. To occupy the disputed areas with German troops would give him the maximum of territory and dramatic success with the minimum of argument. Chamberlain said he was outraged. Fresh demands had been sprung on him. After some discussion of details, and some shouting by Hitler, the first day's meeting ended about 7 p.m.

The subsequent proceedings merely served to confirm Hitler's demands. On the next day (23rd), Chamberlain from his hotel sent a letter to Hitler affirming his belief that the immediate German occupation of the Sudetenland would be an unnecessary display of force which the Czechoslovak forces would be bound to resist and which it would be impossible to commend to British, French, and indeed world opinion. Hitler replied in the afternoon, making it clear that only the forcible procedure 'corresponds to the dignity of a great Power'. At a meeting late that evening he made a few slight changes to the memorandum on the German programme which Chamberlain had demanded. He altered the date of the march from 26 September to 1 October (which of course was the original date for Operation Green). Czech mobilization, agreed to by Halifax on the evening of the 22nd, was announced during the meeting; Chamberlain had thought that this might well produce an immediate German attack, but Hitler, after receiving the news in dead silence, said in a 'scarcely audible voice' that he would not advance while negotiations were in progress. The British party returned to England next morning, Saturday the 24th.[1]

Now war seemed inevitable. On Sunday the Czech government, rejecting the Godesberg memorandum, affirmed its reliance on the 'two great Western democracies'. In London, Chamberlain proposed acceptance of the terms to the inner cabinet, and Halifax agreed. But in meetings on the evening of the 24th and on the morning and afternoon of the 25th, the cabinet argued inconclusively, although Halifax, after a sleepless night, changed his mind and insisted on the rejection of Hitler's terms.[2] No decision was reached as to what to say to the French.[3] Duff Cooper, after urging the need for war, offered to resign: if they accepted the Godesberg claims they would be 'swept out of office and the country would go to war under worse leaders'. But he agreed, on Chamberlain's urging, to take no precipitate action. Then there followed at 9.25 p.m. on the 25th a strange and embarrassing meeting between the four British and two French ministers, with the same supporting officials as on the 18th; Halifax did not speak during the entire proceedings, whereas Simon, supported by Hoare, put searching questions to Daladier as to what precise military action the French proposed to take in the event of war. But at 11.40 the meeting was adjourned for Chamberlain and Daladier to talk alone, and Chamberlain now gave a specific promise of a British expeditionary force for France if France went to war with Germany. The cabinet met about midnight, and accepted the decision; Chamberlain looked 'for the first time, absolutely worn out' and Duff Cooper 'felt very sorry for him'.[4] Next day (26th) Gamelin was brought over, and gave a fairly reassuring review of the military prospects. Sir Horace Wilson was sent off with a final appeal to Hitler and a warning that a refusal would mean that France would fight with British support.[5]

---

[1] B.D., *ibid.*, nos. 1033–73; I. Kirkpatrick, *The Inner Circle* (1959), pp. 110–22; D.G.F.P., *loc.cit.*, nos. 583–4.

[2] Birkenhead, pp. 399–401, quoting Sir Alexander Cadogan's diary.

[3] Templewood says, 'The meeting of the four Ministers at once decided that Hitler's new demands were unacceptable. Our view was strongly confirmed by the Cabinet' (p. 312). Duff Cooper says that Chamberlain on the 24th proposed 'that we should accept (Hitler's) terms and advise the Czechs to do so'; on the 25th, 'the discussion turned mainly on the question whether we should go to the help of France' (pp. 232, 236); cf. Wheeler-Bennett, p. 140; Colvin, p. 261.

[4] B.D., III(ii), no. 1093; Templewood, p. 315; Duff Cooper, p. 237.

[5] B.D., III(ii), no. 1096.

What were the issues at this stage? Everyone agreed that Hitler was an outrageous man, a bully, determined to make war or invade a neighbour. The British and French cabinets, and perhaps the opposition leaders in England, also agreed that a war 'to keep the Sudeten Germans under Czech rule' could not easily be justified, but equally that if Hitler insisted on making the settlement of the Sudeten question an excuse for a military exercise he must be resisted. Where reactions became confused was over the development of lines of action justified by, or necessitated by, this last consideration. Was it right still to work desperately for peace, or to welcome the opportunity for war? As against the first course there was Duff Cooper's argument that any move to accept even a modified version of the Godesberg terms would lead to the government's defeat in the Commons and war under a new and less competent government; to this argument from domestic expediency could be added the view that Hitler really did have Napoleonic ambitions and was at the beginning and not the end of his campaign of expansion. It could be argued (although at the time surprisingly few people, and certainly not Daladier, did so argue) that a general war was inevitable and that it would be better to fight in 1938 than later. There was finally a double point of honour: it was shameful to submit to Hitler's deliberate choice of force; and shameful to allow a small nation to be attacked. 'Small nation' and 'self-determination' ideologies were indeed in direct conflict.

Over the years and in recent weeks Chamberlain had been as angry as anyone at Hitler's conduct; he had stood up to him at Godesberg and he had now (after some wavering) agreed to join France in war. But it must be concluded that he still remained unconvinced on three points, namely that the great war to prevent German hegemony in Europe could be safely embarked on in 1938; that Hitler wanted a great war to secure the hegemony of Europe; and that war would be of any practical help to the Czechs. In the endless talks with the cabinet, the foreign policy committee, the inner four, the French, the Chiefs of Staff, the Foreign Office officials, and the ambassadors, on the basis both of general theory and of elaborate staff memoranda on strategy and war planning, all the eventualities must have been discussed; if there was a fault it was not timidity or drift or ignorance, but over-concentration on a long-term plan based on doubtful premises. One of these was that German grievances explained German conduct. Another was that peace could be saved, and that only he could save it. Another was that time (for rearmament) was on his side.[1] Expediency and his moral duty, thus combined, explain Chamberlain's course on the 26th and 27th. While leaving Hitler in no doubt that France and Britain were prepared to fight, he still wished to avoid public condemnation which might drive Hitler over the edge, and he wished to find a satisfactory procedure, and to persuade both parties to accept it. The letter which Horace Wilson was to present to Hitler stated that the Czechoslovak government regarded the processes of immediate Czech evacuation and immediate German occupation before the terms of cession had been negotiated as 'wholly unacceptable'; Chamberlain therefore proposed a German-Czech conference, with British participation if desired, to arrange for things to be done 'in an orderly manner with suitable safeguards'. On the same afternoon, at 3.30 on the 26th, Churchill was received by Chamberlain and Halifax in the Cabinet Room, and they agreed to his proposal that a communiqué should be issued showing the unity of purpose of Britain, France, and also Russia against German aggression.[2] At 4.10 Chamberlain telegraphed a further message to Wilson. 'Since you left, French have definitely stated their intention of supporting Czechoslovakia by offensive measures if latter is attacked. This would bring us in: and it should be made plain to Chancellor that this is inevitable alternative to peaceful solution.' Wilson, whose calm and firmness in these tense encounters deserve some praise, delivered the first message at 5 o'clock; Hitler could scarcely control himself with rage. Wilson decided to deliver Chamberlain's second message on the following day. On the evening of the 26th Hitler delivered another speech, violently offensive towards Beneš, violently applauded by the well-disciplined audience; Beneš must yield by 1 October, or else; Chamberlain however was praised for his efforts, and again there was the promise that after the regulation of the Sudeten German question, 'we have no further claims to make in Europe'. Just afterwards there came the Foreign Office communiqué saying that the immediate result of a German attack on Czechoslovakia 'must be that France will be bound to come to her assistance, and Great Britain and Russia will stand by France'. Next day, at 12.15 p.m.

---

[1] But with this view the experts agreed. Ironside wrote on 22 Sept.: 'Chamberlain is, of course, right . . . *we cannot expose ourselves now to a German attack. We simply commit suicide if we do.*' (*The Ironside Diaries*, p. 62.)

[2] Churchill, vol. I, p. 242.

on the 27th, Wilson delivered to Hitler Chamberlain's delayed message.[1]

These were the warnings. They were reinforced by the decision on the 27th to mobilize the fleet. Parliament was summoned for the 28th. The other side of Chamberlain's policy was shown in a number of gestures. Just after midnight on the 26th, after a meeting of the inner cabinet, he issued to the press a promise to see that the terms of a settlement were carried out with all reasonable promptitude, providing that the German government accepted the method of discussion and not of force. After receiving Wilson's report on the 27th he and Halifax set to work to draw up a compromise plan which would reconcile the need for an orderly evacuation and the safeguarding of minorities with Hitler's demand for immediate occupation. The result was a set of five proposals[2] which were handed to Krofta and Weizsäcker on the same evening after being approved by Bonnet. Finally Chamberlain made a melancholy wireless speech at 8 p.m.; it is intelligible as the utterance of a weary and upright man, reproaching and warning the intractable German Chancellor, but it was not the rallying cry of a national leader on the eve of battle. It was again the call for appeasement in the tones that were giving that noble word such a bad name. The memorable and unfortunate phrase about 'a quarrel in a far-away country between people of whom we know nothing', was as it happened much less true of Chamberlain than of practically every member of his English audience, but it has reverberated to his discredit down the years. In fact in his quiet, plain language, he did explain and condemn Hitler's behaviour, and asserted the case for war as clearly as he had defined the case for peace. 'If I were convinced that any nation had made up its mind to dominate the world by fear of its force, I should feel that it must be resisted.' He was not prepared to fight for Czechoslovakia; but he was prepared to fight for the great issues. He omitted, to Duff Cooper's exasperation, to mention the mobilization of the fleet. Duff Cooper made the announcement himself at 11.38 p.m.[3]

---

[1] B.D., III(ii), nos. 1097, 1118, 1121, 1126, 1129; Kirkpatrick, pp. 122–6.

[2] They included the German occupation of territory outside the fortified Czech line by 1 October; meeting starting on 3 October of German, Czech, and British plenipotentiaries to arrange for immediate withdrawal of Czech forces, safeguarding of minorities, and instructions to the boundary commission; German entry to a further agreed zone on 10 October; completion of frontier delimitation by 31 October, etc. B.D., III(ii), no. 1140.

[3] Feiling, pp. 370–2; Duff Cooper, pp. 238–9.

What brought Hitler to accept compromise terms at the Munich conference on 29–30 September has been much disputed. The first sign of a disposition to lower his voice and to give the taking-over process a more reasonable air was a written reply to Chamberlain's letter of the 26th; this was received by the Foreign Office at 8.40 p.m. on the 27th. He did not concede much, but in mild and argumentative terms insisted that he was ready for plebiscites, 'a free vote under no outside influence', and for a wide measure of agreement with the Czechs on details. A time limit for the occupation was necessary, he argued, to prevent Czech procrastination. He was now ready to promise a formal guarantee of the remainder of Czechoslovakia. The Americans claimed some credit for this change. Having abandoned the idea of offering himself as a mediator, Roosevelt sent messages on the 26th urging a fair and peaceful settlement by negotiation; he reiterated this view on the 27th. But Hitler seems to have been unaffected by this intervention. The opposition of the German generals, and of some of his close associates such as Goering, to an unnecessary general war was unabated, but he had known their views since Beck's resignation in July. There was evidence that German opinion was unenthusiastic about a major war, whatever its emotions about President Beneš. But this too was not a new phenomenon. What was new was Horace Wilson's insistence that England would fight with France if Hitler refused to budge. Duff Cooper believed that the news of the fleet mobilization 'eventually succeeded in persuading Hitler that we were prepared to fight'. Hitler's letter, which seems clearly to register the change of mood and tactics, was written before the fleet announcement was made.[1]

It is true that Bonnet, desperately anxious to prevent war and therefore to prevent any stiffening of his government's attitude, tried to minimize the extent of the British undertaking to fight, and dismissed the Foreign Office communiqué of the 26th as an unauthorized effort by Vansittart (who had nothing to do with it). He followed up the British five-point proposals with a plan of his own which François-Poncet was to present if the British scheme were rejected, and which offered further concessions, including the occupation of all three zones by 1 October. The French ambassador was quicker off the mark than Henderson, with the result that the

---

[1] Hitler wanted his letter included in the forthcoming White Paper, Cmd 5847 (B.D., III(ii), no. 1144); cf. Duff Cooper, p. 241; Churchill, vol. I, p. 246.

French proposals were in Hitler's hands before the British. But however this may be, Hitler was ready by midday on the 28th to accept the British and French schemes as a basis for a settlement, and Mussolini's opportune intervention enabled him to promise to postpone mobilization (which meant invasion) for twenty-four hours. Mussolini's intervention was prompted by Lord Perth on the morning of the 28th following instructions from London. Much later in the day the American ambassador delivered a similar message from Roosevelt.

Chamberlain was able to announce in the House of Commons just after 4 o'clock that Hitler had agreed to an immediate conference. The reception was enthusiastic, if not unanimous. Churchill, Amery, and Eden were grimly silent; Gallacher, the sole Communist member, made a solitary speech of protest against the dismemberment of Czechoslovakia. But from the ranks of the Tories came applause, and Attlee, Maxton, Lansbury, and Sinclair welcomed the news from the Opposition benches. After this the Munich agreement, signed on the night of 29–30 September, was largely on anticipated lines, although the conflict between Hitler's grabbing propensities and his desire to deceive the British Prime Minister with an appearance of liberality caused some confusion. Next morning, when Hitler was in an irritable mood because of the enthusiastic relief with which the people of Munich had greeted the averting of war, he readily agreed to sign Chamberlain's short statement (based on a draft by Mr. W. Strang), affirming the virtues of consultation.[1]

3. The Aftermath of Munich

During the phase of high crisis plans had been hastily improvised to evacuate 637,000 children from London. 38 million gas masks were distributed and a million feet of trenches dug. There was a 'premature panic migration' of 150,000 people to Wales.[2] An emergency mobilization of the Ministry of Economic Warfare took place. It was agreed that in the event of war British bombers were to drop leaflets, but not bombs, on Germany.

Peace gave Chamberlain an enormous, though momentary, popularity. The Dominions had been kept fully informed and did not dissent at any stage of the crisis. 'Once more', said General

---

[1] Laffan, pp. 437–50; Celovsky, pp. 460–72; Wheeler-Bennett, pp. 171–82; Lord Strang, *Home and Abroad* (1956), pp. 144–8; B.D., III(ii), nos. 1224–8; D.G.F.P., *loc. cit.*, nos. 669–76.
[2] R. M. Titmuss, *Problems of Social Policy* (1950), pp. 29–31

Smuts in Johannesburg, 'the occasion has produced the man. A great champion has appeared in the lists—God bless him!' 'Good man!' telegraphed Roosevelt. He did his best to claim credit for the calling of the Munich conference, and was annoyed that his ambassador in Rome had failed to hurry round to Ciano with the suggestion before Perth. Press judgments in the United States had fluctuated, and there had been a violent reaction against Chamberlain when the Berchtesgaden terms were known, partly on the mistaken assumption that the British government had previously guaranteed Czechoslovak integrity. His popularity returned during the last week of September. One New York paper said that he approached nearer to the founder of the Christian religion than any statesman since Abraham Lincoln. So too the British press in the days from 30 September to 2 October was almost unanimous in praise and relief. 'If we must have a victor, let us choose Chamberlain', said the *Daily Express*. 'There are forces in the world more powerful than the absolute will of a dictator', wrote the *Daily Herald*.[1]

However, the government's parliamentary critics, who had in many cases indulged in untypical displays of approval, soon reminded themselves that it was the Opposition's duty to oppose. George Lansbury and some other Labour members as well as the I.L.P. remained openly favourable, and the others could not find much in their recent attitudes on which to base a convincing alternative programme. The government's policy was endorsed by a decisive majority of 366 votes to 144 after a four-day debate commencing on 3 October. Duff Cooper resigned, and opened the debate with his resignation speech, arguing that the country should have been prepared to fight, not for Czechoslovakia, but to resist Hitler's determination to dominate Europe by brute force.[2] No one else was prepared to demand war, although Churchill, interpreting the events in similar terms of German aggression, told the government in a tremendous indictment that it had suffered a 'total and unmitigated defeat'. It was generally considered that Chamberlain scored a personal triumph by the moderation and sincerity of his winding-up speech, which nearly persuaded some members of the Eden group to vote with the government. But few could bring frankness to the

---

[1] But this was one of the few papers that did not praise the Prime Minister. Fifty papers are analysed in W. W. Hadley, *Munich: Before and After* (1944), pp. 93–110; cf. E. L. Henson, pp. 297–301.

[2] P.D., 5 Ser., HC, vol. 339, 3 October 1938, cols. 29–40.

point of saying with Mr. Maxwell Fyfe that the country would not have supported a war to keep Carlsbad and Marienbad under the Czechs.[1] Nor did anyone argue that Chamberlain should have done less if he had not been prepared to do more.

It is important to recall these uncertain and even favourable judgments on the Munich settlement because of the reckless over-simplification of the issues which developed in later years. Feeling against Churchill in his constituency of Epping was at first so strong that the local Conservative Association debated a motion of 'no confidence' in him which was only narrowly defeated after an impressive fighting speech by its Member. But as Hitler became more and more of a monster in popular eyes, Munich, so thoroughly dramatized, became a symbol of aggression; 'appeasement' became a synonym for surrender, and many who had stood aside and even welcomed the settlement were glad to make Chamberlain and Daladier their scapegoats. But at the time most people felt either that the unpleasant features of the settlement would be worth while if the settlement were permanent, or that Chamberlain could have frustrated Hitler and at the same time avoided war by bolder tactics ('Hitler has always given way to threats').

The adverse turn in opinion came swiftly, but not quite logically, when Hitler proceeded to act on his own theories about British psychology. He had scored a victory, he felt, by his toughness: it must be completed by the final unnerving and discrediting of his critics. During the first ten days of October the Germans could be seen to be screwing the maximum of advantage from the cession of the Sudetenland, bullying the miserable Czechs and treating brutally those Sudeten Germans who were not members of the SDP, thereby dispelling any mistaken notion abroad that the Nazi régime was capable of magnanimity or compromise. Hitler sounded, and no doubt was, thoroughly bad-tempered when in his Saarbrücken speech on 9 October he talked of British arrogance, of the desire of Eden, Duff Cooper, and Churchill for immediate war with Germany, and his determination no longer to tolerate 'the tutelage of govern-esses'. On Ribbentrop's direct instructions a press campaign was launched with the object of splitting public opinion in England so as to discredit those who wanted to face up squarely to Germany 'next time'. The German ambassador's advice against this course was ignored. On 6 November Hitler attacked Churchill in a speech

[1] *Ibid.*, col. 246; cf. The Earl of Kilmuir, *Political Adventure*, p. 51.

at Weimar. The ferocious pogrom against the Jews which followed the assassination of vom Rath in Paris on the 7th caused a new wave of disgust at Nazi conduct in England, yet on the 8th Dirksen was told to launch a campaign against Duff Cooper, Churchill, and Eden in the English press.[1] Chamberlain had announced accelerated rearmament on 3 October, and although he continued to speak of the possibility of better relations he told the Commons on 14 November that no mandates would be returned to Germany.[2]

A Foreign Office official said in later years that in the summer of 1939 the actual weight and strain of responsibility was less difficult to bear than in the crisis of 1938, for there was now no doubt as to what course the country should follow.[3] If we ask what were the basic differences between the two phases of crisis we can perhaps find three that are dominant. The first, and ostensibly the most important, was Chamberlain's conversion to the view, publicly announced on 17 March 1939, that Hitler had finally rejected 'the method of consultation'. And yet, while there was certainly a valid difference between the annexation of the Sudetens and the extinction of Czech independence, there can have been little surprise on Chamberlain's part at this fresh manifestation of Hitler's offensiveness, nor did his reading of Hitler's character appear really to have changed. He continued to think of Hitler as a violent but basically rational man, unbalanced, subject to brainstorms, but not a Napoleon. Because of his growing recklessness, counter-threats were necessary: but Chamberlain still believed, and spoiled much of the force of his policy by the belief, that the problem was primarily one of controlling Hitler's moods. The second difference was the progress of British rearmament: the point of greatest danger, particularly in the air, appeared to be passing, and Britain could now negotiate, and appease, from strength. A third factor was British public opinion, as the government interpreted or misinterpreted it. Chamberlain had doubted in the summer of 1938 whether the British public (or for that matter the German or French) were ready for war, and his belief that he was influencing German opinion against German warmakers made him reluctant to arouse warlike passions at home. By the following spring he had discovered that the public had made up its own mind. The insistence

[1] D.G.F.P., ser. D(iv), nos. 257-9, 258, 264.
[2] P.D., 5 Ser., HC, vol. 341, 14 November 1938, col. 492.
[3] E. L. Woodward, 'Some Reflections on British Policy, 1939-45', *International Affairs*, July 1955, p. 276.

of all critics, to Right or Left, that every Nazi triumph was a direct defeat and humiliation for Chamberlain and England was having its effect, and although the alternative courses suggested were not always convincing, the final conviction of direct menace from Nazi Germany and direct responsibility for meeting it became general during the winter.

And yet, if the Labour movement could agree in deploring the consequences of Chamberlain's policy it could agree on little else. Its pursuit of red (or Red) herrings could not entirely divert attention from the fact that it was always a step behind the government in the various stages of preparation for war. After Munich the party quickly took the line that the imperative need was for a Labour government to replace the National government in order to ensure the rapid mobilization of the country's resources, in the democratic cause. But in January 1939 the Labour party executive repulsed an attempt by Cripps to revive the Popular Front agitation by calling for joint electoral action with all opposition parties, and when the campaign persisted Cripps with his followers, Aneurin Bevan, G. R. Strauss, and C. P. Trevelyan, were expelled from the party.[1] Churchill too, and his group, remained suspect; an attempt by Dalton and Harold Macmillan to bring the Conservative malcontents into a united opposition had failed by Christmas.[2] Churchill's aims were considered by the Labour purists to be right for the wrong reasons: it was felt that he loved battle rather than democracy, and sought the preservation of the British Empire rather than of world peace. The government was not believed to have any aim other than the evasion of its gravest responsibilities, and the protection of its interests and investments abroad.

The government's main concern at the moment was, however, to discern Hitler's intentions. We now know that he had told Mussolini on 29 September 1938 that he intended to fight France and England in due course; he told the German commanders at a meeting on 22 August 1939 that his original plan had been to establish a tolerable relationship with Poland in order to have his hands free to fight England and France 'in a few years' before dealing with the east. If we can take this at its face value it suggests that he would have been satisfied to deal only with Poland in 1939, leaving the fight with the western powers, which had become necessary, until

---

[1] Hugh Dalton, *The Fateful Years* (1957), pp. 208–21.
[2] *Ibid.*, pp. 200–2; M. Foot, *Aneurin Bevan* (1962), pp. 294–9.

1940 or 1941. We have to remember, however, that the Wehrmacht leaders had never been very happy about war in 1938 or 1939, and that he may have referred to war 'in a few years' to suggest that he had been forced into this course. Later in the same speech he elaborated the technical arguments, which he had already thrown out at the Hossbach meeting in 1937, in favour of war in 1939 rather than later, and the actual course of events as we can follow it in the German documentation certainly suggests that he was following a more urgent course than the leisurely procedure of war 'in a few years'. Thus Ribbentrop sounded Poland about the return of Danzig and an extraterritorial road and railway through the Polish corridor as early as October 1938. The Poles at once showed their uneasiness; they not only failed to respond but reaffirmed their non-aggression pact with Russia on 26 November and refused to join the anti-Comintern pact in January 1939.[1]

Again, in the important discussions preliminary to an Italo-German alliance, the plans put forward by the Germans as a basis for discussion visualized war against France and England in the light of the existing armaments position, and not in terms of the relative strengths two or three years later. A plan of campaign on these lines, dated 26 November 1938, was drawn up by Keitel on Hitler's detailed instructions; it provided for war by Germany and Italy against France and England, in which the object would be first to knock out France. As it happened the Italians were ready to quarrel with France but not with England at this point; after Mussolini had withdrawn 10,000 men from Spain early in October the British government agreed to bring the Anglo-Italian agreement of 16 April 1938 into force, and while Ciano's speech to the Italian Chamber on 30 November produced noisy anti-French interruptions to the tune of 'Tunis, Djibouti, Corsica, Nice' there was applause for the British ambassador. Mussolini agreed at the beginning of January 1939 to the German proposal to transform the anti-Comintern pact into a military alliance, but with no intention of an early plunge into war. Even so, things were moving quite speedily towards a fresh crisis. Preparations for the final extinction of the 'rump Czech state' were ordered in December, and in January Hitler endeavoured to talk the Polish foreign minister, Colonel Beck, into an agreement. Keitel's notes of 26 November spoke of Poland's attitude as doubtful and visualized the use of Italian and

[1] D.G.F.P., ser. D(v), nos. 81, 101, 105, 119, 120.

Hungarian forces against Poland if she adopted a threatening attitude.[1]

The British government found the public manifestations of German policy depressing and rather alarming. Although the German plans were supposed to be a close secret, reports of preparations for war with the western powers were circulating widely, and Halifax received warnings from various sources in December and January. On 10 December the German government announced its intention to build up to 100 per cent of the British submarine tonnage. On 11 December the British diplomat, Mr. Ivone Kirkpatrick, was given a secret message by a retired German secretary of state, who claimed to have firsthand information from the German War Office and Air Ministry that Hitler had ordered preparations for a bombing attack on London in peace time.[2] These events brought about a speedy Anglo-French agreement for joint action early in February 1939, and it is interesting to compare its uncomplicated negotiation with the exhausting and fruitless bargaining forced on the two powers by Molotov in the following summer. The problem of indirect aggression was met, following a French suggestion, by assurances from the British to the French and Belgian governments that a German attack on Switzerland or Holland would be regarded as a *casus belli*. Halifax suggested that the staff talks which were going on should be broadened to meet the possibility of war with Germany and Italy combined.[3]

These things show that there was no naive belief in Hitler's good will. They show too the all-sufficiency of the Anglo-French link in the eyes of both governments: there was no approach as yet to Russia. The post-Munich survey of the rearmament programme had produced major changes. The French had offered full military staff conversations, and the British had accepted, knowing that the necessary corollary must be the provisions of large land forces to compensate for the loss of the thirty-five Czechoslovak divisions. This meant in turn the formal abandonment of the 'limited liability' doctrine, which Hore-Belisha proposed in the new year. By the end of February 1939, after long discussions, the Prime Minister and

[1] D.G.F.P., ser. D(iv), nos. 411, 412; (vii), nos. 192, 193; *The Ciano Diaries*, pp. 3–8.
[2] Presumably an echo of the German preparations for talks with Italy. I. Kirkpatrick, *The Inner Circle* (1959), pp. 136–9. Templewood (*Nine Troubled Years*, p. 327) gave much the same account; Halifax a less accurate version of apparently the same episode: *Fulness of Days*, p. 200. Cf. N. Henderson, *Failure of a Mission*, p. 183, and B.D., III(iii), no. 386, 422 and (iv), no. 5.
[3] B.D., III(iv), nos. 40–45, 50, 77, 81, 94, 98 etc.

cabinet had accepted a Regular army of ten divisions with corresponding Territorial reserves. The Chancellor's financial limitation had necessarily to be abandoned at the same time although not his justifiable apprehensions as to the overall limitation of Britain's foreign exchange resources. The Air Staff had virtually freed itself from the financial limitation in the spring of 1938, and its ambitious programme was now accelerated, so that in the new year its output figures were rapidly approaching those of Germany. The monthly total increased in fact from 161 in January 1938 to 348 in September, and to 712 in March 1939. This was mainly an increase in fighter strength; heavy bombers were in production, but were not coming into service until the spring of 1940. In spite of a wide range of continued deficiencies, the rearmament situation seemed sufficient to justify a bolder policy after March 1939.[1]

In the circumstances the Nazi extinction of the rump Czech state on 15 March, after some bullying of the fainting President Hacha on the previous night, was a shock but cannot have been much of a surprise to the British cabinet. It was accepted that the Czech guarantee was not a practicable *casus belli*; the French also had no desire to make it so. There was thus a momentary embarrassment as to how to take the new German aggression. On the 15th Chamberlain said rather fatuously that the state had 'become disintegrated' and on the 16th Simon asked how one could guarantee a state that had ceased to exist. But by the 17th Chamberlain, prompted by strong language in the press and Parliament and by Halifax's advice, and satisfied with the improved armaments position (as he understood it) had made up his mind. Future aggression must be resisted. He announced this at Birmingham in a speech on the eve of his seventieth birthday. Hitler's past aggressions might have been due to 'just claims too long resisted'. This was no longer the case. He hurried back to London with new plans for the cabinet.[2]

4. THE ROAD TO WAR

To understand what followed we must bear in mind that Chamberlain was still seeking peace, and therefore a mode of warning sufficient to deter Hitler but not to madden him. The subsequent

[1] Postan, pp. 53-76; Webster and Frankland, vol. I, pp. 79-85; cf. Chamberlain's remark to Bonnet on 22 March 1939: 'our own difficulties had been successfully overcome and our production was now nearly 600 aircraft a month': B.D., III (iv), p. 463.
[2] Feiling, pp. 398-401; I. Macleod, pp. 272-3; Birkenhead, pp. 432-8.

negotiations were coloured by curious and quite mistaken, but nevertheless very strong, assumptions as to what would and what would not do this.

The new plan was accepted by the cabinet on 20 March after discussions in the inner cabinet. It was that the British, French, Soviet, and Polish governments should sign and publish a formal declaration announcing their intention immediately to consult together 'in the event of action being taken which appeared to constitute a threat to the security or independence' of any European state. There was no desire to exclude Russia, and indeed Halifax on 17 March had already, with commendable but unnecessary promptitude, asked whether the Soviet government would join the western powers in actively helping Rumania, which was wrongly assumed to be threatened. A straightforward statement by the four strongest anti-Axis powers in Europe would have had great psychological and tactical advantage if it had expressed a basic unity of trust and purpose. As a tentative step towards the creation of such a unity it had, however, all the disadvantages of premature publicity.

Hitler was not deterred. Ribbentrop again offered terms to the Poles, hinting on 21 March that they might receive compensation, probably in Slovakia; two days later he even drew up a draft German–Polish treaty which offered part of Slovakia and a twenty-five-year guarantee. This was cancelled on Hitler's orders (probably because a Polish rejection and subsequent publication would have been embarrassing). But in a secret directive to the Wehrmacht on 25 March he announced that he still hoped for a peaceful surrender of Danzig, although he was prepared to annihilate Poland if this were refused. He was at the same time mopping up the advantages that his small neighbours were forced to concede. A German–Lithuanian treaty of the 22nd ceded Memel to the Reich, and on the 23rd treaties were signed with Slovakia and Rumania, the latter conceding many of the German trade demands.[1]

Beck had no intention of giving way on Danzig or the Corridor, but he believed that Poland's survival depended on the deadlock of German–Soviet forces, and that he must continue to balance between the two. He found Chamberlain's plan embarrassingly explicit, and made his reluctance to be associated with Russia clear on the 21st. He offered instead a secret agreement for consultation

[1] D.G.F.P., ser. D(vi), nos. 12, 73, 99.

between Poland and England. For a time it even seemed that he wished to keep the British guarantee a secret from the French. By the 27th the British government had decided to offer Poland and Rumania, 'in view of the "Soviet difficulty"', direct guarantees of help in the event of a German attack, with the promise of reciprocal help if Germany attacked anywhere in western Europe or Yugoslavia. On 29 March Chamberlain announced that the Territorial Army was to be increased to twenty-six divisions, which with the six divisions of Regulars would make up a thirty-two division force for which the French had been pressing. On the 31st it was announced in the House of Commons that if Poland were threatened, the British and French governments intended at once to lend the Polish government all the support in their power.[1]

The tactical disadvantages of an unconditional public assurance given in advance of the final bargaining seem obvious, and they were not ignored because of any trust in Beck's straightforwardness. There were alarmist reports, particularly from the twenty-six-year-old *News Chronicle* correspondent, Ian Colvin, of an imminent German attack on Poland. He was taken by Halifax to see the Prime Minister at 6 p.m. on 29 March, and was asked whether Halifax should replace Chamberlain! There seems to have been little awareness of the touchiness of the Moscovites, and none at all of the vast tactical blunder involved in any published and therefore irrevocable undertaking to fight Hitler over an east European issue before the Russians had been tied down to an agreement. It is fair to say that the plan originated with the ministers, although Vansittart, and Sir Alexander Cadogan too apparently, approved of it.[2] How far was this hurried move due to parliamentary pressure? The Opposition, although well aware of the Polish and Rumanian objections to association with Russia, persisted in regarding any delay in the building of an immediate system of universal security as due exclusively to the procrastination or timidity of the Prime Minister (encouraged by his sinister friends, Simon and Hoare). Eden, Churchill, and thirty dissident Conservatives put down a resolution on 28 March favouring the policy of the 'Foreign Secretary' and the formation of a National government. The Labourites, although still parading their belief in collective security, shrank from the unpleasant realities of the commitment to Poland, but

[1] B.D., III(iv), nos. 446, 459–466, 538, 568; Postan p. 72.
[2] Ian Colvin, *Vansittart in Office*, pp. 298–311.

Maisky reassured them and they accepted the decision in the Commons.[1]

Beck, in discussions with Halifax from 4–6 April, took advantage of the unilateral nature of the guarantee to limit the Polish commitment strictly to a promise of reciprocal aid against a German attack. He would not commit himself over Rumania, or a German attack on the Netherlands, Belgium, Switzerland, or Denmark, and he declined to enter into any agreement with the Soviet government. Halifax was not prepared to conclude a formal agreement on these terms, and the matter remained open throughout the summer. Rumania, like Poland, disliked any public association with Russia; Halifax would have preferred to delay the offer of a guarantee in order to strengthen his bargaining position, but after Mussolini had decided that the moment was as good as any for the seizure of Albania it seemed necessary to guarantee Greece at once, and the French insisted that Rumania must be included. And still Hitler was not deterred. In another secret directive he instructed the Wehrmacht on 3 April to be ready for war with Poland at any time after 31 August.[2]

With these decisions the stage was set for war, and although the next five months are interesting to study from the point of view of national psychology and diplomatic tactics they do not add any major development apart from Russia's decision to stand aside. While Hitler hoped that Poland could be eliminated as a military problem before the major struggle with the Anglo-French forces began, he was willing to risk simultaneous fighting, as he explained to the commanding officers at a meeting on 23 May. His attitude towards Poland in the diplomatic field after the beginning of April was one of ominous silence; there were no further offers, the German ambassador was kept away from Warsaw, and the German press worked up to a steady pitch of fury over alleged and highly improbable Polish atrocities. On 14 April Roosevelt satisfied his long-standing wish to put the dictators on the spot without committing himself; he appealed to Hitler and Mussolini to give

---

[1] He told a Foreign Office official on 29 March that the guarantee 'would increase enormously the confidence of other countries and might have a very great effect'. A Labour group which sought his views (apparently on the 30th) were left in no doubt that the pact would be welcomed by the Soviet government (B.D. III(v), no. 565, and private information; cf. Dalton, pp. 236–9). Maisky in *Who Helped Hitler?* (London, 1964), makes no mention of these conversations, and suggests that he heard of the proposed guarantee for the first time on the 31st, and then gave no approval (pp. 107–8).

[2] B.D., III(v), nos. 10, 11, 16, 17; D.G.F.P., *loc.cit.*, no. 149.

thirty-one nations a ten-year guarantee against attack. Before making his voluminous and crushing reply in the Reichstag on 28 April Hitler used the occasion to denounce publicly the German–Polish agreement of 1934 and the Anglo-German naval agreement of 1935. Italy was finally tied down to a military alliance, the pact of steel, signed on 22 May, but on the understanding, which Hitler seems not to have taken seriously, that she should not have to fight in a major war for a few years. Japan was a disappointment, for she refused to enter a triple military alliance directed against any power except Russia, whereas Hitler wanted to avoid trouble with Russia and use Japan to tie down the British and French. An agreement with the Soviet government had become a distasteful necessity by May if Germany was to avoid a war against major powers on two fronts, or even if she desired a free hand against Poland, for it would scarcely be possible otherwise to conquer Poland without violent Soviet reactions.[1]

On the Anglo-French side the outstanding problem was how to complete the guarantee system by bringing in Russia. After a display of irritability on 18 April Chamberlain gave in to Hore-Belisha's insistence on the need for conscription; having conceded the point he supported it vigorously, and the necessary announcement was made in the Commons on 26 April. His doubts had concerned public opinion, and the Parliamentary Labour party, backed by the trade union leaders, did indeed fight the measure line by line all through May. The State Department was alarmed and fearful that conscription might be 'the straw that breaks the camel's back and goads Hitler into desperation'. Liddell Hart thought the decision an empty political gesture, which by spreading military and industrial resources in the equipment of a mass army of infantry frustrated the early creation of a smaller high quality mechanized force.[2] But the Military Training Bill became law in due course, and the government no doubt hoped that the French, German, and Russian governments would now understand its seriousness of purpose.[3]

It may well be asked nevertheless why they had had to leave everything in their approach to Russia to the last moment, so that so portentous an ugly fairy was absent from the christening of the

[1] D.G.F.P., *loc.cit.*, nos. 424–6, 433, 459, 535; M. Toscano, *Le origini del Patto d'Acciaio* (1956); *The Moffat Papers 1919–1943*, p. 240.

[2] Liddell Hart, *Memoirs*, vol. II, p. 235.

[3] R. J. Minney, *The Private Papers of Hore-Belisha*, pp. 201–6; Templewood, pp. 336–9; Attlee, *As It Happened*, p. 103; *The Moffat Papers*, p. 240.

guarantee system on 31 March. As far as France was concerned the answer is that she had made her contacts with Russia, and also with Poland, long before; there was no need in fact for her even to offer a specific guarantee to Poland. It was Great Britain who had rushed into the guarantee system without diplomatic preparation, and had therefore to work out the details of her relations with Poland, but also with Russia, after the crisis had begun. This can certainly be condemned as a lack of foresight, and the air of improvisation justified searching enquiry and a demand for precise terms by the Russians. But the essential question, unanswerable because of the lack of Soviet documentation, is whether Stalin ever considered fighting Germany, or whether the whole course of the alliance negotiations with the western powers was anything more than a device to bring Hitler to terms, while keeping them in play in case Hitler attacked. Lord Strang, the best informed of the British negotiators, thinks that the latter was probably the main aim throughout, but that the choice between the two courses was one of genuine difficulty.[1] The British had no such alternatives to ponder, but they were greatly puzzled as to how to fit Russia into their system in face of Polish distaste.

There seems nothing to justify the stock Soviet assertion that the western powers were hoping to leave Russia to do all the fighting; on the contrary, their plans (or at least the British) were shaped by doubts as to Russia's military value, and the subsequent Russian defection did not deflect them from their purpose. The reports of the British service attachés from Moscow were consistently gloomy, the usual view being that the Russian forces could not sustain an effective offensive, or survive a prolonged war. The cabinet and Foreign Office accepted this estimate, which remained the predominant opinion until after the German attack in June 1941. Accordingly, although the military value of Poland was not regarded too optimistically, the military value of Russia in April and May 1939 was considered mainly in terms of her ability to supply the Polish forces, and in view of the imperfections of her transport system even this was not thought to be very great.[2] We cannot tell

[1] Lord Strang, *The Diplomatic Career* (1962), pp. 67–70.

[2] Adverse reports by the service attachés: B.D., III(iv), nos. 183, and appendix III; cf. a Foreign Office minute of 22 May: 'It is, however, unlikely that on land their military effort could be of very much effect, and even in the matter of furnishing munitions and war materials their assistance would be limited by the fact that the Russian transportation system is in an extremely backward state' (*ibid.* (v), no. 489). Similarly III(i), nos. 148, 355, 411; (ii), no. 1012; (iii), nos. 286, 529; (iv), no. 498.

how far Litvinov's habit of speaking in scornful terms of British
and French weakness was routine communist one-upmanship or
a reflexion of expert Soviet opinion, but it seems probable that
Stalin took a pessimistic view of both Soviet and Anglo-French
military strength.[1] For some weeks, still hoping that there would
be no war, the British cabinet seems to have feared that a formal
alliance with Russia might precipitate it by driving Hitler finally
over the edge. The happiest solution would be a guarantee by
Russia in strong but general terms of the states covered by the British
and French guarantees; this deterrent might bring Hitler to terms
and make more elaborate measures unnecessary. Such a solution
would also provide an escape from the absurd dilemma which the
two powers faced as a result of the refusal of Poland and Rumania
to accept overt Russian aid. But the British and French certainly
desired an agreement, whatever form it might take.

Litvinov replied to initial British and French suggestions of a
Soviet guarantee by proposing on 17 April a three-power pact of
mutual assistance. It was argued later that the wisest course would
have been to accept this proposal on the spot, while the Moscow
mood seemed cooperative. But some of the clauses were difficult
to swallow, particularly one which provided for assistance to all the
states bordering on Russia without reference to their own desires
in the matter. There was no Soviet offer to guarantee states on the
French frontier. However, before the end of May the two governments had brought themselves to accept what seemed to be the
substance of the Russian programme. A new Anglo-French formula
was first put to Vyacheslav Molotov (who had replaced Litvinov on
3 May); it provided that the assistance of Russia would be immediately available after France and Britain were involved in war on
behalf of Rumania and Poland, and this appeared to remove the
Russian complaint that she might be left to fight alone. The reception however was hostile and challenging. A Tass communiqué on
9 May insisted that the Anglo-French formula was one-sided. In
his reply on the 15th Molotov rejected the Anglo-French formula
on the ground that it did not ensure reciprocity. He demanded a
tripartite pact of mutual assistance, a military convention, and the
inclusion of Finland, Estonia, and Latvia in the guarantee system
with Poland and Rumania. There followed much discussion in

[1] B.D., III(iv), nos. 24, 121, 125, and Stalin's comments at Teheran: *Foreign Relations
of the United States, Conference at Cairo and Teheran 1943* (1961), p. 553. Also to Eden in
December 1941: Avon, *The Reckoning*, p. 302.

London, Paris, and Geneva, where Halifax talked to the French ministers and to Maisky. Finally the British cabinet decided on the 24th to agree to 'a system of mutual guarantees in general conformity with the principles of the League of Nations'. It was assumed that this would meet the essential Soviet demand.[1]

Soviet diplomatists had developed a formidable negotiating technique which was, however, less familiar at this time than it became after 1945. It combined a thorough mastery and exploitation of the traditional diplomatic techniques with a basic disbelief in the existence of common ground with any other power. This was due partly to the permanent ideological isolation of Soviet Russia in an exclusively capitalist world, partly to deeper historical causes; the psychological effect of the revolutionary struggle for existence on the character of the individuals involved must also be remembered. Negotiations were often pursued for propagandist purposes, to confuse rivals, to probe for weaknesses, or merely to mark time; but there were also well-tried tactical devices such as deliberate initial disagreement (staged perhaps on pointless issues such as the form of the agenda) and a systematic trying of the other man's patience even when an ultimate conclusion was not ruled out. Molotov's one-upmanship was physical as well on this occasion: he conducted the negotiations sitting on a raised platform and twiddling with knobs under his desk from time to time. The western representatives had to sit on chairs in a half-circle before him, supporting their papers as best they could on their knees.[2]

Molotov promptly criticized the Anglo-French draft treaty presented to him on 27 May, and produced a redraft of its proposals on 2 June. This Soviet document named Belgium, Greece, Turkey, Rumania, Poland, Latvia, Estonia, and Finland as the states 'whom England, France and the U.S.S.R. have agreed to defend against aggression'. Assistance might also be rendered to any other European state which had requested assistance. Other clauses provided for speedy agreement, military arrangements, the elimination of any dependence on League of Nations procedure, joint agreement in war before concluding an armistice or peace, and a five-year validity.[3] Anxious now to hurry the negotiations Halifax discussed

---

[1] B.D., III(v), nos. 170, 201, 436, 441, 530, 621–5.
[2] G. A. Craig, 'Totalitarian approaches to diplomatic negotiations' in *Studies in Diplomatic History* . . . , ed. A. O. Sarkissian (1961), pp. 117–25; Lord Strang, *Home and Abroad* (1956), p. 175.
[3] B.D., *loc.cit.*, no. 697.

with Maisky a number of expedients, such as an invitation to a Russian representative to visit London and Paris, and decided to call the ambassador, Sir William Seeds, to London for discussion. Seeds, however, was in bed with influenza, and Mr. William Strang, head of the Central Department of the Foreign Office, who was to have accompanied Seeds back to Moscow, was sent off instead. Chamberlain, with his knack of wrong emphasis, announced the appointment (but not the name) in the Commons on 7 June, thus giving too much prominence to the professional labours of a comparatively junior official. The London papers at once started calling him an envoy; the Russians were soon claiming to have been slighted.[1] Seeds in fact remained in charge of the negotiations on the British side, just as the German ambassador conducted parallel negotiations on Germany's behalf. If anything was wrong it was not Strang's appointment, but his instructions.

These included counter-proposals, reasonable perhaps in themselves, which merely gave Molotov another chance to say no, and which were speedily abandoned when he did so. The draft omitted the Soviet provision that the three powers should not make peace except by joint agreement; the British government objected to this commitment before the objects to be secured by such a peace were known. It also included the provision that joint action should be without prejudice to the rights and position of other powers; Molotov chose to regard this as an attempt to condone aggression. The most important clause was one which endeavoured to meet the problem of those states (such as Latvia, Estonia, Finland, the Netherlands, and Switzerland) which were unwilling to be guaranteed. It was suggested that the three powers should consult together if one of them felt that its security was menaced by a threat to the neutrality or independence of any other European power. The other two would at once give help if they 'agreed that such a menace existed'. But the Soviet government would not listen to this, and insisted that the solution of the problem of the Baltic states on its own terms was fundamental, the indispensable condition for any agreement.

Discussions were resumed on 15 June; on the 16th Molotov said that if the British and French governments expected agreement to

[1] B.D., *ibid.*, nos. 716, 719-22, 733-5; W. P. and Z. Coates, *A History of Anglo-Soviet Relations* (1945), p. 611; I. Maisky, *Who Helped Hitler?*, pp. 140-1; P.D., 5 Ser., HC, vol. 348, 7 June 1939, cols. 400-402.

their draft they were treating the Russians as fools and simpletons. He proposed that if agreement could not be reached the best course would be to drop the provisions for guarantee altogether and limit the treaty to the case of direct aggression only. However, there was no response to this suggestion, which would have enabled Russia to stay out of a war arising from a German attack upon Poland. On 22 June he reverted to the Soviet proposal of 2 June. Halifax in some exasperation referred to Molotov's 'inarticulate obstinacy' in a telegram to Seeds on the same day, and on the next day he asked Maisky whether the Soviet government wanted a treaty at all. The ambassador rather ingeniously replied that probably his government had made a mistake in frankly stating at the outset their irreducible minimum. As it was so palpably the irreducible maximum Halifax was not mollified. It was known that the Soviet embassy was feeding the London press and opposition spokesmen with allegations that the British government was preventing the conclusion of the tripartite treaty by unnecessary haggling.[1] Halifax clearly suspected now that the Russians were playing for time in order to bring Germany to a bargain. But Seeds, while not excluding this possibility, believed that there might be a genuine fear of loopholes. Halifax's reply was to give up the point. On 27 June he sent fresh instructions abandoning the provision for the prior consent of the threatened states.[2]

During the war and for long afterwards it was assumed that the negotiations broke down on the question of guaranteeing the Baltic states against their will. In fact, however, this issue was completely settled. It would ease matters if the names of the states to be 'assisted', either with or against their will, were not published; but the British government was now willing to agree even to a published list, as in Molotov's draft of 2 June, if the Russians insisted. However, the faulty tactic of putting forward bargaining points and then speedily dropping them continued. Halifax on his side said that he must require the list, whether published or not, to include states which were of the same interest to Britain and France as the Baltic states were to Russia. These were Belgium, Holland, and Switzerland. The French added Luxembourg. It was decided not to include Portugal and Denmark. When a further meeting took place in

---

[1] This is also the theme of Maisky's book, *Who Helped Hitler?* which makes no mention of his contacts with the Opposition (cf. pp. 116–62).

[2] Strang, pp. 177–8; B.D. III(vi), nos. 122–7, 135, 139, 151.

Moscow on 1 July Molotov, having secured everything that he had hitherto demanded, agreed that the list need not be published, but he objected promptly to the inclusion of Holland and Switzerland, arguing that this would represent a serious addition to the obligations that the Soviet government had already assumed. All he would suggest was that Poland and Turkey might provide compensation for this by concluding agreements of mutual assistance with the Soviet Union. He also complained for the first time that the Anglo-French draft did not cover the problem of 'indirect' aggression and proposed the insertion of the words 'direct or indirect' before 'aggression' in article 1. This raised a quite new difficulty, and he put forward a definition of 'indirect aggression' on the 4th which Halifax felt compelled to reject on the 6th, although at the same time he told Seeds that if necessary, the proposal about Holland, Switzerland, and Luxembourg could be dropped. On 10 July Molotov gave the British and French a further shock by insisting that the political agreement could not come into force until a full military agreement had been concluded.

It was on these two points—the definition of indirect aggression and the military conversations—that the political negotiations came to a standstill. For the next fortnight the delegates in Moscow exchanged definitions of indirect aggression, but the essential deadlock had been reached by 17 July. The Russians sought a form of words which would cover every possible contingency; they wanted it to be laid down in black and white that anything which caused a state to abandon its independence or neutrality, either under threat of force or without threat of force, would justify the intervention of one of the three powers. The British government really could not swallow the words, 'without threat of force'. However, Molotov by this stage was probably seeking merely to keep the discussion open. On his suggestion the political agreement, complete except for this one point, was laid aside while the military discussions took place. The other two governments had hitherto resisted the linking together of the two agreements on the practical ground that delay in signing the political agreement would encourage aggression.[1] No doubt, too, they disliked the revelation of their plans, secrets, and, for that matter, their weaknesses and deficiencies before an alliance had been concluded. But Molotov did not at all take the view that the sole point of military discussions was to pool resources between

[1] B.D., *ibid.*, nos. 225, 253, 378, 413-6, 473; Strang, pp. 177-91.

allies who had loyally committed their fortunes to each other's
care. There was more than a hint that they would have to convince
him of their value as military partners before the final decision to
act together was made.

The Anglo-French military, naval, and air delegates that were
sent to Moscow in August gave the Soviet government a further
opening for accusations of insincerity: they did not rush to Russia
quite as speedily as they might have done, and when they arrived
they had no solution of the problem of persuading Poland to
accept Russian assistance.[1] But in any case Soviet hints of willingness for a Soviet-German agreement had been reaching the German
foreign office since the end of July, and it appears from the Nuremberg documents that Stalin proposed negotiations to Hitler on
12 August, the day on which the military conversations began. In
the meantime British forces had been involved in the Arab revolt
throughout the summer, and in China the Japanese instituted a
blockade of the British concessions at Tientsin on 12 June. The
Japanese case appears from the British documents to have been
rather stronger than it seemed at the time. Nevertheless it was
evident that the Japanese were relying on British distractions in
Europe to push their interests. This particular crisis eased off
during July, and there was one helpful American gesture. On 26
July the United States unexpectedly denounced its trade treaty
with Japan.

From this point there was little that Britain could do except to
await events with what dignity she could muster.[2] Her political and
military ties with France were complete. A joint Anglo-Turkish
declaration on 12 May promised reciprocal cooperation in the event
of an act of aggression leading to war in the Mediterranean. France
made a similar agreement on 23 June. Discussions with Poland
continued during the summer, but Halifax was not prepared to
turn the provisional agreement of 6 April into a formal treaty until
he had seen where the Russian negotiations were leading him.

In the meantime, the futile efforts to save the peace through
some economic *modus vivendi* continued. Memories of 1914 and an
anticipation of future war guilt controversies no doubt explain the
continued efforts of the government to make clear its intention to

[1] The full minutes of the Anglo-French-Soviet military discussions and other
documents, 12–15 August 1939, are printed in B.D., III(vii), pp. 558–614.
[2] Walther Hofer, *War Premeditated—1939* (1955), is a convenient study of the
immediate origins of the war.

fight on Poland's behalf but also its desire to leave no stone unturned in the search for an honourable peace. It was still Chamberlain's desire, as it had been since 1937, to satisfy Germany's legitimate
economic and political aspirations in return for convincing evidence
that she was prepared to renounce war. There were, of course,
conflicting views as to what was legitimate.

A German official, Dr. Helmuth Wohlthat, who was in London
for a whaling conference from 17–20 July, was drawn into talks on
economic policy by R. H. Hudson and Horace Wilson, and Wilson
broached once again the possibility of a comprehensive economic
and colonial agreement, although on the usual condition that
Germany must abandon aggression. News of this got into the
London papers, but talks with other unorthodox German agents,
and in particular Axel Wenner-Gren and Birger Dahlerus, two
well-meaning Swedes whose importance derived from Goering's
patronage, did not become public. Dahlerus warned Goering early
in July that British opinion was resolute and that an attack on
Danzig would lead to war. Chamberlain and Halifax, while offering
no concessions on the basic issue, could not bring themselves to
refuse all sanction to these discussions, just in case there was a
faint chance that Goering meant business. It gradually became quite
evident that he had nothing to offer. So the only result was to
strengthen the wishful German thought that the British government
was desperately seeking escape from its entanglements. Ribbentrop
told the Italian ambassador on 25 July that it was a war of nerves,
and that Germany would get her way if she made no concessions.
Hitler had come to the same conclusion; after asserting on 23 May
that England was a redoubtable opponent and that a war with her
could probably not be avoided he had decided by 22 August that
she probably would not fight.[1]

To make this result more certain he played his greatest diplomatic
card, a speedily negotiated non-aggression pact with the U.S.S.R.,
signed by Ribbentrop on 23 August. This dramatic move had been
recognized in Berlin as a possibility since Molotov's appointment on
3 May, and the trickle of Soviet-German commercial negotiations
had provided a convenient channel for the definite approach when
Hitler had made up his mind (late in July). Evidently the German
move had long been expected in Moscow. The alacrity with which
Hitler accepted all the Russian terms is said to have convinced

[1] D.G.F.P., ser. D(vi), nos. 433, 718, 748; (vii), nos. 192, 193.

Stalin of Hitler's insincerity.[1] Hitler was in great form when he addressed the generals on 22 August; the British and French would probably not fight, and he would then have to dispose only of Poland.

> Close your hearts to pity. Act brutally. Eighty million people must obtain what is their right. Their existence must be made secure. The stronger man is right. The greatest harshness . . .

These histrionics were, however, a little premature.

In England Parliament was at once recalled, and on the 24th Chamberlain reiterated the government's determination to support Poland. The Labour and Liberal opposition parties gave full support. The Emergency Powers (Defence) Bill was passed by both houses and received the royal assent the same night. Halifax in a broadcast speech that evening reaffirmed the government's position. This was unwelcome news for Hitler. He summoned Henderson to see him at 1.30 on the 25th, and while insisting that he must have a free hand against Poland, made 'a large comprehensive offer' to support the British Empire providing that his obligations to Italy and the U.S.S.R. were untouched and his own colonial demands were fulfilled. He gave a similar message to Coulondre. Later that afternoon came the news that the Anglo-Polish agreement had been signed, and that Mussolini would not join in the fight unless supplied with vast quantities of supplies which Germany could hardly spare. Hitler was even more upset, and gave orders postponing the invasion of Poland, which was due at dawn on the 26th.[2]

But he needed the time only for a final manœuvre; while prepared to fight his three enemies, he thought it worth while to give the British and French a last chance to withdraw, if, as he still believed, their hearts were not in the business. There followed a weekend (26–28 August) of intense discussion in the cabinet in London, aided by Dahlerus who had been sent over after talks with Goering and Hitler. In the hope that Hitler's remarks might mean that he was himself seeking a peaceful *dénouement* Dahlerus was questioned closely as to what the German terms were for a Polish settlement, but he could not report any modification of the stock demand for

[1] Peter Kleist, *European Tragedy* (1965), pp. 37, 164.
[2] Henderson, p. 259; B.D., III(vii), nos. 283, 310; D.G.F.P., ser.D(vii), nos. 301, 307; pp. 560–1 (extracts from Colonel-General Halder's notebook).

Danzig and the Corridor.[1] All that Henderson could take back to Germany was Beck's assurance, given on the 28th, that Poland was ready to enter at once into direct discussions with Germany. When he gave Hitler late that night the British cabinet's advice that direct German-Polish discussions should be initiated the response was unpromising: with memories perhaps of his Godesberg tactics Hitler first expatiated on Polish misdeeds, and then said that the terms of his generous offer of March could not be repeated: Germany could now be satisfied with nothing less than Danzig, the whole of the Corridor (not merely an autobahn), and he added for good measure a rectification of frontiers in Silesia. But he promised a definite reply on the 29th. The essence of this was that he would be prepared to start negotiations if a Polish emissary with full powers were despatched to Berlin on the following day (30th).[2]

This was the propagandist trick which Hitler had promised the commanding officers on 22 August. Halder found his master under great strain on the 28th: 'exhausted, haggard, croaking voice, preoccupied'. When Henderson exclaimed that the demand for an emissary looked like an ultimatum, Hitler and Ribbentrop were angry, and a great deal of shouting followed, in which the long-suffering ambassador played a full part. As fighting was to begin on 1 September it is obvious why the emissary had to arrive within twenty-four hours. The calculation was that if a plenipotentiary were sent he would be faced with terms whose acceptance would mean a complete surrender; if he were not sent, then the German government could claim that Poland had wanted war.[3]

It appears that Beck had not the slightest intention (remembering Hacha's fate) to rush to Berlin; in any case Halifax was not prepared to forward the German proposal to Beck until he knew what the German terms were. On the 31st Ribbentrop took the view that as the plenipotentiary had not arrived by midnight on the 30th the proposal had been rejected. He read rapidly to Henderson a list of sixteen points which he claimed were the German terms; as they included provisions for a plebiscite, exchange of populations, and an international commission to examine the complaints of minorities in the Corridor they struck many people as reasonable, but the plain fact was that Ribbentrop had not put them forward until it was too

---

[1] Birger Dahlerus's story is given in *Der Letzte Versuch, London/Berlin, Sommer 1939* (1948), and documents in B.D., *loc.cit.* e.g., nos. 285, 349, 350, 402, 406.

[2] D.G.F.P., *loc.cit.*, no. 421.

[3] Halder's notebook: D.G.F.P., *ibid.*, pp. 563–70.

late for them to be of use. The proposals were broadcast at 9 p.m. on the 31st, with a blatantly propagandist attempt to prove that the Poles had rejected a reasonable settlement.

For once the British government had not fallen into the trap of accepting specious German proposals at their face value. But its attitude lost something in dignity when a declaration of war on Germany was delayed until 3 September. The German armies invaded Poland on the 1st, and it soon became known that Italy would not march; Mussolini, indeed, hoped to mediate and to secure the suspension of operations even at this late hour. While the French and British governments were seriously considering this possibility the French General Staff, fearing air bombardment during mobilization, was adamant in insisting that there must be no declaration of war until forty-eight hours after an ultimatum to Germany. This was the real cause of delay.[1] The British government was being attacked on the point in the Commons, after Chamberlain had made a speech on 2 September so woebegone as to start a fresh round of talk about 'appeasement' (now being used in its derogatory form). In any case the Admiralty wanted speedy action. The Italian proposal fell through when Halifax insisted that Germany must first withdraw her forces from Poland, and it was then decided that the two governments should act independently. Following his instructions, therefore, Henderson presented a two-hour ultimatum at 9 a.m. on the 3rd; no reply was received by 11 o'clock, and at 11.15 Chamberlain broadcast in somewhat mournful terms the news that Germany and Great Britain were at war. The corresponding French ultimatum expired at 10 p.m.

[1] B.D., III(vii), no. 708, etc.; E. L. Woodward, *British Foreign Policy in the Second World War* (H.M.S.O., 1962), pp. 2–6.

10

THE SECOND WORLD WAR

1. TWILIGHT WARFARE

ON one thing the country was agreed: the crisis was due to German aggression, to the 'insane ambition of Germany's rulers', as the Trades Union Congress declared at Bridlington on 4 September in an angry resolution of support for the war. Ignoring as far as possible its own somewhat equivocal record, the Labour party had reached a similar decision on the 3rd, without consulting the Congress.[1] Nevertheless, the party executive and the parliamentary party decided not to join a coalition government under Chamberlain's leadership. The Liberals under Sir Archibald Sinclair also refused. Both told Chamberlain that they felt that they could serve the national cause better from outside. Both told themselves that they did not trust Chamberlain. With politics still running on party lines it was natural for the Tories to close their ranks; Eden entered the Ministry as Dominions Secretary, and Winston Churchill, the man of much delayed destiny, came back to the Admiralty.[2] All the self-governing Dominions except Eire joined in, although in South Africa the decision was taken only by a small majority of thirteen in the Assembly. This brought General Smuts to office as Prime Minister. The dependent Empire came automatically into the war. In India the Viceroy's proclamation to this effect was regarded by the Nationalists as a humiliation.

The commitment to war was irrevocable; German peace feelers, some obscure and difficult to assess, some greatly publicized as in the case of Hitler's speech of 6 October, evoked no confidence and

---

[1] As late as the night of 2 September the party's Parliamentary Executive was divided, Tom Williams, Shinwell, and others being inclined to oppose war if France stayed out. H. Dalton, *The Fateful Years* (1957), p. 265.

[2] Feiling, p. 421; Dalton, pp. 264, 273; Avon, *The Eden Memoirs, The Reckoning* (1963), pp. 61–3; W. S. Churchill, *The Second World War* (1948), vol. I, pp. 317, 320.

usually no response. As in the First World War, it was convenient to accept the theory of long planned aggression and a studied pursuit of world hegemony. This 'Napoleonic' interpretation did not, it is true, quite satisfy those who had been intelligently puzzled by the contradictions in Hitler's behaviour hitherto. The evidence which has become available since 1945 tilts the argument in favour of continuity, but to contemporaries (even among high German officials) Hitler often seemed to be moved more by paranoia than by planning, pushed into irrevocable commitments by the real extremists, the wild men of the party. 'Was Hitler merely talking through his hat, and deliberately deceiving us while he matured his schemes?' asked Chamberlain in his diary on 10 September. 'I don't think so . . . at the last moment some brainstorm took possession of him—maybe Ribbentrop stirred him up—and once he had set his machine in motion, he couldn't stop it.'[1] The brainstorm theory could easily lead to the assumption that a genuine sense of grievance, with the Versailles treaty or other adverse conditions, existed, and that another war guilt controversy was inevitable in the distant future. However, no one believed this at the time.[2] On 9 September it was announced that the British government contemplated a war lasting at least three years, and the country settled down to the task with the sense of purpose, if not in the mood of exhilaration, of twenty-five years earlier.

'The Allies are bound to win in the end', said Chamberlain on 26 November, but this faith in the 'time-on-your-side' programme was tempered by an ill-concealed concern as to the possibilities of a knockout blow. It was still thought that this would be most likely to come from the air. The government, still misinformed by the Air Staff, continued to exaggerate both the size and the hitting power of the German bomber fleet. It doubted the steadiness of civilians under fire, and might have been justified in doing so if the initial premiss had been correct, for death was still contemplated on something like the later nuclear bombing scale.[3] Although the air defences were improving, planned evacuation of the more threatened areas

---

[1] 'With such an extraordinary creature one can only speculate.' He had been speculating since 1933, but always with a leaning towards the theory of madness. Feiling, pp. 417–8.

[2] My own suggestion to this effect at the time was not well received: *British Foreign Policy since Versailles* (1940), p. 298. A. J. P. Taylor argues the case against a long-planned, though not against a dynamic, policy on Hitler's part in *The Origins of the Second World War* (1961).

[3] Feiling, p. 417; Hancock and Gowing, pp. 72, 95. See pp. 337–9 above.

seemed the most practical palliative: 1,473,000 persons, mainly mothers and children, were accordingly moved from the big cities during the first three days of September. Another two million moved out privately, keeping the Health Departments surprisingly in the dark as to their movements. The Germans had neither the power nor the intention to open up the war in this way.[1]

The other form of knockout blow that had to be considered was the more traditional German destruction of the French land forces in a swift attack, although here too the air weapon was expected to play a greater part than in the First World War. For the time being the question was whether a hundred French divisions would be able to hold the same number of Germans in the first furious clash, with little help from Great Britain. Germany used fifty-four divisions, including all her armoured divisions, against Poland, but even so she had been able to keep a third of her 'first-wave' infantry on the western front from 3 September, and had nearly fifty divisions of varying quality there by 21 September, by which date serious Polish resistance had collapsed and Gamelin had achieved no more than preliminary probing operations against the Siegfried Line. Then the best of the élite German divisions were rapidly transferred to the west, and in mid-October after a show of German strength the French forces drew back behind the Maginot defences. British manpower and industrial equipment provided, as at the beginning of the First World War, the largest reserve of unmobilized strength among the belligerents, but could the French hold out until really substantial British help arrived? Four British divisions, organized in two army corps with auxiliary troops, were in France by October; a further eight divisions, including one armoured division, had been promised at intervals between the fourth and eighth months. Four of the available thirty-nine fighter squadrons in actual existence in September were sent to France.[2] In the Anglo-French military conversations after March 1939 the principle of 'limited liability' had been abandoned and the French had been promised the support of thirty-two British divisions within twelve months of the outbreak of war. But Britain's main contribution still lay rather far in the future, and France in the meantime would have to hold the line. The Anglo-French naval position, on the other hand, seemed reasonably satisfactory.[3]

[1] R. M. Titmuss, *Problems of Social Policy*, pp. 9–11, 101–9.
[2] J. R. M. Butler, *Grand Strategy* (1957), vol. II, pp. 27, 36, 61.
[3] S. W. Roskill, *The War at Sea* (1954), vol. I, chap. IV; Butler, vol. II, pp. 24, 96.

In these circumstances the government could not but welcome any postponement of heavy fighting or political crises abroad which would tilt the balance of power against the Anglo-French forces. The National Service (Armed Forces) Act, passed on the outbreak of war, provided recruits; how soon could they be equipped? The startling fact that at this point the Army had only sixty tanks as compared with an estimated requirement of 1,646 must be set against successes in other directions; for example, the output of aircraft was now greater than that of the Germans and naval expansion was being heavily financed. A cabinet committee under Hoare, which examined the matter speedily, presented to the cabinet on 8 September a maximum programme which might well be beyond the country's resources. The four main aims were an army of fifty-five trained and equipped divisions by the end of the second year of war, with at least twenty divisions by the end of the first year; priority for labour and material to complete this programme; and urgent immediate efforts to increase the supply of big guns. But this ambitious programme might drain manpower away from industry, the Navy, and the Air Force. The cabinet accepted the programme as a target, without binding itself to carry it out fully. The French were told that the limit of thirty-two divisions would be exceeded, but not by how much.[1]

So conditions were set for the twilight war. The Royal Navy was active at sea, and a gallant and well-planned action by small cruisers in the South Atlantic forced the pocket battleship *Admiral Graf Spee* to scuttle herself on 19 December. The period until April 1940 was otherwise one of military quiescence during which both sides sought to strengthen their forces for the great main grapple. The country and the world, puzzled by the lull, somewhat uneasy as to its implications, were not too sure as to how they should take the British government's demeanour.[2] The official tone was one of cheery optimism, which was generally followed by the press. 'Herr Hitler has lost the initiative', said Eden on 25 October. 'I do not doubt that time is on our side', said Churchill on 12 November. On 8 October the Secretary of State for War, Hore-Belisha, startled French journalists with the confident assertion that 'in a year we shall have as many men at the front as you'. There seems to have been no more justification for this estimate than for that of R. H. Cross,

[1] *Ibid.*, vol. II, p. 28.
[2] E. S. Turner, *The Phoney War on the Home Front* (1961), pp. 11–18, etc.

the Minister of Economic Warfare, who said on 17 January 1940 that after four and a half months of this war Germany had been reduced by the blockade to something like the same economic straits that she had been in after two years of the last one. And did not the Prime Minister himself say on 4 April 1940 (incautiously summarizing general cabinet opinion) that Hitler had missed the bus?

It is not easy, judging from our knowledge of subsequent events, to acquit the government of some complacency. Too much was being attributed to the blockade, which in the quiescence of the western front had become the country's chief offensive weapon. British bombers flew unmolested over Germany, where they scattered leaflets, but no bombs; the leaflets contained warnings of disaster which were probably taken more seriously by the British than by the German government. Even Churchill, in his eagerness for a new front in Norway and other adventures, showed a very imperfect grasp of the enemy's real strength. More astonishing was the willingness (which the French shared) to accept the risk of war with the Soviet Union as an incidental product of aid to Finland. And there was complacency in some measure in the sedate progress of the industrial effort, which although thorough and well planned gave no hint of the desperate urgency which the situation really demanded.

The performance of the Opposition was also unimpressive. The Labour party limited itself to a more or less automatic criticism of almost every aspect of administrative activity. It asked for more thorough air-raid precautions, better arrangements for the evacuation of women and children, more thorough use of the nation's economic resources, more stringent enforcement of the blockade, and the removal of incidental inconveniences of war connected with such matters as the call-up and anomalies in service pay. It agreed to an electoral, although not a political, truce with the Conservative and Liberal parties. But it showed no real grasp as yet of the basic problem of laying out limited resources of wealth, industry, neutral goodwill, and manpower to the best advantage.[1] Over the Finnish issue it was as ready as the Conservatives to take on the Soviet Union as well as the Nazis. The I.L.P. denounced the war, mainly on the ground that Chamberlain and Daladier were capitalist upholders of imperialistic exploitation. George Lansbury, much distressed by events, died on 7 May 1940. The Communist party in September 1939, ignoring the implications of the Soviet-German

[1] G. D. H. Cole, *A History of the Labour Party from 1914*, pp. 367–82.

pact, promised full support to the war against Fascism, although calling for a 'People's government' to wage it; on 6 October, however, it reversed itself, and denounced the war as imperialistic. Harry Pollitt was removed from the secretaryship of the party four days later.

If there was a mixture of rashness and caution in official pronouncements it was partly due to the freedom given to powerful ministers to run the war according to their own ideas—a partial absence of coordination which emphasized the need for a more dominating leadership. The Treasury stood for caution, and retained its prewar influence. The Chancellor, Sir John Simon, was the sole representative of economic interests in the cabinet, and chairman of the Ministerial Economic Policy Committee. In introducing the special war budget on 27 September he successfully asserted the favourite Treasury doctrine that finance as the fourth arm of defence must be husbanded. He vetoed many proposals for expenditure whose value, direct or indirect, to the war effort could not be denied.[1]

This caution was hard to accept but difficult to criticize in connexion with purchases abroad outside the sterling area. The Treasury estimated that the country in a three years' war could not expend more than £150 million a year from its foreign exchange and gold reserves for the purpose, and although in time additional funds could be raised by the sale of British investments overseas, the process could not be hurried without the risk of bad bargains. It was harder to accept at home, but fear of inflation nagged the Chancellor's financial conscience. Income tax went up to 7s 6d in September 1939, but 49 per cent of the total expenditure for the year had to be met by borrowing, and in spite of appeals for voluntary savings there remained a substantial gap which might have to be filled by an inflation of incomes. A £300 million loan at 3 per cent in March 1940 was depressingly under-subscribed. In the second war budget in April 1940 war expenditure was estimated at £2,000 million, which seemed to many critics a totally inadequate figure, although Simon thought it too big to enable him to hold back inflation. From these circumstances there emerged the 'sterling area' in its more developed form. The Treasury took control of all dealings in gold and foreign exchange at the beginning of the war, and by 1941 the characteristic feature of a single pool of gold and dollar resources had been achieved. In addition, imports were

[1] Hancock and Gowing, pp. 69, 107, 171.

regulated in stages by the Board of Trade to prevent the drain of precious foreign assets on non-essentials, although complete import control was not achieved until June 1940.[1]

The Foreign Secretary also preferred to avoid risks, and was soon to share with Simon the Opposition's charge of missed opportunities. But in diplomacy as in finance considerable circumspection seemed necessary, for among the neutrals there were four great powers and many smaller ones whose active animosity must not be fecklessly provoked. It cannot be said that Halifax, a man certainly of much respected character and even-tempered firmness in negotiation, ever gives an impression of unusual diplomatic ability; he was not a Disraeli or a Canning, apt to achieve nearly impossible results by clever guesswork and shrewd manœuvre. But perhaps the age gives no real scope for these individual skills. Here and there an ambassador was doing well; Loraine in Rome in unsympathetic, Lothian in Washington in sympathetic, surroundings. Sir Alexander Cadogan, Permanent Under-Secretary of State for Foreign Affairs from 1938 to 1946, had already established his reputation as a permanent official of excellent judgment and powers of lucid exposition; under his immediate direction the Foreign Office was coping with an ever-widening field of administrative activity, without giving quite the impression of technical virtuosity and quick wittedness created by the higher officials of the Treasury, if not by the Chancellor.[2] But neither department seemed to be winning the war.

Both were undoubtedly impeding the ambitious plans of the Ministry of Economic Warfare, which regarded itself, and not the Treasury, as the fourth fighting service. Its activities illustrate very well the contradictory tendencies. On the one hand the real, although exaggerated, privations of Germany in World War I and the power of Britain's one major weapon, the Royal Navy, had encouraged thorough preparations since 1933 for blockade in a future war; it

---

[1] R. S. Sayers, *Financial Policy, 1939–45* (1956), pp. 23–44 and *Modern Banking* (1964), pp. 134–44; Hancock and Gowing, pp. 107–120; S. Pollard, *The Development of the British Economy, 1914–1950*, pp. 330–35; A. R. Conan, *The Sterling Area* (1952), pp. 1–14.

[2] E. L. Woodward, *British Foreign Policy in the Second World War* (1962), pp. xxvi–xxx. Space has precluded a discussion of theories which seek to present Halifax as the real author of the war, plotting, like Grey before him, to encircle Germany and to persuade Poland to reject reasonable requests about Danzig and the Corridor between March and August 1939. This is the theme of *Der erzwungene Krieg: Die Ursachen und Urheber des 2. Weltkriegs* (Tübingen, 1964), by the American historian, Professor David L. Hoggan. It follows the official German propaganda line put out by Ribbentrop, von Wegerer, and others during the first year of war. It can only be said that neither his temperament nor his abilities as we know them suggest that Halifax had the capacity for such a positive rôle. This seems also to be his biographer's view: Birkenhead, *Halifax*, chap. 25.

was mainly because inexorable economic pressure could be inexpensively applied that time was thought to be on the Allied side, even in the absence of fighting. On the other hand was the fact that the use of the full range of the Ministry's weapons might have dangerous repercussions. 'Economic warfare' in a 'total' war was visualized as including not only the cutting off of supplies to Germany from all neutral sources but also the carrying of the war behind the enemy's lines by the bombing of industrial targets, sabotage, and the destruction of civilian morale. But was this worth the unpleasant consequences of retaliation? The British heavy bombers were not used against the Ruhr (partly because of the vulnerability of French towns to counter-attack from the air), and the cabinet turned down some of the more ambitious schemes of sabotage, such as the blocking of the Danube by explosives, although attempts to diminish Rumanian oil supplies to Germany by the purchase of tankers had some success. To the agents of the Ministry and other departments, weaving ambitious plans in Bucarest and Belgrade so secretly that they were sometimes unknown to each other, this restraint seemed tepid and disappointing.[1]

The blockade had to be relaxed at times in the pursuit of neutral goodwill. It was not considered expedient to ration the imports by the Italians or other neutrals adjacent to Germany. This led in some cases to the building up of stocks and may have encouraged Italy to enter the war; it certainly provided the Germans a little later with valuable loot in Holland and elsewhere. The United States was regarded as a sympathetic neutral, but she was quick to resent interference with the neutral's way of life. President Roosevelt's proclamation on 5 September 1939 implementing the Neutrality Act of 1937 deprived the Allies of some 79 million dollars-worth of military equipment, and Germany of virtually nothing. The arms embargo in the neutrality legislation was repealed on 4 November but as American ships were forbidden to enter combat zones in Europe the Allies had to use their own shipping for all trade with the United States, and to pay cash: moreover, the Johnson Act of 1934 prohibiting loans to defaulting foreign governments remained in force. Yet when the British government proposed to save dollars by buying tobacco in Turkey and Greece, Cordell Hull protested on 22 January 1940 against the reduction of these traditional exports to Britain, in spite of the fact that the dollar currency saved

---

[1] W. N. Medlicott, *The Economic Blockade*, vol. I, pp. 255–7.

would be used in the United States to buy war equipment. In the Pacific contraband control was virtually non-existent. This avoided trouble with Japan, although she made vigorous protests (as did the United States and other neutrals) at the British seizure of German exports. Negotiations to prevent the re-export of Japanese imports to Germany via the Trans-Siberian railway were prolonged and ineffectual.[1]

It was in northern Europe that the two governments strove to seize the initiative, with unhappy results. Among the politicians these plans were pushed by Churchill on the British side, and Daladier on the French. Expert opinion fluctuated. A great many issues—economic, political, diplomatic, strategic, even ideological —were involved, and combined to give inflated importance to a very risky sideshow. For her industrial survival Germany was heavily dependent on the importation annually of some 10 million tons of Swedish iron ore. The main Swedish fields were in the far north, and she was vitally interested in the supply routes through Narvik in Norway and Lulea on the Gulf of Bothnia. Could not the Royal Navy do something about this? The Foreign Office still had hopes, kept alive by Sir Stafford Cripps's and Maisky's assurances, of a trade agreement with Russia which would check German influence. But the Soviet government was unresponsive, and its demands on Finland led the British cabinet in October to call for an appreciation from the Chiefs of Staff of the consequences of an Allied declaration of war on the U.S.S.R. in defence of Finland.[2]

Thus the problems of Swedish iron ore and Soviet aggression became linked, for the conquest of Finland might lead to the establishment of Russian bases in Norway, German intervention in the south, and a German-Soviet domination of Scandinavia which the allies would be bound to resist. When the Finns, a brave people, held up the invading Russian forces in December, new plans emerged.

It was the delayed shock of the Soviet attack on Finland that completed the disillusionment of Russia's friends in England; even Stafford Cripps shook his head over the attack on Finland. The expulsion of the U.S.S.R. from the League of Nations in mid-December seemed well deserved. From the meeting of the Supreme War Council on 19 December there now emerged a tentative French

[1] *Ibid*, vol. I, pp. 403–11.
[2] *Ibid*, vol. I, pp. 317–20; Butler, vol. II, p. 95.

plan for an Allied occupation of the Narvik area and the Swedish iron ore field as a means of channelling help to Finland and of defending Sweden, and on 5 February 1940 the Supreme War Council agreed to offer Finland 100,000 heavily armed troops. This wildly impracticable scheme continued to be canvassed in secret discussions in Paris and London until the Finnish surrender on 13 March. Nothing came of it, for the British government, although divided on the point, could not agree to act except on the invitation of Norway and Sweden, and all soundings to this effect were received with consternation and rejected with alacrity. Churchill, however, continued to insist to his colleagues that the Allies had everything to gain from the extension of the war to Norway. In a speech broadcast on 20 January 1940 he bitterly condemned the timidity of neutrals who bowed humbly and in fear before German threats of violence, each hoping that if he fed the crocodile enough the crocodile would eat him last.

This episode is the final example of the combination of wishful thinking and technical uncertainty which had so often frustrated British foreign policy since 1937. The point at which the historian can condemn the soldier or the politician for guessing wrong is not always easy to define, although it must be conceded that they guessed wrong rather too often in these unhappy years. Risks were no doubt inevitable in a policy which since 1937 had combined defence and knight errantry, assigning to Britain the rôle of defender of all small nations in distress. In so far as British policy was a mere excuse for throwing troops into the iron ore area it stood condemned for hypocrisy, or for over-ingenuity; but the basic trouble was a miscalculation of all the forces involved. The real Soviet strength was still being underrated, and the risk of war with her had been accepted without any noticeable qualm, by government and opposition alike. German strength had been grossly underrated, as was soon to be seen. The Foreign Office was at fault in its failure to anticipate Norwegian and Swedish reactions. The Chiefs of Staff were at fault, and Churchill very much at fault, in many calculations as to the forces needed and their vulnerability to air attack.[1]

[1] Much has been written on the Norwegian campaign and its political setting. Nils Ørvik, *Norge 1 Brennpunktet* (1953), Part III; T. K. Derry, *The Campaign in Norway* (H.M.S.O., 1952); Woodward, chap. II; Butler, vol. I, chaps. V, VI; Churchill, vol. I, chaps. 20–27; Walther Hubatsch, '*Weserübung*', *Die deutsche Besetzung von Dänemark und Norwegen 1940* (1964).

The Prime Minister's defence in the Commons of the government's attitude towards Finland was not very well received; but the complaint was that too little rather than too much had been attempted. The complicated plans for seizing Narvik and the iron-ore could not be explained. It was, however, announced that the '100,000 heavily armed troops' had been assembled to await the call from Finland which never came.[1] Churchill was not alone in his search for the initiative, but what in him was a natural extremism seemed to be no more than a matter of intellectual conviction in his colleagues. The time was fast approaching when the country must surrender to the extremist—the ruthless (but also *rusé* and technically knowledgeable) leader, the champion who could give his wicked and successful opponents as good as they gave.[2] The Finnish defeat was fatal to Daladier, whose cabinet fell on 20 March. Chamberlain had one last service as scapegoat to perform.

The Norwegian campaign in April destroyed him. Hitler and his advisers had rightly anticipated Anglo-French efforts to cut off the iron ore supplies; in this sense neither party could blame the other for its intentions. The difference between them lay in the German willingness, and Anglo-French refusal, to use force against a small neutral. Hitler struck on 9 April. The essentials of victory were gained on the first day, when the Germans occupied Oslo, Stavanger, Bergen, Trondheim, and Narvik, and the Allied forces which might have been thrown into Norway were unable to sail because the Royal Navy was at sea chasing Germans. It failed to find sufficient of them to deal the German fleet a really crippling blow, although the ultimate German losses were considerable. After the Navy's biggest success, the destruction of all the German ships off Narvik, a small force was landed there, but it was not strong enough to capture the port; in the meanwhile plans were changed and it was decided to try to turn the Germans out of their footholds in central Norway, with converging attacks on Trondheim from Namsos and Aandelsnes. But for this task the Allied forces were never strong enough in numbers, equipment, or air support, and evacuation was decided on and completed by 2 May. General Paget strengthened his reputation through his skilled withdrawal from Aandelsnes. Snow, unsuitable equipment, and the fact that the

[1] P.D., 5 Ser., HC, vol. 358, 19 March 1940, cols. 1834–46.

[2] This of course was anticipated by many on the theory (which is hardly justified by history) that in democratic states the government that starts a war is never the one to finish it.

naval and army commanders were not on speaking terms delayed the capture of Narvik; the town was finally captured on 28 May after the arrival of a new general, C. J. E. Auchinleck.

The Germans, it could be said, had had the advantage in the initiative and certainly in unscrupulousness. But the Allies could hardly claim to have been taken by surprise. The Navy had sown mines in the Vest Fjord on 8 April, an almost meaningless gesture as the iron ore route through the Baltic would soon be open; it was thought that it might impress French opinion. But although they were unable to leave the area alone they failed to anticipate the speed and daring of the German movements. Desperately improvising, the higher direction of the campaign, essentially British, showed grave weaknesses; the capacity of troops inadequately equipped and trained for Arctic conditions was misjudged, the importance of air defence and reconnaissance was underrated, ships were badly loaded, and plans were changed frequently and without adequate warning. At the executive level the coordination of action between the three services largely broke down. Churchill was later to complain that the Chiefs of Staff had inadequate direction from above, but it appears that his own intervention and tendency to exalt the virtues of mere boldness had not helped matters.[1]

Nevertheless it was on Chamberlain that the condemnation of the House of Commons fell in its two-day post-mortem debate of 7–8 May. The Commons were not very well equipped to argue about details of the campaign; but Chamberlain's critics were voicing a general charge of inadequacy when they demanded more foresight and energy and a more ruthless will to victory. Attlee, Sinclair, Lloyd George, Amery, and others all told him to go. There was some gleeful spite in the speeches, although every one professed to be performing a painful public duty.[2]

Churchill wound up the debate; he could do little else in view of his own prominent part in the whole Norwegian policy since September 1939. Remembering the 'dangerous pacifism in former years' of the Labour leaders, and the absence of any past criticism from many of the Prime Minister's now 'abashed and silent' supporters, he did not spare the critics. However, the Opposition vote

---

[1] I have followed J. R. M. Butler, *Grand Strategy*, vol. II, pp. 145–50, in these criticisms of the Norwegian operations.

[2] Dalton refers to Chamberlain as a 'silly old fool', 'showing his teeth like a rat in a corner', etc.: *op.cit.*, p. 305. P.D., 5 Ser., HC, vol. 360, 7–8 May, cols. 1072–1196, 1251–1362.

of censure was defeated by only 281 votes to 200; there were sixty Tory abstentions and thirty voted with the Opposition. On the 10th the German army struck into Belgium and Holland, and Chamberlain resigned, accepting the need for a truly National government which he was not to be allowed to lead.[1] The King sent for Churchill, and the leaders of the three main parties all agreed to serve. When the Commons approved the new government on 13 May the new Prime Minister could offer them nothing but blood and tears and toil and sweat. But he was better than his word, for courage and majestic oratory and a grim, roguish humour sustained them until victory.

The passing of Chamberlain is the real end of the curious epoch in British history which starts with the fading of Lloyd George's magic sometime in the autumn of 1921. For nearly twenty years the country had no taste for adventures; its mood was conciliatory and rather disillusioned, and it had clung to its Tories, satisfied that these cautious and well-meaning gentlemen, pledged to tranquillity at home and appeasement abroad, would do the right thing without too grave a disturbance of normal life. This was not defeatism; there was good will and even idealism in home and foreign affairs, but the emotional temperature stayed down, heroics were at a discount, and to many sly and peaceable citizens Chamberlain had appealed as a clever old gentleman who would out-manœuvre Hitler in the end.[2] All this now collapsed under the threat of an appalling disaster—invasion, enslavement, fate in a variety of forms literally worse than death at Nazi hands.

2. IF NECESSARY ALONE

The second main phase of the war is the year of utmost peril that Britain faced after the French collapse in June 1940. The loss of the French shield gave Englishmen a sense of stark danger unfamiliar since the days of Napoleon, and only the historically-minded could draw comfort from the successful passing of all the

---

[1] He at first suggested Halifax as his successor, thinking that Churchill's trouncing of Labour on 8 May, and perhaps his large measure of involvement in the Norwegian disaster, would have cost him their support. Dalton told R. A. Butler that evening that he and other Labour men were thinking of Halifax. Dalton, pp. 306–7; Churchill, vol. I, pp. 522–7; Feiling, pp. 440–42; Macleod, pp. 290–2. The suggestion gave Halifax a bad stomach ache: Birkenhead, *Halifax*, p. 454.

[2] Among the few satisfying studies of the public mood at this time is Margery Allingham's *The Oaken Heart* (1941), pp. 165–71, describing the reactions of an East Anglian village to the first year of war: 'With Mr. Churchill returned some of the sublime exhilaration hidden in the heart of good fighting'.

'darkest hours' of earlier generations. This one also passed; the Soviet Union came into the war in June 1941, and the United States in December, although the enemy's run of success continued disquietingly throughout 1942. But for twelve months the government faced virtually alone the two problems of immediate survival and—even more difficult—the devising of plans for ultimate salvation and victory.

What was the darkest hour for Great Britain in this war? For the government it was surely the last days of May 1940, when the French collapse seemed imminent and the B.E.F. was confined in the perimeter around Dunkirk. At this point it was doubted whether more than some 20,000 men could be withdrawn, and the British commander was authorized to surrender to avoid unnecessary slaughter when his forces had been reduced to three divisions. On the 27th the cabinet had before it a paper from the Chiefs of Staff which considered the blockade, supported by air power, the only effective weapon if France fell; it did not envisage any offensive rôle for the army. On the 28th Italy's entry into the war was known to be certain, and Churchill warned the country to prepare for 'hard and heavy tidings'; on the 29th the C.O.S. advised the cabinet that invasion was probable and the country inadequately prepared to meet it. After this the news, cautiously announced on 31 May and then triumphantly on the three following days, of the safe withdrawal of over 300,000 men from Dunkirk had the reverberations of a major triumph.

If we look for an explanation of this popular exaltation of spirit we must find it essentially in the deeply satisfying reaffirmation of the country's ability to cope with a crisis. The cheerfulness and good discipline of the troops, the professional expertise of the small warships in dangerous waters, the reliable nurses, tired and soaked to the skin, the swarm of little boats; even the weather seemed to have risen to the occasion. More professionally the saving of a third of a million of trained troops and their officers and N.C.O.s, the air battles, and the quality of British generalship in the skilful fighting retreat (although such names as Brooke, Pownall, Alexander, and Montgomery meant hardly anything as yet to the public) were encouraging. On 4 June, in the greatest of Churchill's war speeches, which finally established his domination of the country, the note was now one of defiant confidence: 'We shall prove ourselves once again able to defend our island home, to ride out the storms of war, and to outlive the menace of tyranny, if necessary for years, if necessary alone'. The splendid invocation to his countrymen pointed the path to ultimate victory, with one curious omission.

We shall fight in France, we shall fight on the seas and oceans, we shall fight with growing confidence and growing strength in the air, we shall defend our island, whatever the cost may be. We shall fight on the beaches, we shall fight on the landing grounds, we shall fight in the fields and in the streets, we shall fight in the hills; we shall never surrender, and even if, which I do not for a moment believe, this island or a large part of it were subjugated and starving, then our Empire beyond the seas, armed and guarded by the British Fleet, would carry on the struggle, until, in God's good time, the new world, with all its power and might, steps forth to the rescue and liberation of the old.[1]

There was again no suggestion that a reconstructed British army could invade and liberate the continent.

It seems that Churchill was genuinely inclined not to rate the chance of success of a German invasion very highly, and was already looking forward to the long phase of baffling struggle between the island fortress power and the master of the continent. That the British did not promptly recognize the situation to be hopeless seems to have been a matter of genuine surprise to the French and Germans.[2] Britain's inability to send any substantial help to France during the first half of June could not but confirm this impression. When Churchill tried to galvanize Pétain by recalling the crisis of 1918 the Marshal replied very quietly that there had then been sixty British divisions in the line.[3] Two extra British divisions were promised, but almost immediately Lieutenant-General Alan Brooke, who had been put in charge of the British troops still in France, had to plan a second evacuation. About 144,000 had been withdrawn by the end of June. Churchill's imaginative offer (apparently originated by Chamberlain) of an Anglo-French union, and Reynaud's appeal for United States help, were fruitless, and it was known in London on 22 June that the French had accepted the German armistice terms.

Dr. Johnson, as Churchill recalls in his memoirs, pointed out that when a man knows he is going to be hanged in a fortnight 'it concentrates his mind powerfully'. The country got down to its

[1] P.D., 5 Ser., HC, vol. 361, 4 June 1940, col. 796.
[2] The French however more than the Germans. Hitler's plans for sea and air attack since 1939 had reckoned on the possibility of a long resistance. Cf. Butler, pp. xviii, 52.
[3] Churchill, vol. II, pp. 136–7. It would have been better to recall the Marne victory of 1914.

anti-invasion preparations with unwonted alacrity. The nine Dunkirk divisions were rapidly re-equipped; vast numbers of civilians enrolled in the Home Guard, which was speedily provided with uniforms, less speedily with arms; an abnormal energy drove up aircraft production; suspected foreign agents, almost invariably innocent, were hurriedly interned and more slowly sorted out and released; the French Navy was crippled in a heart-rending action at Oran on 3 July. Hitler tried a peace offer on 19 July, and then launched the Luftwaffe against the island; the Battle of Britain, after air encounters which had already lasted for over a month, began officially on 13 August. The R.A.F., outnumbered but a more powerful opponent than the Germans had encountered in the Polish or French air forces, won the battle of attrition over southern England, and on 17 September Hitler postponed invasion by sea until further notice. The thoroughness of the German naval preparations and army training show that the invasion threat was no mere bluff; but it was dependent throughout on victory in the air.[1]

In this way Britain survived the first crisis of solitary combat; and at once, though dimly at first, the shape of a new alignment of world forces began to be discerned. If the German attack had been held in France and the war had gone on for the anticipated three years or more as a desperate ding-dong struggle in western Europe, Russia and America would presumably have maintained their equivocal neutralities, benevolent towards one side or the other; Italy might have stayed out (allowing Mussolini a peaceful old age alongside his more astute ally Franco); Japan almost certainly would not have come in. The alternatives are difficult to estimate and the exhaustion of the three main belligerents might have led to a Russo-American domination of the postwar world, complicated by whatever mental attitudes had governed the inevitable intervention of Moscow and Washington in the last stages. But almost certainly the final result would have been less to the advantage of Great Britain than the way things actually turned out.

As it was, the thinking of many states besides Britain's was concentrated powerfully by the French collapse. There was early evidence that few countries in the world except perhaps Bulgaria, Italy, and Japan desired a Nazi victory; Stalin in his cautious way was ready to encourage, although not to assist, the British resistance, and it was soon evident that the United States had abandoned the

[1] D.G.F.P., ser. D(x), pp. 370–4.

policy of the 'eternal question mark', while still insisting on the formula that all aid must be short of war. General Franco's policy behind all its obscurities could only be interpreted as a desire to avoid domination by his Nazi and Fascist allies. North and South America, the surviving European neutrals, Turkey and the Middle Eastern countries were thus unlikely to impede the British use of her sea power and economic machinery for the intensification of the blockade and the supplying of her own population and industries. All this clearly meant that the value of Britain as the front-line fighter of the liberal-democratic world had been advertised by the French collapse; but the American and Russian leaders both knew from this point that England alone could not eliminate the Nazi, Fascist, or Japanese aggressors, even if she could survive alone.[1]

Thus it is not paradoxical to say that defeat in France had been necessary in order to release the forces which made ultimate victory possible. Although the British people and their fighting men and women did many brave and sturdy things during the struggle and strained their resources in a disproportionately heavy contribution to victory, it was the country's contribution to coalition warfare and to the formation of the 'grand alliance' that had the greatest significance for the future. From this new alignment of world forces for the temporary purpose of winning a war there resulted in the postwar era far-reaching changes in the balance of influence and power, and in the process Britain herself ceased to rank as one of the world's strongest states. It has, however, been argued at many points in this book that she had not really had the resources to play the part of world leader or policeman even in the interwar years; and what the events of 1940 finally proved was that a security system for the liberal political and economic state systems of the world would have to depend on wider resources than Britain and France could command.

But for the time being Britain stood alone[2] and the neutral world

---

[1] In a curious three-hour interview with Sir Stafford Cripps on 1 July 1940 (the first with a foreign ambassador since Ribbentrop's visit in August 1939) Stalin encouraged British resistance with the comment that Germany could not establish a hegemony over Europe without the domination of the Seas, which she did not possess and could hardly hope to achieve. He thought however that it would be impossible to restore the old equilibrium in Europe. Churchill (vol. II, pp. 119–20), probably underrated the importance of this gesture.

[2] 'Alone' meant without a major ally. But the embryo coalition already comprised more than the United Kingdom. It included the combined resources of the British colonies and Dominions and the belligerent portions of the French, Dutch, and Belgian empires, enormous if they could be fully mobilized.

was still prepared to offer no more than credit and goodwill. Here the contribution of the United States was decisive, but not unique. In Portugal, for example, while Germany had to pay for her purchases as she went along, Great Britain was allowed to run up a debt of £76 million by the autumn of 1944. The principle of deferred payment was strikingly illustrated too in the sterling area, now more or less coterminous with the British Commonwealth and Empire. Balances amounting to £2,723 million had accumulated by the end of the war; about two-thirds of this debt was incurred in the defence of India, Burma, and the Middle East. But the United States' connexion was the most vital, on account of its enormous productive capacity, access to raw materials, and convenience of transport. The new government met the problem of dollar shortages by ignoring it: as Churchill remarked, from May 1940 onward they followed a simple plan, namely 'to order everything we possibly could and leave future financial problems on the lap of the Eternal Gods'. However, everything received was paid for down to November 1940.[1]

While making use of this precious aid from overseas the government planned the fullest possible exploitation of the country's manpower and economic resources. The strength of the ministry, both in talent and authority, facilitated drastic courses. Churchill became Minister of Defence, and presided over a small war cabinet of only five members, with Chamberlain, Halifax, Attlee, and Arthur Greenwood in addition to himself. The three parties were represented at the Admiralty, War Office, and Air Ministry respectively by A. V. Alexander, Eden, and Sir Archibald Sinclair. On the home front Attlee and Greenwood set out with great reforming zeal but little noticeable success to refashion domestic policy; Attlee became chairman of the Home Policy Committee and the Food Policy Committee, and Greenwood became chairman of the Economic Policy Committee and the Production Council. The activities of these and other committees for domestic policy were at first canalized through the cabinet's home affairs' committee, presided over by Neville Chamberlain as Lord President; but he was found to be suffering from cancer in July, and was succeeded as Lord President by Sir John Anderson on 3 October. It was under Anderson's masterly administration that the Lord President's Committee came to exercise on the home front an authority equivalent to that of

[1] Churchill, vol. II, pp. 492–3; Hancock and Gowing, pp. 111, 119.

Churchill's himself in grand strategy and foreign policy.[1] When Lord Halifax went to Washington as ambassador, following Lord Lothian's sudden death in December 1940, Eden succeeded him as Foreign Secretary. Meanwhile a parliamentary opposition continued to function under the leadership of H. B. Lees-Smith, with such fortuitous front bench associates as Emanuel Shinwell and Lord Winterton, 'arsenic and old lace' according to one commentator. They and Aneurin Bevan made occasional colourful interventions which never seriously shook the government. Yet it is true to say that during the war Parliament retained its ultimate control over the Executive: the parliamentary question proved as usual a potent check on bureaucratic irresponsibility (real or imagined).[2]

Under the new leadership production was forced to remarkable heights; undoubtedly this was industry's finest hour. There was a teasing problem at first of choice between short and long-term programmes, for even the long-term programmes had to be pushed forward with constant urgency. Early in June 1940 the cabinet decided to give priority for five months to the production of fighter and bomber aircraft, anti-aircraft equipment, and fully trained air crews. Lord Beaverbrook as Minister of Aircraft Production carried through this cannibalizing process with the ruthless gusto needed by the times, and not without acrimonious clashes with the Air Ministry, which had its own ideas about how to save the country. Priorities were rearranged after the Battle of Britain. The long-term objective was, as in September 1939, fifty-five divisions trained and equipped,[3] and the Ministry of Supply was set the task of equipping thirty-six of these by September 1941. Thirty-five divisions were to be provided by the United Kingdom, the remainder mainly by the Dominions and India. In view of the lesson painfully learned from Germany's success with heavy tank formations, Churchill insisted on the provision of seven armoured divisions.[4] As air bombing

---

[1] D. N. Chester, *Lessons of the British War Economy* (1951), pp. 5–14.

[2] These and other techniques of wartime parliamentary control are described in *Emergency Powers and the Parliamentary Watchdog . . . 1931–1951* (1957) by John Eaves, Jr. Cf. H. Finer, 'The British Cabinet. The House of Commons and the War', *Political Science Quarterly*, September 1941, pp. 350–60.

[3] These were field divisions. There were large numbers of garrison, depot, and other troops not included in the field army. The field divisions with subsidiary and liaison formations required 42,000 men each. Hancock and Gowing, p. 288.

[4] The single British armoured division had arrived in France too late to take part in the first phase of the fighting in May 1940. According to Captain Liddell Hart the French had more and better tanks than the Germans, but failed in tactics; they were strung out in small groups in the 1918 style. The *Liddell Hart Memoirs*, vol. II, p. 280.

seemed to provide the main hope of really damaging attack a massive increase in bomber output was ordered; by the summer of 1941 a total of 4,000 heavy and medium bombers was being aimed at for the end of 1942. Something had to give way in the ensuing competition for raw material and industrial manpower and this was the Royal Navy, which had to face the demands not only of the other services (with the diversion of armour plate for tank construction) but of merchant shipping. It was found necessary at this period to concentrate on repair work and the construction of lighter ships and to postpone work on long-term projects. The acquisition from the United States of fifty over-age destroyers in exchange for bases was opportune, but there had to be cuts in the building of merchant ships all the same.

Meanwhile a programme of offensive action was beginning to emerge and it dovetailed very well into the plans which American experts were elaborating against the day when they should be involved in war. The situation was discussed freely with American officers who visited England secretly at the end of August 1940. The British plans did not exclude the undertaking of major land operations when the opportunity occurred but their essential feature was the wearing down of Germany by relentless economic pressure, which would be driven home by persistent and ruthless air attack. Thus blockade and air bombing would be major weapons, and the mobility resulting from Britain's amphibious power would almost provide another. The precarious nature of her position in the Far East was also recognized; it was believed that Japan would probably not risk an open breach with the British Empire and the United States until the situation in Europe was clearer, but as Britain could not provide adequate naval forces at Singapore for some time it would be necessary to rely on air defence and to work for a general settlement with Japan; failing that, to play for time. The support of the American battlefleet would clearly transform the whole situation. As far as Germany was concerned the programme was essentially one of softening up the enemy by means of blockade and bombing.

Things began to move in Washington after President Roosevelt's re-election on 5 November 1940, although the destroyer bases deal, some useful supplies of equipment, and a ready acquiescence in the widespread extension of British blockade practices had shown the change of mood immediately after the fall of France. In Roosevelt's pronouncements in December 1940, foreshadowing the Lease-Lend legislation (which became law during March 1941), there was the usual adroit assurance to the American people that they would be kept out of war; he was able to say in a fireside talk on 29 December 1940, 'there is no demand for sending an American expeditionary force outside our own borders'. Churchill was too astute a diplomat, and knew too much about American opinion, to ask for men at this stage, and in his speech of 9 February 1941 he appealed only for the tools to finish the job.[1] It would seem that the self-respect of the President's entourage was irked by the suggestion that they were being helped out by the Prime Minister in this way, and it began to be argued that he really meant what he said and really had the men to finish the job. Later, when the United States was in the war and wanted to start the second front at the wrong time and with the wrong forces it would be argued that he was showing unnecessary restraint. However, the British programme of blockade, bombing, peripheral attack, and the elimination of Italy was accepted in secret Anglo-American staff talks from January to April 1941, and the plans did include the building up of the necessary forces for an eventual offensive against Germany. They were confirmed in December 1941 when the United States was at last in the war as a result of Pearl Harbour. Churchill now labelled the objective the 'closing and tightening of the ring round Germany'.

Although the offensive spirit was bravely paraded in these plans, the actualities of the eighteen months of endeavour after Dunkirk were unimpressive. The Battle of Britain was won but it was followed by the campaign of German night bombing which could not be stopped either by defence or counter-bombing of German targets. After heavy night raids on London the attack was temporarily shifted to Coventry on 14 November 1940. Subsequently London, the Clydeside, the Mersey region, South Wales and the Midlands were among the areas heavily attacked. The offensive began to ease off only in May 1941. Out of over 60,000 civilian deaths in Great Britain during the war from enemy action, 43,685 took place in 1940 and 1941.[2] In the western desert in the three-day

[1] Cf. R. E. Sherwood, *The White House Papers of Harry L. Hopkins* (1948), vol. I, pp. 240–1, which clearly makes too much of a chance remark by Churchill to Hopkins on 10 January 1941.
[2] Titmuss, pp. 23–41 and Appendix 7; B. Collier, *The Defence of the United Kingdom* (1957).

battle of Sidi Barrani (9–11 December 1940) under Wavell's overall command, two British divisions, one armoured, routed seven Italian divisions and followed this with a bold strategic advance which had captured Cyrenaica and taken the British forces into Benghazi by 7 February 1941. With even smaller forces and with an equal mastery of administrative planning two of Wavell's generals, Platt and Cunningham, had destroyed the Italian empire in East Africa by the end of May. A major naval victory was won by Admiral Cunningham off Cape Matapan on 28 March, and the German battleship *Bismarck* was sunk in the Atlantic on 27 May. But against this had to be set three major reverses.

The building up of a great base in the Middle East, the congestion at west country ports in England owing to the closing of those on the east coast, further congestion in the repair yards, and the mounting losses at sea from U-boat sinkings, air attack, mining, and surface raiders, were dangerously reducing imports; at the end of February 1941 the protection of shipping in the north-western approaches was given 'absolute priority' and although the situation improved in the second half of the year there was no decisive victory at sea until the spring of 1943.

Then, too, air bombing of Germany, which it was confidently hoped would bring quick and decisive victories in economic warfare, proved for the time being an almost complete failure. It is a reflection of the still widely exaggerated belief in the destructive power of the bomber that the Air Staff estimated in December 1940 that the seventeen major German synthetic oil plants could be destroyed in four months of continuous air attack. This programme was carried out for some four months in the summer of 1941 but with insignificant results; nor did a further phase of bombing later in the year fare much better.[1]

The most dramatic and disappointing reverse was the collapse of Wavell's fine position in the Middle East. In the early weeks of 1941 a German push was anticipated through the Balkans, engulfing Greece and perhaps Turkey. Wavell was ordered to halt at Benghazi and send the maximum strength to Greece, leaving the minimum to hold Cyrenaica. Here General Rommel, recently landed with a German motorized division, was able to sweep through the weak British defences and to reach the frontier of Egypt by 11 April.

[1] C. K. Webster and N. Frankland, *The Strategic Air Offensive against Germany*, vol. I, pp. 299–306.

In Greece the British and Greek forces, heavily out-weighed in aircraft and armour, could make no stand against the German columns. By the end of the month the British troops had been evacuated from Greece, without heavy losses of men but with crippling losses of transport and artillery. Crete fell on 31 May. Syria now seemed to be threatened, and in Iraq Raschid Ali had seized power and besieged the Habbaniya air base at the end of April. Wavell was ordered to liquidate opposition in both areas and to launch an immediate offensive against Rommel, and although he managed to attempt all three tasks, the first two successfully, he showed plainly that he considered the demand in each case to be unreasonable. Churchill, obstinately convinced that Wavell had lost his resilience and had failed to make adequate and sufficiently foresighted use of the vast resources which he was believed to possess, replaced him by General Auchinleck.

Churchill's eminence as a war leader—perhaps the greatest in British history—does not rest solely on his strategical grasp, which some have questioned. His own professional knowledge, although curious and wide, was not always up to date. One of the British commanders in Norway in April 1940 remarked later that he did not always remember that what was operationally desirable might not be administratively possible. He looked for boldness in his commanders; but boldness is not enough, and it is particularly awkward when a commander's boldness has to be displayed in fighting the Prime Minister himself.[1] Wavell offered to resign on 21 May when he thought that the Defence Committee was interfering too much with his detailed disposition. General Sir John Dill, the C.I.G.S. since the fall of France, a fine soldier but a highly strung man, domestically troubled and of a somewhat melancholy disposition, could make little headway with the Prime Minister, and was posted to Washington in January 1942, where he struck up a great friendship with that courteous American gentleman, General George Marshall. Dill thought that Wavell's only fault had been his failure to resist the pressure from Whitehall with sufficient vigour. This, however, was a difficult requirement of the man on the spot.[2]

---

[1] Butler, vol. II, p. 562; cf. R. W. Thompson, *The Yankee Marlborough*, pp. 295–300.

[2] Dill had been retired on 25 December 1941 on reaching the age of sixty and was succeeded as C.I.G.S. by Sir Alan Brooke, aged fifty-eight. Maj. General A. E. Nye became Vice-Chief of the Imperial General Staff, and Lt. General B. C. T. Paget, C.-in-C. Home Forces. He was succeeded as G.O.C.-in-C. South-Eastern Command by Lt. Gen. B. L. Montgomery. These changes had been announced on 19 November so

The real truth is that the victorious rôle for which Churchill had cast his country was as yet beyond its resources, and he was nagged by the conviction that it was not beyond the capacity of the service chiefs, given sufficient fanaticism and will power. He had rightly assumed the task of continually raising the sights in war production and strategy, with a working assumption that the expert is wrong until he has proved himself to be right; and by these means wars are indeed sometimes won, the miracle sometimes does happen. He was not a megalomaniac like Hitler, although he resembled Hitler in his continued demands for the technically impossible. But after almost intolerable pressure on his advisers he (unlike Hitler) usually accepted their judgments in the last resort. He had greater authority over the service chiefs than Lloyd George ever possessed, but this is partly because they were men of greater forbearance than their predecessors, and put up with a great deal in their desire to avoid the high-level bickering of the First World War. It is not the case that he was always pressing forward while the professionals held back. In the Greek episode there is evidence that they and Eden were more optimistic than he, and while there was general agreement that a point of honour was involved in helping the Greeks there is little to substantiate the view, dear to Churchill's recent American critics, that the operation was due to his craving for Mediterranean adventures.[1]

3. The Bus that Hitler Missed

The whole character of the war was transformed by Hitler's invasion of Russia on 22 June 1941. His chance of total victory, which had received its first setback in September 1940, suffered a second when the momentum of the new attack was insufficient to carry the Wehrmacht to victory in Russia before the winter.[2] Thereafter the mounting German effort could barely keep pace with the vast mobilization of power in the grand alliance that was forming against him. The bus that Hitler had missed by 1945 was not quite the one that Chamberlain had had in mind in April 1940, but as he was thinking in terms of total resources and of convincing the

were not the result of America's entry into the war. A. Bryant, *The Turn of the Tide* (1957), pp. 254–5; Butler, vol. II, pp. 578, 531; J. M. A. Gwyer, *Grand Strategy* (1964), vol. III(1), p. 318; Sir John Kennedy, *The Business of War* (1957), pp. 63–182: sympathetic to Dill, critical of Churchill.

[1] Trumbull Higgins, *Winston Churchill and the Second Front* (1957), pp. 33, 51–3; cf. Avon, *The Reckoning*, p. 217; Churchill, vol. III, pp. 87–93.

[2] J. Erickson, *The Soviet High Command* (1962), chaps. 17, 18.

Germans of the impossibility of victory his anticipation was not entirely at fault.

Hitler believed that the Soviet government could not be trusted and that it was best to destroy it while Britain was still unable to take the offensive. After a swift victory he intended to build up air strength and destroy the island power. He was moved by the sense of urgency implicit in blitz campaigning and a slightly morbid fear of blockade. His deputy, Rudolf Hess, in a 'frantic deed of lunatic benevolence' flew to Scotland on his own initiative on 11 May to warn King George of the wrath to come and arrange an Anglo-German peace; but it soon became evident that he had no authority to speak for his master.[1] Hitler's dream of the central land empire with a slave Ukranian population was elaborated by the planners of the 'Economic Staff East'; they intended that millions of Russians west and north of the rich southern surplus region should be left to die of starvation in order that the whole exportable surplus could go to German Europe.[2] By concentrating his forces for the Russian adventure he threw away the only chance of destroying the British position in the Middle East and North Africa during 1941. It was the end of 'blitzkrieg' warfare. After this Hitler was able to hold off the mighty Allied coalition only because of a phenomenal, but belated, armaments drive which increased German munitions production by more than 300 per cent between 1942 and 1944.[3]

It is evident that Churchill believed that the extension of the roll of belligerents even to the Far East would be favourable on balance to British interests. Hitler's decision not only gave Britain a new ally, following Churchill's prompt offer to Stalin of assistance (not very graciously received) on the evening of 22 June, but it also encouraged the Japanese to a forward move in the south Pacific which brought the United States into the war in December. Since the end of 1940 Britain and the United States had gradually increased their economic pressure by restricting Japanese imports, and in reply to the Japanese occupation of southern French Indo-China in July 1941 the British and Netherlands governments followed the American lead and froze Japanese assets on 26 July.

[1] Churchill, vol. III, pp. 43–9; on the Foreign Office's reasons for secrecy over the affair, Avon, pp. 257–9.
[2] A. Dallin, *German Rule in Russia, 1941–1945* (1957), p. 311.
[3] Mainly the work of Albert Speer, on foundations laid by Dr. Todt. The best study is by A. S. Milward, *The German Economy at War* (1965). H. A. Jacobsen, *1939–1945, Der Zweite Weltkrieg in Chronik und Dokumenten* (1959). pp. 470–503, is a convenient summary of German criticisms of Hitler.

It was not until September that the full potency of this economic weapon appears to have been understood, but Roosevelt then gave instructions that it should not be relaxed.[1] In the meantime there came the sensational news of a meeting between Roosevelt and Churchill at Placentia Bay in August, and a statement of joint aims which was conspicuously innocent of any reference to Japan. The Atlantic Charter was, in form, no more than an affirmation of the ideal bases of a future peace. In practice it was the starting point of the war and postwar United Nations organizations. The Japanese were not prepared to agree to the proposals for a Pacific settlement which Cordell Hull had been deploying, and the British watching somewhat uneasily, since May. The Japanese assault on Pearl Harbour on 7 December 1941 finally removed the gnawing doubt whether the United States would come into the war if the Japanese attacked only the British and Dutch possessions, although Roosevelt had virtually promised this to Halifax on 4 December. 'So we had won after all!' wrote Churchill later, 'Hitler's fate was sealed. Mussolini's fate was sealed. As for the Japanese, they would be ground to powder. All the rest was merely the proper application of overwhelming force.'

But for nearly another year the Axis forces, striking out and striking back with skill and ferocity, held the balance of advantage, and it was by no means certain that with their powerful lead in training and armaments they would not pull off a decisive victory in the nick of time. Allied shipping losses mounted: there was no bar now to unrestricted U-boat warfare. The summer and autumn of 1942 saw another tremendous German advance in Russia, and it was not until Stalingrad had proved itself another Verdun in September-October that the tide really began to turn there. In the Pacific, the Japanese had captured the Philippines, Malaya, and Singapore and were threatening Australia and India when the battle of Midway in June 1942 gave them their first decisive check.

In North Africa the reinforced and re-equipped British forces under Auchinleck had battled their way across Cyrenaica between November 1941 and January 1942, only to be thrown back on Gazala and Tobruk by General Rommel's counterattack. There had then been a lull in the desert war until May, when a further phase of

---

[1] W. N. Medlicott, *The Economic Blockade*, vol. II, pp. 103–23; H. Feis, *The Road to Pearl Harbor* (1950), chaps. 28–30; W. L. Langer and S. E. Gleason, *The Undeclared War, 1940–1941* (1953), chaps. 26–28; R. J. C. Butow, *Tojo and the Coming of the War* (1961), pp. 234–61.

heavy tank fighting began. After initial successes the British tanks were heavily mauled at Sidi Rezagh on 17 June and Rommel, a first-rate soldier who seldom missed his chances, exploited a weakness in the Tobruk defences and compelled the surrender of 33,000 men and vast stores on the 21st. There was nothing for it but to withdraw the remaining British units to El Alamein, a strong defensive position only sixty miles from Alexandria which Rommel's armour, fiercely harassed all the way by the Royal Air Force under Air Chief Marshal Tedder, was not strong enough to penetrate. But it was a galling and exasperating defeat, for not only had Tobruk been considered impregnable, but the British forces were being continually reinforced. Auchinleck took over direct command from General Ritchie on 25 June, but his days were clearly numbered. To set against these things there was little except the occupation of Madagascar in May (to forestall a Japanese attack), and the heavy but not very effective bombing of German cities, now on the 'thousand bomber' scale.

In India the Japanese advance might have been expected to produce a common front against a common danger. But the deadlock remained. The British government through the Viceroy had continued to affirm Dominion status as the ultimate goal for the country. The Indian princes, the Hindu Liberals, and the Hindu Mahasabha had supported the war, and the Muslim League, which had repudiated federation and committed itself to autonomous 'Pakistan' areas in 1940, was prepared to do so as long as the government safeguarded the rights of minorities. The Congress party leaders, on the other hand, refused participation in the defence of India unless independence was proclaimed and a 'national' government formed. Gandhi in any case insisted that such defence must be non-violent. Sir Stafford Cripps was sent to India by the cabinet in April 1942 to offer full Dominion status with the right to secede as soon as the war was over. But after a fortnight the negotiations had broken down over the Congress leaders' demand for an immediate cabinet government with full power, which neither Cripps nor the British government could contemplate while the war was in progress. So he returned, and Churchill was highly embarrassed, but unyielding, when Roosevelt sent urgent secret representations in support of the Congress's most extreme demands. Under continued British rule and with a loyal Indian army of over a million, India stood ready to resist the Japanese invaders.

Yet, though the overall situation was depressing, it was the shape of the final offensives, the 'proper application of overwhelming force', that now mattered most. Britain had little say in the Pacific war, which was America's concern from the start, and even less in Stalin's plans and strategy. But she was still the dominant partner in western European and Mediterranean affairs in 1942 and 1943.

4. PROBLEMS OF COALITION WARFARE

It has been pointed out in a comparison between the two great war leaders, that if Churchill's domestic conditions were easier than those of Lloyd George, the conditions under which he worked with his allies were in many ways less promising. In this third period of the war (until about the end of 1943) he succeeded by tact and good sense and a high degree of forebearance in building up a unique relationship with Roosevelt, whose wayward impulses and basic isolationism must have been decidedly trying at times. By this stage the military committee system, an improved version of Lloyd George's adaptation of the traditional cabinet system to war needs, was functioning effectively at home under his direction and that of the Chiefs of Staff, and he also succeeded in making it the basis of the highly successful working alliance between the British and American forces.[1] Both governments were eager to work together, and until the Americans were ready to play a major part in the land and air fighting against Germany they could do little except help forward the established British plans. But these were based on the processes of peripheral attack and economic pressure which alone seemed consistent with Allied strength at this stage of the war. Impatient Americans and hard-pressed Russians wanted something more direct and dramatic. In war, as in the diplomacy of the prewar years, the British effort was disappointing to those who chose to overrate her power.

The Americans offered fresh ideas on the making of war, in compensation for their own deficiencies in experience. They had a natural desire to do things in a style of their own. Was not the sturdy and elaborate procedure favoured by the Prime Minister a little too deliberate? Could it be that the war was becoming a habit with the British, that they had slipped into the assumption that the existing balance of forces must continue indefinitely? 'How long

[1] J. Ehrman, 'Lloyd George and Churchill as War Ministers', *Transactions of the Royal Historical Society*, 1961, p. 112.

are we going to fight this war in a gentlemanly manner?' one American official asked the British economic warfare experts in Washington 'rather fiercely' in February 1942. In this instance the Americans were more than half convinced that their own system of control at source or 'blockade outside Europe' was more speedy, ruthless, and efficient than the elaborate British system of carefully regulated imports based on economic intelligence. It was with some difficulty that they accepted the view that the surviving European neutrals must be given minimum supplies and that these must be carefully calculated to prevent their complete absorption in the Axis economy and also to prevent their becoming a channel of supply to Germany.[1]

Both governments were also determined to develop amicable working relations with the Soviet Union, although Roosevelt was not unwilling to divert on to Churchill's head any Soviet suspicion or malice against the capitalist world. 'Stalin hates the guts of all your top people', he told Churchill cheerfully in March 1942. 'He thinks he likes me better, and I hope he will continue to do so.' Certainly the gestures of geniality from London created no reciprocal mood of comradely emotion in Moscow; whether Washington was better regarded seems doubtful.[2] Never losing sight of its immediate or ultimate objectives the Soviet government assessed all approaches from its allies in terms of their practical advantage to itself; and as it wanted a great deal, both for Russia's immediate salvation and for her postwar development, all help and offers of help were met by demands for more, presented bluntly, insistently, and even at times with calculated rudeness. Molotov in particular remained unbending and certainly seemed personally hostile to the British. It was not easy to say whether this was due to the natural rigidities of his unattractive character or to the continuance of the anglophobe tradition which he had represented for so long. To the Foreign Office it seemed that things had changed little since the summer of 1939.

Eden promptly agreed to the signature on 10 July 1941 of an agreement promising full mutual assistance and the conclusion of an armistice or peace treaty only by mutual agreement. By the end of September, when Beaverbrook (Minister of Supply) and Averell Harriman visited Moscow to discuss supply questions, large

[1] On the other hand the Americans were less willing than the British to put pressure on Latin American firms and the government of French North Africa. D. L. Gordon and P. Dangerfield, *The Hidden Weapon* (1947), pp. 181–92.

[2] H. Feis, *Churchill, Roosevelt, Stalin* (1957), pp. 6–24; Churchill, vol. IV, p. 179.

quantities of goods had already been sent from England, including all the available stocks of khaki cloth, 3 million pairs of boots, 22,000 tons of rubber, 450 aircraft, and substantial quantities of minerals. The Russians got down to business quickly over further supplies, but showed no desire to exchange information or even to talk with the British service missions or with General Ismay, who had accompanied Beaverbrook to Moscow. On the other hand, Stalin, Molotov, and Maisky repeatedly asked for some diversionary military action by Great Britain, such as a landing in France or the sending of a large British force to the Russian front via Archangel or Iran. Stalin asked in September for a force of 25–30 divisions. Churchill was forced to reply that it was impossible to send such a force anywhere.

The United States government did not like the Foreign Office's attempt to reassure Stalin by an Anglo-Soviet treaty with rather detailed territorial provisions. Proposals on these lines were put to Eden by Stalin in mid-December 1941; they included not only the Curzon line, with the Baltic states, Bessarabia, northern Bukovina, and Petsamo as permanent Russian acquisitions, but also frontier changes for the rest of Europe. Sumner Welles on behalf of President Roosevelt made strong objections to any commitment before the peace conference. The matter was not settled until 26 May, when Molotov accepted a version of the treaty which provided an Anglo-Soviet pact of mutual assistance for twenty years, but made no reference to frontiers. Molotov was the more ready to fall in with this because of the Soviet government's hopes for a 'second front' in France in 1942, which the Americans, in spite of their own inexperience and unpreparedness, were rash enough to promise.

The result was a long and unnecessary controversy, the cause of much irritability on all sides. The first great strategical decision of the United States administration had been to give priority to the war in Europe. The second, taken after Pearl Harbour, was that the best way to win the war was to invade France in force as soon as possible. It was rightly argued that England had incomparable facilities for mounting a major attack, and its choice as a base would save shipping because the convoy system was fully working on the North Atlantic route. General Marshall took up this idea with great singleness of purpose and in April 1942 came to London with Harry Hopkins and presented a plan for a full-scale invasion of northern France in 1943 (Round-up), with a preliminary landing,

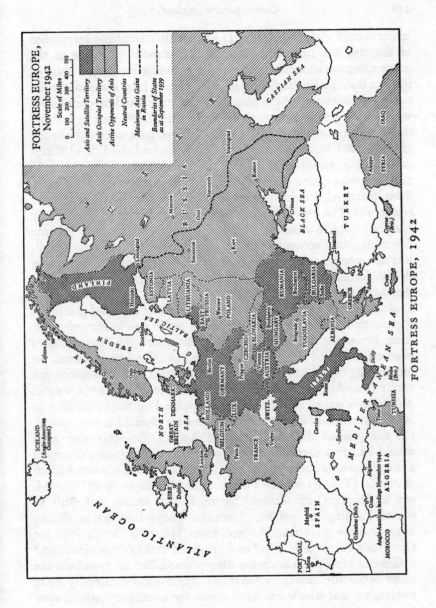

FORTRESS EUROPE, 1942

under certain conditions, in 1942.[1] Churchill's emphatic acceptance of the plan for 1943 was taken as agreement in principle to the much more questionable proposal for a landing in 1942, in spite of the fact that the British Chiefs of Staff seem to have pointed out the technical difficulties of the plan from the start. Landing craft as yet were insufficient to put on shore more than 4,000 men at a time; there were probably at least twenty-five German divisions already stationed in France and the Low Countries, and the United Kingdom, which would have to bear the brunt of the fighting, could not have more than seven mobile divisions ready by September. Two untrained divisions were probably all that the United States could offer. The idea of a 1942 landing had at first been advanced by Marshall only in case the situation on the Russian front became desperate; such action would be 'a sacrifice in the common good'. But as it seemed unlikely that even the destruction of all the available British forces would divert a single German division from Russia the sacrifice would be pointless.

Molotov went on to Washington at the end of May and as a result apparently of his insistence that Russia really was *in extremis* drew from Roosevelt the assurance that Britain and the United States expected to set up the Second Front in 1942. Roosevelt insisted on mentioning '1942' in spite of Marshall's dissent. When Molotov got back to London, however, Churchill took care to give him a written *aide mémoire* stating that everything depended on the availability of landing-craft and 'we can therefore give no promise in the matter'. On the ground that the proposed landing for September 1942 would lead to a disaster without benefit to the Russians, Churchill put to Roosevelt later in June the rival advantages of a North African operation (TORCH) and the President, inclined to be 'leery' (according to Hopkins) of a trans-Channel frontal attack, and with an overriding urge to get the American troops into action during 1942, insisted on a firm decision from Marshall. On 24 July the Combined Chiefs of Staff in London agreed to the African invasion.[2]

General Marshall was deeply disappointed. But he must bear the main blame for raising expectations which were technically quite unjustified, and which tended to create the equally unjustified view that the British, who were forced into the position of saying no,

[1] Woodward, p. 196; Sherwood, vol. II, p. 533.
[2] J. R. M. Butler, *Grand Strategy*, vol. III (2) chap. 24; Ismay, *Memoirs* (1960), pp. 248–60; A. Bryant, *The Turn of the Tide* (1957), pp. 352–62; M. Matloff and E. M. Snell, *Strategic Planning for Coalition Warfare* (1953), pp. 180–9.

were less bold or courageous than their allies.[1] Churchill, with his usual stoutheartedness, undertook to explain the position to Stalin in August, only to be asked why he was afraid of the Germans. Stalin's manners improved later in the conversation when the plans for TORCH were explained to him. Churchill affirmed the plan for an invasion of northern France in 1943 (ROUND-UP).[2]

The essential reason why it did not take place in 1943 is that the build-up of landing craft and U.S. forces in England was almost completely suspended for the next twelve months. Why this happened was never entirely clear to the British, whose insistent reminders of the difficulties of operations in France were meant to stimulate the Americans to send adequate forces, but were regarded in Washington as further proof of British halfheartedness. The slowing down of American supplies seems to have been due partly to shipping difficulties, partly to Marshall's defeatist assumption (announced as early as 24 July 1942) that Mediterranean operations would mean the indefinite postponement of the cross-Channel enterprise, and partly to the diversion of forces, and particularly of landing craft, to the Pacific. A strongly worded note to the C.O.S. on 18 November 1942 shows Churchill's reluctance to accept the argument that TORCH had prevented ROUND-UP in 1943. In another note on 3 December he again insisted on the need for, and feasibility of, an invasion of France in August or September 1943, regretted the contrary opinion of the American Staffs, and urged the need to keep the promise to Russia.[3]

A further reason for not postponing the final assault was that British mobilization and war production were now approaching their peak, and at a ruinous cost which it was not desirable to continue longer than necessary. Aircraft production was over 26,000 a year in 1943 and 1944, as compared with 8,000 in 1939 and 20,000 in 1941, and the motor trade, in addition to its contribution to aircraft production, was called on to supply tanks, tracked carriers, and army vehicles of every description. 600,000 tons of

[1] 'The United States could not go ahead with the 1942–1943 invasion if England played the reluctant dragon.' S. E. Morison, *American Contributions to the Strategy of World War II* (1958), p. 23.
[2] Churchill, vol. IV, pp. 425–45.
[3] Churchill, vol. IV, pp. 582–90. Trumbull Higgins (p. 191), says that Churchill had a 'significant if subconscious fear of an absolute decision in a general war' and 'staved off the continuing possibility of a campaign across the Channel from 1941 to 1944'. Cf. S. E. Morison, p. 36; H. Feis, *Churchill, Roosevelt, Stalin*, p. 51. All the evidence suggests that the British accepted the case for the cross-Channel invasion, but understood the technical difficulties, while Marshall wanted it but did not understand them.

naval and landing craft were launched in 1943, as compared with 260,000 in 1940.[1]

These and similar peaks of production had been attained only as the result of drastic rationing of domestic and non-essential commercial consumption and of manpower. In the end, as stocks accumulated and the shipping problem became easier with the conquest of the U-boat, manpower became the decisive shortage, and the government's manpower budgeting provided the machinery for the central planning of the whole economy during the last phase of the war. The total working population reached its peak at 22,286,000 in 1943, and was to decline to 21,649,000 by 1945. Men and women in the armed forces numbered 4,762,000 in June 1943, and had risen to 5,090,000 by June 1945. In the engineering and chemical industries numbers had risen from 3,106,000 in June 1939 to the peak figure of 5,233,000 in June 1943, and in a second group, including such basic industries as agriculture, shipping, land transport, and coal there had been an increase from 4,683,000 in June 1939 to 5,027,000 in June 1943. These increases had been made possible partly by the conscription of women, which was introduced in December 1941 and applied at first to those between 20 and 30 years of age, then to those between $18\frac{1}{2}$ and $45\frac{1}{2}$ and then, in 1943, to women up to 50. They were also the result of the drastic curtailment of employment in the less-essential industries, including food, drink, tobacco, textiles, clothing, building, civil engineering, banking and others. In these the total figure fell from over 10,000,000 in June 1939 to 6,861,000 in June 1943 and 6,574,000 in June 1944.[2]

These adjustments, which involved constant practical difficulties in the transfer of labour, housing, and the most economical use of key personnel, were handled with great efficiency by the Ministry of Labour. Labour relations were, generally speaking, much better than in the First World War. A great trade union leader was Minister of Labour, and after June 1941 the Communist leaders supported the war instead of harrying the war effort with 'unofficial' movements. Not that strikes could be altogether avoided. Bevin believed that a wave of strikes in the autumn and winter of 1943-4 was politically inspired, sometimes by Trotskyists.[3]

In any case, good administration was not enough. Programmes

[1] S. Pollard, *The Development of the British Economy*, pp. 308-13; Postan, pp. 207-27; Hancock and Gowing, pp. 438-52.
[2] *Ibid.*, pp. 312-4, 351, 456-62.
[3] V. L. Allen, *Trade Unions and the Government*, pp. 143-4.

had frequently to be revised to meet the ever changing character of the war and there was an overall manpower shortage, which Russia and the United States did not suffer or perhaps fully understand. A crisis at the end of 1942 had to be met by cuts in the estimates of the armed services. A comprehensive enquiry by the Lord President had shown a gap of over a million between the demands from the services and industry for additional man (or woman) power for 1943 and the supply. It was evident that the less essential industries could not yield more than half a million without serious damage to the minimum civilian and export requirements. The cuts, which the Prime Minister himself proposed, meant a slowing down of the rate of expansion and not a net loss except in the case of civil defence, which was reduced by 75,000; the Army received an increase of 429,000 instead of 809,000, the R.A.F. 247,000 instead of 472,000, and so on. This manpower budget for 1943 was agreed to in December 1942, with an appeal from the Prime Minister to his colleagues to use 'the best housekeeping ingenuity'.

Fortunately United States help was just becoming a reality in munitions supply, after the first months of American belligerency when it appeared that all supplies and production would be used up in meeting the dramatically high objectives announced by the President in January 1942. In some cases these were vastly in excess of the probable needs and would tie up plant and labour and raw materials unprofitably. In June a Combined Productions and Resources Board was set up charged to work out a joint (Anglo-American) production programme for the two countries which would fulfil, but not needlessly exceed, probable requirements. Even with this careful planning, however, there soon developed new demands and shortages. The casualty rate in the Army mounted with the continuous heavy fighting in the Mediterranean in 1943. But with the overall decline in the country's population the employable portion would fall by 150,000 in 1944.

Thus Britain was fully mobilized by 1943 and her peak mobilization had been admirably timed to bring the war in Europe to an end not later than 1944. If it continued longer the American share would have to be progressively increased both in munition supply and in the field. The War Cabinet decided in the summer of 1943 to work out plans on the assumption that victory would be achieved in 1944. They could do this because in two fields the war had now taken a decisively favourable turn.

The first was at sea. The shipping crisis in the Atlantic was continuous from Pearl Harbour until the spring of 1943; with America's entry into the war the U-boats could attack without restraint, and the British losses were so heavy that only a quarter of them could be met from new British shipbuilding. The inexperienced American defences had been no match for the German submarines, and the Admiralty, at the cost of further reductions in British imports, had had to supply escort vessels to help build up an effective convoy system off the eastern seaboard of the United States. During the second half of 1942 United States shipbuilding on a great scale began to overhaul losses, but these nevertheless continued at a high rate. Admiral Doenitz's fleet, bold and well equipped, more than maintained its own numbers. Allied sinkings rose to 700,000 tons in March 1943. The problem was then rapidly solved, mainly by the short-wave radar device known as H_2S. This was an entirely British invention which had begun to be used with success in the air bombing of Germany, where the longer waves of the earlier radar had been picked up and used by the Germans to detect approaching aircraft. At sea the U-boats had similarly learned to dive in good time. Bomber Command was persuaded to supply Coastal Command with some of these instruments, and with increased firing power began to destroy the U-boats in large numbers —in May 1943 forty were sunk in the Atlantic alone. But if this was the main cause of victory in the battle of the Atlantic it was not the only one. German attacks on the North Atlantic convoys ceased in June, and although Doenitz strove desperately for a comeback he was never able to recover the initiative. In the meantime the President had given a firm promise of sufficient American shipping to carry 7 million tons of imports to Britain in 1943.

The other and more spectacular victory was in North Africa, where Axis military power was finally crushed in May 1943. This was predominantly a British achievement, although the Americans had most of the political limelight. Perhaps the real turn in the Egyptian struggle took place at midnight on 28 June 1942, when the 4th New Zealand Brigade, 'with all its battalions deployed and bayonets fixed' routed its German opponents 'in hand-to-hand fighting under the moon'.[1] The New Zealand Division, freed from Rommel's trap, reassembled in a high state of discipline at the strong El Alamein position, where Auchinleck had successfully

[1] Churchill, vol. IV, p. 382.

withdrawn the Xth, XIIIth, and XXXth Corps, and reinforced them with other troops. The British forces seemed bewildered rather than depressed, exasperated at their recent unexpected reverses. In local counterattacks in July Auchinleck more than held his own against Rommel's depleted forces.

There followed three months of quiescence during which both sides built up their strength; and in Auchinleck's place there were now appointed General Alexander to be Commander-in-Chief in the Near East, with General Gott to command the Eighth Army under him. After Gott's death on 7 August, General Montgomery took his place on the 8th. Auchinleck was offered and declined the newly created post of Commander-in-Chief, Middle East. Alexander, with a justifiably high reputation for his masterly extrication of the British forces from Burma (March-May 1942) and with precious gifts of energy and composure, good humour and drive, inspired confidence at once in the supreme command, while Montgomery, little known to the British public as yet, was soon to vindicate the high expectations of the experts in his skill as a field commander. It is well to remember, however, in fairness to their predecessors, that the British forces were at last in a position to fight with an equality or superiority of strength, in that stage of our wars in which, in Lord Tedder's words, 'after some years of lavish expenditure' the Commander knows that he can more or less 'count on a blank cheque'.[1] Everything now went well: after severe fighting (23 October to 4 November 1942) Montgomery with his heavily armed forces won a grim battle of attrition at El Alamein, and followed it up with a well-planned but somewhat deliberate advance which included the capture of Benghazi on 20 November. He was approaching Tripoli by the end of the year. It may well be, as some critics have argued, that the advance was too slow. But victory was more important than speed; and Montgomery did not wish to make the journey again.[2] In the meantime Torch had been launched with successful landings at Casablanca, Oran, and Algiers on 8 November.

The first experiment in Anglo-American military cooperation had not been brought about without much initial argument between the two governments and their experts. The Americans, overbold in their ideas when it was a question of committing predominantly

---

[1] Tedder, *Air Power in War* (1948), p. 25, quoted Butler, *Grand Strategy*, vol. II, xvii.
[2] M. Carver, *El Alamein* (1962).

British forces to a premature invasion of northern France, drew back with some alarm at the proposal to commit their own forces to operations inside the Mediterranean. General Eisenhower, who was designated early in August 1942 Commander-in-Chief for the TORCH operation seconded by General Alexander (rapidly replaced by Montgomery and then by General K. A. N. Anderson), seems to have agreed from the start to the more extended attack. Churchill's expostulations and the general dictates of common sense brought the President round to the view that there must be landings in strength in both Algeria and Morocco, that is, at Algiers, Oran, and Casablanca. On this basis the plans went forward, with Gibraltar as the only available base. The enterprise was to be entirely under American direction in the first stages owing to the belief that there would be serious resistance only to a British attack. The accidental appearance of Darlan both complicated and simplified matters. The British had little say in the political decisions until the appointment of Mr. Harold Macmillan as Minister Resident in late December.

In the meantime the British First Army was hurriedly pushed forward and captured Medjez-el-Bab and Tebourba, twenty miles from the town of Tunis, on 26 November, but the Germans poured in reinforcements, and for a time the Allied forces could do no more than hold on. In particular the IInd U.S. Army Corps sustained a heavy defeat in February 1943. The arrival of the Eighth Army on the southern border of Tunisia transformed the situation. Under Eisenhower's general command Alexander took charge of all the Allied forces in the field at the end of February, with Cunningham in charge at sea and Tedder in the air. Large forces were involved on both sides, including some twelve British divisions and three American, and the final complete collapse of the German-Italian resistance on 13 May 1943 was a major Allied victory. There were more than a quarter of a million prisoners.[1]

At the Casablanca conference in January 1943 it was agreed without much difficulty that the invasion of Sicily should follow the North African campaign, and that powerful American forces should be built up in England as quickly as possible for the cross-Channel attack (soon to be called OVERLORD), which was to take place if possible in August 1943. Churchill fully supported this last proposal, which was inserted to satisfy General Marshall; Brooke

---

[1] Viscount Montgomery, *From El Alamein to the River Sangro* (1948); A. Bryant, *The Turn of the Tide* (1959), pp. 645-7.

and the British C.O.S., while favouring the cross-Channel attack, believed that it would be impossible for logistical reasons at so early a date. But the conference left unsolved the problem of a continuous offensive in the west. Marshall had been given a date and a definite programme for the movement of troops. But in practice he failed to implement it; of the 80,000 American troops promised by the end of March only 15,000 arrived, and even these had to be brought over in British ships. The bulk of the United States Navy was in the Pacific, with larger land and air forces than had been sent to Europe, and Marshall seems to have acquiesced in this situation, in spite of the 'Europe first' principle. It appears that Marshall would have preferred to close down operations in the Mediterranean, transfer all available divisions to England, and thus abandon all initiative until the date, possibly the spring of 1944, when the cross-Channel invasion could be launched.[1]

Alan Brooke's programme carried the day because it provided for continuous action. He wished to follow the capture of Sicily with an invasion of Italy which would drive her out of the war and draw German forces into Italy and the Balkans, thus relieving the German pressure on Russia and at the same time facilitating the cross-Channel operation. This programme was revealed at the TRIDENT conference at Washington in May 1943. Marshall continued to argue and perhaps to believe that the 'interminable' operations in the Mediterranean would tie up the available forces in a minor sphere, indefinitely delay the build-up for OVERLORD, and perhaps be pursued by the British for political ends, and he still seemed to fear that it would endanger the Anglo-American forces because of a possible German drive through Spain. The more volubly Brooke, who talked much too fast for the Americans, pointed out the technical difficulties of operations in France and the need for the diversion of German forces elsewhere, the more convinced were Marshall and Stimson, the Secretary of State for War, that the British were lukewarm about OVERLORD anyway. But on 19 May it was agreed to prepare some twenty-nine divisions for an entry into France early in 1944, and in the meantime to continue pressure in the Mediterranean.

This satisfied Brooke and half-satisfied Marshall, but there had been nothing to prevent the continued diversion of American

---

[1] Bryant, *ibid.*, pp. 601, 607; Kennedy, *The Business of War*, pp. 276-86; J. Ehrman, *Grand Strategy* (1956), vol. V, pp. 115-8.

assault and landing craft, indispensable to the French and Italian landings, to the Pacific. The invasion of Sicily began on 10 July, and British troops set foot in Italy on 3 September. But at the Quebec conference in August the debate started again. The extent to which the two governments were at cross purposes is shown by the fact that while the British delegation, armed with elaborate plans, were determined to thrash out the practical details of the cross-Channel invasion, the Americans came determined to insist that the invasion should take place. By this stage the British were immersed in ingenious arrangements, elaborated by Cossac during the summer, with plans for mulberry harbours, floating breakwaters, a device of sunken pipes to provide a continuous stream of air bubbles which would diminish wave action, and the rest; they were convinced that a successful invasion would be impossible unless the Americans sent adequate forces and landing craft. The Americans were still saying that unless the British were more enthusiastic it would be useless to send the necessary forces.[1]

The mental processes, which had led Marshall, Hopkins, and others (although not all their advisers) to assume from the first signs of British dissent in May 1942 that matters of political interest and national psychology were involved in the purely technical objections of Brooke and others to SLEDGEHAMMER, were due less to conscious competitiveness than to automatic concentration on a strategy which would most quickly ensure American preponderance. Perhaps it was inevitable, given the national temperament, the vast resources, and the sense of unlimited power to achieve, that when the United States did choose to fight she should think of victory as primarily a function of production: vote the money, fix the necessary figures in tanks, guns, aircraft carriers, divisions, landing craft, planes, and then hurl them in overwhelming force at the enemy as soon as possible, in the most convenient field for their deployment. It is significant perhaps that Marshall, who seemed to the British to be so unconcerned about the more detailed strategical planning, should nevertheless have so satisfied all the Americans as to his adequacy. The reason was that he was doing a fine job at home in raising, training, and equipping great armies: this seemed the supreme task. Where he and those influenced by him seemed to be

---

[1] Bryant, *ibid.*, pp. 692–718; Sir Frederick Morgan, *Overture to Overlord* (1950), pp. 104–22; Churchill, vol. V, pp. 72–6; H. L. Stimson and McG. Bundy, *On Active Service in Peace and War* (1947), pp. 436–40.

at fault was in telescoping the timetable of production, for while they were unable to bring the full American material predominance to bear the more meticulous and more pessimistic British approach, with its juggling with limited forces, retained its validity. The British did not take the view at Casablanca and Quebec that the time for heavy fighting had not yet arrived, but rather that it had already begun in North Africa, and that the momentum must not be relaxed. Nevertheless, it may well be asked whether this intense concentration on the softening-up process was not a partial waste of time, in view of the American ability to steamroller its way forward when it chose to do so.

Brooke's dedication to OVERLORD is sufficiently testified by his readiness to take the command of the Allied forces, which Churchill had promised him. But Churchill now decided that it would be a statesmanlike gesture to offer the command to General Marshall or some other American, on the ground that in due course the American forces would predominate in the operation. He seemed unaware of Brooke's disappointment.[1] Roosevelt accepted Churchill's suggestion at once. The Quebec conference did in the end make detailed plans for the invasion. The date was to be 1 May 1944. The operation was to have first call on the British and American ground and air forces. Divisions and landing craft were to be withdrawn from the Mediterranean according to a fixed timetable. Events in Italy also gave the American leaders a political excuse to retreat from their over rigid attitude to further Mediterranean operations. Mussolini fell on 25 July 1943, and on 15 August the provisional government offered to join the Allies against Germany as soon as Allied armies landed in Italy. The conference therefore decided that Rome should be captured, that Corsica and Sardinia should be seized, and that help should be given to Balkan insurgents.

In the meantime relations with Stalin had not improved. He took badly the decision to invade Italy and postpone the cross-Channel invasion. The failure to bring Hess to immediate trial as a war criminal was considered highly suspicious by the Moscow press. There were rumours at this period of Soviet-German peace feelers.[2]

[1] Ehrman, vol. V, pp. 118–21; Bryant, p. 716.
[2] One of Ribbentrop's personal aides, Dr. Peter Kleist, following an earlier account in German in 1950, describes obscure Soviet approaches in June and September 1943 in *European Tragedy* (1965), but he does not mention the meeting between Ribbentrop and Molotov which is supposed to have taken place at Kirovograd, then inside the German lines, apparently in June 1943 also. Captain Liddell Hart, who was told of this meeting by a German officer who claimed to have been present, has kindly given me

There were said to have been 'scorching' exchanges between Stalin and Churchill in June 1943, and then silence from Moscow in July. The heavy repulse of the final German offensive at Kursh which followed was the beginning of the end for Hitler. Although developments in Italy, culminating in the decision of the new Badoglio government in September to conclude an armistice, were reported to Moscow as fully as circumstances allowed, Stalin again took things ill, and seemed convinced that he had been kept in the dark. Churchill and Roosevelt accordingly felt the need for closer contact with him, and were relieved that the meeting of foreign ministers in Moscow (19–30 October) proceeded fairly amicably. It affirmed the case for the invasion of France in 1944. This was the background of the Teheran conference, which took place amid continued Anglo-American differences over Mediterranean strategy. Although the Germans had rapidly built up their position in Italy to nineteen divisions by mid-October, 80 per cent of the Allied assault shipping and seven divisions were to be withdrawn from the Mediterranean during the following two months, and would then remain idle for six months. Washington finally agreed grudgingly to delay the withdrawal of the assault craft until December, but offered adamantine opposition to Churchill's plan to capture Rhodes.

The Teheran conference (28 November–1 December 1943) was the first attended by all three Allied leaders; the first also at which a broad plan for victory could be drawn up. In spite of this it is the political relationship between the three men that is of most significance today. Roosevelt continued until the end of his life, and his successor continued for a few weeks thereafter, to believe that Stalin had no expansionist aims and that, suitably handled, he would 'work for a world of democracy and peace'. He sought to win Stalin's confidence by nimbly poking fun at Churchill, and hinting at differences of outlook.[1] At the plenary and staff conversations the Russians followed their cue and pleased the Americans by minimizing the value of Mediterranean operations and insisting on the paramount importance of the invasion of northern France. Their

details of this story, which is also referred to in his *Defence of the West* (1950), chap. iv. Kleist's contact in Stockholm brought the conversations to an end by saying that the 'clever Roosevelt' had outbid Germany at Teheran (p. 174).

[1] 'No man of greatness ever placed his temper at the service of a good cause more admirably than Churchill' (H. Feis, *Churchill, Roosevelt, Stalin* (1957), p. 276). 'Though the rôle of attendant listener was uncongenial to him, the Prime Minister played it faultlessly all these days' (Avon, *The Reckoning*, p. 426).

main contribution was to plump for an additional invasion of southern France, a plan which the Americans had considered only tentatively. It can be assumed that the Russians saw clearly enough that the alternative might be an Anglo-American advance from Italy into Austria and the Balkans, which Roosevelt rather surprisingly supported at one stage. The conference had also before it a proposal, resulting from a promise made by Roosevelt to Chiang Kai-shek without consulting the British or his military advisers, for a large amphibious operation (BUCCANEER) in south-east Asia during the next few months. This would involve British forces and take landing craft from the Mediterranean and was clearly incompatible with OVERLORD. And yet, as Churchill told Stalin in a private talk on 30 November which corrected many of the American insinuations, the issue between himself and the Americans was really very slight. There were adequate troops to carry out both OVERLORD and the southern French attack and the British plans in the Mediterranean; the bottleneck was still landing craft.

Stalin spoke frankly when he said that only a landing in France would sustain the morale of the Red Army, and was evidently satisfied with a firm assurance that it would take place 'during' May 1944. On his part he promised to join in the war against Japan as soon as Germany was defeated. The other definite agreements were that the advance in Italy should continue to the Pisa–Rimini line north of Rome and that for this purpose the 68 L.S.T.s due to be sent to the United Kingdom for OVERLORD should be kept in the Mediterranean until 15 January 1944; and that an operation should be mounted against the south of France at the same time as OVERLORD on as big a scale as landing craft permitted. At subsequent discussions between the Combined C.O.S. in Cairo the unwelcome operation BUCCANEER was dropped, and Roosevelt undertook the embarrassing task of breaking the news to Chiang Kai-shek. The Soviet promise to fight Japan had greatly helped the Far Eastern plans with the prospect of bases for bombing the Japanese islands.[1]

5. VICTORY AT A PRICE

It was a reasonable assumption in Allied discussions at Teheran that the Germans had shot their bolt. But Hitler was able to gal-

[1] Ehrman, vol. V, chap. IV; Churchill, vol. V, chaps. 19–22; Bryant, *Triumph in the West*, pp. 68–101; H. Feis, pp. 269–79; *Foreign Relations of the United States: The Conferences of Cairo and Teheran, 1943* (1961).

vanize his battered but still formidable resources, and to counter demands for unconditional surrender with orders for unqualified defiance. He was prepared to die, and for Germany to die with him, amid the ruin of his ambitions; but faith and astrology sustained his belief that he would triumph in the end. Had not Frederick survived a seven-years' battering? The allies as a result were unable to finish the war in 1944.

For Great Britain, as her preparations for the invasion of Europe were increasingly intertwined with those of the United States, there was an embarrassing increase in Anglo-American differences on a number of issues. There was no desire to deny the United States government the preponderant rôle in postwar affairs and even in wartime strategy that Roosevelt had designed for it, but it was possible to question the wisdom of some of the American decisions. Moreover, the signs of reviving isolationism were disquieting.

The Foreign Economic Administration (the final form of the economic warfare machinery) incorporated the Office of Lend-Lease Administration in September 1943 and made no secret of its intention to protect American interests even against the British. In October it was decided that various capital goods, including machine tools and petroleum equipment, were not eligible for lend-lease. The list was later extended to include certain off-shore purchases, pulp and paper, and tobacco for the armed forces. Although in 1942 Britain and the Commonwealth had granted 'reverse lend-lease' on terms which represented a greater sacrifice and a higher proportion of the national income than the American, the British position remained that of 'the dependent partner receiving aid'. The zealous F.E.A. officials were determined to keep the British dollar balances down to the minimum adequate figure, which the President fixed at $1,000 million. The Administration recognized that Britain had an unfunded sterling debt standing at about 10 billion dollars, mainly incurred in paying for goods and services from countries of the British Commonwealth and Egypt with whom lend-lease and mutual-aid arrangements were impracticable. But they did not regard this as America's responsibility.[1]

---

[1] The President's decision involved a reduction from $1,600 million in February 1944. Churchill protested strongly on 9 March, pointing out that these dollar balances were 'our total reserves' and that Britain had 'incurred for the common cause liabilities of at least ten billions'. Also that 'France had at least two billions and no overseas liabilities against them'. *Foreign Relations of the United States, 1944* (1965), vol. III, pp. 45–6.

The new policy took insufficient account of the British need for dollar balances for some classes of wartime expenditure and no account of the disproportionate weakening of British assets abroad during the first three years of the war when the United States was more generous in good wishes than in deeds. The financing of an extensive programme of Anglo-American pre-emptive purchases in Turkey early in 1944 was, for example, hampered on the British side by dollar shortage. The extent of 'reverse lend-lease' was little known. In this as in a number of other fields the American contribution, in proportion to its total resources, was smaller than the British; owing to the acclaim that 'lend-lease' had received in London its extent and liberality were exaggerated. Much greater latitude was given to Soviet Russia by its American suppliers.[1]

It also happened that 1944 was an election year, and Congressional criticism was no doubt feared. There were other embarrassing consequences. Roosevelt refused to associate himself with any arrangement about Poland until after the election. Cordell Hull early in 1944 made a popular issue of the decision that supplies to the small European neutrals should be cut off unless they in turn ceased to supply Germany. As they feared reprisals by Germany, they wished to continue at least token exports. Only after strong messages from Churchill was Roosevelt finally induced to accept compromise terms. An agitation for food relief for civilians in occupied German territory was revived; they were assumed (quite erroneously) to be starving. In March 1944 the Administration decided that it could no longer resist this pressure and Roosevelt telegraphed to Churchill to propose substantial imports, leaving to the British government the onus of refusal. The preparations for OVERLORD made any such import programme quite impracticable. Churchill was criticized nevertheless in the American press and Senate for callousness in this matter.

So these symptoms of Allied tension, due partly perhaps to the mere irritation of prolonged human contact, accumulated as the staffs of the two armies elaborated their plans for the invasion. Here the men at the top excelled themselves in sweetness and *bon-*

---

[1] Medlicott, pp. 413–5; Hancock and Gowing, pp. 243–7. The White Paper of 10 September 1941 (Cmd 6311), under which Britain promised unilaterally not to use materials supplied under lease-lend for production for export, was not allowed to be forgotten by the U.S. officials. Lease-lend itself, by temporarily removing the need for dollar earnings, resulted in the fall of British exports to a bare minimum. Cf. H. Duncan Hall and C. C. Wrigley, *Studies of Overseas Supply* (1956), chap. 8.

homie, and if the continued difficulty of extracting naval units from Admiral King kept some anxieties alive it was hardly possible any longer to make this an Anglo-American issue.[1]

British relations with Russia, on the other hand, had no real warmth, and always seemed on the edge of deterioration. As soon as the Russian forces crossed the Polish frontier in January 1944 the Polish government in exile in London asserted its position as the sole legal steward and spokesman of the Polish nation and its desire for the re-establishment of Polish sovereignty in the 'liberated territories of the Republic'. This was not well received in Moscow, where the Russian government insisted on the Curzon line as the future Russo-Polish frontier. Nor did it show at first any readiness to negotiate with and resume diplomatic relations with the Polish government until it had purged itself of 'pro-fascist imperialist elements'. Churchill, and the Foreign Office following him a little reluctantly, was prepared to accept the Russian case for the Curzon line, although while trying to persuade the Poles to give in on this point he urged Stalin to accept the Polish government, leaving the question of its reconstruction until after its return to Poland. Stalin refused these terms on 3 March 1944, and there was little progress for some months. In April Churchill decided that his 'courteous and even effusive approaches' were actually having a bad effect and that it would be best for the time being to 'relapse into a moody silence as far as Stalin is concerned'. In the meantime the Russian-sponsored 'Committee of National Liberation', set up in December 1943, had established itself at Lublin, and seemed to foreshadow the setting up of a Communist régime; this was denied by the Russian government, but it was ominous that the Polish underground movement, controlled from London, was continually being accused of hostility to the Russian advance.[2]

However, the rather uneasy relations between the Big Three were largely concealed from Hitler and the British public, and the summer brought great military triumphs for all the allied arms. The Anglo-American forces, slogging away in Italy under General Alexander, captured Rome on 4 June 1944 and had reached Florence early in August. On the night of 5–6 June British and American forces, in roughly equal numbers and under the operational command of General Montgomery and the supreme command of General

---

[1] Ehrman, vol. V, chap. VIII.
[2] Woodward, pp. 249–55, 278–90; Avon, pp. 421–42.

Eisenhower, landed on Normandy beaches in the Baie de la Seine. On 10 June on the eastern front, where 300 Russian divisions faced a weakened but still formidable Wehrmacht of some 200 divisions, an offensive against Finland was launched as the first of a series of Russian offensives all along the line.[1]

All the campaigns progressed well, but it was not found possible to overcome the tenacious resistance of the battered German forces in 1944. There was a moment in September when it seemed that Montgomery's northern advance would sweep into the Rhineland and achieve a rapid victory, but the chance, if it really existed, was lost, not without further Anglo-American recriminations. There had been some anxiety after the first landings when the Germans had concentrated strong forces to defend Caen; Eisenhower had fears of a stalemate while Montgomery was quite satisfied to hold the Germans at this point in order to give the American forces corresponding freedom of movement further west. The policy of pinning down the mass of enemy resistance was highly successful. After slow progress for some time in the Normandy bocage General Bradley's forces were able to sweep forward against comparatively light opposition, and then to swing east. As the Germans under Hitler's stringent orders decided to hold their position in the Falaise-Argentan area there followed a great battle of encirclement in August which just failed to become a second Stalingrad, although the Germans lost heavily. They again lost heavily, particularly in equipment, in getting their shattered forces across the Seine.[2]

Montgomery, believing the Germans to be disorganized and off balance, now pressed on Eisenhower the case for a powerful drive of forty divisions into Germany, either north to the Rhine on either side of the Ruhr, or further south to the Rhine between Frankfurt and Karlsruhe. He preferred the former (which he would lead); Bradley pressed the other. It was generally agreed that allied supplies would not be sufficient for both. But Eisenhower now took charge of the grouped forces from Montgomery and decided to advance along the whole broad front. Some emotional and even political factors were involved: American opinion, it would seem, would be

[1] The British share is dealt with expertly by J. Ehrman, *Grand Strategy*, vol. V, pp. 337-47, and by L. F. Ellis, *Victory in the West* (H.M.S.O., 1962). More personal treatments are those of Dwight D. Eisenhower, *Crusade in Europe* (1948); A. Bryant, *Triumph in the West* (1959); Viscount Montgomery, *Memoirs* (1958). Chester Wilmot, *The Struggle for Europe* (first published 1952), is still the most exciting of the shorter accounts.

[2] L. F. Ellis, pp. 491-6.

disgruntled if the American forces were limited for a time to a holding operation similar to that which the British had performed to their advantage at Caen. But the decision was also due in part to the American conception of warfare in which timing was relatively unimportant and victory followed irresistibly the accumulation of overwhelming force. Unfortunately with harbour facilities still inadequate and supply routes disrupted this would take too long; and when Eisenhower did give limited priority to the northern advance, Patton, ignoring or defying the needs of the northern group of forces, continued across the Meuse and attacked Metz. On 22 September Eisenhower decided to shift the main American effort northward to support Montgomery's advance, but by this stage the Germans under Model's rigorous direction had pulled themselves together and the Allied momentum was insufficient for the great breakthrough. By mid-December Hitler had even collected twenty-eight divisions for a counterattack in the Ardennes which caused some anxious moments and was finally held after Montgomery had taken charge, with irritating aplomb, of the Anglo-American forces north of the break through.[1]

The final stage was as much a matter of political as of military manœuvre. Churchill knew—up to a point—what to look for in postwar Europe, and he was increasingly uneasy over Russian aims and American aimlessness. 'When wolves are about the shepherd must guard his flock, even if he does not care for mutton', he wrote later of his complacent Transatlantic allies, and he confesses that in the hour of victory he moved amid cheering crowds 'with an aching heart and a mind oppressed by forebodings'.[2] Having a well-founded suspicion that the Russians would permanently dominate whatever lands they occupied he was concerned to place the Anglo-American forces advantageously at the moment of victory; but the United States soldiers were indifferent to these considerations, and the diplomatists positively alarmed by them. Stalin agreed in May 1944 to a suggestion by Churchill that as Russia was taking the lead in policy in Rumania, Britain should do the same in Greece; but when it appeared that the Americans disliked the proposal, Stalin drew back, and Churchill was annoyed at the 'pedantic interference of the United States'. Since Teheran Roosevelt was visualizing himself more and more as a mediator

[1] Ehrman, vol. V, pp. 379–82.
[2] Churchill, vol. VI, pp. 399–400.

between European rivals of whom the British were possibly the
more sinister. He could see some hope for a future guided by international agreement, and no future for a world which relapsed into
nationalist rivalries; and Stalin seemed more ready at the moment to
talk in these terms than Churchill. But the truth of the matter is
that the Americans had not worked out their plans for Europe as
thoroughly as they had done for the Far East. Thus although the
specific issues that arose were all concerned with Communist
advance westward in various forms Roosevelt seemed to the British
ministers to be curiously unwilling to regard this as a matter of
immediate urgency. He tried without success to interest Stalin in
July 1944 in a tripartite meeting in Scotland, which would have
helped his election prospects. Throughout the autumn of 1944
domestic politics continued to influence American policy in Europe
at many points.

Churchill was profoundly anxious for agreement with Stalin;
his more realistic understanding of Communist aims did not exclude
the hope and belief that in a hard-headed way a permanent *modus
vivendi* could be reached. He had been too loyal to the Anglo-
American partnership to seek to win Stalin's confidence by any
disparagement of the third partner, but was prepared to go a long
way in pressure on the Poles. Russian plans for the postwar Polish
frontiers were therefore accepted in substance, and in July he told
Mikolajczyk, the Polish Prime Minister, that the Russian-sponsored
'Committee of National Liberation' were neither quislings nor
communists. At the same time he urged Stalin to come to terms with
the Polish Underground Movement. Stalin continued to question
the authority and fighting qualities of the Movement and of the
Polish government in London, but he advised Mikolajczyk to come
to terms with the Committee, and disclaimed any desire to 'com-
munize' Poland. Mikolajczyk had three meetings with the Committee early in August, without making any headway.[1]

In the meantime the tragedy of the Warsaw resistance was prepared when General Bor-Komorowski, apparently deceived by a
radio call from Moscow for action, ordered a rising on 1 August
1944. The Russian army was only ten kilometres from the city; it
stayed there for two months while the Germans suppressed the
rising at their leisure. The Soviet reply to appeals from the British
and American governments was to dismiss the rising as the work

[1] Woodward, p. 298.

of criminals and adventurers, and even to refuse facilities for the dropping of supplies for some weeks, although this was agreed to in September, when it was too late to save the rebels. The Soviet advance was resumed on 2 October, the day before General Bor-Komorowski's surrender. Failing Scotland and a visit from Stalin, the British and American leaders and their advisers conferred at Quebec in September and agreed without much difficulty on the future strategy of their forces in Europe and Asia. But the Prime Minister could still not convince the Americans of the urgency of agreement with Stalin in order to provide a satisfactory basis of cooperation in postwar Europe. As Roosevelt could not leave the United States before the election he agreed, not very readily, to an immediate visit by Churchill to Russia, but on the understanding that this would be only a preliminary to a subsequent tripartite meeting.[1]

The Moscow meeting (9–18 October 1944) was nevertheless more important than the Yalta conference (4–11 February 1945) in settling the terms of the watchful Anglo-Russian relationship in the immediate postwar period. The Russian armies were already in Rumania and Bulgaria and showing every intention of taking over full control. The Americans still clung to the theory of tripartite responsibility. On 9 October Churchill suggested to Stalin that Russia should have 90 per cent predominance in Rumania, 75 per cent in Bulgaria, 50 per cent each in Yugoslavia and Hungary, and 10 per cent in Greece; the British, in accordance with the United States, would have 90 per cent predominance in Greece, and elsewhere the balance according to the Russian percentages. Stalin genially agreed; Molotov subsequently secured British assent to an 80 per cent Russian share in Hungary and Bulgaria, although, as the Russian occupation authorities soon showed every intention to monopolize all authority when possible, this haggling had little point.[2]

Churchill perhaps gave a decisive turn to the Polish tragedy by insisting that the London Committee should make with Russia the best terms it could, including the acceptance of the Curzon line, as a condition of continued British support. In Greece Stalin kept the bargain, and when the armed attempt of the Communist-controlled E.A.M.–E.L.A.S. bands to seize power in December was prevented

[1] *Ibid.*, p. 307.
[2] *Ibid.*, pp. 306–13; Avon, pp. 480–8.

by the British occupation forces he accepted the result more readily than the Americans. There was also a sharp difference between London and Washington at this time over Italy. After the British government had made known its objection to the accession to high office of Count Sforza, Mr. Stettinius, the newly-appointed Secretary of State, issued on 5 December what was virtually a public rebuke to the British for interfering in the internal affairs of Greece and Italy. Some stiff exchanges followed in which recent American policy in Argentina and Sweden did not escape comment.[1]

So, as victory approached, its uncomfortable consequences were becoming evident to the British ministers, and were a damper on hopes of an easy future. Nevertheless, the blue prints of a better world, both at home and abroad, were being sedulously prepared. Plans for a postwar 'Welfare State' were advanced by the co-operative efforts of all the parties, although Labour had gone a long way towards establishing itself as its genuine begetter. Sir William Beveridge presided over the committee of experts which produced the famous Report on *Social Insurance and Allied Services* in November 1942.[2] Its purpose was to abolish all the known causes of want by a complete range of insurance benefits, and it foreshadowed a national health service and family allowances to complete the welfare structure, together with the necessary development of administrative responsibility and the provision of adequate benefits at all stages. A Minister of Reconstruction, Lord Woolton, was appointed in 1943. The government hesitated to accept the level of adequate benefits laid down in the Beveridge proposals, although its own scheme in 1944 was otherwise not greatly different. Beveridge had indeed guarded against excessive cost by an agreement with the Treasury that in the early years the state obligation of the scheme should not exceed £100 million a year. The government showed in its White Paper on *Employment Policy* of 1944 (Cmd 6527) that it preferred to approach the postwar social problem from the standpoint of a full employment policy, which linked up with the need for a great increase in productive effort to raise the level of exports. Beveridge's own plans for full employment, set out in 1944, were considered daring in their promise of a reduction of the postwar unemployment figure to 3 per cent, although in fact

[1] Churchill, vol. VI, 258–9; Woodward, p 402–6
[2] Cmd 6404.

this figure was soon to prove unduly pessimistic.[1] There were new plans and objectives, too, for education and housing.[2]

But it was evident that the country would have to look for international cooperation on a more generous scale than in the prewar years if its economic strength was to be restored and its political influence maintained, and indeed if the welfare state itself was to become a reality. This pointed to a dependence on United States' understanding and goodwill, which was distasteful to some of the isolationists of the Labour party: scouting such pessimism, Aneurin Bevan, in May 1945, issued his own declaration of independence with the observation that the country was, after all, made of coal and surrounded by fish.[3] The Treasury, worried by false optimism in high places, protested in 1944 that 'the time and energy and thought which we are all giving to the Brave New World is wildly disproportionate to what is being given to the Cruel Real World'.[4] Certainly the new international machinery could not be regarded, from Britain's angle, entirely without misgiving.

The United Nations conference at Bretton Woods in the summer of 1944 was the most important in a long series of discussions and negotiations aimed at removing the typical prewar barriers to international trade. Provision was made for the setting up of an International Monetary Fund and a Bank for Reconstruction and Development. The first was intended to solve the problem of international liquidity by establishing a fund to which states would contribute in their own currency and gold in accordance with their economic strength, and from which they could draw proportionately in foreign exchange as needed, subject to safeguards against persistent borrowers and (in America's interest) an overall limit to the availability of dollars. The Fund excluded long-term loans, which were to be the concern of the Bank. The result was to a large extent a triumph for J. M. Keynes's economic ideas and skilful negotiation over a period of years; after that it was essentially an Anglo-American achievement with useful Canadian support. Yet Keynes did not get his way on all points, and in the parallel discussions over commercial policy it was considered that the Americans were taking advantage of their strong financial position to

---

[1] W. H. Beveridge, *Full Employment in a Free Society* (1944); S. Pollard, pp. 348–55; W. K. Hancock and M. M. Gowing, pp. 534–46.
[2] See pp. 564–6 below.
[3] M. Foot, *Aneurin Bevan. A Biography* (1962), vol. I, p. 504.
[4] Hancock and Gowing, p. 542.

attack and castigate the British system of imperial preferences while maintaining the rightfulness of their own system of high tariffs. These negotiations, often highly technical and involving many nations, led to the General Agreement on Tariffs and Trade (G.A.T.T.) of 1947, and much heartburning in the loan negotiations which the Labour government had to conduct after the war.[1]

The special relationship of Britain and the United States had been forged in war; it must continue, although the stronger partner appeared unrealistic and exigent at times. In February 1945 at the Yalta conference Roosevelt seemed wayward and uncommunicative to the British ministers, determined to consolidate his footing with the Russians; he sanctioned substantial Soviet acquisitions in the Far East at China's expense and without previous consultation with either Churchill or Chiang Kai-shek, and Eden advised Churchill not to sign the agreement. The Prime Minister did so, however, for he felt that Britain's authority in the Far East would suffer if she did not participate.[2] Undoubtedly Roosevelt believed that Soviet Russia was not an expansive (this is, an 'imperialistic') power, and that the best way to restrain the Soviet Union's possible heavy-handedness against small powers was to ensure its entry into the world security organization. The British government was thinking more at this time of the importance of ensuring the entry of the United States, remembering her last-minute defection from the League of Nations in 1920. It readily agreed, therefore, that the conference to set up the United Nations Organization should take place on American soil. This was held at San Francisco from 25 April to 26 June 1945; Eden, supported by Attlee and Halifax, led the British delegation and the Charter was signed on 26 June.

With Hitler's death (30 April) and VE day (7 May)—the end of the war in Europe—the country could at last adjust itself to the blessings and austerities of hard-won peace. Wartime deaths were lighter than in the First World War, lighter too than those of Soviet Russia and Germany. According to the official figures the total did not exceed 400,000 (303,000 in the armed forces; 60,000 civilian air-raid victims; 30,000 in the merchant navy). But her economic

---

[1] R. F. Harrod, *The Life of John Maynard Keynes*, pp. 573–85; R. S. Sayers, *Financial Policy, 1939–1945*, pp. 456–64; A. J. Youngson, *The British Economy*, pp. 154–7; R. N. Gardner, *Sterling-Dollar Diplomacy* (1956).
[2] Woodward, chap. 28; Avon, pp. 511–18; H. Feis, *Churchill, Roosevelt, Stalin*, pp. 497–558. By this stage the American army in Europe was two-and-a-half times as large as the British, and the preponderance was much heavier in the Far East.

effort had been ruinous; unlike the United States she could not sustain it indefinitely, or even meet her immediate peacetime needs. The war had proved that Great Britain still had the political flair, the personal authority, the industrial know-how, and the military capacity for a major rôle in world affairs. What she no longer commanded was the balance of resources which would enable her to do so on a true basis of equality with the two greatest powers.

II

COLD WAR AND WELFARE:
LABOUR TAKES CHARGE

1. GENERAL ELECTION

LABOUR had made it clear that it did not wish to continue the partnership with the Conservatives after victory. The situation was the same as in 1918 in some respects: the country wanted the good things of life after the hardships of war. But there were some vital differences. In 1918 there had been a tendency to exaggerate the attractions of 'the good old days' of pre-war England, whereas in 1945 there was a tendency to exaggerate the hardships of the bad old times of the nineteen-thirties. The masses had a much more clearly defined alternative before them in 1945. In both cases the escapist mood made them intolerant of warnings about the certainty of postwar austerities, and in both cases the postwar government lost its popularity rather speedily in consequence.[1]

Both parties offered programmes of social reform. The Conservative Four-Year Plan dated from 1943, and took in the essentials of the Beveridge plan and the educational programme put forward by Mr. R. A. Butler in the 1944 Education Act. It promised an export drive and a firm handling of international affairs. Churchill on 15 March 1945 also promised 'mental toil and physical sweat'. Labour speakers for the most part avoided this stark realism.[2]

In this campaigning the Labour party derived strength and a suggestion of restless mental vigour from its diversified composition and uninhibited freedom of expression as an opposition party before the war, although these conditions, as so often happens

[1] Cf. David Thomson, *England in the Twentieth Century* (1965), pp. 217–19. It is doubtful, however, whether the Labour supporters looked back nostalgically in 1918.
[2] J. D. Hoffman, *The Conservative Party in Opposition* (1964), pp. 33–43.

in reformist politics, produced corresponding internal tension after the achievement of power. The alliance between organized trade unionism and the radical groups was in excellent working order during the later war years. A shrewd recent analysis has distinguished as many as ten of these radical strains, ranging from the aristocratic Catholic radicalism of Lord Pakenham to the intellectual neo-Marxism of the radical publishers.[1] An early exposition of the party's objectives, more a pamphlet than a policy statement, had been issued in 1942 under the title, *The Old World and the New Society*. This had been followed during the next two years by a long series of reports from the party's Reconstruction Committee which elaborated the plans in many directions, although with notable gaps. This material was the basis of *Let Us Face the Future*, virtually an election manifesto, which in April 1945 set out briefly and clearly the programme for the postwar period. It included the nationalization of the Bank of England and of such key industries as fuel and power, transport, iron and steel; a planned economy in both industry and agriculture with the necessary controls; and a national health service, houses, and comprehensive social insurance. There was little reference to the international situation apart from expressions of vague goodwill, and no explicit recognition of the extent to which foreign trade and investment, indispensable to prosperity at home, had been damaged by the war.

The success of Labour was greatly helped by aggressive pamphleteering, which went on in spite of the electoral truce. Mr. Victor Gollancz had not joined the government, and his firm continued the Left Book Club tradition with such publications as *Guilty Men* (1940) by 'Cato', which had sold 250,000 copies by 1945. *The Trial of Mussolini* (1943) by 'Cassius' (Michael Foot), *Tory M.P.* (1939) by Simon Haxey, and *Your M.P.* (1944) by 'Gracchus' were other examples. The general theme of the last of these was that most of the Tory M.P.s were wealthy men, defeatist or even pro-German in proportion to their wealth. There was much explicit detail as to their property, directorships, private fortunes, membership of the Anglo-German Fellowship, and opposition to the Catering Wages Bill (in 1943). There was one effective answer from Captain Quintin Hogg in *The Left was Never Right* (1944). He recorded the Labour

[1] Others include Fabian radicalism, Nonconformist radicalism, the regional radicalism of South Wales and other areas, and the 'emotional populism of the self-educated worker'. See D. C. Watt, *Personalities and Policies* (1965), p. 58.

party's persistent opposition to rearmament, and pointed out that of the M.P.s who had served in the war 136 were Conservative and only fourteen were Socialists, and of these ten Conservatives but no Socialists had lost their lives. The *Daily Herald* seemed 'rather touchy about these facts'. But this was the voice of the more articulate Conservatism of the nineteen-fifties; for the most part the Tory party during the war suffered the gibes of their party opponents in injured (or complacent) silence. On the other hand there seems little justification for the view that the Conservative party abandoned political activity or allowed its constituency organization to lapse during the war.[1] The small Common Wealth party, led by Sir Richard Acland, was also not bound by the electoral truce; its programme was remarkably like that of the Labour party.

In the general election on 5 July 1945 Labour won 393 seats and the Conservatives 213, a gain for Labour of 239. The Liberals won eleven seats, and failed to win 295. The Communists won two, and failed to win nineteen; twelve of their candidates lost their deposits. Although the balance of seats as usual favoured the stronger party there was no mistaking the voting figures: Conservative and National voters numbered only 9,988,306 as compared with 11,995,152 for Labour. There were still 759,000 Liberal National, and 2,248,226 Liberal, voters, but no one credited the Liberal party, united or disunited, with a future.

The Labour victory is no surprise to the historian except in connexion with Churchill's position. Although the pendulum of party popularity may not swing quite so rhythmically as some imagine a Labour majority was overdue; the party had gathered strength in 1935 after the 1931 electoral débâcle, and it had had five years of effective opposition followed by five years of creditable responsibility. The coalition was not so much a Conservative as a Churchill government; as a party, Labour had been equally prominent, and indeed, apart from the Prime Minister himself, it is probable that Attlee, Bevin, Morrison, and perhaps Cripps caught the public eye more than any Tory minister.[2]

In spite of doubts about the servicemen's vote, the Conservatives, and no doubt Churchill himself, seem generally to have been confident that his past prestige and popularity would give his party

[1] The assertions of R. B. McCallum and A. Readman to this effect in *The British General Election of 1945* (1947), pp. 2–4, are challenged by J. D. Hoffman, pp. 54–62.
[2] This was also true of the election campaign: cf. R. B. McCallum and A. Readman, p. 128.

a comfortable majority.[1] The 1918 election was in everyone's mind. But there was an essential difference. Lloyd George had separated himself from the failing cause of the Asquithian Liberals; Churchill had not separated himself from the discredited Chamberlainite Conservatives. Lloyd George had formed an alliance with the party favoured by the electoral swing; Churchill had no desire, and still less opportunity, to lead a coalition composed of Labour and dissident Tories. And yet his own opposition to Chamberlain down to 1939 remained a colourful memory; did he really belong to a party that he had castigated so soundly? His status as a war leader also placed him above party, to some extent. It was thus not so difficult for the voter to cheer the man and vote against his party. Many of the servicemen wanted him out of office before he sent them on fresh campaigns. And the great war leader, so tough and forceful, did not look much like a great social reformer: it had long since been forgotten that he had once vied with Lloyd George in this rôle. Churchill's hurriedly prepared election speeches, with half-humorous warnings against a socialist gestapo which were primly reproved by Attlee, offered no attractive alternative to the heady delights of high wages, full employment, abundant food, houses, and medicine guaranteed to all by socialist planning and efficiency. They also concealed the fact that the Conservatives were offering much the same programme.

So Attlee came to power at the head of a strong government. Tenacious and underrated, he showed remarkable gifts for the management of abler and more dynamic colleagues. If he had no favourites or special friends he had no particular enemies, whereas they had many: in this sense no one could take his place.[2] Like Bonar Law, he seemed dim after his effulgent predecessor; unlike Bonar Law, he had a policy. Ernest Bevin and Hugh Dalton, after a last-minute change of mind and exchange of offices on Attlee's part, went to the Foreign Office and Treasury respectively. Herbert Morrison, whom the egregious Harold Laski had tried to substitute for Attlee as Prime Minister, became Lord President and Leader of the House of Commons.[3] Cripps went to the Board of Trade, and

---

[1] Trygve Lie, the Norwegian foreign minister, warned Eden on 23 May of the strength of left-wing views in the army, and argued that the Conservatives would have a better chance if Churchill retired. Oliver Stanley among others agreed. Avon, *The Reckoning*, pp. 538, 539, 553–4.

[2] C. R. Attlee, *As It Happened* (1954), p. 169; G. Mallaby, *From My Level* (1965), pp. 57–9.

[3] Lord Morrison, *Herbert Morrison, an Autobiography* (1960), pp. 245–6.

the party's rather younger *enfant terrible*, Aneurin Bevan, became Minister of Health, to do his best with housing and the doctors.

The ministry was to do some courageous and imaginative things, and it had outstanding achievements in ensuring full employment and a major revision of Britain's external relations. But luck was against it. Wartime shortage and postwar stringency had led to a severe state of crisis in both external and domestic affairs by the autumn of 1947, and although things improved after this in some measure the public felt cheated of the good things and good times which it had so unreasonably demanded in 1945. In the process the main panacea, nationalization, lost glamour, although criticisms of it were largely irrelevant. Undoubtedly the party had been unwise to create false hopes by telling the electors only what they wanted to know.[1] But to some extent they may have genuinely misread the situation through the all too familiar assumption that the exceptional influence enjoyed by the country in world affairs (at its height in the moment of victory) implied a corresponding measure of permanent power or of foreign goodwill.[2]

2. ATLANTIC MISALLIANCE

Great Britain's rôle as a world power after 1914 had been played among states of medium strength. By 1943 Russia and the United States had mobilized resources sufficient to put them into a small, exclusive class of super-states, although the British war record and Churchill's personality had enabled the country to rank as one of the 'Big Three' until the end of the war. Dalton tells us that he thought that the Russians, Americans, and British would find it easy enough to agree on a common policy during the first years of peace. His colleagues were less optimistic. It was the competitiveness rather than the cameraderie of the later war period that at once became evident, partly a sign that in Washington and Moscow as in

---

[1] Cf. G. D. H. Cole, *A History of the Labour Party from 1914*, p. 424. He remarks that he pointed out the realities of Great Britain's difficult international position in *Great Britain in the Postwar World* (1942), and in a pamphlet, *A Word on the Future to British Socialists* (1942) which he drafted for the Fabian Society, but what he had to say was 'too unpalatable to be given serious attention'.

[2] For the period of recent history since 1945 the reader will find ample near-contemporary surveys of international affairs in the (more or less) annual volumes of the Chatham House *Survey of International Affairs*, under the successive editorships of P. Calvocoressi, Geoffrey Barraclough, and D. C. Watt. The indispensable equivalent for British history is *The Annual Register*, ed. I. S. Macadam, which gives a strictly annual survey, published punctually every May following the year under examination, together with good accounts of Commonwealth and other developments.

London, Great Britain was still regarded as an equal in world politics, with the strength and ambition to push her 'imperialist' interests.[1] As a result the new government speedily ran into trouble. The first shock came in the field of international economics.

After the German collapse in May 1945 the war had to continue until the defeat of Japan, which at first was expected to involve another eighteen months of fighting. British forces were to take part, and their dependence on American lend-lease supplies would continue. We have seen that already during 1944 the U.S. Treasury and F.E.A. officials were trimming the lend-lease programme in order to force the British to spend the dollar balances accumulating from American spending in Britain. After the Quebec conference in October 1944 Keynes was able in negotiations in Washington to secure some relaxation of this strict bookkeeping, and it seemed that the need for some further American aid to cushion the transition to peace in Britain had been recognized. On 8 May 1945 Truman signed without reading an order for the cutting back of lend-lease supplies as soon as Germany surrendered; this produced an immediate embargo on all such shipments to Europe and ships at sea were even called back for unloading. Although the Russians protested loudest the British were hardest hit. Truman then read the order and rescinded it. But it was a warning. The end came quickly to Japan; the first atom bomb killed 60,000 people in Hiroshima (6 August); there was an even more devasting raid on Nagasaki. The Russians just managed to issue their declaration of war before the Japanese asked for terms on 14 August. The immediate discontinuance of lend-lease was announced on the 21st, although the instrument of unconditional surrender was not signed until 2 September.[2]

Meanwhile the new Parliament had assembled on 1 August. Labour wished to 'go off with a big rush, and win public confidence while the Tories were still stunned'.[3] The governmental ranks were in no way shaken by Opposition criticisms, or by Mr. Quintin Hogg's rousing denunciation of them as 'Lobby fodder, infinitely patient, all enduring, well-whipped, and very gullible Lobby-

---

[1] Roosevelt's views on this matter continued after his death to be echoed by his wife, who had wide influence as a columnist. Truman also echoed them faithfully during his first weeks of office. 'I was trying to get Churchill in a frame of mind to forget the old power politics.' *Year of Decisions 1945* (1955), p. 164.

[2] Harrod, pp. 590–1; Truman, p. 145; Sayers, pp. 478–86.

[3] Hugh Dalton, *High Tide and After* (1962), p. 481.

fodder'. The King's Speech on the 16th foreshadowed nationalization for the Bank of England, the coal industry, and civil aviation;
a national health service; increased social security; housing and
food production drives, repeal of the Trades Disputes Act, and
financial provision to meet the heavy cost of all these plans. After
Truman's abrupt announcement it was the Labour leaders who
were stunned, and Attlee spoke of Britain's 'very serious financial
position' in the Commons on the 24th.[1]

There were three reasons for concern. The first was the suddenness
and completeness of the American action, which did not allow a few
months or even a few weeks in which to make other arrangements.
The second was the basic difficulty of the British position, which
even the most sympathetic of the American officials seemed unable
really to grasp. Between 1936 and 1938 there had been an excess
of imports over exports in the average U.K. balance of payment
figures of £388 million, but this had been nearly balanced by income
from shipping, overseas investments, commissions, insurance, and
other sources. Investment income of some £203 million had been
sufficient by itself to cover the annual imports of meat, dairy
produce, and tobacco. This balancing was now impossible. Britain's
war effort had exceeded 50 per cent of the national income for four
years.[2] During the war she had borrowed heavily abroad, liquidated
foreign investments, and reduced her export trade to about one-third
of its prewar level, often to the advantage of American competitors.
Her industry had been heavily adapted to, and disrupted by, the war,
and would take some years to reconvert. The loss of physical assets
was estimated at £5,000 million; debts, principally in the sterling
area, amounted to over some £3,500 million;[3] overseas investments
sold off (one quarter of the total) were valued at over £1,000
million. Her total merchant shipping tonnage had been reduced by
about 28 per cent. The terms of trade (the cost of imports as against
compensating exports) had also turned severely against the country.[4]

---

[1] P.D., 5 Ser., HC, vol. 413, cols. 956, 1048.

[2] A rate, as Sir Keith Hancock points out, which could not be sustained. The United
States' effort reached 40 per cent, a rate which, on the other hand, she could sustain
indefinitely. *Studies in Peace and War*, p. 28.

[3] Not 'between three and four million pounds' as Truman suggests (*Year of Decisions*,
p. 414).

[4] In all, about one-quarter of Britain's prewar national wealth (£30,000 million)
was estimated to have been lost in the war. *Statistical Material Presented During the
Washington Negotiations* (Cmd 6706, 1945). R. N. Gardner, *Sterling-Dollar Diplomacy*
(1956), pp. 178–9; P. D. Henderson, chap. 3, in G. D. N. Worswick and P. H. Ady,
The British Economy, 1945–1950 (1952), pp. 62–71.

The third cause for concern was that some revival (in perhaps new and disguised forms) of the American economic isolationism of the interwar years would exclude anything but hard-fought commercial bargaining.

As things turned out the Marshall Aid programme of 1947 and all that it implied checked and reversed this last tendency, but in the meantime the American negotiators saw no reason why they should not use the embarrassment of their ally to further their own international programme. Roosevelt's death had been followed by the retirement of Morgenthau and others of his close associates, leaving what he had slightingly called the 'economic Royalists' largely in control of policy. The British intention was to increase exports in volume to at least 175 per cent of the prewar figure in order to bridge the gap caused by diminished investments, sterling debts, and the other difficulties. In negotiations for aid in Washington which began in September 1945 they asked at first for a credit of $6,000 million dollars as a gift to cover the period of estimated dollar deficiency. This was refused, as was also an interest-free loan, and in the end they settled for a loan of $3,750 million dollars at 2 per cent interest, repayment not to start until 1951. For a commercial loan these terms were not unfavourable, although the _Economist_ spoke for many Englishmen who had convinced themselves that too hard a bargain had been struck. 'In moral terms we are creditors; and for that we shall pay $140 million a year for the rest of the twentieth century. It may be unavoidable; but it is not right.'[1] With the addition of a Canadian loan for $1,250 million the British experts considered the funds to be just barely sufficient to cover the total adverse balance of £1,250 million which it was anticipated would have accumulated by 1951. In fact, the dollar loan was nearly exhausted by August 1947, less than two years after the signing of the loan agreement in December 1945, and only a year after it actually became available in July 1946.

The Americans had refused to accept the more gloomy estimates of the British position to the point of insisting that the British government would be able to bring the liberal and multilateral features of the Bretton Woods system into full operation within a year of the signing of the loan agreement. This meant the abandon-

---

[1] _The Economist_, 8 December 1945, quoted Youngson, p. 162. There is a good account of the British reaction to the loan in Gardner, _op.cit._, pp. 224–36. Cf. R. A. Brady, _Crisis in Britain_ (New York, 1950).

ment of British Empire preferences and full convertibility for sterling without the promise of any corresponding liberalizing of the United States system, with its high tariffs and huge export surplus. Britain was also required to settle with her sterling creditors before 1951, which would free them, if they chose to do so, to buy in the dollar market. The negotiations at Savannah in March 1946 for the setting up of the International Bank and Monetary Fund supplied further evidence of the determination of the United States authorities to 'railroad' their own plans through the international discussions, and led to some angry exchanges between Keynes and Mr. F. M. Vinson, the Secretary to the Treasury.[1]

Yet the future, Britain's future at least, made Anglo-American agreement imperative. Both governments had to re-educate themselves rapidly under the pressure of swiftly deteriorating conditions and although the undercurrent of mutual exasperation between them never quite disappeared it ceased to be stormy after 1947 (until perhaps 1956). The dependence on the United States was partly domestic and financial, in view of the temporary upheavals of the British economy, but partly political and economic in foreign affairs as a result of the stubborn offensiveness of Communist policy. Direct competitiveness and business rivalry remained. In spite of all this the new government was determined not to allow its bold social policy to be defeated by the depressing conduct of its difficult allies.

3. Welfare and the Commanding Heights

In the first eighteen months of its existence the Labour cabinet took the basic steps for setting up state control of the commanding heights of industry and the social services. Herbert Morrison, Lord President, was made chairman of a 'committee on the Socialization of Industries' and was in general charge of the nationalization programmes until 1951. The normal procedure was to appoint national or central boards to administer each concern as a 'public corporation' and after the process, sometimes lengthy, of working out legislative details a 'vesting date' was fixed for each board to take control. The first of these were for the Bank of England on 1 March 1946, for civil aviation on 1 August 1946, and for the coal

---

[1] Harrod, pp. 625–39; Gardner, chap. XIII. Lend-lease to Britain since 1941 was valued at $29,000 million, and reverse lend-lease at $6,000 million; the balance was cancelled, except for $650 million, added to the loan, to settle outstanding debts.

industry and cables and wireless on 1 January 1947. Later came the vesting dates for transport (1 January 1948) and gas (1 May 1949).[1]

For a reform which had been so widely heralded as the triumphant realization of Socialist progress nationalization turned out to have been vaguely conceived and to be decidedly limited in scope. Mr. Shinwell, who as Minister of Fuel and Power was responsible for the mines, tells us that after talking about nationalization for twenty-five years he had believed, as had other members, that in the Labour party archives a blue print for the takeover would be ready. But he found that 'nothing practical and tangible existed'.[2] Labour spokesmen who had so confidently demanded it in the past had to some extent confused ends with means, for they felt bound to affirm continually that the mere change in ownership and control would eliminate 'waste and inefficiency' resulting from 'a jostling crowd of separate employers', as Sidney Webb had put it in 1918. The rank and file of the party, while listening readily to advocates of production for use (with assured output unaffected by the profit motive) were no doubt mainly allured by the prospect of high and guaranteed wages. It was not for them to argue that there could be no incompatibility between production for profit and production for use if full employment were to be maintained in the industries concerned; indeed, production would have to continue in such circumstances even if the goods were socially undesirable.

Inside the movement, however, the socialist advocates of full-scale national planning had had from the start to face the somewhat inarticulate reservations of the older trade union leaders, and in the later thirties the younger school of academic economists had found in the Keynesian social economics a more sophisticated, more intellectually stimulating, and more practicable approach to the problem.[3] The five years of the Attlee administration were to see on the whole the triumph of this latter group, chary of sweeping commitments now that their own party was responsible for the consequences. In theory, perhaps, this was no more than gradualness again, but at least it meant a step by step advance rather than the immediate replanning of the whole economy 'from the ground up', as the election manifesto had promised. The public corporations

---

[1] The structure and appointment of the boards are described in H. Morrison, *Government and Parliament* (1954), pp. 247–62. His autobiography is silent on the subject.
[2] E. Shinwell, *Conflict without Malice* (1955), p. 172.
[3] See p. 270 above.

and not the state—this was Morrison's distinctive contribution—were to control the nationalized industries. A working arrangement with the private sector in a 'mixed economy', acceptable to the Conservatives and the basis of what was called 'Butskellism'[1] in the fifties, became the standard policy of the party, although never without challenge.[2]

Accordingly, apart from mining, the government was in no hurry to take control of the production of goods for consumption. State control was limited mainly to services on a national scale—transport and aviation, cables and wireless, gas and electricity, the Bank of England—although steel was on the list. It meant that some 20 per cent of the economy was taken over, but most of the profit-making industry was left untouched.[3] There was little that was new in principle. Nationalization began in the sixteenth century with the Church; and this was followed in the seventeenth century by state control of the armed forces, and the development of royal arsenals and dockyards; the police and the post office and a national education system were added in the nineteenth century; before 1939 gas and electricity were largely run by the local authorities, B.O.A.C. had been created, and the railways had either already become public corporations (as in the case of the London Passenger Transport Board of 1933) or were closely supervised[4]. The state could not but benefit from a comprehensive national control of these services, although it also had to face difficult problems of management and labour relations which had hitherto been shouldered by local authorities or private companies.

The Opposition, although cautious in its first criticisms of these reforms, soon had grounds for scepticism; the miners in particular did not seem at all responsive to Herbert Morrison's appeal to them to rise to the occasion, shed their understandable inhibitions, and emancipate themselves from 'the mentality thrust upon you by a

---

[1] A term indicating the common ground between the policies of the two Chancellors, Hugh Gaitskell and Mr. R. A. Butler.

[2] Cf. the authoritative but critical study by R. Kelf-Cohen, *Nationalisation in Britain, the End of a Dogma* (2nd edn., 1961), pp. 5, 25–6, and E. Eldon Barry, *Nationalisation in British Politics* (1965), pp. 294–364. J. C. R. Dow, *The Management of the British Economy* (1965), pp. 7–13.

[3] S. Pollard, pp. 388–91.

[4] The use of the public corporation was familiar from the setting up of the Central Electricity Board in 1926, the British Broadcasting Corporation in 1927, and the British Overseas Airways Corporation in 1939. In local government examples were the Metropolitan Water Board (1902) and the Port of London Authority (1908). Cf. M. Abramovitz and V. F. Eliasberg, *The Growth of Public Employment in Great Britain* (1957), pp. 86–90.

crude capitalism'. Output remained disappointing, and the building of a centralized national organization, however desirable in theory, meant the loss to the industry of most of the managerial and technical staff employed by the former colliery companies.[1]

The most popular of the government's measures were those to increase social security, mainly by implementing the proposals of the Beveridge Report. 'A shield for every man, woman and child in the country against the ravages of poverty and adversity', in the words of James Griffiths, was to be provided as rapidly as possible, and the frequent reference to the 'mean and shabby treatment' of the poor by prewar Conservative governments left no doubt that Labour meant to complete the setting up of the Welfare State and to have the exclusive credit for doing so. Yet the Beveridge proposals were a development of long-established lines of prewar policy. Beveridge in politics was a Liberal, and all parties in the Coalition had accepted the principles of the Report. How much a Tory government would have done in this field cannot be said, but it would have done a great deal.

The two essential features were the National Health Service and the Social Insurance scheme. Conservative opposition was limited in the main to criticism of reckless financing or administrative confusion. It was the proud aim of the National Health Service to provide medical care and treatment without charge for all (including even foreign visitors), whether insured or no. The old system of National Health insurance was abolished. The National Insurance scheme provided cash benefits for sickness, unemployment, maternity, widowhood, retirement and the like in return for regular weekly contributions. The cost of the health service was to come mainly from taxation. When Aneurin Bevan, not the most conciliatory of Attlee's ministers, introduced the bill to implement the new service the Opposition objected to its complete subordination of every doctor to the State, the destruction of the doctor's primary responsibility to his patient, the taking over of voluntary hospitals, overlapping, and the vast bureaucratic powers of the Minister of Health. The bill passed, but Bevan had a long fight on his hands with the British Medical Association.

How was the government to finance both the export drive and

[1] Kelf-Cohen, pp. 25–26. Roy Harrod, *The British Economy* (1963) criticizes the nationalized industries less for inefficiency than for difficulties arising from the government's failure to make proper provision for the financing of their capital requirements (pp. 10–11, 105–111).

cost of the new social services at home?[1] In some respects the two aims were incompatible, for while imports from hard currency areas might either be absorbed at home or used in the production of goods for sale abroad they were not sufficient to give full satisfaction for both. The dollars of the 'line of credit' were drawn on far more rapidly than had been anticipated, and were nearing exhaustion in the autumn of 1947 instead of lasting until 1951. Nearly three-quarters of the dollar credit was used in Britain. Yet it could not be said that the standard of living, which was roughly that of 1938, was a great inducement to increased productivity, and to provide incentives in the forms of more abundant consumer goods and services would divert yet more output into the home market.[2]

The Chancellor's chief and most controversial expedient was the cheap money policy. Following its practice since 1932 the Treasury continued to maintain low interest rates, and the arguments for and against this were sometimes highly technical. For the government it had the advantage of providing ample funds at low costs for the reconstruction programme; with the existing system of controls, funds could be directed to such desirable ends as the financing of housing by local authorities and the expansion and re-equipment of the export and other basic industries. In an unfortunate phrase Dalton exclaimed in his budget speech on 9 April 1946 that he made this provision 'with a song in his heart'. But it was essentially a device to counter a possible depression, and was likely to have inflationary effects as a monetary weapon in a period of full employment.[3] Altogether the honeymoon of Labour and Welfare on Uncle Sam's money was nearing its end by the beginning of 1947. After the Chancellor's *annus mirabilis* of 1946 there followed a year of sharp crisis and fundamental policy changes which mark the real beginning of Britain's postwar era.

The winter of 1946–47 was the worst since 1880–81 and until 1962–63. But even before the big freeze began late in January 1947 the approach of crisis conditions in the fuel industry had been

---

[1] The general course of British economic development in the post war era is covered fairly fully but tentatively in the standard works of Dow, Pollard, Youngson, and G. C. Allen. The section on 'Finance, Trade, and Industry' contributed to the *Annual Register* annually by the Midland Bank Intelligence Department since 1948, is useful for both trends and statistics.

[2] Pollard, p. 360; Youngson, p. 164.

[3] C. M. Kennedy in Worswick and Ady, pp. 195–202; Pollard, pp. 368–9; Youngson, p. 160; Dalton's defence: *op.cit.* pp. 93, 110; P.D., 5 Ser., HC, vol. 421, 9 April 1946, col. 1807.

revealed on 13 January by Sir Stafford Cripps's plan to cut the basic coal allocation of industry by half in order to keep the electricity stations going. Labour relations, which had been comparatively easy in 1946, worsened in mid-January with a widespread transport strike in London; the government had to bring in troops to move food supplies. Ministers appealed without much effect to the commonsense and goodwill of the workers. Aneurin Bevan warned them that all social improvements depended on higher productivity. Then the bad weather spread from Europe and from 23 January and throughout February Britain froze. Railways were blocked; coal movements were held up by land and sea; factories closed; the Cripps plan, in itself a crisis measure, had no chance, and on 7 February more drastic measures of fuel economy announced by Shinwell put 1,800,000 men out of work in the following week. Although some Labour members sturdily attributed the crisis to the prewar carelessness of the Tories the country probably preferred Lord Swinton's verdict that it was due, not to an act of God, but to the inactivity of Emanuel. It is only fair to recall that the fuel situation was gradually ·improved by extra output and a great effort on the part of the railway staffs to move coal through the country. But the final result was heavy though temporary unemployment, and a disastrous drop in production with an estimated loss of £200 million worth of exports.

This contributed to the exchange crisis which was now becoming acute. A further £80 million had been drained from the dollar reserves in 1946 to finance imports into the British zone of occupation in Germany; invisible earnings were disappointing, and a severe worsening of the terms of trade in the summer of 1947 was followed by the convertibility crisis in the early autumn. Only £250 million of the American loan, and £125 million of the Canadian loan, were left at the end of July. It will be remembered that as a condition of the loan, sterling currently earned (although not the accumulated balances) had to be made freely convertible, in accordance with the Bretton Woods conditions, after 15 July 1947. This was done, with no anticipations of disaster on the government's part. Yet the inevitable result was that most of Britain's foreign creditors hastened to convert their sterling into dollars; only $400 million of the loan was left when Dalton announced the suspension of full convertibility on 20 August. Both the fuel and the convertibility crises had been mismanaged.

So ended the first phase of Labour's over-confident planning. The domestic economy was faltering, with low productivity and widespread apathy resulting from shortages, lack of incentive, and the tendency to take things easily after the war. The export drive, which was taken seriously enough by the government, had also failed by 1947 to bridge the gap between the cost of the import programme and the external debt on the one side and the diminished yield of foreign currency on the other. Lacking direction, the country seemed to be drifting towards disaster. Permanent 'full employment' still seemed an unlikely achievement.[1] In some quarters the government was even suspected of deliberate inaction in order to ensure the failure of the convertibility arrangements.[2] From the party itself there now came demands for 'leadership not leaders'. In May 1947 the publication of a pamphlet entitled *Keep Left*, under the signatures of R. H. S. Crossman, Michael Foot, Ian Mikardo, Geoffrey Bing, S. Swingler, Woodrow Wyatt and others, marked the crystallization around Mr. Crossman of an influential dissenting group within the Labour ranks. The pamphlet followed the earlier line taken by this group in criticizing Bevin's foreign policy, but its theme was more particularly the absence of a unifying purpose in both foreign and domestic affairs. It demanded more overall planning, further nationalization, compulsory measures for coordinating and rationalizing private industry, together with emancipation from the economic assistance and anti-Communist campaigning of the United States government.

Although the Keep Left Group was asking, and was to continue to ask, too much of the leaders, it was generally agreed that an urgent and obvious need for better coordination of planning between departments existed. But it was not until 29 September that the appointment of Sir Stafford Cripps as Minister of Economic Affairs was announced. One cause of delay was a cabinet crisis starting late in July in which Cripps and Dalton had sought to substitute Bevin for Attlee as Prime Minister. Bevin was uncooperative, but some ministerial reshuffle, and if possible a scapegoat, were clearly needed. Cripps' appointment led Churchill to forecast measureless misery and tribulation as the result of totalitarian compulsion, but the country was soon to feel the benefits of

[1] Cf. A. G. B. Fisher, *International Implications of Full Employment in Great Britain* (1946), pp. 12–30; he considered Beveridge's limit of 3 per cent of unemployed optimistic.

[2] Youngson, p. 167.

Labour's capacity to think again and to learn from its mistakes. Dalton was a self-appointed scapegoat in November. It was in the wider context of external policy, however, that the fortunes of Britain now began to mend.[1]

4. THE NEW COURSE IN FOREIGN POLICY

Bevin faced the triple task of handling Britain's immediate post-war difficulties, evading the more impracticable plans of his Labour party colleagues, and devising a satisfactory long-term framework for the anti-Communist, western forces. As Foreign Secretary he undoubtedly had a touch of greatness. A sturdy trade union figure, he has nevertheless been compared by a close and well-informed admirer to Castlereagh.[2] Apart from assets of robustness of character he had the supreme political gift of recognizing the point of advantage in confused political situations, and of seizing the moment of decisive action which might never recur. We must not be deceived by some resounding affirmations of faith in world federation and open diplomacy, and his shocked rejection of power politics and manœuvre; these things had to be said for the edification of the rank and file of the Labour party. He showed himself to be a power politician of some distinction when the need arose.[3]

Outside the cabinet, Labour members were looking for some form of a 'socialized' foreign policy. Attitudes ranged widely as the party tried to adjust itself to the international implications of its ambitious domestic programme. The vision of a Third Force interposing itself between Soviet Communist and American capitalist positions soon appeared. It was hoped that the radically inclined Congress party in India, with which Labour had close links, and the socialist governments of Australia and New Zealand, together with a general leftish trend in some other parts of the Commonwealth, might make possible a linking of European democratic socialism and the emergent members of the Commonwealth. Neither of these approaches was pleasing to American opinion. There were also possibilities of Anglo-American tension in the preference of the Labour government for long-term bilateral commodity and bulk buying agreements designed to eliminate fluctuations in international

---

[1] David Marquand, 'Sir Stafford Cripps', in *Age of Austerity 1945–1951*, ed. M. Simons and Philip French (1964), pp. 174–6.
[2] Lord Strang, *Britain in World Affairs* (1961), p. 344; cf. Mallaby, p. 189.
[3] Cf. F. S. Northedge, *British Foreign Policy* (1962), p. 62.

trade, cutting across the American pursuit of multilateralism. The 'Keep Left' group tended to be the focus for these and similar trends towards an independent line in foreign policy.[1]

While the Labour ministers, like the Tories, never doubted that close Anglo-American cooperation must be the basis of Britain's postwar policy they were disconcerted for a time, not so much by divergent views inside the party, as by the evidence that the United States government itself had different ideas. Truman inherited Roosevelt's conception of Britain as an expansive, imperialist power, and this complete misreading of the whole trend of British thinking on the Commonwealth did not alter when Attlee replaced Churchill, although the new Prime Minister was clearly a sober man, pledged to imperial devolution, Test cricket, and collective security. In March 1946, after contemplating India's uncertain attitude and Russia's threat to the Middle East, Attlee was thinking in terms of retreat to an imperial line of defence across Africa from Lagos to Kenya, with a strong concentration of defence forces and many industries in Australia.[2] Labour's socialist inclinations were distrusted by the more conservative elements in America, while in Left-wing and Zionist circles it was assumed that the new government would be radical at home but reactionary abroad.[3]

While the attitude of the Truman administration was partly no doubt just an attempt to win the votes of zealous American liberals and Zionists it was also due to eagerness to eliminate a major obstacle to the expansion of its own influence and business interests. Although Roosevelt had revealed the rather less amiable sides of his character in his demands for oil concessions in the Middle East in 1944[4] it was probably the former impulse that explained the uncooperative attitude towards the Palestine problem. In the Pacific area there was no mistaking the American determination to eliminate British competition. British participation in the Far Eastern war was not welcomed. A treaty concluded in November 1946 between the United States and Nationalist China was intended to give

---

[1] D. C. Watt, pp. 59–62; M. A. Fitzsimons, 'British Labour in search of a Socialist foreign policy' (*Review of Politics*, April 1950).

[2] Dalton, p. 105.

[3] 'The old Labour politicians know how to preserve the empire against the threat of progressive forces in an age of revolution. To this end the British government will use every means at its disposal—force, diplomatic pressure, chicanery, treaty-breaking, and violence of solemn pledges' (Saul K. Padover, in *P.M.* (New York, 21 August 1946); L. D. Epstein, *Britain—Uneasy Ally* (1954), pp. 120–3; H. C. Allen, *The Anglo-American Predicament* (1960).

[4] Woodward, pp. 396–401; *F.R.U.S., 1944* (1965), vol. V, pp. 8–37.

America a political ally and also a great free market in the Far East; each party was to open its doors to the trade and investment of the other. There were jubilant prophesies in the American press as to the vast future gains of American exporters in India and the Far East, mainly at Britain's expense. This pipedream ended with the complete Communist victory and Chiang Kai-shek's expulsion from mainland China in 1949. A later example of the desire to conjure the imperial relationship out of existence was the exclusion of Great Britain from the Pacific Security agreement of September 1951 between Australia, New Zealand, and the United States.

Now, to understand the paradoxical and at times chequered course of Anglo-American relations since the war we must recognize that although the United States government swiftly changed its mind about Soviet Russia, it never quite succeeded in doing so about the Commonwealth.[1] But as the anti-Communist preoccupation became all-powerful, America had perforce to acquiesce in the British handling of Commonwealth affairs and of many aspects of economic policy, although with obstinate recurrent indications of dissent. Each power needed the other; and although Britain's need was greater she could stand up to her ally if she did so with good judgment and without rocking the boat too much, as she tended to do in the fifties. In Commonwealth affairs the United States persisted in regarding the imperial link as wedded misery, a bondage which could end only with the divorce of the partners, for which she had been waiting since 1783. When India, Pakistan, and Ceylon became independent within the Commonwealth in 1947, to the accompaniment of sober rejoicings in Labour circles in London over the government's enlightened and progressive behaviour, American commentators appeared to regard the event as merely a further proof of Britain's declining power. In the British conception, which was beginning to find surprisingly wide favour in the Labour party, the divorce should certainly take place when the parties were ready for it, but they could and should live happily together ever after. In practical terms this meant a transition to new régimes friendly to the ex-colonial power and prepared to continue its administrative tradition and economic contacts. These new relationships soon began to be labelled 'neo-colonial' or 'neo-imperialist' in both the American and Communist worlds, and the result was certainly to prevent Communist takeovers, and to safeguard British

[1] M. Donelan, *The Ideas of American Foreign Policy* (1963), pp. 42–6.

investments and the great trading companies whose evolution had been a result and a symptom of the colonial régimes.[1]

A *modus vivendi* with the Soviet Union would make life easier for the Labour ministers. There was some wishful thinking behind confident statements in the general election that they understood better than the Tories how to cooperate with Russians. In December 1945 Bevin offered to extend the Anglo-Soviet treaty of 1942 from twenty to fifty years. The immediate response was lukewarm in England (as also in America) when at Fulton in Missouri in March 1946 Churchill called for a revival of the alliance of the English-speaking peoples against Soviet-Russian machinations. Bevin at this time was hoping for an international consortium (including Russia and the U.S.A.), for the Ruhr, and permanent occupation by an international force. Attlee in June 1946 protested his desire for understanding with Russia, and dislike of the prospect of exclusive eastern and western blocs. Bevin echoed these sentiments in December. The Labour leaders were, no doubt, also affected, as were the Americans, by the general popular upsurge of admiration for Russia and her achievements, ideological considerations apart. There were also those who argued that security was a sufficient explanation of her conduct. In this view her defensive glacis of satellite states threatened no one, and any attempt by the western powers to denounce, contain, or reverse this system branded them as the real authors of the Cold War.[2]

With German power in ruins the massive Soviet defensive system would not, however, be needed except on the assumption that the victorious British and American allies were the immediate enemy, and the Communist theory of revolution taught, moreover, that capitalistic economies, always tottering on the edge of disaster, were most likely to topple over in periods of postwar uncertainty. Certainly to the British cabinet the tough, uncompromising, surly acquisitiveness of Soviet policy did not suggest apprehension so much as a determination to grab while the grabbing was good. Bevin felt that he must stand up to Stalin, and with the United States seemingly anxious for a year or more to withdraw from Europe as soon as possible the early clashes in the Security Council and the Foreign Ministers' conferences were mainly between the British and Russians.

[1] M. B. Brown, *After Imperialism* (1963), pp. 289–95, 208–11; the argument is developed in chap. 7; cf. Anthony Hartley, *A State of England* (1963), pp. 105–10; John Strachey *The End of Empire* (1959), pp. 195–200.
[2] Thus D. F. Fleming, *The Cold War* (1961), vol. I, pp. 249–61, 445–50.

Bevin moved with great assurance and good judgment among these contradictory impulses in 1947 and 1948, and achieved a major adjustment of Britain's rôle in world affairs. After the Suez crisis in 1956 there were increasing calls for a drastic reappraisal of this rôle from many who were only just waking up to the fact that her position in the world was not what it had been at some not very clearly defined point in the past. But under Attlee and Bevin, the three essential conditions of Britain's new position had already been recognized and accepted (following indeed much anxious anticipatory discussion among all the party leaders in the war years). The first condition was that Empire and Commonwealth strategy would soon have to be conducted without the resources (but also without the responsibilities) derived from direct control of India, Ceylon, and Burma. The second was the new position, strategical and economic, created by the fact that the United States was at last willing to play a part in world affairs commensurate with her strength. The third was the appearance of a continental threat in the form of Russian Communism which could not be conjured away by any of the conciliatory devices which had inspired Britain's semi-isolationism in Europe in the prewar years. To these essentially political conditions some would add as a fourth the need for a new economic policy. But except for the adoption of many of the Keynesian devices the external economic policy of the government followed the traditional expedient of boosting exports in order to improve the balance of payments within the framework of the sterling bloc; it was not until ten years after the war that the problem of a choice between the Commonwealth preferences and entry into a European common market began to be seriously faced. On the issue of European integration the Labour government was cautious and insular when the matter was first broached in 1950. In the three other fields, however, its innovations were drastic enough, and in the process many of the fundamental problems of British foreign policy during the previous thirty years were resolved.

Palestine was Bevin's greatest, and perhaps his only, failure, and it involved in some measure all the contemporary dilemmas of British foreign policy. On India the American attitude was critical and ill-informed but passive; the Zionists, however, had a direct quarrel with the British authorities and a good press. In 1942 the Zionist Organization, at a Congress in the United States, had pledged itself in the Biltmore programme to work for the transfer of immigration from the British authorities to the Jewish agency, and for British agreement to the establishment of a Jewish state as soon as a Jewish majority had been achieved. In subsequent discussions the rights of the existing Arab population in accordance with the mandate were either ignored or briefly dismissed with the impatient comment that there was ample room for the Arabs elsewhere. But the British government, still pledged under the Balfour declaration to reconcile a Jewish national home with Arab interests, and vividly recalling the costly Arab revolt of 1936–39, had also to face the active opposition of the newly formed Arab League to anything resembling the Biltmore policy.

Both of the British political parties before the general election had been rather free in their expressions of sympathy for the Jewish cause. Churchill had condemned the White Paper of May 1939 (Cmd 6019) which had put an upward limit of 75,000 a year during the next five years to Jewish immigration. The Labour party conference of December 1944 had actually agreed to the principle of immigration sufficient to give a Jewish majority in Palestine, the Arabs being 'encouraged' to move out 'as the Jews move in'. It is obvious that Bevin was soon convinced by the Foreign Office that unrestricted immigration would mean civil war and the destruction of the British standing in the Arab world,[1] and the State Department gave Truman similar advice, although he waved aside the opinion of these 'striped pants boys' after only a week in office.[2] He continued to press on the British government the Zionist demand for the admission of 100,000 Jewish immigrants into Palestine from West Germany, without showing any willingness either to share in the military problem of enforcement or to facilitate a substantial entry of refugees into the United States. While disorder and terrorism mounted during the autumn of 1945 Attlee followed Churchill in trying to keep the problem on a basis of inter-allied discussion, and Truman could not refuse in November 1945 to agree to an Anglo-American committee of inquiry. But when its report was presented on 29 April 1946 his attitude was again unhelpful. He promptly endorsed its recommendation of the issue of 100,000 visas, without committing himself to any of the accompanying conditions.

---

[1] Cf. Richard Crossman, *A Nation Reborn* (1960), violently critical of Bevin's policy.
[2] In April 1945: Harry S. Truman, *Year of Decisions*, pp. 71–2. After this the memoirs are silent on this question. Some of his advisers believed that the loss of the Jewish vote in certain key states would be fatal to Truman's prospects in the next presidential election. *The Forrestal Diaries*, ed. W. Millis (1951), p. 363.

Truman also rejected the British 'Morrison Plan' of July 1946, which envisaged a federal Palestinian state comprising an Arab province, a Jewish province, a district of Jerusalem, and a district of the Negeb. Each province would have had local autonomy with control of land grants and immigration, and the central government under a British High Commissioner would have been responsible for defence, foreign affairs, and customs, and would control immigration (starting with the immediate admission of the 100,000) but on the basis of recommendations from the provinces. Finance was to be provided from American, Jewish, and German sources. It was a serious attempt to square the circle. But as it assumed the continuance of British trusteeship and failed to set up the Jewish state, it had the inevitable hostile press in America. Truman's rejection encouraged the Jewish Agency in October to boycott discussions. In the meantime systematic Jewish violence, including the blowing up of the King David Hotel with over 150 casualties in July 1946, was intended to stampede British opinion. Devices for implementing the Morrison plan continued to be discussed without any real progress for some months, and in February 1947 it was decided to refer the matter to a special session of the General Assembly. Since August 1946 Churchill had been urging that if the United States were not prepared to share the burden of the Zionist cause, the British government should return the mandate and evacuate Palestine.

From the international point of view the importance of the Palestine problem was the danger that it would split the Anglo-American front on other issues, and indeed one of the arguments used by the pro-Zionist press in harrying the Truman administration was that it was weak on the Palestinian question because it needed the British Empire as a bulwark against Russia.[1] In fact, the administration's progressive disillusionment with Soviet policy did little to modify its policy elsewhere. It is difficult to define the exact point at which the two governments abandoned hope of a *modus vivendi* with Communism, but they had no difficulty in keeping in step with each other in doing so. The deterioration was visible both in the conflicting occupation policies of the victorious powers in

---

[1] e.g.: 'We have supported the thesis that the Russians must be held back, which has meant in practice maintaining the British position throughout the world. No matter what official American policy has been, the State Department has followed that course.' Alexander H. Uhl in *P.M.*, 25 August 1946; similarly Sumner Welles in *Washington Post*, 9 August.

Germany, and in the international discussions in which Molotov said no to almost everything.

The control machinery, as it was finally defined at the Potsdam conference in August 1945, provided that the supreme authority in Germany should be exercised by each of the four commanders-in-chief, British, Soviet, American, and French, in his own zone, and by all four acting together as the Control Council, whose decisions were to be unanimous, for questions affecting Germany as a whole. But if they agreed on the need to stamp out any revival of Naziism they agreed on little else, and it had become evident by the spring of 1946 that the Russian zone, a roughly rectangular area stretching from the Oder and Neisse rivers on the east for varying distance of 100 to 200 miles westward, was being thoroughly Sovietized by the elimination of any party leaders or party organizations that were not entirely subservient to Russian interests. The same process was being ruthlessly advanced in Poland, Hungary, Rumania, and Bulgaria; but Finland was spared, and Yugoslavia soon proved obstreperous.

The Soviet iron curtain became rapidly more opaque as allied representatives were denied contacts in, or even access to, the Soviet-controlled countries. Vast movements of refugees completed a process which had begun with Hitler's brutal resettlement in conquered Polish territory of all the German minorities west of the new Soviet frontiers of 1939. Ten million German refugees had been forced into one or other of the western occupied zones by the middle of 1947. Soon further waves of immigrants were flowing from the Soviet zone into the British and American. This ethnic revolution had an air of permanence to everyone except the West German irredentists who continued to dream of a united Germany.[1]

For the British government the ultimate aims of Soviet policy might be puzzling, but the immediate consequences were financially disastrous. The British zone in north-west Germany, with a population of 19 million constantly reinforced by refugees, and with a high degree of industrialization, had been a food deficiency area even before the war, and now had to surrender a proportion of its

---

[1] 'The total effect of these sweeping and devastating transfers of population in Eastern Europe was to cancel the ethnic effects of a thousand years of German, Polish, and Lithuanian conquest and colonization, and to restore the ethnic map to something like the *status quo ante* A.D. 1200.' A. J. Toynbee in *Survey of International Affairs 1939–1946:*, *The Realignment of Europe* (1955), pp. 3–8, a good brief account; E. M. Kulischer. *Europe on the Move* (1948), pp. 255–6; E. Wiskemann, *Germany's Eastern Neighbours* (1956)

current output and capital equipment, mainly to France and Russia, as reparations, without receiving from the Soviet-controlled zone equivalent food imports. Any surplus in the Russian zone was sent east into Russia and not west into Germany. Yet the Potsdam agreement had provided that Germany should be treated as a single economic unit during the occupation. The result was that in the British and American zones supplies, mainly of food, had to be imported; this was the main reason for the £80 million drain in occupation costs on British dollar resources in 1946.[1] Twelve months of Allied occupation had thus shown the two governments that it was not they who were imposing a hard peace on Germany, but Russia who was imposing a hard peace on all three. General Clay's decision to suspend reparation deliveries from the United States zone on 3 May 1946 was followed by the fusing of the British and American zones into a single economic unit, 'Bizonia'. While this did not mean any immediate reduction of British obligations it made possible a sufficient degree of economic recovery for the area to cease to be an economic liability in a few years.

In the eastern Mediterranean countries a similar development of financial embarrassment against a background of Communist aspiration (although, in fact, the Soviet government remained for the most part a sardonic onlooker), also helped to shape a new Anglo-American relationship. The big freeze at home during the first three months of 1947 coincided with the rapid announcement of a series of surrenders of British commitments throughout the world and also with the culmination of the wave of vituperation in America against British policy excited by the Zionist crisis. It was perhaps inevitable in these circumstances that the revolutionary shedding of Commonwealth responsibilities should be attributed by American opinion and perhaps also the American government to mere weakness; although American politeness led to some tributes to Britain's enlightened conduct there was certainly no tendency to place the Labour leaders on any sort of pedestal. It was about this time that American commentators stopped talking about the Big Three, and thought henceforth in terms of a bipolar, Russo-American, setting for world politics. The practical result was to reverse the American trend towards isolationism in Europe and the Middle East, without underwriting the Commonwealth elsewhere.

Bevin had offered in May 1946 to evacuate all British troops

[1] Lord Morrison, *Herbert Morrison, an Autobiography*, pp. 255-7.

from both the Nile Valley and the Suez Canal zone; this did not produce a complete Anglo-Egyptian agreement, for the Egyptian government was determined to assert its sovereignty over the Sudan, whose rights of self-determination the British government wished to protect. It was, however, announced on 27 January 1947 that British troops would, after some sixty years' occupation, be withdrawn from Egypt. On the following day Mr. Attlee announced that Burma was free to leave the Commonwealth, or stay in it as a self-governing and equal Dominion. When it seemed that the sincere efforts of the government to find a solution of communal differences in India as a preliminary to independence were merely sharpening rivalries and perpetuating accusations of continued 'divide and rule' tactics it was decided to end all uncertainty by fixing an unalterable date for independence: 'divide and quit' as Jinnah put it. So on 20 February 1947 Mr. Attlee announced to the House of Commons the government's historic decision to hand over power to one or more Indian governments not later than June 1948.[1] There followed an announcement on 21 February which foreshadowed the termination of British financial aid to Greece and Turkey after the end of March, and by this stage the decision to refer the question of Palestine to the United Nations similarly foreshadowed the possible surrender of the British mandate.

Bevin's steps seem to have been excellently timed to consolidate a western security system at the right moment. The British government had been in favour of such a grouping since the end of the war, but it was not financially strong enough to underwrite all the devastated western European and Mediterranean countries. United States backing was essential, but for a time impossible while the American press, and the State Department more circumspectly, continued to regard even the British support of Greece and Turkey as reprehensible power politics. There were also the more theoretical American objections to regional groupings (except the Pan-American). However, in December 1946 Bevin on a visit to New York detected an inclination on the part of James F. Byrnes, the Secretary of State, to favour economic (but not at this point military)

---

[1] The Indian Independence Bill, providing for the setting up from 15 August 1947 of two independent Dominions to be known as India and Pakistan, was in fact introduced in the House of Commons on 4 July (1947). The last Viceroy, the Earl Mountbatten, whose mediation had attenuated some of the worst dangers of the struggle for power in the peninsula, left India on 21 June 1948. Mr. Rajagopalachari became Governor-General on the same day. Labour's goodwill throughout the negotiations is well brought out by Vera Brittain, *Pethick-Lawrence* (1963), pp. 134–91.

aid to Greece and Turkey. The announcement of 21 February is naturally linked with Britain's dollar crisis; but we know that the British cabinet had been, if anything, over-optimistic about the financial position up to this point, and they continued to carry far heavier commitments elsewhere. It looks very much as if this was really a tactical device to bring the Americans into the eastern Mediterranean.[1] Bevin also showed his capacity for good timing by signing a fifty-year treaty of alliance, the Dunkirk treaty, with France on 4 March 1947, ostensibly against Germany. This was a vital first step towards the western system, and he completed the essential negotiations swiftly in January while the friendly Léon Blum was in office for a few weeks.[2] On 12 March 1947 President Truman followed the British notice of withdrawal from financial and military obligations in Greece and Turkey with the enunciation of what became known as the Truman Doctrine. The more specific side of this was a request to Congress for $400 million to give financial assistance to Greece and Turkey, but the accompanying declaration of an intention to support any free people resisting sub-jugation by armed minorities or outside pressure meant a general assumption of leadership of anti-Communist forces. At Harvard on 5 June 1947 the new Secretary of State, George Marshall, gave these proposals a definite programme in an offer of American aid for the economic recovery of Europe.

But Marshall and his advisers insisted that the initiative must come from Europe, and Bevin was quick to grasp with both hands, as he himself said, the task of organizing the European response.[3] It has, nevertheless, been argued that it was the political, rather than the economic, implication of the Harvard speech that excited him: the latter was to be used to consolidate a strong Anglo-French bloc, with American backing.[4] Talks with M. Bidault on 17 and 18 June 1947 were at once followed by an invitation to Molotov, and the three ministers met in Paris from 27 June to 2 July. While Bevin still thought it expedient to keep open the line to Moscow

---

[1] J. F. Byrnes, *Speaking Frankly* (1948), p. 300; there is a good discussion of Bevin's tactics in Roy E. Jones, 'Reflections upon an eventful period in Britain's foreign relations' (*International Relations*, October 1963; cf. pp. 529–31). Cf. Dow, p. 22.

[2] Bevin told Blum, during the course of the discussions, that he agreed with Duff Cooper on only one point, namely that the danger still came from Germany rather than from Russia. Duff Cooper, *Old Men Forget*, p. 371.

[3] Francis Williams, *Ernest Bevin* (1952), pp. 264–5.

[4] Duff Cooper says that Bevin was even talking at this time of an Anglo-French customs union, with common currency. Jones, p. 533; Duff Cooper, p. 376.

Marshall is said to have made his offer only after an assurance from Mr. George Kennan that the Soviet government would reject it.[1] Bevin started by pressing the case for the full utilization of European resources before asking the United States to give aid. But Molotov objected to any all-embracing European plan. His preference for something like an improved version of the wartime lend-lease system (America in effect to give each individual state whatever it claimed that it wanted) was essentially a rejection of the Marshall programme, and he was supported by the Polish and Czechoslovak governments, which had at first accepted the invitation to all European states to confer in Paris.

Virtually all European countries outside the Communist bloc did take part in the discussions which led to a speedy result—the setting up of the Committee of European Economic Co-operation on 15 July. So was launched, not a moment too soon economically, the programme of Marshall aid which also served America's political purpose in the Cold War by strengthening the internal resistance of western European states against possible Communist subversion. The British government seems to have been happier about the economic than about some of the political implications.

5. CONTAINMENT AND RECOVERY

That it was no more than a relative improvement is clear from the gravity of the continued crises abroad and from the behaviour of the British electorate, which showed its disillusionment by giving the Conservative party its unprecedented run of office after 1951. Widespread Tory gains in the 1947 municipal elections showed that the glory of Attlee was already fading. But full employment and an exports boom, together with the decisive entry of the American champion into the European prize ring, were positive gains, even although they created some new difficulties and left others unsolved. Dalton called the year 1947 *annus horrendus* and so it was for him, although not for Bevin.[2]

Not quite fairly perhaps his replacement at the Treasury by Sir Stafford Cripps on 13 November 1947 was accepted with general relief, although it was austerity rather than comfort that he had to offer. He had already taken charge of economic policy after Morrison's attack of thrombosis early in 1947. The ablest, the most

[1] C. M. Woodhouse, *British Foreign Policy since the Second World War* (1961), p. 20.
[2] Dalton, p. 110; F. W. Paish, *The Post War Financial Problem* (1950), pp. 4–34; 43–51.

awkward, and one of the wealthiest of Labour's political eccentrics in the prewar period, when he had fallen rather too readily for the over-simplifications of Popular Front propaganda, Cripps had only risen to his full stature after 1942, when he had been called on to deal with the specialized problems of a series of government departments. He was clearly a persuasive and courageous and probably disinterested man; Churchill thought him the one man of outstanding intellectual ability in the Labour party, but he also thought that the more facts he had to deal with the better. After an excellent term at the Board of Trade he was appointed Minister of Economic Affairs on 29 September.[1]

In his first pronouncements austerity predominated. The problem was essentially to replan trading policy in agreement with the rest of the sterling area, which now had a total adverse balance with America of some $10,000 million. While Bevin pointed out one path to salvation from the dollar bondage by robust appeals to British workers to produce more, Cripps was planning revised export targets for 23 groups of industries, and on 23 October announced his programme to the Commons. To buy time while home and imperial production grew, there were to be drastic cuts in imports (including food and tobacco), in the costs of the armed forces, and in capital expenditure (at the expense of housing and factory building). After this Dalton's interim budget, introduced on 12 November, seemed to many of his critics to be almost a sedative, and raised a momentary doubt as to his capacity for agreement with Cripps. This, however, was unfair: it was he who took the major political decision of raising an extra £200 million in tax so as to cut back inflation,[2] but he resigned on the following day, after the leak of a budget secret to *The Star*.

Cripps's appointment as Chancellor thus removed the danger of a clash between planning and finance. He took with him to the Treasury the bulk of the staff which had just been appointed to plan the nation's economy at the Ministry of Economic Affairs. Once more, as under Simon in the late thirties and Neville Chamberlain to some extent in the middle thirties, the Chancellor was the powerful figure on whom economic policy mainly depended. The country, although experiencing a milder winter than the preceding, shivered in anticipation of draconic legislation, and was barely reassured

---

[1] D. Marquand, pp. 174–95; Colin Cooke, *Life of Richard Stafford Cripps* (1957), p. 364.
[2] Cf. I. M. D. Little in Worswick and Ady, p. 172; Dow, pp. 28–9.

by the Chancellor's *sangfroid* in taking his wife to the theatre on the evening of his appointment. Apart from the import and food restrictions—the bacon ration was halved and the purchase of American tobacco stopped in October, while potatoes were rationed in November—nothing had created a greater stir than the government's revival in October of the wartime practice of directing labour. Direction had indeed been foreshadowed in the *Economic Survey* for 1947, published in February, which regarded the anticipated labour force of 18,400,000 available in December 1947 for the home market and exports as inadequate for the purpose; but the shock was great. The T.U.C. loyally accepted the plan, after profuse assurances of moderation by Mr. George Isaacs, the Minister of Labour, who, however, complained of the spivs and drones, not to say eels and butterflies, who flourished in the luxury trades. His attempt later to enforce the registration of those engaged in betting and street trading led the street traders of Southwark to affiliate themselves to the Conservative organization. However, as things turned out the need to dragoon and direct the economic forces of the country on something like wartime lines soon became less urgent.

This was partly because the Treasury itself much preferred to rely on financial methods of control, and to exercise influence during the next few years mainly through the budget; but the basic cause was the stimulus to the economy of the second dollar injection through the Marshall Aid programme.[1] With this went a gratifying expansion of exports which, although producing a somewhat hand-to-mouth prosperity, enabled the government to relax rather than tighten its direction of the economy. The first of these developments went smoothly ahead. The Committee of European Economic Co-operation, representing sixteen nations, presented in its report of 22 September 1947 a programme of agricultural and industrial expansion which with American aid and the maximum of self-help would have eliminated the wartime dislocation of the western European economies by 1951. After discussions in Washington between British, American, and other experts in November President Truman presented an outline European Recovery Programme (E.R.P.) to Congress in December, and Congress approved the completed programme in April 1948, with cuts which were restored by the Senate in June.

Until Marshall Aid had become a reality the British government's

[1] Pollard, p. 374.

interim emergency measures had to continue, and they included a once-and-for-all capital levy in Cripps's first budget in April. But by September 1948 the precise figures had been arrived at; Great Britain was to receive $1,263 million Marshall Aid out of a total of $4,875 million; of this, $312 million was to be set against equivalent British grants to other European countries, and she, on the other hand, was to receive a grant of $30 million from Belgium. All sterling balances of members were to be frozen, but the United Kingdom was to release $230 million of the Greek and Italian sterling balances. With these adjustments Britain became the second largest recipient (after France) of Marshall Aid. The benefits of this opportune measure were well understood and well publicized by government organs. The *Board of Trade Journal* on 16 October said that without Marshall Aid cotton goods would have disappeared from the home market, tobacco consumption would have been cut by three-quarters, rations of butter, sugar, cheese, and bacon would have had to be cut by over a third; most serious of all, supplies of raw materials for industry would have been affected. The unemployment figures might well have reached 1,500,000.

Nevertheless, the conditions suitable for a world boom existed independently of Marshall Aid, and it was true of other countries as of Great Britain that the achievement of a satisfactory industrial output for export was primarily a matter of domestic policy. The steps which the government had been taking since 1945, somewhat accelerated by the near panic of the last months of 1947, were continued during 1948, with further import restrictions and a preference where possible for non-dollar sources of supply. Above all the strong pressure to expand output in the capital goods and export industries was now producing results. The most spectacular case was that of the motor-car industry, which was able to profit from the shrinking of American competition owing to the dollar shortage and from the slower pace at which western European production was recovering from the war. Output in 1950 had reached over 900,000 units (cars, vans, tractors, etc.) as compared with 526,000 in 1937, the prewar peak year. There were also substantial increases in the output of bicycles and motor cycles. Apart from vehicles the heavy increases were in engineering and shipbuilding, metal manufacture, and chemicals.[1]

[1] G. C. Allen, *British Industries and their Organization* (1959), pp. 34–5, 145, 158, 202–10; Pollard, pp. 376–85.

Thus the goal of increased output had been decisively attained; the *Economic Survey* for 1948 announced 150 per cent, and Mr. Attlee 160 per cent of the 1938 volume, as the target to be reached by the end of the year and, in fact, 136 per cent was actually followed by 151 per cent in 1949. It was also satisfactory that this net increase of exports was to be more or less maintained, in spite of many crises and uncertainties, throughout the later forties and fifties, so that the exhaustion of the postwar boom was not followed as in the nineteen twenties by prolonged depression. This was partly because British industry was very much more ready to adventure into the 'growth' sections of world trade instead of relying on time to achieve a revival of demand for traditional and declining commodities.[1]

But it was still a rather precarious prosperity, and if we look at the economic record as a whole, domestic and external, we can understand the sense of popular frustration which was industriously exploited by a hard-working Opposition. National solvency, registered conveniently but misleadingly by the state of the balance of payments, was dependent on a whole range of factors only partially under the government's control. After 1948 the Labour party appeared to have lost some confidence in its ability to handle them.[2] The boom conditions were obviously transitory. At any moment a run on sterling, or a drop in the demand for British goods, might cause a crisis in view of the relatively small reserves. Although a substantial surplus on the current account was being secured, and continued indeed to be maintained with only two exceptions during the next ten years, the building up of large reserves was not easy; there was a constant tendency to invest new capital abroad, mainly in the Commonwealth, and it was necessary to meet the demands of holders of the sterling debt accumulated during the war. And the dollar problem remained, for not only was Marshall Aid transitory, but there was no desire to remain dependent on it longer than necessary. In these circumstances one possible expedient would be the devaluation of the pound, and Britain's problems were sufficiently well understood abroad for there to be considerable speculation in 1948 as to when this would take place. Although during 1948 Cripps firmly denied any intention to devaluate, the anticipations continued.[3]

[1] *Ibid*, p. 363.
[2] A. Shonfield, *British Economic Policy Since the War* (1958), p. 160.
[3] *Ibid*, pp. 84–6; Youngson, pp. 168–71.

Still with all this 1948 was a good year for the economy, and the
Marshall initiative in its political repercussions meant a solid reinforcement of the British position in many of the diplomatic
fields in which Bevin had struggled in 1946 and 1947. With the
revival of the wartime Anglo-American alliance a new relationship
began, with the United States as the undisputed leader but with a
slowly growing awareness of the extent to which the leader is the
servant of his followers. The unsolved problem of American
foreign policy was soon to be that of commending to American
public opinion those allies whose policy the State Department was
not prepared to underwrite in some spheres but whose goodwill
must be retained to secure their cooperation in others. McCarthyism
was, in this aspect at least, an explosive reassertion of earlier isolationist simplifications. Anglo-American collaboration had now
become a reality in Europe; elsewhere it still hung fire.[1]

There was also a growing campaign against 'colonialism' among
the non-colonial powers who constituted a majority of the United
Nations, with proposals in the General Assembly for the extension
of the trustee provisions to cover all dependent territories. The
United Kingdom was the chief subject of this pressure, and found
little support in her resistance to plans to transfer to the United
Nations the right to decide when, in fact, the time for the grant
of self-government had arrived. The new turn in the foreign policy
of the United States after 1947 involved, however, a growing
recognition of the fact that newly independent states could not
always stand alone and that more was involved in arranging for the
independence of ex-colonies than a simple act of repudiation. While
there was continued suspicion that the British and other governments might be clinging to authority for too long there was also a
dawning awareness that they might, through exasperation or mere
weakness of will, be tempted to abandon it too soon.

This was illustrated by the somewhat startling American proposal
in the Security Council on 19 March 1948 for a temporary trustee-
ship for Palestine, a belated recognition of the fact that the United
Nations had no means of enforcing the partition plan except with
Soviet participation. It was also due no doubt to the discovery that
a continuance of singleminded support of the Jewish as against the
Arab cause might not be to America's own best interests. As the
British government had no intention to enforce partition or to carry

[1] M. Donelan, pp. 84–7.

on the mandate without the consent of all the parties there was nothing to do but to leave the rivals to fight the issue out. The British mandate accordingly ended at midnight on 14–15 May 1948, a few hours after the proclamation of the establishment of the State of Israel and its immediate recognition by the United States. Not the least of everyone's miscalculations in this sombre affair was the military strength of the two sides; the converging Arab forces were decisively defeated, and thus had no reason to thank Great Britain for the military assistance which they had received from her.

The partition of Germany, however, was the powerful corrective of tendencies to Anglo-American disunity elsewhere. Partition became inevitable with the failure of the Council of Foreign Ministers, sitting in London from 25 November to 15 December 1947, to agree. While the Soviet delegate, Molotov, insisted on the continuance of the existing reparations arrangements for the Russian occupied zone, the British and American delegates demanded an east German contribution to the economy of their own zones; they also insisted that an economic agreement must precede a constitutional settlement, and that the future government of Germany must be a federal one. As neither side could risk the loss of its own German area to the other, each had to abandon for the time being the idea of German unity under four-power control and to consolidate separate east and west German states. This was a temporary measure which showed every sign of continuing indefinitely, and with it the existing extraordinary situation of the four zones in Berlin had to continue too.

At the end of December (1947) the United States took over the entire dollar responsibility for Bizonia, and during 1948 the constitution of a West German Republic was evolving. The basis of this was set out in the six main provisions of the London agreement of 2 June 1948, but it was not until 12 May 1949 that the 'Basic Law' or constitution for the 'Federal Republic of Germany' was approved, with some reservations, by the three allied military governors. In the meantime a Communist *coup d'état* in Czechoslovakia in February 1948, with every sign of Soviet contrivance, further tightened nerves in the west, and the Soviet zone was organized into close subservience to Moscow under the Communist-controlled Socialist Unity Party. However, Stalin did not intend tamely to acquiesce in the partition of Germany. Soviet agencies instituted a propaganda campaign in favour of German unity, and in June Marshal Sokolovsky vigorously and publicly denounced the currency reform of the three western zones as a further violation of the Potsdam agreement. Thereafter the Soviet blockade of the three Allied zones of Berlin, which had been interrupting traffic with increasing thoroughness since January, became complete.[1]

Britain's part in these crises was the strictly practical one of finding means to supplement the United Nations organization in order to deal with the Communist problem; but this involved profound adjustments in the British approach to foreign policy. Although Bevin emphatically denied any incompatibility with the aims of the United Nations Charter the criticism that British policy was in this respect contributing to the consolidation of rival power blocs was put by a few who equated the United Nations with the rule of law, or who thought in a more down to earth way that the Soviet leaders were more sinned against than sinning. There were a few isolationist voices in Congress which similarly denied the logic of America's position in a bipolar world. Nevertheless it was with the general approval of both the main British political parties that Bevin acted.

On 22 January 1948 he announced to the Commons plans for the 'consolidation of western Europe' which took the form of invitations to the Benelux powers and France to discuss mutual assistance.[2] The Brussels treaty which followed was signed by Britain, France, Belgium, the Netherlands, and Luxembourg on 17 March, and provided a fifty-year pact of mutual and collective military aid against any aggression and specifically against a revival of aggression by Germany; it was not confined to Europe and it also visualized economic and social co-operation to ensure 'a firm basis for European economic recovery'. Steps were quickly taken to set up a permanent organization, and also to bring in other powers. The United States, as it had been hoped, showed its readiness to join when the Senate on 11 June passed the Vandenberg Resolution favouring aid in suitable cases to those who had entered into defence pacts. The ultimate result was the signing of the North Atlantic treaty on 4 April 1949. The United States, with Canada, Iceland, Norway, Denmark, and Portugal, joined the five Brussels powers with a pledge to aid one another in the event of attack and to consider an armed attack against any one of them as an armed

---

[1] Philip Windsor, *City on Leave* (1963), chaps. 3–5.
[2] P.D., 5 Ser., HC, vol. 446, 22 January 1948, cols. 395–7.

attack against all. This led in turn to the North Atlantic Treaty Organization (N.A.T.O.), a most powerful military alliance with a Supreme Headquarters Allied Powers in Europe (S.H.A.P.E.) and a corresponding naval command.

No doubt this was Bevin's greatest achievement and we must remember its broader implications, which were not much stressed at the time. The fifty-year commitment at Brussels symbolized a permanent abandonment of the guarded and circumscribed attitude to continental interventions of the pre-1939 era, but equally the bringing in of the United States as the predominant partner in European affairs meant a recognition of a paradoxical but vital change in the balance of power. Britain could now do or risk more because her comparative contribution to European security was less in the great shared partnership of N.A.T.O. than it had been in the Anglo-French framework of the interwar years. Whereas in 1939 the Polish guarantee had seemed to many a quixotic and ill-judged venture beyond the country's restricted strength, now Great Britain could play a notable part in a distant enterprise such as Operation Plainfare, the air lift which beat the Russian blockade of Berlin. What was described by the Air Minister, Arthur Henderson, as 'the biggest single task which the R.A.F. has ever been called upon to undertake in peacetime'[1] ended on 11 May 1949 after two and a half million people had been kept supplied for nearly eleven months. Great Britain contributed the bulk of the ground organization, a quarter of the tonnage of supplies, and a third of the flights.

The new freedom made possible by the North Atlantic treaty also influenced British policy outside Europe, where before the war the refusal of the United States or any other western power to risk war with Japan had had a correspondingly inhibiting effect on British policy. Now the United States had so firmly taken charge in the Pacific that the British could afford the luxury of disagreement with her on occasion, while concentrating strong forces for the attainment of limited objectives such as the suppression of the Chinese Communist threat to Malaya. Great Britain retained her wide influence, and her power of manoeuvre was increased because her associates in the work of peace were better organized and better adjusted mentally to the task than they had been before the war.

[1] *Ibid*, vol. 462, 15 March 1949, cols. 1936–8.

6. Paradise Lost

But this respectable record abroad may not have greatly helped the fortunes of the government at home. It is more than probable that there had developed by 1949 something of the popular revulsion against involvement in continued foreign crises which had destroyed the Lloyd George government four years after the First World War. The Tories did not on this occasion blame the Prime Minister for the absence of tranquillity abroad, and with no strong political lead the feeling remained submerged, but it may have contributed to the government's declining popularity. This was clearer in the domestic field. On 12 May 1949 the Atlantic treaty was approved in the House of Commons by 333 votes to six. But at the same time local, municipal, and parliamentary elections were taking place which marked a further swing against Labour. While the old London County Council, for example, had had 90 Labour, 28 Conservative, two Communist, and two Liberal members, the new Council had 64 Labourites and 64 Tories (with one Liberal), and the Socialists were only just able to keep control.

Labour had exhausted its mandate. In office it had shown a willingness to experiment and sometimes to think boldly, but it had by now run through the range of its novel expedients without satisfying its own exigent followers—let alone the rest of the world—that the good life 'based on social justice' was being attained by control of 'the main factors in the economic system'.[1] The 1949 version of the good life was not good enough, or was not felt to be worth the cost. All the exasperating pitfalls of state planning were compactly illustrated at this time in the groundnut fiasco, a source of much election humour in the following year. The scheme took its place among a number of plans to increase the self-sufficiency of the sterling area. The effort to produce 800,000 tons of groundnuts a year from Tanganyika towards the annual United Kingdom deficit of $1\frac{1}{2}$ million of oils and fats was vast, imaginative, and, it seemed, practicable according to the best advice—that of the experts of the United Africa Company. It was launched in accordance with the recommendations of a mission of enquiry in September 1946. By 1949 it had virtually collapsed, amid recriminations and resignations, charges of maladministration, and unhappy explanations of the technical difficulties involved.[2] The historian's

[1] C. R. Attlee, *As It Happened*, pp. 162–3.
[2] Peter Ady in Worswick and Ady, pp. 561–72.

general verdict may well be that this was an able government which could not easily have done better in the difficult circumstances. But the great rosy dawn of 1945 had faded into the light of common day; it was an austere and regimented Paradise that remained.

Or so it seemed to the government's increasingly vociferous critics. At what point the Conservative party recovered sufficiently from its electoral shock of 1945 to think at all confidently of an early return to power is not altogether clear. But it had presumably satisfied itself by the end of 1947 that Labour was by no means in office for ever. Angela Thirkell's novels, depicting the bewildered gentry of brave Barsetshire waiting to see what 'They' would do next, reminded the British and American public of the more endearing qualities of the upper middle class, the Conservative party's most faithful members. County life and the conservative virtues in an increasingly disintegrating and caddish world were in some measure the theme of many other writers from Evelyn Waugh to T. S. Eliot, and there was a marked Conservative swing among politically-minded students in the universities.[1] The Conservative party, under the chairmanship of Lord Woolton, showed great energy in reforming its ranks and refurbishing its image. New names were appearing. R. A. Butler, as chairman of the party planning committee responsible for new policy statements, was helped by Iain Macleod. He, with Edward Heath and Reginald Maudling, entered Parliament in 1950. Peter Thorneycroft led a group which produced a 'Design for Freedom' in 1947, based on modified planning and industrial cooperation; although this was not far removed from the moderate socialist position it was sympathetically viewed by some ex-ministers including Harold Macmillan and Oliver Stanley. An *Industrial Charter*, produced under Butler's direction and published in May 1947, aimed to provide 'a system of free enterprise which is on terms with authority'. Meanwhile much was done by Woolton and the Maxwell Fyfe committee to improve the party machinery. A very large and strong Young Conservative association was built up. Debates in the Commons showed a steady revival of Tory spirits after the rather depressing first year of Labour exultation.[2] Nevertheless it seems probable

[1] David Pryce-Jones, 'Towards the Cocktail Party, the Conservatism of Post-war writing', *Age of Austerity*, pp. 221-7.
[2] *Memoirs of the Rt. Hon. the Earl of Woolton* (1959), pp. 331-55; Viscount Hailsham, *The Conservative Case* (1959), pp. 142-4; Earl of Kilmuir, *Political Adventure*, pp. 157-66; Hoffman, chap. 5.

that the ultimate Conservative victory in 1951 owed more to Labour's unpopularity and mistakes than to the attractiveness of the new Tory image.

The government was losing ground in spite of the fact that the energetic young President of the Board of Trade, Harold Wilson, was getting rid of controls as fast as prudence allowed. During 1948 food rationing could not be abolished, and Britain was considered by an American charity in March to be the worst-fed nation in Europe bar one. But potato rationing ended in the spring, bread rationing in July, and jam rationing in December; clothes rationing was eased, footwear ceased to be rationed altogether; and on 4 November 1948 Wilson was able to say that the need for 200,000 licences and permits had been removed since February. On 22 March 1949 came the further announcement that the Board of Trade would remove the need for 900,000 licences a year. This 'bonfire of controls' included the end of all clothes and textile rationing in March 1949, the removal of restriction on midweek greyhound racing, and the doubling of the basic petrol ration for the summer months. On the other hand, meat remained dreadfully short, largely because of the Argentine government's attempt to double-cross the British consumer by doubling the price for meat provided in the Andes agreement of 1948. At the end of March 1949 the carcass meat ration was the lowest ever. But clearly it was far from being the case that the Labour government was clinging tenaciously to all controls for their own sake. The trouble was that many restrictions remained, and controversies within the party made it all too easy for critics to ask whether there was any intention to remove them.

There were many who, relying on the obvious fact that recent economic recovery, the welfare state, and the promise of future prosperity had only been made possible by a greater measure of government interference with society than had been practised before the war, argued that it must be continued in order to achieve the ultimate goal—the complete socialist state.[1] With varying degrees of emphasis and passion the members of the Keep-Left Group, although more prominent in the field of foreign policy, urged the party to keep left at home. Some ministers also took the uncompromising line, and belied their genial and law-abiding characters by injudicious exercises in platform toughness.

The best known of these were gratefully publicized by the press

[1] A. A. Rogow, *The Labour Government and British Industry*, pp. 181–4.

and the Tory Central Office. 'We know that the organized workers of the country are our friends, indeed it could not be otherwise,' said Shinwell at Margate on 7 May 1947. 'As for the rest, they don't matter a tinker's cuss.' 'No amount of cajolery can eradicate from my heart a deep, burning hatred for the Tory party,' said Aneurin Bevan on 4 July 1948; 'so far as I am concerned they are lower than vermin.' A year later, in a somewhat roundabout way, he was apparently threatening revolution: a Tory majority would mean that Britain had said to the world, 'All roads are closed except the roads to civil war; all roads are closed except to the blood bath that is the history of mankind.' The lesser stars also had their picturesque moments. 'I don't care two hoots at any time if the other side is not all right; I don't care if they starve to death' was Mrs. E. M. Braddock's contribution in February 1946, and Tom Braddock, M.P. for Mitcham, writing in July 1949, said that the workers must have everything. 'There is no surplus for the cultured few, for the royal and noble few, for the wealthy few. All these must be stripped of their rents, of their interest, of their profit and of their inflated salaries and expense accounts.'

After a certain point the Englishman's well-founded inclination not to take what politicians say too seriously begins to wilt under bombardment, and it appears that the valuable marginal suburbanites and others were beginning to be shaken by this barrage. Herbert Morrison was the leading voice in support of a more moderate and conciliatory platform, which would woo the indecisive elements. From time to time ministers remembered to say that the middle class were workers too. But on balance it was the tougher line that prevailed in the election programme.

It may well be, however, that what was disillusioning was not the possibility of future governmental activity—which after all the electorate had accepted with alacrity in 1945—so much as the conviction that the cabinet did not really know what to do with the powers that it had. It was all very well to acquiesce in the direction of the economy under a system of overall planning, providing that the plan was acceptable: but the plan itself seemed ill-defined. The programme of nationalization had been completed in essentials by 1948, but there were few signs as yet that anyone was the better for it. The recovery of 1948 was evidence that in the conditions of postwar crisis and scarcity the continuance of the wartime control machinery—which the government had had the good fortune to inherit intact—had been entirely beneficial. But the advantages were becoming less and less obvious as the period of genuine scarcity passed and both the consumers and the manufacturers preferred to make their own choice. There were further severe crises in external payments in 1949 and 1951 which again seemed proof that the government had found no way of avoiding these recurring difficulties.

In fact nationalization, limited to the control of only 10·3 per cent of the British working population and with no designs on the bulk of the profit-making sector of industry, scarcely justified either the ideological fervour of the Socialists or the anathematizing of Tory critics. But the system was so fundamental to the Socialist programme as to necessitate faithful defence and injudicious demands for its extension from the loyal party member ; without it (and the pacifist ideology of prewar days which had now been abandoned) what remained of the typical Labour party objectives ?[1]

It was therefore with a sound political instinct that the Conservatives attacked. 'Socialism, with its vast network of regulations and restrictions and its incompetent planning and purchasing by Whitehall officials, is proving itself every day to be a dangerous and costly fallacy', said Mr. Churchill, rumbling into the attack at Wolverhampton on 23 July 1949. 'Every major industry which the Socialists have nationalized, without exception, has passed from the profitable or self-supporting side of our national balance sheet to the loss-making debit side.' The Conservative case, elaborated on election platforms throughout the country in 1950 and 1951, was that the vices inherent in monopoly would not be reduced by the fact that the monopoly was state-owned. The consumer would no longer have the effective safeguard of competition. The employee would find himself faced with an employer more remote and more inhuman than any private employer. The tax-payer would have to carry the burden of the inefficiency of the nationalized industries.[2] There was a sufficient element of plausibility in these assertions (combined with the inevitable problems of the running in of the new machinery) to drown the counter-assertion that full employment was guaranteed by the capacity of the government to expand

---

[1] Cf. Kelf-Cohen, pp. 317–22; Abramovitz and Eliasberg, p. 85.
[2] These arguments were prominently canvassed in *The Campaign Guide 1950*, pp. 93–154, published by the Conservative and Unionist Central Office in October 1949 for the benefit of its candidates, and were repeated with even greater assurance in the sequel, *The Campaign Guide 1951*, pp. 41–72.

investment in the publicly owned industries at the first signs of a depression.[1]

The Labour programme for the next election was published on 12 April 1949, under the title, *Labour Believes in Britain*. It showed that the advocates of 'consolidation', led by Herbert Morrison, had had to give way at many points to demands for a further leftward movement, with a long list of additional industries due for nationalization.[2] In general, the plan was to complete the control of the vital sections of production by nationalizing the steel industry, and to extend control to the field of distribution. The timing of the programme was unfortunate for it followed a fresh dose of austerity on 6 April in the budget. Cripps, while pointing to some hopeful developments in 1948, emphasized the continuing dollar problem, which must be solved by 1952. There was a dollar deficit for the sterling area of £423 million for the second half of 1948. He believed that they had reached about the limit in the possibility of redistributing national income by way of taxation; 'for the future, we must rely rather upon the creation of more distributable wealth than upon the redistribution of the income that exists'. In short, harder work from those who received, and he proposed to hold food subsidies firmly at £465 million, to allow supplementary estimates in future only to cover major changes of policy, to increase postal and telephone changes, to tax pool betting and large bequests more heavily, and to devote the surplus to the increased costs of defence and the social services. The trade union leaders, steadily opposing Communist-inspired unofficial strikes and the abandonment of wage restraint, felt let down after their hopes of an easy budget. A Liberal spokesman, Mr. Edgar Granville, called it 'another budget of taxation and tears in ten years of austerity'.[3]

But sterling was running into a fresh crisis which excluded complacency. In spite of the 1948 boom the balance of payments position had remained precarious, and it had not been found possible to strengthen the reserves to any extent. The new troubles were due primarily to a mild American recession which had, however, resulted in 4 million unemployed and a fall in commodity prices with a consequent drop of 7 per cent in the value of imports,

[1] *Speakers' Handbook 1949–50* (October 1949; prepared by the Labour Party Research Department), chap. 5, 'Public Ownership', is brief and undogmatic on this point.

[2] Specific proposals included water supplies, cement, certain minerals, sugar, the wholesale meat trade, and industrial assurance.

[3] P.D., 5 Ser., HC, vol. 463, 6 April 1949, col. 2119.

and therefore in the demand for goods from the sterling area. As a result the dollar deficit rose from £82 million in the first quarter of 1949 to £157 million in the second, at which point the gold reserve of the sterling area had fallen nearly £100 million below the safety level of £500 million that had been maintained in the previous estimates. The existing level of Marshall Aid could not make up the difference, and in any case this was to end in 1952. The more permanent difficulties of selling more to the United States across the high tariff barrier, and the drastic American restriction on imports of raw rubber (a major dollar-earning asset of the sterling area hitherto) together with the reciprocal problem of the continued need for imports from the dollar area, pointed once again to devaluation. But the dollar drain was increased by a decision, urged by Belgium and accepted by France and America, that the drawing rights of debtor countries under the Marshall plan should be freely convertible into dollars. Cripps succeeded only with difficulty on 1 July in getting the extent of the transfer limited to 25 per cent, in the face of some nasty comments in the Belgian press. A speculative attack on sterling, partly in anticipation of devaluation, followed. Cripps now fell ill, retired to a Swiss clinic for six weeks, and announced the devaluation of the pound from $4·03 to $2·8 on 18 September 1949.

After this, as Professor Youngson remarks, nothing could be the same.[1] The extent of the devaluation—30·5 per cent—called for much comment, and was greater than that of other countries at the time. Cripps told a press conference on 19 September that he had been driven to it by 'a series of crises as each expedient became exhausted'. But if it had taken place earlier, perhaps in April, it would have been considered a deliberate and not a crisis move. In essentials it meant the abandonment of the policy which the government had followed since 1945. It was alarming that such an extensive drop should follow what everyone insisted on calling a 'slight' American recession. What would follow a major recession? The purpose of the drop was evidently to make British exports fully competitive, and to demonstrate to the world the government's determination to do this. But it could be argued that exports were being held back not so much by high costs as by restricted produc-

---

[1] Youngson, p. 172; cf. Dow, pp. 38–45. He suggests that at first Cripps could not believe that financial manipulation of this sort was not too easy to be effective (p. 42, fn. 1).

tion, and that the existing controls were all that was necessary to hold back imports.[1] What was certain was that prices must rise at home as a result of the greater cost of imports, and this would lead in turn to the abandonment of wage restraint and to other inflationary developments. The alternative of unemployment, lowered wages, and in due course lowered prices, was indignantly denounced by James Griffiths on 19 September as the only alternative and the only Tory solution. The Tories, however, blamed the mishandling of the sterling balances. The government, it was argued, had been much too ready to allow creditor countries (particularly India and Egypt) to receive large quantities of goods from Britain for no return, thus limiting sales to the dollar market.[2] A further essential step by the government was an economy programme announced by Attlee on 24 October, which was to produce eventually a disinflationary effect of £250 million a year. And there was to be a charge of one shilling for prescriptions under the National Health Service.

All things considered, Cripps had served his country well. During his three years of office the British economy had recovered from the war; there had been a 60 per cent rise in exports which more than balanced the modest (14 per cent) rise in imports; inflation of prices and wages had been held to a moderate figure. It was found possible to announce the end of Marshall Aid in December 1950. Austerity had triumphed; but it had also to be its own reward.[3]

Looking back to these events it is perhaps surprising that the government should have gone to the polls on 23 February 1950 with so much confidence. It claimed, fairly enough, that it had fulfilled all the pledges made to the electorate in 1945. It had not lost a single by-election. While 'controls' were irksome, goodwill had been accumulated from full employment and the great advance in the social services. Foreign policy had been prudent but firm. But evidently the government had lost more ground than it realized. There had been remarkably few by-elections in the genuinely marginal seats, but the trend of the local elections since 1947 might have been a warning. The Conservatives had replied to *Labour Believes in Britain* with *The Right Road for Britain* (July 1949), which to

[1] Pollard, pp. 361–2.
[2] *Campaign Handbook 1951*, pp. 9–14.
[3] 'Inflexibility had perhaps been both his weakness and his strength.' Dow, p. 53; pp. 29–54 of this work provide the best available study of Cripps's Chancellorship.

the unprejudiced observer did not seem very different, apart from a built-in prejudice in favour of private thrift and free enterprise.[1] In January 1950 there appeared the Labour party's manifesto, *Let Us Win Through Together*, giving a reminder of the doleful thirties, promising 'work for all', listing proposals for more public ownership, emphasizing the benefits of the social services, and omitting virtually all reference to external affairs, including devaluation.

The dissolution was on 3 February 1950 and some rather sedate campaigning followed. Uncertainty had been caused in November 1949 by Herbert Morrison's hint that the campaign carried on by Tate and Lyle and other firms threatened with nationalization might infringe the Representation of the Peoples Act of 1948.[2] This led to some suspension of activities in December and January, but it was not a substitute for effective Labour counter-propaganda. During the campaign the leaders did their accustomed duties in their familiar but contrasted styles. Aneurin Bevan, perhaps warned by an explosion of 'Vermin Clubs' among Conservative supporters, said nothing very dramatic, and on the Tory side there was none of the 'election stunts' which Labour supporters somewhat nervously anticipated until the last moment. Churchill did, however, rattle his opponents a little with promises of an increased petrol ration and a summit meeting with Stalin. But if the contest was decorous the electorate was not indifferent: there was an 84 per cent poll, the heaviest in British history, $10\frac{1}{2}$ per cent more than in 1945. The total votes numbered 28,772,671 (nearly 4 million more than in 1945), and it was reckoned that those cast against 'anything left of Liberalism' totalled 15,124,115 to 13,358,276. There was a national turnover of 3·3 per cent as compared with 1945.[3] The fine Labour majority was swept away, and in the new parliament 315 Labour M.P.s faced 297 Conservative (and allied) members. For once membership was almost exactly in proportion to voting strength. There were nine Liberals and two Irish Nationalists.

Where had Labour lost support? Mainly it would seem in dormitory suburbs and housing estates and other urban areas in the Home Counties and the south, and in some parts of the industrial

[1] Hoffman, pp. 192–5.
[2] H. G. Nicholas, *The British General Election of 1950* (1951), pp. 21, 71–4.
[3] The detailed figures for the main parties were: Labour, 13,266,592; Conservative, 12,502,567; Liberal, 2,621,548; Communist, 91,746. There are detailed analyses in Nicholas, pp. 306–333, and the *Annual Register, 1950* (1951), pp. 13–23. I have followed the Butler/Freeman figures.

north. Labour's hopes of gain in these constituencies had been strong. They also failed to make inroads into the rural areas. All the Independents failed; so did all the 100 Communist candidates, including Gallacher and Piratin; 97 of them lost their deposits. So too did 319 of the 475 Liberal candidates.

As he listened to the results Dalton longed, he tells us, for a Tory victory if the winners were to have a lead of less than ten. Leaving out the Speaker and the Irish Nationalists, Attlee had a majority of eight, sufficient to enable him to keep going precariously for a time, insufficient to enable him to attempt controversial legislation.[1] The nationalization of steel was the most obvious casualty. To hold office was difficult with so slight a majority, when the calls of public business, missions abroad, sickness and the like must continually sap the government's full voting strength and give many headaches to the whips, but the party made up in discipline what it lacked in the inspiration of a challenging programme. Perhaps it helped matters that the party had shed some of its awkward squad; recently expelled rebels such as Lester Hutchinson, Pritt, Solley, Platts-Mills, and Konni Zilliacus had lost their seats, although Aneurin Bevan was still there.

The first session of the new Parliament was in these circumstances something of a triumph for the government.[2] Cripps's budget, introduced on 18 April 1950, was cautious and avoided electioneering devices; he limited food subsidies to £140 million and reduced income tax on lower incomes as an incentive to overtime, while levying higher taxes on petrol and commercial vehicles. He was able to report improvements in exports and the dollar reserves, and although the Opposition attacked vigorously there was not much for it to go on. The government maintained its fragile majority in divisions in June on the main tax increases, and generally took care to avoid controversial legislation; in fact the revoking of the Control of Engagement Order on 11 March and of a considerable list of food rationing orders during the following weeks drew protests mainly from the Labour benches, uneasy at the prospect of price increases. Edging its way along like this from week to week it could look forward to a well-earned respite until mid-October after the House rose late in July. The Opposition, in two motions at the end of June, unsuccessfully challenged the government's

---

[1] Dalton, p. 346.
[2] Joan Mitchell, *Crisis in Britain 1951* (1963), chap. 6.

isolationist reaction to the Schuman Plan and could not entirely conceal the Conservative party's own reservations on the question of European economic integration.

But this issue was immediately dwarfed by dramatic news from Korea. North Korean forces invaded South Korea on 25 June; on the 27th President Truman ordered full United States support to be given to the South Korean troops. Mr. Attlee immediately promised British assistance in United Nations action. The British naval forces, approximately equal in strength to those of the United States in Far Eastern waters, were placed at President Truman's disposal. For a time these decisions strengthened the government's position. But they brought fresh economic strains which added to the government's discomfiture, and although it remained in office until the Conservative victory in October 1951 it had by now lost much of its initiative in the fields which it had wished to make its own.

12

CONSERVATIVE COMEBACK

1. LABOUR FADES OUT

THE battling forties were followed by a decade of somewhat improbable domestic prosperity which carried the Conservatives, rather to their own surprise, through a long series of external retreats and reverses. The debate abroad as to Britain's place in the world, and as to whether she was a first or a second or a third class power, scarcely ruffled the ordinary British citizen. It was at home, and not abroad, that he had 'never had it so good', and he was content to return the party to power with its third successive majority in 1959. Thus it was seen that earlier patterns of party development were being repeated, and that the British electorate, treating the reformist Labour government of Mr. Attlee as ungratefully as it had treated Liberal reformist governments in the past, had decided to entrust the Tories with a long spell of office.

This was a great disappointment to Labour, which had anticipated an indefinite spell of power in 1945. However, the pendulum did not swing very far at first. The last year of the Attlee administration strengthened the impression of divided counsels and of technical inability to cope with the economic problem, but this was probably balanced by some rallying to the government as a result of its Korean policy and by lingering distrust of the Tories surviving from earlier Labour propaganda.[1] So the Conservative majority in 1951 was small, and the future doubtful.

As a symbol of Anglo-American solidarity the British entry into the Korean war was more apparent than complete. The Labour government shared the American apprehensions over the advance of Communism in Asia and had welcomed the American initiative

---

[1] Aided perhaps by rather indifferent Tory tactics in opposition. Hoffman, pp. 250–69.

in Pacific affairs. But its approach to each phase of crisis in the area since 1945 had been empirical and cautious, adjusting old positions and (if the Commonwealth was to have any meaning in the future) still vast present responsibilities as circumstances demanded. We have seen that after the war the Americans, while approving the British withdrawal of troops from Indonesia and Indo-China in 1946, frowned on their retention of Malaya, Singapore, and Hong Kong. The British for their part were sceptical about the prospects of Chiang Kai-shek's Nationalist régime in China, on which the Americans set high hopes. They did not feel the intense animosity towards the Chinese Communists which the Americans displayed after the Nationalist defeat in 1949; some British journalists and even perhaps some British Labour politicians had been comforting themselves for a time with the belief that Mao Tse-tung's men were liberally-inclined patriots and not true Communists at all. The United States government approved the British military measures in and after 1948 to prevent the capture of the new Federation of Malaya by the left-wing and predominantly Chinese Council of Joint Action. This was a major effort which was costing Britain over £50 million a year at its height, and using over 100,000 British troops, although the gravity of this problem was unfamiliar to Americans generally. But the State Department looked with distaste on the British inclination to accept the accomplished fact of the Chinese People's Republic.

The British recognition of the new government on 6 January 1950 and willingness to support the admission of Communist China to the United Nations met with so surly a response from Peking that no progress was made with the restoration of diplomatic relations. Nevertheless, the Attlee government, while sending a token force to Korea, and providing substantial naval help to the brilliant American amphibious operation at Inchon on 14 September, was convinced that it should restrain its ally from any extension of the Korean war into a major world conflict. Attlee's visit to Truman in Washington in December 1950 for this purpose was generally applauded, although it was probably unnecessary.

In the existing state of electoral tension it was impossible to avoid some party conflict over the worsening international situation. The two Opposition parties approved the Korean decisions, but during July 1950 Churchill strongly criticized the government's defence preparations, and on the 27th, after failing to secure a secret session, publicly proclaimed the dangerous weakness of the west—with only twelve divisions and almost no armour against Russia's eighty divisions, of which twenty-five at least were fully armoured.[1] Responding as it was believed to strong American pressure the government announced in September a massive rearmament programme, which was to cost £3,600 million in three years and establish six to ten regular divisions. Recruiting was to be stimulated by an extra expenditure of £68 million on pay, and compulsory service was increased from 18 months to two years. Liberals and Conservatives again approved, but Churchill continued to insist that the ministers lacked 'forethought, conviction, and design'. So in their turn Labour men began to talk darkly of warmongering, and in the defence debate in February 1951 Aneurin Bevan said that the decoy of the Tory party was now their Jonah; the Tories were glumly watching their ship going nearer and nearer to the rocks 'in charge of a captain who appeared to be witnessing the scene with increasing enthusiasm'.[2] But Bevan could never adapt his wayward dialectical brilliance to the task of capturing power, and it was on balance the government rather than the Opposition which was weakened and divided by the new programme.[3]

The ship of state was certainly approaching some financial rocks which had to be faced with resolution if not with enthusiasm. The new rearmament programme would involve stockpiling and a deterioration in the terms of trade and would mean at home the diversion of energy from some important industries (such as engineering and building). Greater output for the export industries would be at the expense of the civilian consumer, and there would be some increase in the cost of living. Independently of this, however, there was a slowly growing dissatisfaction in the cabinet with the expense of the National Health Service, which Bevan jealously defended in spite of its mounting cost and faulty estimating. How far should expenditure on the social services be considered sacrosanct? It was bound in the circumstances to be a natural subject for economies, and it did not ease matters that a new Chancellor of the Exchequer applied restraint.[4] Some thought that Bevan was aggrieved when Hugh Gaitskell, aged forty-five, succeeded Cripps as Chancellor on 19 October 1950, and again disappointed

[1] P.D., 5 Ser., HC, vol. 478, 27 July 1950, cols. 701-2.
[2] *Ibid*, vol. 484, 15 February 1951, col. 732.
[3] Dalton, pp. 358-9; Joan Mitchell, pp. 171-3, 283.
[4] Cf. Asa Briggs in Worswick and Ady, pp. 377-380.

when Herbert Morrison succeeded Ernest Bevin as Foreign Secretary on 9 March 1951. Bevan was moved instead to the Ministry of Labour, where he showed no enthusiasm for the task of demanding harder work and increased output from the unions. He resigned, along with Harold Wilson and John Freeman, on the ground that Gaitskell's first budget, opened on 10 April 1951, marked the beginning of the destruction of the social services in which Labour had taken a special pride.[1]

The resignation was a political blunder of the first magnitude, whether we regard it from the point of view of Bevan's ultimate personal ambitions or of the immediate prospects of the Labour party. It had just lost Cripps and Bevin, its two ablest men. Morrison, Dalton, and Attlee were near to retirement.[2] A period in the wilderness with a triumphant return at the right moment is sometimes good tactics for a potential party leader, but time was against Bevan. In the circumstances of the nineteen-fifties he was not quite young enough at fifty-two to wait, as Churchill had waited for eight years after his rebellion at the age of fifty-six in 1931. On Attlee's retirement Bevan's admirers were to find, as the Lloyd-Georgeite Tories found after Bonar Law's departure in 1923, that a dark horse from the Treasury had won the race. Not that Gaitskell's solitary budget had not caused criticism for its ill-judged optimism. His increases in the profits, entertainment, and purchase taxes and an additional sixpence on the income tax fell far short of producing the amount needed to cover the anticipated increase in governmental expenditure, mainly on defence. But he resisted Trade Union pressure in favour of increasing the ceiling for subsidies and he placed a ceiling on National Health expenditure, with a charge which made most of the patients pay about half the fee for spectacles and dentures; moreover the ease and tact with which he stated his case and the firmness with which he resisted the scorn of the Bevanites were pleasing to many. Unfortunately the party could not fail to suffer from such a public revelation of internal differences.[3]

The impression of divided counsels was increased by indecisive handling of foreign affairs and the deteriorating economic situation.

[1] They were replaced by Arthur Robens, Sir Hartley Shawcross, and Michael Stewart. Dalton, pp. 358–9; Morrison, *Autobiography*, pp. 266–7. Attlee was in hospital, and presumably favourable to Gaitskell, but does not say so: *As It Happened*, p. 206.
[2] Bevin died on 14 April 1951, and Cripps on 21 April 1952.
[3] Joan Mitchell, pp. 179–89; Dow, pp. 59–62.

Herbert Morrison's career as Foreign Secretary was short but disastrous; it was remembered chiefly for the showy defiance of the British government and the Anglo-Iranian Oil Company by the Iranian Prime Minister, Dr. Musaddiq, who added to the humours of the situation by expropriating the company in the name of nationalization. Musaddiq and his fanatical supporters were wrong both in their denial of the advantages that the company's vast payments had brought to the state in the past and in their belief that they could themselves run the oil industry successfully and profitably in the future. They did not control the tanker fleet or marketing organization which would enable them to sell their output overseas, and the American companies were not prepared to help them. The right course was undoubtedly the one that the company and the British government followed—namely to wait until Musaddiq and his experiment collapsed. But in the meantime Morrison seemed very much at sea.[1] His speeches in the Commons on this and other matters of foreign policy generally made a poor impression.

To this had to be added a further deterioration in Anglo-Egyptian relations, which had remained in a state of deadlock under Bevin. The Foreign Office tried again on 11 April 1951 with a further offer of conditional withdrawal of British troops in return for the coordination of defence measures with the Egyptian forces, but this was rejected flatly on 24 April, and no progress was made during the summer. The Egyptian government promptly refused an invitation to join the Allied Middle East command as a founder member. Instead, Egyptian decrees of 8 October repudiated the Anglo-Egyptian treaty of 1936 (due to expire in 1956) and proclaimed Faruq King of the Sudan. It was generally believed that this action was inspired by Musaddiq's defiance. Morrison protested on the 9th. Meanwhile there was a long, confused, and unpleasant campaign of violence against the British troops, establishments, and civilian employees. No doubt there was little that Morrison or Attlee could do, but they were not doing it very well. Nor did the Opposition like British exclusion from the A.N.Z.U.S. pact concluded between the United States, Australia, and New Zealand in September 1951 for the maintenance of security in the Pacific. The abrupt departure of two young Foreign Office officials, Burgess and Maclean, to their spiritual home in Moscow on 25 May 1951 could also not be blamed

[1] He says in his autobiography (pp. 281-3) that he favoured 'sharp and forceful action'.

on Morrison, but it did reflect on the security arrangements for which his predecessor had been responsible.[1]

The Festival of Britain, declared open by the King on the steps of St. Paul's on 3 May, was intended to mark the centenary of the Great Exhibition of 1851 and to provide 'a shaft of confidence cast forth against the future'. But faith in the nation's future had to struggle against depressing reality as the government ran into the third great economic crisis since the war. Once more the balance of payments was worsening steadily, and in the third quarter of the year the sterling area as a whole had a dollar deficit of $638 million, accentuated by gold repayments of $106 million to E.P.U. and by the need for heavy dollar purchases of oil. As usual, some of the adverse influences were seasonal and non-recurrent. But the effects of the rearmament programme were not yet being seriously felt and economists were more inclined to attribute the extent of the crisis to conditions at home which Gaitskell had clearly not anticipated in his budget. These included a large round of wage increases which raised home demand and frustrated hopes of an early increase in exports, while at the same time import prices were rising more rapidly than export prices, and the terms of trade were thus moving unfavourably just when large purchases abroad were needed to replace stocks. The government's counter-measures of dividend and price control seemed remarkably inadequate.[2] Anyway, a fresh election could not be postponed much longer. The King, after his recovery from a serious operation, was able to sign the proclamation dissolving Parliament on 5 October 1951. Churchill set the tone of Tory electoral pessimism by saying on 8 October that 'it will take all our national strength to stop the downhill slide and get us back on the level'.

2. The Second Churchill Era

The Tories in fact seemed a little overawed by the problems facing them, and not inclined to make any very bold promises in their election manifesto, *Britain Strong and Free*. The most striking assurance was that 300,000 houses a year would be built. Labour dismissed this impatiently as a piece of rank electioneering.

Those defenders of the Conservative position who had been seeking to devise a body of doctrine for their party had found it

[1] *Ibid.*, pp. 274–8.
[2] 'It seemed that the planners in Whitehall had now tried every club in the bag without success.' Youngson, p. 174.

easier to say what it was not than what it was trying to do. Defining Conservatism in 1947, Quintin Hogg had said that it was not so much a philosophy as an attitude, a constant force, performing a timeless function in the development of a free society, and corresponding to a deep and permanent requirement of human nature itself. As it did not believe that man (apart from the grace of God) was perfectible it did not expect to found a society in which a perfected human nature would function contentedly, requiring no more attention than a well-oiled machine. He did not find it necessary to alter this definition in a second and very much more self-confident edition of his pamphlet in 1959. The Conservatives, he said, had seen the end of many, and more dangerous, opponents—Roundheads, Whigs, Chartists, Radicals, Irish Nationalists, Liberals—and could confidently expect, 'unless disaster overtakes our country first' to attend the obsequies of the Labour party.[1] This was all very well, and it was possible to bring in groundnuts and a few other fiascos to give point to the argument that in trying to plan Utopia Labour had merely given the country bad government. But it left the Tories with no convincing counterplan or alternative philosophy. They offered themselves simply as the more likely providers of good government, directed towards maintaining the true foundations of a free society.

Since the most characteristic field of activity under the leadership of Churchill and Eden might well be foreign affairs, the Labour leaders, who did not expect to regain the votes that they had lost in 1950 over their domestic policy, believed that some of the public could be scared by hints of Tory bellicosity. The *Daily Mirror* asked, 'Whose finger on the trigger?' The vigour with which the Conservatives criticized the Labour misfortunes, 'Abadan, Sudan, and Bevan' in Churchill's words, may thus have played into their opponents' hands by concentrating attention on the 'war and peace' issue, and Labour spokesmen were not reticent in asserting that in these matters they possessed superior judgment and temperament.

It was probably for this reason that the public opinion polls, after moving steadily against Labour for some time, did in fact show a last minute swing in favour of Labour during the campaign, and the Conservative lead had been narrowed to $2\frac{1}{2}$ per cent three days before polling. But it became known during the course of 26

---

[1] Quintin Hogg, *The Case for Conservatism* (Penguin, 1947), pp. 12–14; Viscount Hailsham, *The Conservative Case* (Penguin, 1959), p. 16.

October 1951 that Churchill would have a workable overall majority. There had been a slight but remarkably uniform swing throughout the country which gave the Conservatives and allied groups 321 seats, Labour 295, and the Liberals 6, with three Irish members. This meant a Conservative gain of 23, and a Labour loss of 20 seats. Eighty-two-and-a-half per cent of the electorate voted, with 13,717,538 for the Conservative and 13,948,605 for Labour; but after making allowance for uncontested seats and Conservative support to Liberals it could be concluded that the two parties had almost exactly equal support throughout the country, to the detriment of all the smaller groups.

Was there now any essential difference between the parties? The issue might well be no more than one of capacity and temperament, for while Labour had lost virtually all its prewar pacifist tinge it had imposed an increased measure of state control and planning techniques on the country which the Conservatives had more or less accepted, and which neither party proposed at the moment to carry much further. But if this position were accepted permanently, Labour would have lost the ideological battle, as the Bevanites well knew; it would have accepted the Conservative's 'timeless function in the development of a free society' and the existing one at that, as its ultimate purpose. Attlee was no hand at the recasting of ideologies, and failed to reconcile party differences in a new reform-ist programme, a task which was ultimately attempted, without complete success, by Gaitskell. A reformist era had once more ended with the satiation of the electorate, and with the Labour party eschewing innovation for the time being there seemed no reason why the Conservatives should not stay in office indefinitely providing that they could give the blessings of peace, tranquillity, and full employment that the country evidently craved. Perhaps to their own surprise, aided by some good luck and genuine com-petence, they did this.

As a result the second Churchill administration (1951–55) was by a long stretch the most successful peacetime ministry that the country had seen since 1918. A certain splendour and authority was a legitimate asset of a government presided over by the great, if somewhat autumnal, figure of Winston Churchill, even although some of his admirers, remembering the last ministries of Chatham, Palmerston, and Gladstone, wondered uneasily whether return to office at an advanced age might not impair a great reputation.

Would there be a hankering after old ideas, as there certainly was after the old faces?[1] In fact there was soon to be a new Queen to typify vague hopes of a national renaissance and to conjure away recent depressions. King George VI, a much respected figure whose rôle had been made more prominent—or so many believed—by the Attlee government as a counter to Churchill's popularity, died on 6 February 1952 at the comparatively early age of fifty-six. Princess Elizabeth and the Duke of Edinburgh were called back from Kenya, where they were en route to Australia. The lying-in-state and ten days of mourning were reinforced by the B.B.C. with a loyal extrusion of all frivolity and an impressive broadcast oration by Churchill. In turn the Coronation on 2 June 1953 seemed, in spite of the pouring rain, to focus not only a wave of admiration for the elegant, dedicated young woman who had come to the throne as Elizabeth II, but the urge to bring back some glory and high confidence to the national life. There was talk of a new Elizabethan age. And it was just at this point that a general improvement in the nation's affairs was vindicating the new government's promise of a freer life.

After so much talk about setting the nation free it was evident that the new government must launch some attack on Socialist controls, and it fell largely to the new Chancellor, Mr. R. A. Butler, and his Treasury advisers to work out in due course a convincing programme of 'anti-planning'. But the country saw very little change for the first year. The situation in November 1951 called for drastic action, and the government proceeded to tighten the existing restrictions in several directions. There was growing inflation at home and a general balance-of-payments crisis abroad; for October alone the loss of gold and dollar reserves had been $320 million, and for the last quarter of 1951 the deficit amounted to $1000 million, easily the heaviest on record. To check the drain the Chancellor on 7 November announced immediate measures to reduce imports by £350 million a year, to curtail the strategic stock-piling programme, and to cut the allowance for tourist travel abroad by half to £50 a year. As the outflow continued, more drastic steps followed; in succeeding months there were further cuts in imports and the travel allowance was again halved. £600 million was thus

---

[1] Cf. Mallaby, *From My Level*, p. 36. The affectionate but discriminating picture by Lord Kilmuir, *Political Adventure*, pp. 166-8, 190-5, suggests that these fears were unnecessary in 1951.

saved on the import bill. These might be described as routine precautions; more significant and constructive was a series of steps
marking a return to the more traditional methods of monetary
control and the end of the cheap money policy. The first moves
included the raising of the bank rate from 2 to 2½ per cent and the
'funding' of £1,000 million worth of the public debt. The purpose
of these and similar measures was to check the danger of inflation
by restricting credit. It was considered that the ratio of liquid assets,
including Treasury bills, held by the banks was too high in proportion to deposit liabilities, and that the traditional safe minimum
ratio of 30 per cent should be restored.[1]

But things continued to look grim in the early months of 1952,
and the budget, opened unusually early on 11 March 1952, contained further examples of Tory austerity. Its aim was to ensure
that the home consumer enjoyed no more of the country's resources
than in the previous year, and that a reduction of some £400
million in the resources available for home consumption and
investment would be balanced by increased production and government economies. Food subsidies were cut from £410 million to
£250 million, the increase in the cost of food being only partially
balanced by tax concession and increases in allowance. Hire purchase
sales were restricted, the bank rate was raised to 4 per cent, and the
rearmament programme slowed down. After this however it
gradually became evident that the economic storm was being
successfully weathered, and as it died away the benevolent if slightly
confusing glow of Tory economic liberalism began to lighten the
political skies.

There seems no reason to think that Tory anti-planning had been
worked out in advance with any more detail than Labour planning,
for both were dependent on changing circumstances and the
expertise of government officials. Nor was the Conservative party
without its own tradition of paternalism. In the first months the
new government seemed to be moved not so much by a doctrinaire
belief in the virtues of a free market as by the desire to woo the
working classes. Efforts were made to put relations with the trade
unions on an easy footing, and some thought that this was the sole
reason for the immediate imposition of an excess profits tax to
operate during the period of rearmament. On the other hand Mr.
Macmillan's ambitious housing programme, at a time when building

---

[1] Dow, pp. 68–73; Youngson, p. 175; *Annual Register* for 1951, p. 433.

materials might be needed for urgent industrial development, was condemned by the *Economist* as a shocking example of playing politics. It was announced in February 1952 that the standard subsidy for ordinary houses would be raised from £22 to £35.12s, and that extra houses would be built for miners.

Two conditions encouraged the government, after its successful survival of the 1951–2 economic crisis, to make another and more wholesale bonfire of controls. The first was that the ordinary citizen, who had acquiesced in rationing during the war and immediate postwar period when it ensured fair distribution in times of genuine shortage, was increasingly irked by accounts (sometimes rather imaginative) of consumers' paradises abroad. The second was that the national economy ran quickly into a prolonged phase of prosperity which turned the risks of decontrol into rewards for liberal virtue. The rapid improvement was due primarily to a favourable turn in the terms of trade; that is to say, a drop of as much as 25 per cent in the cost of British purchases abroad was combined with restricted imports and a tendency for the price of British manufactures sold abroad to rise. The *Economic Survey* for 1953 noted at the beginning of the year that confidence in sterling had been restored;[1] a year later there could be no doubt about the boom, and the *Economic Survey* for 1954[2] recorded that production and consumption were both at record levels, unemployment was low, a remarkable degree of price stability had been maintained, and the recovery of the home market had not given rise to new inflationary tendencies.

These favourable conditions continued into 1955. So it was safe to commence the systematic derationing of food in 1953, and it was completed in 1954, while the zest for the abolition of official intervention extended to other spheres. In 1953 the two major denationalization measures, the Iron and Steel and the Transport Acts, became law; official trading in various raw materials ended; and controls were relaxed in a wide range of industries. In 1954 the Ministry of Materials and the Raw Cotton Commission were abolished, the international commodity markets reopened, hire purchase trading eased, and some surviving wartime building restrictions were removed. The situation had its obvious dangers, which were pointed out by the scandalized occupants of the Opposition front bench; but the intoxicating fact was that business

[1] Cmd 8800.　　[2] Cmd 9208.

men seemed to do better and better the more they were left to themselves, and if there was a moderate rise in prices and the cost of living it was proportionate to the rise in wages and an increase of production in the factories of 5 per cent in 1953 and 4 per cent in 1954.[1]

Not until 1955 did things begin to go wrong, and by this stage the Conservatives had strengthened their hold on the confidence of a significant sector of the electorate, and re-established their own self-confidence. They could claim that full employment and an expanding economy were more readily assured by Tory freedom than by Socialist regimentation. They had no quarrel with the unions. In fact there were still plenty of Conservative controls, and if Labour had been in office it would have benefited equally from the good luck of falling commodity prices abroad. But for the time being socialist planning was out of favour; nationalization had become an embarrassment and something of a bore.

In foreign affairs the situation was different. International tensions were somewhat eased between 1952 and 1954 through British intervention, but there were no spectacular successes to record. The new government did not seek to challenge the broader lines of policy laid down by Attlee and Bevin, although they could, indeed, after the Morrison interlude, bring more practised hands to the conduct of diplomacy. The ultimate task was to put on the most favourable footing possible the three vital relationships—with the Commonwealth, the United States, and the Communist world— which had each taken a new form since the war and which were, in their present forms, so new as possibly to be quite transitory.

The essential basis of action continued to be close cooperation with the United States, whose assumption of responsibility for defence against Communist aggression anywhere in the world was now the pivot of all world politics. But there were growing doubts as to what the Communist forces were really aiming at and whether the State Department had discovered the best tactics for dealing with them. The new Eisenhower administration after 1952 was pledged to end 'Truman's war' in Korea but it was soon reeling under the emotional shock of McCarthyism, and the Secretary of State, John Foster Dulles, had dedicated himself to the task of containing the new menace of expansive Chinese Communism. Churchill and Eden evidently felt uneasy over this fierce con-

[1] Shonfield, pp. 183-5; *Annual Register* for 1954, pp. 414-15, etc.

centration on immediate targets, which might lead to an avoidable clash with the Sino-Soviet forces or to some injudicious show of exasperation against hesitating friends. Accordingly Eden worked hard to secure some *modus vivendi* with the Communist forces and a satisfactory relationship with the Western European Union, not without some tension with the United States.[1]

This was due partly to the care with which Churchill and Eden, like their predecessors, sought to develop relationships with the new Dominions into ties as close as those with Australia and New Zealand, in the face of American indifference or even hostility. Moreover, Britain retained in the Middle East and in South-East Asia her vast and profitable economic interests and the bases in these regions which in the past had flanked her central military position in India. The troubles in the Far East offered a natural field for collaboration. It was not at all clear how far the Dominions would respond. Several incidents since the war had shown that even Australia, and to a lesser extent New Zealand, were no longer prepared to follow the British lead in foreign affairs as automatically as they had done in the past. Both continued to support British policy in the Middle East but they were taking their own initiatives in Pacific affairs. Australia, however, had given a welcome lead in her proposals in 1950 for economic collaboration in Asia known as the Colombo plan. Canada had gone her own way earlier, in a number of fields. Cricket, parliamentary procedure, the British infantry training manual, the sterling area, the British administrative routine, the monarch as a symbol of community, the British public school and university systems at home and in many Commonwealth replicas, the external degrees of the University of London, the habit of consultation—were these the bases for any genuine political collaboration in the modern world?

The Americans did not think so. They were expecting the final demise of the Empire, and now the ghost was proposing to walk under a new name. Long-term British capital investments were flowing overseas, mainly into the sterling area, at a higher rate than in any previous period except the years just before 1913.[2] India too

---

[1] *The Memoirs of Sir Anthony Eden: Full Circle* (1960), pp. 84–9 (cited as 'Avon'). Useful short surveys are by F. S. Northedge, chaps. 5–9, and C. M. Woodhouse, chaps. 2 and 3.

[2] Gross private capital exports were officially estimated at £4,000 million for the period 1946–1959: cf. M. B. Brown, *After Imperialism*, who suggests higher figures, pp. 254–66.

was taking rather too objective view of the Korean war for America's liking, and there was little interest in the sedulous efforts of the British government to bring the Asiatic Dominions into the Far Eastern discussions. On the other hand the United States was quite willing to bring the Commonwealth countries on her own terms into her own security system, replacing the Commonwealth or even the British link. The A.N.Z.U.S. pact of September 1951, coolly received in London, had been the first formal example. Britain was excluded, ostensibly because her inclusion would involve Malaya, but she was refused even observer status.

Yet she had voluntarily limited herself to observer status in the negotiations for European unity, ostensibly through loyalty to the Commonwealth, though also through the sheer little-Englandism of the dominant figures in both parties. The assertion in some Labour circles that European economic integration might interfere with the progress of the socialist programme in Britain may have been no more than a rationalization of this basic escapism. Certainly the Labour government had been lukewarm towards the Council of Europe, created in 1948, and encouraged (with more reservation than was at first apparent) by Churchill and a few of his French-speaking friends. The government gave a cautious blessing to the Schuman Plan of May and the Pleven Plan of October 1950. The first led to the setting up by six powers (Holland, Belgium, Luxembourg, France, Germany, and Italy) of the European Coal and Steel Community in April 1951, and the second resulted in the signature by the same six powers of the E.D.C. (European Defence Community) treaty of May 1952. In neither case was the British government of the day prepared to join and so to accept the obligation to submit its economy or armed forces to the decision of a foreign majority vote.

This was abruptly made clear on 28 November 1951. A few hours after Sir David Maxwell Fyfe had read an agreed cabinet statement to the consultative assembly of the Council of Europe at Strasbourg promising 'thorough examination' of any proposals for a European army, Eden in a press conference at Rome said flatly that British forces would not participate, although there might be some other forms of association.[1] This meant that Britain, while

---

[1] Lord Kilmuir (formerly Maxwell Fyfe) speaks of his 'humiliation' (*op. cit.*, p. 187). General Eisenhower had advised Eden against participation on 27 November. Avon, pp. 32–3.

continuing to play a part in western defence, must be free if necessary to withdraw her forces to meet challenges elsewhere. If this happened France, having merged her armed forces in those of the six, might find herself overshadowed by a stronger Germany. Germany too, under Adenauer's intelligent leadership, saw the danger of almost inevitable Franco-German tensions unless Britain joined the six as a balancing force. But there was no change of heart while Eden remained in power. Five of the six ratified the treaty of May 1952, but France postponed her decision for more than two years, finally refusing ratification in August 1954. Plans for a federation of the Six went ahead under M. Spaak's leadership.

Thus the harmonious development of the anti-Communist coalition was not being very easily attained. The few pro-Europeans in the Tory cabinet felt powerless against the enormous authority in foreign affairs of Eden, who was backed 'hesitatingly but inevitably' by Churchill.[1] Meanwhile the negotiations for an armistice in Korea had made such slow progress since 1951 as to strengthen the suspicion that they were being used to gain time for the building up of the North Korean forces. The Communists were able to prolong the deadlock mainly by demanding the repatriation of all prisoners, willing or otherwise. Although Churchill and Eden in January 1952, after a visit to Washington, affirmed that Great Britain would join the United States in retaliation if the truce were broken, there was continued uneasiness lest American impatience should draw Communist China into a major war, a possibility which seemed to have drawn nearer with the bombing of Chinese installations over the Yalu river in June. The British government encouraged Indian attempts at mediation, which the Americans mistrusted, and after the armistice was finally signed at Panmunjom on 27 July 1953 some sense of irritation at Britain's lack of passion over the Korean issues seems to have lingered in the State Department. However, Eden had been seriously ill since April, and Churchill was incapacitated for some weeks by a stroke in June.

In French Indo-China an open and more fundamental difference between Eden and Dulles developed as the French position crumbled. The northern areas of Vietnam and Laos, independent members with Cambodia of the French Union since 1947, were readily accessible to penetration by Communist bands and supplies from

---

[1] 'Winston was determined not to oppose his successor.' Kilmuir, p. 193.

southern China, and strong French forces had been unable to cope effectively with guerrilla problems very similar to those of the British in Malaya. When the French forces were on the verge of collapse in the decisive battle of Dien Bien Phu in April 1954, the United States government proposed to secure the Chinese withdrawal with a threat of naval and air action by the U.S.A., France, Britain, and other interested powers against the Chinese coast, together with a threat of active intervention in Indo-China itself. Eden was in agreement with Churchill in rejecting this plan with a wide range of arguments based on the unlikelihood of Chinese agreement and the possibility of joint Sino-Soviet resistance; and although Dulles modified the proposal a week later the British ministers were agreed that nothing short of a general war, with the use of ground forces, could prevent large parts of Vietnam from falling into Communist hands, and that the best hope of a peaceful solution lay in partition. Nor, incidentally, could they otherwise hope to hold Hong Kong, their hostage to fortune.[1]

Dulles seemed to be convinced that China was poised for a career of international aggression as Japan had been when she took Manchuria in 1931 and Hitler when he entered the Rhineland in 1936. A better analogy would probably have been the position of the early Bolsheviki, hitting out at enemies or imagined enemies abroad in 1920 in the last phase of revolutionary consolidation. The British government was less agitated over the immediate situation. There seemed a good chance that the present phase of Chinese expansionism could be sealed off, if only because Mao Tse-tung had much to do at home. Eden welcomed Dulles's idea of an organization for collective defence in South-east Asia, but could not convince him that India and other Asiatic Commonwealth countries should be invited to join. In the end, however, the settlement largely followed Eden's proposals, with some unexpected help from Molotov.

A conference in Berlin in January 1954 was abortive as far as German affairs were concerned, but it arranged for the calling of a conference at Geneva in April on Asian affairs. Here Dulles and Chou En-lai, the Chinese Foreign Minister, glowered at each other for the first week, after which Dulles returned to Washington and his place was taken by the more amicable Assistant Secretary of State, Bedell Smith. Eden was still complaining in mid-June that neither

[1] Avon, pp. 89–105.

the French nor the Americans had established any contacts with the Communist representatives, while he had to act as an intermediary and bring forward proposals for which he was continually being criticized, particularly in the American press. The final agreement, which provided for the partition of Vietnam and separate agreements ensuring neutral status for Cambodia and Laos, seemed to have been felt by Dulles as a defeat at Eden's hands. He refused to be associated with the settlement. The British view was that a drift into an impossible situation had been stopped. Eden had kept in close daily touch with Nehru and other Commonwealth members. India, Pakistan, Ceylon, Burma, and Indonesia were in conference at Colombo and were not represented at Geneva.[1]

Faced with protests from both American political parties against the creation of another Korea in Indo-China and also against any compromise with Communist China, Dulles probably found Eden a useful scapegoat. On a three-day visit to the United States (25–28 June 1954) Churchill had an excellent reception when he explained the British point of view at a televised press conference, but the net result of the Geneva settlement seems to have been a growing distrust of Dulles's somewhat enigmatic attitude. 'My difficulty in working with Mr. Dulles was to determine what he really meant and in consequence the significance to be attached to his words and actions', Eden wrote in his memoirs.[2] This, as he points out, was unfortunate for Britain, the weaker partner. But still they were partners, and the puzzle is greater as they were agreed about so much.

They were certainly agreed as to the need for a defence treaty for South-East Asia, although Eden successfully opposed Dulles's plan to announce it on the eve of the Geneva conference, partly at least because of the need for preparing the ground with the Commonwealth countries assembled at Colombo. The treaty creating the South East Asia Treaty Organization (S.E.A.T.O.) was signed at Manila on 8 September 1954 by representatives of Great Britain, France, the United States, Australia, New Zealand, Pakistan, Thailand, and the Philippines, and although India and others declined to depart from their policy of 'non-alignment' it seemed important to Eden, and a matter of indifference to Dulles, that their coy reactions should have been so politely handled. The two

---

[1] *Ibid.*, pp. 67–76; 107–45.
[2] *Ibid.*, p. 63.

governments again appeared to be in broad agreement about the Middle East, but each underrated the other's reservations.

In the Iranian oil dispute Musaddiq had been able for a time to play off the Americans against the British by hinting that without American aid he would have to go over to Communism. Eisenhower and Dulles seemed to fear this possibility at least as strongly as Truman and Acheson had done. The British view that Musaddiq's authority was becoming increasingly shaky was ultimately justified by events, although not before the Iranian oil industry had been brought to an almost complete standstill and the Iranian Treasury almost to bankruptcy. The Shah's authority was restored by a *coup d'état* in August 1953, after Eisenhower had taken the risk of refusing economic aid in May. An international consortium, in which the British company held 40 per cent of the shares and sold the rest for £214 million to American and other companies, was set up in October 1954. The Foreign Office's waiting game had thus been justified; and the State Department's tendency to be stampeded by fear of offending nationalist forces and politicians in the Middle East had again been demonstrated.

This probably accounted for the devious course of American diplomacy with regard to the Baghdad pact. There was much to be said for the view that the pact tended to create the problem—Russian interference in the Middle East—which it was designed to remove, for it could hardly be maintained that Stalin had shown any obvious interest in the area after the Soviet withdrawal from northern Iran in 1946. Nevertheless, the United States government undoubtedly encouraged the formation of a defensive group, which seemed the natural complement to the American-inspired N.A.T.O. and S.E.A.T.O. After Turkey and Pakistan had signed a treaty of mutual consultation for defence in April 1954, Iraq decided to join Turkey in a similar treaty early in 1955, and as the Iraqi government wished to bring to an end the Anglo-Iraqi treaty of 1930 the British government thought that a multilateral pact, concluded with the other two in April 1955, would be the best alternative. Iran and Pakistan joined the pact a little later. But the pact displeased Egypt (as a source of Arab disunity), Syria (and therefore France), Israel, India, and of course the Soviet Union. So the United States drew back, and for a time sought credit for doing so in Cairo and other capitals, although later it drew nearer to the pact group and gave it supplies. 'An ounce of membership would have been worth all the havering and saved a ton of trouble later on', was Eden's subsequent comment.[1]

There was again some criticism of Dulles for his impatience with France's dithering over E.D.C. It was in this connexion that he threatened in December 1953 an 'agonizing reappraisal' of America's relations with Europe should the European army not come into being. Eden, while not liking the method, was not inclined, as were the French, to dismiss the threat as an American bluff. In any case he shared Dulles's concern lest Germany should become disillusioned with the European idea, and seek release from the existing allied restrictions. He therefore joined in the pressure on France, but it finally became clear during the spring and summer of 1954 that France was not ready, without at any rate far greater guarantees of support than Britain and the United States would offer, to surrender her sovereignty to a supranational authority in the way that E.D.C. required. It was Eden who finally discovered a way out of this impasse by bringing the Federal German Republic into a revised version of the Brussels treaty of March 1948. He secured the consent of the five, and the virtual consent of France, to this plan in a quick tour of four capitals (Brussels, Bonn, Rome, and Paris) and the matter was clinched in a conference at Lancaster House from 28 September to 3 October 1954.[2]

The London Nine-Power agreement was signed on 3 October 1954 by representatives of the six and of Great Britain, the United States, and Canada. It is a landmark of great importance in postwar diplomacy, for it not only provided the permanent political basis of western defence but also registered, after much uncertainty and embarrassment, a certain advance in mutual trustfulness by all of the signatories. For Germany the occupation régime was to end and she was to make a contribution to European defence not exceeding the twelve divisions and the tactical air force fixed under the E.D.C. treaty. She would join N.A.T.O. Great Britain promised to continue to maintain four divisions and a tactical air force, and it was this promise, with guarantees against withdrawal considerably more binding than she had ever offered in the E.D.C. discussions, which Eden introduced in a well timed speech, and which was accepted by the French as a decisive breakthrough. Italy joined the Brussels organization, and both Canada and the United States

[1] *Ibid.*, p. 336.
[2] *Ibid.*, chap. 7.

agreed to continue to provide forces for European defence. There were further negotiations in Paris, and the French Chamber, hoping for further concessions, delayed its approval until 29 December. But what became known as the Paris agreements finally came into force in May 1955.

These foreign developments, although insufficiently dramatic to stir the patriotic ardour of the newspapers, were vaguely reassuring to the public, which no doubt found diplomatic issues too technical and complicated for precise judgment. It was enough that peace continued, and that Eden and his aged leader were usefully active in the cause. They carried the bulk of the Tory backbenchers with them, although as early as 1952 a dissident group was beginning to contemplate resistance to the government's Suez policy. At home prosperity and high employment, red meat in the shops and confectionery galore with an abundance of household goods and cars, were the decisive counts, and the argument that the government's *laissez-faire* policy was unsound and that retribution was just around the corner was likewise too technical for the public, which judged by results. It could observe other successes, such as the housing drive. In the census of April 1951 13·3 million houses and flats were shown to be occupied by 14·5 million private households throughout Great Britain. Harold Macmillan, who was succeeded as Minister of Housing by Duncan Sandys in October 1954, had announced the target of 300,000 houses a year in 1951, and with 327,000 completed in 1953 and 354,000 in 1954 this figure was attained and exceeded.[1]

At the same time the country was not so escapist as to be free of apprehension about external dangers, and was ready to accept the comfort of massive rearmament now that Mr. Butler had shown so brilliantly that it could be paid for. As far as the public could judge it was developing well. The Labour government's defence programme had had to be spread over a longer period because of industrial shortages, but £1,513 million was actually expended in 1952–53, and the 1953–54 estimates promised a higher figure. Military aid from the United States meant in practice substantial dollar relief to sterling; it was fixed at $300 million for 1951–52. Against this had to be set contributions, rising to 11½ per cent of the total, to the 'N.A.T.O. common infrastructure', which meant capital investment in facilities such as military headquarters, air-fields,

[1] G. D. H. Cole, *The Post War Condition of Britain* (1956), pp. 357–62.

signal systems and the like. In this period of rearmament the strength of the British armed forces (including the reserves) rose from just over 800,000 to nearly 1½ million. Things in general were going well for the government. But the good times might not last. An early general election would be sensible.[1]

The disintegration of the Labour party leadership was from the Tory point of view a further reason for an early election. It was all very well for the old guard to deplore the brashness, self-seeking, and fratricidal publicity methods of the Bevanites, but the Labour movement faced a serious dilemma of policy which Attlee was doing nothing to resolve. What was to be the place of private enterprise in the national economy? If the patience of the electorate with rationing and governmental regulations was coming to an end with the shortages which justified it, should the Labour party enter into competition with the Conservatives in the abolition of controls? If it did, would not this be the end of planned economy? If not, would its chances of a return to power be other than remote?

The Bevanites on these issues were insistent but unhelpful. Their aim was 'democratic socialism'; the gains in social welfare already achieved must not be thrown away; rather was it necessary to press on to complete the revolution. In April 1952 Bevan set out his programme in an ambitious essay entitled *In Place of Fear*. He rejected Morrison's platform of 'consolidation'; 'the relations between public and private enterprise have not yet reached a condition where they can be stabilised'. They had still to create 'a purposive and intelligible design for society'; this was 'no place in which to halt'.[2] He was supported by Harold Wilson, Driberg, Mikardo, and others. There had been a strong pro-Bevanite swing at the annual conference at Scarborough in October 1951. A year later at the annual conference at Morecambe six Bevanites and the popular near-veteran, James (Jim) Griffiths, captured the seven seats on the National Executive. Bevan headed the voting. Morrison, Dalton, Gaitskell, Callaghan, and Shinwell were among the defeated. But Bevan's popularity, strongest with the constituency parties, decreased as he approached the centre of power. He could not dominate the Labour shadow cabinet, and resigned from it in April 1954; in the autumn he was defeated by Gaitskell in competition for the party treasurership. He was nearly expelled from the

[1] C. M. Woodhouse, pp. 82–3; *Britain, an Official Handbook* (1956 edn), pp. 96–102.
[2] A. Bevan, *In Place of Fear* (1952), p. 118.

Labour party after openly attacking Attlee in the House of Commons in March 1955 in a debate over defence, which led fifty-seven Labour members to abstain from voting.[1]

His vociferous complaints as to the lack of leadership helped to discredit Attlee without endearing Bevan to the majority of the party. The Conservatives on the other hand could go to the polls with the psychological advantage of a new leader. Sir Winston Churchill—increasingly handicapped by the weight of years and deafness and perhaps some insensitiveness to sudden new domestic (but not foreign) problems—announced what was apparently a very reluctant retirement on 5 April, 1955, after entertaining the Queen and the Duke of Edinburgh at 10, Downing Street on the 4th. Sir Anthony Eden accepted office as Prime Minister on the 6th. The experts could see signs of a new sterling crisis from the beginning of 1955, but nothing had happened as yet to upset the electorate. The general election was announced for 25 May. Butler's fourth budget, presented on 19 April, reduced the standard rate of income tax by sixpence, freed 2,400,000 taxpayers from income tax altogether, and halved purchase tax on non-woollen textiles for the benefit of the Lancashire cotton industry. A fortnight later the remaining purchase tax on these goods was removed. A busy round of strikes, which paralysed all the London newspapers from 26 March to 21 April, and brought out busmen, miners, dockers, bargees, and the footplate men, did not help Labour's cause. Nor did the promise—or threat—of further nationalization.

In the election Conservatives and associates secured 345 seats, Labour 277, Liberals 6, and Sinn Fein 2. The overall Conservative majority thus rose to sixty (including the Speaker). The total poll was 76·8 per cent as compared with 82·6 in 1951; this meant that the Tory vote fell by 421,000 and the Labour vote by 1,543,000. A reasonable conclusion from these figures was that the marginal voter, even if his earlier sympathies had been leftward, was content to leave the Conservatives in office. And if the Labour party began to give itself a more youthful appearance when Gaitskell defeated both Bevan (seventy votes) and Morrison (forty votes) for the leadership in December 1955, it had still to recapture the moment of glory of 1945.

---

[1] Cf. Dalton, pp. 408–9.

3. Eden, Sterling, and Suez

It can seldom have happened in democratic politics that recently attained power seemed more richly deserved or more firmly assured than in the case of Sir Anthony Eden in May 1955. Was his retirement twenty months later, after a curious diplomatic fiasco, proof of a sudden adverse turn in Britain's fortunes or of an unexpected collapse of his own political skill and judgment? Was this the rather tragic case of an adroit and experienced diplomat suddenly losing his head when he had attained the highest office?

The real cause of his resignation was, we must remember, a serious illness. Apart from this the explanation of his policy in the Suez crisis is to be found less in any improbable plunge out of character than in the maturing of a fresh series of challenges to existing assumptions about Britain's place in the world. The years 1955–56 have been called 'a spiritual climacteric for the Conservative Party'.[1] After the wide adjustments to new world conditions in the immediate postwar period a phase of relative stability for British interests had followed. There had been no major changes in the Commonwealth since 1947; complicated international machinery under United States direction had been functioning for some years as a barrier to world Communism; the Communists since Stalin's death in 1953 seemed content to glare at their opponents with rather static ferocity; and in domestic affairs the Tory freeing of the market had allowed three years of expansion without strain. But too many dynamic or merely restless forces had plans for profit at some cost, direct or incidental, to British interests, and the government's posture was, in the first instance at least, defensive.

Eden's tendency to mark time led him to postpone major cabinet changes until December. This was unfortunate for Butler, who was feeling the strain of four hard years at the Treasury. He was not at his best in handling the renewed financial difficulties of the later months of 1955. During the happier years of his chancellorship it had seemed possible, in defiance of experience, to achieve both the full carrying out of British commitments abroad and the continued development of production at home by *laissez-faire* methods—by leaving the economy to adjust itself. The Bank of England favoured—or was widely believed to favour—the full convertibility of sterling with a measure of deflation, although by

[1] Shonfield, p. 196.

the summer of 1955 the Treasury, warned by adverse winds, was increasingly opposed to such risks.[1] The new difficulties were due to rapid inflation, resulting from rising wages assisted by a heavy round of major strikes, and a deterioration in the balance of payments, assisted by the expansion of imports, including steel. Increases in exports had hardly been sufficient to maintain the balance even during the first half of the year. Two rises in the bank rate and some restrictions on hire purchase were thought to have righted the situation, but a more severe turn came in July. It was accompanied by a prolonged speculative attack on sterling, for which the rumours of deflation and convertibility were partly responsible. Butler had to make explicit statements in July and at the meeting of the I.M.F. at Istanbul in September, denying any intention to depart from parity of $2·80 to the pound, before this attack was halted. The credit squeeze was tightened in July, with more discriminating hire purchase restrictions; then came a highly unpopular supplementary budget in October, designed to limit public capital expenditure and private investment, to encourage savings, and to discourage the citizen from spending orgies on furniture and bedding (hire purchase again). This 'pots and pans' budget was brilliantly assailed by Gaitskell. Macmillan went to the Treasury in December, after stipulating that this must be regarded as a step towards, and not away from, the premiership. Selwyn Lloyd succeeded him as Foreign Secretary, and Butler became Lord Privy Seal and Leader of the Commons.[2]

The reconstruction of the cabinet came too late to save Eden from a remarkable round of hostile press criticism which even made it necessary for him to deny on 7 January 1956 that he was planning his retirement. But the Treasury could not greatly help him. Butler had rightly insisted that there was no real economic crisis in 1955; the curbs imposed later in the year had speedily righted the balance of payments. But while the domestic situation could be controlled effectively by government action, the chronic vulnerability of sterling in any fresh crises of speculation or confidence abroad remained. Mr. Macmillan and the influential Financial Secretary to the Treasury, Sir Edward Boyle, were not convinced that *laissez-faire* methods were adequate, and there was some tendency in 1956

[1] 'Like the cavorting of an elephant under a dust-sheet the Government's intentions remained wrapped in a species of obscurity.' Dow, p. 80.
[2] Kilmuir, pp. 255–7.

to revive the Treasury's function of policy direction almost on Crippsian lines. In February the bank rate was put up to 5½ per cent and at the same time hire purchase arrangements were tightened, food subsidies were cut by £38 million, investment allowances were restricted, and the investment programme for the nationalized industries cut by £50 million. Capital expenditure by government departments was also reduced. The cabinet is said to have discussed seriously, and nearly accepted, an increase of sixpence in the standard rate of income tax in the budget in April.[1] Nothing much could be done at the moment however about the external financial problem, which required the country with its precarious balance of payments and inadequate gold and dollar reserves to make continued heavy and often unexpected payments abroad. Thus an additional burden of £50 million had recently been added to the balance of payments to finance the stationing of British troops in Germany under the Paris agreements.

The Suez crisis later in the year was to show that the United States government, faced with a certain unresponsiveness to its exigent standards as a result of the nuclear deadlock, was developing a deliberate cat-and-mouse technique of economic coercion as a substitute. The offering and withholding of economic aid to potential friends and obstreperous satellites was also an increasingly favoured weapon of the new Soviet régime. This was one aspect of a major series of changes in the cold war struggle which neither Eden nor Dulles on the one side nor the new Russian leaders, Malenkov and Khrushchev, on the other were able to turn to full advantage, although the Russians gave signs of greater imagination and agility. After replacing Malenkov in February 1955 the Bulganin-Khrushchev régime had at first sought to prevent the ratification of the Paris agreements and West Germany's entry into N.A.T.O., and had then countered it with the setting up of a unified East European command, at the same time annulling the Anglo-Soviet treaty.[2]

Nevertheless there were persistent appeals from Moscow for the easing of east-west tensions. The 'summit' meeting at Geneva in July 1955 achieved this up to a point, although the foreign ministers' conference which followed in November provided no

---

[1] Shonfield, pp. 228–9.
[2] G. Barraclough and R. F. Wall, *Survey of International Affairs, 1955–1956* (1960), pp. 218–29, 241–9.

reconciliation between the Russian demand for a system of collective security for all Europe and the western demand for German re-unification. But by this stage the Soviet government had jumped over the political-military defences of N.A.T.O. by carrying the cold war into the Afro-Asian countries, with visions of economic aid to free them from dependence on capitalist-colonialist-imperialist warmongers and exploiters. A general offer of Soviet aid to the Middle East was made in October. At the end of the year the two Russian leaders visited India and south-east Asian countries, freely denouncing 'British imperialism'. They had a rather silent reception from curious British crowds and hosts when they toured the country, following an invitation from Eden, in April 1956, and they had one stormy passage with the Labour leaders. Thus co-existence was a continuation of the cold war by other means. Eden warned Khrush-chev that Britain would not abandon her interests in the Middle East, but it was here that the main showdown, as far as Britain was concerned, almost at once occurred.

The British quarrel with Colonel Nasser, a man of boundless ambition and self-assurance, owed its peculiar course to Soviet-American intervention, for neither of these two great powers was prepared to regard Egypt as any longer an exclusively British sphere of international interest. There were the usual references (even in Washington) to colonialism, but this had little relevance (apart from its derogatory implications) to the Anglo-Egyptian issues in 1956. It had already been arranged, under an agreement of 12 February 1953, that the Sudan was to become completely self-governing, with the withdrawal of British and Egyptian forces in three years, while the Anglo-Egyptian treaty of 27 July 1954 had provided for the withdrawal of British forces from the Suez base within twenty months, the maintenance of the base by civilians, and its reactivation only in the event of an armed threat to Turkey or to any member of the Arab League, including Egypt.[1]

But in spite of the apparent settlement of the outstanding prob-lems Great Britain remained the target for the campaign against foreign control which was basic to Nasser's popularity and survival. He needed successes, partly because he was at first less popular than the displaced General Neguib, partly because of the economic dis-

---

[1] This was accepted by all parties, although twenty-five Tory M.P.s, out of about forty members of the 'Suez Group', voted against the ratification of the agreement in the Commons. Major E. A. H. Legge-Bourne resigned the Conservative whip. L. D. Epstein, *British Politics in the Suez Crisis* (1964), pp. 42–5.

contents of the Egyptian masses, partly to satisfy the army officers who wanted to avenge defeat by Israel. He seems at first to have thought of himself more as an internal reformer—a new Ramasses or Muhammed Ali—than as a leader of the Arab world. By 1954 he had decided, as he says in a book of memoirs, 'that in the Arab circle there is a rôle wandering in search of a hero'.

There seems to have been no major difference of aims between London and Washington. Both agreed that the base, although less important under nuclear conditions, ought to be available to the western defence system; both also agreed that it was now impossible to link its maintenance with a Middle Eastern defence pact, which Egypt had rejected in 1951 and 1954. Eden and Dulles were both convinced of the need to work with the new Egyptian régime, and although the Americans seemed more willing to take Egyptian protestations at their face value the two agreed as to the need to provide substantial economic aid, mainly American. This was just sufficient to restrain Nasser from complete absorption in the dynamic, anti-western, anti-Israeli, pan-Arab campaign for which he evidently hankered.

Instead he favoured for a time a policy of ostensible neutralism which was rather too obviously designed to stimulate competitive bidding by the two great-power blocs. A treaty of friendship with India and attendance at the Bandung conference in April 1955 associated him with the growing self-assertive neutralism of the Afro-Asian countries; a visit to Moscow in August was followed by an arms deal with Czechoslovakia which freed him from dependence for military aid on the western powers and seemed to be the prelude, with Soviet connivance, to a concentrated attack with other Arab states on Israel. The United States and Britain countered this move by agreeing later in 1955 to help finance a vastly expensive scheme for a High Dam at Aswan on the Nile. But Nasser proceeded to demonstrate his independence by other gestures such as his recognition of the Chinese Communist government on 16 May 1956.

In the end the effect was the opposite of that intended, for while it inclined Eden to the view that Nasser was beginning to look very much like a small Hitler or Mussolini it convinced Dulles that the High Dam scheme was no longer a viable proposition. This was partly because the Russian arms had to be paid for out of some or all of the funds earmarked for the dam,[1] but also because Nasser

[1] There were various estimates as to the cost. As against a minimum of $1,300 million

let it be known that he hoped to add a Soviet loan to that of the west. Dulles said in May that in that case the United States would not participate, and on 19 July, following an expression of doubt by the Senate Appropriations Committee, he announced that the American offer was withdrawn. Britain did the same: both governments acted without considering any of the political implications of these ostensibly economic questions.[1] The Bank's offer lapsed, and on the 26th the Egyptian President, in a two-and-a-half hour speech, announced that Egypt had nationalized the Suez Canal Company and would use the revenue to build the dam. The shareholders would be compensated at the market rate. How this was to be done if the revenue was devoted to the dam was not explained.

This was the setting of the Suez crisis, certainly the most dramatic, although not the most important, episode in Britain's postwar foreign relations. Sir Anthony Eden's own account has been given, with every appearance of frankness, in his memoirs. As the governments concerned acted under the maximum arc lamps of modern publicity much is known of the day to day negotiations, but many of the exchanges between the governments necessarily remain obscure.[2] It was, however, evident from the start that there was widespread and genuine alarm among the canal users at the Egyptian action, but that there was even greater alarm on the part of most of them at the prospect of any action which would lead to war. After diplomatic protests by the French and British governments on 27 July Egypt's sterling assets were frozen, Gaitskell told the House of Commons that the Labour party deeply deplored Egypt's 'high-handed and totally unjustifiable step',[3] and the twenty-four signatories of the 1888 Suez Canal convention were invited to confer in London. In mid-August Dulles's proposal for a Suez Canal Board which would provide for the international operation of the canal was accepted by eighteen states, and Mr. Menzies, the

---

it was proposed that Egypt should supply $900 million in materials and services, while the World Bank had promised $200 million. Initially the United States and Britain were to supply $56 million and $14 million respectively. As Nasser had earmarked the cotton crop to pay for the Czechoslovak-Soviet arms its seemed likely that the western powers and the World Bank might be saddled with the whole cost of the dam.

[1] Kilmuir, p. 267.

[2] A good account of the crisis, incorporating all the then available material, is that of G. Barraclough, *Survey of International Affairs 1956–1958* (1962), pp. 3–71. In Lord Avon's memoirs, *Full Circle* (1960), pp. 419–584 deal with the crisis. M. and S. Bromberger, *The Secrets of Suez* (Eng. translation, 1957) offers some startling, but rather unconvincing, disclosures from French sources. These are amplified by Terence Robertson, *Crisis, the Inside Story of the Suez Conspiracy* (1965).

[3] P.D., 5 Ser., HC, vol. 557, 27 July 1956, cols. 777–8.

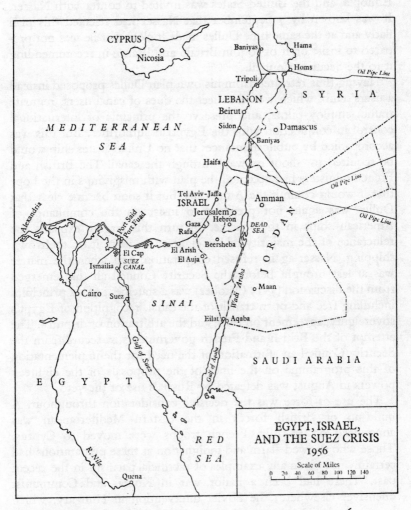

EGYPT, ISRAEL, AND THE SUEZ CRISIS, 1956

Australian Prime Minister, with representatives of Persia, Sweden, Ethiopia, and the United States was invited to confer with Nasser. It was known by 7 September that Nasser had rejected this plan flatly and at the same time Dulles made it clear that he was not prepared to insist on it or to join Britain and France in recommending it to the Security Council.

Having thus retreated from his own plan Dulles proposed instead a users' club, which would collect the dues of canal users, regulate traffic, employ pilots, and preserve the principle of international control in conjunction with the Egyptian authorities. But this was accompanied by public assurances that no United States ship would be required to 'shoot its way' through the canal. The British and French ministers had accepted the plan with misgivings in the hope that it would commit the Americans, but it soon became clear that Dulles was again not prepared to insist on the compliance of American ships in the scheme. In turn this largely explains the reluctance of the majority of the eighteen to force it on their own shipping. Nasser again refused cooperation, and when the matter was at last brought before the Security Council all that emerged from the discussion (5–13 October) was a statement of six principles including free and open transit of the canal, recognition of Egypt's sovereignty, agreement on tolls, and the arbitration of disputes. The attempt of the British and French governments to secure from the Security Council an affirmation of the need for the implementation of this programme on the lines of the proposals of the eighteen powers in August was defeated by Russia's use of the veto.

The use of force was the decisive consideration throughout. A build-up of British forces in the eastern Mediterranean was announced on 30 July. French troops were moved to Cyprus. Those who showed alarm and indignation at these preparations had certainly not given any examples of sacrificial pacifism in the recent past. There had been a major war in Korea, and Communist offensives elsewhere; the Soviet intervention in Hungary, which began on 24 October, was soon to show the determination to maintain positions behind the Iron Curtain. As in similar earlier periods of great-power deadlock, brinkmanship flourished; it was tempting to take risks, relying on the other party to give way at the eleventh hour. In January 1955 Eisenhower had asked Congress for authority to take military action against the Chinese mainland if the concentration of Chinese forces there were such as to constitute an immediate threat to the security of Formosa and the Pescadores. Dulles claimed later that the fact that such an attack did not take place was due to the warning. Did not the forcible seizure of the canal by Nasser threaten British and French interests more immediate than the American interest in Quesmoy?[1] It was not brinkmanship but the possibility that they did not intend to stop at the brink that alarmed Dulles. He told Selwyn Lloyd at the beginning of October that he 'once more' recognized the Anglo-French right to maintain the threat of using force, and did not even rule it out as an ultimate resort, although he was convinced that its use in the immediate future would be a mistake.[2]

He was in fact saying, realistically if not very heroically, that in the existing circumstances they and he could not get away with it. There are three practical considerations which clearly justified this view. First, the British and French forces were geographically outside the area of possible operations; an existing footing or a local invitation (as in Kashmir, Malaya, Hungary, Korea, Tibet, Guatemala and elsewhere) was necessary for effective intervention unless indeed it was backed by an unusually powerful wave of world opinion. Secondly, however provocative and offensive, the Egyptian action was economic and not military in character, and any form of armed retaliation seemed disproportionately severe to influential bodies of opinion throughout the world, including the United States voters on the eve of a presidential election. Thirdly, there was the aura of colonialism, so irrelevant and yet so pervasive; although the Anglo-French action was in defence of the international rights of the canal users it was assumed with scarcely a second thought in the Communist and Afro-Asian countries that these rights were a relic of earlier colonial bondage and that the angry reaction of the two powers was due to their inability to abandon older attitudes of dominance. Krishna Menon, the Indian delegate to the United Nations, took the lead in organizing Afro-Asian condemnation in the harshest terms of Anglo-French action, and continued to fan the embers as long as possible.[3]

---

[1] Cf. the letter of A. L. Goodhart to *The Times*, 3 November 1956, asking this question. In 1954 American military and naval assistance had secured the forcible overthrow of the pro-Communist government in Guatamala, with the acquiescence of the British government.

[2] Avon, pp. 502–3. Dulles's policy and tactics are severely condemned as detrimental to American interests and misleading to America's allies by Herman Finer, *Dulles Over Suez* (1964), pp. 491–512.

[3] Robertson, pp. 304–5.

With the reverberations of this debate in our ears it is easy to forget that the short phase of Anglo-French intervention at the beginning of November was due to a new development and was not, ostensibly at least, an attempt to reverse the nationalization of the canal company. Indeed, there is no doubt that after the success of Nasser and the State Department in dragging out the negotiations for over three months any such attempt would have been impracticable, particularly as the company had erred badly in claiming that the withdrawal of its pilots would paralyse the Egyptian attempts at navigation. The new development was the Israeli attack on Egypt starting on 29 October. It was outstandingly successful, and Eden comments in his memoirs that 'the marked victim of the garrotter is not to be condemned if he strikes out before the noose is round his throat'.[1] That a noose existed and was about to be tightened seemed a reasonable assumption from the signs of increased self-confidence on Nasser's part following the frustration of the canal users, the renewal in October of *fedayeen* raids, the setting up on 25 October of a joint armed command under supreme Egyptian direction of the Egyptian, Syrian, and Jordanian forces, and a Jordanian announcement that the time had come.

These developments and the Egyptian build-up of its forces with £150 million worth of Soviet equipment were certainly not invented or concocted in London or Paris to justify Anglo-French intervention. Yet much of the subsequent debate turned on the question of 'collusion', either between Israel and France, or between both and Great Britain. In its crudest form this means that France instigated and undertook to support in some form the Israeli offensive. Britain was generally assumed to have had some idea as to what was going on, but not to have been actively involved,[2] although there are persistent assertions about secret meetings and assurances which await verification from the official documents. Much of this seems in any case to be making a mystery out of nothing, or very little. Since Mr. Ben-Gurion's return to office as Prime Minister early in 1955 retaliatory raids against the *fedayeen* had been stepped up, and it was obvious that the fiercely efficient Israeli army might hit out at any time. But the British government had good reason for not welcoming such an Israeli offensive in spite of the grudge

---

[1] Avon, p. 523.

[2] Robertson, pp. 146–67, elaborates the theme of Anglo-French connivance; Lord Kilmuir, a member of the cabinet, says that the 'wild accusations of collusion' had 'absolutely no foundation in fact' (*Political Adventure*, p. 278).

Conservative Comeback

against Nasser. Support of Israel would finally lose them all Arab regard, even in Iraq, and an Israeli attack on Jordan would, under the existing treaties, compel Britain to intervene in Jordan's, and therefore Egypt's, defence.[1] The Israeli operations in Sinai were so successful that the Egyptian forces east of the canal had been largely destroyed in six days, and from one point of view it might have been better to risk allowing the fighting to go on, with a possible overthrow, and certainly the discrediting, of Nasser's government. But this might have brought the rest of the Arab countries into the attack on Israel, and again involved the British treaty with Jordan, among other things.

The explanation of the British government's policy which most closely fits the facts is that its moves were defensive throughout a crisis in which, in spite of its resolute bearing, it did not really control the course of events. Eden had never plunged readily into great decisions and adventures; as a diplomatist his expertise had been mainly exercised in skilful negotiation designed to repair, frustrate, or benefit from the impetuosity of others.[2] In the present crisis the initiative had been held successively by Dulles, by Nasser, by Dulles again during the 'canal users' phase, by the Security Council, and then by the French, allegedly in connivance with the Israeli government. If, as seems probable, Eden did not share in the 'collusion', this again emphasizes the extent to which the initiative was held by others. The decision that was now taken, in the form of an Anglo-French ultimatum of 30 October, was, from the British point of view at least, an attempt to prevent a worse, rather than to secure a better, position. It called on the two belligerents to retire to positions ten miles east and west of the Suez canal. Failing agreement within twelve hours, British and French forces would enforce compliance.

When Egypt refused, intervention followed; but it was called off on the initiative of London against the French wishes as a result of angry and horrified pressure from Washington and New York six days later. The ultimatum is said to have favoured Israel in that it left her in occupation of most of the Sinai peninsula. But she

---

[1] Robertson, pp. 146, 163, 369–70.
[2] e.g. his reaction to Germany's occupation of the Rhineland in 1936, foreign intervention in Spain in 1937, Chamberlain's plans for agreement with Italy in 1938, and the situation in French Indo-China in 1954. In the second World War the great decisions were essentially Churchill's; the supporting and consolidating diplomatic rôle as Foreign Secretary suited Eden admirably.

had already victoriously established herself over most of this area, and the ultimatum while preventing her further advance did nothing to guarantee her permanent possession. It may well have saved Nasser from defeat and supersession. The decision to make the canal the dividing line was intended to ensure its availability to international traffic, and the two powers also maintained that with their special interest in the area their intervention was justified by the chronic failure of the United Nations in the past to solve the Israeli border problem or to ensure the passage of Israeli ships through the canal. Nevertheless the action in its international setting was clumsy in the extreme. If collusion were really involved, the moment when Americans were being asked to vote for Eisenhower the peacemaker was the worst possible one to choose.

The effect of the crisis on British public opinion will probably remain a puzzle to the historian, for any possible electoral consequences were soon to be mixed up with an unfavourable economic turn and indeed the government was losing constituency support before the crisis broke. The party debate was violent, but not clear cut. On the Conservative side some M.P.s were shocked by the government's intervention, and some by its retreat. The former included two ministers outside the cabinet, Sir Edward Boyle and Anthony Nutting, Minister of State to the Foreign Office, who both resigned. Eight 'anti-Suez' Conservative M.P.s abstained from supporting the government on 8 November, but the bulk of the anti-Suez dissidents (estimated at between twenty-five and forty) did not challenge the government. Similarly the Suez group, also estimated at between twenty-five and forty-five members, limited their protest at the withdrawal of troops in December to speeches and some abstentions.[1] On the other hand a Labour M.P., Mr. Stanley Evans, resigned both his seat and his membership of the Labour party because of his approval of the government's policy, and one or two of Labour's elder statesmen were markedly sympathetic.[2] Labour spokesmen in the Commons had at first condemned Nasser's seizure of the Canal, and there was a growing satisfaction among some ex-service elements and working men at the government's tough line with the Egyptians. When Parliament was recalled for a two-day debate on 12 September it was evident that the Opposition

---

[1] Epstein, pp. 87–94.

[2] 'Eden did not deserve the hysterical abuse hurled at him during the Suez controversy. Neither did the brave State of Israel, which had been repeatedly threatened by Nasser.' Morrison, *An Autobiography*, p. 298.

had decided on a policy of all-out attack, and on 1 October a resolution at the Labour party conference evoked such expressions of sympathy for President Nasser as to lead even Gaitskell to give a warning against playing into Tory hands. His own wireless speech on 3 November, with an emotional, high-pitched call to Eden's followers to depose him, sounded decidedly 'party-political' to many who wanted a measured judgment, and the Opposition's boos and catcalls in the Commons debates after Parliament reassembled on the 6th may have strengthened the marked swing of public opinion in the government's favour. According to one public opinion poll support for Eden increased from $48\frac{1}{2}$ per cent on 30 October to $60\frac{1}{2}$ per cent on 21 November; according to another, from 40 to 53 per cent in the fortnight ending 14 November. The government had had a sensational setback in the Tonbridge by-election on 7 June, when the Conservative majority in a safe seat fell from 10,196 to 1,062; now in another by-election in another safe seat at Chester on 15 November the Conservative poll fell by only 5 per cent.[1]

4. RETHINKING CONSERVATIVE POLICY

Mr. Harold Macmillan's appointment as Prime Minister on 10 January 1957 was no more than an indirect result of the Suez crisis; Sir Anthony Eden's colleagues seem to have been agreed that his retirement was politically inexpedient at this moment,[2] but he had to accept the unanimous advice of his doctors. With several more years of high office he might well have placed his premiership in a different perspective, for the lessons of the Suez crisis were not all unfavourable. Under his unflappable successor the Conservatives did indeed enjoy another spell of fair fortune and popularity similar to that of the 1951–54 years.

The immediate result of the Suez crisis in the diplomatic field was the hasty despatch by the United Nations of an international police force, something which had been much talked about and never achieved hitherto; the Israeli army returned to base, the Anglo-French forces were withdrawn, Egypt's military weakness, in spite of the expensive Soviet equipment (much of which had passed

---

[1] Avon, p. 546; *Annual Register* for 1956, p. 56.
[2] Cf. Avon, p. 583. Churchill in mid-December considered the situation 'a magnificent position to fight back from' (p. 575). Retirement would be interpreted in some quarters as a confession of embarrassment or shame for which sentiments there seems little evidence. Selwyn Lloyd continued in office as Foreign Secretary until July 1960.

into Israeli hands) had been demonstrated, and although the Egyptian government did its best to treat the whole affair as a resounding victory it acquiesced in the patrolling of the Gaza strip and the opening of the port of Eilat, two developments of great benefit to Israeli nerves and economy. If the crisis had shown that the British government could not intervene in the Red Sea and western Mediterranean region as freely as it had done in the past it had also shown that the highly equivocal attitude of Britain's Nato allies towards Middle Eastern affairs would have to be modified in their own interest. Moreover, if we are thinking in terms of the general balance of military power in the world, we must not exaggerate the significance of the Anglo-French retreat. It has never been true that a great power is free to throw its weight about at will; tensions along the international frontiers between the major power blocs in the world have made the coercion of small neighbours an extremely hazardous affair in most circumstances, although it remains easy in others. The U.S.A. could intervene in South Korea, but not in North Korea; in Guatemala but not in Cuba. Soviet forces could dominate Hungary but not West Berlin. Foiled in Egypt, the British sent troops into Kuwait and the Buraimi oasis area during the next few years.[1] All the evidence seems to show that the Soviet threat of nuclear intervention was treated lightly, while the violent reaction of the United Nations Organization made a deep impression.

Thus the problems that faced the new Prime Minister were in some respects less formidable than some of the government's critics hopefully imagined. Macmillan's undoubted political flair, combined with a more forthcoming attitude by the United States government, led to a fairly rapid *dénouement* of the Suez affair. On 5 January 1957 Eisenhower announced a new 'doctrine' for the Middle East: the United States would accept an invitation to protect any Middle Eastern state against Communist aggression up to a figure of $200 million. Congress agreed, and although there were complaints from some quarters about the cost and from others about the lateness of the decision, it had been made clear that the State

---

[1] It is, at any rate, unwise to generalize from the Suez episode as to Britain's reduced power in the world. In 1895, when according to some historians she was ruling the world and the waves, she was prevented from having her way in a diplomatic dispute with Venezuela by the intervention of a misinformed American President. She was continually harassed by other powers in carrying out her Egyptian policy between 1882 and 1904.

Department had abandoned its punctilious adhesion to the frustrating machinery of the United Nations as soon as the presidential election was over.[1] Dulles returned to his more typical policy of energetic maintenance of the world front against Communism, exhorting and bolstering his friends and allies in the struggle with phrases of a calculated toughness which just stopped short of incitement to violence. Talks in Bermuda (21-24 March) between Eisenhower, Macmillan, Dulles, and Selwyn Lloyd re-established personal contacts and reaffirmed the Security Council's resolution of October 1956 about the freedom of the Canal. There were provisions for strengthening the nuclear defences of western Europe, and the United States somewhat modified its equivocal attitude to the Baghdad pact. The Queen accompanied by Prince Philip visited the United States in October after a state visit to Canada, and immediately afterwards Macmillan went to Washington and signed with the President a Declaration of Common Purpose.

Nevertheless the new Prime Minister was no more ready than his predecessor to accept the full rigidity of the Dulles policy of containment. In the struggle with Communism as well as in the related fields of economic policy, western European integration, and Commonwealth relations, there were already signs before the end of the year of a new approach to many problems of external policy. At home, where recurrent economic crises had kept alive so much uneasy speculation as to the ultimate viability of the welfare state, there was an equal need for a study of new expedients. The results began to show themselves more clearly after the election of 1959 had given the Conservatives another five years of office. But there had been a start, deceptively promising perhaps, in 1957 and 1958.

A fresh economic crisis was successfully handled in 1957, although the dilemma remained. It was agreed that trading conditions were generally good. The terms of trade had shown no appreciable deterioration since a small setback in 1953; some heavy losses and a fall in the reserves, due to the Suez crisis and expenditure to meet the oil losses, were rather speedily restored. The gold and dollar reserves indeed increased by $297 million between February and June 1957. But after this they plunged again, with losses of $225 million in August and $292 million in September, to a total of only $1,850 million in September 1957. It was again a crisis due primarily

[1] And before the announcement of Sir Anthony Eden's resignation.

to the behaviour of foreign speculators, influenced this time by anticipation of sterling devaluation in September. It did not ease the Treasury's embarrassment that as usual the speculator was for the most part anonymous, the gnome in the bank in Zürich or some other foreign capital; the government's vast decisions had to be based on what the gnome might be expected to believe. On this occasion the reason seemed to be in the main a doubt as to whether Great Britain would be able to hold her economic position in the world against the competition of the thumping new prosperity of West Germany, whose D-mark was expected to be upvalued. Instead of devaluation the bank rate was raised on 19 September 1957 to 7 per cent, the highest since 1920. This dramatic move was an emphatic resumption of monetary leadership which caused quite a sensation and effectively checked the outflow of gold and dollars. The reserves began to rise again.[1]

But the dilemma was not resolved. The expansion of British industry was being hampered by the determination of the government to maintain, for essentially political reasons, what some regarded as an outmoded external financial policy.[2] In this view investment was being held back at home and encouraged to go abroad to the detriment of British industry and even of the arts; exports had to be boosted at the expense of domestic needs in order to earn foreign exchange for political ends, such as the maintenance of garrisons throughout the world from Bermuda to Hong Kong. The 1955 crisis had shown that it was not enough to rely merely on adjustments in the rates of interest and exchange to determine the level of economic activity at home and ensure a satisfactory balance of payments abroad. Macmillan's expedients in 1956 had had some success, measuring success by the holding back of industrial production in order to ensure solvency abroad. In the process the demand for labour had been reduced, with ominous criticisms of any policy of planned unemployment. But a major cause of the crisis was also seen to lie in the field of government expenditure.

The Conservatives had continued the Labour practice of making vast funds available for state-supported schemes, while urging the banks to show restraint in giving credit to private borrowers. This expenditure by creating incomes and fostering many industrial and

[1] Dow, pp. 94–102; Youngson, pp. 179–85.
[2] 'There was a good deal of vestigial imperialism—of a civilized twentieth-century type—in this ideology.' Shonfield, p. 253, and chap. 10 generally for a stimulating analysis, and comments by M. B. Brown, *After Imperialism*, pp. 311–20.

other developments was itself a major contribution to the inflationary spiral. Thorneycroft, the Chancellor of the Exchequer, in a statement accompanying the bank rise of 19 September, accordingly announced the maintenance of the exchange parity of the pound even at the expense of something less than full employment and of extra controls on the supply of money. This was worked out during the following weeks, in a programme whereby governmental expenditure was to be held 'within the level attained this year'. The Chancellor was not prepared to eat these brave words when their practical implications were challenged. Some of his cabinet colleagues, evidently supported by the Prime Minister, asked for some elasticity, and Thorneycroft resigned on 6 January 1958. The new Chancellor was Heathcoat Amory, who had been a successful Minister of Agriculture. He announced at once that the government's policy had not changed. The incident passed, owing to Macmillan's superb handling, without any sense of crisis. Many thought that the unchallenged ascendancy over the party which he attained dated from this moment.[1]

It was the policy of carefully balanced regulation in both the domestic and foreign sectors of the economy, with no final solution of the problem of reconciling domestic and external economic objectives, which characterized the government's policy during the next two years. There were no fresh crises, and it became evident in the general election of 1959 that a significant section of the industrial working class was satisfied with the way in which things were ticking over. The balance of payments was highly satisfactory in 1958, and smaller, although still very favourable, in 1959. It was found possible to lower the bank rate by stages during the year from 7 to 4 per cent, and to turn from a policy of restricting business activity to the promotion of expansion. This was mildly foreshadowed in the budget in April 1958, which gave some small reliefs in taxation and increased initial depreciation allowances on plant, machinery, and industrial building; but the main advance came in July, with the easing of restrictions on bank lending and thus of the credit squeeze. Industrial production increased a little in 1958, and rather more in 1959; unemployment gradually fell to the low figure of 421,000 in December 1959 (1·9 per cent). In the 1959 budget the Chancellor felt it safe to announce substantial reductions in the income tax (ninepence off the standard rate) and purchase

[1] G. Mallaby, *From My Level*, p. 63.

tax, and twopence off the price of beer, together with the restoration of allowances for investment and for new plant, machinery, and industrial building with as much as 40 per cent allowance for new mining works.

It could not be said that the foreign scene, as the Englishman viewed it with continued uneasiness in the late nineteen-fifties, presented any outstanding triumph for the government. Although the Russians had not been particularly forthcoming during 1958, Mr. Macmillan evidently retained hopes that their frequent requests for a summit meeting might lead to some easing of tensions if not to any major settlements; but as Soviet diplomacy concentrated more and more urgently on the 'solution' of the problem of West Berlin, from which the western powers were not prepared to budge, the deadlock continued. Nevertheless, the Prime Minister's visit to Russia (20 February to 3 March 1959) was popular in England, although unwelcome to West Germany and France. Meanwhile the orderly devolution of Britain's Commonwealth commitments was complicated by all the subtle variations in attitude of her friends, allies, and outspoken critics in the United Nations. Rather too many people at home and abroad were seeking the credit of pushing the government along rather faster than it could safely go.

Macmillan's tour of India, Pakistan, Ceylon, Malaya, Australia, and New Zealand at the beginning of 1958 was memorable in many ways, and it was followed on his return by an eloquent reaffirmation of belief in the 'mysterious and almost incredible development in the structure of the Commonwealth, which has strengthened it instead of weakening it'. This meant in practice a firm decision to complete the movement towards self-government and independence even of those parts of the British Commonwealth in Africa which had seemed the least suited for it only a few years earlier; it meant in due course the parting of the ways with South Africa; and it meant a faith in the ability of experienced British and largely inexperienced African administrators to improvise institutions, administrative élites, and habits of cooperation at desperately short notice. If the new Nigeria, independent within the Commonwealth in October 1960, was a vindication of these methods, the tragedy of the too-hasty devolution of Belgian rule in the Congo a few months earlier was a warning. The death of eleven Mau-Mau detainees at the Hola camp on 3 March 1959, together with the rioting and violence throughout Nyasaland in February and March, were reminders of the physical realities of government in a period of transition. Mr. Justice Devlin's report on the Nyasaland disturbances agreed that the government was justified in taking action if it was not to abdicate, but questioned the existence of an organized conspiracy by the African National Congress. This was seized on by the government's critics, and Gaitskell was also critical of the government's past record when a settlement of the triangular British–Greek–Turkish animosities in Cyprus was announced to the Commons on 19 February 1959.

And yet in these conditions the task of the leader of the Opposition was not easy. The country was showing a decided inclination to be content, if not delighted, with its lot. The general trend of the by-election figures was puzzling rather than encouraging to Labour. Although the Conservative vote had fallen dramatically in the Tonbridge election in June 1956 the Labour vote had remained almost the same. In a series of contests during the next twelve months the Conservative vote was generally down, and the Labour vote generally up, but not sufficiently to promise a general-election victory. It seemed that Tory voters, through apathy or dissatisfaction, were withholding support from their party without giving it to Labour; sometimes they gave it to the Liberals. At Edinburgh South in May 1957, and at Gloucester in September, the appearance of an effective Liberal candidate led to a Tory loss and Liberal gain in each case of over 20 per cent of the poll; the Labour vote hardly changed. The Liberals gained a moral victory (with second place and 17,603 votes) at Rochdale in February 1958, and an actual victory over a 'National Liberal and Conservative' candidate at Torrington in March. In both cases Labour polled less than in 1955. After this the Liberals did less well, and the Conservatives seemed to be holding their positions with figures not much below those of the last general election.

This meant that the Opposition was forced to attack at a disadvantage; with the tide still running against socialist plans of control there was no great policy platform for the Labour party, and the tactics of making an industrious hullabuloo about current problems might easily miscarry against so circumspect an opponent as Macmillan. Thus the Opposition persisted in airing suspicions of a Treasury leakage over the raising of the bank rate in September 1957 in spite of their dismissal by the Lord Chancellor as of no significance; Macmillan finally appointed a tribunal under Lord

Justice Parker which rejected the allegations in January 1958, and left the Opposition with its mare's nest.

But still there were hopes of an electoral swing, for the government had had its setbacks, including Suez; moreover, Labour had closed its' ranks. In October 1956 Aneurin Bevan was elected Treasurer of the party, narrowly defeating Mr. George Brown, and with his agreement to act as Labour's Shadow Foreign Secretary the feud with Gaitskell seemed to have ended. Bevan showed himself during the next three years to be increasingly willing to identify himself with the Labour Establishment, and in the process he almost ceased to be a Bevanite. At the 1957 Labour party conference at Brighton he secured with Frank Cousins's support the defeat of a motion condemning the manufacture of the H-bomb by Britain, and it was said that the ghost of Bevin had come back to earth. When at the same conference Harold Wilson and Gaitskell secured overwhelming acceptance for the plan to increase government investment in industry it was believed by some critics, prematurely as it turned out, that this device had secured the essentials of nationalization without the stigma.

The theme of under-investment was taken up by Mr. Roy Jenkins in *The Labour Case*, a 'Penguin' published on the eve of the election in 1959. He was able to show that Butler, Macmillan, and Thorneycroft had restricted facilities for industrial private investment by various devices in 1955, 1956, and 1957, and he considered that the restoration of the investment allowance in the 1959 budget had come too late. But there was no effective counter to the Conservative rejoinder that the internal economy had to be restricted in the interest of the country's external economic relations. The Labour party's election programme concentrated instead on the government's record abroad, and there was much talk of the scandal of Suez, of Hola and Devlin, and of the government's dubious record or intentions elsewhere. There were also ambitious plans for the expansion of the social services. Labour published a National Superannuation plan in 1957. An alternative Conservative plan was revealed a year later, and was on the Statute Book by the time of the 1959 election. Labour's final proposals for the health service were published on 25 August 1959.

The Tories prepared for battle with professional assistance in the arts of publicity; their campaign, skilfully directed by Lord Woolton, capitalized the virtues of 'Super-Mac', and Macmillan himself made legitimate play with a loan from his American phrase book, 'you've never had it so good'.[1] Each side seemed to be hoping for a gaffe from the other and it was the Labour leader who fell into the trap of over-definition. That all election programmes are self-contradictory can be taken almost as an axiom of democratic politics, for any popular programme of promises must have its unpopular counterpart of means and costs. Gaitskell seems to have been uneasy from the start lest the social reforms promised in his party's manifesto should frighten the electorate with the spectre of increased taxation, and on 28 September he gave a pledge at Newcastle that there would be 'no increase in the standard or other rates of income tax under the Labour Government so long as normal peacetime conditions continue'. He appears to have meant that the money would come from the yield of increased industrial output. His opponents naturally argued that if direct taxes were untouched, indirect taxation, which fell heaviest on the poor, must be substituted. 'A bribe a day keeps the Tories away', was Butler's comment on 2 October. The elections took place on 8 October 1959, and resulted in another decisive victory for the Conservative party, which increased its lead over Labour and Liberals to 102 seats. It also had a clear majority over Labour in the total votes cast (13,749,830 to 12,215,538). The Labour vote fell by 189,000, the Conservatives increased by 463,000. The Liberals, however, gained nearly a million votes, although as they had put up candidates in 106 more constituencies than in 1955 some of this could be expected.

The lesson seemed easy to read. The government lost votes in those industrial areas which had not had it so good; it gained, and gained on balance, in those in which prosperity continued. Thus it was mainly in Lancashire and parts of industrial Scotland that there was a swing towards Labour in 178 constituencies, whereas the swing to the Conservatives, which took place in 436 constituencies, was most clearly marked in the very prosperous Midland and London suburban areas, associated with the flourishing motor and allied industries. The highly paid workers were perhaps voting against nationalization, or, as some suggested, were registering their annoyance with unofficial strikes. What was clear was that the election had not been swayed by attacks on the government's

---

[1] In a speech at Bedford on 20 July 1957. But he went on to ask whether this prosperity could be maintained in the face of rising prices. 'Can we control inflation? This is the problem of our time.'

external policy; indeed, it was the opinion of James Griffiths that
many Labour candidates had lost support through the whisper that
they were more interested in Africa than in their own country.
Lord Morrison said more bluntly that the Labour party had given
the impression that it was 'rather anti-British'.[1] Roy Jenkins
however read the lesson in terms of domestic politics. He put
forward five causes of defeat on 4 November. These were fear of the
consequences of Labour's financial policies; dislike of unofficial
strikes; the restrictive practices of some local Labour authorities;
Labour's class basis; and continued dislike of nationalization. Some
of these objections were now of long standing. Others were disquietingly recent, and while the Labour party began a prolonged
post-mortem, the Tories could think with unhurried self-satisfaction
of their plans for the nineteen-sixties.

[1] Morrison, *An Autobiography*, pp. 318–19.

13

INTO THE NINETEEN-SIXTIES

IT could scarcely be denied that the state of the nation in the early sixties was one of remarkable stability and prosperity. The capitalistic system, so discredited in the thirties, seemed now a guarantee that, under intelligent direction, the public well-being might continue indefinitely. Was there also a tendency to be bored with pleas for more productive effort and foresight? The public mood was not easy to judge. After so much trial and tribulation since 1914 men were finding life easier, with few fundamental issues to distract them. The nuclear deadlock was as much a reality as full employment. And yet the Prime Minister was unable to deny that there was still much to do, and his opponents did their best to dispel any easy confidence that he or his Conservative colleagues could be relied on to do it. His tone was defensive when he told the Foreign Press Association on 29 May 1963 that in absolute terms Britain's military power and prosperity had never been greater.

The chiding voice of a Labour spokesman on the same occasion did not suggest that there was anything amiss with Britain's own position: nevertheless, 'tremendous problems' must soon be faced. 'We have', said Mr. George Brown, 'to be less selfish, to think rather less of ourselves, rather more of the kind of society that we want the world to be, rather more of what we can give than what we can take.' Perhaps the British public felt that it had done enough for the world. Opposition attacks during the next twelve months helped to destroy the image of Tory all-sufficiency, without creating a decisive swing in favour of Labour.

The major political task now facing the parties was to discover new programmes and slogans and even fresh crises after the consummation of so many earlier efforts. The country had made good its retreat from some of the untenable positions that it had previously held abroad. Its version of a capitalistic economy called for increasingly skilful and sophisticated handling but not for abolition.[1] Thus the new orientation of policy had to be sought in the less expected and less desirable consequences of the revolution in the country's domestic and external affairs: there was no serious desire to reverse the revolution itself.

1. MEDIOCRITY AND MERITOCRACY

There were certainly no second thoughts about the country's living standards. The advance since 1945 amounted to a major social revolution, and there was more to come. The expectation of life at birth in 1958–60 was now 68·1 years for males and 73·9 for females, as compared with 45·8 for males and 52·4 for females at the beginning of the century. Infant mortality rates had fallen from 138 per 1,000 live births in 1901–05 to 21 per 1,000 in 1961. The population of the United Kingdom rose correspondingly from 38·2 million in 1901 to 52·8 million in 1961. But the increase in numbers had not resulted in any deterioration in public health. It has been remarked that when we talk today of malnutrition we think of underdeveloped countries; in the nineteen-thirties the term applied nearer home, where half the population was considered to be living on an inadequate diet.[2]

The improved expectation of life brought new problems and opportunities. Men and women could work longer. On the other hand the numbers of aged people and the problem of their maintenance increased too. There were significant changes in the activities of women. Families continued to be small, and marriages were taking place earlier. As a result, many married women had their children off their hands before they reached middle age. This, with the constant demand for labour in both industry and the professions, led many women to resume careers for which they had been trained before marriage, and it was evident that the opposition to their employment (which had been widespread in the teaching profession for instance before the war) was lessening. This was essentially a by-product of full employment, and the increased expectation of life meant that older women could settle down to

[1] A. Shonfield's *Modern Capitalism* (1965) is a notable assertion of the view that prosperity can continue under the existing system, subject to a more energetic deployment in Britain of public planning of the private sector of the economy.
[2] G. M. Carstairs, *This Island Now* (1963), pp. 29, 40; Lord Boyd Orr, *Food, Health and Income* (1937).

twenty or thirty years of a career. Domestic service attracted fewer and fewer, but the married couple, with double salaries or pay packets, could to some extent solve the domestic problem with labour-saving kitchens, tinned or deep-frozen food, drip-dry clothing, and other civilized devices.[1] With men too in continuous steady employment the effect of the consumer revolution was to transform the working class into the outward semblance of the middle class, or at least to start it moving in that direction—after all, there was no alternative model. With the blessings of regular employment and hire purchase the washing machine, television set, vacuum cleaner, car, holidays with pay, hair-do's and nylon stockings for women, standardized and ubiquitous lounge suits, felt hats, and beach wear of the ready-made clothiers for men, were as much symbols of social egalitarianism as the privilege, now shared by all, of queueing, sometimes for hours, in doctors' waiting rooms for 'free' medical attention. If there were still poor people there was no longer 'the Poor'. By the early sixties the social problem was that of knowing how to satisfy the vast numbers who had had time to discover that the new prosperity could bring with it new embarrassments, horizons, and frustrations.[2]

There was full (which was not the same as complete) employment, there were good wages which were continually becoming less attractive with rising costs, and some problems of welfare had not been solved—retirement pensions and annuities, for example, could not keep pace with the inflation.[3] The unemployment figures, low but fluctuating, were sufficient after 1960 to cause some concern as to new areas of distress, particularly in the north. In June 1960 the number of wholly unemployed persons was only 290,000; in February 1963 it had risen to 878,000, the highest since 1947, although it had fallen again by the end of the year to 450,000. Still, this represented a fluctuation of between only one and two per cent out of a total working population which had increased from 24·44 million in June 1960 to 25·11 million in December 1963.[4] Unemployment was not a major political problem. More important in political terms was that while the big pay packets of the regularly

---

[1] Carstairs, pp. 61–72. The interesting book by R. and K. Titmuss, *Parents Revolt*, published in 1942, shows how little these developments were anticipated during the second world war (cf. pp. 95–100).
[2] Harry Hopkins, *The New Look, A Social History of the Forties and Fifties in Britain* (1963), pp. 342–3, 349; G. D. H. Cole, *The Post War Condition of Britain* (1956), chap. 3.
[3] Cf. Youngson, *The British Economy, 1920–1957*, p. 218.
[4] *Annual Register*, 1963, p. 514.

employed workers in the booming industrial areas were an inducement to them to move away from risky Labour panaceas, the pinch
of relative hardship was leading many of the middle class to withdraw their support of the Conservatives, without going Labour.
But within the 'middle class' too there was a process of transformation which was leading new sections to draw ahead of the rest.

Full employment, with the consequent expansion of business and
the continued drawing power of professional and managerial
opportunity, had also strengthened the 'solid superstructure' of
Britain; it is not fanciful to assume a diversion into the City and the
professions at home of many bold spirits who would have found
careers abroad in the heyday of the Empire. In his brilliant and
exhaustive study of the superstructure, Mr. Anthony Sampson has
described the unchanging strength and characteristics of the main
elements, the aristocracy, the City, the industrial corporations; but
even between the first and second editions of his book (1962 and
1965) there were noticeable changes. In part these were familiar
problems of all capitalistic countries, but they were accentuated
by the continuity of British traditions. The reader can explore these
contrasts in Mr. Sampson's crowded pages. The impact of the new
'meritocracy' on the old aristocracy, the emergence of a more
thrusting and self-ambitious young generation of managers, and
the continuing gap between prestige and power, are clearly constant
features of the whole post-1950 era.[1] One result was that the technological revolution, made possible by, and essential to, the
expansion of mass production and a widening range of related
service occupations, was a solvent of middle-class as well as of
working-class traditions.

The section of the middle class with the traditional education and
social background continued to enter many of the traditional
occupations but found these to be less well regarded by the state and
society and relatively less well remunerated than before. It was this
section which saw itself, as it had also done after 1919, as the 'New
Poor', and the chief victim of the Labour government's transfer of
national wealth to the workers, who in many cases seemed no longer
to need it (as in rate-subsidized housing estates with car-owning and
well-salaried occupants). And yet, while the differentials in favour
of the white-collar as compared with the manual worker—the bank
clerk or school teacher as compared with the coal miner or dustman

---

[1] Anthony Sampson, *Anatomy of Britain Today* (1965), pp. xiii-xv and *passim*.

—were constantly narrowing, there had been a 50 per cent growth between 1938 and 1951 in the proportion of the population in professional occupations. This could be seen in the much greater size of the Civil Service as compared with prewar days, and in the continued expansion of engineering, scientific, and technological staffs in industry, the great increase in the numbers of managerial and administrative posts, of accountants, production experts, market researchers, advertising men, public opinion pollsters, and even the shadier fringes of 'spivs, eels, and butterflies' that flourished along the highways and by-ways of the distributive system. Interesting statistics showed that industrial workers might not now predominate even in the typical industrial towns; in England and Wales the proportion of directly productive workers to those in service occupations was estimated at 53:47 in 1951.[1] This new middle class of technocrats and business experts had to live on its wits and the ability to produce results and it was being paid accordingly, instead of following the staider progress of the older professional career, with its greater security, fixed rewards, and smaller chance of either triumph or disaster.

These changes were on balance healthy tendencies of a dynamic economic system. The Conservative party could make out a good case for an overall advance in real income during its long spell of office. Between October 1951 and October 1963 wage rates were estimated to have risen by 72 per cent and prices by 45 per cent. The total income of professional people had risen from £228 million in 1951 to £372 million in 1962, according to the National Income Blue Book, and percentage increases in salaries in every profession were greater than the fall of 30–40 per cent in the purchasing power of money. Moreover it could be argued that many middle-class families had been adversely affected, sometimes in very indirect ways, by mass unemployment before the war; this had ended, income tax had been reduced, and they had benefited too as a class by higher allowances for children staying on at school or going to the university.[2] The Labour party hardly attempted to rebut these claims, although they talked darkly about the bribing of the electorate in orgies of ostentatious, useless expenditure. R. H. S. Crossman was reported to have said in a speech in Oslo in April 1960

---

[1] Professor K. C. Edwards, quoted Hopkins, pp. 157–8.
[2] These and similar arguments were deployed in *The Campaign Guide 1964*, pp. 172–8 issued by the Conservative and Unionist Central Office.

that British workers had been given 'an extent of luxurious living probably unequalled since the Roman Emperors in their heyday'.

Symptoms of the partial commingling of newer and older class groupings were numerous. While new ranges of consumer goods spread downwards in the social scale with the new prosperity, and state medical treatment upwards with the Health Act, housing and rehousing on a vast scale was treated, theoretically at least, as largely a classless public service.[1] This and the planning by the public authorities of entirely new towns and suburbs gave a new look to the housing drive, although this was also very much concerned with the older mysteries of insatiable demand and perennial slums. In spite of wild accusations of neglect by their opponents, both parties put great energy and thought into the campaign. Labour made a good start with the repair and patching-up of war-damaged property and the provision of useful pre-fabs. Following the reports of two commissions—that of Sir Montague Barlow in 1940 on the redistribution of the industrial population and of Lord Justice Scott in 1942 on land utilization in rural areas[2]—the New Towns Act of 1946 gave the Ministry of Town and Country Planning authority to set up corporations which would develop entirely new towns or expand existing ones. Twelve corporations had been appointed for England and Wales, and two for Scotland, down to 1950. The main work of developing these towns fell to the Conservatives, who had made sufficient progress to be able to provide in the New Towns Act of 1959 for the transfer to the usual local authorities of the functions of corporations whose work was completed.[3] Skelmersdale in Lancashire (1961), Dawley in Shropshire (1963), and a number of other new towns were then designated.

Elsewhere too an enormous amount of house and flat building was going on; after triumphantly raising the annual figure from around 200,000 to 318,779 in 1953, the Conservatives were able to keep building at approximately this level. Over $4\frac{1}{2}$ million new permanent homes, including those of the new towns, had been completed between 1945 and the end of 1963. It was, of course, not enough: it never is. The Minister of Housing, Sir Keith Joseph,

---

[1] The Labour party's Housing Act of 1949 deleted from the Conservative party's Housing Act of 1936 the reference to 'the working classes', thereby authorizing the local authorities to build, with subsidy, houses for all classes of person, irrespective of income.

[2] Cmd 6513 and 6378.

[3] A. C. Duff, *Britain's New Towns* (1961), pp. 11–33.

claimed in a television speech on 19 June 1963 that in spite of a population increase of 3½ million since 1951 the number of households and houses were about in balance—16½ million in each case. This did not prevent a slightly hysterical competition between the parties at the 1964 election which pushed up the promised annual figure to 400,000 new houses 'as soon as possible'. There were, no doubt, substantial local shortages, and much older property—some beautiful but inconvenient, some slummy and primitive—to be bull-dozed and profitably replaced.

In education, too, from nursery schools to universities, there were great developments, much new building, salary improvements for teachers and vast increases in public assistance for students. This was again a field in which the social revolution was very marked, and in which long-term aims, as they were mirrored in the Fisher Education Act of 1918 and fully developed in the Butler Education Act of 1944, were approaching their full realization by the early sixties. And as in other cases there was a sudden upsurge of disillusionment, partly due to the electoral struggle, but partly again to the tendency for achieved ends to channel attention on to fresh problems. The 1944 Act, apart from setting up a Ministry (in place of the Board) of Education and charging it in a broad way with responsibility for education of the people of England and Wales, caught attention mainly by its dramatic promise of 'free secondary education for all'. This on the face of it was a worthy companion of Beveridgeism and full employment in the building of a progressive, unified modern society. In place of 'all-age' schools the two stages of education, primary and secondary, must be provided in separate schools. To cater for differing aptitudes and abilities there were to be three types of secondary school, grammar, technical, and modern. To determine the child's suitability for entry to one of these types of school a variety of tests, comprehensively labelled the 'eleven-plus', were provided by local educational authorities. But the necessary vast range of secondary schools did not at first exist, and while it was being laboriously and expensively provided, educationalists discovered that too many children wanted to go to the grammar schools, and that too few parents were content to accept the verdict of the eleven-plus judgment day.[1]

During the fifties and early sixties local authorities and the government went ahead with the creation of new schools; 4,017

---

[1] H. C. Dent, *Growth in English Education, 1946–1952* (1954), pp. 67–75.

new primary and 2,397 new secondary schools were provided between 1945 and 1963 (3,518 and 2,260 respectively since 1951), and while older buildings and over-large classes remained, the gap between plans and actuality was narrowing. Costs went up too, and the supply of teachers was progressively increased (with 50,000 in training in 1963–4), but was never enough to cope with the increased demands and rising numbers of school entrants (resulting from the higher birth-rate) and delayed leavers (resulting from the raising of the school-leaving age). And all the time the storm of dissatisfaction with the system itself was blowing up. Both parents and children felt the nervous strain of the eleven-plus exam, in an age when government was expected to provide welfare freely and for all; only about a third of the secondary schools were grammar schools, and the numbers of places varied from one district to another. In any case, was the system democratic? An L.C.C. manifesto remarked that although the aristocracy of wealth had gone out of fashion an aristocracy of brains had taken its place, in the form of those who excelled in book learning. An aristocracy 'of those who excel in the art of social living' was needed.[1]

Thus the grammar schools now began to take the place of the public schools (which remained strangely immune for the time being from interference)[2] as the target of class-conscious criticism: the comprehensive school, incorporating the three streams, admitting all and so removing the need for the formal entrance test, solved all difficulties. Or perhaps not quite all. As one local authority after another took up the comprehensive school idea, the arguments against it were also being aired: would not the tone in these vast and glassy barracks become that of the lowest common denominator, with the clever boys and girls swamped and derided by the mediocre majority? Was this the best way to marshal the alpha-plus talent which had to be driven into new and expanded universities 'to make England great again'?

Two famous educational reports put forward detailed proposals

---

[1] Hopkins, pp. 145–8; cf. A. Hartley, *A State of England* (1963), on the 'social' versus 'intellectual' issue: pp. 199–203. Anthony Sampson thinks that the debate about comprehensive schools has had one startling effect: it is eroding the old rivalry between public schools and grammar schools. *Anatomy of Britain Today*, pp. 206–7. But if the old-boy network is loosening, the Oxbridge network remains strong.

[2] Nevertheless they found some critics in the crisis talk of 1963: cf. Elizabeth Young, 'Against the Stream' (*Encounter*, no. 118), who remarks that in education 'the buyable element is cancerous on the system as a whole', and a reply by Alan Barker, 'Independence and the Public Schools' in *Rebirth of Britain* (1964).

for a better educated and technically equipped population, very much in tune with the pre-election mood of compulsive planning. The Newsom Committee[1] advocated on 17 October 1963 the raising of the school-leaving age to sixteen and many improvements for the average and sub-average child. It was, however, the Robbins Committee, in a Report[2] published six days later, that really captured the headlines with plans for rapid university expansion which would raise the number of full-time places to 390,000 by 1973. Six new universities were called for, the status of colleges of advanced technology was to be raised, and money found on an appropriate scale. The Report made a plausible case for the view that there was enough untapped talent in the country to man the new universities without loss of quality. It did not explain how the indifference to higher education among large sections of the English working classes—the chief reservoir of talent—was to be overcome.

2. WINDS OF CHANGE

It was not only in the social sphere that the country and the political parties were becoming conscious in the early sixties of new problems inherent in the solution of the old. This was particularly true of the whole range of external problems—diplomatic, strategic, and economic. It was more usual and more easy now to talk realistically about the limitations of British power than had been the case before 1939, and few stopped to ask whether the power that was supposed to have been lost had ever been held. The simple truth is that it was not power, but the willingness of the United States (in the main) to use it, that had changed. Britain's 'power' in eastern Asia for example was no greater in 1931 than it was in 1951: there was successful resistance to aggression because the United States was prepared to act in a big way in Korea in 1950 as she had not been prepared to act in Manchuria in 1931. It has been the argument of this book that after the first world war Britain assumed a range of responsibilities which, if fully carried out, would have been beyond her strength. As a result, much of the politics and diplomacy of the interwar years had represented an attempt, which could usually not be talked about too openly, to husband weakened resources and fend off further commitments. The all-out effort of the second world war had shattered these prudential

[1] *Half Our Future.*
[2] Cmd 2154.

policies, but although Britain had emerged from the war with some glory it was with the knowledge that drastic changes were now inevitable in her economic and political-strategic relationships.

It could be said that the Attlee government, not always quite aware perhaps of the full implication of its innovations, had come to terms with this much-changed world. The three essential bases—a new Commonwealth strategy, the acceptance and support of American leadership, and formal peacetime military commitments in Europe and beyond—were designed primarily to meet a world-wide menace in the form of Communism; they compare favourably with the extent and cost of her prewar obligations. The fifty-year commitment at Brussels in 1948 meant the permanent abandonment of the guarded and circumscribed attitude towards continental interventions of the pre-1939 era. It fell to the Conservative government after 1951 to work out the full implications of these innovations, and in some respects this had been an encouraging experience, for the combination of a bolder line with a narrowed range of exclusive responsibilities had worked well enough in view of the willingness of the United States and other powers to play a more active part than before the war. The policy of interdependence was clearly established by the mid-fifties as an attempt to play a major part in each of the three overlapping fields of European, Atlantic, and Commonwealth affairs without giving exclusive attention to any one; it was a mode of diplomatic activity which seemed to satisfy some old and deeply rooted traditions of British foreign policy, offering obvious parallels with the position before 1914.

But in the new phase of public discussion of foreign policy that begins in the early sixties the starting point was an assumption that in each of the three spheres British influence was shrinking, owing to the greater self-sufficiency of the other powers in each group; the conclusion was evidently that she should throw herself more ardently into one of them. It was also widely asserted that her own relative strength (as compared with other powers in the western alliance) was declining, mainly for economic reasons. Both views were questionable, and hard to prove or disprove. Undoubtedly the freedom with which such assertions had been made abroad for many years provided handy material for similar speculation at home. One American professor, A. G. Mazour, wrote in 1956 that Britain's economic, naval, and political force was all in the past: 'Britain virtually lives on America's dole.' It was in 1962 that

Dean Acheson discovered that Britain had lost her rôle.[1] English publicists now gave this theme a good airing. Mr. Anthony Hartley, writing on the 'condition of England question' in 1963, considered that her loss of power was demonstrated by her inability to resist an attack from Russia without the help of the U.S.A.:[2] but to this it could be replied that all the powers, including Russia and the United States, shared this new degree of vulnerability to nuclear weapons, and Britain did retain some deterrent power of her own. Mr. John Mander, a young ex-Etonian socialist, in a 'Penguin' also published in 1963,[3] conveniently put the case of those who choose to regard Britain's attempt to play a leading part in each of the three spheres of policy as proof of a general lack of national purpose.

If Britain had indeed been as powerless or aimless as some of these sweeping judgments suggest she could hardly have played the lively rôle that her impatient critics still seemed to expect of her. But in fact she was active enough when the occasion arose. The state of world politics was itself largely one of deadlock, but a good deal could be done within the existing international framework. In May 1961 Macmillan set himself a sufficiently ambitious programme when he said that the two greatest problems were those of the European Common Market and Africa. During the first two years of his second term of office he had also busied himself with disarmament and given much thought to the possibility of a *détente* with Soviet Russia.

The first step in this direction was his official visit to Moscow in March 1959 which had started off a train of uneasy speculation in Bonn as to British 'appeasement'. From 29 November 1958, when he announced his intention of liquidating the occupation status of Berlin, until the Cuba crisis in 1962, Khrushchev seems to have been conducting a planned offensive comparable to that carried on by Stalin from 1947 to 1952. The probable aim was the liquidation of the Berlin situation and whatever broader Soviet and Communist advances would accrue incidentally; and the plan failed essentially because the United States government refused to budge. At the

---

[1] H. J. Morgenthau, *Politics among Nations* (1948), p. 274, estimated Britain's strength in 1948 at one-seventh of that of the United States, and he believed that if it were removed from the American side and added to the Russian the balance would still be in America's favour. He modified this view somewhat in 1954. Cf. the comments of Lord Strang, *Britain in World Affairs* (1961), pp. 376–7. Professor Mazour's outburst is from *World Affairs Quarterly*, July 1956, p. 116.

[2] A Hartley, *A State of England*, pp. 58–9.

[3] John Mander, *Great Britain or Little England?*

same time Macmillan was pressing on with plans for a test ban treaty, and seemed in sight of this when a ten-power disarmament conference was agreed on for 1960. A new Soviet-British trade agreement was signed in May 1959 and a cultural agreement in the following December.

No progress was in fact made in 1960, for Khrushchev's reaction to the U 2 episode killed the Paris summit conference; there was reason to think that he preferred to avoid talking business with Eisenhower in the hope that the presidential election would shortly result in a more malleable successor. The ultimate crisis in October 1962 over the installation of rocket bases in Cuba may thus have been a misjudged attempt on Khrushchev's part to find the basis for a bargain over Berlin. The purpose of British diplomacy was essentially that of keeping the door open for discussion between East and West, while supporting the firm line taken by President Kennedy in Washington. There is ample evidence that this facilitated Khrushchev's rather numerous tactical withdrawals. What emerged was the Berlin wall and the nuclear test ban treaty, signed by Britain, the United States, and the U.S.S.R. in Moscow on 5 August 1963. The latter was very much a success for Macmillan's personal efforts.

The problem of Africa, and with it that of Commonwealth relations generally, was essentially one of keeping pace with the advance of colonial nationalism, but the pace was now rapid and it generated fresh doubts as to the viability of the whole structure. There had been a passing fear in 1951 that the Tories after their return to power would reverse the trend towards colonial self-government; 'good-bye to Colonial freedom!,' wrote one West African newspaper. But the new government had hastened to affirm its progressive intentions. The Colonial Secretary, Lennox-Boyd, remarked in November 1956 how different it would be 'if only nationalism were a patient, gentle, amenable creature—a kind of political cocker spaniel!' Since it was not, and since the frustrating of local demands would merely advertise extremist leaders hungry for martyrdom, it was best to complete an inevitable process as speedily as possible, subject to the setting-up of satisfactory governmental machinery in each case.[1]

Ghana (6 March 1957) and Malaya (31 August 1957), followed by Nigeria (1 October 1960), became independent within the Common-

---

[1] P.D., 5 Ser., HC, vol. 522, 16 December 1953, col. 410.

wealth and were sufficiently well-endowed with western-trained native talent to produce stable, although not uncontentious, governments. In East and Central Africa the situation had at first seemed somewhat different owing to the much smaller size of the native professional class, the presence of hitherto dominant white minorities, the absorption of the great majority of the native populations in tribal rule and economy, and the warning from the Belgian Congo in the summer of 1960 as to the dangers of a relapse into chaos after a too-precipitate withdrawal. Nevertheless in these areas too the idea of independence was becoming the outstanding political force at such a rapid pace after the middle fifties as to surprise even the African leaders themselves in some cases.

The significance of Macmillan's approach to these problems, as it was symbolized in the 'wind of change' speech at Cape Town on 3 February 1960, was not that it continued the process of colonial devolution but that it cleared the way for its completion. By the same process it cleared the way for a possible retreat from Commonwealth commitments and an approach to the European common market. After visiting Ghana and Nigeria early in January he made a rapid tour of central and southern Africa with masterly speeches which, if they were encouraging to African aspirations, were apparently not distressing to the white settlers. The speech to the joint meeting of the two Houses of Parliament in Cape Town was however a long and quite explicit statement that Britain could not support apartheid. Fifteen years ago, he said, the movement of national consciousness spread through Asia. Today, the same thing was happening in Africa. The wind of change was blowing through the continent. 'Will the great experiments in self-government that are now being made in Asia and Africa, especially within the Commonwealth, prove so successful, and by their example so compelling, that the balance will come down in favour of freedom and order and justice?' He had to tell them frankly that there were some aspects of South African policy which Britain could not support 'without being false to our own deep convictions about the political destinies of free men'. This was the parting of the ways: and Macmillan with a succession of colleagues set out to complete the revolution which had commenced with Attlee and Bevin.

Sierra Leone became independent within the Commonwealth on 27 April 1961, and Gambia on 4 October 1963; British Somaliland left the Commonwealth on joining the new state of Somalia on

19*

1 July 1960. Tanganyika, after a slower start than its neighbours, was considered to have progressed so promisingly that independence was celebrated on 9 December 1961; a year later it became a republic within the Commonwealth, with Mr. Julius Nyerere as President. There was more contention elsewhere. Uganda had no problem of white settlement, but there was dispute between the advocates of a unitary and of a more federal constitution, which would preserve the authority of the Kabaka of Buganda and other rulers. After conferences in London in 1961 and 1962, it became independent within the Commonwealth on 9 October 1962, with a constitution of carefully contrived compromises, and a year later a president was substituted for the Queen as head of state. Zanzibar became independent within the Commonwealth on 10 December 1963, and moved Left after a revolutionary coup some months later. Kenya became the eighteenth sovereign member of the Commonwealth on the 11 December 1963, with the usual brave oratory, but with justifiable concern as to its racial and economic stability. Security measures following the seven-years long Mau Mau emergency did not end until 1960, and the substantial European, Arab, and Asian minorities had to recognize the fact that in the elections of January to March 1961 K.A.N.U. (the Kenya African National Union), relying strongly on the support of the large Kikuyu tribe, had pulled ahead of its rivals. Led by Jomo Kenyatta the party rejected the plans of its rival K.A.D.U. (the Kenya African Democratic Union) for a federal constitution, and got its way at the decisive London conference in October 1963. Outside Africa, Malaya, which had become the tenth independent member of the Commonwealth in August 1957, was able to terminate the 'emergency' campaign against Communist rebellion on 31 July 1960, and a momentous speech by Tunku Abdul Rahman on 27 May 1961 foreshadowed a 'Greater Malaysia' plan for closer political and economic links with Singapore and the British territories of Sarawak, Brunei, and North Borneo.

Did all this mean that the Commonwealth idea was becoming merely a Commonwealth myth? Certainly the new member states, while retaining the formal link, repeatedly proclaimed their non-alignment with Great Britain in foreign affairs. They went further and openly challenged the British government's handling of the remaining problems of imperial devolution in such issues as those of Central African federation and South Africa. On a number of occasions the Afro-Asian bloc in the United Nations, usually with Ghana as the prime mover, brought before the General Assembly or the Security Council abrupt and highly publicized demands for the rapid completion of independence, with scant regard for the complexities of some of the issues involved. One such proposal in September 1963, alleging that the situation in Southern Rhodesia constituted a threat to international peace, forced the British government to use the veto in the Security Council for only the third time in its history.

The tenth Commonwealth Prime Ministers' conference since the war began on 8 March 1961, and gave a dramatic demonstration of the new Commonwealth relationships. South Africa had decided, by a very small majority in a plebiscite of October 1960, to become a republic. Dr. Verwoerd invited the views of his fellow Prime Ministers as to South Africa's racial policy before deciding whether to press for his country's continued membership of the Commonwealth, and when he found that at least half of them were hostile he announced in a dignified speech that he would withdraw the application. Mr. Diefenbaker (Canada) firmly aligned himself with the Afro-Asian members in this debate. On 16 March Mr. Macmillan spoke with obvious distress of the breaking of the Commonwealth ties with South Africa after fifty years. It was announced that South Africa would stay in the sterling area, and Dr. Verwoerd reciprocated Mr. Macmillan's hopes for future cooperation 'in all possible ways'. During the next three years the construction of Bantustan went on in South Africa in spite of the cold war and iron curtain set up by the many world critics of apartheid; it could not be said that the new republic, after a first phase of dismay at its isolation, showed anything but a sturdy, if wrong-headed, imperviousness to criticism.

Further north the Federation of Rhodesia and Nyasaland was the next to provide a field for Commonwealth dissension. The Federation, set up in 1953, had had everything to commend it in the economic field. Dr. Banda's Malawi Party in Nyasaland opposed it for precisely this reason: they regarded the economic argument as a device to perpetuate white supremacy. In March 1962 Mr. Macmillan announced a reconsideration of the Federation's future, and Mr. R. A. Butler was entrusted with overall responsibility for Central African affairs. The process of enquiry thus started meant the ultimate dissolution of the Federation in spite of accusations of broken faith

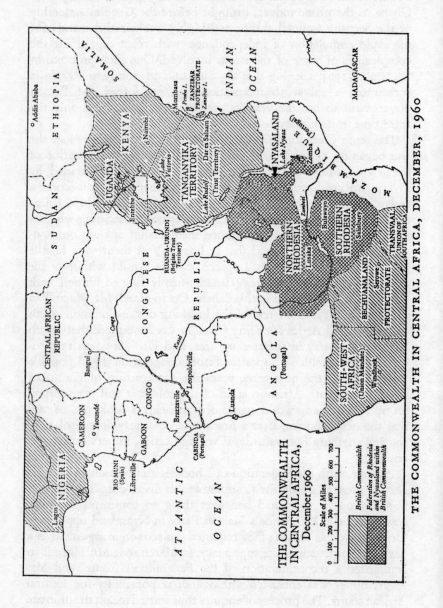

THE COMMONWEALTH IN CENTRAL AFRICA, DECEMBER, 1960

THE COMMONWEALTH
IN CENTRAL AFRICA,
December 1960

Scale of Miles
100 0 100 200 300 400 500 600 700

British Commonwealth

Federation of Rhodesia
and Nyasaland within
British Commonwealth

by Sir Roy Welensky, the Federal Prime Minister.[1] Nyasaland's desire to secede was nevertheless accepted by the British government in December 1962, and the right to do so of Northern Rhodesia, where an African majority was certain, was recognized in April 1963. In Southern Rhodesia, where there was a much larger white population. and an acceptance of the existing constitutional position by the tribal chiefs, the request of the Prime Minister, Mr. Winston Field, for an assurance about independence had a different look. The British government had to reply that, as in other areas, independence could not be granted until all necessary conditions had been arranged.

Here things rested for the time being, although the sense of suspended crisis everywhere south of the Zambesi was increased by Dr. Salazar's flat refusal to modify the colonial status of Angola and Mozambique, the spectre of U.D.I. (unilateral declaration of independence) in Rhodesia, and the tough self-sufficiency of Dr. Verwoerd. In its broadest perspective, however, the problem of political independence in the Afro-Asian world, and certainly in its Commonwealth setting, had been solved. Many problems of economic viability, domestic stability, and the pending population explosion had not.

3. OUT OF EUROPE

Are we to assume that the British government's application for membership of the European Common Market, which took place at the height of these transactions on 10 August 1961, meant the substantial abandonment of its Commonwealth commitments? It was denied in very strong terms that this was the intention, and the failure of the negotiations can, up to a point, be regarded as supporting evidence, for it followed the defence of Commonwealth agricultural interests. On the other hand the innermost thoughts of Macmillan and his cabinet have not yet been revealed, and the strength of right-wing Conservative opposition to any weakening of the Commonwealth, combining curiously with the cherishing of Commonwealth loyalties by the Labour party, must have precluded frank speaking. At the Conservative party conference in October 1961, the Secretary of State for Commonwealth Relations, Duncan Sandys, certainly denied that there was any question of choosing between Common Market and Commonwealth; but he

[1] The Federation was dissolved on 31 December 1963.

indicated a change of priorities. Since the creation of a Commonwealth customs union and huge internal market were impracticable, Britain would seek the advantage of joining those of the Six,[1] but with the promise that she was to be a more effective Commonwealth country as a result.

Ostensibly at any rate this attempt to hold an advantage in both spheres spoiled her case, but again we are largely in the dark as to the ultimate strength of resistance to her participation. Since the formation of E.F.T.A.[2] on 21 July 1959 the British government had appeared content to await developments for a time; little had been heard of European problems in the election campaign in October 1959 or in parliamentary debates for nearly two years thereafter. But in the meantime business men of the Six seemed exhilarated by the task of handling former competitors as future customers, and the programme of tariff reduction was speeded up; thus whatever need there might have been for United Kingdom membership was correspondingly reduced. All the same, for a year after the negotiations for Britain's inclusion began in November 1961 there seemed a likelihood that satisfactory arrangements would be worked out. Progress was bound to be slow in view of the fact that the Six had first to negotiate on every issue among themselves in order to present a united front to the British. The essential problem was that of ensuring that Britain's traditional Commonwealth suppliers of wheat and other temperate-zone produce should not be too hard-hit by the Community's high tariffs on agricultural imports. Special treatment for New Zealand was conceded, but otherwise the Community was not prepared to promise more, in the earlier negotiations, than fair opportunities for those outside the Common Market. Two other outstanding issues were the British desire for nil tariffs on industrial raw materials and for the avoidance of an abrupt ending of British farm subsidies. The Commonwealth Prime Ministers' conference, in September 1962, naturally showed great alarm over these issues, although it revealed no inclination on the part of the members, new or old, to develop anything resembling a Commonwealth Common Market. Indeed, it came as a shock to the British government when the new African members, with the exception of Sierra Leone, all rejected the offer of

[1] E.E.C.: European Economic Community (Holland, Belgium, Luxembourg, W. Germany, France, and Italy).

[2] The European Free Trade Association, consisting of Austria, Denmark, Norway, Portugal, Sweden, Switzerland, and the United Kingdom.

'Associated Overseas Territory' status which the British negotiators had succeeded in securing for them on the same terms as those of the former French colonies.

Although the negotiations seemed to be circling with heavy-footed tact around a number of immovable obstacles the rather abrupt termination of the talks by General de Gaulle in January 1963 came as a shock and was treated as an offence. The other five still seemed genuinely anxious for British admission. De Gaulle told a press conference on 14 January that the question was simply whether Great Britain could give up all preferences in regard to the Commonwealth, cease claiming that her agriculture should be privileged, and abandon all her undertakings to the countries of the free trade area. This was a rejection of all compromise and phased adjustment, and on 29 January, after a final insistence by the French foreign minister, M. Couve de Murville, the British negotiator, Edward Heath, was told that no agreement had been found possible as to future procedure. Macmillan on the 30th said on television that the decision was 'bad for us, bad for Europe, bad for the whole free world'. But it did not appear that de Gaulle shared these qualms. There was much talk about the determination of this vain and difficult man to repay wartime slights at British and American hands. Earlier in the month Britain had been described in de Gaullist circles as the Trojan horse of American influence in E.E.C. The fact was, however, that France was hoping for the best of both worlds; while she consolidated her position as the leader of little Europe by excluding Anglo-American influence she knew that the massive strength of N.A.T.O. would still be behind her, in spite of her gestures of isolationism. But Britain hoped for the best of both worlds too, in de Gaulle's opinion.[1]

These developments seem to have created doubt in some quarters as to the continuance of the Anglo-American relationship in its existing form. The second, and perhaps the major, reason for de Gaulle's decision in January 1963 was thought to be Macmillan's failure to offer France any cooperation in the nuclear field. He had said nothing about these matters when he met de Gaulle at the château de Rambouillet on 15–16 December 1962, but at Nassau in the Bahamas, 18–21 December, he had reached agreement with President Kennedy whereby Britain would receive Polaris missiles

[1] Miriam Camps, *Britain and the European Community, 1955–1963* (Princeton, 1963), pp. 499–506.

in compensation for the American decision to abandon the Skybolt missile on the ground of expense. An offer of Polaris missiles on the same terms to France was haughtily rejected. While these events had for the time being thrown Britain and the United States closer together, it was argued that if the Six consolidated themselves under de Gaulle's leadership the United States government might be forced to come to terms with them, leaving the British high and dry.

All that could really be said, however, was that the advance of the Six was beginning to create a new situation which could take many different forms in the future, and not necessarily to Britain's disadvantage. The 'special relationship' with the United States, much talked about at this time, might be modified thereby; but had the term any particular meaning anyway? The two powers spoke the same language and had been mixed up together in the wartime grand alliance and in continuous normal personal contact in all the phases of postwar diplomacy; by contrast, all the other major governments had been hostile, disorganized, or otherwise a problem just when the American leaders, assuming tremendous new responsibilities, perhaps needed someone to talk to on world affairs. The wartime links of Churchill, Eden, Attlee, and Macmillan with Eisenhower, Harry Hopkins, Harriman and others had thus been a useful starting point for postwar relations, and had been followed by the good relationship of Mr. Macmillan and President Kennedy, helped by the presence in Washington of an ambassador, Sir David Ormsby-Gore (Lord Harlech), who had known Kennedy for twenty-five years. He was reported to have said, 'I trust David as I would my own cabinet ministers'. All this would mean little if a real divergence of interests appeared.

But in fact it had not done so. The British government accepted the need for an Atlantic community, it welcomed United States armed power and its deployment, and while maintaining for reasons of prestige and political interest its own substantial forces and nuclear programme was ready to coordinate its resources with those of the senior partner. De Gaullist France had rejected a similar relationship, without building up an independent complementary organization on a western European basis. Similarly in non-European affairs the continued responsibility of the British government for Commonwealth defence was in no way incompatible with American anti-Communist preoccupations, particularly in south-east Asia, while de Gaulle practised an ostentatious neutralism in this area.

There was ample evidence before the general election of October 1964 that the official leadership of the Labour party had accepted this position. Harold Wilson said on 4 March 1964, after a visit to the United States, 'We have always been a world power; we should not be corralled in Europe'. Some weeks later he elaborated these views in a television interview, in which he defined Britain's defence function as that of 'putting out brush fires all over the world', and he firmly asserted that 'our Commonwealth associations and naval tradition will enable us to play a big part in stopping big wars'.[1] Foreign policy as formulated by both the leading parties was still that of the useful, but not exclusive, rôle in the three interlocking circles: to recognize that conditions in each might rapidly change does not appear to have greatly disturbed the professional self-confidence of politicians and officials in their capacity to adapt policy to circumstance.

4. END OF AN ERA?

However, continuities in foreign and domestic policy were not readily stressed as the parties approached another general election. Tension mounted during the years of decision, 1963 and 1964. There were signs of uncertainty in both the main camps as to how the conflict could best be joined.

The floating voter was flirting with Liberalism, but was not greatly enamoured of Labour. The most tangible cause of discontent seemed to be irritation by the suffering middle class at a lack of progress in the midst of apparent plenty: at any rate, there seemed to be plenty for the aristocrats of labour and of big business —the powerful unions and the expense-account plutocracy. 'Stop-go' economics, the policy of judiciously mixing planning and freedom in accordance with the doctrines of J. M. Keynes, had had a successful run as 'Butskellism' throughout the nineteen-fifties. But while it could be defended in prosperity as the best empirical means of extracting advantage from the fiercely competitive and expanding world economy, it had a diminishing attractiveness when the time came for emphasis on restraint. Even in the later fifties the willingness to leave business and industry to the free play of self-interest, subject to a minimum of deft regulation of the flow of money by the banks and the budget, had caused uneasiness in the minds of many officials and academic economists. There was a growing urgency in

[1] Cf. Kenneth Younger, *Changing Perspectives in British Foreign Policy* (1964), pp. 70, 108.

the advocacy of government encouragement of a higher rate of investment at home in plant and equipment.[1] Many argued, with strong support from the Board of Trade, in favour of the stimulus of increased competition, including tariff cuts and the ending of resale price maintenance, and above all the bracing challenge of membership of the Common Market.

But still a new phase of external strain was met by the Chancellor, Mr. Selwyn Lloyd, in 1961 with expedients along traditional lines, very much it would seem under the inspiration at this period of Professor Frank Paish.[2] There had been a deficit in the overall balance of payments for the two previous years, accentuated by the revaluation of the German mark and the Dutch guilder, while at home incomes were rising more rapidly than industrial production, which was only slightly higher in 1961 than it had been in 1960. Following a counter-inflationary budget in April, additional measures had to be introduced in a 'little budget' in July 1961, including further restrictions on bank lending and on government expenditure; the bank rate was increased from 5 to 7 per cent. More dramatic was the Chancellor's call for a 'pay pause', less so a surcharge of 10 per cent on customs duties and purchase tax; most dramatic of all, perhaps, was the decision in August to apply for entry into the Common Market. Undoubtedly the Chancellor showed courage in this counter-inflationary pressure on wages and salaries, and the budget of April 1962 had the same broad purpose. But by this stage the trend of criticism was changing, and there were complaints of slackness in the economy, of spare industrial capacity—in short, unemployment—and of declining industrial investment. By the summer steps were being taken to reverse the previous policy of restriction.[3]

But this was something more than a decision to turn again from stop to go: it represented a turn away from the stop-go technique itself in favour of a planned promotion of economic growth. This was certainly a bold new venture (or death-bed repentance) on the part of the Conservative party, and it appears to have had enthusiastic support among its expert advisers. The T.U.C. on the other hand was hesitant, and the business world

[1] Cf. A. Shonfield, *British Economic Policy Since the War*, pp. 243–7.
[2] One cabinet minister called it 'the reign of King Paish at the Treasury': S. Brittan, 'Economics à la mode: Butskell to Beeching' (*20th Century*, no. 1018, pp. 27–32). His own views appear in *Studies in an Inflationary Economy* (1962).
[3] Roy Harrod, *The British Economy* (1963), pp. 209–12.

cautious. The new approach had its origin in Mr. Selwyn Lloyd's own proposal in July 1961 to set up a body for the 'joint examination of the economic prospects of the country stretching five or more years into the future'. The result was the National Economic Development Council (N.E.D.C. or, not very affectionately, 'Neddy'), which had ambitious objectives: first, to coordinate the plans of the government and the private and nationalized industries; second, to prescribe, and thirdly, to remove the obstacles to a faster rate of growth. The T.U.C. finally agreed to join in January 1962, after airing its objection to wage restraint as the solution of Britain's economic difficulties. The pay pause ended officially on 31 March 1962, but in February the government urged that wage and salary increases should be limited to the likely rate of growth in productivity of 2 to 2½ per cent. In May N.E.D.C. adopted 4 per cent as the annual rate of growth to be aimed at in the gross domestic product for the period 1961–66.

But the merit of these new initiatives was evidently lost on the electors. Throughout 1962 the Conservatives had cause to be worried by a prolonged gust of mid-term unpopularity. At the Orpington by-election on 14 March 1962 the Liberal candidate, Eric Lubbock, turned the Conservative majority of 14,760 in 1959 into a Liberal majority of 7,855. The Labour candidate fared even worse. Apart from boredom with the Tories after eleven years of office the result reflected the revolt of white-collared workers in an outer suburb where everyone was depressed by the losing battle of salaries against inflation. The Pontefract by-election on 22 March represented virtually no change from Conservative to Labour; no Liberal was standing. But the Conservative poll was down by 18·5 per cent at Stockton on 5 April; on 6 June Labour captured the Tory seat of West Middlesbrough and nearly captured the traditionally safe Tory seat of West Derbyshire; on 14 June the Conservative candidate lost his deposit at West Lothian. On 12 July at Leicester North-East the Conservative poll fell by 23·9 as compared with the 1959 election.

The Prime Minister, who had been urged for some time from many quarters to reshuffle his cabinet, now did more: on the day after the Leicester North-East result he discarded a third of them, and offered the country a galaxy of comparative youth (under fifties) in part exchange. The seven to go were the Lord Chancellor, Lord Kilmuir, Selwyn Lloyd, J. S. Maclay (Secretary for Scotland),

Harold Watkinson (Defence), Dr. Hill (Housing and Local Government), Sir David Eccles (Education), and Lord Mills (Minister without Portfolio). Among those replacing them in the cabinet were Reginald Maudling as Chancellor (aged 45), Sir Keith Joseph as Minister of Housing (aged 44), and Sir Edward Boyle as Minister of Education (aged 38). Henry Brooke became Home Secretary; Peter Thorneycroft returned to the forefront of politics as Minister of Defence; Lord Dilhorne became Lord Chancellor. A week later nine more ministers, outside the cabinet this time, were replaced with such youthful figures as Edward du Cann, Nigel Fisher, David Price, and C. J. Chataway (aged 31) among the under-secretaries. There was a suggestion of desperation about these moves. The abrupt discarding of the able Lord Kilmuir seemed rather pointless,[1] and there was sympathy for the loyal and dedicated Selwyn Lloyd. Five by-elections on 22 November 1962 and one on the 23rd showed a slight overall reduction in the swing from Conservative to Labour as compared with the summer, but the figures suggested a Labour majority of over 100 at a general election.

And yet few Opposition parties in British history had less to offer in the way of alternative policies than the Labour party at this period. The country was back to the mid-Victorian conditions under which the absence of major political issues had left the parties little to quarrel about except the morality, statesmanship, or intelligence of the party leaders. It was almost inevitable in the circumstances that the Labour party, in its pre-election campaign, should adopt the theme of the exhausted Prime Minister, bankrupt of ideas, clinging to office while the country stagnated. In a future age anthropologists may study the myth of the dying Prime Minister, and note the strange persistence with which these tough and resourceful men are considered to have rendered themselves due for political death or suicide after about six years of office.[2] The 'state of England' question was discussed more generally with remarkable thoroughness and gloom by a wide range of writers at this time.[3]

---

[1] 'Loyalty was the Tories' secret weapon', but 'I doubt if it has ever had to endure so severe a strain'. Kilmuir, *Political Adventure*, p. 324.

[2] Just before their final retirements Asquith, Baldwin, MacDonald, Chamberlain, and Attlee were all supposed rather suddenly to have become tired men; was it merely the electorate that was tired? Bonar Law (1923) and Eden (1957) were genuinely ill. Lloyd George in 1922 and Churchill in 1945 were not, nor could their rampant vitality justify the insidious rumour that they were not very well; it was considered, however, that they had suddenly lost their touch.

[3] In a special number of *Encounter* (July 1963), entitled 'Suicide of a Nation', eighteen authors conveniently summarized a wide variety of criticisms, starting with Arthur

The Labour party owed to its still rather youthful leader, Hugh Gaitskell, the united front which enabled it to wait with confidence the coming of high office. This had not seemed a likely development just after the 1959 election: his attempt to reappraise party policy led indeed to some fierce quarrelling. He was defeated in an attempt to get rid of the more embarrassing features of clause IV of the party's constitution, by which Sidney Webb had committed them long ago to common ownership of the means of production, distribution, and exchange.[1] Everyone knew that nationalization was discredited, a certain vote-loser, and he put the case for revision persuasively to the special post-election conference of the Labour party at Blackpool on 28 November 1959. 'We have long ago come to accept a mixed economy, at least in some form—for the foreseeable future—in which case had we not better say so instead of going out of our way to court misrepresentation?' There was some support from Douglas Jay and others of the right wing, but from Michael Foot, Anthony Greenwood, Mrs. Barbara Castle, and others came the cry that Socialism was in danger. A new draft advanced by Gaitskell in March 1960 was swept away when the National Executive reaffirmed the inviolability of clause IV on 14 July 1960. Harold Wilson had dissociated himself in February from the movement for revision. There was an even greater crisis in the party over defence.

Since Attlee's day the official policy had affirmed the need for an independent nuclear deterrent, essentially, as Gaitskell claimed in the Commons on 1 March 1960, through 'fear of excessive dependence upon the United States'. However, a growing minority inside the Parliamentary Labour party, and a strong movement among the party's left-wingers, pacifists, and unilateralists, much stimulated it would seem by the starry-eyed zealots of C.N.D., now declared war on the party leadership on this issue. At the Scarborough conference of the Labour party in October 1960 Frank Cousins in a long and prosy speech moved a resolution from the T.G.W.U. demanding the complete rejection of any defence policy based on the threat or use of nuclear weapons. Gaitskell's reply, fluent,

Koestler, who complained of the 'psychological *apartheid* between the bourgeoisie and the proletariat'. The general theme was the need for greater overall direction of the economy and greater uniformity in education. These views were criticized by the Institute of Economic Affairs, in *Rebirth of Britain* (1964), also with essays by eighteen authors. They wanted maximum competition, with the strengthening of the law against monopoly and other restrictive practices.

[1] See p. 101 above.

emphatic, and uncompromising, called the critics 'pacifists, unilateralists, and fellow travellers', and said that there were those who would 'fight and fight and fight again to bring back sanity and honesty'. Cousins carried his motion. Gaitskell had shown his powers of decision. He was safe in the leadership of the Parliamentary party. Harold Wilson, generally regarded as the second most prominent figure in the party since Aneurin Bevan's death in July 1960, allowed himself to be nominated for the leadership on 20 October, and was decisively defeated ten days later, although the respectable minority vote (81 to 166), included more than the unilateralists (with whom he disagreed). There were also those who detected in him a more ruthless streak and a more authentic note of power than in Gaitskell; also perhaps a more flexible attitude to party dissensions. He did not weaken Gaitskell's position, but in spite of George Brown's election as deputy leader his stature was not diminished. The shake-up at Scarborough was followed in February 1961 by a somewhat confused redefinition of Labour's defence policy which accepted membership of N.A.T.O. but said that Britain should cease the attempt to remain an independent nuclear power.

From this point, however, the unity of the party improved, mainly perhaps because the turn in Tory fortunes had a pleasantly steadying influence on Labour's prospects. The resolution of Gaitskell and his parliamentary supporters, who refused to accept defeat by the unilateralists and domination by trade union bosses, strengthened this inclination to close the ranks. They won a complete triumph at the Labour party conference at Blackpool early in October 1961, when proposals for more precise nationalization plans and for a reaffirmation of the unilateralist creed were convincingly rejected. The curiously uphill struggle of the Conservatives in 1962 to persuade the country that they were still capable of doing useful and constructive things—and they were indeed taking a positive enough line in Africa and Europe—undoubtedly strengthened Labour confidence that its own hour of destiny was approaching. In fact the electoral setbacks of the Tories did not yet mean a decisive swing to Labour; nor had the party as yet found a convincing platform to replace that of the Conservative party or of its own 1945 programme. Labour's domestic policy was laid down in *Signposts for the Sixties* (published on 28 June 1961), which placed the emphasis on planning nationally rather than on doctrinaire loyalty to nationalization or other time-honoured expedients. But the two parties were really well in step, for now the Tories were also planners, although they professed to see a world of difference between planning by consent and the Socialist yearning for compulsory controls and regimentation. Gaitskell was not to lead his party into the promised land. He died on 18 January 1963 at the age of fifty-six as a result of complications following an attack of pleurisy.

This might have been a grievous setback for the party: the record, however, suggests the reverse. In this most curious phase of political restlessness, experience in leadership seemed to be almost at a discount. Gaitskell's virtues were familiar, his image a little battered, his ability to offer a dramatic and exciting alternative to Harold Macmillan more than doubtful. He was suceeded by Harold Wilson, who defeated the mercurial George Brown decisively on 14 February 1963 on a second ballot.[1] A successful young academic of middle-class industrial Yorkshire background before the war, Wilson had certain remarkable assets. He had, after all, been the youngest cabinet minister since Pitt when he became President of the Board of Trade at the age of thirty-one. About him there was the indefinable suggestion of prime-ministerial timber, recognized, however reluctantly, by his opponents in both the Labour and the Conservative ranks. He soon showed that he could handle the party differences deftly. He was not an orator of George Brown's stature but he maintained an effective, rasping, ironical flow of nagging criticism as the leader of an increasingly self-confident Opposition front bench.

After the forced landing in January 1963 which followed their unhappy reconnaissance of Common-Market Europe, the government found it increasingly hard to get off the ground. Unemployment was rising again, particularly in the north. Shipbuilding was doing badly. Bitter winter weather brought building and construction work to a standstill. Neddy (N.E.D.C.) in its first report on 28 February 1963 seemed to have the right ideas: it called for an annual growth of 4 per cent for the period 1961 to 1966, but the problem was to achieve such a figure while keeping incomes in step. The government had set up a National Incomes Commission on 26 July 1962 but found it impossible to persuade the trade

---

[1] Although he had been beaten by Brown in November 1962 by 133 votes to 103 in the contest for the deputy leadership of the Labour party.

unions to cooperate in an incomes policy. In January 1963 the
T.U.C. notified all trade unions of its advice to the building unions
to boycott the commission, and in October confirmed its opposition
to wage restraint. The thing itself was evidently distasteful to them,
and the failure of the government to provide a dramatic restraint
on dividends and even expense accounts gave an excuse and perhaps
a justification for refusal.

On 3 April the new Chancellor of the Exchequer, Reginald
Maudling, sought in his first budget to reconcile economic expansion with anti-inflation, and offered a mixture of tax reliefs and
incentives to investment; it was not badly received by the shadow
Chancellor, James Callaghan, who, however, took the opportunity
to make his own contribution to economic policy by proposing a
reform of the whole tax system, apparently based on a wealth tax.
This suggestion aroused little enthusiasm, but Labour talked more
and more emphatically of the need for an incomes policy when it
was seen that the Tories would not achieve it. Another round of
substantial wage increases made nonsense of the modest 3 to $3\frac{1}{2}$ per
cent rate of increase that the Chancellor had suggested. On the other
hand, while the economy still seemed rather unresponsive to direction, trade was improving. Exports increased gratifyingly throughout the year 1963, and although the rate of expansion was decreasing
after the autumn, there was, for the year as a whole, an increase of
5 per cent in volume and 8 per cent in value as compared with 1962.
The cost of imports (mainly because of increasing food prices) was,
however, also rising.

The patient efforts of the government to soar once again in
public esteem were now largely frustrated by a curious round of
security scares and personal scandals. It was not too difficult for
the opposition and the press to link them to the theme of tiredness
and failing efficiency. Security was in people's minds because of the
conviction in October 1962 of William Vassall, an Admiralty clerk
who had been spying for Russia. A judicial tribunal under Lord
Radcliffe presented a report on 25 April 1963 which completely
vindicated Mr. Thomas Galbraith, a former Civil Lord of the
Admiralty, and Lord Carrington, the First Lord, who had been
victims of Fleet Street's no-smoke-without-fire reporting technique.
But in the meantime, Mr. John Profumo, the Secretary of State for
War, had denied in the House of Commons on 22 March any
impropriety in his relations with a certain Miss Christine Keeler

and a former Russian naval attaché, Captain Ivanov. After pressure by Wilson the Prime Minister asked Lord Dilhorne to make a private enquiry into the affair; and it ended with a confession by Profumo that his statement on 22 March was untrue. He resigned, and the government, so recently jubilant after the Radcliffe report, came under damaging attack from the Opposition leader on 17 June. The theme was inefficiency: why had security failed? And why had Macmillan not personally investigated Profumo's case, instead of leaving the matter to others? The suggestion of failing grasp seems unwarranted: every Prime Minister must delegate authority, and Macmillan remained a man of vast energy, political flair, and splendid debating power. And yet his own party was restless: 27 Conservative back benchers refrained from voting against the motion of censure.

The Profumo affair was kept alive in the public mind by the trial of Dr. Stephen Ward, with many salacious details of sex and sin in high places. There was a chance link between one of the young ladies in the case and Peter Rachman, a slum landlord who before his death (which some questioned) in November 1962, had become the symbol of racketeering and extortion in the Paddington area. A virulent attack on the government's alleged housing delinquencies arising from the 1957 Rent Act was launched by Mr. Wilson on 18 July. Sir Keith Joseph's reply was that the Paddington case was not typical; moreover, safeguards had already been introduced in the 1961 Housing Act. But he set up an independent committee of inquiry under Sir Milner Holland into London housing conditions. If his reply satisfied the Conservatives it did not abate the Labour party campaign against Rachmanism, the Rent Act, and alleged Tory responsibility for both. All these things certainly shook the self-confidence of the government's supporters, and there were further anxious speculations as to whether Macmillan would go—or not go. But whatever his judicious weighing of the position in August and September there seems no doubt that he had decided, well before the Conservative party meeting at Blackpool, to stay on and lead the party in the general election. And then a sudden and untoward event upset everyone's careful calculations. He departed for hospital and an operation which would incapacitate him for some weeks, and the day after the opening of the conference on 9 October he felt compelled to resign the leadership.

The Conservative government continued in office for another

year, but there was now little that the parties could think about except their own electoral prospects; a process trying enough no doubt to everyone's nerves. This is not the place to say much about the manoeuvres. The Tories surprised everyone, including themselves, by showing at Blackpool a sudden yearning for Lord Home as Prime Minister. After some hurried but rather haphazard efforts by the supporters of Lord Hailsham and R. A. Butler, soundings of the cabinet members led the Chief Whip to advise Macmillan that the preference was for Lord Home, and he in turn advised the Queen. Lord Home then agreed to try to form a government, secured Butler (as Foreign Secretary) and Maudling while losing Iain Macleod and Enoch Powell, kissed hands, surrendered his title, and after winning the seat at Kinross and West Perthshire on 8 November took his seat in the Commons as Sir Alec Douglas-Home on 12 November. Selwyn Lloyd was brought back as Lord Privy Seal and Leader of the House. It was perhaps natural that the new Prime Minister should be inclined to postpone the date of the general election as long as possible. He had to make himself known to the electorate, and to allow time to repair the Tory image, which had undoubtedly suffered from the political setbacks of 1963.

It was hoped that the reviving prosperity of 1963 would continue, with a boomlet to carry the Tory party safely into port. Pledged now to an ambitious programme of modernization, the party expounded its plans zealously, although its opponents could ask why so much remained to be done after thirteen years of office. The government accepted the main proposals of the Robbins report, and promised to finance them, whatever the cost. In other directions there was a heavy bill which was to be met over the years from the profits of successful industrial expansion. The government's crash regional programme had removed any chance of a revival of the serious unemployment of the early months of 1963; there was actually a labour shortage in the summer of 1964. But the economy behaved oddly. There was the puzzling fact that industrial production, in spite of increased employment, did not reveal a corresponding expansion. Above all, there was the disconcerting tendency for imports to get ahead of exports, and January 1964 produced the unprecedented gap of £164 million. On the assumption that this was explained by industry's stocking up of raw materials as a necessary preliminary to export expansion the Chancellor refrained from applying the traditional restraints;

the exchange rate was allowed to take the strain and there was sufficient expansion in exports for some time to justify hopes that things would all come right soon. In presenting his budget in April 1964 the Chancellor still seemed mainly concerned lest the rate of expansion should be too great. After this, however, exports fell back relative to imports, and the trade gap increased steadily and alarmingly. In June it was £113 million, with a continuing rush of imports. In October the balance of payments deficit for the year was estimated at over £700 million.

As a partial counter to alarmist views the Bank of England published in March 1964, for the first time on record, an estimate of Britain's total long-term capital assets and liabilities abroad. Although there were important items on both sides for which figures were not available the broad picture was that assets amounted to about £13,000 million as against international liabilities of just over £11,000 million. As Mr. Graham Hutton commented in two articles in *The Times* in September, no country save the United States could show an 'immediate' creditor position of such magnitude. His conclusion was that the country could easily cope with any imaginable short-term run on sterling and hold the $2·80 rate of exchange indefinitely, as long as it preserved the internal United Kingdom purchasing power of the pound. This meant maintaining full employment and continued economic growth, while avoiding the recent excessive inflation of incomes which was out of line with lagging production and exports.[1] Other voices warned against an uncritical acceptance of the view that economic miracles had occurred in Germany, France, and Italy, while Britain lagged behind. Comparisons were misleading, but did not support the view that the three countries had cheaper labour, poorer social services, or longer working weeks. Working hours were indeed longer in the United Kingdom, and labour costs almost the same in all four countries. But it could well be argued that an essential difference existed in the postwar tendency in Britain to prefer status to contract.[2] The country, too, was said to have the worst record of unofficial strikes in the world.

Absorbed in these difficult and ambiguous discussions, the two

---

[1] The balance sheet, based on the Bank of England *Quarterly Bulletin* for March, was given in *The Times* on 9 March 1964; two articles by Graham Hutton in *The Times*, 8 and 9 September.

[2] As in the case of the worker whose job depended on his trade union membership rather than the quality of his performance. Cf. Jossleyn Hennessy, 'A British "Miracle"?' in *Rebirth of Britain*, pp. 242–55.

main parties had singularly little to say during the election about foreign affairs. Hardly any reference was made, except by the Liberals, to Europe and the Common Market, and only the need for an independent nuclear deterrent, very much Sir Alec's own preoccupation, had a thorough airing. It was finally decided to hold the general election in October 1964, leaving Labour's election campaign, which had apparently been planned to come to its climax in June, rather out of steam for the moment. The welcome given to British troops which were keeping the peace between the Greek and Turkish communities in Cyprus and, with Gurkhas, defending the frontiers of Malaysia, helped the government's reputation and showed that there was a Commonwealth rôle still to be played; British troops had also been asked to assist in handling disturbances in Tanganyika, Kenya, and Uganda in January 1964. In August the Prime Minister found himself a little ahead of Mr. Wilson in the public opinion polls.

But Labour's greatest asset was undoubtedly the predisposition of a significant sector of the electorate for change, and the ability of Harold Wilson to suggest a reasonable chance that the change might be for the better. The clarion call for modernization more than balanced any lingering whispers as to a revival of austerity and financial ineptitude on the Attlee model. Efficiency, which Wilson's matter-of-fact, no-nonsense, dedicated eloquence seemed to guarantee, would above all make British industry, fully using automation and the trained brains of the technologists, dominant in the export markets; and it would solve the balance of payments problem by a competitive development of import-saving industries. Nationalization was not in fact discarded, and steel nationalization was still a point of honour with the party; nevertheless, the feeling, with the Labour party as with the Conservatives, was that public ownership should be regarded as an expedient rather than a philosophy. At last polling day came, on 15 October 1964; as the returns came in it looked at one point as if the hopes of Labour would once more be disappointed. But the final figures gave the party an overall majority of five, and as it turned out the support on the main issues of the Liberals, whose number rose by the following spring to ten, meant that this was a working majority for the time being.

When all is said and done, the most significant feature of the election to the student of history is the absence of any fundamental issues between the parties, and the absence of any problem of apparent crisis proportions (apart from finance) facing the country. In October 1964 the country was at almost the same distance in time from VE day of 1945 as it had been in September 1939 from the moment of the signing of the peace of Versailles. No similar international crisis threatened now; the nuclear deadlock was not even news, and certainly no party anticipated its end. And although the balance-of-payments problem was a sizeable and legitimate election issue it was essentially a crisis of prosperity, with no major difference of ideology or even practical politics to divide the parties over its treatment. Planning, an incomes policy, greater productivity, a mixed economy, modernization, bigger universities, more technologists, the manning of Commonwealth outposts, close ties with America, a guarded friendliness towards the Common Market, a watchful scepticism towards Communist manifestations of all varieties, an honourable rôle in the global war against backwardness and poverty—in these and similar matters it was difficult to find a fundamental difference between the party programmes.

There was no case for complacency in this situation. Britain was once again, as in 1914, a major supporting power in a world divided by fundamental antagonisms. Her relative contribution to the western alliance in 1964 would probably have been smaller in a crisis than her contribution to the entente strength of 1914, although her commitment was more precise. But the fundamental antagonism seemed likely to remain quiescent in the second case whereas it had not been possible to postpone it in the first. The peculiarity of the nuclear deadlock only partially explains this paradox; there is also something to be said for the view that the U.S.A. and U.S.S.R. were basically satiated powers in view of their size and achievements, although it was equally evident that some of the potential giants—Communist China and Indonesia—were not.

It was an age, some were saying, of economic optimism and political pessimism; for if the fundamental political clashes were progressively postponed they also seemed insoluble, whereas economic tangles were deemed to be readily susceptible to rational handling, given the necessary expertise. The position had been rather the reverse in the thirties. The continued primacy of economic issues during Mr. Harold Wilson's first year as Prime Minister emphasized in turn the need for a self-assured handling of the more technical aspects of the subject by the Opposition leader. The day of the grammar school boy had evidently dawned (although not only for this reason), and within the year Mr. Edward Heath replaced Sir Alec Douglas-Home as leader of the Conservative party. Political passivism and economic experimentation thus seemed the likeliest prospect for the years ahead: but the historically-minded, conscious of the rôle in human affairs of the contingent and the unforeseen, could well remind themselves that the outlook had not been so very different in the weeks before our story opened on the eve of the sudden crisis of late July 1914.

EPILOGUE

1964–1974

During the ten years which followed the Labour victory of October 1964 the country's political and strategical responsibilities —and the accompanying worries—were greatly diminished; the balance of payments, rather than the balance of power, was becoming the major preoccupation. But crisis conditions never seemed to be absent for long and it was still the case, as it had been in so many spheres since 1914, that national policy, although now mainly concerned with the economy, was governed by the impact of external challenges.

Certainly Mr. Wilson and the new Chancellor, Mr. James Callaghan, facing a deficit of £800 million for the year 1964, were well aware of the need to revive overseas confidence in sterling, although the new government may itself have worsened the economic situation by its crisis talk and the apparent desperation of some of its own early measures. These included a 15 per cent surcharge on imports and the raising of the bank rate to 7 per cent in November 1964. While Mr. Wilson and the Chancellor fiercely rejected the devaluation of sterling, they did not appear enamoured of the deflationary alternative; at any rate, plans for a wide range of increased social benefits went ahead. There were great hopes of the new Department of Economic Affairs, headed by Mr. George Brown; its National Plan, published on 16 September 1965, aimed at a 25 per cent increase in the gross domestic product in six years. But its relations with the Treasury, the traditional director of economic policy, had still to be defined. The pound remained vulnerable, although funds were beginning to flow back to London by the end of 1965. Mr. Wilson's reputation still stood high, and the general election which he called for 31 March 1966 was excellently timed: the Labour party increased its seats to 363 (with

253 Conservatives and 12 Liberals), giving the government an over-all majority of 97. But it was soon being said that the election had been won on a false prospectus.[1] For the teasing basic dilemma of Britain's economic policy was unresolved. As a great exporting country but one relatively poor in raw materials she needed a high level of imports to maintain her domestic consumption and visible exports; growth, while benefiting exports, would increase wage packets and strengthen home demand, thus promoting inflation and upsetting in due course the balance of payments; a phase of deflation in some form would then have to follow. The fact that inflation and the overheating of national economies was happening elsewhere lessened the force of anti-British criticism while complicating Britain's problems. The crisis had not been solved in time for the 1966 election; the balance of payments was the over-riding problem for another three years.

The continued opposition to the devaluation of sterling made foreign speculators, who expected it, suspicious and jittery. The selective employment tax (S.E.T.), introduced by Mr. Callaghan on 3 May 1966, was intended to favour the exporting and manufacturing at the expense of the service and distributing industries, and also to raise revenue and check inflation; but it penalized some dollar-earning industries such as catering, and seemed rather in the 'try anything' spirit. A devastating seamen's strike, from 16 May to 1 July 1966, made it necessary on 23 May to declare a State of Emergency; this triggered off another run on sterling, not halted by support for the pound by the Basle group of central bankers. Drastic steps had to be taken in July. A further rise in the bank rate on 14 July merely engendered more heavy selling. On the 20 July Mr. Wilson announced the 'July measures'. These included a six-months' standstill on wages, salaries, and dividends, to be followed by six months of 'severe restraint'; a £50 foreign travel ceiling; and cuts in foreign aid and defence and in nationalized industry and local government expenditure. This savage deflation of the economy meant the end of George Brown's hopes of a 25 per cent expansion; after resignation talk he became Foreign Secretary on 10 August 1966.[2]

Meanwhile the state of the economy was having its effect on military and political strategy abroad. Defence cuts in February 1966, mainly in the interest of saving, placed an annual ceiling of £2,000 million

[1] R. Rhodes James, *Ambitions and Realities* (1972), p. 32.
[2] H. Wilson, *The Labour Government 1964–1970* (1971), pp. 256–72; George Brown, *In My Way* (1971), chap. 6.

expenditure on defence and foreshadowed the end of Britain's peace-making role east of Suez, although Mr. Wilson seemed reluctant to admit the fact. He was active in seeking to honour British obligations in Africa by negotiations on the Rhodesian problem, culminating in a provisional but ultimately abortive agreement with the premier, Mr. Ian Smith, on the cruiser *Tiger* early in December. He also irked the Left-wing and anti-American elements in the Labour party by his steady support for United States policy in Vietnam, where he sought, although without success, to arrange, through the enigmatic Russian leaders, a ceasefire between the contending forces. When he decided that a second application for membership of the European Common Market should be launched in November 1966 there was noticeably less opposition to it in both the major parties than there had been in 1961–2; there was, however, no diminution of disapproval in Paris, and on 27 November 1967 General de Gaulle cited Britain's economic difficulties as sufficient ground for keeping her out.

For all the admiration aroused by Mr. Wilson's energy, dexterity, and political flair there remained doubts as to the clarity or consistency of his political thinking; his critics dismissed his policies as entirely opportunistic, gimmickry raised to a fine art. But in his three-year battle against devaluation there is sufficient proof of his capacity for stubborn (and indeed injudicious) consistency. The July measures had been a massive bid for a balance of payments surplus, and during the first four months of 1967 the prospects of achieving it by the end of the year seemed quite promising. But there was a fresh setback in the sterling marking after the middle of May, and the six-day Israeli-Egyptian war (6–10 June), with an embargo on oil supplies to Britain, the closing of the Suez Canal, higher freight charges, and other immediate and remoter consequences, gave it a further major blow. Even more dramatic was the effect of 'unofficial' dock strikes in Liverpool and London, which held up exports and produced a trade deficit for October 1967 of £162 million. The situation now began to get really out of hand, with heavy selling of sterling reaching almost panic proportions by mid-November. A 14·3 per cent devaluation of sterling (from $2.80 to $2.40 to the pound) was announced on Saturday, 18 November. Mr. Callaghan, who had given so many assurances against devaluation, resigned on 29 November, and was succeeded by Mr. Roy Jenkins.

The situation remained gloomy during 1968, with a £398 million deficit. But the new Chancellor, who as Home Secretary had made a high reputation outside the sphere of financial policy, was winning confidence by his singleness of purpose in righting the payments balance. There was a convincing surplus of £387 million in 1969, ensured by the expansion of the export industries resulting from devaluation and favourable world conditions, together with the restriction of imports following continued deflationary measures. So national solvency was won, but it was at a cost. Unemployment was the highest since the war—averaging 565,000 in 1968, with only a slight drop in 1969. Unofficial strikes tended to cancel official union restraint over wage demands. And the discontent of Labour supporters was registered in a long series of by-election disasters for the government during 1968 and 1969.

One result was Mr. Wilson's decision in June 1969 that in face of the opposition of the TUC and the threatened revolt of even the loyalest of Labour back-benchers the government must abandon the rather bold plans for trade union reform which Mrs. Barbara Castle was sponsoring in the House of Commons. But they had shown courage in pursuing the attempt this far. Mr. Callaghan, now Home Secretary, also showed resolution and good judgment in handling the crisis which had been escalating in Ulster since 1968. The increasing violence, with the intervention of the I.R.A. and of Protestant extremists, the sending in of British troops, and patient negotiations with Dublin and the Ulster leaders for a constitutional solution, did not become a matter of party conflict at Westminster. This was the one relatively happy feature of a problem which remained unsolved by both the Labour government and its successor.

Price and income restraints had already been virtually abandoned in the budget of April 1969, and in view of the imminence of a general election something of the Chancellor's austerity had to be further relaxed. The result was the beginning of a wage explosion which did not, however, blow Labour to victory at the general election on 18 June 1970. Completely refuting the prophesies of the opinion polls and the Labour party, the Conservatives were returned with a safe majority of 330 seats over Labour with 287 seats and the Liberals with six.

The Conservatives had been preparing themselves very thoroughly for office since 1965, with an overall strategy aimed at achieving a dynamic, expansive economy, with the reduction and reform of taxation, legislation on industrial relations, and entry into the E.E.C. as the main objectives. Later it was argued that the programme had taken shape at too early a date, and failed to take sufficient account of the fact that by 1969 price stability had become the main priority.[1] Pre-occupied with rising costs, the British people failed to respond very readily to the call for thrustful action. Meanwhile the party struggle was bitter, and bipartisan only over Northern Ireland; no similar charity was extended to Conservative policy over Rhodesia and Europe. 'Will Labour rat?' 'Will the Tories grovel?', represented the level of much of the debate on the E.E.C. terms.

Nevertheless, the new government made good progress towards its planned objectives during 1970 and 1971, in spite of continued concern over inflation and the strike wave. The budgets of the new Chancellor, Mr. Anthony Barber, replaced S.E.T. and purchase tax by the Value Added Tax (V.A.T.), simplified surtax, estate duty, and the capital gains tax, and made plans for an overall saving of £1,100 million on public expenditure by the financial year 1974–5. An Industrial Relations Bill, published on 3 December 1970, became law on 6 August 1971 after bitter Commons' debate; it covered much of the ground of the abortive Labour legislation of 1969. It provided for the registration of trade unions, strengthened the rights of employees, and provided for the setting up of an Industrial Relations Court empowered to determine rights, require the attendance of witnesses, and enforce its own decisions. It could delay strike action up to sixty days or order a strike ballot. The government's crowning success was the signing on 22 January 1972 of the treaty of accession establishing Britain's membership of the E.E.C.; it was ratified in the House of Commons by 309 to 301 votes on 17 February. Labour at once denounced the terms as humiliating, and announced its intention of re-negotiating them.

By this stage, however, the Cabinet was increasingly aware of the inadequacies in existing conditions of its vision of a free market economy. A major dock strike had greeted the new government in July 1970, and had been followed by those of the dustmen and electricity workers. 1971 was another bad year for lost working days. The number of registered unemployed reached 620,000 at the end of 1970, 923,000 a year later, and went over the million mark in January 1972, in spite of confident Treasury prophesies that the rate would fall in 1971. This led to insistent demands from many quarters for reflation and the Chancellor called for a 5 per cent growth rate, which

[1] Ralph Harris & Brendon Sewill, *British Economic Policy 1970–74* (1975), pp. 29–35.

he sought to facilitate by substantial tax reductions and other measures in his 1971 and 1972 budgets. At the same time, unemployment did not act as a check on the steep rise in prices, which was accelerated by further massive wage settlements. Early in 1972 a miners' strike with aggressive picketing at power stations led to the government's surrender to the miners' terms on 23 February, a position quickly emphasized by other inflationary settlements. One result was a run on sterling in June and the decision that the pound should be allowed to float. Accordingly, after much anxious cogitation and the breakdown of tripartite talks between the government, the C.B.I. and the T.U.C., the Cabinet made its famous 'U turn', in the form of a statutory prices and incomes policy starting in November 1972. There was to be a ninety-days' freeze, which was to be followed by two Stages of controlled wage increases. Economists did not fail to argue that the government's policy was gravely inconsistent, with the anti-inflationary purposes of the prices and incomes policy frustrated by the credit expansion and deficit budgeting on an exceptional scale of the reflationary drive.[1]

Nevertheless, things seemed to go much better for a time in 1973, with the growth rate at 5 per cent and a falling level of unemployment. External as well as internal difficulties finally frustrated the government's determination to soldier on. There was a big rise in the cost of imported foodstuffs (38 per cent) and of many industrial raw materials, which added some £2,000 million to the import bill for the year. The oil producing states heavily increased their prices between October and December. Above all, there was strong union defiance of Stage III of the incomes plan, announced at the end of October. This allowed for a basic 7 per cent in pay rises, with some flexibility to allow for anomalies and incentive schemes and for 'threshold' payments (to meet rises in the retail price index). From this point the rapidly deteriorating fuel and power situation, complicated by rail and gas workers' strikes and a heavily adverse turn in the balance of payments which led to a record bank rate of 13 per cent, brought the country to something like siege conditions.

Accepting the miners' challenge, Mr. Heath announced drastic economies on 13 December in the use of power, which put much of the country's industry and commerce on a three-day working week from 31 December. But the crisis continued, and the government

[1] Lord Robbins, *Aspects of Post-war Economic Policy* (1974), pp. 24–5.

decided that it must submit its case to judgment in a general election on 28 February 1974. The appeal for a powerful demonstration of support in the national interest was not quite successful. Labour secured 301 seats and the Conservatives 296, although they had a small lead of 308, 481 votes in the country as a whole.

So Labour was back in office, and at a critical moment for its future and that of the country. Mr. Wilson, like MacDonald and Attlee before him, certainly wished to prove that the party could be one of government as well as of protest, and could think and act in office for and with the country as a whole. Yet the party and its trade union supporters had a long established strategy of withdrawal of co-operation or approval in order to force concessions from the class rivals—a comprehensive category including employers, capitalists, Tory politicians, Whitehall and Brussels bureaucrats and the like. When Labour in office wished to work with the same establishment figures the more exasperating features of this approach were revealed. Still, fraternal goodwill had hitherto kept Right and Left wings of the movement in fair harmony. The question now was whether an extra degree of militancy, both in the trade unions and in the parliamentary party, did not mean that the Left was no longer prepared to conform. Was the country now facing what Mr. Andrew Shonfield called a negative dictatorship of the proletariat, under subversive leaders seeking the breakdown of the system to secure socialist objectives? Five members of the Cabinet voted against acceptance of the revised terms of British membership of the E.E.C., which Mr. Callaghan had negotiated in 1974; and on 9 April 1975 the government's proposal that the terms should be submitted to a referendum was actually opposed by a majority of the Labour party in the House of Commons, although the proposal was carried with Tory support.

On 6 March 1974 the new government had quickly settled the miners' demands on the miners' own terms; this set the pace for a round of staggeringly high wage increases, which were clearly the main, though not the only, cause of a galloping inflation. By April 1975 average wage earnings were 30 per cent higher than they had been a year earlier, and the increase in the retail price index for the year was the highest on record at 21·2 pence in the pound. Although both major parties called for wage restraint, they regarded support for a statutory incomes policy as outside practical politics; the Liberals, however, continued to demand it. The government did something to restrain food prices with subsidies, but the Chancellor, Mr. Denis

Healey, took increasingly the view that yet heavier taxation, with large cuts in public spending and a consequent rise in unemployment, was the price to be paid for inflation at the existing levels. The balance of payments deficit for 1974, due largely to oil purchases, was £3,800 million. And yet the country did not seem greatly perturbed by all the crisis talk, or in a hurry to blame the government: after another well-timed dissolution, Labour at the general election of 10 October 1974 increased its majority to 319 seats (as compared with 276 Conservatives, 13 Liberals, and 26 for members of sub-nationalist parties). In February 1975 the Conservative party found a new leader in Mrs Margaret Thatcher, but a new policy was harder to come by.

To leave our survey of the course of British history at this point is, at first sight, to end on a rather dismal note. And yet the country could perhaps take comfort from its survival of numerous monetary and other crises since 1914. It remained the fifth largest trading nation in the world. It could hope, with North Sea oil and gas, to be independent of all foreign sources of energy by 1980. And perhaps, too, the Common Market, after the 'Yes' vote in the referendum of June 1975, would at last fulfil its promise. The story was not finished.

NOTE ON BOOKS

Good bibliographical guides to the period are numerous, and the purpose of this note is simply to call attention to some of the key works on which a further study of the period might profitably be based.

1. SOURCE MATERIAL

In response to press and parliamentary pressure or in merely forwarding the transaction of its current business the government continually offers accounts and explanations of its activities, supported as the need arises by reports, white papers, official histories, diplomatic correspondence, and statistical information of all kinds. All writing about more or less recent public policy is necessarily based on this material. Guides to it include, apart from the annual lists published by H.M. Stationery Office, P. and G. Ford's *A Breviate of Parliamentary Papers, 1917–39* (1951) and *1940–54* (1961), together with R. Vogel's *A Breviate of British diplomatic blue books 1919–1939*. Official publications include the *Documents on British Foreign Policy, 1919–1939*, edited by E. L. Woodward, R. Butler, W. N. Medlicott and others; 43 volumes have so far appeared. Official histories, based on unpublished official documents, include over forty volumes on the military, naval, air, and blockade aspects of the first world war, a series that was incomplete when world war II began. For the latter the various series range wider, for there are not only the usual detailed histories of action by the armed forces, but some 25 volumes on the civil history of the war as well. In 1958 the opening of the archives of government departments to historians was fixed at fifty years after the date of the documents; this period has now been shortened to thirty years. Thus historians will in future be able to check progressively the information already made available for the half-century since 1914 and decide whether it was misleading or intended to deceive. They will also be able to use for this purpose many of the private papers of public men and women. Access to these is sometimes governed by the fifty (now thirty) year rule, sometimes by the discretion of the owners, sometimes by the timetable of memoir writers. Most of the numerous political biographies of the period embody some material of this sort. Official series of foreign documents, German, Belgian, French, Italian, and American are valuable for their point of view on British diplomacy.

2. GENERAL WORKS AND BIBLIOGRAPHIES

No other work quite covers the whole of the period dealt with in this volume. For the interwar years C. L. Mowat, *Britain between the Wars, 1918–1940* (1955) is detailed and perceptive, strongest on social and economic developments, but adequate on all. It has a full bibliography. So too have A. J. P. Taylor's *English History, 1914–1945* (1965), in the Oxford History of England series, and Arthur Marwick's *Britain in the century of total war: war peace and social change, 1900–1967* (1968). Recent shorter works include Henry Pelling, *Modern Britain, 1885–1955* (1960), and David Thomson, *England in the Twentieth Century* (Penguin Books, 1965). *British Politics since 1900* (1950), by D. C. Somervell, readable, good-tempered, and a little out of date, finds good points in the Tory record. W. G. Truchanowski, *Neueste Geschichte Englands 1917–1951* (Berlin, 1962), is the German translation of a substantial work by a Soviet historian who shows how different it all looks through Marxist-Leninist spectacles. A good American survey is that of A. F. Havighurst, *Twentieth-Century Britain* (1962). C. L. Mowat's *British History since 1926* (*Helps for Students of History*, 1960) and H. R. Winkler's *Great Britain in the Twentieth Century* (1960) are critical bibliographies primarily intended for the use of teachers, while the *Annual Bulletin of Historical Literature*, published by the Historical Association, enables bibliographies to be kept up to date.

3. OTHER STUDIES

Party politics can best be followed in the memoirs and auto-biographies, apart from some notable works on special aspects and periods. Among the former the war memoirs of Lloyd George and Churchill for world war I and of Churchill for world war II embody much official material. There are biographies of most of the Prime Ministers, based on private papers, varying in frankness; they include those of Bonar Law (by Robert Blake), Asquith (J. A. Spender and C. Asquith; Roy Jenkins), Lloyd George (Malcolm

Thomson; Frank Owen; Tom Jones), Baldwin (G. M. Young) and Neville Chamberlain (Feiling; Iain Macleod). Most of the greater cabinet figures, and some minor ones, have their 'standard' biographies. Apart from these, Ivor Bulmer-Thomas, *The Growth of the British Party System* (2 vols, 1966), covers the period in the latter part of volume one and in volume two. R. T. McKenzie, *British Political Parties* (1963), W. I. Jennings, *Parliament* (1957) and *Cabinet Government* (1959), and K. B. Smellie, *A Hundred Years of English Government* (1950) deal with the machinery of politics. There is the detailed and reliable *History of the Labour Party from 1914* (1948) by G. D. H. Cole, and a more sketchy history of *The Communist Party* (1958) by H. Pelling, but no comparable party history for the Liberals and Conservatives.

Foreign policy is consecutively treated by W. N. Medlicott, *British Foreign Policy since Versailles* (1968) and P. A. Reynolds, *British Foreign Policy in the Interwar Years* (1954), then by E. L. Woodward, *British Foreign Policy in the Second World War* (1962), and finally by C. M. Woodhouse, *British Foreign Policy since the Second World War* (1961), and F. S. Northedge, *British Foreign Policy, The Process of Readjustment, 1945–1961* (1962). The three volumes of Lord Avon's memoirs are based heavily on unpublished Foreign Office material for the years 1931 to 1957. W. Strang, *Britain in World Affairs* (1961), chaps 13–16, usefully combines first-hand experience with shrewd analysis.

Fairly short general surveys of economic developments are those of A. J. Youngson, *The British Economy 1920–1957* (1960), and the relevant chapters of W. Ashworth, *An Economic History of England 1870–1939* (1960); more detailed is S. Pollard's authoritative work, *The Development of the British Economy* (1962). G. C. Allen, *British Industries and their Organization*, first published in 1933, is now in its fourth edition (1958), with a survey of both trends and individual industries. The various phases can otherwise be studied in A. C. Pigou, *Aspects of British Economic History 1918–1925* (1947), and E. V. Morgan, *Studies in British Financial Policy 1914–1925* (1952); L. Robbins, *The Great Depression* (1934), J. H. Richardson, *British Economic Foreign Policy* (1936), and H. V. Hodson, *Slump and Recovery, 1929–1937* (1938); K. Hancock and M. M. Gowing, *British War Economy* (1949); G. D. N. Worswick and P. H. Ady, *The British Economy, 1945–1950* (1952), and J. C. R. Dow, *The Management of the British Economy* (1965).

Finally the revolutionary changes during the period in social conditions, class structure, the managerial and professional superstructure, nutrition, health, and the national ethos, have had numerous and sometimes rather puzzled interpreters. A few examples, varied but representative, are G. F. C. Masterman, *England after War* (1922); M. Muggeridge, *The Thirties* (1940); R. Graves and A. Hodge, *The Long Week-End* (1940, a more serious work than its title suggests); R. M. Titmuss, *Problems of Social Policy* (1950), and his earlier *Parents Revolt* (1942); H. Hopkins, *The New Look, a Social History of the Forties and Fifties in Britain* (1963); G. M. Carstairs, *This Island Now* (1963); A. Hartley, *A State of England* (1963); and Anthony Sampson, *Anatomy of Britain Today* (1965).

For the period since 1964 Harold Wilson's apologia, *The Labour Government 1964–1970* (1971), is massively informative on its chosen themes; George Brown, *In My Way* (1971), is slighter and livelier. There is not much yet on the Heath administration, but two biographies, George Hutchinson's *Edward Heath* (1970) and Margaret Laing's *Edward Heath, Prime Minister* (1972), are useful for background and personality. Robert Rhodes James, *Ambitions & Realities, British Politics 1964–1970* (1972), shrewdly assesses the two leaders and their respective embarrassments. C. J. Bartlett, *The Long Retreat* (1972), is an important study of recent defence policy down to 1970. F. S. Northedge, *Descent from Power, British Foreign Policy 1945–1973* (1974), expands his earlier work, mentioned above. Roy E. Jones, *The Changing Structure of British Foreign Policy* (1974), is stimulating and analytical. *Britain 1975, An official handbook* (1975), is the twenty-sixth volume in a series published by H.M.S.O. and providing information about every aspect of British public life and national administration.

INDEX